Leabhar breathnach annso sis : the Irish version of the Historia Britonum of Nennius – Primary Source Edition

James Henthorn Todd, fl 796
Nennius, A 1792–1855 Herbert

85.B

Leabhar breathnach annso sis.

THE IRISH VERSION

OF THE

HISTORIA BRITONUM OF NENNIUS.

EDITED, WITH A TRANSLATION AND NOTES,

BY JAMES HENTHORN TODD, D.D., M.R.I.A.,

FELLOW OF TRINITY COLLEGE, DUBLIN, ETC.

THE INTRODUCTION AND ADDITIONAL NOTES

BY THE HON. ALGERNON HERBERT.

DUBLIN:

PRINTED FOR THE IRISH ARCHÆOLOGICAL SOCIETY.

MDCCCXLVIII.

EDITOR'S PREFACE.

THE Text of the following work is taken principally from a collation of three MSS., which are referred to in the Notes by the letters D., B., and L.

1. The first of these, denoted by D., is a miscellaneous volume, containing various tracts and fragments of the fourteenth, fifteenth, and sixteenth centuries; it was formerly in the possession of the celebrated antiquaries, Duald Mac Firbis and Edward Lhwyd, whose autographs it possesses; and it is now preserved in the Library of Trinity College, Dublin, Class H., Tab. 3. No. 17.

The volume contains a copy of the celebrated code of Brehon Laws called the Seanchus Mor[a], with a copious gloss of great value. This is followed by several other tracts and fragments of tracts on Brehon Law, of different dates, and by various scribes, some of whom have given their names.

After

[a] For an account of the Seanchus Mor, with several extracts from this very MS. of it, and from another copy also in Trinity College, see Dr. Petrie's Essay on Tara Hill, in the Transactions of the Royal Irish Academy, vol. xviii. pp. 71-80.

After the Law Tracts follow several miscellaneous pieces on historical and religious subjects, short anecdotes of Irish saints, poems, and historical romantic tales. Of these the most curious are : 1. The tract called Seanchuṗ na ṗelec, or the History of the Cemeteries, containing an account of the most celebrated burial-places of the Pagan Irish ; 2. The History of the plebeian Tribes called Aitheach Tuatha, who were subjugated by King Tuathal Teachtmar, in the second century of the Christian era; 3 A List of the ancient Tales or historical Romances which were wont to be recited by the Bards at Entertainments, in presence of Kings and Chieftains, 4 A List of the celebrated Women of Antiquity ; with many other tales, tracts, genealogies, and poems, of the greatest value for the illustration of Irish history, language, and topography.

The copy of the Leabhar Breathnach, or British Book, contained in this MS, occurs in p 806[b], and was probably written in the fourteenth, or early part of the fifteenth century

This is the copy of the Irish version of the Britannia of Nennius, which has been made the basis of the text of the following work, and is denoted by D in the notes. Its errors, however, have been corrected, as far as the Editor was able to correct them, by collation with the other MSS to which he had access ; and such interpolations as occurred in the other MSS, when judged of any value, have been inserted in their proper places All these deviations from the text of D have been mentioned in the notes

2 The second MS (denoted by B) is the copy of the Irish Nennius, which is contained in the Book of Ballymote, in the Library of the Royal Irish Academy, written in the fourteenth century

The

---

[b] Or rather *column* 806 The MS is written some parts of it in double columns and some parts not the whole has been paged by Edward Lhwyd, each column, wherever columns occurred, being counted for a page.

The order of the sections in this MS differs considerably from that of D, and it also contains several interpolations The Editor has numbered the sections in the printed text of the work, in order to enable him with greater facility to refer to them.

The order of the copy in the Book of Ballymote is as follows It begins with the section *Ego Nennius,* marked sect I. p 25, *infra* Then follows the chapter " On the Origin of the Cruithnians," which has been given in the Additional Notes, No XX., p xci. After which follow sections II, III, and IV., as in the printed text

After section IV. this MS interpolates the prose account, sections XXVII and XXVIII, followed by the poem on the Origin and History of the Picts or Cruithnians, which has been published section XXX p 126, *infra.*

Then follow sections V. to XIV, inclusive, in the same order as in the text; but after section XIV. is interpolated the Legend of St Cairnech, which will be found in the Appendix, No I, p 178

After this we have the history of the Saxon conquest, sect XV ; the miracles of St German, sects XVI, XVII ; and the story of Ambrose Merlin and the Druids, sects. XVIII, XIX ; followed by the history of the wars of Gortimer (or Gortighern, as he is called in this copy), sects XX. to XXIV, inclusive, in the same order as in the text.

At the end of this last section recording the battles of Arthur, and briefly noticing the conversion of the Saxons to Christianity, the copy of this work in the Book of Ballymote ends . and its completion is notified by the words ꝼiniꞇ ꝺo'n ḃꞃeaꞇnocaꞃ, which are literally " Finit to the Breathnochas," where the scribe evidently wrote *Finit* for *Finis* It appears also from this note that the title then given to this book was " The Breathnochas," which would be equivalent to *Britanismus,* if we may be permitted to coin such a word

b 2

3. The

3   The next authority which has been employed in the formation of the text is the copy of this work in the Book of Lecan, a MS written in the year 1417[c].   To this copy is prefixed, but in a more recent hand, the title Leabap bpeacnach annpo pip, which has been adopted in the title page of the present volume, and which expresses what the Irish understood by the Latin titles, " Eulogium Britanniæ," and " Historia Britonum "

This copy, which is denoted by L in the notes, begins with sect II., *Britannia insula*, &c., p 27, *infra*, omitting the list of British cities. Then follows the chapter on the origin of the Picts, which will be found in the Additional Notes, No XX. p. xcii   Section III is omitted altogether, and then follow sects IV to VIII, inclusive Sections IX and X. are omitted in this place.   Then comes the account of the adventures of the Gaedhil, sects XI to XV, inclusive[d], followed by another copy of the history of Roman and Saxon Britain, sects. V., VI, VII., VIII., which is headed, Oo peancup bpeacan anopo booeapca, " Of the history of Britain, here follows," but the title prefixed to sect VIII, in the former copy of this chapter, is omitted here.

Then follow sects IX, X. with the title Oo ʒabalaib Epenn amail inoipeap Nemiup [*sic*] annpo, as in the text, p 42   After which comes another copy of the history of the adventures of the Gaedhil, sects. XI.–XIV., with the title Oo imcheachcaib ʒaeioeal anopo booŗ ca, but a portion of sect XIV is wanting after the words cuʒŗacap leo iapoain caipechou, p 72 line 9.

About

---

[c] This date may be collected from the MS. itself See also Mr O'Donovan's note to the Annals of the Four Masters, at the year 1417

[d] The account of the sons of Cruithne, in section X., differs considerably in this copy from that given above, p 50   See Additional Notes, No XX, p. xciv, where the more important variations are noticed

About ten leaves are here wanting in the Book of Lecan, which is now preserved in the Library of the Royal Irish Academy, although it originally belonged to Trinity College[e], where nine of the missing leaves were discovered by Mr Curry, bound up with other MSS, (Class H Tab 2. No. 17). One leaf, however, which contained the continuation of sect. XVI. is lost, and the next page begins with the words ιρ ιn lo.nζeαρ ριn ταιnιζ α ιnζeαn co h-Ɛnζιρτ, p. 84, l. 16, to the end of sect. XVII

Then follows the account of Dun Ambrose and of the contest of Ambrose Merlin with the Druids, sects. XVIII. XIX., then the wars of Gortimer or Gortighern, sect XX. to XXII., with the short account of St. Patrick, sect. XXIII, and the remainder of the history of the Saxons from the death of Gortighern (sect XXIV.) to their conversion to Christianity

This was also regarded by the scribe who copied the Book of Lecan as the conclusion of the work, for he has written the word ριnτ at the end of sect. XXIV. But there follow immediately the tracts on the wonders of Britain, sect XXV., and on the wonders of the isle of Man, sect. XXVI

After this begins what seems to have been intended as a new edition of the work[f] It commences with the chapter *Ego Nennius*, sect I, followed by the chapter on the origin of the Picts, which has been given in the Additional Notes, No. XX, p. xcv.

Then

---

[e] The Book of Lecan is entered among the MSS of Trinity College in the Catalogus Manuscriptorum Angliæ et Hiberniæ, published at Oxford, 1697 (No. 117, p 22), and still bears the Library marks, D 19. It was carried off in the reign of James II to Paris, but was restored to Ireland at the instance of General Vallancey, and by him deposited in the Library of the Royal Irish Academy. See O'Reilly, Trans Iberno-Celtic Society, p cxvii, Mac Geoghegan, Hist. d'Irlande, tom 1 p. 39

[f] This new edition appears, from its contents, to have had special reference to Pictish history.

Then follows "*Britannia insula,*" &c , sect ii , with the list of cities, and sections III IV , as far as the words mic lapeth, p. 32, line 11.

Next we have the account of the origin of the Picts (sects XXVII. to XXIX, inclusive), with the title Do Chpuichnechaib anopeo, oo peip na n-eolach[g] Section XXIX, containing the account of the manner in which the Picts, after their settlement in North Britain, obtained their women from the Milesians of Ireland, is peculiar to the Book of Lecan.

Then follows the poetical account of the Picts, sect XXX, wanting, however, the last two stanzas.

With this poem the second copy of the Irish Nennius in the Book of Lecan concludes

4. A fragment of this work is also to be found in the remains of the Leabhar na h-Uidhri, preserved in the Library of the Royal Irish Academy It begins on the first page of the second leaf now remaining in that MS, with the words act ceana ol pe, &c , p 94, line 15, and concludes at the end of sect XXIV, which in this MS. was also the termination of the work This fragment is referred to in the notes, pp. 95–113, by the letter U The Leabhar na h-Uidhri is a MS of the twelfth century

5 Another copy of the Leabhar Breathnach is to be found in the Book of Hy-Many, or the Book of the O'Kellys, as it is called by O'Reilly, a MS of the early part of the fifteenth century, transcribed by Faelan Mac an Gabhan, whose death is recorded by the Four Masters at the year 1423 This MS is not now accessible to Irish scholars in Dublin, and it has not been possible to consult it for the present work, although it is believed to be in existence in the possession of a private collector in England In O'Reilly's time it belonged to Sir William Betham

We

* See p 120, note [c].

We learn from O'Reilly[h], that at the commencement of this copy of the work there is or was " a memorandum," stating " that Nennius was the author, and that Giolla Caoimhghin translated it into Scotic."

Giolla Caoimhghin died about A. D. 1072, or shortly after, as has been inferred from his chronological poem, beginning Annalaiꝺ anall uile, which brings down the series of events to that year.

If, therefore, he is to be taken as the original translator of Nennius[i], we may probably fix the middle of the eleventh century as the earliest period at which the " Historia Britonum" appeared in an Irish version

In its original form, the work, as we have seen, terminated at the end of sect XXIV.; and all that follows must be regarded as subsequent interpolations, although, probably, added at the same period as the translation or edition, put forth by Giolla Caoimhghin

The first of these additions contains the section on the Wonders of the Island of Britain, and that on the Wonders of the Isle of Man This is also found added to some copies of the Latin of Nennius[k], with a chapter, omitted in all the Irish copies, on the Wonders of Ireland

The tract on the history of the Picts (sects. XXVII–XXIX), with the curious poem (sect. XXX), now for the first time printed, is also to be regarded as an addition made to the original work The Book of Ballymote, although it omits the Mirabilia, has preserved these sources of Pictish history, of which the prose portion was known to Pinkerton, through a very faulty transcript, and still more erroneous

[h] Transactions of the Iberno-Celtic Society, p cxxii

[i] Mr Herbert, however, has shown that there is some reason to attribute the first attempt at a translation of the Historia to an earlier author —See his remarks, Introd. p. 21

[k] See Mr. Herbert s note [m], pp 113–114.

neous translation, but the poem appears to have escaped his notice
Although the text is corrupt in many places, in both the MSS. that
have been employed in editing it, yet it is hoped that its publication,
even in the imperfect state in which we have it, will be regarded as
a service of some value to the student of Scottish history

The next interpolation or addition is an Irish version of the document already known to the readers of Innes and Pinkerton, under
the title of the " Chronicon Pictorum." This curious fragment occurs
only in the manuscript D.; but another copy of it has been given in
the Additional Notes[l], from a MS in the Bodleian Library[m] which
preserves a considerable fragment of the Psalter of Cashel, and evidently contained formerly a copy of the Leabhar Breathnach, or Irish
version of Nennius, of which the leaf containing the Pictish Chronicle is now the only remnant.

Next follows (sect xxxiii. p. 168), an abridged translation of the
beginning of the history of the Venerable Bede. This document occurs
also immediately after the Pictish Chronicle, in the Bodleian MS It is
of very little value, but as it appears to have been connected with the
work, and to have been regarded as a part of it in the manuscript
D. which has been principally followed, it was thought right to include it in the present volume.

The Appendix contains some other documents of the same kind,
not so immediately connected with the Leabhar Breathnach in any
of the MSS, but tending to illustrate the history to which it relates,
and the traditions prevalent at the period when it was compiled
The first of these documents is the Legend of St Cairnech, which,

as

[l] No XVIII p lxxv

[m] See an account of this MS, by the
Editor, in the Proceedings of the Royal
Irish Academy, vol ii p 33; and some

further remarks on it by Mr. O'Donovan,
in his Introduction to the Book of Rights,
published by the Celtic Society, p xxviii
et seq.

as we have seen, occurs only in the Book of Ballymote, having been
interpolated in the copy of the Irish Nennius there preserved, immediately after the account of the final conquest of Britain by the
Romans   It relates to the history of the sixth century, although it
is evidently a compilation of a much later period.

The next document inserted in the Appendix is an account of
the Wonders of Ireland, chiefly from the Book of Ballymote.   This
tract is not without interest, as a curious collection of ancient fables
and traditions, not very unlike the celebrated *Otia imperialia* of Ger-
vase of Tilbury, and compiled probably about the same period   It
proves, incidentally, that the stories of Irish wonders told by Giraldus
Cambrensis, for which Lynch has so severely, and, as it now appears,
so unjustly censured him, were not his own inventions, but copied,
with some embellishments of his own, from the genuine traditions of
the Irish people.

The poem of Maelmura of Fathain, on the history of the Milesian
or Gadelian invasion of Ireland, is now published for the first time,
and it was thought worth while to add to it the contemporaneous
poem on the history of the Albanian Scots, known under the name
of the "Duan Albanach," although this latter poem has already been
published by Pinkerton, by Doctor O'Conor, and more recently by
Mr Skene, in the "Collectanea de Rebus Albanicis," edited by the
Iona Club

Thus the present work will be found to contain three specimens
of the bardic sources of British and Irish history, written, one of them
in the ninth, and the others probably in the eleventh century, containing the traditions, as they were then currently received, of the
origin of the Pictish and Milesian tribes, and the succession of the
early kings of Scotland   Two of these poems are now published
for the first time; and the third is presented to the reader in, it is

hoped, a very much more correct version than those which accompanied the former publications of it.

In conclusion, the Editor has to acknowledge his very great obligations to Mr O'Donovan and Mr. Curry, for the invaluable assistance they have afforded him throughout the following work. Without them he could not have executed it, and to them he is indebted for the greater part of the historical and topographical information which is collected in the notes. For many valuable references to ancient Glossaries, and other MSS, containing philological and historical illustrations of obscure or obsolete words and phrases, he is specially indebted to Mr. Curry.

The Editor has preserved the orthography of the original, without any attempt at correction, or even at uniformity; and in the case of proper names, he has retained, even in the English translation, the spelling of the Irish. This seemed necessary, in order to give the English reader a fair representation of the age to which the original belongs. Thus the Picts are called Cruithnians, the Gaels, Gaedhil; Ireland, Eri; and Scotland, Alba".

The Notes marked (*H.*) have been contributed by Mr. Herbert For those marked (*T.*) the Editor is responsible.

JAMES H TODD

TRINITY COLLEGE,
April 8th, 1848.

" In some few instances this rule, from inadvertence, has not been adhered to — See pp 41, 43, 47, 53, 59

CONTENTS.

ADDITIONAL NOTES

INTRODUCTION.

HE Irish MS. of which a translation is here given professes to be, and after a fashion is, translated from the Historia Britonum by Nennius. Little is known of that author (if not rather, editor), and, as usual, the less we know the more we are obliged to say; for knowledge soon tells its tale.

That the Historia Britonum sometimes bears the name of Gildas, may be sufficiently accounted for by these circumstances: that the first genuine tractate of St. Gildas, concerning the Britons, was commonly called his Historia; and that a fabulous history of the Britons was formerly extant under that name. But it can be further explained by the nature of that title, for name indeed it is not, but an Irish title, so liberally bestowed upon the religious and learned, that Dr. C. O'Conor said there were not less than 1000 persons adorned with it. Script. Rerum Hib. 1, 198. Therefore, when we have shewn its original author to be closely connected with Ireland, we shall have removed any wonder at his being entitled Gildas. Its total dissimilitude to the works of St. Gildas of Ruiz is apparent;

and it also differs in its contents[a], and in some portion of its spirit, from that other fabulous history which is cited with admiration in Geoffrey of Monmouth by the name of Gildas   Its printed editions are by T Gale, Oxon, 1691; by C Bertram, jointly with St Gildas, and a production given by him to the world under the name of Ricardus Corinæus, Copenhagen, 1757, in the title, and 1758 in the colophon, by the same, with 1758 in the title, and without colophon, which edition I have never seen; by W. Gunn, B D, London, 1819, and by Jos Stevenson, London, 1838

The Historia Britonum[b] had two or more publishers in succession That is to say, transcribers of it made more or less of change and addition; and sometimes took no pains to inform the world that they were mere transcribers, and not the authors   The edition rendered into Irish is that by Nennius, styling himself a disciple of St Elbod or Elbodug, and styling the priest Beulan his master   Some copies have a long Prologus, which declares that he published his work "in A D 858, being the twenty-fourth year of Mervyn, King of the Britons." Mervyn Vrych or the Speckled, King of Man in his own right, and of Wales in that of Essyllt his queen, reigned over the latter country from 818 to his death in 843   See Powell's Cambria,

PP

[a] As to its contents the matters cited by Geoffrey were there related *satis prolixè*, therefore they were no casual paragraphs, missing out of our MSS Galfrid lib 1 cap 17, ii cap 17   And as to its spirit, it evidently sought to magnify the Britons at the expense of the Romans, from which temper our Historia is nearly exempt, iv cap. 3   It is not cited by name in cap. 4, but the identity of the sources is pretty obvious   I know not whether the references to Gildas are by Geoffrey, a free translator, or by his original   In i cap 17, the Welch copy called Tysilio omits the reference, p 116 But in ii cap 17, it quotes Gildas by name, p 139   Neither can we say with entire certainty in what language it was, but probably in Latin.

[b] The Archdeacon of Huntingdon in one place cites it as *quidam author*, and in another as Gildas Historiographus. Henr Hunt p 301-13, in Script post Bedam, Franc 1601.

pp 24–8; Warrington, 1, pp 205–10, Brut y Tywysogion, pp 475–8
He alone of that name was *Rex Britonum;* though Mervyn, third son
of Rodri Mawr, held Powys from 873 to 877[c] The year 858 fell fifteen years after his death, which argument would prove the forgery
of the Prologus, were it not for the ignorance, then so prevalent,
of the current year of our Lord. It is, however, a mere swelling out
and amplification of the shorter prologue, in a bombastic phraseology
which Nennius did not employ, and it is not credible that both are
genuine. But the shorter prologue, or Apologia, is to be received as
genuine It begins, as in the Irish version, "Ego Nennius Sancti
Elbodi discipulus aliqua excerpta scribere curavi," &c., but it is interpolated from the longer prologue, and otherwise altered. in that
version. It is to be received, first, from the absence of internal evidence to its prejudice, secondly, from the absence of internal evidence And I wonder that Mr. Stevenson should urge, for such, that
it occurs not in MSS anterior to the twelfth century; when from
his own shewing we collect, that there exists only one MS. anterior
to circiter 1150; one, not two, for the MS of Marcus Anachoreta
could not contain it, and is not strictly to the purpose The document
cannot suffer from the silence of MSS that do not exist Thirdly,
there is no motive for the forgery Great or even well-known names
have been assumed, in order to give currency to fictions, such as
Orpheus, Berosus, Ovid, Tully, Ossian, and (if you please) Gildas
But Nennius was nobody at all, his name does not exist elsewhere,
and no other works belong to him What was to be gained by in-
venting his name? The fabricator of a work may invent an ideal
author for it But here we must suppose, that the genuine work of
some other man was by forgery ascribed to a Nobody, to an unknown
person, claiming no rank or distinction, and made to avow his modern
date

---

[c] Brut y Tywysog, p. 481–2. Others give other years, but the question is not relevant.

date   The rejection of this document would therefore appear to me uncritical, and needlessly destructive of fact and document Falsehood is most usually built upon a basis of truth; and the Apologia or lesser prologue was the substratum upon which the larger one was erected   That fiction was, however, partly founded upon the contents of the book itself, which, in cap xi Gale, p. 14, Stevenson, purports to be published in A D $437 + 418 + 3 = 858$, and in the same chapter makes mention, though irrelevantly to that date, of King Mervyn, and of the fourth year (not the twenty-fourth) of his reign   Such are the sources of the false Prologus.

The name, which Geoffrey, Archdeacon of Monmouth, writes Nennius, is Nynmaw or Nynyaw in all the Welch copies of the chronicles   But it is not a name, whereof the etymon or significancy appears   Those chronicles have a legend, that one Nennius was brother of Cassivellaunus, fought against Cæsar, and took his sword from him, slew Labienus, but died himself of his wounds in fifteen days after   Galfrid Monumet iv cap 3–4; Brut Tysilio &c, p 173–6   To connect those statements with our historians would have exceeded all effrontery, but that of John Bale   That centuriator maintains, that Nennius, brother of Cassivellaunus, wrote a beautiful history of the origin and progress of the Britons, which another Nennius, Abbot of Bangor, translated into Latin and continued   Cent 1, fol 13, fol 36, 7th ed 1548 Mr Gunn's observation, that Nennius is described by Geoffrey, 1 cap 17, iv, cap 3 and 4, and by Tysilio, Coll Cambr pp 30 and 75, as a British historian, was made inadvertently, being at variance with the fact   Gunn's Preface p 19 Geoffrey's author makes no allusion to Nennius the historiographer, though he has borrowed things, either from the Historia, or from sources common to both   This name (written Ninnius and Ninius in some copies) is in all probability the same as that of Ninia, the Apostle of the South Picts, and founder of the Church of Candida Casa, so called by William

William of Malmesbury, and Nynia by Alcuin and Beda *Vide* Ussher, Brit. Eccles p 161, or ed. ii p. 137. Ninianus has been his common appellation among subsequent writers He had a brother, St. Plebeias. Johan. Tinmuth, ap Ussher addenda, p 1059, or ed ii p. 506 Two kings were said in the Welch mythologies to have formerly reigned over part of South Wales, and to have been transformed into oxen for their sins Their names were Nynniaw and Peibiaw See Mabinogi of Kilhwch, p 281, note, p 351. Some genealogies of King Arthur include the name of this Nynniaw From Nynniaw and *Peibiaw*, John of Tinmouth, or those to whom he was indebted, probably derived the idea of the brother saints Nynniaw and *Plebiaw* St Finnian of Maghbile was sent in his youth to a place in Britain called Magnum Monasterium, by John of Tinmouth, Rosnat, Alba, and Monasterium Album, in Colgan A SS i, pp 438–9, and civitas quæ dicitur Candida in Colgan, *ib* 634 Its abbot is styled Monennus, Monennius, Nennius, and Nennio Colg *ib* Ussher, p 954 or 494. But Finnian's instructor at Candida is called by his biographer, and in ancient hymns, Mugentius Colg *ib* 634 In the life of St. Eugenius he is called Nennio, qui Mancenus dicitur, de Rosnatensi monasterio Colg *ib* p 430 num 4 Dr Lanigan concluded that Mo-nennius or Nennio was no other than Ninia, the founder of Candida Casa, who was confounded with the existing abbot by reason of its being called his monastery See Lanigan's Eccles Hist i, 437, ed ii The address of Alcuin's epistle was, *Ad Fratres S Niniani de Candida Casa* Besides the coincidence of *candida* and *alba*, it might have been added that the Gaelic name Rosnat, *promontory* of learning, agrees with the Whithern or Whithorn, candidum *cornu*, of the Northumbrians Of the various Irish saints named Ninnidh or Nainnidh, and sometimes Latinized into Nennius, I take no account, as they belong to another nation; and it is uncertain if it be the same name, the more so as the Gaelic appellation

of

of St Ninia is Ringen or Ringan   Ussher, p 661 , Chalmers's Caledonia, 1 135.   Nor do the Irish copies of the Historia seem to recognize the name of Nennius, as having a known equivalent; for they give it, Numnus, Nemnus, Nemnius, Neimnus, Nemonus, and Nenammis   I do not know if the name in question hath any historical instances, besides those of the Apostle of the Picts and our historian.

His discipleship unto St Elbod now demands consideration The four chronicles annexed to that of the kings of Britain do not clearly define Elbod's date   He is said to have flourished in 755 and 770   Brut y Tywysog. p 473, p 391.   Warrington fixes his appointment to the primacy of North Wales (seated at Bangor) about A D 762   The Bonedd y Saint, p. 42, says that he was son of Cowlwyd, and bishop [of Caergybi[d] or Holyhead] in 773   He died in 800, according to the Brut y Tywysog p 392, and John Brechva, p 474; and in 809 according to the Brut y Saeson, p 474, Brut y Tywysog *ibid*   The Annals of St David's, carried down to 1285, say, *anno* 770, *Pascha mutatur apud Britones emendante Elbodu homine Dei*, and A D 811, *Elbodu* (sic) *episcopus Venedotiæ obiit*.   Anglia Sacra, 11, p 648   The date of 755 related to North Wales, and this of 770 perhaps relates to South Wales, another South-Welchman, Ieuan Brechva quotes it   Elbodu (whence Elvodugus) is no doubt Elbod Ddu, i e Elbod the Black, meaning either swarthy or black-haired   Godwin, in his book de Præsulibus, has not numbered him among the bishops of Bangor, which he might have done   He seems, by these accounts, to have been in activity towards the middle of the eighth century, and to have departed this life in the first, or ninth, or at latest eleventh year of the ninth century   But the book
of

[d] H. Llwyd, in his Commentariolum, p 85, note, observes that Caergybi was   his birthplace, and erroneously described   as his see.

of Nennius exhibits the date of A. D. 858, in its eleventh chapter, as being the third year of the existing cycle of nineteen years or forty-fifth cycle from the Nativity, and the actually current year. His professed acquaintance with the Roman annalists and chronographers, and with those of the Angli, which must include Beda himself, and his computation of it by the Paschal cycles, give to his statement of the *annus Domini* a credit, which is wanting to quotations of that æra by other editors of the Historia Britonum; and in the same sentence he correctly states, that St. Patrick visited Ireland in the twenty-third cycle[e]. Therefore I believe him not to have been far, if at all wrong; and to have written in the reign of Rodri Mawr Nennius was also an author not far advanced in years, for his magister or teacher Beulan, was not only living, but still actively influencing his conduct Therefore there appears a disparity of date between Elbod and his disciple

But I do not deduce from his words, that Nennius did learn under Elbod or Elbodu, or even that he was born when that person died Mere individuals can have only personal disciples, but founders of a rule, like Benedict, or of a doctrine, like Arius, are said to have disciples in those who espouse their systems Now St Elbod was the author of the greatest revolution known in the Welch Church between the fifth and sixteenth centuries By his influence and authority the churches of Wales were first led into conformity with the Latin communion; and the celebrated Paschal schism, after 350 years of duration, began to be abandoned But this

[e] I would not take his words (xxiii cycli decemnovennales usque ad adventum S Patricii in Hiberniam, et ipsi anni efficiunt numerum 437 annorum) so rigidly, as that Patrick came in 437, at the ex-pination of the cycle, but rather as the fact is. For if he had been as ignorant as the other British chronologists, he would probably have missed the true cycle

this change (which, contrary to the order of events in Ireland, began in the north and was most resisted in the south) was not suddenly completed, nor without violent dissensions among the clergy and people; to which cause may be ascribed the various years in which this affair is said, either generally, or with distinction of north and south, to have been decided, viz 755, 768, 770, 777   Yet though " in A D. 777, Easter was changed in South Wales" (Brut y Tywys p 474), that change was not as yet realized there in 802.   See Ussher, Index Chronol.   And the death of Elbod, in 809, is said to have been a signal for fresh disputes on the subject   Brut y Tywys p 475.   Between[f] 842 and 847, it was still a topic of private discussion, though perhaps no longer of national contention.   The memory of their old ritual was long cherished among the Welch, who erroneously imagined that their discipline had been that of St. John and the Seven Churches of Asia, and therefore paid a peculiar honour to that apostle, and sometimes called their religious peculiarities *the ordinances of John*.   See Beda, Hist Eccl iii cap 25; Probert's Triads, p 79; Triodd Doethineb Beirdd, num 219, p 314, Llewelyn Vardd, Canu y Gadvan, v 5, ab ult   In the spurious prologus, Nennius is made to entitle himself *Dei gratiâ, S Elbodi discipulus*, and I think its writer understood Nennius as I do, not meaning to thank God for giving him, personally, so learned a tutor; but to profess, that by God's grace he was reunited to the catholic communion of the west, which the Paschal differences had disturbed for several centuries   He was not a disciple of John, but a disciple of Elbod   It is observable that Nennius (as distinct from Marcus) computes his own date by the decemnovennal or Latin cycle, as that established

---

[f] Vita S Johan. Chrysostomi, cit Rice Rees on Welch Saints, p 66, note.   That Britain, not Ireland or Scotland, was the scene of those discussions, appears from the date.   For even Iona had then conformed 130 years

established in his country when he wrote; and we verify thereby the fact, that he was an Elbodian.

It is commonly said, that Nennius was a monk or even abbot of Bangor is y Coed, studied under the celebrated Dunawd Gwr or Dionotus, and was one of those who escaped from the massacre of the monks by Ethelfrid, King of Northumbria, in 607 There is not a single date in any of the various copies of the Historia, which lays claim to an earlier century than the ninth. And the chief motive for reverting to this obsolete idea is to observe, that the entire notion of his belonging to Bangor, and his title of Nennius Bannochorensis, was probably a mere delusion, founded upon his being a disciple of Elbod, who was styled Archbishop of Gwynedd, and was Bishop of Bangor Vawr in Arvon, a place remote from the abbey of Bangor is y Coed in Cheshire, or, more correctly speaking, in Flintshire I have detected no indications of his town or province.

He had for instructor a priest by name Beular, or rather Beulan[g], of whom a little more has been said than he merits. "I omitted (saith Nennius) the Saxon[h] genealogies, cum inutiles magistro meo, id est Beulario presbytero, visæ sunt." Cap 65. Some have called him Samuel Beulan ; but others will have it, that Beulan had, by his wife Læta, a son Samuel, who wrote commentaries upon Nennius Gale repeatedly speaks of this Samuel as an interpolator ; Mr Bertram of Copenhagen becomes quite impassioned on the subject; while the oracles from Mr. Pinkerton's tripod pronounce that both Nennius and Samuel are equally vile But neither father nor son have any historical existence, other than what the former owes to the

above

[g] Peu llan, *regio ecclesiæ,* or *regio culta.*

[h] That omission is supplied in some MSS. at considerable length We are probably not to understand that they were composed subsequently to Nennius, but that, being then in existence, the Saxon genealogies were not received by him into his compilation ; at least, they appear to me to mention no person subsequent to the eighth century

above text of Nennius, and both of them to notes in prose and verse
appended to one or two of the MSS. The principal record of Samuel is in the following production, contained in a Cambridge MS. of
about the beginning of the thirteenth century, marked Ff. 1 27, p. 20;
which Mr Stephenson (Pref. p xxvi.) has printed in a form meant
to be explanatory, but rather needing explanation   I believe I have
restored them to the form in which the document exhibits them.

"Versus Nennini ad Samuelem filium magistri sui Beulani presbyteri, viri reli-
giosi, ad quem historiam suam scripserat

"Adjutor benignus caiis doctor effabilis fonis',
      i Samueli
"Gaudium honoris isti katholicâ lege magni,

"Nos omnes precamur, qui ros sit tutus utatur.
      i Beulani
"Xpiste¹ tribuisti patri Samuelem, letâ matre
    i mater   i Samuel
"Ymnizat hæc semper tibi longævus Ben servus tui

"Zonâ indue salutis istum pluribus annis".

      "Versus ejusdem Nennii

"Fornifer qui digitis scripsit ex ordine trinis
Incolumis obtalmis sitque omnibus membris
En vocatur Ben notis litteris nominis quini."

Then follows the false statement about the twenty-fourth year of
Mervyn Vrych, extracted from the spurious Prologus   The initials
of the *words* in the first three lines, from *adjutor* to *utatur*, go
through the alphabet to U, and the initials of the last three *lines* go
on to Z, the change occurring at the sacred initial X   How to construe
them ; what *fornifer* can mean , what Ben⁹ means, who is so called,
and why , and what the *nomen quinum* is , are mysteries   The only
thing plain from them is the origin of Samuel's mother *Læta*, in verse 4,
                                                        lætâ

¹ Fonis for the Greek φωναις
² *Sic*   The p in Xpiste is the Greek
Rho
" This verse stands thus in the MS ,
Zonâ indue salutis istum *tis* pluribus annis
The *tis* begins a line, and the writer

thought he had closed the preceding one
with *istum salu* —   Mr Stevenson has
erroneously printed *Amen*, for annis.
⁹ Gualtherus in his Alexandreis lib. iv
says, "Successit Ben Num Moisi post
bella sepulto."

lætâ matre, his mother being glad! In spite of these obscure sayings it is not apparent to me, that Samuel, son of Beulan and Læta, is a different person from Nennius himself For the words added to cap 3 in one of Gale's MSS, wherein Samuel's name occurs (and wherein alone it occurs, so far as I am made aware, with the exception of those verses) are these. " I, the Samuel, that is to say the child, of my master, that is to say of Beulan the priest, wrote it in this page, yet this genealogy was not written in any volume of Britain, but was in the writing of   writer" Gale, p 119. Bertram, p. 187. "Samuel, id est infans, magistri mei, id est Beulani presbyteri, in istâ paginâ scripsi," &c Here we see, that Samuel is only a figurative phrase for one dedicated to divine studies from his tender years " And the child Samuel ministered to the Lord before Eli" But there is an obvious delicacy in not saying " Eli mei" instead of " magistri mei," for the priest and kind patron of Samuel was a feeble and imperfect character The youth of Nennius, and his not having passed the inferior orders, may also be inferred from this passage; as well as from cap 65 Therefore the writer of the verses could not mean Nennius, but might mean Beulan, by longævus Ben If these things be so (and I see them no otherwise) we shall be quit[k] of Samuel Beulanus, Samuel Beulani filius, Samuel Britannus, &c , and Beulan himself remains, only known for his contempt of Saxon genealogy

But another man besides Nennius, and before him, had published the Historia Britonum, Marcus the Anachoret To him that Historia is ascribed in the famous MS of the tenth century, published by Mr Gunn It was penned in A D 946, being the fifth and last year of Edmund, King of England pp 45, 62, 80 The frequent repetition

[k] See Bale, Cent fol 37, *a*, 38, *a* Med et Inf Latin vi p 417, in *Samuel* Leland de Script Brit. cap 48 Fabrich Pitseus cit *ibid*

repetition of this date, and some changes in the catalogue of cities, shew the writer to have been an Englishman or Anglo-Saxon. Mr Gunn, in his title page, says it was edited by Mark in the tenth century But Mark flourished early in the ninth, and it is only his transcriber, who gives us his own date in the tenth Marcus was a Briton born, and educated in Ireland, where he was for a long time a bishop, but he settled in France, where (for aught that appears) he ended his days Heric of Auxerre (in a prose Life[1] of Germanus, which mentions an event of A. D. 873, but was certainly published before October, 877) reports, that he and divers other persons had formerly heard, from the lips of Marcus, a narrative concerning Germanus; which Heric retails, with as little variation[m] from the same narrative in the Historia Britonum (Marcus, pp. 62–5; Nennius, cap 30–4), as could be expected in such oral repetitions Therefore the heading of the Petavian MS. derives potent confirmation, from the fact that Marcus could repeat the substance of it by heart Mr Stevenson's adverse supposition is not an absurd one, that the transcriber of A. D 946, having read Hericus de Miraculis Germani, and seen there the substance of this story, thence inferred that Marcus wrote the Historia, and so asserted it It may be replied that, if he did read Hericus he would have seen that he quoted no book, but only conversations; and that Marcus himself in those conversations, referred

---

[1] Heric also formed, out of the most ancient Life of Germanus, by his cotemporary Constantius Monachus, a poem which entitles him to a high rank among modern Latin versifiers; upon the strength of which Mr Stevenson has dubbed him Constantius Hericus Præf. p. xiii.

[m] Nothing is more natural, than for Heric, after many years, to substitute natio Britonum for the phrase, so strange to his ears, of regio Porcysorum. The main discrepance is the expulsion of the tyrant, instead of the burning him with fire from heaven. It is astonishing that Gale should annotate "Vide Ericum in Vitâ Germani, quem hæc ex Nennio sumpsisse constat," when the contrary is declared in such very express terms.

referred to no such historical work, but to the original sources of it "The aforesaid bishop, whose probity whosoever hath experienced will by no means hesitate to believe his words, assured me, with the addition of an oath, that these things were contained in *Catholicis litteris* in Britanniâ" But the words *litteræ Catholicæ* do not apply to such a compilation as this, but to the *acta* or *gesta* of their saints, which were preserved in particular churches

However, there are broader reasons to be considered, than the mere assertion of the MS The Historia is the work of a Briton None other is likely to have been in possession of so many British traditions; and the Irish, in particular, seem to have held[n] opposite traditions Besides, he plainly signifies himself such, in a phrase which the Anglo-Saxon scribe cannot have introduced, where he quotes British legends "ex traditione *nostrorum veterum*" Marcus, p 53 Yet the work of this British man is that of an Irish author, addressing himself peculiarly to the Irish people, and exclusively Irish in the religious part of his feelings This appears in his notices of Irish history; in his copious notice of St Patrick; but chiefly and most demonstratively in the fifty-third page of Marcus[o] There the epochs of Patrick, Bridget, and Columkille, the three patrons of all Ireland, are commemorated; whereas the whole work does not contain the name of David, Iltutus, Dubricius, or any British saint whatsoever. Nothing can be more certain than the author's close connexion with Ireland This truth was appreciated, or perhaps was known, by those transcribers[p] who assigned the Historia to Gildas Hibernicus; for its author, though not an Irishman, was really an Hibernian Gildas, or man of religion and learning But all

[n] For they derived the Britons from Britan Maol, son of Fergus Red-side, son of Nemedius.

[o] Cap 11, Gale, 16, Stevenson.
[p] See Casimir Oudin, Script. Eccl. ii p. 73.

all the premises are true of Marcus, who was *natione Brito*[q], *educatus vero in Hiberniâ*, and had been an Irish bishop. For though Heric's words, "ejusdem gentis episcopus" are equivocal, the doubt is solved by those of the Ekkehards or Eccards of St Gallen[r]. "Marcus *Scotigena episcopus* Gallum tanquam *compatriotam suum* Româ rediens visitat" So that if we determine to reject Marcus, the alleged author of this production, it will only be to seek for some other man precisely corresponding in circumstances Nennius, on the other hand, is neither recorded, nor doth he seem, to have had connexion with Ireland; he was not an Irish religionist, but an Elbodi discipulus, and he refers to the scripta Scotorum Anglorumque as to things equally foreign to himself

We have now to compare the date of Marcus with that of the Historia After mentioning *Britannia insula*, Heric proceeds to mention the holy old man Marcus, a bishop of the same nation, who was by birth a Briton, but was educated in Ireland, and, after a long exercise of episcopal sanctity, imposed upon himself a voluntary pilgrimage, and having so passed into France, and being invited by the munificence of the pious King Charles, spent an anachoretic life at the convent of Saints Medard and Sebastian, a remarkable philosopher in our days, and of peculiar sanctity Eccard Junior explains to us that his pilgrimage was to Rome, and that on his return from thence he visited the Abbey of St Gall His sister's son, Moengal, accompanied him, whom they afterwards named Marcellus, as a diminutive from Marcus At the request of Grimaldus the Abbot of St Gallen, and at the persuasion of his nephew, he consented to

tarry

[q] Hericus de Mirac Germ ap Labbe, Bibl Manuser 1, p. 555

[r] Ekkehardus Junior de casibus Monast Sangallensis ap. Goldasti Rerum Alamannicarum, tom 1 p 12 In Ekkehardi Minimi Vita Notkeni, cap 7, *ibid* p 230, there are similar words

tarry there, which raised a mutiny among their servants, who desired to return home   But they pacified their retinue by distributing among them the bishop's money, mules, and horses   The commencement of this sojourn fell between A D 841 and the June of 872[s], such being the limits of Grimald's abbacy   After a time Marcellus was made master of the abbey school and of the boys who were training up to the monastic life, including Notkerus, who was afterwards called Balbulus, in which situation he distinguished himself in music and other sciences   But Marcus afterwards seceded to the abbey of St Medard at Soissons   At the time, between 473 and 477, when Hene was writing this, Marcus was no more; for Labbe's reading, *exercebat ritum*, though changed by the Bollandists to *exercet*, is confirmed by " multis coram referre *solitus erat*," by the phrase *nostro tempore*, and by the description of him as having then been " sanctus *senex*." But his entire sojourn at St Gallen succeeded his sojourn at Rome   And his journey to Rome was undertaken " post *longa* pontificalis sanctitatis exercitia;" the commencement of which exercitia could not, canonically, have preceded the completion of his thirtieth year; but cannot, according to the laws of probability, be fixed to its earliest possible epoch   From all which circumstances, it is by no means improbable, that the birth of Marcus ascended into the eighth century

Such

[s] Ratpertus de Monast S Gallensi, pp. 6–9, *ibid*   Notker the Lisper was placed under Marcellus, when a boy. But Notker died in 912, *nimiâ ætate ingravescente,* and *in senectâ bonâ plenus dierum beato fine deficiens,* consoling himself with the reflection that " man's days at the most are an hundred years "—Ecclus xviii. 9. Therefore I place his birth at least eighty years before, or in 832, and if he was a boy of fifteen when Marcellus took him in hand, the latter was master of the abbey school in 847   If Notker died at 85, 84, 83, &c., we shall draw so much nearer to 841, our chronological limit   But he could scarcely be appointed, before his uncle and he had made some considerable sojourn at the abbey. See Ekkehardi Minimi Vita Notkeri, cap 32

Such being the chronology of Marcus himself, we require the date of the book ascribed to him   Here it must be observed, that during and before the first half of the ninth century, the æra of Christ[t] was recently introduced and ill understood, among the British and Irish , whereat we need not complain, seeing how imperfectly it was worked out by Beda himself   " The Christian æra (saith Mr. Carte) was not then, at its first coming into use, so well understood as it hath been since" Their use of the two Christian æras or years of redemption, viz the Nativity and the Passion, sometimes one, sometimes the other, and sometimes both, increased the confusion of their Dominical dates   But the plain root of the evil was, that they did not know, and could not tell, what year of our Lord the current year was   If the Christian æra were now of recent introduction, seldom mentioned, and not to be found in one book out of a thousand, few of us could tell what year thereof it is.   It would be a fact of learned and not obvious attainment, and was more so to those whose learning was scanty   They knew how many years the reigning prince had reigned; but they did not know what year of Christ that was   So the English transcriber of Marcus gives us his date sufficiently, viz , the *quintus Eadmundi regis Anglorum*, but absurdly adds that it was A D P 946 and A D N 976; and twice again states, that it was 547 years after A D P 447, which makes[u] A D N 1024   Yet this imbecility does not affect the date, which is consistently given   Marcus nowhere gives an *express* date, that we can convert into the *Annus Domini*   But we have his assertion that,

" from

---

[t] Upon this subject see the learned preface to the Ogygia, and O'Conor in Script. Rer Hib. xi p. 20   And, for specimens of absurd anachronism in that æra, see Gale's second appendix to Nennius. p 118, and the Æræ Cambro-Britannica an-nexed to Moses Williams's edition of Lhwyd's Commentariolum

[u] According to his computation, which allows only thirty years between the Nativity and Passion

"from the time when the Saxons came into Britain, unto the fourth year of King Mervyn, 428 years are computed," being in truth about fifty-one years too many Now the fourth year of Mervyn Vrych, or 822, was no epocha, either in general or local history; and no motive can be conjectured for his computation stopping at that year of the reign, except that it was the then current year We must, therefore, dismiss entirely his miserable attempts at Christian chronology, and take the plain fact, that he was writing *quarto Mermeni* [*Mervini,* Nenn] *regis.* p. 53 Therefore the book was in progress of composition in the year 822, which agrees sufficiently well with what we know of Marcus It equally agrees with the date' of 820 *et deinceps,* assigned to Gildas Hibernicus The Historia seems to have been originally composed, whilst a certain Fernmael, son of Tudor, was Lord of Buellt and Guortigerniawn, from which passage and others, I conjecture the author to have come from those parts of Wales, and to have had some acquaintance or connexion with that descendant of Vortigern All copies agree that Fernmael was eleventh in descent from Pascent, youngest son of Vortigern Therefore if we suppose Pascent's son, Briacat, to be born at the time of Vortigern's death, which Owen calls 481, and Blair 484, and we may call 480, then Fernmael's birth, at thirty years to the generation, will fall upon 780, and the forty-second year of his life will coincide with 822 Therefore this date, which our ignorance when Fernmael lived and died deprives of any direct utility, seems at least to be consistent with the *quartus Mervini regis,* or 822 It is remarkable, that while Nennius retains the assertion that Fernmael was actually reigning (*regit modò*) the text of Marcus exhibits *regnavit* p 78 Nennius, cap 52 But that is the handywork of the scribe of 946, who was particularly tenacious of his own date, and would not have Fernmael for his
contemporary

' Cave de Script Eccles ii, p. 16, ed. 1745

contemporary The year 822 is, therefore, the lowest date of the original Historia. But it is also the highest, unless we are disposed to look for some other nameless Brito-Hibernian, anterior to Marcus, as a tortoise for the elephant That such a one may have existed is, of course, possible; but perhaps criticism, having found exactly what it wants, will do better to acquiesce

It results, that Marcus compiled this credulous book of British traditions, for the edification of the Irish, *circ* A. D 822; and one Nennius, a Briton of the Latin communion, republished it with additions and changes, *circ* A D 858. We should, however, keep in mind, that we have not the text of Marcus upon which Nennius worked, but a text which was tampered with about ninety years after Nennius wrote, and, therefore, the Marcian text of the Petavian MS. is not, in every trifling instance where they differ, the oldest of the two

But another edition or revisal of the Historia succeeded that of Nennius; and its author has introduced his own date with precision, yet with an utter ignorance of the Christian æra What more he introduced besides the date does not appear, but perhaps nothing of moment It occurs in the enumeration of the six ages of the world, that precede the British history "From the Passion of Christ 800 years have elapsed, but from his Incarnation 832, down to the thirtieth year of Anarawd, King of Mona, who now rules the region of Venedotia or Gwynedd"[w]" In truth Anarawd or Honoratus, son of Rodri Mawr, reigned over Gwynedd from 876 to 913, and the thirtieth year of his reign was the year 906, and the same in which that scribe was writing, being just seventy-four years out of his reckoning Brut y Tywys p 482–5 And as he republished with an interpolated

[w] "Wenedociæ regionis, id est *Guer-met,*" apud Gale, malè. In the Cambridge manuscript, Ff. 1 27, it is Guernet.

terpolated date the Nennian edition, so (we have seen) did another person, in A D 946, send forth again the older Marcian edition

It will strike every reader, that this work was peculiarly dealt with It was treated as a sort of common land, upon which any goose might graze Mere transcribers seem to have played the editor, if not the author The dates thrice introduced by the Petavian scribe are not annexed in the way of colophon, but are interwoven into the solid text, in complicated sentences, and with elaborate miscalculation Nennius himself no where states, that he was republishing, with a limited amount of change and addition, the Historia of the Brito-Irish compiler It seems to have been regarded as the album or common-place book of Britannia, to which any one might laudably add such passages as he knew of; and elucidate or obscure, according to his ability, what he found already there It was no rule to expunge what the predecessors had stated, even when stating the contrary, from which cause inconsistencies disfigure the text So Marcus having stated that St Patrick went to Ireland in A.D 405, Nennius has faithfully republished it; but almost in the next sentence of the same chapter he states, that there were twenty-three decemnovennal cycles unto St Patrick's advent, in a true sense, I believe, but certainly in one utterly discordant with the previous text In like manner, Fernmael, son of Tudor, continued to be living and reigning in 858, and in the thirtieth of Anarawd, or 906, and was not killed off till 946. This common-place book of Britain seems rather analogous to the histories about St Patrick, which Tirechan has strung together under the name of *Annotationes* The Historia Britonum merits such a title equally well, and the like of it is signified by its writers in their phrase of *Experimenta*, cap 1, 3, and 12, Gale, pp 48, 53, Gunn This state of the case tends to absolve Nennius from the charge of imposture in appropriating the labours of another, for the mode of proceeding with this book seems

to

to have been understood. In his Apology he speaks of his own work or publication, as being one, " quod multi doctores atque librarii scribere tentaverint," authors and transcribers classed together, and complains, that "nescio quo pacto difficilius reliquerint," each transcribing doctor leaving it less intelligible than he found it; which misfortune he ascribes to frequent wars and pestilences, instead of the more proximate cause, viz : the accumulated blunders of ill-instructed men. He apologizes for presuming " post tantos hæc tanta scribere," and he can scarcely apply the words " post tantos" generally to the historians of Britain, for he had complained that there were next to none; but the " *hæc* tanta" is to be taken literally for the very book in hand In his concluding chapter he mentions his omission (at Beulan's suggestion) *to write* the Saxon genealogies, seemingly of earlier date than his own, " nolui ea scribere," adding, " but I have written of the cities and remarkable things of Britain, as other writers wrote before me" The same observations apply to this passage Lastly, when he says of a Trojan genealogy[x], " hæc genealogia non est scripta *in aliquo volumine Britanniæ*, sed in scriptione scriptoris fuit," he clearly means " in any previous copy or edition of this *book of Britain,*" and in fact it is absent from the text of Marcus. The Irish version now published, is actually entitled, in the Books of Lecan and Hy-Many, " Leabhar Breathnach," i e. *Volumen Britannicum,* or Book of Britain. The vast avidity with which Geoffrey of Monmouth was received by the world prevents our wondering that transcripts of this book had been multiplied within about thirty-six years, as seems to have been the case.

This condition of affairs offers a great excuse for our Irish translator, if he be found to introduce many things illustrative of British history, that were not in any transcript of the Latin book from
which

[x] Cod Bened in Gale, Var Lect. p. 119.

which he professes to take his own, or as Nennius hath it, "in aliquo volumine Britanniæ." It were indeed more hard to excuse him, for giving expressly "as recorded by Nennius" certain details of Irish history which Nennius did not record, but for the great likelihood that the same thing happened in Ireland as in Britain, viz: that the successive editorial transcribers of the Irish Nennius inserted words of their own. In which case, that false heading may not have been the work of any man who knew it to be false. There is some reason to think, that the Irish translation was made by a certain Guanach, and that the text, as now printed, was revised by a later hand. For after a translation of considerable closeness and fidelity from Nennius, it is written, "it was in this way that our noble elder Guanach deduced the pedigree of the Britons, from the chronicles of the Romans." Infra, p 37. But a work, actually commencing with the words "Ego Nemnius [Nennius] Elvodugi discipulus," could never mean to rob that author of his matter, and falsely ascribe it to a certain Guanach. It is, therefore, apparent that Guanach was either the Irish translator, or an editor of the translation, and that this annotation proceeds from an editor of junior date and calling him his elder.[v] The "chronicles of the Romans," employed by Guanach, are nothing more than the Latin copies of the Historia Britonum, which is stated by Nennius himself (in the Irish translation, as well as in the original, of his Apologia) to be partly collected from the Annals of the Romans and the Chronicles of the Saints. The earliest MS of the Irish Nennius, so far as is known to its editor, is of the twelfth century. But the epoch

---

[v] According to O'Reilly (*Irish writers*, p. 120) there is a memorandum prefixed to the copy of the *Leabhar Breathnach*, in the Book of Hy-Many, which says that Nennius was the author, and Giolla Caoimhghin (who died in 1072) the translator. This would furnish increased evidence to the employment of a plurality and succession of hands. The Book of Hy-Many has passed into the hands of some private collector, and is no longer accessible.—(*T*)

epoch of the translation does not seem to transpire from any internal evidence.

A. H.

P. S — A partial elucidation of the very obscure verses in page 10 is due to the kindness and ingenuity of the Rev. S. R. Maitland, who observes that the last line, if we read it " En vocatur Ben notis litteris nominis *quinis*," not *quini*, will apply to the name Benlanus (though not to Beulanus), which spelling is mentioned in Fabricius, and that of Benlanius in Pitseus. For Benlanus, understanding (notis, i. e subintellectis) the other five letters, lanus, will leave Ben ; or, by changing notis to motis, i e removed, the sense becomes more explicit Indeed the MS, which has Beulani plainly written in red ink, has another *u* written above in black ink, and the red *u* scored under with black; which shows that attention had been attracted to the first syllable of the name Benllan signifies Caput Ecclesiæ. Mr Maitland thinks that magni in the second line had its origin in magri, the contraction of magistri. And also that the inexplicable word formifer should be formiter, i e. " recté, secundum formam vel legem." Du Cange. Upon the whole, a more obscure and enigmatical composition will scarcely be met with.

A. H.

* It is written in the MS. qni; and trinis, tnis.

Leabhar breaᴄhnach annso sis.

Leabhar breathnach annso sis.

Ego nemnnṡelbḋuġ ḋiṗcipuluṗ aḣ-
qua excerpta ṗcṁpeṗe cupauṁ .ɪ. ṗo ḋeɪṫniɡeṗ
ɡo ṗa ṗɡṁbaɪnḋ aṗaɪle ḋo lamaṗta, ⁊ me Nenam-
nip ḋiṗɡɪbaɪl Cluḋaɪɡ, ḋaɪɡ ṗo ḋeṗmaɪḋ beaṗ ⁊ aɪmeaɡna ɪn
ceneoil

[a] *Liber Brittanicus.*—Leaḃap bṗeṫnaċ, "the British Book;" this title is given to the following work in the Books of Lecan and Hy-Many. The initial words, Ego Nemnɪuṗ Cloọuɡɪ, are a fac-simile from the Book of Lecan.—(*T.*)

[b] *Ego Nennius, &c.* Numnus, D., Nein-nius, B., Nemonus, D., *a secunda manu.*—(*T.*) The following are the true words of the Apologia Nennii : "I Nennius, a disciple of St. Elbod, have taken the pains to write certain extracts, which the dulness of the British nation had cast aside, because the doctors of the island Britannia had no skill, and did not place any commemoration in books. But I have collected all that I could find, as well out of the Annals of the Romans, as out of the chronicles of the holy Fathers [that is, Jerome, Eusebius, Isidore, Prosper, in-terpol. in some MSS.], and from the wri-tings of the Scots and Angles, and from the traditions of our own ancestors (*ve-terum*); which thing (*quod*) many doctors and scribes have attempted to write, but have left more difficult ; I know not wherefore, unless it be on account of the frequent mortalities and continual disas-ters of war. I beg that every reader, who reads this book, will forgive me, that I have ventured to write such considerable things as these after such considerable per-sons, like a chattering bird, or like some incompetent judge (*invalidus arbiter*). I defer to him, who may know more in this branch of knowledge than I do." That

LIBER BRITANNICUS[a].

GO Nemnius[b] Elvodugi[c] discipulus, aliqua[d] excerpta[e] scribere curavi, i. e. I have taken pains[f] to write certain fragments, and I am Nenamnis[g] a disciple of Eludach[h], because the folly and ignorance[i] of the nation of Britannia have given to oblivion the history and origin of its first people, so that they are

reterum means ancients or ancestors, not aged men, appears from cap. 13, Gale and Bertram, 17 Stevenson. I conceive *invalidus arbiter* to mean a judge, acting without the limits of his jurisdiction.—(*H.*)

[c] *Elvodugi.*—Elodugi L. See the Introductory Remarks, p. 6.—(*T.*)

[d] *Aliqua.*—ᚕᚔᚂᚔᚐ, D., for *alia;* Irish scribes frequently write Latin words in conformity with the rule of Irish orthography called Caol le caol, ᚐᚌᚒᚄ ᚂᚓᚐᚈᚐᚅ le leaᚈan; of this we have another example here in the word cuᚇᚐᚒᚔ for *curavi.*—(*T.*)

[e] *Excerpta.*—Oᚔᚄᚉᚓᚇᚈᚐ, L., Oᚔᚄᚓᚇᚈᚐ, B.—(*T.*)

[f] *I have taken pains.*—Oeᚔᚈᚔᚒᚅᚔᚌᚔᚒᚄᚐ, B., Oeᚔᚉᚑᚇᚔᚌᚓᚇᚐ, L., from ᚈᚔᚌᚔᚅᚔᚅᚓ, care, diligence.—(*T.*)

[g] *Nenamnis.*—Nemnuᚄ, B. The Book of Lecan does not give the name in this place.—(*T.*)

[h] *Eludach,* or Eludag. ᚓᚒᚂᚑᚈᚐᚌ, B. ᚈᚓᚄᚉᚔᚒᚂ ᚐᚔᚂᚓ ᚄᚑᚈᚐᚔᚌ, L.—(*T.*)

[i] *Folly and ignorance.*—ᚈᚓᚐᚄ ᚐᚌᚒᚄ ᚐᚓᚅᚓᚉ, B., where ᚐᚓᚅᚓᚉ is probably for ᚐᚔᚅᚈᚓᚔᚉ or ᚐᚔᚅᚓᚑᚂᚐᚉ, ignorance. ᚈᚐᚄ ᚐᚌᚒᚄ ᚓᚌᚅᚐ, the habit and knowledge, D. The Latin copies read "quæ hebetudo gentis Brittanniæ," &c. The reading in the text is from L.—(*T.*)

ceneoil bpeatainia peancapa ⁊ bunadana na cetdaine cona pilit [i ɼopaiɾme] a ɼ̇ṁbandaib nac a lebɼaib Meɼɼe iṁopɼo, ɼo comɾinoilɼa na pencapa puapapa in analɾaib na Roman, aɼ na cɼoinicib na ɼɼuiɾhe noeb .i. Aɼɼuioiɼ ⁊ Cipine ⁊ Eaɼebii, in analɾaib Saxan ⁊ Ʒaeoil, ⁊ ina ɼuapaɼ o ɾionocol aɼ n-apɼa pein.

II bpiɾonia inɼola a bpiɾinia pilio Ipocon dicɾa eɼc .i. o bpiɾan paɾeɼ iniɼ bpeɾan, no aɾbepaio apaile ʒomao o'n ɾi aɼ bpuɾaɼ no paɾea .i. an ceo conɼal ɼo bai a Romancaib Albion iṁopɼo ɼo b'e ceo ainm inoɼi bpeaɾan Ocht ceo mile cemeno ɼoɾ inoɼi bpeaɾan Da ceo mile cemino ina leɾeɾ Ocht pɼim-cath-ɼaca xx inoɾe, ⁊ aɾe anoɼo a n-anmanda [do ɼeiɼ eolach bɼeɾan].

Caeɼ

ᴶ *Commemorated* —Ɑ ɼopaiɾhmeach, L Omitted in D. "Neque ullam commemorationem in libris posuerunt"—(*T*)

ᵏ *Brought together.* — Comɾhiniol, L, Coimɾinoiliuɼ, B, "concervavi"—(*T*)

ᴸ *Isidore* —The Irish always corrupted foreign names Thus Isidore is Eɼuioiɼ, L., Eɼɼuioiɼ, B Jerome is Cipene, L, Cipine, B (the C having probably been aspirated to represent *Hieronymus*) Eusebius is Ebɼeniuɼ, L, Euɼebiuɼ, B The readings of D are given in the text The Latin adds *Prosper*, who is not mentioned in any of the Irish copies.—(*T*)

ᵐ *Gaels* —It is worthy of note that the Latin word *Scoti* or *Scotti*, is uniformly translated Ʒaeoil, Gadeln or Gaels, throughout this work. Ʒaeoil is the name by which the Irish and Highlanders of Scotland designate themselves to the present day The Welch also call themselves Gwydhil, and their country Tir Gwydhil.—(*T*)

ⁿ *Tradition* —The word ɾionocol is here evidently used to represent the Latin "ex *traditione* veterum nostrorum" It signifies, *conveyance, handing down from one to another, tradition;* the verb ɾiodnacaim, *to deliver,* is in use in modern Irish Ɑ h-analɾaib Ʒaeioel puapuɼ o ɾhionocol h-e iaɼ n-apɼandaib, L Ocuɼ ina ɼuapuɼ o ɾionacul aɼ n-aɼɼaɾa, B —(*T*)

ᵒ *Britonia insola* —This section is repeated twice in L first at the beginning, and again near the end; the readings of the former of these copies will be denoted by L¹ those of the second by L² The second alone contains the list of cities —(*T.*)

ᵖ *A Britinia* —Omitted L¹; a bɼeɾone, L², a bɼiɾone, B —(*T*)

ᑫ *Dicta est* —Daeanɾa, D, the Irish equivalent word put instead of the Latin. —(*T*)

ʳ *Or some say   named* —Omitted,

are not commemorated[j] in writings nor in books   But I have brought together[k] the histories that I found in the Annals of the Romans, out of the chronicles of the learned saints, viz : Isidore[l], and Jerome, and Eusebius, in the Annals of the Saxons and Gaels[m], and what I discovered from the tradition[n] of our own old men

II. Britonia insola[o] a Britina[p] filio Isocon dicta est[q], i e   the island of Britain is named from Britan, or some say that it was from one Brutus it was named[r], i e the first consul[s] that was of the Romans; but Albion[t] was the first name of the island of Britain   Eight hundred thousand paces *is* the length[u] of the island of Britain.   Two hundred thousand paces *is* its breadth.   Eight and twenty principal caers [or cities] *are* in it, and these following[v] are their names, according to the learned of Britain[w].—

Caer-Gortigern

B L². No aобepaiо apoile ir o бpicuр po h-ainmnizeaо, L'.   The name of Britain is here derived from Brutus the first Roman consul, but in another part of this work it is said to have been derived from Brutus, son of Silvius, son of Ascanius, son of Æneas —(*T.*)

[s] *The first consul.*—*First* is omitted in all the Latin copies, and rightly   For L Junius Brutus is not here alluded to, and consul is said, in a general way, for a person of power and dignity   See Mr Gunn's note vi. p. 94, &c.; Du Cange in *Consul* and *Consulatus;* Galfrid. Monumet 1 cap 13, x. cap 4, &c. Marcus Anachoreta, p 80. Tywysawg appears to be the British equivalent, Bruttus Tywysawg o Ruvein, Hanes Grufudd ab Cynan, p 584.   The fable of Brute the Trojan was not devoid of a slight foundation in the Roman tra-

ditions, for Junius Brutus was descended from a Trojan who accompanied Æneas, but the name Junius, rather than the surname Brutus, was Trojan.   See Dion Hal. Ant. iv. cap. 68 —(*H*)

[t] *Albion.*—This name does not occur in any of the Latin editions   It is not of Latin origin, and has no reference to the Latin word *albus,* nor is its origin and meaning known   It does not appear that the Greek geographers gave any explanation of their word Ἀλουΐων —(*H*)

[u] *Eight hundred   .   .   the length —* Omitted, B L² Cemenо omitted B L'. L² —(*T*)

[v] *These following —*Ir iaо po rir. B L' (*T*)

[w] *According to the learned of Britain —* This clause occurs only in L²   B adds here, cecuр —(*T.*)

Caeꞃ Ꝡoꞃꞇiꝷeꞃnn. Caeꞃ Ꝡꞃuꞇuꞃ. Caeꞃ Menceꞃꞇ. Caeꞃ Luill Caeꞃ Meꝺꝷuiꝺ. Caeꞃ Colun. Caeꞃ Ꝡuꞃꝺiꞃꞇ. Caeꞃ Abꞃoꝷ. Caeꞃ Caꞃaꝺoꝷ Caeꞃ bꞃuꞇ Caeꞃ Maꞔoꝺ. Caeꞃ Lumainꝺ. Caeꞃ Oen. Caeꞃ Iꞃanꝷin Caeꞃ Pheuꞃ. Caeꞃ Ꝺon. Caeꞃ Lonmopeꞃuiꞃc. Caeꞃ Ꝡꞃuꝷan Caeꞃ Sanꞇ Caeꞃ Leꝷun. Caeꞃ Ꝡmiꝺiuꝺ. Caeꞃ bꞃeaꞇan Caeꞃ Leimꝺoin Caeꞃ Penꝺꞃa Caeꞃ Ꝺꞃuiꞇhꝷolꝷoꝺ Caeꞃ Luiꞇicoiꞇ Caeꞃ Uꞃnochꞇ Caeꞃ Eilimon.

III Iꞃiꞇ imꝺa a caꞇhꞃaca ꝷenmoꞇa ꞃin, [ꝺiaꞃmeꝺe a ꞃaꞇa ⁊ a caiꞃꞇel cumacꞇa] Ceiꞇhꞃi cenela aiꞇꞇꞃeabaiꝺ iniꞃ bꞃeaꞇan, .i. Ꝡaeꝺil ⁊ Cꞃuiꞇhniꝷ ⁊ bꞃeaꞇnaiꝷ ⁊ Saxain Inꝺꞃi Ꝡuꞇa ꞃia aneaꞃ, Abonia amaꞃ eꞇaꞃꞃu ⁊ Eiꞃe .i. Manainꝺ, ⁊ inꝺꞃi Oꞃcc ꞃia aꞇuaiꝺ [Aꞃenaiꝺ h-Eꞃe ꞃeac iniꞃ bꞃeaꞇan ꞃiaꞃ ꝺeaꞃ co ꝼoꞇa.

---

a *Caer-Gortigern.*—The names of the cities are given in B thus C Goirthirgirnd C Gutais, C Luaill, C Meguaid, C Colon, C Gustint, C Abroc, C Caratoc, C Graat, C Machuit C Ludain C Ceist, C Giraigon, C Pheus, C Mincip, C Leomaiphuise, C Grucon, C Sent C Legion C Guent, C Breatan, C Lerion, C Pensa, C Gluteolcoit, C Luiteoit, C Urtach, C Cehmeno The names, as given in L², are C Gorthigearnd C Gutais, C Luaill, C Meagnaid, C Cholon, C Gustaint, C Abrog, C Charadoc, C Graad, C Macaid C Lugain, C Cose, C Girangon, C Peus, C Minchip, C Leoanaird puise C Grugoin, C Sent, C Legion, C Guhent, C. Bretan, C Lergum, C Pennsa, C Druithecolcoit. Luiteoit, C Urtocht, C. Ceilimon Most of these variations are doubtless attributable to error or ignorance in the transcribers, but they are worth preserving as it is possible sometimes, even from a blunder, to obtain a clue to the true orthography—(*T*)

The twenty-eight caers do not occur till the close of the Latin Nennius, but, in the corresponding place of the MS of 945 from Marcus, the names of thirty-three cities occur, p 46 As Nennius gives one name Verulam which is not in that copy, the latter must have given six which Nennius did not receive, but the confusion of texts prevents my saying which they were Caer Guiroc and Caer Teim (Thame?) were two of them Archbishop Usher has commented upon this catalogue in his Primordia, pp 59, 65, or 33–5 of edit 2, (Works, vol v p 82). The Irish translator has, in some cases, left it difficult to identify his names, and, on the other hand, many of the explanations by Llwyd,

Caer-Gortigern[x]. Caer-Grutus Caer-Mencest Caer-Luill Caer-Medguid. Caer-Colun Caer-Gusdirt Caer-Abrog Caer-Caradog Caer-Brut Caer-Machod. Caer-Lunaind Caer-Oen Caer-Irangin Caer-Pheus Caer-Lonmoperuisc Caer-Grugan Caer-Sant Caer-Legun Caer-Gnidiud Caer-Breatan Caer-Leiridoin Caer-Pendsa Caer-Druithgolgod Caer-Luiticoit Caer-Urnocht. Caer-Eihmon

III Numerous are[y] its caers [*or cities*] besides these; innumerable its raths [*or forts*] and its fortified castles[z] Four races inhabit the island of Britain, viz. the Gaels, the Cruithnachs[a] [*Picts*], the Britons, and the Saxons The island Guta[b] *is* to the south of it, Abonia[c], i e Manaind, is on the west between them and Eri [*Ireland*], and the islands of Orck *are* to the north of it Eri extends beyond the

Camden, Ussher, and earlier authors, are light and vague conjectures —(*II.*) See Additional Notes, No. 1

[y] *Numerous are —*Ipic (or Ipao, B L²), a synthetic union of the assertive verb, ip, *it is*, and iao or iac, *they* See O'Donovan's Irish Grammar, p. 161.—(*T*)

[z] *Innumerable   . castles.*— This clause is inserted from B L² L². reads ocup no bo oiaipmichi a pacha, &c The Latin reads "In ea sunt viginti octo civitates et innumerabilia promontoria, cum innumeris castellis ex lapidibus et latere fabricatis." It is evident, therefore, that the Irish translator understood *promontoria* to mean *raths* or *forts,* for nothing was more common than to convert a promontory into a fort, by casting up an intrenchment across the narrow neck that united it to the main land. The remains of many such are still to be seen in Ireland. The word *promontorium,* however,

is sometimes used to denote *a mound* or *hill,* and therefore may have signified also a fort of the ordinary kind See Du Cange, *in voce* —(*T*)

[a] *The Cruithnachs —*The well-known Irish name for the Picts or ancient inhabitants of Scotland Duald Mac Firbis considers the word as synonymous with the Latin *Pictus.* See Additional Notes, No. II —(*T*)

[b] *Guta —*Ꝿuceao, B Ꝿuechpia, L. —(*T*) Guta is the Isle of Wight, in Latin Vectis or Vecta, in Welch Gwyth The Latin Nennius says, "Gueid vel Guith, quod Latinè *divortium* dici potest" However Ynys Gwyth is simply the Channel Island "Three principal islands are united to Ynys Prydain, Orc, Manaw, and Gwyth" Triads 3id series, No 67 —(*II*)

[c] *Abonia —*Ꝼbon Mania, B Ꝼbonia, L The Isle of Man —(*T*) See Additional Notes, No. III

ṙoṫa   ḃenaiḃ imoṙṙo iniṙ ḃṙeaṫan ṙeaċ h-Eṙinn ṙaeṙ-ṫuaiḋ co
cian]

Ḋiaiṙmiṫe [ono] a loċa [aguṡ a ṙṗoṫa] Ḋa ṗṙim-ṙṙuṫh inḋṫi
i Ṫamuṙ ⁊ Saḃṙainḋ; iṡ ḟoṙṙa-ṙaiḋein ṙeolaiḃ longa ⁊ ḃaṙica
iniṙ ḃṙeaṫan [co ṙeḋaiḃ ⁊ go mainiḃ inḋṙe ḃṙeaṫan uile]

Ro linṙaṫ ḃṙeaṫain in n-iniṙ uile aṙ ṫúṙ ḋia clanaiḃ, o muiṙ
n-Iċṫ co muiṙ n-Oṙc [⁊ ṙo allaḃ ⁊ aiṙḃeṙcoṙ]

IV Iaṙ n-ḋiliṅḋ ṫṙa ḋa ṙanḋaḃ in ḋoman a ṫṙi [iḋiṙ ṫṙi
maccu

---

[d] *But the island . north east.*—This
passage is inserted from B L. The verb
benaiḃ signifies to draw out, to prolong
O'Reilly (Dict v beanaim) quotes a passage from the Leabhar Mac Partholain,
in which the word is applied to drawing
a sword —(*T*)

[e] *And its rivers.*—Inserted from B L.
as is also the expletive particle ono, *vero,
autem* —(*T*)

[f] *Sabraind.*—The Sabiina or Severn
King Locrine (saith the Galfridian Chronicle) deserting his wife Gwenddolen, took
a concubine, Estrildis, by whom he had
a daughter, Sabrina But Gwenddolen,
levying war against her husband, slew
him, and flung the two ladies into the
river, the younger of whom bequeathed to it her name Lib ii. cap 5 But
Havren (the name of Sabrina and of the
Severn) signifies *a harlot;* and therefore
cannot refer to the innocent daughter,
but relates to Estrildis herself This
renders it probable (as Mr Carte suspect-
ed) that the fable, in its existing shape,
was composed in Armorica , where the
word havren does not seem to be known

The real etymology of the Sabriana or
Sabrina, Celticè Havren, is, no doubt, from
hau, (Irish, ṡam or ṡampa) summer;
part of the adjoining country being
called the Gwlad yr Hav, or Land of
the Summer, Anglicè Summersetshire
This passage of the Historia is taken
from the words of Gildas in cap i, including that melancholy word which is
omitted in the Irish, " per quæ *olim* rates
vehebantur," &c —(*H*)

[g] *Upon them.*—Iṡ ḟoṙṗu-ṙṗḋein, B Iṡ
ṙoṗo-ṙaiḋe, L. " It is upon these very
rivers " The emphatic ṙaiḋein or ṙiḋein,
gives an additional force, " upon the *self-
same* rivers " The word is not to be found
in the common dictionaries, but it is the
ancient form of ṙean or ṙan Ḟoṙṗa-ṙiḋein
would be written, in the modern Irish
language oṗṗa-ṙan —(*T*)

[h] *With the jewels . Britain.*—
This clause is added from B L The word
uile occurs only in L. The Latin copies
read " per quæ olim rates vehebantur ad
portandas divitias pro causa navigationis "
—(*T.*)

the island of Britain far to the south-west But the island of Britain extends beyond Eri far to the north-east[d]

Innumerable are its lochs and its rivers[e]. Two principal rivers *are* in it, viz Tamus and Sabraind[f]; it is upon them[g] that the ships and barks of the island of Britain sail, with the jewels and wealth of the whole island of Britain[h]

The Britons at first filled the whole island with their children, from the sea of Icht[i] to the sea of Orck, both with glory and excellency[j]

IV. Now after the deluge the world was divided[k] into three

parts ,

---

[i] *From the sea of Icht, &c.*—Understand from the British channel, or sea of the Portus Iccius or Itius, to that of Orkney. "Dathi went afterwards, with the men of Erin, across Muir n-Icht (sea of Icht) towards Leatha (Brittany)," &c—*Genealogies, &c. of Hy-Fiachrach,* p 19 So in the Duan Albanach, verse 10, (Pinkerton's Inquiry, ii 321), "Britus tar n'huir n'Icht" Where Adamnan speaks of St. Germann's crossing the Sinus Vallicus (Channel of Gaul) to visit Britain, he gives a Latin equivalent Vita Columb ii cap 34. The Portus Iccius has been confounded with Calais and Boulogne, but is now conjectured to be the same as Vissent or Witsant, a neighbouring village. Some of the Latin copies have it, "from Totness to Caithness," but others have no termini assigned.—(*H*)

[j] *With glory and excellency.*—This passage is inserted from L.—(*T.*)

[k] *Was divided.*—Ro panoao, B L In the text oa or oo, as it is often spelt,

is used for no.—(*T.*) This chapter is made up from chapters 13 and 14 of the old Latin editions, at pp. 53-4, of the Marcian. The three sons of Alanus are, Ihisicion, Armenon, and Neugio or Negno. The former is probably Tuiscon, father of Mannus, from whom all the Germans derived themselves Tacit Germ cap 2 For he is said to be father of Francus and Alamannus, for which latter our translator has improperly put Albanus Armenon relates to Armenia, Negno or Neugio (here Negua), from whom he derives the Saxons, to I know not what. It is scarcely worth while to mention the Rugn. Cibidus or Cebidus (here Cebetus) to the Gepidæ. Walagothus (here Uilegotus) either to the Balti or Amali (Visigoths or Ostrogoths), but nothing indicates to which In the genealogy from Alanus to Lamech, inclusively, the Latin copies give twenty names, and the Irish only sixteen, but it is useless to supply such mere gibberish.—(*H*)

maccu Nae] ı Eopaıp ⁊ Affraıc ⁊ Appıa Sem an n-Aᴘıa Cam
an Affraıc Iafeth an Opaıp Ire cet fear do ril Iafeth taınıc
[ap tur] ın n-Eopaıp ı Ɑlanıur co n-a tpı macaıb ,ı Ipacon ⁊
[Ꝺothur no] Apmıon ⁊ Neᵹua Ceıthpı meıc aᵹ Ipacon ,ı Ffan-
cur, Romanur, bpıtur, Ɑlbanur Apmon [umoppo] u meıc laır,
Ꝺotur, Uıleᵹotur, Cebetur, bupᵹanour, Lonᵹobapour Tpı
meıc Neᵹua, Uandalur, Saxo, [boarur Saxo mac Neᵹua ır uada
ataıd Saxaın] bpıtur, ımoppo, ır uad bpeataın, mac raıdeın
Ipacoın, [mıc Ɑlanı], mıc Fethuıp, mıc Oᵹamaın, mıc Taı, mıc
buıob, mıc Semoıb, mıc Ɑtact, ınıc Ɑoth, mıc Ɑbaıp, mıc Roa,
mıc Appa, mıc Iobaıth, [mıc Ioban], mıc Iafeth, mıc Nae, [mıc
Laımıach] Ir amlaıd rın at pıadap a peancaraıb bpeatan

V Inıırdap ımoppo a n-analtaıb na Romanach Ɑenıar
ınac Ɑnacır do tıachtaın ıap toᵹaıl Tpaı co h-Eataıl, ⁊ tuᵹapdaıp
Lauına

¹ *Between* ... *of Noe* —Inserted from
B L —(*T*)

ᵐ *At the beginning* —Inserted from L¹.
where the words are in a different order
Ceo fear thanıc ın n-Eopaıp ap tur do
ril Iafed In B the clause ap tur do ril
Iafed is omitted There are two copies
of this section in L , both very corrupt
—(*T*)

ⁿ *Gothus or Armıon* —The words Ꝺo-
chur no are inserted from L¹ Ɑpmenon,
B Ɑpmen, L¹ Ɑpmeon, L²—(*T*)

ᵒ *Now* — Umoppo, inserted from B
L¹ L² —(*T*)

ᵖ *Burgantus* —bupᵹanour, B L¹ L²
Pungandtus in D is evidently an error of
the scribe for Burgandtus The Latin
copies of Nennius read *Burgoandus* —(*T*)

ᑫ *Boarus* . . . *descended* This

clause is inserted from B L¹ L² Its
omission in D is an evident error of the
scribe —(*T*)

ʳ *He is the son of Isacon* —Saıdeın
is for pıı or é pen, which signifies *he*
The insertions between brackets in the
Irish text are from B and L Ioban,
son of Japheth, occurs in B. L¹ and L²,
but Jobaıth is omitted. In the Latin
copies Semoıb is called Simeon, and Mair
is inserted between him and Aurthach,
who is evidently the same as Athact (or
Ethacht, B L¹ or Echtaeht, L²) in the
Irish copies, whose name is written *Etha*
in some MSS. of the Latin Between
Asra, or Ezra, and Iobaath, the Latin
copies insert Izrau and Baath, which are
most probably corrupt repetitions of Ezra
and Jobaath.—(*T*)

parts; between the three sons of Noe[l], viz.: Eoraip, Affraic, and Asia. Sem *was* in Asia, Cain in Affraic, Jafeth in Eoraip The first man of the race of Jafeth that came into Eoraip at the beginning[m] was Alanius, with his three sons; viz · Isacon, Gothus or Armion[n], and Negua Isacon had four sons, Francus, Romanus, Britus, Albanus Now[o] Armion had five sons, Gotas, Uilegotas, Cebetus, Burgandus[p], Longobardus Negua *had* three sons, Vandalus, Saxo, Boarus It is from Saxo, son of Negua, that the Saxons are *descended*[q]; but it is from Britus the Britons *come* He is the son of Isacon[r], the son of Alanius, the son of Fethuir, the son of Ogaman, the son of Tai, son of Boidhbh, son of Semoibh, son of Athacht, son of Aoth, son of Abar, son of Raa, son of Asra, son of Iobaith, son of Ioban, son of Japeth, son of Noe, son of Laimiach Thus it is recorded in the histories of Britain[s].

V. Furthermore[t] it is related in the Annals of the Romans[u], that Aenias the son of Anacis arrived in Italy after the destruction of Troy, and took to wife Lavina the daughter of Ladin, son of Pan, son

of

[s] *The histories of Britain* In the Latin, " Hanc peritiam [*al.* genealogiam] inveni ex traditione veterum, qui incolæ in primo fuerunt Brittanniæ "—(*T*)

[t] *Furthermore* —Here we revert to the third chapter of Nennius, from which chaps v, vi, vii., above are translated Essare is Assaracus, and Airic or Airictondus is Erichthonius Britan exosus is that same son of Silvius (viz Brutus), who, as the Druid had prophesied, would be "exosus omnibus hominibus" The account in Marcus, pp 48, 50, is different, and a more obscure composition—(*H*)

[u] *Annals of the Romans* —The whole of this and the next two chapters occur twice in the Book of Lecan; the readings of the two copies shall be referred to as L¹ and L². In B. and L¹ the reference to the British histories is separated from the foregoing chapter, and united to this, L² reads Cio tra acht ir amlaio feo atfiaoar Sencur Breatan a n-anoalaib na Roma The reading of D, which is followed in the text, agrees with the Latin copies, in which the history of Æneas is begun thus: "In annalibus autem Romanorum sic scriptum est. Æneas post Trojanum bellum,' &c.—(*T*)

Lauina ingean Laoin mic Puin mic Pic mic Saouipno ⁊c   iap
mapbao Tuipno ⁊ iap n-eg Laoin in pig po gab Aeniap pigi
Laoianoai, ⁊ po cumoaigeo in cathpaig Albalonga la h-Apcan
mac Aeniapa, ⁊ tugapoap peitig, ⁊ pugapoaip mac oo i Siluiup,
[po cetoip]

Siluiup iapoain tugapoaip peitig, ⁊ po ba toppach, ⁊ aopet
oo Apcan bean a meic [oo beit toppach, i] alachta, ⁊ po paio
teachta co [a] mac co po paioio a opuio oo tabaipt apomepa
ap a mnai co peapao in po ba mac, nó'n po ba h-ingean po teacht
Oo coio in opuio, ⁊ aobept [iap tiáčtian] in opuio pe h-Apcan
conao mac oo bai 'na bpoino; ⁊ aobept comao tpen, ⁊ co muipi-
peao a athaip ⁊ a mathaip, ⁊ comao mipgneach la cach.   Mapb
tpa a mathaip oia bpeith   Ro h-ainmnigeao poin .i. bpitip, ⁊ po
h-aileo iapoain

VI   bpitup [oin] mac Silui mic Apcain mic Aeniapa mic
Anacip, mic Caipen, mic Eppaic, mic Tpoip, mic h-Aipic, mic
louip, mic Oapoain, mic lob, mic Sapoain, mic Ceil, mic Polloip,
mic Gopaptpeip, mic Meppaim, mic Caim, mic Nae, pilii male-
oicti pioenteip patpem, mic Nae

Tpop

ᵛ *Shortly after*—Added from B, L²
reads (instead of pugapoaip mac oo .i.
Siluiup), innipteap cop b'i mathaip Seil-
biup po cheooip.—(*T*)

ʷ *It was told*—B L¹ and L². read (instead of aopet) innipteap.—(*T*)

ˣ *Was pregnant*—The words oo beit
toppach, i aic added from B and L².
The Latin copies read here "nunciatum
est *Æneæ*, quod nurus sua gravida esset," but one of the MSS collated by Mr.
Stevenson has *Ascanio* instead of *Æneæ*,
in conformity with the Irish version,

which is manifestly the true reading   In
L¹. and D, the word used to denote pregnant is aluicta, which in B. is given as
an explanation of toppac.—(*T*)

ʸ *Druid*—Nennius says, cap 3. "ut
mitteret *magum* suum.—(*T*)

ᶻ *After his return*—Added from B L¹.
L².—(*T*)

ᵃ *That it was a son*—Cop bo mac po
bai ina bpoino, L¹ L²   Ro boi mac po
boi in a bpoin, B.—(*T*)

ᵇ *Hated by all*—Nennius says, "et erit
exosus omnibus hominibus."—(*T*)

of Pic, son of Saturn, &c. After having slain Turn, and after the death of Ladin the king, Aenias took the kingdom of Ladianda, and the city of Alba-longa was founded by Ascan, son of Aenias, and he married a wife, and she bare him a son, viz Silvius, shortly after[v]

Silvius afterwards married a wife, and she became pregnant, and it was told[w] to Ascan that his son's wife was pregnant[x]; and he sent a messenger to his son *to say* that he would send his Druid[y] to give an opinion on his wife, to know whether it was a son, or whether it was a daughter she was about to bring forth The Druid went, and after *his* return[z] the Druid said to Ascan, that it was a son[a] that was in her womb, and said that he would be powerful, and that he would kill his father and his mother, and that he would be hated by all[b] In fact his mother died in giving him birth He received a name, viz. Britus, and afterwards he was nursed[c]

VI Now[d] Britus *was* the son of Silvius, son of Ascan, son of Aenias, son of Anacis, son of Caipen, son of Essarc[e], son of Tros, son of Airic, son of Idus, son of Dardain, son of Jove, son of Sardain, son of Ceil, son of Polloir, son of Zororastres, son of Mesrain, son of Cam (filii maledicti ridentis patrem), son of Noe[f].

Moreover,

[c] *He was nursed*—The Latin is, " et nutritus est filius, et vocatum est nomen ejus Bruto "—(*T*)

[d] *Now*—Ò in inserted from L¹. Ona, B Òno, L².—(*T*)

[e] *Son of Caipen, son of Essarc*—These two generations, inserted between Anchises and Tros in all the Irish copies, do not occur in the Latin. Essarc, is evidently Assarracus, and is written Araree, B. Arainʒ, L¹. Arainʒ, L².—(*T*)

[f] *Son of Noe*—In the remainder of the genealogy from Tros to Noah, the Irish copies differ from each other and from the Latin They agree, however, in tracing the pedigree to Cham or Ham, and not to Japhet, as in the Latin copies. L¹ gives the pedigree thus, mic Thnoir, mic Epechtoniur, mic Òanòain, mic Ioib, mic Shaòannn, mic Ceil, mic Palloir, mic Sorerronrrnear, mic Merrain, mic Caim ercono mic Naei (i e the accursed son of Noe), mic Caimiach L². thus mic Thnoir, mic Epectoiniur, mic Òanòain, mic Ioib, mic Shaòuinn, mic Pheil, mic Phalloin, mic Sonaroirrnear, mi

F 2

36

Cpoy [ιmoppo] mac Οιριετοπουρ δα mac laιp ι llιum ⁊
Οραρcup, ιp leιp po cumδαιξεδ llιum ι. Cpoι, ιp δο po bα mac
Caιnιδoιn, αcηαιp Ρριαιm. Οραρc ιmoppo αcηαιp Capen, Caιpen
αcηαιp Οnacιp, Οnacιp αcηαιp Οεnιαρα, Οεnιαρ αcηαιp Οp-
caιn ρen, αcηαιp bpιcaιn εχορι ι. bpιcaιn mιρξnech. Ιp amlaιδ
ριn cuξαρδαιp αp ρenoιp-ne uαραl ι ξuanach, ξεmιlach bpεαcαn
α cpoнιcιb na Romanac.

Μεαρραιm, mιc Caιm εαρcoιncι, po
ηιb ιm a αcηαιp, .ι. ιm Nαε mac Caι-
mιach (ι. e Caιm the accursed, who
laughed at his father, ι e. at Noe, son of
Lamech) B gives it thus, mιc Cηopιp,
mιc Θρεccoнι, mιc Dαρδαιн, mιc loιb,
mιc Sacuιpb, mιc Palloιp, mιc Sopaρ-
cpeρ, mιc Μερραιm, mιc Caιm ερcoιncι
po bιch ιmm [a] αcηαιp, ι ιm Noe,
mιc Caιmpιach ⁊pl Where the description of Caιn is the same as in L² for
bιch is an evident error of the scribe
for ηιb.

In D, instead of the clause describing
the curse of Ham, which in the other
copies is given in Irish, the same thing is
given in Latin as in the text The words
mιc Nαε are repeated unnecessarily, and
are therefore omitted in the translation
Mr Stevenson mentions three MSS of the
Latin, which have a genealogy of Brutus
and of Tros in the margin, and in which
the genealogy of Brutus is made to end
thus "filii Jupiter de genere Cain
[Cam?], filii maledicti videntis et ridentis patrem Noe"

The Latin copies make Tros the son of
Dardanus, son of Elise, son of Juvan, son

of Japhet It will be seen, however that
the Irish version is more nearly authentic,
for classical authorities make Tros the son
of Erichthonius, son of Dardanus, son of
Jupiter, son of Saturn, son of Cœlus It
would seem probable also that the text
was corrupted by British transcribers,
anxious, for the honour of their country,
to deduce the ancestry of Brutus from the
race of Japhet rather than from the accursed Ham. Pallor, the father of Ceil
(who is evidently Cœlus) is probably a
corruption derived from the genitive case
of Tellus —(T)

ᵍ Moreover —Ιmoppo, added from B,
L¹ and L² —(T)

ʰ Airic-tondus, i. e. Erichthonius, mac
Θρεccaιнι, B , mac Οιριετoнιup, L¹ L¹
omits this name —(T)

ⁱ Asaracus, i e Assaracus, Οραιριc, L
Οραρc, B Homer gives Tros three sons,
(Iliad υ 230)
Τοῶα δ' Ἐριχθόνιος τίκετο Τρώεσσιν ἄνακτα
Τρωὸς δ' αὖ τρεῖς παῖδες ἀμύμονες ἐξεγένοντο,
Ἴλος τ', Ἀσσάρακός τε, καὶ ἀντίθεος Γανυμήδης
D reads corruptly Ilam, both as the name
of the son of Tros and of the city. B.,
L¹, and L² read Ilium in both places,

Moreover[g], Tros, son of Airictondus[h], had two sons; viz, Ilium [Ilus] and Asarcus', it was by him [i e. by Ilus] was founded Ilium, i e Troy[j], he had a son, Laimidoin, the father of Priam. Assarc, moreover, *was* the father of Capen, Capen *was* the father of Anacis, Anacis the father of Aenias[k], Aenias the father of Ascan, the grandfather of Britan exosus, i e of Britan the abhorred[l]   It was in this way that our noble elder Guanach[m] deduced the pedigree of the Britons, from the Chronicles of the Romans

VII

but L² instead of ir leir ro cumoaiӡeo, reads n-il ir e ro cumoaiӡ —(*T*)

[j] *Troy.*—Τρος, H. Τροι, B. L'. Αpochachaip na Τpe, L² —(*T*)

[k] *Aenias* —Homer makes Æneas give this genealogy thus

Ἰλος δ' αὖ τεκεθ' υἱὸν ἀμύμονα Λαομέδοντα
Λαομέδων δ'ἄρα Τιθωνὸν τίκετο, Πριαμόν τε
Λάμπον τε, Κλυτίον θ', Ικεταονά τ', ὅζον Ἄ-
ρηος
Ἀσσάρακος δὲ Κάπυν   ὁ δ' ἀρ' Ἀγχίσην τεκε
παῖδα
Αὐτὰρ ἐμ'' Ἀγχίσης   Il ύ. 236, sq —(*T*)

[l] *The abhorred* —Sean-ucuip ὁριτι εχorri in τ-Αρcain rin, .i ὁριτan mironech, B, which may be translated thus "the grandfather of Britus exosus, i e of Britain the abhorred, was that Ascan."—(*T*)

[m] *Our noble elder Guanach.*—In B and L this reference to Guanach, and the Chronicles of the Romans, is written so as to relate to what follows, not to what precedes, but the words ir amlaio rin and the sense of the whole passage are inconsistent with this supposition, and therefore D has been followed Guanach is not mentioned in the Latin copies of Nennius; and therefore, as well as from his being called "*our* noble

elder," we may perhaps conclude that he was an Irish historiographer, but no such Irish writer is known, nor is the name Irish, unless we suppose it to be the same as Cuan or Cuana (in the genitive case Cuanach), which was a common name among the ancient Irish   An historiographer of this name is frequently cited in the Annals of Ulster, thus "sic in libro Cuanach inveni," at A. D. 467, 468, 471, 475, 552, 600, 602, 628, or "sic est in libro Cuanach," A. D. 610, or "ut Cuana scripsit," A D. 482, 489, "ut Cuana docet," A D. 598; ' secundum librum Cuanach," A D. 543. As no reference to Cuana occurs in these annals after the year 628, Ware supposes the writer so named to have flourished about that date, and Colgan doubtingly identifies him with S Cuanna, Abbot of Lismore, Ware's Writers, by Harris, p 26; Colgan, Acta SS ad 4 Feb, p 251. All this, however, is simple conjecture, for we know nothing of the writer quoted in the Annals of Ulster except his name, unless he be the same as the Cuana, who is called "Scriba Treoit," or of Drogheda, and

VII Iap n-il bliaᵭnaib iapᵭain, ᵭo peip papᵭine in ᵭpnaᵭ, ᵭo
pala ᵭo bpiṫup beiṫ ag paiȝᵭeopaċt a piaᵭnaipi in piȝ ɪ a
aṫaip, co pamȝ in ṫ-paiȝeᵭ uaᵭa a ṫoll apiaċ in piȝ, ⁊ ȝop
mapb in piȝ po cetoip ainnpin ɪ a aṫaip pein, ⁊ co po h-inᵭapbaᵭ
pon [o'n] h-Eaṫail iapṫoin pop inᵭpib mapa Coppian, ⁊ inᵭapbaᵭ
Ȝpeiȝ h-e ap na h-inᵭpib a ȝ-cinaiᵭ Cuipnn ᵭo mapbaᵭ ᵭo Aeniap.
Canȝ a Fpancaib iapᵭain, [ocup] po cumᵭaiȝeᵭ leip Copinip, [⁊
nip puilnȝeaᵭ anᵭpin h-e], ⁊ canȝ iapᵭain a n-inip bpeatan, copo
ȝab a piȝi, ⁊ co po h-ainminȝeᵭ in inip [uaᵭ], ⁊ ȝo pop lin ᵭia claino
⁊ ᵭia cineᵭ poin   [Aȝup conaᵭ h-epin] topaċ a ṫpebe, ᵭo peip
na Roman

ᵭe Riȝaib Roman [anᵭso].

VIII Ianup ɪ Ian piȝ na n-Epepᵭa, ipe ceᵭ piȝ [po ȝab] Romanchu, [aȝup] ip uaᵭ ainminȝep nil enaip   Saᵭupnᵭ iapᵭain
Ioib iapᵭain   Dapᵭan mac Ioib iapᵭain. Piccup mac Ioib [iap-
ᵭain]   Funup [mac Piccup] ɪɪ [bliaᵭain]. Laᵭin a mac .l.
[bliaᵭan]. Aeniap a iii   Apcan a xxxiiii. Siluiup xii. cona po
mapb

---

whose death is recorded A. D. 738 (Annals of Ulster), 739 (Tighernach).—(T.)

ⁿ His father.—For ɪ a aṫaip, B and
L¹. read .ɪ Siluɪ   L² adds after a aṫaip,
ɪ Siluiup.—(T)

ᵒ The temple.—Collapach, the hollow
of the temple, in front of the ear.—(T)

ᵖ Died—his own father.—The reading
here followed is that of B   D reads
aȝup ni apaenlop ȝop mapb in ṫ-aṫaip
annpin. L¹ reads aȝup ni poenlup co po
mapb a aṫaip annpin   And L² aȝup
nip aenlop cop mapb a aṫaip annpin
The meaning of all these readings seems

to be, ⁊ ni po an lap co po mapb, &c,
"and he stopped not (was not restrained)
until he had killed his father."—(T)

ᵠ By Aenias.—L¹ adds here, aȝup ɪ
pean-choċat ȝpec aȝup Cpoiann pein,
and L² adds, ocup ip e cocaᵭ ȝpec ocup
Cpoianᵭaċ co pin anuaip.—(T)

ʳ Torinis.—Coip-inip, B   Caṫaip ɪ.
Copinip, L². The city of Tours is intended
—(T)

ˢ He was not suffered to remain there.—
This clause is added from L¹ and L².—(T)

ᵗ Here.—Anᵭpo is added from B and L¹.
—(T.) The first paragraph of this chap-

VII After many years subsequently, according to the prophecy of the Druid, it happened to Britus to be shooting arrows in presence of the king, i e his father[n], and an arrow from him pierced the temple[o] of the king, and the king died immediately there, i e his own father[p]; and afterwards he was driven out of Italy, to the islands of the Torrian [Mediterranean] sea, and the Greeks expelled him out of the Islands in revenge for Turnn, who had been killed by Aenias[q]. After this he came to France, and Tonnis[r] was founded by him, and he was not suffered *to remain* there[s], but came afterwards into the island of Britain, where he took possession of the kingdom, and the island was named from him, and became full of his children and his descendants And thus was it first peopled, according to the Romans

Of the Kings of the Romans here[t]

VIII. Janus, i e Jan, King of Eperda[u], was the first king that took possession of the Roman territory, and it is from him was named the month of January[v] Saturn after *him* Joib [Jove] after *him* Dardan, son of Joib, after *him* Piccus, son of Joib, after *him* Faunus, son of Piccus, *reigned* twenty years[w] Latin, his son, fifty years. Aenias, three years Ascan thirty-four years. Silvius twelve, until

ter, down to "son of Aenias," does not appear totidem verbis in any part of the original The residue is gleaned from the fourth, fifth, tenth, and twenty-eighth chapters of Nennius —(*H*)

[u] *Eperda* —Eᴘᴘeᴘᴅᴀ, L² Hesperia was an ancient name of Italy. Hor Od lib. iii. 6, v 7; lib iv 5, v 38 —(*T*)

[v] *January*—Mic Ianuaip, L².; the other copies all read mi enaip. The words po ᵹab, are inserted from B. L¹. L². Aᵹuᴘ from L¹ L².—(*T*)

[w] *Twenty years* —L¹. and L². read cpica bliaᴅan, i. e. thirty years. The insertions between brackets in this passage are from B, L¹., and L². Instead of Aeniaᴘ a.[i. e annos] iii. Apcan a ᵹᵹᵹiiii, the other copies read Aeniaᴘ iii. bliaᴅan, Apcan, ᵹᵹᵹiiii Other variations in orthography are not worth noting —(*T*)

mapb a mac, ıı ᵇbpıτuρ, [amaıl ρo paıτρeamap] Sıluıuρ aınım
ᵹach pıᵹ o ροın [ılle], co τοpacht Romaʟ mac ριᵒeın Rea Sıluıae
ınᵹeıne Numıτaıρ, mıc Pροıc Sıluıı, mıc αuenτıne Sıluıı, mıc αρ·
aımuʟıρı Sıluıı, mıc αᵹρaıppae Sıluıı, mıc τıbeρne Sıluıı mıc αl·
baıı Sıluıı, mıc αρcaıı Sıluıı, mıc Pορτaıme Sıluıı; bρaτhaıρ ρıᵒe
⁊ bρıτıρ ᵒa mac Sıluıı mıc αρcaıı mıc αeıııaρa ıaτ.

Pορτοmuρ a ρıᵹı Romaıı xxxıx. bρıτaρ a ρıᵹı [ınoρ·ı] bρeaτaıı
xxx bʟıaᵒaıı Pορτοmıορ a bρaτhaıρ a ρıᵹı Romaıı uτ ᵒıxımuρ
heıle ρaᵹaρτ ba plaıth mac n-Iρρıaτheʟ, ⁊ ıρ'na coımaıρ ρuᵹaᵒ
ınᵒ aıρe ıρın ᵒaıρe, ⁊ τuᵹaᵒ ρo ceᵒoıρ

O ᵹabaıl bρıτaıρ ᵹo ᵹabaıl Cρuıthneach a n-ınoρıb Oρcc
ᵒ. cccc [bʟıaᵒaıı] ; ⁊ ρo ᵹabρaτaıρ ın τρıan τuaıρᵹeaρτach
                                                            ınᵒıı

 ˣ *As we have said* —Added from B
Lᴵ Lᴸ —(*T*)

ʸ *Of every king from that time* —In ceτ
pıᵹ, B ; but the other MSS. all read ᵹach
oı cac pıᵹ Ille is added fıom Lᴵ —(*T*)

ᶻ *Numitor, son of Pıoc Sylvius.*—Heım-
τuıρ. Numıτuıρ, B Lᴵ Lᴸ *Pıoc*, for
Procas, it will be obseıved that ın the
Iıısh form of the propeı names the termı-
nations *as, es us,* are unıfoımly omıtted
Lᴵ ıeads Pıc heıe, and Lᴸ Pıcc, ınstead
of Pρoıc, which, howeveı, is evıdently
the true ıeadıng. The lıst of the Sılvıı
which follows appeaıs to have been taken
fıom the Chıonıcon of Euscbıus, although
with some vaııations and ınaccuracies.
The genealogy, as gıven by Euscbıus, is
as follows Numıtor, son of Procas Sylvıus, son of Aventınus Sylvıus, son of
Aremulus S., son of Agrıppa S, son of
Tıbeıııus S, son of Caıpentus S., son of

Capıs S, son of Athys or Egyptıus S, son
of Alba S, son of Æneas S, son of Pos-
thumus S, brother of Aıcanıus and son
of Æneaı See also Dıon Hal and Lıvy.
Our Iıısh author has omıtted three gene-
ratıons betwcen Tıberınus and Alba, and
ıt ıs pıobable that *Ascan Sylvıus,* whom
he makes the son of Posthumıus, ıs a mıstake of the scrıbe (although ıt occuıs ın
all the MSS.) for *Æneas* He also makes
Sylvıus Posthumıus the grandson, ınstead
of the brotheı, of Ascanıus, foı which
there ıs no authoıity, although Lıvy
makes Posthumıus the son, not the brother, of Ascanıus —(*T*)

ᵃ *Thıty-nıne yeaıs* —Probably a mıstake for *twenty-nıne,* which ıs the number
of yeaıs assıgned to the ıeıgn of Posthu-
mus by the Chronıcon of Eusebıus. Lᴸ.
ıeads τρıcha bʟıaᵒaıı aıle, *thırty other
yeaıs,* but omıts the next clause contaın-

until his son, viz, Britus, killed him, as we have said[x]   Silvius was the name of every king from that *time*[y] until the coming of Romul, himself the son of Rea Silvia, daughter of Numitor, son of Proc Silvius[z], son of Aventine Silvius, son of Aramulus Silvius, son of Agrippa Silvius, son of Tibern Silvius, son of Alban Silvius, son of Ascan Silvius, son of Postam Silvius, he and Britus were brothers, *and they were* the two sons of Silvius, son of Ascan, son of Aenias

Postomius *was* sovereign of the Romans, thirty-nine *years*[a]. Britus was sovereign of the island[b] of Britain thirty years   Postomios his brother, was sovereign of the Romans as we have said   Heli, the priest, was prince of the children of Israel[c], and it was in his presence the ark was taken into captivity[d], and was brought back soon after.

From the conquest of Britus to the conquest of the Picts in the islands of Orc[e], were nine hundred years, and they took the northern[f] third

ing the length of the reign of Britus, so that there is reason to suspect that a line may have been overlooked by the scribe, and that the thirty *other* years really belonged to the omitted reign of Britus.—(*T.*)

[b] *Island* —ιnσρι is added from B.—(*T*)

[c] *Children of Israel*—Flaith mac naρo Iρραel, B   Flaith ρoη macaιb h-Iρραel, L'. Iomaρ ρa h-uaρal ρacaρτ ρoη macaιb Iρραel, L[2].—(*T*)

[d] *Into captivity*—This clause relating to the captivity of the ark is omitted in all the MSS except D, but it occurs in the Latin "quando regnabat Bruto in Brittannia, Heli sacerdos judicabat in Israel, et tunc archa Testamenti ab alienigenis possidebatur;" and these words seem taken from the Chronicon of Eusebius, where the capture of the ark is thus recorded "Mortuo Heli sacerdote archa testamenti ab alienigenis possidetur."—(*T*)

[e] *Orc*—Єριcoαo, L' Oρcατ, L[2] Oρecατ, B.—(*T*)

[f] *Northern*—In the Latin "in sinistrali plaga Britanniae." Anciently the north was considered to be on the left hand side, and the south on the right, looking east, as the ancient Christians did in prayer   And the same language is still used in Irish, for τuαιo is properly the left hand, as well as the north, and oeaρ signifies the right hand and the south. See Ussher, Primordia, pp 80, 1021.—(*T*) Likewise in British go-gledd, quasi-sinistralis, the north, and deheu-barth, pars dextra, the south.—(*H.*)

ınoṗı bṗeaṫan aṗ eᵹın o bṗeaṫnaıb, ⁊ aıṫṫṗeabaıṫ ann coṗ anoıu

Ᵹaeoıl ıaṗoaın ṗo ᵹabṗaṫ ın ṗano ceṫna na Cṗuıṫneaċ, ⁊ oo ṗonṗaṫ aenṫaıᵹ ṗe Cṗuıṫnıb a n-aᵹaıo bṗeaṫan

Saxaın ṗo ᵹabṗaṫ ıaṗoaın ınıṗ bṗeaṫan a n-aımṗıṗ Maṗcıaın ın ṗıᵹ Ᵹoṗṫıᵹeaṗnn [ona] ba ṗıᵹ bṗeaṫan ann ı Luċṫ ṫṗı lonᵹ ṫanᵹaṫaṗ aṗ ın Ᵹeaṗmaın ım oa bṗaṫaıṗ ı Oṗṗ ⁊ Aıᵹeaṗṫ ᵹo ṗo oıcuıṗṗeaṫ bṗeaṫnu ın-ımlıb na h-ınoṗı

oe ᵹabaıl eṗenn amaıl ınoısıs nemnus

IX. Ceıo ṗeaṗ oo ᵹab Eıṗıno ı Paṗṗṫalon cum mıle hommıbuṗ ı mıle ıṫıṗ ṗıṗṗ ⁊ mna, ⁊ ṗo ṗoṗbṗıṫeaṗ a 'n-Eıṗı na n-ıl mıleaoaıb, coṗaṗ maṗb a n-aen ṫ-ṗeaċṫmaın oo ṫam, [a n-oıᵹaıl na ṗınᵹaılı oo ṗoınoı ṗoṗ a ṗaṫaıṗ aᵹuṗ ṗoṗ a maṫaıṗ].

Nemeao

<hr>

[g] *Marcian the king*, i.e. the emperor Marcian, A D 450–457 The Latin reads 'Regnante Gratiano secundo Equantio, Saxones a Guorthgirno suscepti sunt," but some MSS read, "Regnante Martiano secundo quando Saxones, ' &c.—(*T*)

[h] *The crew of three ships.*—The story is thus told in the Latin, "Interea venerunt tres enulæ a Germania expulsæ in exilio, in quibus erant Hois et Hengist, qui et ipsi fratres erant."—(*I*)

[i] *Island.*—Na chṗıoċ, Lᵉ The repetition in the Book of Lecan ends here —(*T*)

[j] *The first man, &c.*—See Additional Notes, No IV

[k] *With a thousand men.*—Aᵹuṗ mıle maılle ṗṗıṗ, B L Keating quotes Nen-

nius, out of the Psalter of Cashel (which, very probably, contained a copy of this work), as his authority for the number of Partholan's companions After giving the names of Partholan's wife and three sons, he says that there came with him an army of a thousand men, mıle oo ṗluaᵹ ı maılle ṗıu, oo ṗeıṗ Nennıuṗ, amaıl leuᵹṫoṗ a Pṗalṫaıṗ Caıṗıl, "according to Nennius, as we read in the Psalter of Cashel" Mr Dermot O'Conor, in his translation of this passage, has transformed Nennius into *Nunus*.—(*T*)

[l] *They multiplied.*—Ṗoıṗbṗeaṗṫaṗ, B. Ṗoıṗbṗeaoaṗ, L.—(*T*)

[m] *In one week.*—This event, as Keating tells us, from the Psalter of Cashel, took place 300 years after the arrival of Par-

third part of the island of Britain by force from the Britons, and they dwell there unto this day.

Afterwards the Gaels took the same division *occupied by* the Picts; and they made a treaty with the Picts against the Britains.

The Saxons afterwards took the island of Britain in the time of Marcian the King[g]. But Gortigearn was then King of Britain, i. e. the crew of three ships[h] came out of Germany under two brothers, viz., Ors and Aigeast, so that they drove the Britons into the borders of the island[i].

OF THE CONQUEST OF ERI, AS RECORDED BY NENNIUS.

IX. The first man[j] that took Eri was Parrtalon, with a thousand men[k], i. e. a thousand between men and women; and they multiplied[l] in Eri, into many thousands, until they died of a plague in one week[m], in judgment for the murder that he committed on his father and on his mother[n].

Nemed

tholan; see also the Annals of the Four Masters, who give A. M. 2820 as the date of this plague, and 2520 as the date of Partholan's arrival. Keating fixes the arrival of Partholan in the twenty-second year before the birth of Abraham, on the authority of an ancient poem, or 300 years after the Deluge. It never seems to have occurred to these ancient historians to explain how all this minute knowledge about Partholan and his followers could have been preserved, if they had *all* perished in the plague. O'Flaherty (Ogygia, p. 65) places the birth of Abraham in A.M. 1949, and the arrival of Partholan in A. M. 1969, on the authority of the Annals of Clonmacnois, and Giolla Coemhan's poem beginning Epe app, of which there is a copy in the Leabhar Gabhala.—(*T.*)

[n] *In judgment . . . . . his mother.*—This clause is added from L. The double parricide of Partholan is not mentioned in the Latin copies. Keating speaks of it thus: Ap i cuip umma o-cainig Papthalon a n-Epinn ɼne map oo maɼḃ ɼe a aɼaip, aʒuɼ a ṁaɼaip, aʒ iappuiṫ piʒe o'a ḃɼaɼaip, ʒo o-cainiʒ ap ceicioḃ a ɼionʒaile, ʒo painiʒ Epe. ʒonaṫ aipe pin oo cuṁ Dia plaiʒ ap a pliocc, pep maɼḃaṫ naoi mile pe h-aoin peaceṁain oioḃ, a m-ṫeinn Coaṁ. "The cause why Partholan came into Eri was because

Nemead iarsain ros gab [sen in Eirinn] Mac saidein araile Agnomain; ro aittreab a sil re ré cian [in Eirinn], co n-deacadar co h-Earbain, for teitead [in cissa] na Muiride i na Fomorac.

Uiri bullorum i Firbolg iardain 7 Uiri Arminorum, i. Fir Gaileoin, 7 Uiri Dominiorum i. Fri Domnann, sil Nemid annsin.

Ro gab in n-Eirind iardain Pleber Deorum i Tuata de Danann

he had killed his father and mother, in order to obtain the kingdom from his brother, after which murder he departed, and came to Eri, but on this account God sent a plague on his race, by which were killed nine thousand men of them in one week, at Ben Hedar," now Howth The Four Masters, ad A M. 2820, place this event "at the old plain of Moynalta, on the Hill of Edar," or Howth,—for sen maig Ealta Edair, and they add, that a monument in memory of it was erected at Tallaght, near Dublin, thence called Tamleacht muintire Partholan, the Tamhleacht, or plague monument of the posterity of Partholan —(*T*)

[o] *Eri* —The words sen in Eirinn are added from L The arrival of Nemed is dated by the Four Masters, A M 2850, and by O'Flaherty (Ogygia, p 65) A M 2029 Gab, when followed by a preposition, has a neuter signification —(*T*)

[p] *In Eri.*—Added from B L —(*T*)

[q] *The tribute* —Added from B L For an account of the Irish traditions about the Nemedians, their contests with the Fomorians or mariners, and the oppressive tribute imposed upon them, see Keating's History of Ireland O'Flaherty dates the flight of the Nemedians, A M 2245. The Fomorians were "men of the sea," for so the name signifies, i. e they were *pirates*. Keating says As aire do gairti Fomoraig diob, .i. o na m-beit ag deunam fogla ar muir. Fomoraig. i fo muirib "For this reason they are called Fomorians, because they used to commit robbery on the sea *Fomorians*, i e on the seas"—(*T*)

[r] *Viri Bullorum* —Uirnd, in D, is a manifest error of the scribe for Uiri. D is the only one of the three MSS. that gives the Latin names here *Bullum*, in the Latinity of the middle ages, signified, according to Du Cange, *Baculum pastoris*, which suggests a derivation of the name Fir-Bolg, that the Editor has not seen noticed Keating derives it from bolg, a leathern bag, or pouch, and others think that this colony were Belgæ. See O Brien's Dict *in voce* bolg, and O'Flaherty (Ogygia, p 73), who fixes the date of the arrival of the Fir-Bolg, A M 2657. The Four Masters place this event under A. M. 3266 —(*T*) See Ad. Notes, No.V.

[s] *Were the race of Nemid*—Viri Ar-

Nemed afterwards inhabited Eri°. He was the son of one Agnoman; his race dwelt long in Eri[p] until they went into Spain, flying from the tribute[q] *imposed on them* by the Muiridi, i. e. the Fomorians.

The Viri Bullorum[r], i. e. the Firbolg, afterwards, and the Viri Armorum, i. e. the Fir-Gaileoin, and the Viri Dominiorum, i. e. the Fir Domnann: these *were* the race of Nemed[s].

Afterwards the Plebes Deorum, i. e. the Tuatha De Danann[t], took Ireland;

morum is a literal translation of Fir-Gaileoin, for ᵹaıllan signifies *a dart* or *spear*. (See O'Brien *in voce*). The Fir-Domnann are supposed to be the same as the *Damnonii* or *Damnonii*, and the fanciful derivation of their name given by Keating, is far less probable than that suggested by our author; although both are, most probably, wrong. Keating's account of these tribes of the Fir-Bolg is as follows. After noticing the five leaders of the Fir-Bolg, he says: Ⱥp ꝺo na τaoıpıoċaıb pe ᵹo na b-ꝼoıpnıb ᵹaıpᵹıop Ꝼıp bolᵹ, Ꝼıp Ꝺhoṁnann, aᵹuꝛ Ᵹaıleoın. Ꝼıp bolᵹ, ımoppo, o na bolᵹaıb leaᵹap ꝺo bıoꝺ aca pan nᵹpeıᵹ, aᵹ ıomċop uıpe, ꝺa cop pop leacaıb loma, ᵹo n-ꝺeunꝺaıoıp moıᵹe mıon-pᵹoꝛaċa po blaꝛ ꝺıob. Ꝼıp Ꝺhoṁnann o na ꝺoıṁne ꝺo ċoċlaıoıp an uıp pe na h-ıomċop ꝺ'ꝼeapaıb bolᵹ. Ᵹaıleoın τpa o na ᵹaıb po h-aınmnıᵹeaꝺ ıaꝺ, ꝺo b·nᵹ ᵹupab ıaꝺ ꝺo bıoꝺ a n-apm aᵹ copnaṁ caıċ an τan ꝺo bıoıp aᵹ ꝺeunam a bpeaꝺṁa, aᵹuꝛ o na ᵹaıb, no o na pleaᵹaıb pa h-aıpm ꝺoıb, po h-aınmnıᵹıoꝺ ıaꝺ. "It was these chieftains, with their followers, who were called the Fir-Bolg, Fir Dhomhnann, and Gaileoin. Fir Bolg, from the leathern bags that they had with them in Greece, for carrying mould, to lay it on the flat-surfaced rocks, so as to convert them into flowery plains. Fir Dhomhnann, from the deep pits (*doimhne*) they used to dig to obtain the mould to be carried by the Fir-bolgs. And the Gaileoin were so called from their spears; because they used to be under arms to protect them all when they were performing their task; and it was from the spears (*gaibh*), or from the lances (*sleaghaibh*) which they used as arms, that they were so called." See also the Poem beginning Ⲉpe apap na n-ıopᵹal, by O'Mulconry of Cruachain, in the Leabhar Gabhala (O'Clery's copy, Royal Irish Academy, p. 34), which was most probably Keating's authority.—(*T.*)

[t] *Plebes Deorum*, i. e. *Tuatha De Danann.*—The name *Tuatha De Danann* signifies "the people of the Gods of Danann." Danann, daughter of Dalbaoit, (whose genealogy, in thirteen descents up

nann is dib ro badar na prim eladnaig Edon Luchtenus Artifex Credenus Figalus. Dianus Medicus. Eadan [dna] filia eius .i. muimi na filid Goibnen Faber Lug mac Eithnega rabadar na h-uil-dana Dagda [mor] (mac Ealadan mic Dealbaith) in rig Ogma brathair in rig, ar e a ranig litri na Sgot

Is iad na fir seo ro brisead cath mor for na muireadaib .i. for na Fomorcaib, ⁊ cor taetsadar romra ina tor i dun ro daingean

to Nemed, is given by Keating), is fabled to have had three sons, Brian, Iuchar, and Incharba, famous for their sorceries and necromantic power, who were therefore called De Danann, or the Gods of Danann, and from them the people who venerated them received the name of Tuatha De Danann See Keating O'Flaherty dates the invasion of the Tuatha De Danann, A M. 2737. The Four Masters, A M 3303 —(*T*)

[u] *Goibnen, faber*—In B and L the trades or arts practised by these "chief men of science" of the Tuatha De Danann, are given in Irish, not in Latin as in the text, and their names are also somewhat varied Luctand saer Credne cerd Diancecht liaig. Etan, dna, a h-ingein side .i. buime na filead Goibnend goba, B Luchra in saer, agus Creidne in cerd, agus Dianceacht in liaig, agus Eadandana a ingean sin, .i. muime na filed, agus Goibneann in goba L i. e "Luchtan (or Luchra), the carpenter (or mechanic), Credne, the artist, Dianceacht, the leech (or physician), Etan (or Edandana) *was* his daughter, viz the nurse of the poets; Goibnenn, the smith" These personages (with the exception of Etan "the nurse of poets") are all mentioned by Keating Etan is thus noticed by O'Flaherty, "Etana poetria, filia Diankecht filii Asaraei, filii Nedu, Lugadii regis amita, et soror Armedae medicae, fuit mater Dalbocthii regis," &c —*Ogygia*, iii. c 14, p 179 See also the Leabhar Gabhala (O'Clery's copy, R I A) where she is thus mentioned, p. 45 Eattan baneccer ingen Diancecht mic Esairg bric, mic Neitt, and again, p 49 Eatan .i. an bainfile, matair Coirpri Airmed an banliaig di ingin Diancecht isidside —(*T*)

[v] *With whom*, i e who had a knowledge of all the arts —Occai ro badu, B Uair is aici ro badar, L This Lugh was Lugh Lamh-fhada, or the Long-handed who instituted the games at Taillten, now Telltown, in East Meath Keating makes him the son of Cian, son of Diancecht, &c See also Leabhar Gabhala, p 48, and O'Flaherty's Ogygia, part iii ch. 13, p 177 —(*T*)

[w] *Son of Dealbaeth.*—This short gene-

Ireland; it was of them were the chief men of science; as Luchtenus, artifex; Credenus, figulus; Dianus, medicus; also Eadon, his daughter, viz. the nurse of the poets; Goibnen, faber[u]. Lug, son of Eithne, with whom[v] were all the arts. Dagda the Great (son of Ealadan, son of Dealbaith[w]) the king. Ogma, brother of the king; it was from him came the letters of the Scots[x].

It was these men that defeated in a great battle[y] the mariners, i. e. the Fomorians, so that they fled[z] from them into their tower[a], i. e.

alogy does not occur in L. or B. Moꞃ is added from L. The genealogy of these chieftains is thus given in the Leabhar Gabhala (p. 48): Eochaıꝺ Ollaċaꞃ, ꝺıaꞃ bo h-aınm an Ꝺaᵹꝺa, mac Ealaċaın, mıc Ꝺealbaoıċ, mıc Neꞇ, mıc Ionꝺaoı, ceıꞃe ꝼıcıꞇ blıaꝺan. "Eochaidh Ollathar, who had the name of the Dagda, son of Ealathan, son of Dealbaoth, son of Net, son of Iondaoi (reigned) fourscore years." Ꝺealbaoıċ mac Oᵹma Ᵹꞃıanoınn, mıc Ealaċaın, mıc Ꝺealbaoıċ, mıc Neıꞇꞇ, mıc Ionnꝺuı, ꝺeıċ m-blıaꝺan. "Dealbaeth, son of Ogma Grianoinn, son of Ealathan, son of Dealbaet, son of Ned, son of Iondai, (reigned) ten years. See also O'Flaherty, Ogyg. iii. c. 13, p. 179.—(T.)

[x] *The letters of the Scots.*—The ancient occult methods of writing were called *Ogham.* Ogma was surnamed Ᵹꞃıan-eıᵹıꞃ, the resplendent poet, which O'Flaherty Latinizes into Ogma Griananus (Ogyg. iii. c. 14, p. 179).—(T.)

[y] *Defeated in a great battle.*—Lit. "broke a great battle upon the mariners." Instead of caċ moꞃ, L. reads caċ Muıᵹı

Ꞇuıꞃeaꝺ, but the Irish traditions represent the battle of Moy Tuireadh as having been fought between the Tuatha De Danann, and the Firbolg; so that this reading is probably an error of some scribe.—(T.)

[z] *They fled.*—Ꞇaeꞇꞃaꞇ, H. Ꞇhaeꞇꞃeaꝺ, B. Ꞇheıchꞃeaꝺaꞃ, L.—(T.)

[a] *Into their tower, &c.*—This is stated as of the Milesians by Nennius; and the tower is said to have been of glass. The legends of glass towers, houses, ships, &c., are capable of two solutions: the one natural, and referring to a time when glass windows were a great rarity; and the other mystical, and analogous to Merlin's *prison of air,* whereof the walls, though invisible and transparent, were for ever impassable. See Roman de Merlin, cvvviii. On that principle, every magic circle described by a wand of power is a tower of glass; and a circle of triliths or of stones, though it be a half-open enclosure (a point harped upon in almost every combination of British words), is a perfect and inviolable structure. From the

ꝺaingean ꝼoꞃ muiꞃ   Co n-ꝺeachaꝺaꞃ ꝼiꞃ Eꞃenn ina n-ꝺaᵹaiꝺ co
muiꞃ, coꞃo cathaiᵹꞃeat ꝼꞃiu co ꞃoꞃ ꝼoꞃꞃo ꝺo ᵹlaeꞃeat in muiꞃ
uile act lucht aen luinge, ᵹoꞃ ᵹabaꝺaꞃ in n-iniꞃ iaꞃꝺain   No co-
maꝺ iaꝺ clann Neimiꝺ im Ƒeaꞃᵹuꞃ leiꝺ-ꝺeaꞃᵹ mac Neimiꝺ ꝺo
ꞃoᵹailꞃeat in toꞃ, 7c

X Tainiᵹ iaꞃꝺain ꝺám ochtaiꞃ, cona och[t] lonᵹaib, iꞃ co ꞃo
aittꞃeabꞃat a n-Eiꞃinn, 7 co ꞃo ᵹab ꝼ{iand} moꞃ ꝺe.

Ƒiꞃ bolᵹ imoꞃꞃo ꞃo ᵹabꞃat Manainꝺ 7 aꞃaile inꞃi aꞃceana,
Aꞃa 7 Ili 7 Rachꞃa.

Clanꝺa Ᵹaileoin, imoꞃꞃo, mic Eaꞃcail ꞃo ᵹabꞃat inꞃi oꞃc i
Iꞃtoꞃeth

Preiddeu Annwvn (Spoils, or Herds, of the
Abyss) we may cite this passage " I
shall not win the multitude   [Under] a
veil [is] the leader of hosts   Through
the enclosure of glass (caer wydyr) they
discerned not the stature (or length,
gwrhyd) of Arthur   Threescore bards
(canwr) stood upon the wall   It was
difficult to parley with its sentinel "—i
29-32   The name of Bangor Wydrin or
Glaston, belongs to this notion of vitreous
castles or sanctuaries, whatever be its
true origin —(H)

b Closed upon them.—Coꞃ aꞃoib ꝼoꞃaib
in muiꞃ, L   Coꞃ ꝼaꞃ ꝼoꞃ ꝺiuclainꝺ in
muiꞃ, B —(T)

c Ship —ꝺaꞃꞃe L —(T)

d Or according to others —The second
account of this event is found only in D.
and is more in accordance with the Irish
traditions   See Keating and the Leabhar
Gabhala   The tower, called Conaing's
Tower, from Conaing, son of Faobhar,
is said to have been on the island on

the north coast of Ireland now called
Toꞃinꞃ, 1 e Tower Island, corrupted into Tory island   After the destruction of
the Fomorians, another body of pirates
commanded by More, son of Dela, with
a fleet of thirty (some copies of Keating
read sixty) ships from Africa, again occupied the island, and were again attacked
by the Nemedians, but the tide coming
upon them unperceived during the battle,
the Nemedians were all drowned, except
the crew of one boat   Nennius, as has
been said, attributes this exploit to the
Milesians   It would seem as if two or
three different stories had been confounded together in the accounts of it that
now remain   See O'Flaherty, Ogygia, iii
c 7. p 170 —(7) Fergus Leithdearg
was one of the four sons of Nemed, and
father of Britan, from whom the Irish
deduced the name of Britain and the
pedigree of St Patrick —(H)

e A company of eight —Ꝺam ochtaiꞃ,
so written in D. and L   B. reads Ꝺa-

a very strong fortress on the sea. The men of Eri went against them to the sea, so that they fought with them until the sea closed[b] upon them all, except the crew of one ship[c]; and thus they [*the Irish*] took the island afterwards. Or, *according to others*[d], it was the descendants of Nemed, with Fergus Leith-dearg [*the red sided*], son of Nemed, that destroyed the tower, &c.

X. Afterwards came a company of eight[e], with eight ships, and dwelt in Eri, and took possession of a great portion of it.

But the Firbolg seized upon Mann, and certain islands in like manner, Ara, Ili, and Rachra[f].

The children of Galeoin[g], also, the son of Ercal [*Hercules*], seized the

inoċċop, as if it were intended for Da-mochtor, a proper name, as in the Latin copies; but the verb ṫanʒaḃap, which is the third person plural, shews that in this MS. also the words meant a company of eight. L. and B. read only cona lonʒeap or ʒona lonʒip, *with their ships*, omitting oċṫ. Some of the Latin copies read *Clam Hector, Clan Hoctor*, and some merely *Hoctor*; a word which in Irish signifies *eight men.*—(*T.*)

[f] *Ara, Ili, and Rachra.*—Apa ⁊ Ila ⁊ Reċċa, B. Apa ⁊ Ile ⁊ Raċċa, L. The islands of Ara, Ila or Islay, and Rachlin or Rathlin, are intended. In the Latin we read "Buile autem cum suis tenuit Euboniam insulam, et alias circiter." Eubonia is the Isle of Man, and Buile is most probably a corruption of ḃolʒ or Fip ḃolʒ.—(*T.*)

[g] *The children of Galeoin, &c.*—That is to say the Fir-Galeoin before mentioned; being that tribe of the Firbolg who ob-tained Leinster. The original merely says, that Istoreth, son of Istorin, occupied Dalrieda, i.e. Argyle, Lorn, and their vicinage; and has nothing about the Ork-neys. The translator, in this instance, has only heaped confusion. For the name of Agathirir, grandfather of Istorin, means Agathirsus, i. e. Pictus; yet he is made a Ferbolg, and distinguished from the race of Cruithnich or Picts, in which occurs another Istoreth. I suppose the name Istorinus of Nennius to be the Irish name Starn, which occurs in the brother of Partholan (Ogygia, part i. p. 4) and the father of Simon Bree (Keating, p. 37); and which has been derived from *stoir*, history. See Wood's Primitive Inhabitants, pp. 14, 118. The name Historeth of Nen-nius, transferred by our translator to the Picts, is quoted as son of Agnamhan, but Starn, father of Simon Bree, was grandson of Agnamhan, which has been interpreted *Song.* See Wood, *ibid.* p. 13.—(*H.*)

Iṛcoṗeċ mac Iṛcoiṗine mic Aizine mic Azaċiṗiṗ ṗo ṛzailṗeac
aṗiṛ a h-inoṗib Oṗcc .i. oo cuaio Cṗuiċne mac Inzu mic Luiċhe
mic Ṗaiṗce mic Iṛcoṗeċ mic Aznamain mic ḃuain mic Maiṗ
mic Ṗaiċheaċc mic Iauao mic Iaṗeċh ; conao ṗo zaḃ cuaṛceaṗc
innṛi ḃṛeacan, ⁊ co ṗoinoṛeac a ṗecc macu a ṗeaṗann a ṗeacc
ṗannaib, ⁊ aṗé ainm cacha ṗiṗ oib aca ṗoṗ a ṗeaṗann.

Seacc meic Cṗuiċniz .i. Ṗib, Ṗioaċ, Ṗoclaio, Ṗoṗcṗᶜnn,
Cac, Ce, Ciṗiz [Uc oiṗic Colam cilli

Moiṗṗeiṗeaṗ oo Cṗuiċhne claino
Roinoṗeo Alḃain a ṗeaċc ṗaino
Caic, Ce, Ciṗeaċh cecaċh clano,
Ṗib, Ṗioaċh, Ṗocla, Ṗoiṗṗeano]

Azuṗ co ṗo zaḃ Aenḃeazan mac Caicc mic Cṗuiċhni aṗoṗize na
ṗecc ṗano Ṗinacca ba ṗlaic n-Eiṗenn iṗ in ṗe ṗin, [azuṗ] ṗo
zaḃṗac ziall Cṗuiċhneach

Do cuaoaṗ coicṗeaṗ imoṗṗo, oo Cṗuċhancuaċhib a h-inoṗib
oṗcc

<hr>

ⁿ Son of Agathan —hiṛcoiṗeno mac hiṛcoṗiṗ, mic Azoiṗ, mic Azaċiṗṗi, B Iniṛcoiṗeano mac Iṛcoiṗini, mic Aznuinna, mic Azaċuiṗṗi, L The Latin reads, "Istorith, Istorim filius, tenuit Dalrieta cum suis" It will be observed that the Fir-Galeoin, who a little before were supposed to have derived their name from galian, a spear, and who were therefore called viri armorum, are here derived from Galian, the name of a man These inconsistencies at least prove that the present work was compiled from various ancient sources, which were copied blindly by the compiler, without any attempt to make them hang together consistently —(T)

ⁱ Again —Aṗiṗioi. L Ooṗioiṗi, B —(T)

ᵏ Cruithne —Cṛuithne is here made to be a man's name ; his genealogy is thus given in L Cṗuiċhne mac Inze, mic Iuchca, mic Ṗaṗiċalon, mic Aznon, mic ḃuain, mic Maiṗ, mic Ṗhaċhecc, mic Iauao, mic Iaċhṗeċh, mic Nae in B thus· Cṗuiċhne mac Cinze, mic Iuccai, mic Ṗaṗcai, mic hiṛcoṗeċh, and it will be seen that in another part of B the genealogy is given in another form more nearly agreeing with L —(T)

ˡ To his own portion —Literally, "and it is the name of each man of them that is on his land" This clause is omitted in this place in B.—(T.)

ᵐ As Columbkille said —This short poem

the islands of Orc, i. e. Istoreth, son of Istorine, son of Aigin, son of Agathirir[n], were dispersed again[i] from the islands of Orc, *and then* came Cruithne[k], son of Inge, son of Luithe, son of Pairte, son of Istoreth, son of Agnaman, son of Buan, son of Mar, son of Fatheacht, son of Javad, son of Japheth; so that he seized the northern part of the island of Britain, and his seven sons divided his territory into seven divisions, and each of them gave his name to his own portion[l]

The seven sons of Cruithne are Fib, Fidach, Fotlaid, Fortrean, Cat, Ce, Cirig. As Columbcille said[m]

> Seven of the children of Cruithne
> Divided Alban into seven portions;
> Cait, Ce, Cireach of the hundred children,
> Fib, Fidach, Fotla, Foirtreann.

And Aenbeagan[n], son of Cat, son of Cruithne, took the sovereignty of the seven divisions Finacta[o] was Prince of Eri at that time, and[p] took hostages of the Cruithnians

Now five men[q] of the. northern Cruithnians, i. e five brothers of their

is inserted from L and from B (where it occurs in another place) B in this place agrees almost exactly with D. Immediately after the genealogy of Cruithne, L adds · Ir h-e achaip Cpuichnech aзup cet bliaꝺain inpize. Seacht meic Cpuichne inꝺpo ı Fiꝺ, aзup Fioach, aзup Focla, aзup Fopzpeann, Caiz, aзup Ce, aзup Cipic, uz ꝺixiz, &c, as in the text. After Columbkille's verses follows, Co po poinꝺpeaz ı pecz pannaib in peapann, aзup ir e ainm cach pip ꝺib pil pop a peapanꝺ, uz epz Fib, Ce, Caiz, 7c̄. xiii ꝑii con зobpaꝺ ꝺib poppo, aзup зabaip Onbecan mac Caiz mic Cpuichne aipꝺpiзi na pecz penn pin. Then follows Finꝺacca pa

ꝼlaich n-Epenn, &c, as in the text, with only some trivial variations —(*T*)

[n] *Aenbeagan* Onbecan, L B.—(*T*)

[o] *Finacta*.—This must be Finacta, son of Ollam Fodla, who became king of Ireland on the death of his father, A M. 3276 according to O'Flaherty, 3923 according to the Four Masters, and 3112 according to Keating.—(*T*)

[p] *And*—Aзup, added from L—(*T*)

[q] *Five men*—Coiccap, D Coiзeap, B Coicpeap, which is the reading of L, shews the true etymology of this class of personal numerals. See O'Donovan's Irish Grammar, p 125.—(*T*)

oȝcc ı cuıc bȝachȝı achaȝ Cȝuıcne co Fȝancaıb ȝo ȝo cumbaıȝ-
ȝeao cachaıȝ ann ı Pıcccacuȝ no Inȝıccuȝ, o na ȝınncaıb aınmnıȝeaȝ; ⁊ co canȝaoaȝ ooȝıȝ oocum na h-ınnȝı ı oocum na h-Eȝenn,
co ȝabaoaȝ ȝe cıan ann, ȝo ȝaȝ oıcuıȝȝeac Ȝaeoıl caȝ muıȝ oo
cum a m-bȝachaȝ

Clanna Lıacaın mıc Eaȝcaıl ȝo ȝabȝac ȝeaȝann Oıeımcoȝum ⁊
Ȝueȝ ⁊ Ȝuıȝelle, ȝo ȝaȝ ınnaȝb Coheno a co [a] macaıb a bȝeacnaıb

oe ımcechcaıb ȝaeoeal aNNso sıs.

XI IS amlaıo ȝeo ımoȝȝo acȝıaoaıc na h-eolaıo na n-ȝaeoeal
ımceachca

r *Pictatus oı Inpictus*.—Or perhaps we should translate, "Pictatus or the Pictus" L reads Pıccabıȝ, and B Pıcca-uıȝ, without the second name The city of Augustoritum, or *Poictiers*, capital of Pictavia, oı Poictou, in France, is evidently the city meant The fable is invented to suit the similitude of names Keating, quoting the authority of the Psalter of Cashel, makes the Cıuithneans a people of Thrace, and supposes them to have founded *Pictaı ium* in the couı se of their migrations, *befoı e* their arrival in the British isles See Keating, at the reign of Heremon —(*T.*)

s *From the pick-aı es*.—Instead of o na ȝınncaıb aınmnıȝeaȝ, B and L read simply a h-aınm —(*T*)

t *To theıı bı ethı en*.—The substance of this section, with some additional matter (the length of the reigns, foı example, of the sons of Cruithne, and the cıties where they reigned), is given in another copy, near the beginning of this Tract, in both B and L —(*T.*)

u *Sons of Liathan*.—This is a literal version of Nennius ' Filu autem Liethan obtinuerunt in regione Demetorum, et in alus regionibus, ı e Guir et Cetgueli, donec expulsi sunt a Cuneda, et a filus ejus, ab omnibus Britannicis regionibus."—(*T.*) The names, Liathan and Ercal, variously disfigured in the Latin, are, perhaps, corrected here On the otheı hand the names of Denetia or Dyved, ı. e Pembrokeshire, Gwyr or Gower, in Glamorgan, and Cydweli or Kidwelli, in Caermarthen, as well as that of king Cynedda, are further corrupted See Humph Llwyd Commentariolum, p 100 —(*II*)

v *Dieimptoı um and Guer and Guigelle*.—Oıeımcoȝum aȝuȝ Cuheȝ aȝuȝ Cuȝeıllı, L. Oıamcoȝao aȝuȝ Ȝueȝ aȝuȝ Ȝuȝellı, B.—(*T*)

w *Cohenda*.—Cuanna, L Cuaıoa, B —(*T.*)

x *Expelled*.—Innaȝb, II. Inoaȝbaȝcaȝ, B Innaȝbȝaoaȝ, L —(*T.*)

y *As folloı es*.—So much of this Gadelian

their father Cruithne, went from the islands of Orc, to the Franks, and founded a city there, viz., Pictatus or Inpictus[r], so called from the pick-axes[s]; and they came again to this island, i. e. to Eri, where they were for a long time, until the Gaedil drove them across the sea to their brethren[t].

The sons of Liathan[u], son of Ercal, seized the country Dieimptorum, and Guer, and Guigelle[v], until Cohenda[w] and his sons expelled[x] *them* out of Britain.

OF THE ADVENTURES OF GAEDEL, AS FOLLOWS[y].

XI. The learned of the Gaels[z] give the following account of the adventures

or Milesian story, as belongs to Nennius, is culled from his ninth and seventh chapters. The Altars of the Philistines are the Aræ Philænorum, between Leptis Magna and Barce,

"Qua celebre invicti nomen posuere Philæni,"

two Carthaginian brothers, whose patriotic self-devotion is recorded in many writers, especially in Sallust's Jugurtha, p. 126. Delphin. 1674. The Lacus Salinarum (here Salmara) must signify the salt-marshes near the Syrtis Major, called in maps Salinæ Immensæ ; and not the lake anciently called Salinæ Nubonenses in the Mauritania Sitifensis ; for otherwise the Gaels would be retrograding eastwards to Rusicada. The city of Rusicada (here Ruiseagdæ) was near the modern Stora, to the west of Bona, and had a Donatist bishop Victor, and a Catholic bishop Faustinian. See Optatus a Dupin, p. 14, p. 369. Antwerp. The Montes Azaræ (here Mount Iasdaire) are the

Mons Aurasius, stretching S. W. of Rusicada. The River Malva is now the Enza, at or near the division of the Algerian and Maroquin states. The Mediterranean Sea is the Mare Terrenum, or Land Sea, of Marcus, pp. 52 and 49, and of Tirechan in his Annot. p. xix. Wherever (as in Nennius, cap. ix. Galfrid. Monumet. 1, c. 12, and in the Lives of St. Patrick) the Tyrrhenum æquor is spoken of by writers of these islands, it is a corruption of Terrenum, and means the Terranean or Medi-Terranean. It is worthy of observation, that learning, neither inaccurate nor very common, has found its way into this geography of the Historia Britonum. It has been copied, in an ignorant manner, by the Archdeacon of Monmouth, or by the original author whom he rendered. Galfrid. Monumet. 1, cap. 11, 12.—— (*II.*)

The learned of the Gaels.—" Sic mihi peritissimi Scottorum nunciaverunt.——

ımceachca a n-appaıde coıreac. Ro baı apaıle peap poceanolach
pop loıngeap ı n-Eıgıpc, ıap na h-ındapba a pıgı Sgeıchıa, ın n-
ınbaıd cangadap meıc Ippachel cpe Muıp Ruaıd, ⁊ po baıdead
Popand cona pluag In pluag cepna ap gan badad, po h-ınnapbpac
a h-Eıgıpc ın loıngpec [poıcenelach] ud, ap ba chamaın pıum do
Popand do baıdead ann ı Popann Cíncpıp

Ro apcnadap ıapum ın Sgeıcheagdaı co na clann ıp a n-Qppaıg,
co h-alcopaıb na Peılıpdınach co cuıcıb Salmapa, ⁊ eıcıp na Ruıp-
eagdaıb ⁊ plıab ıapdaıpe, ⁊ cap ppuch mbaılb cpıep ın pec
muıpıde co colamnaıb Epıcaıl cap nıuncınn Gaıdıdoın co h-Eappaın;
⁊ po aıccpeabaıd [ın Eppaın] ıapdaın, co cangadap meıc Mılead
Eappaıne co h-Eıpınd co cpıchaıc cuıle, co cpıcha lanamaın cach
cuıl, a cınd da blıadan ap mıle ıap ın-badad Popaınd [ım muıp
puaıd].

Rex hautem eopum meppup epc .ı. po baıdead ın pıg ı Donn ag
cıg

Quando venerunt per mare Rubrum filii
Israel," &c—*Nennius* See Additional
Notes, No VI Two copies of this section are to be found in different parts of
the Book of Lecan —(*T*)

[a] *Noble*—Soıcenelach added from B
L¹ L²—(*T*)

[b] [i] [c] *Forann Cincris*—These words
occur only in D In the Chronicon of
Eusebius we read, " Iste est Pharao Chen-
cres qui contradixit per Mosen Deo, atque
mari rubro obrutus est "—(*T*)

[c] *The wells of Salmara*—Salmapum,
B L¹ Salmapıum, L². In the Latin
" per lacum Salınarum, or "Palınarum,"
as some MSS of Nennius read erroneously —(*T*)

[d] *The Ruiseagdir*—Na Ruʀcecdu, L¹
na Roıʀcıcdu, L² na Roʀcıcdu, B. In
all the Irish copies this word seems given
in a plural form as the name of a people
The Latin reads, " ad Ruʃıcadam "—(*T*)

[e] *Mount Iasdune*—Slebe Eapcaıp, L²
Slebe Qpcape, B L¹ The Latin reads,
" Montes Azarıæ ." but some copies read
" Syrıæ," and Gale's edition reads Araıat
—(*T*)

[f] *The River Mbalb*—D reads cap plıab
Mbalb ı. ppuc, where the words ı. ppuc,
are manifestly the correction of plıab, and
introduced by the ignorance of the copyist
into the text B and L² read ppuch
Maılle L¹ reads ppuch Maılb The
Latin is " per flumen Malvam "—(*T*.)

adventures of their ancient chiefs. There was a certain nobleman in exile in Egypt, after he had been banished out of the kingdom of Scythia, at the time when the children of Israel passed through the Red Sea, and Forann [*Pharoah*], with his host, was drowned. The army that escaped without being drowned, banished out of Egypt the aforesaid noble[a] exile, because he was the son-in-law of the Forann that was drowned there; i. e. Forann Cincris[b].

Afterwards the Scythians went, with their children, into Africa, to the altars of the Philistines, to the wells of Salmara[c], and between the Ruiseagdæ[d], and Mount Iasdaire[e], and across the River Mbalb[f], through the Mediterranean Sea[g] to the pillars of Hercules, beyond the sea of Gadidon[h] to Spain; and they dwelt in Spain[i] afterwards, until the sons of Miled (*Milesius*) of Spain[k] came to Eri, with thirty boats, with thirty couples in each boat, at the end of a thousand and two years after Forann was drowned in the Red Sea[l].

Rex autem eorum mersus est, i. e. the king, viz., Donn, was
drowned

[g] *The Mediterranean Sea.*—Set muipine, literally *semita marina*, the sea path or way, which must here signify the Mediterranean. The Latin is " transierunt per maritima."—(*T.*)

[h] *The sea of Gadidon.*—This is not mentioned in the Latin. Muincino Citedan, B. (the aspirated ჳ omitted.) Muincino Ჶaioioonou, L. The word muincino or muincinn, signifies the top or surface; the level plain (here of the sea). In the Leabhar Gabhala (p. 3), it is explained in a gloss by uactar, surface. Or muincinn [.i. uactar] mapa main Caipp; "Over the surface of the Caspian Sea." O'Reilly, in his Dictionary, al-

though he refers to this passage, has entirely misunderstood it.—(*T.*)

[i] *In Spain.*—Added from B. L¹. L². (*T.*)

[k] *Miled of Spain.*—This occurs in another part of the Latin copies, " Et postea venerunt tres filii cujusdam militis Hispaniæ" (Mileao Carpaine, where the proper name, *Miled* or *Milesius*, appears to stand for *miles*), " cum triginta ciulis apud illos, et cum triginta conjugibus in unaquaque ciula." The word cuil or cul, (cubal, L.) is evidently cognate with the Anglo-Saxon *ceol*, a long boat, the root of our present English word *keel*. See Du Cange v. *Ceola, Ciula.*—(*T.*)

[l] *In the Red Sea.*—Added from L. D.

τις Όuінο.   Τρι banóé ın n-ınbaıo ρın a ρlaıċıuρ Єρenn, Ϝolla, ┐
banba, ┐ Єıρe, coρo moıóeaóaρ τρι caṫa ϝoρρo ρe macaıb
Mıleaó.   Coρo ʒabaóaρ meıc Mıleaó ρıʒı ıaρóaın

Conτenρıo maʒna ϝacτa eρτ ı. ρo ϝaρ coρnam [mоρ] eτeρ óa
mac Mıleaó ımon ρıʒe co ρo ρıóıρτaρ a m-bρeıṫam ıaτ ı Ụmaıρ-
ʒeın [ʒlun ʒeal mac Mıleó, ┐] ba ϝılıó eıρıóen óna, ┐ ıρ e ın
ρıo óo ρoınóe ı. ρaınó Єρenn a n-óo, ┐ ρoʒab Єbeρ [ın leaṫ]
τeaρ, ┐ Єıρemon [ρa leaṫ] τuaıʒ, ┐ [ρo] aıττρeabaıó a clanna
an n-ınóρı [ρeo cuρ anóıu]

XII bρeaτaın τρa ρo ʒabρaταρ ın n-ınρı ρeo ıρ ın τρeaρ
                                                aımρeaρ

reads ıaρ m-aoao for ıaρ m-baóaó, omitting the eclipsed initial letter, a very common omission in that MS —(*T*)

 [m] *Tıgh-Duınn.*—Heber Donn, one of the
eight commanders of the Milesians, was
shipwrecked at Teach Duınn, i e the
House of Donn, in Kerry. Ogygia in
cap 16, p 182   This is the name still
given by the peasantry of the neighbourhood to one of the three islands commonly
called the Bull, the Cow, and the Calf,
off Dursey island, at the south entrance
of Kenmare Bay.   Keating speaks of
Teach Duınn as being near sand banks,
Uρ an ρo baıτoıó ıao aʒ na óumacaıb,
ρe ρaıττıoρ Τeaċ Όuınn, ı n-ıaρταρ
Muman, aʒuρ ıρ o Όhonn, mac Mıleaó,
óo baτaó ann, ʒaıρτıoρ Τeaċ Όhuınn
óe " The place where they were drowned
was at the sand banks which is called
Donn's House, in the west of Munster ,
and it is from Donn, son of Milesius, who
was drowned there, that they are called

Donn s House." He also cites the following verses from a poem by Eochy
O'Flynn

Όonn, ıρ bıle, ıρ buan a bean,
Όıl, ıρ Uıρeaċ, mac Mıleaó,
buaρ, bρeaρ, ıρ buaıʒne ʒo m-bloıo,
Όo baτaó aʒ na Όumacoıb.

" Donn, and Bile, and Buan his wife,
   Dil, and Aireac, son of Milead,
   Buas and Breas, and Buaighne renowned,
   Were drowned at the sand banks "—(*T*)

 [n] *Three goddesses* —That is to say, three
princesses of the Tuatha De Danann, for
that tribe were called the Gods   They
were the wives of the three grandsons of
the Daghda —(*H*)

 [o] *Folla, Banba, and Ene*—Ϝoτla, B
L[1] L[2]   Her name is commonly spelt
Ϝoóla   See the story in Keating —(*T*)

 [p] *The kingdom* —Τρı ρıʒı ρoρτ, L , i e
the three kingdoms of Fodhla, Banba, and
Eri   Rıʒe ϝoρρo ρoρτ, B   The Latin

drowned at Tigh-Duinn[m]. Three goddesses[n] at that time held the sovereignty of Eri, *namely*, Folla, and Banba, and Eire[o], until three battles were gained over them by the sons of Milead, so that the sons of Milead afterwards took the kingdom[p].

Contentio magna[q] facta est, i. e. there grew up[r] a great dispute between the two sons of Milead, concerning the kingdom, until their Brehon[s] pacified them, viz. Amergin of the white knee, son of Milead; and he was their poet[t]. And this is the peace which he made[u], viz., to divide Eri into two *parts*, and Eber[v] took the northern half, Herimon the southern half, and their descendants inhabit this island to the present day.

XII. Now the Britons took possession of this island[w] in the third age

words, or abbreviations for them, *et, vero, sed, post*, often occur in Irish MSS., but they were always read by their Irish equivalents, just as we read the contraction " & " *and*, although it is really an abbreviated mode of writing the letters *et*.—(*T*).

[q] *Contentio magna, &c.* — The Latin words at the beginning of this paragraph appear to intimate that our Irish compiler was copying from some Latin original. They occur only in D. There is nothing corresponding in the Latin copies of Nennius.—(*T.*)

[r] *Grew up.*—Ꞃo oꞃ, D. B. for ꞃo ꞃaꞃ, omitting the aspirated initial. Coꞃ ꞃaꞃ cocaꝺ moꞃ, L[2]. Coꞃꞃam moꞃ, B. L[1].—(*T.*)

[s] *Their Brehon.*—D. reads co ꞃo ꞃꝺaɩꟃꞃeac a m-bꞃeɩcɩmaɩn, "until their Brehons pacified them:" but this, being inconsistent with what follows, is an evident mistake, and the reading of L[1]. L[2]. and B.

has therefore been followed. The words inserted between brackets after Amergin's name in the Irish text, are added from L[1]. and L[2].—(*T.*)

[t] *Their poet.*—The word ꝼɩleꝺ implied much more than a poet. See O'Flaherty, Ogyg. iii. c. 16. p. 183, who says, "Amerginus sub fratribus suis supremus vates fuit. Quo nomine (Filedh, quasi Philosopho) non poetæ tantum, sed etiam aliis scientiis apprime versati audiebant."—(*T.*)

[u] *He made.*—Instead of the words aꟃuꞃ ɩꞃ e ɩn ꞃɩꝺ ꝺo ꞃoɩnꝺe (which are inserted from L[1].) D. reads ɩꞃ ꞃe ɩn, leaving the sense imperfect. B. reads aꟃuꞃ ɩꞃ e ɩn ꞃɩꝺ. L[1]. reads ɩꞃe ɩn ꞃɩch.—(*T*.)

[v] *Eber.*—Eɩmbeꞃ, D. The insertions between brackets in the text are from L[2]. D. reads clann instead of clanna. In ɩnoꞃɩ cuꞃ anꝺɩu, B. In ɩnoꞃɩ ꞃeo cuꞃ anɩu, L[2]. In n-ɩnꞃɩ co ꞃɩꝺ, L[1].—(*T.*)

[w] *This island.*—Here our Author, trans-

aimrear in domain. Irin ceatramad aimrear in domain imorro
ro gabrat Gaedil Erinn; ir in aimrir cenna ro gabratar Cru-
ichnig tuarceart indri Breatan; ir in treired aimrear imorro
tangadar Dal-riada co ro gabrat raind na Cruitneach, ⁊ ir an
aimrir rin ro gabrat Saxain a raind a Breatnaib

Iar n-il aimrearaib tra ro gabrat Romain apo flathur in domain, ⁊ ro raedreat teachtaire co h-inir Breatan do cuingid
giall ⁊ eitire, amail tugrat ar gac tir [n-aile]. Do cuadar imorro
na teachta [co] dimdach gan giall; ro feargaidead in rig imorro
i. Iuil Cerain re Breatnu, ⁊ tanig co lx cuile co h-indbear rpo-
cha Tamair. beallinor imorro ba rig Breatan in n-indaid rin
Do cuaid imorro Dolabeallur air conrul rig Breatan a com-
dail Iuil [Cearain], ⁊ ro teargda milid in rig, irin aimrir rin
ro brir donino ⁊ anrad a longa, ⁊ do rathcuir in rig gan cor-
gur

lating a British authority, probably Nennius, uses the words *this island*, to signify Britain. Nennius (cap 10,) says,
"Brittones venerunt in tertia ætate
mundi ad Brittanniam Scotti autem
in quarta obtinuerunt Hiberniam." The
six ages of the world are given in the
various editions of the Historia (and with
some difference in Tahesin's Divregwawd,
p 96), but are omitted by this translator. The third age was from Abraham
to David, the fourth was from David to
Daniel, and the sixth is from John Baptist
to Doomsday Some anachronisms of Nennius are corrected in this passage.—(H)

ˣ *Age.*—Aer, L². Air, B L¹.—(T)

ʸ *Sixth age.*—In teired aimrir, D. in
reread air, L². in reread aimrir, L¹.—
(T)

ʳ *The Romans.*—Here we pass to the
fourteenth chapter of Nennius, "Romani
autem dum acceperunt dominium totius
mundi, ad Britannos miserunt legatos,"
&c.—(T)

ᵃ *Other.*—n-aile added from L¹ L².—
(T)

ᵇ *Displeased.*—Dimgach, D Co dimdach, L¹. L¹ go dimdach, B.—(T)

ᶜ *Sixty ships.*—Co xl ciule, D lx cu-
baile, L¹ lx. ciuile, B L¹. "Tunc
Julius Cæsar . . . . iratus est valde,
et venit ad Brittaniam, cum sexaginta
ciulis, et tenuit in ostium Tamesis," &c.—
Nennius.—(T)

ᵈ *Tames.*—B. reads go h-inber rpota-
mer, which is evidently a mistake for
rpota Tamer.—(T.)

ᵉ *Proconsul.*—Air conrain, D, an evi-

age of the world. But it was in the fourth age[x] of the world that the Gaels seized upon Eri In the same age the Cruithnians took the northern quarter of the island of Britain But it was in the sixth age[y] that the Dalriada came, and took the district of the Cruithnians, and it was at that time *also* that the Saxons took their portion *of the island* from the Britons.

But after many ages the Romans[z] took the sovereignty of the world, and they sent an ambassador to the island of Britain, to demand hostages and pledges, such as they had taken from every other[a] country The ambassadors, however, went away displeased[b] without hostages ; and the king, viz , Julius Cæsar, was enraged with the Britons, and came with sixty ships[c] to the month of the river Tames[d] Now Belinus was king of the island of Britain at that time And Dolabellus, pro-consul[e] of the King of Britain, went to meet Julius Cæsar[f], and the soldiers of the king were cut down ; in the mean time[g] tempestuous weather and storm broke his ships, and the

dent mistake Enconꞃul, B L[1]. Ɑꝓo-chonꞃol, L[2]. This last reading would signify chief consul , but the Latin calls Dolobellus "proconsul regi Brittanico " Some take "Dolobellum" in the Latin to be the name of a town, an interpretation which has the authority of Geoffrey of Monmouth , it will be seen, however, that our Irish author considered it as the name of a man—(*T.*) Nennius has contra Dolobellum, and Marcus, apud Dolobellum. Camden quotes it, ad Dole bellum, "a battle at Deal ," but neither states where he found it, nor how the rest is to be construed. In this passage of the Historia, Beli Maui ap Manogan is represented as still king of Britain ;

though he was clearly dead, being father to Cassivellaunus —Galfrid iii. cap. 20. But Beli Maur was a sort of patron hero to Britannia, which was called his island. Taliesin, Dirge of Pendragon, p 73 Perhaps the passage may be restored in this manner, which brings into play both the *apud* and the *contra:* " pugnabat *apud* Dolo[n] *contra* [Cassi]bell[an]um, qui erat proconsul regi Britannico, qui et ipse rex Belinus vocabatur, et filius erat Minocam "—(*II*)

[f] *Cæsar.*—Added from L[2].—(*T.*)

[g] *In the mean time* —Ro ꞇeꝛcꞇa milio ꝓiᵹ iꞃ ino amuꞃ ꞃin, B. Ro ꞇeaꝛᵹoa mile, D Ro ꞇecóa miliᵹ ino ꝓiᵹ in n-ꝺamuꞃ ꞃin L[1] Ro ꞇeꞃcaoan miliᵹ

ʒup oıa τıp   Ͳanıʒ ımoppo apıp a cınn τpı m-blıaoan co τpı
c lonʒ cop ın -ınobeap ceona, po puıoıʒıpoap ımoppo Oolobel-
lup beapa ıapaıno ın n-aτha na h-abann apa cıno ın caτha, co
τopcpaoap na mıleao pomanach τpep ın n-enʒnam neamaıcpıoe
pın ı τpep na ʒpaımb caτha.

Co po τıneoılıo o luıl, ┐ co τapoao caτh ıp ın feapann oıa-
nao aınm Ͳınuanopıum, co pemaıo poıme ın caτ pın ┐ ʒo po ʒab
pıʒı na h-ınopı uıı m-blıaona χl pe ʒeın Cpıpτ, ab ınıτıo muınoı
ū χχχ ıı

XIII luıl ona ın ceo pıʒ Roman po ʒab ınıp bpeaτan po map-
                                                          ban

ın pıʒ ıp a n-ınbao pın, L² Ͳepcτa ıs
the old form of the passive participle,
τa being the termination, which in the
modern Iiish is ao—(T)

ʰ *Without victory* —Can ʒıall, without
hostages L² —(T)

ⁱ *Thiee hundred* —Ͳpıchao, D Ͳpı c
L ccc, B "Cum magno exercitu, tre-
centisque ciuhs "—*Nennius* —(I)

ʲ *Seeds of battle* —This passage is very
obscure, and the Irish text in all the MSS
corrupt. The Latin (Stevenson's text) is
as follows "Et ibi mierunt bellum, et
multi ceciderunt de equis et mihtibus
suis, quia supradictus proconsul posuerat
sudes ferreas et semen bellicosum, id est,
Cetilou, in vada fluminis, quod discrimen
magnum fuit militibus Romanorum, et
ars invisibilis" Here it would seem that
the ʒpana caτha of the Irish is an attempt to translate *semen bellicosum*, which
was probably a name given to the spikes
or caltrops cast or *sown* in the river for the
annoyance of the enemy. See Additional

Notes, No VII. Cethilou, Cetilou, Cathilou, Catheleu, Cechilou, Cethilo, Ceth-
locium, for in all these forms it is found
in the MSS of Nennius, seems to have
been a British word, identical in signifi-
tion with *semen bellicosum.* Ͳpep ın n-aı
cenaıcpıoe, L² "Through invisible knowledge," translating *ars invisibilis* B is
altogether corrupt, τpep ın n-aʒ nec
mac pıoı L¹ reads τpı pın n-aʒ neamaıcpıoe D has naʒpıoe, where n is
probably a contraction for neam —(T.)

"Seeds of battle" is literally rendered
from 'semen bellicosum' "Dietus proconsul posuerat sudes ferreas et semen
bellicosum, quæ calcitramenta, id est
cethilocium [cethilou, cethilou, cethilou,
cathilou cechilou, catheleu] in vada fluminis, etc" The only clue to this mangled
British is the Latin translation of it,
which shows that caltrops, or the like
thereof, were called the seed of battle,
and consequently that *cad* or *cat*, battle,
is the beginning of this word, and perhaps

the king was driven back without victory[h] to his country. He came again, however, at the end of three years, with three hundred[i] ships, to the same bay; but Dolobellus put spikes of iron in the fording place of the river, in preparation for the battle, so that the Roman soldiers fell by this invisible stratagem, i. e., by the seeds of battle[j].

Notwithstanding, a rally was made[k] by Julius, and battle was given in the land which is called Tinnandrum[l], so that he broke[m] that battle before him, and took the sovereignty of the island, forty-seven years before the birth of Christ, ab initio mundi 5035[n].

XIII. Now Julius, the first king of the Romans, who took the island

heu, sowing, its termination. *Catheu* is too short, and gives up the *l* in which all readings agree. *Catol-heu* is exactly "semen bellicosum." It is a strange criticism that, with the Latin actually given, passes it over unnoticed, and invents things alien to it! See Owen Pughe's MS., apud Gunn's Nennius, p. 127. Roberts' Tysilio, p. 78.—(*II.*)

[k] *A rally was made.*—Co n-ɒeaꞃnaɒ a ꞇinol, L[1].—(*T.*)

[l] *Tinnandrum.*—Ꞇꞃinuabann, L[2]. Ꞇꞃinouanɒ, B. "Gestum est bellum tertio juxta locum qui dicitur Trinovantum." *Nennius.* Coꞃo no Ꞇꞃinouonnꞃum, L[1]., where coꞃo seems a mere mistake—(*T.*)

For Tinandrum read Trinovantum (the Troynovant of Geoffrey), by which name London is denoted. I believe that name had its origin in a mistranslation of Orosius, "Trinobantûm [gen. pl.] firmissima civitas .... Cæsari se dedidit." vi. cap. 9.

Cæsar died B. C. 45, not 47, as stated; the statement immediately following in cap. xiii., concerning A. D. 47, has arisen out of the former by some unaccountable confusion. In Marcus, forty-seven years *after Christ* are made the duration of Claudius' reign.—(*II.*)

[m] *He broke*, i. e. he won the battle.—Co ꞃo meabaiɒ, L[1]. Co ꞃo main, L[2]. Ʒu ꞃo aemiɒ, B. which last reading is evidently corrupt.—(*T.*)

[n] *Ab initio mundi, &c.*—This date is omitted in L[2]. u. m. xxxu. a ꞇhoꞃach ɒomain co ꞃin in n-aimꞃiꞃ ꞃin, L[1]. ll.xxxu. bliaɒan o ꞇoꞃaċ ɒomain, B. "Et accepit Julius imperium Brittanicæ gentis quadraginta septem annis ante nativitatem Christi, ab initio autem mundi quinque millia ducentorum quindecim."—*Stevenson's Nennius.* In D. the reading is ū. xxxu. as in the text, where ū. is for um.—(*T.*)

bao ina h-aipeċc h-ṗein, ⁊ iſ na h-amoiſ ſo h-ainmniṫeaṫ Romain
mi luil a cinṫ uii m-bliaṫna ꝉ. iaſ n-ṫein Cṗiſṫ.

.ií. Cluiṫ in ſiṫ ṫanaiſꝺe ſo ṫab iniſ bſeaṫan, [a cinṫ cheaṫ-
ſacaṫ bliaṫan aṫuſ a ceaṫaiſ iaſ n-ṫen Cṗiſṫ], ⁊ ꝺo ſaṫ aſ moſ
aſ bſeaṫnaib, ⁊ ſainiṫ iniſ Oſicc iaſ coſ áiſ a munnṫiſe, ⁊ iaſ
moſ ꝺiṫ a muinnṫiſe laſ in ṫoiſeach ꝺianaṫ ainm Caiſebeallunuſ;
ṫſi bliaṫna ꝺeṫ ⁊ .uíí míſ a ſiṫe, co n-eſbailṫ im Maṫnanṫia h-i
Lonṫbaſꝺaib aṫ ꝺola ꝺo Roim [a] h-iniſ [bſeaṫan]

Iaſ .uíí. m-bliaṫna ꝉ. aſ ceṫ o ṫein Cṗiſṫ, ſo ſaiſeaṫ in ſiṫ
⁊ in Papa .i. Ealiṫuheſiuſ ſſuiṫhe uaiṫib co n-ebiſlib co Luciuſ
co ſiṫ bſeaṫan, co ſo baiſꝺiṫea in ſiṫ, co ſiṫaib bſeaṫan aſ-
ceana.

íii. Suaſeiſ in ṫſeaſ ſiṫ ṫainiṫ a m-bſeṫnaib; iſ leiſ ꝺo ſo-
naꝺ

---

[o] *In his own senate* —In a oiſeċṫ ṗein,
L¹ O na aiſeaċṫaib ſen, L², "by his
own senators" The word Aiſeaċṫ, or
Oiſeaċṫ, signifies an assembly. It was
the common name given to the assemblies
of the people in Ireland at which the native Brehons administered justice, and
it would seem that it is in this sense our
author applies it to the Roman senate
In Anglo-Irish documents of the period
of Hen III. to Eliz, it was commonly
anglicised *Eriott*, and *Iraghte* as in the
letter of J. Alen to the Royal Commis-
sioners (1537), "And in any wyse some
ordre to be taken immedyately for the
buildeing of the castell hall, where the
lawe is kept, for yf the same be not
buyldeid, the majestie and estimation of
the lawe shalle perryshe, the justices being then enforceid to minister the lawes
upon hylles, as it were Brehons or
wylde Irishemen, in their Eriottes"—*State
Papers*, ii p 501. See also Battle of
Magh Rath, p 92, note [e] —(*T*)

[p] *Forty and four years* —This clause is
added from B L¹. L² The Latin reads
forty-eight "Secundus post hunc Claudius
imperator venit, et in Britannia impe-
ravit, annis quadraginta octo post adventum Christi, et stragem et bellum fecit
magnum," &c B L¹. and L². read Cluiṫ
in ſiṫ ṫanaiſṫe ṫainic, (instead of ſo
ṫabe) i e "the second king that came to
Britain."—(*T*)

[q] *He brought* —Do ſaṫ, B. L¹ Do
ſaṫaṫ, L² —(*T.*)

[r] *His people*,—A mileaṫ, L¹. a-mbiṫ-
baṫ, his enemies, L². a maiṫe aṫuſ a
mileaṫ, his chieftains and his soldiers,
B.—(*T*)

island of Britain, was killed in his own senate°; and it was in his honor that the Romans gave the month of July its name, at the end of seven and forty years after the birth of Christ.

ii. Cluid [Claudius] *was* the second king that took possession of Britain, at the end of forty and four years[p] after the birth of Christ, and he brought[q] a great slaughter upon the Britons, and he penetrated to the islands of Orc, after causing a slaughter of his people, and after a great loss of his people[r] by the chieftain whose name was Cassibellaunus. He reigned thirteen years and seven months[s], when he died in Magnantia[t] of the Longobards, as he was going to Rome from the island of Britain[u].

After one hundred and forty-seven years[v] from the birth of Christ, the Emperor and the Pope, viz., Eleutherius,[w] sent clerks from them with letters to Lucius King of Britain, in order that the king might be baptized, and the *other* kings of Britain in like manner.

iii. Severus[x] *was* the third king *that* came to Britain ; *and* it was

by

---

[s] *Seven months.*—Τρι bliaδna δεc δο αχυρ οἐc μιρ, B. L². The Latin also reads, "regnavit autem annis tredecim, mensibus octo."—(*T.*)

[t] *Magnantia.*—For Magnantia it is Magantia in Nennius, and in Marcus, Moguntia, which are Latin modes of writing Mentz.—Nennius, cap. 17. This erroneous statement arises from a misconstruction of the words of Eutropius, vii. cap. 13. "Post hunc Claudius fuit, patruus Caligulæ, Drusi *qui apud Moguntiacum monumentum habet* filius."—(*II.*)

[u] *Britain.*—Added from L¹. L².—(*T.*)

[v] *Forty-seven years.*—The Latin reads "Post centum et sexaginta annos.—(*T.*)

[w] *Eleutherius.*—Ϲυleceηιυρ, B. Ϲυleceηιυρ, L¹. δeleceηιυρ, L². The Latin reads, "missa legatione ab imperatoribus Romanorum, et a papa Romano Eucharisto." Mr. Stevenson mentions a MS., in the margin of which is added by the original scribe, "Mentitur, quia primus annus Evaristi fuit A. D. 79, primus vero annus Eleutherii, quem debuit nominasse, fuit A. D. 161." The Irish translator, therefore, seems to have corrected this mistake of the original.—(*T.*) For some remarks on the legend of King Lucius, see Additional Notes, No. VIII.

[x] *Severus.*—Sebeηιυρ, L¹. Seueηιυρ, L¹. B.—(*T.*)

,ao clao Saxan a n-aᵹaio na m-baᵱḃaᵱoa ı Cᵱuıṫneaċu oa
ın. xxx aᵱ .c. ceımenn ına ᵱao, ⁊ aᵱe aınm ın claıo ᵱın la ḃᵱeaṫ-
ıaċu Ᵹuaul, ⁊ ᵱo ᵱoᵱconᵹaıᵱ clao aıle oo oenam ın n-aᵹaıo Ᵹae-
oeal ⁊ Cᵱuıṫneaċ ı Clao na muıce, ⁊ oo ᵱoċaıᵱᵱın [ıaᵱᵱın]
la ḃᵱeaṫan co n-a ṫoᵱeaċuıḃ

.ıııı. Caᵱauᵱıuᵱ ıaᵱoaın ṫanıᵹ co cᵱaou oo oıᵹaıl Seuıᵱ aᵱ
ḃᵱeaṫnaıḃ co ṫoᵱcaıᵱ ᵱıᵹ ḃᵱeaṫan leıᵱ, ⁊ co ᵱo ᵹaḃ aeoᵹu ᵱıᵹ uıme
ṫaᵱ oıoen ın ᵱıᵹ ı ın ṫ-ımᵱeᵱ; conao ᵱo maᵱḃ Allecṫuᵱ coᵱaıo
Romanac, ⁊ co ᵱo ᵹaḃ [ᵱıoe] ᵱıᵹe ıaᵱṫaın ᵱᵱıa ᵱe [cıana]

.u. Conoᵱanṫınuᵱ mac Conᵱṫanṫın ınoıᵱ mıc Aılına ᵱo ᵹaḃ
ınıᵱ ḃᵱeaṫan, ⁊ aoḃaṫ, ⁊ ᵱo aṫnaċṫ a Caıᵱᵱeᵹınṫ .ı. Mınanṫıa .ı.

aınm

¹ *Guaul*—The wall of Severus, from
Tinmouth to the Solway, is stated by
Nennius, after Orosius, to be 132 miles
long, but the distance given by Spart-
ianus, in his Life of Hadrian, who first
drew that line of defence, viz., 80 miles,
is nearer to the truth. Camden, Britt. ii
189, Gibson. That which is here mentioned, 2130 paces, is absurd and unaccountable. In Arabic numbers, we might
have supposed the translator to have read
213 passuum, without the *millia* (213
being a transposition of Orosius' 132),
and to have lengthened that extremely
minute extent by addition of the cipher.
But as he employs a mixture of Roman
numerals and words, "two M. xxx and
C." we are in a manner cut off from that
solution.

The second wall ascribed to Severus by
the translator, and called by him Cladh
na Muice, must be the line of Agricola
and Antoninus Pius, which Severus did

not restore, but Theodosius afterwards
did. Perhaps he was led into this interpolation by mistaking *propterea* for *præ-
terea*.

The MSS. of Nennius confound the
wall of Severus with that of Antoninus,
both in their original description of it,
and in their assertion that Carausius repaired it; for the latter, if true of any
wall, relates to that of Antonine, cap. xix.
The fable of the violent death of Severus
is given at large in Galfrid Monumet. 5,
cap. 2—(H)

² *Cladh na muice*, i. e. the pig's ditch,
or the "swine's dike." It is remarkable
that a very similar fosse and rampart, in
the counties of Down and Armagh, which
formed the ancient boundary between
the territories of Oriel and Uladh or
Ulidia, is called by the native Irish,
"*Gleann na muice duibhe*," or the black
pig's glen, and by the Anglo-Irish,
"the Dane's cast." See an account of it

by him was made the Saxon ditch against the barbarians, i. e. the Cruithnians, 2130 paces long, and the name of that ditch among the Britons was GUAUL[y]. And he commanded another ditch to be made against the Gaels and the Cruithnians, i. e. Cladh na muice[z], and he was afterwards[a] killed by the Britons, with his chieftains.

iv. Carausius afterwards came bravely[b] to avenge Severus on the Britons, so that the King of Britain fell by him, and he assumed the royal robes in spite of the king, i. e. of the emperor; so that Alectus, the Roman champion, killed him, and he himself[c] [viz. *Alectus*] seized the kingdom afterwards[d] for a long[e] time.

v. Constantinus, son[f] of Constantine the Great, son of Helena, took the island of Britain, and died, and was buried at Caersegeint, i. e. Minantia, another name for that city; and letters on the grave-

stone

in Stuart's Armagh, App. iii. p. 585, and Circuit of Muircheartach, p. 31. There is a village called *Swine's Dike*, on the line of the Roman wall of Antoninus, which runs from the Frith of Clyde to the Frith of Forth. Horsley (Britannia Romana, p. 172), speaking of this wall, says: "After it has crossed a brook, it leaves the parks and passes by a village called *Langton*, which stands about three chains south from it, and next by another village called *Swine's Dike*, where the track of the ditch is clearly discernible."—(*T.*)

[a] *Afterwards.*—Added from L¹. L². B. —(*T*).

[b] *Bravely*—Co τοραἐτ, D. Co ἐoρατα, L¹. ᵹo cυρατα, B. The Latin reads, "in Brittaniam venit tyrannide." —(*T.*)

[c] *He himself.*—Added from B.—(*T.*)

[d] *Afterwards.*—Aρ α ᾽ailε, B. Iαρρm, L¹. p. [for *postea*], L².—(*T.*)

[e] *Long.*—Cιανα, added from B.—(*T.*)

[f] *Constantinus, son, &c.*—It should be "Constantius, father," &c., as in Gale's edition. The tomb of Constantius is said to have been discovered at Caer Segeint, close to the modern Caernarvon, in 1283. The discovery of a tomb in that year is consistent with there having been a more ancient tradition to the same purpose. But Constantius did really die at York, the "Caer Ebrauc . . . . . alio nomine Brigantum" of Gale's Nennius, and beyond reasonable doubt was buried there; not at Caer Segeint, as in Marcus and the translation. "Obiit in Britanniâ Eboraci," Eutrop. 10, cap. i. Brigantum is the translator's Minantia, and Marcus's Mimanton.—(*H.*)

66

ainm aile do cachpaiz pin; 7 paillpizio litpi [i cloich] in aonacail
a ainm, 7 poppazaib tpi pila ip in n-paitce op in catpaiz pin, cona
pil pocht ip in cathpaiz pin.

.ui Maixim ano peipead impep oo zab bpeatain [ip na aimpip
pin po] tinocpnao conpaileacht az Romancaib, 7 nip tozpao Ce-
papi pop piz eile o pin amach. Ip a na aimpip Maximin po bai an
t-apptal uap aipiminoeaċ .i. naem Maptain; [oo Zaillia la Uleicpip
uoboven].

uii Maximain po zab pizi bpeatan, 7 puz [ploza] bpeatain a
Romancaib co topcaip laip Zpaoian in t-impep, 7 po zab pein
pizi na h-Coppa , 7 [ni] po leiz uao na pluaiz puz leip oocum a
m-ban 7 a mac nach a peapann, act oo pao peapanna imoa ooib
[o tha in loch pil immullach Sleibe loib] co Canacuic buoeap 7
piap co ouma Oichioen ait a puil in chpop apzna, 7 ip iao pin
[bpeatain

---

[8] *Point out his name.*—Foillpizio litpi
puippi ainm in piz pin i cloich in aonа-
cuil, B   L¹ and L² omit puippi. The
Latin reads, "Sepulcrum illius monstra-
tur juxta urbem quæ vocatur Cair Segeint ut literæ, quæ sunt in lapide tumuli,
ostendunt "—(T)

[h] *He left three seeds* —L¹. and D. read
pop azaib [for pazaib] tpi pila D. adds
ip in catpaiz pin n-aioce, and L¹, ipa
n-aitce [for n-paitce, the *green* or open
space of a village, which is, no doubt, the
correct reading] op in catpaiz. B reads
Fop a cleib tpi pila ip in n-aioci uap in
catpaiz ; and L² reads, Fopaclib 7 tpi
pila ip in aiochi uap in catpaio pin.
The Latin is " Et ipse seminavit tria se-
mina, id est, auri, argenti, ærisque, in
pavimento supradictæ civitatis, ut nullus

paupei in ea habitaret unquam   et vocatur alio nomine Minmauton [*al.* Mimian-
tum]."—(T.)

[1] *Maxim*—See Add. Notes, No IX

[3] *He was of Gaul of Uleus.*—This clause
is added from L², it is not in the Latin.
In the text (which is from D), St Martin
is called apptal, an apostle, a word which
in Irish often signifies no more than a
prelate , in the other MSS. he is merely
called eaj poz, a bishop. boven is the
old form of the emphatic pronoun pein,
he himself , it occurs in ancient MSS. in
various forms, uoben, boben, paoein,
fooen, from which, by aspirating, and
then omitting the o, comes the modern
form pein. We find it also in the forms
paoepin, and buoepin See O'Donovan's
Irish Grammar, p. 130 —(T) The words

stone point out his name[g], and he left three seeds[h] in the green of that city, so that there is not a poor man in that city.

vi. Maxim[i] *was* the sixth emperor *that* took Britain. It was at that time that the consulship was begun among the Romans, and no king was called Cæsar from thenceforth. It was in the time of Maxim that the noble venerable prelate St. Martin flourished; he was of Gaul of Ulexis[j].

vii. Maximian took the kingdom of Britain, and he led the armies[k] of Britain against the Romans, so that Gratian, the emperor, fell by him, and he himself took the empire of Europe; and he did not suffer the armies he had brought with him *to go* back to their wives and their children, nor to their lands, but gave them many lands, from *the place* where there is the lake on the top of Mount Jove[l], to Canacuic[m] on the south, and westward to the Mound Ochiden[n], a place where there is a celebrated cross[o], and these are the Britons of Letha,

"Gaul of Ulexis" are evidently corrupt. The name of the river Ligeris upon which, or that of Lugugè or Liguè (Locociagum) at which Martin at different times sojourned, may be latent. If any one prefers to see here the name of Ulysses, he must have recourse to the verses of Claudian,

"Est locus extremum pandit qua Gallia littus
Oceani prætentus aquis, ubi fertur Ulysses
Sanguine libato populum movisse silentem."
In Rufin. 1, 123.——(*H.*)

[k] *The armies.*——Added from L[1]. L[2]. The Latin reads, "Et ipse perrexit cum omnibus militibus Brittonum a Brittannia, et occidit Gratianum regem Romanorum, et imperium tenuit totius Europæ."——(*T.*)

[l] *From the place* ..... *Mount Jove.*——Added from L[1]. L[2]. B. The Latin reads

"a stagno quod est super verticem montis Jovis, usque ad civitatem quæ vocatur Cantguic."——(*T.*) See additional Notes, No. X.

[m] *Canacuic.*——Canchuic, L[1]. L[2]. Cancuic, B.——(*T.*)

[n] *The Mound Ochiden.*——"Usque ad Cumulum occidentalem, id est, Cruc Ochident." This passage settles the signification of the word ꝺuma, which enters into the composition of many topographical names in Ireland, and which O'Brien, and after him O'Reilly, explain, "a place of gaming." Its true meaning is *a mound, a tumulus.* The word *Cruc* is explained by Davies, *lippus, tumulus.*——(*T.*)

[o] *Cross.*——D. reads ɪnꝺeɪchnoꝑ aꝛᵹna, which is evidently corrupt; the reading

[Breatain Leta] ⁊ tarastair tear dogres, ⁊ is aire sin ro gabsadair eachtar-cineada tire Breatan, ⁊ ro marbtha Breatain a n-imlib a fearaind

Gradian imorro, cona brathair .i. Ualentinen a comrigi .ui. bliadna, is n-amsir ro bai in t-espoc uasal i Medolen forceallaid na cathlagda .i. Ambros

Ualanentinen ⁊ Teothas a comflatus ocht m-bliadna, is na h-aimsir ro tineolaid in searad i Constantin .i. l ar tri ccc do sruitib do dicur iris Maiccidoin .i. diultad in Spirid naem, ⁊ is 'na aimsir ro bai Cirine uasal sagart i m-Beithil [Iuda] in t-eidirceartaig cathlagda

Gradian ceana mar dubramar ⁊ Ualenten h-i rigi co ro rigad Maximen o na mileadaib a n-inis Breatan, ⁊ co n-deachaid tar muir a Francaib, ⁊ co ro fosuaslaigid in rig Graidian tre brath magisoreach

adopted is from L¹ L² and B. There is no authority in the Latin for this mention of a cross, unless we suppose the word *crue* to have been in some way confounded with *crux*. See Mr O'Donovan's note, Hy Fiachrach, p. 413.—(*T*)

p *The Britons of Letha.*—Added from L¹. L² B. L² reads, Breatain letan. The Latin is "Hi sunt Brittones Armorici."—(*T*) See additional Notes, No XI

q *Prelate.*—D reads easpol, perhaps for easptol, *apostle*. Espoc, *bishop*, is the reading of L¹, L², and B. D also reads Ambros, omitting the b. The Latin is "et Ambrosius Mediolanensis episcopus clarus habebatur in Catholicorum dogmate."—(*T*)

r *Macedon, &c.*—The second Œcumenical Council of Constantinople is here correctly stated to have had especial reference to the opinions of Macedonius, who denied the personality of the Holy Ghost. But the Latin copies do not make mention of that heresiarch.—(*H*)

s *Judah.*—Added from L². Teacht teastaig, D. This notice of St Jerome is taken almost verbatim from Prosper's Chronicon, ad A D 386.—(*T*.)

t *As we have said.*—dogramar, D, an evident error of the scribe. The reading followed is that of L¹, L², and B.—(*T*)

u *Went.*—Neachadar [for n-deachadar], D. The reading of B., L¹, L², has been followed.—(*T*)

v *Set at liberty.*—Fuaslaigead, L¹ forbaisligead, L² fosuaislighead, B.—(*T*)

w *Master of the soldiers.*—All the Irish copies make Parassis the prænomen of

Letha[p], and they remained in the south ever since, and it was for this reason that foreign tribes occupied the lands of the Britons, and that the Britons were slaughtered on the borders of their land.

But Gratian, with his brother Valentinian, reigned conjointly six years. It was in his time lived the noble prelate[q] in Milan, a teacher of Catholicity, viz. Ambrose.

Valentinian and Theothas [*Theodosius*] were in joint sovereignty eight years. It was in their time was assembled the synod in Constantinople of three hundred and fifty clerks, to banish the heresy of Macedon[r], viz., the denying the Holy Ghost. And it was in their time the noble priest Cirine [*Hieronymus*] flourished at Bethlehem Judah[s], the catholic interpreter.

The same Gratian, as we have said[t], and Valentinian, reigned until Maximen [*Maximus*] was made king by the soldiers in the island of Britain, and went[u] across the sea to France; and the king, Gratian, was set at liberty[v] by the treacherous counsel of the master[w] of the soldiers

this magister militum : the Latin, as printed by Bertram, reads Parasius, as an agnomen of Gratianus; and Mr. Stephenson gives it thus: "Gratianus Parisiis, Meroblaudis magistri militum proditione, superatus est, et fugiens Lugduni captus atque occisus est." But the Irish makes Meroblaudes treacherous towards Maximus, not towards Gratian, which appears to have been the historical fact.—(*T.*) Parassis is a corruption of Parisiis, *ut Paris*. Merobaudes magister militum was faithful to Gratian, and is said to have therefore suffered death at the hands of Maximus. "Quòd si cui ille pro cæteris sceleribus suis minus crudelis fuisse videtur, vestrum is, vestrum, Ba-

lio triumphalis et trabeatæ Merobaudes, recordetur interitum; quorum alter, *&c.*, alteri manibus satellitum Britannorum gula domi fracta, et inusta fœmineæ mortis infamia, ut scilicet maluisse vir ferri amantissimus videretur laqueo perire, quam gladio."—*Drepanius Pacatus Paneg. Theodosii*, cap. 28. It seems to have been an affair like Pichegru's and Captain Wright's, and may have happened as Pacatus intimates. But the character of Maximus was not vile, and cannot be estimated from the rhetoric of Pacatus. The words of Nennius, imputing treachery to the faithful Merobaudes, are copied from those in the Chronicle of Prosper Aquitane, page 637, ap. Roncalli Latinorum

maṁ ṁoṗeach na milṁo .ṁ. Paṁaṗṁṗ Meaṗoblaoṁṁ ; co ṗo ṁeiċ
ṁn ṗṁȝ co Luȝṗon, co ṗo ȝabaṁ ann, ꝛ co ṗo maṗbaṗ

Maxṁmen ꝛ a mac Uṁċṁoṗ a compṁȝṁ. Maṗṁaṁn a Ṫoṗṁnṁṗ ṁn
n-ṁnbaṁṁ ṗṁn. Maxṁmen ṁoṗṗo ṗo ṗaṁbaṁȝṁṁ leṁṗ na conṗalṁ o eṁȝṁ
ṗṁȝṁa .ṁ. la Ualenṁṁnen ꝛ la Ṫeoṁaṗ ṁṗ ṁn ṁṗeaṗ lṁcc on caṁaṁṗ
Eṁȝṁlṁa, ꝛ ṗo ṁamnaṁȝeṁ o cṁnn ṁṗ ṁn luȝ ṗṁn   Ṁo ṗoċaṁṗ ṁṁoṗṗo
a mac ṁ Uṁċṁoṗ h-ṁ Ṗṗancaṁb laṗ ṁn comṁṁ ṁṁanaṁ aṁnm Aṗȝuba
O ṁuṗ ṁomaṁn u. m ṁc. xc, [co ṗṁn, ṁo ṗeṁṗ cach cṗoṁṁce ṗṁn.]

XIV IS amlaṁṁ ṗṁn ṁnṁṗṁo aṁṗṗanṁa na ṁṗeaṁan .ṁ na. uṁṁ
n-aṁṗṗṁȝa ṁo Romancaṁb ṗoṗ ṁṗeaṁan. Aṁbeaṗaṁṁ ṁoṗṗo Ro-
mancaṁṁ ṁṗ nonṁuṗ uaṁoṁb ṗoṗ ṁṗeaṁnaṁb ṁ. ṁn ṁ-ochṁmaṁ ṁn Seueṗṁ
ṁanaṁṗṁ, aṁbaṁh aȝ ṁul ṁo Roṁm a h-ṁnṁṗ ṁṗeaṁan   Conṗṁanṁṁn
.xuṁ blṁaṁna ṁ ṗṁȝṁ ṁnṗṁ ṁṗeaṁan co n-eṗbaṁlṁ   Naṁ m-blṁaṁna
ṁṗa aṗ cccc ṁo ṁṗeaṁnaṁb ṗon cṁṗ Romanac   Ro h-ṁnnaṗbṗaṁ
ṁṗa

Chronica   But that of Prosper Tiro,
p 679, correctly gives it, not "*Merobaudis
magistri* militum proditione superatus,"
but "*Merobaude magistro*" In his preface,
p xvii, xviii., Roncalli expresses himself
sceptically upon the text of Prosper, but
not upon the fact of Merobaudes's inno-
cence.—(*Il*)

ˣ *Lugdon*—Luṁon, D. Loȝṁon, Lᶜ. The
reading of Lᶜ B has been followed —(*T*)

ʸ *Stone* —ṁṗ ṁn ṁṗeṗ blṁaṁaṁn luȝ ṁn
caṁaṁṗ, Lᶻ. ṁṗ ṁn ṁṗeaṗ luȝ ṁn caṁaṁṗ, D The reading of Lᶜ. and B has
been followed as most in accordance with
the Latin, which is "Post multum intervallum temporis a Valentiniano et Theodosio Consulibus, in tertio ab Aquileia
lapide spoliatus indumentis regalibus sis-
titur, et capite damnatur." This is taken
word for word from Prosper's Chronicle.
See note ᵃ infra —(*T*)

ᶻ *His head was cut off* —Lit. "he was
separated from his head," ṗo ṁiċeanṁaṁ,
Lᶜ. ṗo ṁiċeanṁa, Lᶻ   ṗo ṁiċeannaṁ,
B , all different spellings of the same
word, *he was beheaded* —(*T*)

ᵃ *Arguba*—Aṗȝubuṗ,Lᶜ. Aṗȝoboṗ,Lᶻ.
Aṗȝubaṗ, B   The Latin reads, "Ab
Argobaste comite interfectus est." The
authority is Prosper's Chronicon, where
the fact is thus recorded, "Maximus
Tyrannus a Valentiniano et Theodosio
imperatoribus in tertio ab Aquileia
lapide spoliatus indumentis regis sis-
titur, et capite damnatur Cujus filius
Victor eodem anno ab Arbogaste est
interfectus in Gallia" Ad A. D., 389.—
(*T*)

soldiers, Parassis Merobladis; and the king fled to Lugdon[x], and was taken there and put to death.

Maximen and his son Victor reigned jointly. Martin *was* at Torinis at that time. But Maximen was stripped of his royal robes by the consuls, i. e. by Valentinen and Theothas, at the third stone[y] from the city Eigilia [*Aquileia*], and his head was cut off[z] in that place. His son Victor also fell in France by *the hand* of the count whose name was Arguba[a]; from the creation of the world *are* 5690[b] *years*, to this *event*, according to all the chronicles.

XIV. It is thus the elders of the Britons have recorded *their history*, viz., that *there were* seven Roman emperors[c] *who had dominion* over Britain. But the Romans say that *there were* nine of them over the Britons: that is *to say, that* the eighth *was* Severus the second[d], who died as he was going to Rome from the island of Britain. *The ninth was* Constantine, *who was* sixteen years in the kingdom of the island of Britain when he died. Four hundred and nine years[e] were the

[b] 5690.—ıııı. ɔc. χχ., D. u. mile. ɔccc., B. The reading of L[1]. and L[2]. has been followed, as being in accordance with several MSS. of the Latin. The words in parentheses which follow are added from L[2]. —(*T.*)

[c] *Seven Roman emperors, etc.*—It should be observed that this Historia, as well as the Galfridian Chronicles, is framed upon the plan of dissembling the island's permanent subjection and provincial character, and of representing those Roman emperors who visited it as the only ones who ruled it. By this means the Britons of the fifth century appear as the continuing possessors of an ancient monarchy, which seven (or nine) Roman intrusions had chequered and interrupted, not as revolters against a long-established dominion. I believe Constans to be the last emperor, not depreciated by the epithet of "tyrannus," who was in Britannia.— (*H.*)

[d] *Severus the second.*—See additional notes, No. XII.

[e] *Four hundred and nine years.*—B. and L[2]. read *three hundred*. D. reads Nɑı m-bɫıaɔnɑ ɔpɑ ɑɲ ɔɲı cccc., where the word ɔɲı is a manifest blunder. The reading of L[1]. has been followed, as it coincides with the Latin "Hucusque regnaverunt Romani apud Brittones quadringentis et novem annis."—(*T.*)

τρα bρeατnαιξ ιαρoαιn neαρτ Romαnαch ⁊ nι ταρoραo cír na cαιn
oοιb, ⁊ ρο mαρbρατ na h-uιle ταιρeαchu Romαncu ρο bαoαρ a
n-ιmρ bρeαταn

Ατραchτ ιmορρο ρο ceoοιρ neαρτ Cρυιτneαch ⁊ Ƨαeoeαl oαρ
hροιno bρeαταn ⁊ ρορ ιnnαρbρατ coρ ιn n-αbαιno oιαnαo [αιnm]
Cιn. Do cuαoαρ ιαρoαιn τeαchτα bρeαταn ι Romαncαιb co noubα
⁊ co τορρι mοιρ, co ροταιb ρορ a ceαnoαιb ⁊ co ρeαταιb ιmoαιb
[leo], na ρο oιξlαoιρ ρορρο [na τοιριξ Romαnchu ρο] mαρbαo oοιb
Cuξρατar leo ιαρoαιn τοιρeαchou ⁊ conραlnu Romαncu ⁊ ταιρn-
ξαιρρξτ co na luξa oo ξeboαιρ ιn mαm Romαnαch cιαmα τριοm

Do ροchαoαρ ιαρoαιn na mιleαoα Romαncu ⁊ ρο h-ορoαιξτeα
τοιρξ ⁊ ριξu ρορ ιmρ bρeαταn, ⁊ oo cooαρ na ρlοιξ ιαρoαιn oιa
τιξιb Ro ξαb ρeαρξ ⁊ τορρμu bρeατnu αρ τριmα ιn cíρα ⁊ ιn
mαmα Romαnαιξ leo, co ρο mαρbρατ na τοιρeαchu ρο bαoαρ αcu
a n-ιmρ bρeαταn oοn oαρα cuρ. Cu n-eρuchτ αcu neαρτ Cρυιτh-
neαch ⁊ Ƨαeoel ταρ bρeατnu oορoαιρ coρ bo τριmα ιna ιn cαιn
Roman, αρoαιξ a n-oιcuρ [uιle] αρ a ρeαραιn ρο bαιl oo Cρυιτ-
eαnτuατ ⁊ oo Ƨαeoιlαιb

Do cuαoαρ ιαρoαιn bρeατnαιξ co τρμαξ ⁊ co oeαρραmαch [ιn
αιρeαcτ na Romαnαch], αρ αmlαιo ατ ριαταρ a n-oul [⁊ a] n-oρo-
mαnna ροmρu αρ ιmnαρe, ⁊ ταιnιξ ροchραιoe mορ leo ι ρluαξ oι-
αιρmιτhe oo Romαncαιb, [⁊] ρο ξαbτhα τρα ριξι ⁊ τοιρeαc ρορο
ιαρoαιn

f *But afterwards   Roman power* —
L² omits this clause, which leaves the
sense imperfect —(*T*)

g *Name* —Added from L¹, L². B The
name of the river is given Din in L¹., and
Inti in B L² and D read Cin —(*T*)

h *Along with them* —The word leo is
added from B, L²—(*T*)

i *Chiefs of the Romans* —Added from
L¹., L²., and B. Here L² abruptly stops,

there being a defect of perhaps two leaves
in the MS —(*T*)

k *Put to death by them* —L¹. and B².
omit oοιb, and read ρο mαρbρατ (*active*)
"whom they put to death"—(*T*)

l *Promised* —L¹ ιnξeτραo.—(*T.*)

m *Than* —B L¹ αnoα—(*T*)

n *Because* —L¹ and B Uαιρ ιρ e.—
(*T*)

o *To the Roman Senate* —Added from

the Britons under Roman tribute. But afterwards the Britons drove out the Roman power[f], and did not pay them tax or tribute, and they killed all the Roman chiefs that were in the island of Britain.

Immediately, however, the power of the Cruithnians and of the Gaels advanced in the heart of Britain, and they drove them to the river whose name[g] is Tin [*Tyne*]. There went afterwards ambassadors from the Britons to the Romans with mourning and great grief, with sods on their heads, and with many costly presents along with them[h], *to pray them* not to take vengeance on them for the chiefs of the Romans[i] who were put to death by them[k]. Afterwards Roman chiefs and consuls came back with them, and they promised[l] that they would not the less willingly receive the Roman yoke, however heavy it might be.

Afterwards the Roman knights came, and were appointed princes and kings over the island of Britain, and the army then returned home. Anger and grief seized the Britons from the weight of the Roman yoke and oppression upon them, so that they put to death the chieftains that were with them in the island of Britain, the second time. Hence the power of the Cruithnians and Gaels increased again over the Britons, so that it became heavier than[m] the Roman tribute, because[n] their total expulsion out of their lands was the object *aimed at by* the northern Cruithnians and Gaels.

After this the Britons went in sorrow and in tears to the Roman senate[o], and thus we are told they went with their backs foremost for shame; and a great multitude returned with them, i. e. an innumerable army of Romans, and sovereignty and chieftainry was assumed[p] over

them

L¹. and B.—(*T.*)

[p] *And sovereignty and chieftainry was assumed over them.*—Aᴈuꞃ added from B. L¹.; ꞃıᴈı ⁊ ᴛⱥıꞃıᴈ D.; ꞃıᴈ ⁊ ᴛⱥıꞃıch, L¹.; ꞃıᴈ ⁊ ᴛoıꞃeach, B. Rıᴈı, *kingdom*, would

require ᴛoıꞃıᴈeachᴛ, *sway*, not ᴛⱥıꞃeⱥc, *a chieftain*; but if we read ꞃıᴈ ⱥᴈuꞃ ᴛⱥıꞃeⱥc, the passage will signify "a king and governor was set over them."— (*T.*)

ιαρραιη. ба τροm τρα le δρεατηu ιαρραιη ιη ειρ Romαηας, cορ
mαρбρατ α ριζα ⁊ α ταιριζυ ιη τρεαρ ρεαςτ

Τανζαραρ ιαρραιη ρlαιτι Roman ταρ ηιυιρ cορ ρεmαιρ ςατ
ριmορ ρompo ρορ δρεατηu, ζορ ριζαιlρ́τ αηαιρ [α η-ραιηε] ρορρο,
⁊ cορ lomαιηζρ́τ ιmρ δρεαταη ιm α h-ορ ⁊ ιm αh-αιρζεαρ, co ρυζ-
ρατ leo α ρριοl ⁊ α ρριιζ ⁊ α ριρα ⁊ α leαρραιη οιρ ⁊ αιρζιρ, co
ηρεαςαραρ co m-бυαιρ ⁊ coρςαιρ ρια τιζ

ре ζαбαταιр SACSAN [ρορεαςτα] AHHSO.

XV. Do ραlα τρα ιαρριη ςατ ραmραιτε ⁊ ιαρ mαρбαр ηα
τοιρεαςαρ Romαηρυςα ба τρι lα δρεατηu ιαρ τοςαιτηιm ροιб
ρον ειρ Romαηας ccccᵗᵒʳ quαρραζιητιηουem αηηορ. Ζορτι-
ζειρηр mαc Ζυραιl ρο ζαбαιl αιρρριζι δρεαταη ⁊ co τορτρomτα
h-e o υαιηαη Cρυτηηεαςhu ⁊ Ζαεрel ⁊ o ηιρτ Ampoρ ριζ Fραης
⁊ δρεαταη leαςα

Τανζυραιρ

q *Gained.*—Lat "broke a very great battle before them upon the Britons" L¹ reads ρο moιρ B ροιmιр —(*T*)

r *Of their people.*—Added from B and L¹ —(*T*)

s *Silk.*—All the copies here read α ριριζ αζυρ α ριρα, but these words both signify silk, ριριζ or ριριc being the corrupt Latin, and ριρα the corresponding Irish word. added, perhaps, originally as an explanation of the other —(*T*)

t *With victory.*—L¹ reads co m-бυα-ραιб, *with victories;* and B omits "victory and triumph," and reads only αζυρ co η-ρεαςαραρ ρια ταιζ, "and so they returned home" This paragraph is a translation of the following in Nennius " Romani autem ad imperium auxilium-

que, et ad vindicandum, veniebant, et spoliata Brittannia auro argentoque, cum ære et omni preciosa veste, et melle, cum magno triumpho revertebantur." For "ad vindicandum," some MSS read, "ad vindictam propinquorum," which seems to have been the reading adopted by the Irish translator

Immediately after this section, B has a long interpolation, containing the Legend of St Carnech, which will be found in the Appendix —(*T*)

u *Here follows.*—Fορεαρτα, added from B. This word is often written бυρορτα, and more commonly, in modern Irish, ρεαρρα, it signifies *hereafter, henceforward.*—(*T*)

v *Three times by the Britons.*—ба τρι,

them afterwards. But again the Roman tribute became oppressive to the Britons, so that they slew their kings and chieftains the third time.

Afterwards there came Roman chieftains across the sea, and gained[q] a very great victory over the Britons, so that they vindicated the honour of their people[r] upon them, and they plundered the island of Britain of its gold, and of its silver, and took from it its satin, and its silk[s], and its vessels of gold and silver, so that they returned home with victory[t] and triumph.

Here follows[u] of the Conquest of the Saxons

XV. Now it came to pass after the aforesaid battle, and after the slaughter of the Roman chieftains three times by the Britons[v], after they had been four hundred and forty-nine years[w] under the Roman tribute, *that* Gortigern, son of Gudal, took the chief sovereignty of Britain, and he was oppressed by the fear of the Cruithnians and Gaels, and by the power of Ambrose, King of France[x] and Letavian Britain.

There

D. bao chpi, L'. for pa chi, three times. B. reads comba pi ōpezan, "that there was a king of Britain."—(*T.*)

[w] *Four hundred and forty-nine years.*— ix bliaoan .xl. ap .cccc. L. B. reads ix m-bliaona .xl. ap .ccc., and the same variation between three hundred and four hundred, is to be found in the Latin copies of Nennius.—(*T.*)

[x] *King of France. etc.*—Aurelius Ambrosius, with his brother, Uthyr Pendragon, are said to have taken refuge in Britanny, and to have sailed from thence to Totness, when they declared against

Vortigern; but Aurelius is not elsewhere described as having any sovereignty in Gaul. The Latin has merely " necnon et a timore Ambrosii." But even those words are so inconsistent with what follows, as to make them suspicious, though all copies are agreed in them. For there are two schemes concerning Ambrose, one identifying him with Merlin, and another making them distinct persons. But Nennius adopts the former (which is the bardic) scheme, and accordingly introduces the prophet Ambrose in the form of a young boy, at a period subsequent to that

L 2

Τangabap τρι cuile aρ in Ƶeaρmain ı. τρι baρca ρoρ mbaρba
ı ρababap na bo bρaτaıρ ı. Oρρ 7 Єnƶıρτ o ρuılıτ Saxaın ; ıρe
ρeo ımoρρa a nƶemealac ı. Oρρ 7 Єnƶıρτ ba mac Ƶuecτılıρ,
mıc Ƶuıƶτe, mıc Ƶuechτaı, mıc Ƶuτa, mıc boben, mıc Fρealaıb,
mıc Fρeboılb, mıc Fınτe, mıc Fρeann, mıc Folcball, mıc Ƶaeτa,
mıc Uanle, mıc Saxı, mıc Neaƶ

bρıταρ mac Olonn o ταıτ bρeaταın ın Leaτha, mıc Єolonn,
mıc

in which Vortigern is said to be in dread of him as a warrior. Therefore, there is interpolation in all the transcripts, unless we conclude the author not to have known what he was talking about.—(*H*)

' *Three ciula*.—The word *chiulo* or *cyula*, seems to be the same as *keel* in English, German *kiel*, Swedish *köl*, Icelandic *kioll* or *kiøll*, Anglo-Saxon *cœle*. They were the boats used by the Germans. Mr. Turner supposes each to have carried one hundred men ; and Layamon asserts their number to have been such, ''three hundred eighten.' History Anglo-Sax. i. 245. Layamon, *ut ibid.* Nennius, however, had previously in cap. xi. (vii. Gale) described a chiula as carrying but sixty persons. The three boats could evidently bring over no force capable of influencing the fortunes of Britannia, whose shores and northern frontiers were continually assailed, and of whose petty princes, sometimes called kings, the number must probably have exceeded that. Therefore, we must either understand that the arrival of the three cyuls was a mere personal introduction of Hengist to Vortigern, and so became the basis of a more extensive subsidiary treaty, or we must discredit the statement.

In point of fact, the statement has no other authority than what it derives from an involved sentence of Gildas, which, as pointed in the editions (Mr. Stevenson's included) has no grammar or meaning ; but which reads thus, with a long parenthesis. "Tum erumpens grex catulorum de cubili læænæ barbaræ tribus ut lingua ejus exprimitur *cyulis* nostra lingua *longis* [navibus interpolated I believe, the kiul of the low Dutch being the llong of the British language. If navibus be not (as I suppose) a simple interpolation it should have run thus, ' Latiná veró, navibus'] secundis velis, secundo omine augurisque (quibus vaticinabatur certo apud eum præsagio quod ter centum annis terram, cui prioras librabat, insideret, centum veró quinquaginta, hoc est dimidio temporis sæpius quoque vastaret) evectus primùm in orientali parte insulæ, jubente infausto tyranno, terribiles infixit ungues, quasi pro patriá pugnaturus, sed eam certiùs impugnaturus."—Cap. 23. If this sentence contains the statement in question, that statement exists ; but if it be

There came three ciulæ[y] out of Germany (i. e. three barks) into exile, in which were the two brothers, Ors and Engist[z], from whom are the Saxons; this is their genealogy, viz. : Ors and Engist *were* the two sons of Gueetilis, the son of Guigte, son of Gueeta, son of Guta, son of Boden, son of Frealaif, son of Fredolf, son of Finn, son of Freann, son of Folebhall, son of Gaeta, son of Vanli, son of Saxi, son of Neag[a].

Britas, son of Olon, from whom are the Britons of Leatha[b], *was the*

---

not expressed in this sentence, it hath no real existence, however many may have repeated it. The inflated phrase, "terribiles infixit ungues," seems to speak of some effective force, rather than of a trifling retinue; and, therefore, a doubt may exist, whether *de cubili* is governed by *grex*, or whether we should not punctuate it "grex catulorum, de cubili leanæ barbariæ *tribus*" (nom. case), a tribe. The less elegant arrangement of words is a minor objection, in a work of such obscure and rugged Latinity, and in a sentence which actually appears to have undergone some alteration. If this be not so, that first arrival of Hengist was merely a diplomatic, not a military, affair.—(*H.*)

[z] *Engist.*—Gızıp, L'. D. reads Gızıpt and Gızıpt, throughout, which is evidently a transcriber's blunder.—(*T.*)

[a] *Neag.*—This genealogy is given in B., with no variation except in the spelling of some of the names, thus:—Ors and Engist, Guechtiles, Guigte, Gueeta, Gutta, Uoden, Freolap, Freodulb, Finn, Frend, Folebhall, Getta, Vanli, Saxan, Negua. In

L'. it is given thus: Hors and Eigis, Gueetilis, Guiti, Guitechtai, Gutai, Uoden, Frelab, Reaulb, Finn, Freann, Boleull, Gota, Uanli, Saxi, Negua. In the Latin copies, Frend, Vanli, Saxan, and Negua are omitted, and after Geta is added, "qui fuit ut aiunt filius Dei. Non ipse est Deus Deorum, Amen, Deus exercituum, sed unus est ab idolis eorum, quæ ipsi colebant."—(*T.*)

[b] *Britas, son of Olon, from whom are the Britons of Leatha.*—These words are omitted in L'. and B., and the genealogy here given to Britas follows on as a continuation of the genealogy of Ors and Engist; the names are given thus in B.: Alan, Fethur, Ogaman, Tho, Bodhb, Semobh, Etacht, Aoth, Abir, Raa, Erra, Joban, Jonan, Jafeth, Noe. In L'. they are given thus: Alan, Fetur, Ogaman, Dai, Bodb, Semoth, Etacht, Athacht, Abir, Raa, Esra, Joban, Jonan, Jafeth. See the genealogy of Britus already given sec. IV, *supra*, where, besides some variations of spelling. Isacon is inserted between Alawn and Britus.—(*T.*) Alawn,

mic Feitiuir, mic Ogamain, mic Tai, no Teo, mic Boib, mic Semboib, mic Atheact, mic Aoth, mic Abair, mic Raa, mic Earra, mic Ioban, mic Ionan, mic Iafeth, mic Nae.

Goirtigernn tra ro gabasdair h-i sid [a Roman] neart Cruithneac, ⁊ do rad doib inn inis dianad ainm Teineth, Roinn imorro ainm Breatnach. Gradian ⁊ Aequit i rige Roman an inbaid sin. O gein Crist imorro .i. ccc.xlvii. annos, ⁊ in aimsir in rig sin .i. Gortigernd, tainig Gearman naem do proicept a n-inis Breatan, [agus do rigni Dia fearta agus mirbaile imda ar in clerec sin in inis Bretan], ⁊ ro ic sochaide ⁊ dos fug fo baithis ⁊ creidim

DE FEARTAIB GEARMAIN ANN SO SIS.

XVI. Iar tiachtain do Gearman in n-inis Breatan do cuaid do dunad in corad dianad ainm Benli do proceapt do. Tarar-dair

there written Alanus, and here Olon or Eolonn, was a famous name among the Armorican Britons, though less used among those of the island.—(*H.*)

[c] *Son of Eolonn.*—This is an erroneous repetition, Olon and Eolonn are obviously the same.—(*T.*)

[d] *Now Gortigern, etc.*—The Latin has nothing about Vortigern governing the Picts. But the Galfridian chronicle represents him as indebted to Pictish mercenaries for his crown. vi. cap. 7. Whence Gale conjectured him to have been genere Pictus, p. 129.—(*H.*) The words a Roman, are added from B.—(*T.*)

[e] *Roinn.*—Printed also Ruoihin, Ruichun, Ruoichin, Ruithina, etc., etc. Mr. J. Lewis supposes that Thanet was called Inis Ruochinn, from the town of Ruoch, now Rich, or Richborough.—History of Tenet, p. 2.—(*H.*) B. reads, Tenet and Rohin. L. Teneneth and Ropin. The Latin (Stevenson's text), is "et tradidit eis insulam, quae in lingua eorum vocatur Tanet, Brittannico sermone Ruoihin."—The verb, radaim, bears a remarkable resemblance to the Latin, *trado*, which it is here used to translate. But the Irish rad, rat *to give*, is a simple root, and *trado* a compound of *trans* and *do*.—(*T.*)

[f] *Gradian and Aequit.*—Gratian agus Equit, B. Graidian agus Eigeth, L. Gratianus (the first emperor of the name) and Equitius were consuls, A. D. 374. See Baron. (in anno) n. 1. But the true read-

the son of Eolonn[c], son of Feithiver, son of Ogaman, son of Tai, or Teo, son of Bob, son of Sembob, son of Athacht, son of Aoth, son of Abar, son of Raa, son of Eassa, son of Joban, son of Jonan, son of Jafeth, son of Noe.

Now Gortigern[d] held in peace, under the Romans, the government of the Cruithnians, and he gave up to them [i. e. *to the Saxons*], the island whose name is Teineth [*Thanet*], but Roinn[e] *is* its British name. Gradian and Aequit[f] *were* in the sovereignty of the Romans at that time. But it was from the birth of Christ, three hundred and forty-seven years ; and *it was* in the time of that king, viz., of Gortigern, that Saint German came to preach in the island of Britain, and God wrought[g] miracles and many wonders by this ecclesiastic in the island of Britain, and he healed many, and brought them under baptism and faith[h].

OF THE MIRACLES OF GERMAN HERE.

XVI. After the arrival of German in the island of Britain, he went to the fortress of the warrior whose name was Benli[i], to preach

ing of the Latin is Gratiano Secundo, or Gratiano Secundo Æquantio. See Gale's Edit. c. 28, with the var. Lect., and Additional Notes, No. XII. In this manner the anachronism is mitigated by 33 years. In the date which follows, L[1]. reads, ᵽeαċe mbliαöna .xl. αp. ccc., but B. reads, ᵽeċᴅ m-bliαöna .ccl. αp .ccc., where .ccl. is an evident mistake for .xl. Mr. Stevenson, in the text of his edition of Nennius, reads 447, and mentions in the note that the MSS. read variously, 337, 448, 400. and 347.—(*T.*)

[g] *God wrought . . . . . island of Britain.* —This clause is added from L[1]. and B. The mission of St. German to Britain was undertaken for the purpose of checking the Pelagian heresy, and is recorded by Prosper in his Chronicle, under the year 430.—(*T.*) See Additional Notes, No. XIII.

[h] *Faith.*—For ᵽo baiċhiᵽ αᵹuᵽ cᴘeιᴅιm, L[1]. reads ᵽo baiċhiᵽ baιᴅoι ᴅo ᵹᴘeᵽ, where baιᴅoι seems redundant ; ᴅo ᵹᴘeᵽ signifies, *always, for ever.*—(*T.*)

[i] *Benli.*—ᴅeιnoli, D.—(*T.*)

oaip Ʒeapman co ra ppuithib in n-oopup in ounaio ; oo coio in
ooippigi cop in pig im caingen in cleipig, po paio in pig co na luigi
oia m-beth na cleipig co ceno m-bliaona in n-oopap in ounaig ni
toippio apoeach. Cainig in ooippeoip cop in ppeagpa pin oo cum
Ʒeapmain Cainig Ʒeapman o'n oopap amach tpath feapcaip,
ㄱ ni pioip conaip no paga Cainig aen oo mogaoaib in pig ap in
caithpig amac. ㄱ po taipbip a piaonaipi Ʒeapmain, ㄱ pop pug leip
oo cum a boithe co cain agup co pailio, ㄱ ni poibe aigi oo cpoo act
aen bo co na laeg. ㄱ po mapb in laeg, ㄱ beapib, ㄱ oo pao oo na
cleipcib Agup po paio Ʒeapman na po bpipoip a cnama , agup
ap na maipeach tpa po maip in laeg a piaonaipi a inathap.

Oo coio Ʒepman oo oopup na caitpac iap na maipeac oo
h-eapnaioi agallaim in pig Ip ann pin tainig feap i n-a pith, ㄱ pé
lan oo allap o cino co bono. ㄱ po taipino oo Ʒeapman ; atbeapt
Ʒeapman

---

j At the door of the fortress —I n-oopup
an ouine, B in nopup in ounaio, D., omitting the eclipsed o in the word n-oopup
Oun, which signifies a fort or fortress,
and which occurs in the composition of
so many topographical names in Ireland,
is inflected ouine, and also ounaio or
ounaig, in the genitive this latter form
occurs in D throughout, and has been
retained in the text B adopts the form
ouine. This word seems cognate with
the English ton, or town, and with the
Welsh Din, Dinas —(T)

k The king said with an oath —B omits
the clause, po paio in pig cona luigi
oia m-beth na cleipig, to the manifest
loss of the sense —(T.)

l To German —Oocum in Ʒepmain
ceona, B 'To the same [or the afore-

said] German "—(T)

m Came away —B reads Cainic fep-
cup noine pai, agup nip peopaoaip cio no
pagaoaip, which is more close to the
Latin, ' Dies declinabat ad vesperum, et
nox appropinquabat, et nesciemunt quo
irent —(T)

n One of the servants, etc.—The word
mog, servus is generally used to denote
a labouring man, a slave, a hewer of wood
and drawer of water, one of the lowest
class —(T.)

o Out of the fortress —Ap in catpaig
amach The Latin is, "e medio urbis"
The Irish word cataip, which is here used
to translate the Latin urbs, is employed
in ancient MSS to denote a stone fort It
afterwards was applied to a walled town,
as Limerick, Waterford, &c , and is now

to him. German stopped with his clerics at the door of the fortress[j]. The porter went to the king with the message of the clergyman; the king said, with an oath[k], that if the clergy were to remain until the end of a year at the door of the fort, they should not come in. The porter came with this answer to German[l]. German came away[m] from the door in the evening, and did not know what road he should go. But one of the servants[n] of the king came out of the fortress[o], and bowed down[p] before German, and brought him with him to his cabin kindly and cheerfully[q]. And he had no cattle[r] but one cow with her calf, and he killed the calf, and boiled it, and gave it to the clergymen. And German ordered that its bones should not be broken; and on the morrow the calf was alive[s] in the presence of its dam.

On the next day German repaired to the door of the fortress to pray an interview[t] with the king. And then there came a man running

used to denote *a city*, as distinguished from baıle, *a town*, or baıle móp, *a large town.*—(*T.*)

[p] *Bowed down*—po caıpbıp in D., and po ꞃleċꞇ in B., to translate the Latin, "inclinavit se." The verb caıpbıp, *to prostrate*, or bow down the body, is now obsolete, and is not explained in any of the Dictionaries; but ꞃleċꞇ, *to kneel*, or, as now written by the moderns, ꞃleaċꞇ or ꞃleuċꞇ, is still in use.—(*T.*)

[q] *Brought him . . . . . cheerfully.*—Roꞃ ꝼuᵹ in D., and poo ꝼuc, in B. are only varied spelling of the same words, and signify "he brought." In modern Irish, po ċuᵹ. D. reads co caın ꝼuıꞃeach. B. reads co ꝼaılıó, which has been substituted in the text for ꝼuıꞃeach. Co ꝼaılıo (in modern orthography ᵹo ꝼaoı-

lıó) means joyfully, cheerfully. The Latin is *benigne*, which is more nearly rendered by co caın.—(*T.*)

[r] *He had no cattle.*—Nı po baı acca oı cꞃuó, B. The Latin is " Et ille nihil habebat de omnibus generibus jumentorum." The word cꞃuó or cꞃoó here used, signifying *cattle*, is the origin of the word *Cro, Croo,* or *Croy,* in our old laws, denoting a fine, mulct, or satisfaction for murder, manslaughter, or other crimes, such fines having anciently been paid in cattle. See Du Cange *in voce* Cro; Jamieson's Scottish Dictionary *in voce;* and Ware's Irish Antiquities, by Harris.—(*T.*)

[s] *Was alive.*—Ro baı ın laeᵹ beo, B. —(*T.*)

[t] *An interview.*—Ⱥcallmaı, B.—(*T.*)

Ӡeaɼman ın cɼeıoı ın naem τɼınnoıo. Cɼeıoım oıɼɼe; ɼon baıɼo
Ӡeaɼman ⁊ oo ɼaτ ɼoıc oo, ⁊ ɼo ɼıaıo ɼıɼ, eıɼıӡ, anoɼa aτbela, aτaıτ
aınӡıl Oe aӡ τ' uɼnaıoe , ⁊ oo [coıo] ɼaelıӡ ıɼın n-oun, ⁊ ɼo maɼbao
laɼ ın ɼıӡ ; oaıӡ ba béɼ leıɼ ın ɼıӡ maɼbao cach ouıne oıa muınn-
τıɼ no τoıτceao ɼe τoɼӡabaıl ӡɼeıne oe oeanaım obɼe ın oúıne.

Ro caıτ Ӡeaɼman ın la co h-aıocı a n-ooɼuɼ ın oúnaıo, co τo-
ɼaτ an moӡ ceona. Aτ beaɼτ Ӡeaɼman ɼıɼ, ɼomna, ɼoınna na
ɼoıb neac ooo muınoτıɼ ıɼ ın oun ɼo anochτ. Τuӡaɼoaıɼ ɼo cea-
ooıɼ ın nonbuɼ mac oo [baı occa] ɼa oun τall, ⁊ ɼuӡ ın cleıɼeach
leıɼ oıa τıӡ [ooıɼı], ⁊ oo ɼonɼaτ uıle ɼɼıchaıɼe. Co τamıӡ τeıne
Oé oo nım ɼo ceooıɼ ıɼ ın n-oun coɼ loıɼc [lucτ na caτɼac] eτeɼ
ınnaıb ⁊ ɼıɼu, mılı ouımı aɼ ɼeıɼӡ Oe ⁊ Ӡeɼmaın ; ⁊ ıɼ ɼaɼ coɼ amu.

Iaɼ na maıɼeach ımoɼɼo, ɼo baıɼoıo ın moӡ uτ co n-a macaıb
⁊ co luchτ ın τıɼe aɼceana, ɼo beanoachτ Ӡeaɼman [e] co n-a
claıno. Caıτeal a aınm, ⁊ bao ɼıӡ [e], ⁊ baoaɼ ɼıӡa a meıc τɼe
bɼeτhıɼ

u *From head to foot* —O h-ıno, D In
modern Irish the orthography would be,
o ceann ӡo bonn.—(*T.*)

v *Knelt.*—Slecτ, B See note ʸ D
reads τaıpıno, which is perhaps a form
of the old verb τaıɼbıɼ used before, unless there be some error of the MS The
Latin is ' ınclınavıt," and B. reads ɼo
ɼlecτ ın both places —(*T*)

w *I believe.*—D reads here Cɼeıτ oo,
corruptly, and omits ın before naem Τɼı-
noıτ the text is corrected from B B
reads olɼe —(*T*)

x *Said unto him* —Aτbeɼτ ɼnıɼ, B.

y *He went into the fortress.*—D. omits
the essential word coıo B reads Oo
coıo ɼaılıo ıɼ ın ounao D has ıɼ ın nun,
corruptly for ıɼ ın n-oun.—(*T.*)

z *Was accustomed* —Literally, ' It was a
custom with the king" oo'n ɼıӡ, B —(*T*)

a *Did not come* —Τoıɼɼeuo, B —(*T*)

b *Before sunrise* —Re τuɼӡabaıl nӡɼe-
ne B The Latin is "*ante solis ortum,*"
from which it is plain that the preposition ɼe is here used for ɼıa or ɼoım,
before Τuɼӡabaıl ӡɼeıne is a phrase
which is now, as Mr O'Donovan informs
me, obsolete in every part of Ireland; but
it was in use in Keating's time, who in
his Treatise Eochaıɼ ɼӡıaτ ın Aıɼɼɼınn,
has, o τuɼӡabaıl ӡɼéme ӡo a ɼuınıo,
" from the rising of the sun to its setting." Keating also sometimes uses ɼe
in the sense of ɼıa, as ɼe n-oılınn, " before the deluge "—(*T*)

c *Till night* —B reads, Ro caıτ Ӡeɼ-

running, and full of sweat from head to foot[u]; and he knelt[v] to German, and German said, "Dost thou believe in the Holy Trinity?" and he replied, "I believe[w]." And German baptized him and gave him a kiss: and he said unto him[x], "Arise, now thou shalt die, and the angels of God are awaiting thee." And he went cheerfully into the fortress[y], and was put to death by the king, for the king was accustomed[z] to put to death every one of his people that did not come[a] before sun-rise[b] to do the work of the palace.

German passed the whole of that day till night[c] at the door of the fortress, until the same [i. e. *the first mentioned*] servant came; and German said to him, "Take care, take care[d] that none of thy people be in this fortress this night." He immediately brought out with him the nine sons he had in the fortress, and he brought the clergyman with him to his house again; and they all kept watch. And the fire of God[e] immediately came from heaven upon the fortress, so that it burned the people of the fortress, both men and women, one thousand persons, through the anger of God and of German; and it remains a ruin to the present day.

On the following day this servant[f], with his sons and the people of the district, in like manner were baptized; and German blessed him and his children[g]. His name was Caiteal, and through the word

---

main co h-oióci. D. has no caié Ⓖerman in la con aiche, which is corrupt. The text has been corrected from both MSS.—(*T.*)

[d] *Take care.*—Fomnai, B., which is not repeated. The Latin is "Cave ne unus homo maneat de hominibus tuis in istâ nocte in arce." The words enclosed in brackets in the Irish text are all supplied from B. —(*T.*)

[e] *Fire of God.*—Ⓒene oo nim, B., which

exactly translates the Latin, "ignis de cœlo." Ⓒeine De, "the fire of God," is used to denote *lightning*, and is sometimes written ceine Diaic, *ignis Divinus.*—(*T.*)

[f] *This servant.*—B. reads, no baipc Ⓖerman in fecqi pin; "German baptized this man." The Latin is, "In crastino die ille vir, qui hospitalis fuit illis, credidit, et baptizatus est," &c.—(*T.*)

[g] *Him and his children.*—The pronoun [e] is here supplied as necessary to the

bρethiρ Ʒeaρmain, ⁊ a ρil o ρin ale, iρ in ρeaρann ðianað ainm Poʒuρ, uc ðicicuρ iρ na ρalmain, [Suρcicanρ a ceρρa inoρem, ec ðe ρceρcoρe eρⁱʒenρ pauρeρem.]

XVII. Saxain imoρρo in n-iniρ Ceineth, ⁊ Ʒoρciʒeρinn occa m-biachað ⁊ ʒa n-eiciuð Saxain co caithaiʒρec ðaρ a cenn ρe Cρuicencuach. Oρo imðaiʒiðaρ [cρa] Saxain, ρoρeimðρeac bρe-cain a m-biachað nac a n-eiðið, acc ρo ρoʒaiρρeac bρeacnaiʒ [ðoib] ðulaρ uile.

Ro ρρeaʒaiρ [ðoib immoρρo] Enʒiρc, ρeaρ ρaiʒe ρoρcʒe, cuai-ceall, ρoill, aρ ac connaiρc ρe bρeacnu co ρann ʒan miliða ʒan aρma, iρ ρeað ρo ρaið ρρiρ in ρiʒ Ʒoρciʒeρinn ðo cρunρað Ðe-nam ðeʒ comaiρli, ciaʒaρ uainð iρ in nʒeaρmain aρ ccað mileað co ρabam ρochaiðaiðe a n-aʒaið aρ namað. Acbeρc Ʒoρci-ʒeρinn a n-ðola na ceachca aρ cenn mileað; [⁊ ðo coað]; ⁊ ðo ρochρaðaρ occ lonʒa ðeʒ [co] miliðaib coʒaiðe aρ a Ʒeaρmain. Iρ in loinʒeaρ ρin cainiʒ a inʒean co h-Enʒiρc, iρ iρiðe ba caime ðo mnaib Cochlainðe uile.

iaρρin

sense   B omits e con-a claino, so that the meaning will be in that MS, "and German blessed the people of that coun-try" Instead of Caiceal a ainm, B reads, Caicel ainm in ρiρ ρin   in what follows [e] is supplied after ρiʒ from B, and baðaρ instead of bað, the reading of D B omits a meic after baðaρ ρiʒa, which is evidently corrupt—(T)

ʰ The word —bρiacaρ (in the dative or ablative bρeiciρ) when thus applied may signify either a blessing or a curse. That it signifies sometimes a curse is evident from the following quatrain which occurs in a MS in Trinity College, Dublin (H 1 17 fol 97 b)

" O ρéimior Ðiaρmaða Ðuinn,
Mic Feaρʒuρa, mic Chonuill,
O bρéiciρ Ruaðain ð á coiʒ,
Ní ρaib ρiʒ a ð-Ceamρaiʒ"

" From the reign of Dermot, the brown haired,
Son of Fergus, son of Conall,
On account of the word [curse] of Ruadan to his house,
There was no king at Tara '

—(T)

ⁱ Pogus —Pauʒuⁱ, B   In the Latin, " Regio Povisorium," Povus —(T)

ᵏ Pauperem Ps cxii 7. The Latin words within brackets are supplied from B, being omitted in D —(T)

ˡ The Saxons.—Occa, from B, is sub-

word[n] [i. e. *blessing*] of German, he became a king, and his sons became kings, and their seed have ever since been in the land called Pogus[i]; ut dicitur in the psalms, suscitans a terrâ inopem, et de stercore erigens pauperem[k].

XVII. Now, the Saxons *remained* in the Isle of Teineth [*Thanet*], and Gortigern was feeding and clothing the Saxons[l], that they might fight for him against[m] Pictland. But[n] when the Saxons had multiplied, the Britons *not only* refused to feed or clothe them, but the Britons warned them all to go away.

But Hengist[o], who was an experienced, wise, cunning, and subtle man, made answer to them (for he saw that the Britons were feeble without soldiers, without arms), and he said to the King Gortigern in private[p]: " Let us make good counsel; let us send into Germany for soldiers, that we may be numerous[q] against our enemies." Gortigern answered, " Let ambassadors go for soldiers ;" and they went[r]; and there came eighteen ships with chosen soldiers out of Germany. In this fleet[s] came his daughter to Hengist: she was the fairest of the women of all Lochland[t].

After

stituted for co, D. D. also reads co neoir corruptly, for which 'ᵹa n-eιᴣιuᴅ, which literally means, " a clothing them," is substituted from B. For caιᴄɦαιᵹreᴄ, both D. and B. read caιᴄɦαιᵹeaᴄɦᴄ.—(*T.*)

[m] *Against.*—Re, for which D. reads ᴘιᵹ, a manifest slip of the scribe. Cᴘuιᴄeᴨ-ᴄuαιᴄ, Pictland, the country of the Cruith-nigh. In D. Cᴘuιᴄneaᴄh-ᴄuαιᴄ.—(*T.*)

[n] *But.*—The words within brackets in this sentence are inserted from B.—(*T.*)

[o] *Hengist.*—Θιᵹιrᴄ, D. For ᵹeaᴘ ᴘαιᵹe. B. reads corruptly, ᵹᴘιᴘιᴅe ; ᴘαιᵹe would be more correctly written ᴘιᴅe.—(*T.*)

[p] *In private.*—Ιn ᴄαnᴘuᴅ, B., " in par-

ticular." D. reads ᴅo ᴄunᴘαᴅ, for ᴅo ᴄ-ᴘunᴘαᴅ, omitting the eclipsed letter.—(*T.*)

[q] *Numerous.*—Soᴄᴘαιᴅe ᴅun α n-αᵹαιᴅ, B.—(*T.*)

[r] *They went.*—Ðo ᴄoαᴘ (generally written ᴄuαᴘ) added from B., where we read ⁊ ᴅo ᴄoαᴘ, ⁊ ᴅo ᴘoᴄᴄαᴅαᴘ. Co is also added from B. before mιlιoᴄιb.—(*T.*)

[s] *In this fleet.*—Here the imperfection in the Book of Lecan ends. The text has been corrected from the three MSS. which read, Ιr ιn loιnᵹ, D. Ιr ιn loιnᵹιᴘ, B. Ιr αnᴅᴘα loιnᵹeαᴘ ᴘιn, L.—(*T.*)

[t] *Lochland.*—This name is here evi-

Iarrin imonna do nizne Enzirt pleav [mon] do Ꝺonzizennn ⁊
dia pluaz ir in tiz [niz] dianad ainm Centic Elmit ; ⁊ ni poibe in
Saxrain-benla az neoch do bneatnaib act az aen fean. Ro zab
imonno inzean Enzirt pon dail na pleidi .i. pina ⁊ piccena a leap-
tnaib oin ⁊ ainzid, comtan menzda meadancain na pluaiz ; do
cuaid tra demon i nꝽonzizennn im znad inzeine Enzirt, ⁊ nola in
benlaid dia naizid dia cuinze d'on niz do h-Enzirt, ⁊ no naid ciobe
cunzear 'na tochna do beannan do. Ró naid Enzirt tni comanle
Saxan tuctan duind in feanand dianad ainm Conzanlona 'rin
benla Saxan, Ceint imonno ir in benla bnetnuch. Do nad doib
Ꝺonzizennn

dently intended for some part of Germany, although generally applied by the Irish to Denmark and Norway See O'Brien's Irish Dict in v. *Lochlannach*.—(*T*)

ᵘ *Great banquet*—Fleiz, D pleid B pleud mon, L ; this last reading has been followed In the next line L reads pluazaib uile, for pluaz niz has been added from L and B. The name here given to this royal house is in the Latin Nennius given to Gortigern s interpreter "Fecit convivium Hengistus Guoithgirno regi, et militibus suis, et interpreti suo qui vocabatur Cerdicselmet"—Bertram, c. 36 and the name is variously given *Cerdic Elmet Ceretecc, Cerdic, Ceretic,* and in the Irish copies, Celetielmed, L Ceneticelemet, B. Centic Elmit, D The reading of B has been followed in the text, and it is very probable that the original meaning of the Irish translator was, that the banquet was given "in the house of the king, whose name was Cereticus Elmet, i.e. Cereticus king of Elmet," although, as

the Irish text now stands, it must be translated as above.—(*T*)

All this, however, is a mistake A certain Ceretic of Elmet was Hengist's interpreter, being acquainted with the British and Saxon languages See Nennius, cap 36 Marcus, p 66. There is an Ulmetum or Elmet in Yorkshire, called Elmed-setna in Gale's Hidæ Cis-Humbranæ, apud xv Scriptores, p. 748, from which Leeds was anciently Loidis in Elmeto, and where Berwick in Elmet now remains, a place at or near which the Northumbrian kings once had their palace It is the Silva Elmete of Beda, Hist ii cap 14 Camden Brit ii. 90, i Thoresby's Ducatus by Whitaker, p 232. Building on this passage of the Historia Britonum, the author of Bertram's Supplement, p 142 says, that Edwin, son of Ella, "regnavit annis xvii, et ipse occupavit Elmet, et expulit Certec regem illius regionis" But Edwin's reign was no earlier than 616-33 There must have been

After this Hengist prepared a great banquet[u] for Gortigern and his army in the royal house, which is called Centic Elinit; and none of the Britons knew the Saxon language except one man only. The daughter of Hengist proceeded to distribute the feast, viz., wines and ales, in vessels of gold and silver[v], until the soldiers were inebriated and cheerful[w]; and a demon entered Gortigern, from love of the daughter of Hengist[x], and he sent the linguist to Hengist to ask her for the king; and he said[y], that "whatever he would ask for her dowry should be given to him." Hengist, by the advice of the Saxons, said, "Let there be given to us the land which is named Congarlona[z] in the Saxon language, and Ceint in the British language,

elm forests in Britain, besides that in Deira, which makes the situation not certain. Cerdic being a Saxon name, and Ceretic a known way of writing Caredig, it is not obvious of which nation the interpreter was; but the transcribers of Nennius take him for a Briton, and indeed his being of a given place implies he was a native.—(*H.*) Hengist's name is spelt Eızıᵹırᴄ in L. throughout, and Aıᵹırᴄ in D.—(*T.*)

[v] *Gold and silver.*—No mention of these costly vessels is found in the Latin. The word comᴄap is an ancient mode of writing co m-baoap. It is spelled comoap in B. and L.—(*T.*)

[w] *Cheerful.*—Meopach, L. Meaopaıᵹe, B.—(*T.*)

[x] *Daughter of Hengist.*—L. adds, ᴄpe comaıplı Saxan, which is a mistake copied from what follows. In the next words B. has been followed. L. reads

oo pala ın belaıo, and D. po paᵹ ın bepla, which is manifestly corrupt. B. and L. omit oı a paıᵹıo, and read, oıa cuınoıᵹ pop Enᵹırᴄ. B. oıa cuınoıᵹ pop Eᵹırᴄ, L.—(*T.*)

[y] *He said.*—This clause, from oo paıo to beapᴄap oo, is omitted in L. B. reads oo paıo Enᵹırᴄ, which is an evident mistake. D. reads oo beapᴄap oı, "should be given to her," but the whole tenor of the story shews that oo, "to him," is the correct reading. The orthography in B. is Cıbeo cuınoᴄep na ᴄoćmapc oo bepap oo.—(*T.*)

[z] *Congarlona.*—Conᵹaplon, B., L.— (*T.*) This should be written Cantwarland, or the land of Kent.—(*H.*) Ceno, L. Cenᴄ, B. It appears from the Latin that Gurangona (Ᵹupanᵹopo, B., Cupancopo, L.) is the name of the king who then ruled over Kent: "et dedit illis Gnoiranegono regnante in Cantia".—(*T.*)

Ͷoptigepnn go paelte plaith Ͷupangona ⁊ po pac lap in n-ingein ⁊ pop cap go mop.

Agup paid Engipt pe Ͷoptigepnd bid mipi t' athaip ⁊ do comapleid ⁊ dia ndeapnda mo comaple ni caempat na cineadaig eile ni duit; ⁊ pagap uampea i Lochlaind ap ceand mo meic ⁊ meic peathup a matup ⁊ cathaigpid a n-aigiona namad do pochpadap co mup gual. Atbept Ͷoptigepnd a tocuiped, ⁊ do cop ap a ceand, ⁊ do pochtadap Ochta mac Engipt ⁊ Ebipa co. xl. long; ⁊ po aipgpead indpi Opcc ic tiachtain a tuaid; ⁊ po gabpat peapanna imda cop in muip Fpipeagoa, .i. in muip pil a leith ppi Ͷaedealu po tuaid. No teigoip teachta ó Engipt ap ceand long pop, ⁊ no tigoip pluaig nuad cacha bliadna cucu, co po popbappead, ⁊ go po linpat o inip Tened co Cartapboig.

Ba beag la diabul de ulc do poinde Ͷoptigepnd co tapd paip a ingen pein do tabaipt, co pug mac do. Od cualaid Ͷeapman naem [pin] tainig ⁊ cleipech dia muintip .i. Bpeatnach, do caipi-

ugud

---

a Loved her much.—Rop egap co mop, L. The word *egar* is still in use to express endearment, and is often found even where the Irish language has entirely ceased, and in the lips of those who never spoke a word of Irish, in the form "a haygur"—(*T*)

b I will send.—Act pacaip uaimpea, B L.—(*T*)

c The wall. Gual.—Mup gpadul, D mup gaulup, B. In L mup guub, which is probably a mere slip for gual, which, as the Latin proves, is the true reading. See pp. 64, 65.—(*T.*)

d There arrived Ochta.—Roctadap imoppo mac Engipt ⁊ Ebipa, B. Rocht

Ochta mac Eigipt ⁊ Eigi da, D. Rocht ocht meic Eigipt [the eight sons of Engist] ⁊ Ebipa, B The Latin is "et invitavit Ochta et Ebissa".—(*T.*)

e The Frisey Sea, etc.—"Mare Fresicum, quod inter nos Scotosque est, usque ad confinia Pictorum." The author had a very indistinct notion of the position of Friesland. The Gaidheal or Scoti here mean Ireland.—(*H.*)

f To Cantarborgh.—The whole of this passage is very corrupt both in the Latin and Irish copies: ⁊ po teigoip tecta o Engipt ap cenn long pop, ⁊ po tigoip pluaig nuad gaca bliadna cucu, co popbpipet, ⁊ co po linpat o inip Tened co

guage." Gortigern cheerfully gave them the dominions of Gurangona, and he lay with the daughter and loved her much[a].

And Hengist said to Gortigern: "I will be thy father and thy counsellor, and if thou takest my advice the other tribes will not be able in any way to molest thee; and I will send[b] to Lochland for my son, and for the son of his mother's sister, and they will fight against the enemy who have reached as far as the wall Gual.[c]" Gortigern said, "Let them be invited;" and they were invited; and there arrived Ochta[d], son of Engist, and Ebisa, with forty ships; and they plundered the Orkney islands on coming from the north, and they took many lands as far as the Friseg sea[e], that is the sea which is to the north of the Gaedhal. And ambassadors were further sent by Hengist for more ships, and a new force used to arrive every year, so that they increased, and filled *the land* from the island of Teneth to Cantarborgh[f].

The devil deeming it but little the evil that Gortigern had done, induced him to cohabit with his own daughter, so that she bare him a son. When German[g] heard of this, he went, accompanied by a clergyman

---

CᴀnᴢᴀꝚbonᵹ, B. ┐ no ᴢheɪᵹoɪꝚ ᴢeᴀchᴢᴀ o Eɪᵹeꝶᴢ ᴀꝶ ceᴀno lonᵹ boᴜꝶ, ┐ no ᴢɪᴄoɪꝶ ꝶlᴜᴀɪᵹ nᴀᴀ cᴀchᴀ blɪᴀonᴀ chᴜcᴜ co ꝶᴀ ꝶoɪꝶbꝶɪꝶeᴀo, ┐ co ꝶo lɪnꝶᴀo o h-Eneꝶ Cenocᴄh co Ceᴀnoᴀꝶbꝶoᵹ, L. ᴎo ᴢeɪᵹoɪꝶ ᴢeᴀchᴢᴀ o Eɪᵹɪꝶᴢ ᴀꝶ ceᴀno lonᵹ bᴜꝶ, ┐ no ᴢɪᵹoɪꝶ ꝶlᴜᴀɪᵹ nᴜᴀó cᴀchᴀ blɪᴀonᴀ cᴜcᴜ, co ꝶo ꝶoꝶbᴀꝶꝶeᴀo, ┐ ᵹo ꝶo lɪnꝶᴀᴢ o ɪnɪꝶ Ꝺꝶeᴀᴢᴀn co ᴢᴀnᵹᴀoᴀꝶ bᴀꝶᵹ, D. This latter reading, however, is evidently corrupt.—(*T.*)

[g] *German.*— German took his final leave of Britain in 447, and Vortigern is said to have died circa 484, which is consistent with his having a child some years old, at that time. But it is evident that his unpopularity commenced several years later, when he attached himself to the Saxons, whose original invitation was subsequent to St. German's death; and so far from being an unpopular act, was not even the king's act, but one resolved upon by all the consiliarii.—Gildas, cap. 23. Therefore these statements are false; and the entire charge of incest is open to doubt.—(*H.*)

uᵹ̇no ⁊ do coṗᵹ Ḃoṗᵹiᵹeṗno, ⁊ ṗo ᴄinóiliu laiᴄẏ ⁊ cleiṗiᵹ Ḃṗeaᴄan uile imon cainᵹen ṗin, ⁊ im cainᵹin na Saxan, ⁊ aᴄbeṗᴄ imoṗṗo
Ḃoṗᵹiᵹeṗno ṗe ẏ-inᵹein, Aᴄẏᴄ co ᴄi caᴄẏ a n-aen baile ᴄabuiṗṗea
do mac a n-uᴄẏᴄ Ḃeaṗman, ⁊ abaiṗ coṗob é a aᴄẏaiṗ, ⁊ do ṗaiu
in n-inᵹean Ro ᵹab Ḃeaṗman ⁊ aᴄbeṗᴄ ṗiṗ in mac, biu miṗi
ᴄ'aᴄẏaiṗ ol ṗé, ⁊ ṗo cuiuiᵹ Ḃeaṗman alᴄain, ⁊ uemeaṗ, ⁊ ciṗ, [⁊ a]
ᴄabaiṗᴄ alaim na nauen, ⁊ ᴄuᵹau, ⁊ auḃeaṗᴄ Ḃeaṗman A mic
ᴄabaiṗ ṗin a laim ᴄ'aᴄẏaṗ collaiue; ⁊ auṗaᴄẏᴄ in naiue ⁊ do ṗau
in ciṗi ⁊ in uimeaṗ ⁊ in n-uilᴄim a laim Ḃoṗᴄiᵹeṗno, ⁊ auḃeṗᴄ, A
mo ṗoba, ol ṗé, ḃéna mo beaṗṗau, áṗ iṗ ᴄu m'aᴄaiṗ collaiue,
Ḃeaṗman imoṗṗo m'aᴄẏaiṗ cṗeiuim Ro ẏ-imueaṗᵹau im Ḃoṗᴄiᵹeṗno, ⁊ ṗo ᵹab ḟeaṗᵹ co ẏ-auḃal, ⁊ ṗo ᴄeiᴄẏ aṗṗ a n-uiṗeaᴄẏᴄ, ⁊
ṗo mallaᴄᴄ in popul Ḃṗeᴄnaᴄẏ uile, ⁊ ṗo n-eaṗᴄain Ḃeaṗman [ue
uuobuṗ].

DO DUN AMḂROISS ANNSO AᵹUS DIA ᴄAᵹRA ḞRIS NA
DRAIᴄẏAIḂ

XVIII. Ro ᴄocuiṗṗuaiṗ iaṗuain Ḃoṗᴄiᵹeṗno cuice ua uṗuiu
ueᵹ, co ṗeaṗau uaᴄẏib a ní bo coiṗ uo ueanam. Do ṗaiuṗiu ṗiṗ
na uṗuiui, Síṗ imli imṗi Ḃṗeaᴄan, ⁊ ṗo ᵹeba uun uainᵹean uou
uiuean aṗ in cinél n-eaᴄẏᴄṗann uia ᴄaṗᴄaiṗi uo ᴄíṗ ⁊ uo ṗiᵹe, uaiᵹ
nou múiṗṗiu uo namau, ⁊ ᵹébaiu uo ᴄíṗ ⁊ uo ᴄalam ᴄaṗ ᴄ'éiṗ.
Ro ᴄoᴄẏleaṗuaiṗ Ḃoṗᴄiᵹeṗno co n-a ṗluaᵹ ⁊ co n-a uṗuiuib ueiṗ-
ceaṗᴄ

<hr>

ʰ *A clergyman* —The reading adopted
is that of L   D. reads ᴄainᵹ aᵹuṗ cleiṗiᵹ Ḃṗeaᴄan   B reads ᴄainᵹ in clepec
Ḃṗeaᴄan uile   The Latin is ' venit cum
omni cleio Brittonum "—(*T*)

ⁱ *British people* —Popal na m-Ḃṗea-
ᴄan uile, D pobul m-Ḃṗeaᴄnaᴄẏ. L B
ue uuobuṗ added from B and L —(*T*)

ʲ *The fortress of Ambrose* —Do uun
Ampoiṗ, D Do uun Amḃṗoiṗṗ, B   In
Welsh, *Dinas Emris*, the fortress of Emrys
or Ambrose —(*T*)

ᵏ *The Druids said* —Aᴄḃeṗᴄauaṗ a
uṗuiu ḟṗiṗ imle Ḃṗeaᴄin uo iaṗṗain, B.
auḃeṗᴄauaṗ ne uṗuiu ṗiṗ, ṗiṗ imli cṗiᴄẏi
Ḃṗeᴄan, L.   In what follows the ortho-

clergyman[h] of his nation, i. e. British, to criminate and check Gortigern; and he assembled all the laity and clergy of Britain for this purpose, and also for the purpose of *consulting about* the Saxons. But Gortigern told his daughter, "When they are all assembled together, give thou thy child into the breast of German, and say that he is his father." And the daughter did so. German received the child, and said unto him, "I will be thy father," said he ; and German asked for a razor, scissars, and a comb, and gave them into the hands of the infant; and this was done; and German said: " My son, give these into the hand of thy carnal father;" and the infant advanced, and gave the comb, the scissars, and the razor, into the hand of Gortigern, and said, " O my master," said he, "do thou tonsure me, for thou art my carnal father. German is my father in the faith." Gortigern blushed at this, and became much enraged, and fled from the assembly; and he was cursed by all the British people[i], and excommunicated by German also.

Of the fortress of Ambrose[j], and of his contest with the Druids.

XVIII. And afterwards Gortigern invited to him twelve Druids, that he might know from them what was proper to be done. The Druids said[k] to him, " Seek the borders of the island of Britain, and thou shalt find a strong fortress to defend thyself against the foreigners to whom thou hast given up thy country and thy kingdom, for thine enemies will slay thee[l], and will seize upon thy country and lands after thee." Gortigern, with his hosts and with his

graphy of D. is very corrupt; the text has been corrected from B. and L., but it will only be necessary in these notes to mention the more important various readings.—(T.)

[l] *Will slay thee.*—B. and L. read do maippead do namaid. For do talam, B. reads do ceneoil; L. do cheneli, "thy race," " Cum universa gente tua;"— *Nennius.*—(T.)

ceapc innṗí bpeacan uile, co paŋgaḃap Ẑuineḃ, ⁊ po ṗippeaḃ ṗliaḃ
hepep uile, ⁊ conaḃ anḃpin ṗuapaḃap in ḃinḃ oṗ in muip, ⁊ ṗeap-
anḃ ḃaiŋgean, coṗ cumḃaiᵹeᵹ h-e , acḃepcaḃap a ḃpuiḋi ṗiṗ, Ḋéan-
aṗu ṗunḃa ḃu ḃun, ol ṗiaḃ, aṗ ni caeinnaᵹaiṗ ní ḃo co bṗacḣ
Cuccḣa ṗaiṗ iapḃain ⁊ po cinolic anḃaiṗ in ḃun eiciṗ cloicḣ ⁊
cṗanḃ, ⁊ ṗuᵹaḃ aṗ uile in comaḃḃaṗ a n-aen aiḃce, ⁊ po cinolic ṗo
cṗí inoṗin in comaḃḃuṗ ṗin ⁊ ṗuᵹaḃ aṗ ṗo cṗi Ocuṗ po ṗiaṗṗaiᵹ
[cṗa] ḃia ḃpuiḃcib ciḃ ḃia ḃa in c-olc [ṗa] aṗ ṗé; po ṗaiḃṗeac a
ḃpuiḃe, cuinᵹiḃ mac na ṗeaṗ a acḣaiṗ ⁊ maṗbcaṗ leac ⁊ eaṗṗain-
ceṗ a ṗuil caṗ in ḃun; [⁊] aṗ ainlaiḃ conn icṗiḃeaṗ a cinḃacḣ

Ro laice ceacḣca uaḃ ṗo iniṗ bpeacan ḃ'iaṗṗaiḃ mic ᵹan acḣaiṗ,
⁊ po ṗippeac co maᵹ Eilleice a ciṗ Ẑleuiṗic, iṗ anḃ ṗin ṗuapaḃap
na macu aᵹ imain, co capila ḃeaḃaiḃ eciṗ ḃa macain ḃib, con
n-eḃaiṗc in mac ṗṗia aṗaile, aḃuine ᵹan acḣaiṗ, ní ṗil maic aᵹuḃ
eoiṗ Ro h-iaṗṗaiᵹṗeac na ceacḣca ciḃ ḃia ḃo mac in ᵹilla ṗiṗ a
n-aḃṗe ṗiuḃ? Acḃepc lucḣc na ṗaicḣe, ni eacainaṗ, ol ṗiaḃ [ca
a macḣaiṗ

m *Guined*—B reads co Neḃ corruptly ,
L has Ẑuineḃ; the Latin reads Guoie-
net —(*T*)

n *Herer*—The text is here corrected
from B, in conformity with the Latin
D omits hepep, and L corrupts the
words ṗliaḃ hepep to ṗalu aiṗep Snowdon is the mountain meant.—(*T*)

o *A Dinn*—In the Latin *arcem.* The
word *Dinn*, which is found in many names
of places in Ireland (as Dinn Righ, near
Leighlin), and in the name of the ancient treatise Dinn-Senchus, (the History
of *Dinns*) is synonimous with *Dun*, a fort
It seems to be here used in its original
signification of a high or naturally fortified hill. It is explained cnoc, a hill, in
old Glossaries —(*T*)

p *Carried away*—Similar traditions exist in connexion with the erection of
many churches in Ireland, viz, that what
was built in the course of the day was
thrown down at night by some unknown
power Mr O'Donovan found this tradition told of the church of Banagher, in
the county of Derry, and has given an
account of it in a letter preserved among
the Ordnance Survey papers, Phœnix
Park, Dublin —(*T*.)

q *Whose father is unknown.*— Nacḣ
ṗinḃcaṗ a acaiṗ, B , L , i e whose father
is not known "—(*T*.)

r *Let his blood be sprinkled*—Eaṗṗain-
ceṗ, L., has been substituted in the text,

his Druids, traversed all the south of the island of Britain, until they arrived at Guined[m], and they searched all the mountain of Herer[n], and there found a Dinn[o] over the sea, and a very strong locality fit to build on; and his Druids said to him, "Build here thy fortress," said they, " for nothing shall ever prevail against it." Builders were then brought thither, and they collected materials for the fortress, both stone and wood, but all these materials were carried away[p] in one night; and materials were *thus* gathered thrice, and were thrice carried away. And he asked of his Druids, " Whence is this evil?" said he. And the Druids said, " Seek a son whose father is unknown[q], kill him, and let his blood be sprinkled[r] upon the Dun, for by this means only it can be built."

Messengers were sent by him throughout the island of Britain to seek for a son without a father; and they searched as far as Magh Eillite[s], in the territory of Glevisic, where they found boys a hurling; and there happened a dispute between two of the boys, so that one said to the other, " O man without a father[t], thou hast no good at all." The messengers asked, " Whose son is the lad to whom this is said?" Those on the *hurling* green[u] said, " We know not,"

said

---

for ꝺeiꝗiᵹꝺeꝓ, D., which signifies, "let it be spread." B. reads eꝓꝓaiꮓeꝓ, " let it be sprinkled." The Latin is aspergatur or conspergatur.—(*T.*) See Additional Notes, No. XIV., for some remarks on the practice here alluded to.

[s] *As far as Magh Eillite.*—Ꝼo maᵹ Eilliꮓꝺe, D. Co maꝺ Elleꮓi, B. Co maᵹ Eilleiꮓe, L. This last reading has been adopted.—(*T.*) See Additional Notes, No. XV.

[t] *O man without a father.*—ꓥ ꝺuine ᵹen aꮓꧥaiꝓ ni h-uil aꮓꧥaiꝓ aᵹaꝺ, D. ꓥ ꝺuine can aꮓꧥaiꝓ ni ꝼuil in aꮓꧥaiꝓ occa, L., i. e. " O man without a father, thou hast no father." The reading in the text is taken from B., as it coincides with the Latin.—(*T.*)

[u] *Hurling-green.*—Ꝼaiꮓꙅi, B. ꝼaiꮓꙅi, L. This word, which occurs frequently in composition in the names of places in Ireland, signifies a green field; and in the county Kilkenny is still used to denote a fair-green, or hurling-green; as Ꝼaiꮓꙅi an aonaiᵹ; Ꝼaiꮓꙅi na h-iománu; ꙅé an ꝼeaꝓꝓ iꝓ ꝼeaꝓꝓ aꝓ a' ꞗ-ꝼaiꮓꙅi é. See

a maṫaıp punn, op pıaö]   Ro ıappaıöpeaꞇ öıa maꞇaıp cıö öıap
bo mac an ᵹılla   Ro ppeaᵹaıp ın maꞇaıp ın eaöap-pa, oıpı, aꞇaıp
oᵹa, ꞅ nı eaöap cınöap öo pala ım bpoınö eıꞇıp   Ꞇuᵹaꞃöaıp ꞇpa
na ꞇeacꞇa leo ın mac pın co Ꝝopꞇıᵹepın, ꞅ po h-ınöıpöaıp amaıl
puapaöap e

XIX ıap na maıpeac po ꞇınolıꞇ [ın] pluaıᵹ copo mapbꞇa ın
mac, ꞅ ꞇuᵹaö co pın pıᵹ ın mac, ꞅ aöbepꞇ ppıp ın pıᵹ, cıö ap naım
ꞇuᵹaö-pa cucaıb, ap pé? Ro paıö ın pıᵹ öoö mapbıöpa, ap pé, ꞅ
öoö copcpaö, ꞅ öo copepᵹuö ın öuın pea öoö puıl Aöbepꞇ ın mac
cıa po h-ıncoıpc öuıö-pıu pın? Ɱo öpaıöe, ap ın pı. Ꝝaıpꞇep alle
ol ın mac, ꞅ ꞇanᵹaöap na öpuıöı Aꞇbepꞇ ın mac pıu, Cıa po paıö
pıbpı na cumöaıᵹep ın öun po no co coıpeacapꞇa [öo m' puıl-pea] ap
ꞇup? ꞅ nı po ppeaᵹpaöap   Öo eaöappa, ol pé, ın ꞇı öom paöpa
cucaıb öap bap n-aıceöö ıp e öo paö popaıb-pı ın bpéaᵹ öo canꞇaın
Acꞇ ceana, a pıᵹ, ol pé, poıllpıᵹpeaö-pa pípınöe öuıö-pıu, ꞅ pıappaı-
ᵹım öuö öpaıꞇıb ap ꞇúp, cıö aꞇa a polac po'n n-úpláp po ın ap pıaö-
naıpı Ro paıöpeaö na öpuıöı poc n-eaöamap ap pıaö Ro eaöap-
pa ol pé· aꞇá loch uıpce ann, péachap ꞅ claeꞇep. Ro claeöeö
ꞅ ppıꞇh [ın loc anö] A paꞇe ınö pıᵹ, ap ın mac, abpaıö cıö aꞇa
ın meöon ın loca⸲ Nı peaöemap, ol pıaö Ro peaꞇappa, ol pé,
aꞇáıꞇ öá clap cıpöı mopa ann ın n-aᵹaıö a n-aᵹaıö, ꞅ ꞇucꞇap ap
[ıaꞇ; ꞅ peaᵹꞇap ꞅ ꞇucaö ap;] ꞅ a öpuıöe ap ın mac, abpaıö cıö
aꞇa eꞇıp na clap leapꞇpaıb uö? nı eaöemap, ap pıaö. Ro pea-
öappa,

note [h], p 66 *supra*. In Cormac's Glossary (*voce* plu), it is employed to translate the Latin word *platea*.—(*T*)

[v] *His mother is here, said they*.—Added
from L B reads aꞇꞇ aꞇa maꞇaıp pun-
öa occaı olpıaꞇ—(*T*).

[w] *To them*.—Fpıp na öpaıᵹıb, D pıu
ın B and L.—(*T*)

[x] *With my blood*.—Supplied from B
and L Other corrections of the text have
also been made from the same sources,
but the variations are not worth noticing,
being, for the most part, mere differences
of orthography.—(*T*)

[y] *This he*.—The meaning seems to be
this "The person who induced you to

said they, " his mother is here," said they[v]   They asked of his
mother whose son the lad was   The mother answered, " I know
not," said she, " that he hath a father, and I know not how he happened *to be conceived* in my womb at all " So the messengers took the
boy with them to Gortigern, and told him how they had found him.

XIX On the next day the army was assembled, that the boy
might be killed.   And the boy was brought before the king, and he
said to the king, " Wherefore have they brought me to thee ?" said he
And the king said, " To slay thee," said he, " and to butcher thee, and
to consecrate this fortress with thy blood " The boy said, " Who instructed thee in this ?" " My Druids," said the king. " Let them be
called hither," said the boy And the Druids came The boy said to
them[w], " Who told you that this fortress could not be built until it
were first consecrated with my blood?[x]" And they answered not " I
know," said he , " the person who sent me to you to accuse you, is he
who induced you to tell this lie[y], howbeit, O king," said he, " I will
reveal the truth to thee; and I ask of thy Druids, first, what is concealed
beneath this floor before us ?" The Druids said, " We know not," said
they " I know," said he ; " there is a lake of water there ; let it [the
floor] be examined and dug."   It was dug, and the lake[z] was found
there " Ye prophets of the king," said the boy, " tell what is in the
middle of the lake ?" " We know not," said they   " I know," said
he, " there are two large chests of wood face to face, and let them be
brought out of it "   It was examined, and they were brought forth[a]
" And O Druids," said the boy, " tell what is between those two
wooden

---

tell this he will be the cause of your disgrace " Here begins a fragment of this
work in the Leabhar na h-Uidhri, which
shall be referred to in the following notes
by the letter U.—(*T.*)

[z] *The lake* — The words in loc ano
are added from U.—(*T*)

[a] *Brought forth* — The words within
brackets are added from B   U. and L
read ר דuraᵭ aר, only —(*T.*)

ʋaᵽᵽa, aᵽ ᵽé, áᴄa ᵽeol bᵽaᴄ [anⱱ ; ⁊ ᴄuᴄᴄaᵽ aᵽ, ⁊ ᵽᵽiᴄ in ᵽeol]
ᴄimmaᵽᴄᴄé eᴄiᵽ na ⱱa claᵽ ᴄiᵽⱱi.   Abᵽaiⱱ, a eolcha, aᵽ in mac,
ᴄiⱱ aᴄa a meaⱱon iii n-éaⱱaiᵹ ⱱⱱ ? ⁊ ni ᵽo ᵽᵽeaᵹᵽaⱱaᵽ, [aᵽ ni ᵽo
ᴄhucᵽaᴄaᵽ]   Aᴄaiᴄ ⱱa cᵽuim ann, ol ᵽé, .i. cᵽuim ⱱeaᵽᵹ ⁊ cᵽuim
ᵹeal ; ᵽcailᴄeaᵽ in ᴄ-eaⱱach.   Ro ᵽcaileⱱ in ᵽeol bᵽaᴄ, [⁊] ᵽo
baⱱaᵽ na ⱱa cᵽuim na cⱱⱱlaⱱ ann   [Ro ᵽaiⱱ in mac] ᵽeacaiⱱ-ᵽe
a n-ⱱiᵹnaiⱱ anoᵽa na biaᵽⱱa.   Aⱱᵽuchᴄ cach ⱱib co aᵽaile co
ᵽaibe ᴄeᴄᴄaᵽ ⱱe ic ᵽᵽaineⱱ a ceile, ⁊ [co ᵽobaᴄaᵽ] ic imleⱱᵽaⱱ,
⁊ ic imiᴄhe, ⁊ no h-innaᵽbᴄhaⱱ in cᵽuim ⱱib aᵽaile co meⱱⱱii in
ᴄ-ᵽiuil, ⁊ in ᵽeachᴄ aile co imell   Do ᵽonᵽaᴄ ᵽa ᴄᵽí ᵽon n-inⱱuᵽin
In cᵽuim ᵽuaiⱱ ᴄᵽa ba ᵽanⱱ aᵽ ᴄuᵽ, ⁊ ᵽo h-innaᵽbᴄaⱱ co h-imeal
iii n-eaⱱaiⱱ ; in cᵽuim ᴄaiᵽneamach imoᵽᵽo ba ᵽann ᵽo ⱱeⱱiᵹ, ⁊
ᵽo ᴄeich iᵽ in loch, ⁊ ᵽo ᵽineaᵽⱱaiᵽ in ᵽeol ᵽo ceⱱⱱiᵽ   Ro h-iaᵽ-
ᵽaiⱱ in mac ⱱo na ⱱᵽaiⱱib ; inniᵽaiⱱ aᵽ ᵽe, ciⱱ ᵽaillᵽiᵹiᵽ in ᴄ-inᵹnaⱱ
ᵽa ? Ni eⱱⱱamaᵽ, aᵽ ᵽiaⱱ   Do ᵹéan-ᵽa [aᵽ in mac] a ᵽaillᵽiuᵹaⱱ
ⱱo'n ᵽiᵹ   Iᵽ é an loch ᵽlaiᴄhiuᵽ in ⱱomaii uile, ⁊ iᵽé in ᵽeol ⱱo
ᵽlaiᴄiuᵽiu a ᵽiᵹ   Iᵽiaᴄ na ⱱa cᵽuim imoᵽᵽo [na ⱱa neaᵽᴄ] i ⱱo
neaᵽᴄ ᵽo co m-bᵽeaᴄnaib, ⁊ neaᵽᴄ Saxan   In cᵽuim ᵽuaⱱ, iᵽ i
ⱱo h-inⱱaᵽbaⱱ aᵽ ᴄúᵽ ⱱo'n ᵽlaiᴄhiuᵽ ⱱo neaᵽᴄ-ᵽo ; neaᵽᴄ Saxan
imoᵽᵽo in cᵽuim [ᵹel] ᵽo ᵹab in ᵽeol uile acᴄ beaᵹ .i. ᵽo ᵹab iᵽ
bᵽeaᴄan acᴄ beaᵹ, co ᵽo h-inⱱaᵽbᵽaᴄaᵽ i eaᵽᴄ bᵽeaᴄan ᵽo ⱱeⱱiᵹ
Ꜩuᵽa imoᵽᵽo, a ᵽiᵹ bᵽeaᴄan, ciᵽiᵹ aᵽ in ⱱun ᵽo, aᵽ ní caemaiᵽ a
cumⱱach, ⁊ ᵽíᵽ iiᵽ bᵽeaᴄan, ⁊ ᵽo ᵹeba ⱱo ⱱún ᵽéin   Ro ᵽaiⱱ in
ᵽiᵹ, caiⱱe ⱱo comainiiᵽiu a mic, ol ᵽe, ᵽo ᵽᵽeaᵹaiᵽ in ᵹilla, Am-
bᵽoᵽ,

b *Was found* —The words within brackets are added from U and B In the next
lines the clause aᵽ ni ᵽo ᴄucᵽaⱱaᵽ is
added from U and L , and Ro ᵽaiⱱ in
mac from U., L , and B —(T.)

c *Alternately.*—D. reads, in cᵽuim ᵽuaiⱱ
ᵽᵽiuᵽ, i e "the red maggot was first driven to the middle of the sail." But U ,
B , and L all read as in the text, which
also agrees with the Latin—(T)

d *Kingdom* —D. reads, in ᵽlaiᴄhemnaᵽ ;
U , B , and L all read ᵽlaiᴄiuᵽ, without
the article. The words na ⱱa neaᵽᴄ,
"the two powers," in the next line, are

wooden chests?" "We know not," said they. "I know," said he; "there is a sail-cloth there." And it was brought forth, and the sail was found[b] rolled up between the two wooden chests. "Tell, O ye learned," said the boy, "what is in the middle of that cloth?" And they answered not, for they understood not. "There are two maggots there," said he, "namely, a red maggot and a white maggot. Let the cloth be unfolded." The sail-cloth was unfolded, and there were two maggots asleep in it. And the boy said, "See now what the maggots will do." They advanced towards each other, and commenced to rout, cut, and bite each other, and each maggot drove the other alternately[c] to the middle of the sail and again to its verge. They did this three times. The red maggot was at first the feeble one, and was driven to the brink of the cloth; but the beautiful maggot was finally the feeble one, and fled into the lake, and the sail immediately vanished. The boy asked the Druids: "Tell ye," said he, "what doth this wonder reveal?" "We know not," said they. "I will reveal it to the king," said the boy. "The lake is the kingdom[d] of the whole world, and the sail is thy kingdom, O king. And the two maggots are the two powers, namely, thy power in conjunction with the Britons, and the power of the Saxons. The red maggot, which was first expelled the kingdom, represents thy power; and the white maggot, which occupied the whole sail except a little, represents the power of the Saxons, who have taken the island of Britain, except a small part, until ultimately driven out by the power of the Britons. But do thou, O king of Britain, go away from this fortress, for thou hast not power to erect it, and search the island of Britain and thou shalt find thine own fortress." The king said, "What is thy name, O boy," said he. The youth replied, "Ambrose," said he, "is my name." (He was Embros Gleutic[e], king of Britain.) "Tell thy

bꞃoꞃ, ol ꞃe, m'aınm-ꞃe (ıꞃ é ꞃın ın Cmbꞃoꞃ Ꙅleuꞇıc ꞃıꞅ bꞃeaꞇan.)
Can ꝺo cenel aꞃ ıꞃ ꞃıꞅ. Conꞃul Romanach, ol ꞃe, m'aꞇaıꞃ-ꞃe, ⁊ bıꝺ
e ꞃeo mo ꝺun. Ro leıꞅ ꞇꞃa Ꙅoꞃꞇıꞅeꞃnꝺ ın ꝺun ꝺo Cmbꞃoꞃ, ⁊ ꞃıꞅe
ıaꞃꞇaıꞃ bꞃeaꞇan uıle, ⁊ ꞇaınıc co n-a ꝺꞃaıꝺıb co ꞇnaıꞃꞅeaꞃꞇ ınꞃı
bꞃeaꞇan, ı ꞅuꞃ an ꞃeaꞃann ꝺıanaꝺ aınm Ꙅunnıꞃ, ⁊ ꞃo cuımꝺaıꞅ
ꝺun ann, .ı. caeꞃ Ꙅoꞃꞇıꞅeꞃnꝺ a h-aınm

ꝺo caıꞇhıꞅhecꞇ ꙄoıꞃꞇhımıR.

XX. ıaꞃꞇaın ꞇꞃa aꞇꞃachꞇ Ꙅoꞃꞇhemıꞃ coꞃcꞃaċ, mac Ꙅoꞃꞇı-
ꞅeaꞃnꝺ, co na bꞃaꞇhaıꞃ, .ı. Caıꞇceaꞃnꝺ, ın n-aꞅaıꝺ Cnꞅıꞃꞇ ⁊ Oꞃꞃa.
[⁊] ꞃo caꞇhaıꞅꞃeaꞇ bꞃeaꞇnaıꞅ maꞃaen ꞃıu co h-amnaꞃ, co ꞃo
h-ınꝺaꞃbꞃaꞇaꞃ

U. Cmꞃuꞃ Ꙅleꞃıꞇıc, L.—(T.) That is
to say, Emmrys Wledig, which means
Ambrosius Sovereign of the Land. But
Gwledig seems also, for some unknown
reason, to have been conventionally an
equivalent for Aurelius, since not only
Emmrys Wledig is Aurelius Ambrosius,
but Cynan Wledig is Aurelius Conanus.
Nennius and Taliesin identify him with
Merlin, the bard and prophet, called
Merddin Emmrys. Two structures bore
his name, viz., the Stonehenge, called the
Cor Emmrys and Gwaith Emmrys, Circle
of Ambrose, or Work of Ambrose, and
the Dinas Emmrys, in Snowdon, here spo
ken of. The latter is a roundish mound
of rock, difficult of access, on the top of
which are two ramparts of stone, and
within them the ruins of a stone building, ten yards in length. Hard by is a
place said to have been the cell of Vortigern's magicians.—Pennant's Journey to
Snowdon, p 174. The mount is said to
have been called Brith,

"And from the top of Brith so high and wond'rous
    steep,
Where Dinas Emris stood,' &c
                        Drayton, cit ibid p 175

In Triads 53 and 101, the Dinas
Emmrys is called Dinas Faraon, that is,
Enclosure of the *Higher Powers* or *Spiritual Beings*. The last of these Triads
states, that an eagle's pullet, brought
forth by a sow, was intrusted to the
keeping of Brynach the Irishman of Dinas Faraon. It was clearly a building
appropriated to magical uses.—(H)

† *Gunnis.*—So all the Irish MSS. read.
The Latin MSS. vary considerably.—(T)
The translator, having begun the story by
stating that Gwynedd (or North Wales),
and Mount Eryri (or Snowdon), were in
the South of Britain, seems to repeat the

thy race," said the king "My father," said he, "was a Roman consul, and this shall be my fortress." Then Gortigern left the fortress
to Ambrose, and also the government of all the west of Britain, and
went with his Druids to the north of the island of Britain, that is, to
the land which is called Gunnis[f], and built a fortress there, which
city is named Caer Gortigern[g].

Of the warfare[h] of Gortimer

XX After this, Gortimer[i] the victorious, son of Gortigern, with
his brother Catigern[j], rose up against Hengist and Orsa, and the
Britons fought fiercely along with them, so that they drove the Saxons
to

name of Gwynedd, in the travestied form
of Gunnis, and place it in the north. In
the first place the Latin copies have Gu-
oienit and Guenet, and in the second,
Gwnnessi, Gueness, and Gueneri Probably the same name is meant in both
instances, for Gwnnessi is said to be in
the sinistral or northern part of Britain
But it is false that Caer Guortigern was
either in Gwynedd, or any where in the
north. And the whole sentence, "et ipse
cum magis suis ad sinistralem plagam pervenit," etc , seems to be an ignorant interpolation.

[g] *Caer Gortigern*, ı Caeɲ Ꝺoɲcıȝeɲɲ
ıɲɲoeın, B. .ı. caeɲ ȝoɲchıȝeɲɲo, U. ı.
Caeɲ Ꝺoıɲchıȝeɲɲɲ, ꝋ ɲo ba la h-Cmɲ-
ɲoɲ ın ꝺun, ı ꝺun Cmɲoıɲ, L —(*T*.)

[h] *Of the warfare* —B reads ꝺo cacaı-
ȝecc Ꝺoɲcıȝeɲn anꝺɲo ɲıoɲ. L reads ꝺo
chachaıb Ꝺoıɲmchıȝeɲn anꝺɲo ɲıɲ —(*T*)

[i] *Gortimer.*—The reading of U. has been

adopted as being in accordance with the
Latin D reads Ꝺoɲcımȝeɲno. The other
MSS. read Ꝺoɲmchımeɲn, L. Ꝺoɲcı-
ȝeɲno, B.—(*T*.)

[j] *Catigern.* — This name occurs here
in D only. The Latin makes no mention of the brother, but reads, "et cum
gente illorum" There is much confusion
in the Irish copies about these names,
and even in the same copy uniformity is
not preserved For Gortimer we find,
*Gortingernd, Gonmthigern, Gonmthimern
Gontimper, Gorthemir, &c.* For Catigern, *Caithgearnn, Cantigern, Cern*, &c It
has been thought better, however, to pre-
serve uniformity in the translation.—(*T*)
The Catigern of the Latin copies is Cyndeyrn in Welsh, to which Kentigern is the
equivalent, both meaning *Chief Prince*,
but Cathigern, *Battle Prince*, is quite
a distinct word, which discrepancy is un-
accounted for—(*H*)

h-inoaṗḃraṫap Saxana co h-inip Ceineṫ, ⁊ po gaḃrat ḃpeatain po tpi poṗno in n-inip, co topaċt coḃaip cucu ap in Ḟeapmain, ⁊ po caiṫaipgeat ṗip ḃpeatnu cac tan ba leo copcap, tan aile ba poṗno

Ocup vo po pav Ḟoipṫemip ceiṫpi cata vóiḃ, i. caṫ pop ḃpu Deipgḃeint ⁊ caṫ pop ḃpu Reṫenepgaḃail ⁊ ip ann vo poċaip Oppa ⁊ Catigepnn mac Ḟoptigepnn, ⁊ caṫ pop ḃpu mapa iċt, ⁊ taipnigṫep Saxain co a longaiḃ mulieḃpitep, [⁊ caṫ pop ḃpuaig Epippopt] Maṗb imoṗpo Ḟoptimpip [iap n-aimpip m-bic] ocup a voḃaipt ṗpia ḃpeatnaiḃ gap pé n-ég a avnacail pop ḃpu mapa ⁊ ni tiepaitip guill et p in inopi iapvain. Ni veaprarat ḃpeatain in ní pin. Avpact peapt Saxan iap pin, ap ba capa voiḃ Ḟoptigepnv ap vaig a mna

[^a] *Dengbeint.*—That this battle of the Darent was distinct from that of Crayford (which, in fact, is not on the Darent), appears from Henry of Huntingdon, p 310, 311 Ailsford, on the Medway, is supposed to be the Saxon Eppisford and the British Set Theigabail Sathenegabail, or Rit Hergabail of Nennius Being a Vadum, Rit is clearly right, and Saisenagaball, *destruction of the Saxons*, is perhaps the title of that ford. But Camden unless he had other copies, incorrectly states that Nennius hath told us it was so called, because of the Saxons being vanquished there—i. p. 260 Gibson The last of these battles was at the " *Lapis Tituli super ripam Gallici maris,*" which the most probable conjecture places at Folk-stone, whereof the name almost implies that the people had some rights,

sanctions, or usages (some titulus) connected with a stone.—(*H*)

[^b] *Episfort.*—The text of this passage is very corrupt in all the MSS, and is here given chiefly from U , the following are the readings U. reads i caṫ pop ḃpu Deipguipt, ⁊ cat pop ḃpu Reṫene gaḃail, ⁊ ip ano poċaip Opp ⁊ Catigepno mac Ḟoptigepnn, ⁊ caṫ pop ḃpu mapa icc, ⁊ taipnitip Saxan co a longaiḃ, ⁊ cat pop ḃpuaig Epippopt D reads i caṫ pop ḃpu Deipgḃeint, ⁊ caṫ pop ḃpu Raceapgaḃail, ⁊ ip ann pio vo poċaip Eigipt ⁊ Catigepnn, mac Ḟoptigepnn ⁊ caṫ pop ḃpu peitepga mapa icht, ⁊ taipnigep Saxain co longaiḃ mulieḃpitip. Here three battles only are mentioned, as in Bertram's Nennius, cap 45. The word *muliebriter* is inserted from the Latin, " et ipsi in fugam usque ad

to the island of Teineth, and the Britons took this island thrice from them; so that forces arrived to their assistance out of Germany, and they fought against the Britons, and were one time victorious and another time defeated.

And Gortimer gave them four battles, viz., a battle on the bank of the Deirgbeint[k]; a battle on the bank of Rethenergabail, in which Orsa and Catigern, son of Gortigern, were slain; and a battle on the shore of the Iccian sea, where they drove the Saxons to their ships, muliebriter; and a battle on the banks of Episfort[l]. Gortimer died soon after[m], and he said to the Britons shortly before his death, to bury him on the brink of the sea, and that the strangers would never afterwards come into the island. The Britons did not do this[n]. After this the power of the Saxons increased, for Gortigern was their friend on account of his wife.

XXI.

chinlas suas reversi sunt, in eas muliebriter intrantes." This is the only MS. which makes Hengist, instead of Orsa, be killed in one of these battles. .ı. Cαċh ꝼoꝛ bꝛu Ɗeꝛᴄoᴜınᴅ, ⁊ ᴄαċ ꝼoꝛ bꝛu Reċhene Renᴈαbαıl, ⁊ ıꞅ αnꝺꝛαᴅe ᴅo ꝛoċαıꝛ Oꝛꞅ ⁊ Ceꝛn nıαc Ᵹoıꝛċhıᴈeꝛn, ⁊ ᴄαċh ꝼoꝛ bꝛu mαꝛα ıcċ, ⁊ ᴢαıꝼꝛıᴈċheαꝛ Sαꝗαın ᴄo lonᴈαıb, ⁊ ᴄαċh ꝼoꝛ bꝛu Cıᴈeꝛıꝼoꝛċ. B. reads .ı. Cαċ ꝼoꝛ bꝛu Ɗeꝛᴈᴜınᴅ, ⁊ ᴄαċ ꝼoꝛ bꝛu Reċheꝛe ᴈαbαıl, ⁊ ıꞅ αnꝛıᴅe ᴅo ꝛoċαıꝛ Oꝛꞅ ⁊ Cαnᴢıᴈeꝛn nαc Ᵹoꝛċıᴈeꝛn, ⁊ ᴄαċ ꝼoꝛ bꝛuαıᴈ, Cꝛıꝼoꝛċ. In the Latin, Episford is made identical with the second battlefield: "super vadum quod dicitur in lingua eorum Episford, in nostra autem lingua Sathenegabail."—Bertram. "Rit Hergabail."—Stevenson.—(T.)

[m] Soon after.——Instead of the words within brackets, which are supplied from U., B., and L., and are a literal translation of the Latin post modicum intervallum, D. has paulopost.—(T.)

[n] The Britons did not do this, etc.——Gortimer is the Vortimer of Latin, and the Gwrthevyr of Welsh, history; celebrated both as a saint and a warrior, and surnamed Bendigaid, or the Blessed. What the Britons are here, and in Geoffrey, said not to have done, they are elsewhere reported to have done. The bones of Gwrthevyr Vendigaid were buried in the chief ports of the island, and whilst they were concealed, the oppression of the island was impossible. But Vortigern of the Perverse Mouth revealed his bones, out of love for Ronwen, daughter of Hen-

XXI. Do ṗala imoṙṙo, iaṙ n-eg Ᵹoṙthemiṙ ⁊ iaṙ ṙío Enᵹiṙt ⁊ Ᵹoṙtiᵹeṙnn, do ṙonṙat Saxain meaḃail ṙoṙ ḃṙeatnaiḃ, .i. ḃṙea-tain ⁊ Saxain do tinol in n aen ḃaile [amail ḃiḋ do ṙíᵹ .i. Enᵹiṙt ⁊ Ᵹoṙtiᵹeṙn] ṗo comlin ᵹen aṙmaiḃ ac cachtaṙ nai[ḋiḃ], act tuᵹṙat Saxain ṙceana etuṙṙa ⁊ am maelana, ⁊ ṙo maṙḃṙat na ḃṙeatnaiᵹ ḃaḋaṙ annṙin uili oct Ᵹoṙtiᵹeaṙnn na aenaṙ, ⁊ ṙo ceanᵹlaḋaṙ Ᵹoṙtiᵹeaṙnn, ⁊ do ṙaḋ tṙian a ṗeaṙainḋ taṙ ceanḋ a anma, i Allṙaxan ⁊ ṙutṙaxain ⁊ mitilṙaxan.

No ṙoṙcanaḋ imoṙṙo Ᵹeaṙman in ḋí Ᵹoṙtiᵹeaṙnn co ṙo léiᵹeḋ a mnai [.i. a inᵹen]. Ro teich ⁊ ṙo ṗolaiᵹ ṙé n-Ᵹeaṙman iṙ in ṗeaṙann ḋianaḋ ainm Ᵹoiṙtiᵹeaṙnmain, ⁊ do cuaiḋ Ᵹeaṙman co cleṙciḃ ḃṙeatan, ⁊ ṙo ḃai cetṙaca la ⁊ aiḋce ann . ⁊ do cuaiḋ aṙiṙ Ᵹoṙtiᵹeaṙnḋ ṙoṙ teicheḋ na cleṙeach co a ḋun, ⁊ do cuaḋaṙ na ḋiaiᵹ, ⁊ ṙo ḃaḋaṙ tṙi la ⁊ tṙi h-aiḋci annṙin in n-aine, ⁊ ṙo loiṙc teine Ḋe do nim [in ḋi] Ᵹoiṙtiᵹeaṙnn anḋ ṙin co n-a h-uile muinn-teṙi.

gist the Saxon —Triad 53, Series 3 The history of this person is involved in ob-scurity, and his date and age agree but ill with the chronology of Voitigern. See Rice Rees' Welsh Saints, p 135 It has been doubted if any such man was his son —Carte's History, i p 193 — (*T*)

° *In peace* —The clause within brackets is added from L , B , and U —(*T*)

ᴾ *Sandals* —According to the Latin, the Saxons were diiected by Hengist to bring each an artavus, or small pocket-knife, "in medio ficonis sui," i e in his shoe or boot.—(*H*)

ꟼ *Sparing his life.*—" Pro redemptione animæ suæ," Nennius. Ḋaṙ cenḋu mna, U. Aṙ ḋaiᵹ a mna, " On account of

his life," L For *one third* (tṙian) of his land, the translator ought rather to have said three parts; "tres provincias."— *Marcus* In the names of these three provinces, which are evidently Essex, and Sussex, and Middlesex, the MSS are very corrupt. Caxaxum, ⁊ Sutxaxum, ⁊ Mulṙaxum, B La Saxum, ⁊ Sut Saxum, ⁊ m-ṗuil Saxain, L Alṙaxum, ⁊ ṙutṙaxum ⁊ mitilṙaxum, U. Allṙax-an, ⁊ ṙutṙaxain, ⁊ mitilṙaxan, D —(*T*)

ʳ *Gortigern* —Literally, " the person," or " the man Goitigern," in i, D in ni, U, L. in ḋi, B This prefix is not to be understood as implying any contempt or depreciation of Gortigern, but rather the contrary —(*H*)

ˢ *His own daughter* —These words are

XXI. Now it came to pass after the death of Gortimer, and after the peace between Hengist and Gortigern, that the Saxons committed an act of treachery upon the Britons; that is, the Britons and Saxons were assembled together in equal numbers in one place, as if in peace[o], viz, Hengist and Gortigern, neither party having arms; but the Saxons carried knives concealed between them and their sandals[p], and they killed all the Britons who were there except Gortigern alone, and they fettered Gortigern, and he gave the one-third of his land for the sparing of his life[q], viz, All-Saxan, and Sut-Saxan, and Mitil-Saxan

Now German had admonished Gortigern[r] to put away his wife, that is, his own daughter[s]; but he fled away from German, and concealed himself in the land which is named Gortigernmain, and German, with the clergy of Britain, went *after him*, and remained there for forty days and nights; and Gortigern fled again[t] from the clergy to his fortress, and they followed him and tarried there three days and three nights fasting And the fire of God from heaven burned Gortigern[u] there, with all his people. Others assert that

he

inserted from U, B, and L The incest of Gortigern is only mentioned in the MS edited by Mr Gunn, and in the margin of the Cottonian MS Cahgula, A. viii See Stevenson —(T) This whole affair is very doubtful See p 89. But here the falsehood is manifest, for the plot of knives is usually attributed to the year 473, and at any rate German died one year before Hengist's first arrival in 449.—(H.)

[t] *Fled again* —There is a confusion here, from its not being clearly expressed that Gortigern had two places of refuge. First, he went to the district of Guorti-

gernmawn, where it is not doubted Caer Guortigern was situate, and, being pursued by Germanus and his priests, and dreading their power, he removed thence to another fort of his called Din Gortigern, in Dyved or Demetia, on the banks of the Tivy. So it is styled in Gale's text, but Mr Gunn's has "Can Guorthegirn juxta flumen Tebi,' which I conceive to be erroneous —(H)

[u] *Gortigern* —Literally, "the person Gortigern" See above, note[r], in ni, U. in bi, omitted in D L does not name Gortigern here, but reads in ꞇⁱᵹᵉⁿꞁ ᵃ ꝑꞁⁿ.—(T.)

teri Adberat araile is do dércaínnud adbat for faenduil a llog illog Adbert araile is talam do sluig in agaid ro loisced a dun

XXII. Robadar immorro, tri meic oca .i. Gortimper, is eside ro cathaid fri Saxann; Caitigearnn; Pascannt, is do side do rat, Ambros ri Breatan, Bocuelt ⁊ Gortigearnmain iar n-eg a athar, Faustus noem, mac a ingene. ⁊ Gearman ro m-baisd ⁊ ro n-ail ⁊ ro forcan; ⁊ teachtaid in cathraig for [bru] srota Raen Nemnus adbert so

Fearmael fil anora for fearann Goirtigernomain, mac tedubre

[v] *Died of grief and tears, etc*—But certainly far advanced in years His reputed tomb, called the Bedd Gwrtheyrn or Grave of Vortigern, is still seen at Llanhaiarn in Carnarvonshire, and was found to contain the bones of a man of lofty stature. See Carte i 196 The Beddau Milwyr, st. 40, says that the tomb in Ystyvachau is supposed by all men to be that of Gwrtheyrn or Vortigern—(*H.*)

[w] *Three sons*—That is to say, Vortigern had three legitimate sons, or such as the British recognised for princes Nothing is known of this Saint Faustus, nor doth there seem to be any church or convent of his invocation The Reins or Reins, at which Faustus (not Germanus, as here) built a *locus magnus*, has been conjectured to be the Rumney, dividing Glamorgan from Monmouth.—Ussher, Brit Eccl. Primord. Appx p. 1002. One manuscript calls him S Faustus Secundus A Briton of the name of Faustus was bishop of Riez, in Gaul, and honoured as a saint (Vide Aub Miræum in Gennadium, cap 61), though by some condemned as heretical He flourished in the days of Vortigern, and kept up a correspondence with Britannia. See Sidonius Apollinaris, Lib ix Epist 9 A fourth son ascribed to Vortigern is Gotta, whom his Saxon wife, Rowena, is said to have borne to him and to whom Vortigern is said to have given (i e limited in succession) the crown of Britain—Triad. 21, series 3. Lastly, Mr R Rees mentions three saintly sons of Vortigern, St. Edeyrn, who formed a convent of 300 monks at Llanedeyrn, near the Rumney abovementioned, St Aerdeyrn, and St Lldeyrn—Essay on Welsh Saints, p 186 All these names are formed, like Gwrtheyrn's own, upon *teyrn*, a prince. Pascent is the most authentic of his imputed progeny—(*H*)

[x] *Who fought*—Is e ro chathaid re Saxain, D. "Qui pugnabat contra barbaros"—*Nennius.*—(*T.*)

he died of grief and tears[v], wandering from place to place. Another *authority* asserts that the earth swallowed him up the night on which his fortress was burnt

XXII He had three sons[w], viz, Gortimper, who fought[x] against the Saxons ; Catigern , Pascant, to whom Ambrose the king of Britain gave Bocuelt and Gortigernmain, after the death of his father, Saint Faustus[y], his son by his own daughter, and whom German baptized, fostered, and instructed, and for whom he built a city on the brink of the River Raen[z] Nennius[a] said this

Fearmael[b], who is now *chief* over the lands of Gortigern, is the

son

[y] *Saint Faustus*—D reads ꝼaupꞇup pancꞇup all the other MSS have ꝼaupꞇup noem or naem.—(*T*)

[z] *The River Raen* See note[u]—ꝼon bno ꞃpoꞇa, L , B. ꝼon bno ꞃpoꞇa Roen, D ꝼon bno ꞃpoꞇa Rein, U —(*T.*)

[a] *Nennius*—Henup, B Nemnep, L. Neamnop, D Nemnup, U —(*T*)

[b] *Fearmael*—Fernmael (Strong-ankles), Firmwail, or Fermail, was a petty prince, reigning when the Historia was compiled The same name occurs in Fernwail, Fernael, or Fermael, son of Idwal, in the Brut Tywys and Saeson, p. 391, 473, and (as I conceive) in King Farinmagil, slain at the battle of Deorham.—Henr Huntingd p 315 Feinmael I take to be the true form and etymon, according to the orthography of these days His genealogy (which Gale attributes to that bugbear, Samuel) is in every copy and edition. Pascentius, son of Vortigern, was permitted (as the Historia has already told us) to retain Buellt, a district of Rad-

noi, where stood the ancient Bullæum Silurum, and Guorthigernmawn or Gwrtheyrniawn, i e the Jurisdiction of Vortigern or Gwitheyrn, a district adjoining the other in the direction of Rhaiadrgwy, whereof the name yet survives in the ruined castle of Gwrthrenion

This patrimony of Pascent ap Gwitheyrn descended from him, through ten intermediates, to Feinmael, son of Theodore or Tudor All copies exactly agree in the pedigree, save that one or two have mistaken Vortigern's opprobrious surname, Gwrthenau, Perverse-Mouthed, for a separate person It is not likely that such particular accounts should be given of the fate of Vortigern's estates in Radnorshire, and of the descent of their actual owner, save by a person specially acquainted with those parts But that impression rises into conviction, when we find that every copy of the catalogue of the twenty-eight cities of Britannia, including that copied into the Harleian

oubne, mic Paincceann, mic Joonoicann, mic Mopuc, mic Alltao, mic Elooc, mic Pauil, mic Meppic, mic bpiacac, mic Papcent, mic Jopcijeapino, mic Juacail, mic Juacuilin, mic Jloa. bonup 7 Paulup 7 Mupon cpi meic [oile] Jloa, ip epioe oo poine in cacpaij Caipjlon 1 Jlupepcep pop bpu Sabpainoe Oo cuaio Jeapman oia cip.

XXIII. Paopaic cpa in n-inbaio pin 1 n-oaipe 1 n-Eipino ic Miliuc, 7 [ip ip in aimpip pin] po paioeao Pleoiup cum n-Eipeann oo ppoicepc ooib Oo cuaio Paopaic o'pojlaim bo oeap, co po léij in canoin la Jeapman Ro h-inoapbao Pleoiup a h-Eipinn, 7 cainij co pa pojain oo Oia 1 Popoun ip in Maipne Cainij Paopaic oo cum n-Eipino iap pojlaim, 7 po baipc pipu Epeann. O Aoam co baicip pean n-Eipeann, u m ccc xxx Feapca Paopaic oo muipin oaibpi a pipu Epeann, ip upce oo loch annpin, [7 ip haicep

---

MS of pedigrees, places Caer Guortigern the capital of Guortigerniawn, first in the list of cities, before London, York, Caerleon upon Usk and upon Dee, and whatever was most famous in the island! The place in question was, on the face of it, no older than the fifth century, and, from its wild and mountainous site, could have been little more than a military fastness This is such palpable exaggeration and flattery as may best be accounted for by supposing Guorthigerniawn to have been the author's native land, and Fernmael his lord and patron —(II)

c *Tedulie son of Paistcenn* —That is to say, Theodore or Tudor, son of Pascent. The authenticity of this pedigree from Vortigern derives some support from the recurrence of Pascent's name At least, if it be a fiction, it throws back the invention of it to Fernmael's grandfather, or rather to that grandfather's sponsors —(II) This genealogy is given in the MSS with great variations in the spelling of the names D is followed in the text U gives them thus Fearmael, Tendubri, Pascent, Guodicator, Moiut, Eldat, Eldoc, Paul, Meprit, Biiacat, Pascent, Gorthigeind, Gintail Guitolin, Glou L gives them thus Fearmael, Teudbii, Pasceand, Guodicatur, Muiriud, Eltaid, Eltog, Paul, Mepret, Biicad, Pascent, Goithigern, Gutail, Gutolin, Golu B has them thus Fermael, Teudbri, Pascenn, Guodicant, Muriut, Eldat, Eldoc, Paul, Meprit, Bricat, Pascent, Gorthigern, Gutail, Gutolin, Glou

son of Tedubre, son of Paistcenn^c, son of Guodicann, son of Morut, son of Alltad, son of Eldoc, son of Paul, son of Mepric, son of Briacat, son of Pascent, son of Gortigern, son of Guatal, son of Guatulin, son of Glou Bonus, Paul, and Muron were three other sons of Glou, who built the city of Caer Glou^d, i e Glusester, on the banks of the Severn. German returned *home* to his *own* country^e.

XXIII At this time Patrick was in captivity in Eri with Miliuc, and it was at this time that Pledius was sent to Eri to preach to them. Patrick went to the south^f to study, and he read the canons with German Pledius was driven from Eri, and he went and served God in Fordun in Mairne. Patrick came to Eri after studying, and baptized the men of Eri From Adam to the baptizing of the men of Eri *were* five thousand three hundred and thirty years To describe the miracles of Patrick to you, O men of Eri, were to *bring water*

For Gloucester we have Gluseghter, B Gluserether, L. Glusester, U., D —(*T*) For some remarks on Gorthigern, son of Guatal, see Additional Notes, No. XVI

^d *Caer Glou.*—This statement is not in all the Latin copies, and is deservedly accounted fabulous. For Caer Glour or Gloucester is the Glevum of the Itinerarium Antonini, a work not later than the fourth century And the idea of Glour building cities east of the Severn implies a measure of Celtic independence and sovereignty which did not exist in the days of the Itinerary, nor in those of Vortigern's grandfather —(*H*)

^e *To his own country* — Dí acallaim, B, L. U omits this clause altogether. In the Latin it is "Sanctus Germanus reversus est post mortem illius ad patriam suam."—(*T*)

^f *To the south* —In the Latin, " Romam usque perrexit;" but there is no mention there of Patrick's studying the canons with German In describing the mission of Palladius, the Latin adopts the words of Prosper in his Chronicle " Missus est Palladius episcopus primitus a Celestino episcopo et papa Romæ ad Scottos in Christum convertendos "—(*T*) The translator of Nennius deservedly rejects his sketch of St Patrick's life and miracles, as a mere drop of water or grain of sea-sand. But he is himself much at variance with the popular hagiography, if he conceives Patrick to have been still a captive to Miliuc Mc Cuboin, the Dalaradian magician, at the time when Palladius was sent. The mission of St Patrick to

P 2

liaiτep ȝainein mapa ano pin, ⁊ lecfeao oaib pechaino co pe can cimaip ⁊ can faipneip inoipin co leicc]

XXIV Ro ȝab τpa neapτ Saxan pop bpeaτaib iap n-eȝ Ȝopτiȝeapno. Ro ȝab Ochτa mac Enȝipτ, piȝi foppo Ap a uioi no caτhaiȝio Apτup ⁊ bpeaτain piu co calma, ⁊ oo pao oa caτh oeaȝ ooib, i in ceo caτh in n-inobeap Ȝlein; in τanaipτe ⁊ in τpeap ⁊ in

Ireland falls upon the Annus Mundi 4382, and not on 5330, according to the Hebrew chronology of O'Flaherty —(*H*)

⁸ *To a lake* —Upce fo chalman, L Upce oo loch, U., D. Upei fo lap ⁊ licip ȝaneam mapa, B. The clause which follows, within brackets, in the text, is inserted from L —(*T.*)

¹¹ *Arthur and the Britons* —Mr Bertram's edition insert, before the mention of Arthur, "hic expliciunt gesta Britonum a Nennio conscripta," from which some have thought this history was originally silent as to Arthur But all MSS agree in containing his legend, and the mistake arose thus :—That colophon is subjoined to the Acts of St. Patrick ; but in some copies, particularly the Marcian or Mr Gunn's, those Acts form the conclusion of the Historia, and some of the editorial copyists, while transferring them to the middle, took along with them the *expliciunt* or colophon —(*H.*) In the following account of Arthur's battles, the text of all the MSS of the Irish is very corrupt, particularly D ; it has been corrected by the help of the Latin from B, L., and U., but it would be a waste of time

to specify all the variations, most of which are the blunders of mere ignorance. The names of the several battle-fields are very variously given in the Irish MSS. The following is a list of them The first was at Inbuip Ȝlein, U Inobep Ȝlein, L Ȝlein, B Inobep Ȝlain, D. In the place of the next four all agree. The sixth at bpu bappa in B and L. bapa, D. bpu bapa, U. The seventh at Caill Caillioin i caiτ coiτ Cleiouman, D Caill Cailioin i caiτ coiτ Cleoeb, U Chaτain i caiτ coiτ Cleb, L Caill Caooin i caiτ coiτ Cloceb, B The eighth at lep Ȝuinneain, U Ceipc Cuimpein, L Ceipc Ȝumooin D (It should be mentioned that D apparently omits the seventh and gives the eighth twice, but this is a mere slip of the scribe, who wrote a h-ocτu, when he ought to have written in pecτmao) Cep Ȝuimpeain, B After the eighth battle D. inserts the clause which in the other copies, and in the Latin, follows the twelfth, —Ip ann pin oe po imopcoip Apτup oeccil in aenlo, ⁊ ba leip copcap inoτib peo uile,—and then goes on (as in the text) to speak of his having there carried the image of the Virgin

water to a lake[g], and they are more numerous than the sands of the sea, and I shall, *therefore*, pass them over without giving an abstract or narrative of them just now

XXIV After the death of Gortigern, the power of the Saxons prevailed over the Britons Ochta, the son of Hengist, assumed government over them Arthur, however, and the Britons[h] fought bravely against them, and gave them twelve battles[i], viz, the first battle at the

---

The ninth battle was at Caʒpaiʒ ino Ceomain, U , L , B Caɔhpaiʒ ino Ceʒoin, D , which agrees with the Latin The tenth at Robpoiɔ, U , L , B Robpuio, D The eleventh is omitted in all the Irish MSS , nor do they name the twelfth , in what they say of it they all agree with the text except D., where the scribe wrote a ɔo ɔeʒ ip ann po maɲb, and there stopped short without finishing the sentence.—(*T.*)

[i] *Twelve battles* —This was the favourite and mystic number of the British nations St. Patrick is made (by the author of the very barbarous productions bearing his name) to boast of having gone through *duodena pericula* It is unknown where these battles were fought, and it is mere guess-work, from resemblance of sound and other trifles I Gleni, or Glein, is a name consistently given, and therefore not to be treated *ad libitum*. The river Glem by Glemford, in Lincolnshire, is recommended by Gale. There is also the Glen of Glendale, in Northumberland, *fluvius Gleni*, in which Paulinus baptized multitudes Bede, Hist. ii , cap 14.—II., III.,

IV.,V The river Duglas or Dubhglas may be the dark green or blue (for *glas* is either), or rather the dark stream, from the Gaelic *glaise*, a stream It is said to be the Dowglas in Lancashire, that runs by Wigan — R. Higd Polychron p 225, Gale But if so the regio Linuis, Linnuis, Linuis, or Limus, cannot be Lindsey, Lindissi of Bede, in Lincolnshire Indeed, the Archdeacon of Huntingdon calls it *regio Innis*.—Hist ii. p. 313 Mr Whitaker speaks of a local tradition that three battles were fought near Wigan, but omits to observe, that the tradition probably came from those very chronicles, of which it is therefore insufficient to determine the sense.—Hist. Manchester, ii p. 36, 43. There is also the river Douglas, in Clydesdale, more famous for the family who took its name, than for its own dark waters. VI. Bassas of Nennius, Lusas of the Marcian manuscript, is unascertainable But a place called Eglwysau Bassa, the Churches of Bassa, is prominently mentioned in Llywarch's Elegy upon Cynddylan Near that place, Cynddylan and Elvan of Powys were slain by the Lloegrians, or Britons west of

ın ceατhραmαδ ⁊ ın cuıceαδ cατ ρορ bρu Ɖubɣlαıρı; ın ρeıρeαδ
cατ ρορ bρu bαρρα; ocuρ ın ρeαccmαδ cατ α Cαıll Cαıllıδoın .ı.
cατ Coıτ Cleıδumαn, ın τoccmαδ cατ ım leρc Ʒuımδoın; ıρ αnδ
ρın ρo ımαρcoρ Ɑρτuρ δelb Muıρe ρορ α ɣuαlαınδ, ⁊ ρo τeılɣıρταρ
nα Ραɣán   Ɩn nomαδ[cατ] ı cατhραıɣ ınδ Leɣoın, ın δechıneαδ
ın

Seveın, and were buried ın the Eglwysan,
of which the plural number ındıcates some
great establıshment, probably conventual
Owen's Llywaıch, p 82–84 Llywaıch,
apud Arch. Myvyı p. 109, 110 However, Mr Carte has ımagıned the Bassas
to be the rıver of Basıngstoke and Basıng,
ın Hants, ı p 205 VII The seventh
was *cad coed Celyddon*, the battle of the
wood of Forests Celyddon ıs a general
name for any tract of woodlands so exten-
sıve as to furnısh shelter and baffle pur-
suers, of whıch the ancıent orthography
was expressed ın Latın, Caledonıa or
Calıdonıa —See Florus, cap xı. Thıs battle may have been fought ın any celyddon or vast forests, ın the sylva Caledonıa
of Cæsar ın Florus, ın Caledonıa north
of Clyde, or where the fortress of Pen-
sarle-coed was buılt Geoffrey of Monmouth, ıx. cap 3, places the battle of
Nemus Caledonıs ın Lındsey, near Lın-
coln, but as he clearly mıstakes the
posıtıon of Caer Lрод Coed, hıs rectı-
fied sense would place ıt ın the Sylva Elmete of Leeds VIII Castellum Gunnıon,
Gunnıon, Gunnеr Thıs place ıs sımply
unknown. The Vınovıum of Ptolemy,
Vınovıa of Antonınus, and Vınonıa of

Ravennas, ıs mentıoned ın Messrs. Gunn's
and Stevenson's Notes. It ıs now called
Bınchester, ın Durham. There ıs also a
Vennonıs (Hıgh-Cross), otherwıse Vıno-
nıum, ın Antonınus Gwynnawn, ın modern spellıng, ıs probably the word ıntended by Nennıus, whatever place he may
have meant An ınterpolatıon (absent
from Mareus and varıous other MSS,
as well as from thıs translatıon), adds
to the portraıt of the Holy Vırgın an
account of a wooden cross made at Jeru-
salem, whereof the relıques were preserved
at Wedale, near Melrose IX Urbs Le-
gıonıs or Caer Lleon, was a name commonly applıed to two cıtıes, that upon
the Usk ın Gwent or Monmouthshıre,
and that upon the Dee, now called Ches-
ter. It does not appear whıch ıs specı-
fied, but northern places seem rather to
be ın questıon. X. Upon the rıver Trat-
treuroıt, Trath-trevroıt, Trıbruıt, Rı-
broıt, or Ardent, ıt may be observed
that the four first readıngs represent the
same, and the real appellatıon; whıle the
ıntrusıon of the celebrated, but not Ar-
thurıan, battle of Arderydd ıs an ımper-
tınence. A trath or traeth ıs not properly
a rıver, but an ınlet of the sea, a tract of

the mouth of the *river* Glein ; the second, the third, the fourth, and the fifth battle, on the brink of the *river* Dubhglas , the sixth battle on the brink of the Bassa ; the seventh battle in the wood of Callidon, that is, Cait Coit Cleiduman ; the eighth battle at Lesc Gunnidon ; it was here Arthur carried the image of Mary on his shoulder, and drove out the Pagans; the ninth battle at the city of Legion ;

marsh, or other shallow and sandy place usually covered with water; such as the Traeth Mawr, Traeth Bychan, and Traeth Artro in Merioneth, and Traeth Taffe in Glamorgan , and the word *traeth-llyn* (ap Camden, ii 46), a quagmire " Dicitur autem Traeth linguâ Cambricâ sabulum mari influente longius, et se retrahente, nudatum."—*Giraldus Camb. Itin. Cambr.* ii cap 6. Of Traeth Trev there is no room for doubt; but the difficulty is to meet the analogies of the ancient Welsh spelling, which is preserved in *roit* and *ruit* Perhaps Traethtrevrhwydd (the frith, or marshy channel, of the open or unenclosed habitation) is the name. But the name is easier found than the place. XI. The eleventh battle (here omitted) was at Agued Cathregenion, Cath-Bregion, or Thabregomion, or, as Marcus has it, " in Monte Breguoin . . quem nos Cat Bregion appellamus." Humfrey Llwyd says, " Edenburgum, Scotorum regia, olim ab Eboraco Britannorum rege condita, et Castell Mynydd Agned, id est, Castellum Montis Agneti, posteà verò Castellum Virginum, dicta."—*Comment.* p. 62 That suffices for the place. As to its additional name, we see clearly from Marcus, as well as from the reason of the thing, that the Cat is added in consequence of the battle; and I believe that Agned Brechion, Agnetum Maculis-distinctorum, was simply expressive of the nation to whom that fortress is said to have belonged. Edinburgh of the Picts XII. The place, which is omitted here, was Mons Badonis " Ad annum obsessionis Montis Badonici, qui prope Sabrinum ostium habetur, novis simæque ferè de furciferis non minimæ stragis."—*Gildas Hist.* cap 26 Landsdowne Hill, above Bath, is supposed to be signified , and no doubt can exist of Badon being Bath, or, more strictly, *the Baths.* Mr. Carte's conceit, that Mount Badon is Badbury Hill, on the borders of Wiltshire, towards Berkshire, is fully confuted by " prope Sabrinum ostium " The " novissima ferè strages" of Gildas suggested to the Historia Britonum its *duodecimum* bellum, or last battle.—(*II*) For the history of Arthur and his twelve battles, see " Assertio incomparabilis Arthuri autore Joanne Lelando, Antiquario." Lond 1544 Reprinted in Leland's Collectanea, vol v p. 17, &c —(*T*)

ın Robɼuıɒ, a ɒo ɒeaʒ ıɼ ann ɼo maɼbaɒ [la láım Aɼτúıɼ xl. aɼ occ
ceτaıb ı n-aen lo, ⁊ ba leıɼ coɼcuɼ ınτıb ɼeo uıle]   No chuınoʒıɒıɼ
ımoɼɼo Saxaın na ɼoɼτacτ ɒoıb a Ʒeɼmanıa ⁊ ɼıʒı ɼoɼo, co h-lɒa
ıɼ eıɼıɒe ceɒ ɼıʒ ɼo ʒab uaɒɼıb ıɼoɼ ınɒbıɼ Onıc .ı. ɼɼı Umbɼıa,
aτuaıɒ   lɒa ɼılıuɼ Gabba. Enɼleɒ ɼılıa Gɒuınnı τoıɼeac ɼıam ɼo
baıɼτeɒ ɒo Saxanaıb ın n-ınıɼ bɼeaτan

INCIPIT ɒO h-INƷANTAIƆ INɒSI ƆREATAN AND SO SIS.

XXV In ceɒ ınʒnaɒ ınɒɼı bɼeaτan Loch Lomnan; lx ınıɼ
ann, lx caɼɼaʒ ⁊ lx ɼɼuτ ınɒ, ⁊ aen ɼɼuτh aɼ, ı Leamaın.

                                                          In

---

[j] *Eight hundred and forty men, &c*—So all but Gunn's MS, which is represented as having DCCCCXL   This statement is less hyperbolical, though it may be more mysterious, in its real than in its apparent sense. Like 7 to the Hebrews, 12 was to the Britons the absolute number, significant of perfection, plenitude and completeness   But they had also a way of expressing that number by various other numbers, of which the cyphers added together make 12   So, at his great synod of Llan-Ddewi Brevi, St. David assembled 7140 saints, at the battle of knives, or of Hengist's banquet, Eidiol Gadian, with the branch of a roan tree, slew 660 Saxons ; and here, Arthur, with his own sword, slays 840   In some remarkable instances the numbers 147 and 363 were so employed, and from each number deductions of seven and three were made respectively, the object of which affected deductions was to shew the principle; for 7 from 147 leaves 1 and 4, 1 e. 5, being the remainder of 7 from 12, and in the like manner 3 from 363 leaves 9   The direct demonstration of the fact is found in the statement, where twelve years of well-known chronology (the reign of one king) are termed *ten blynedd trugein a thrychant*, 363 years—Cyvoesi Merddin st 106 The motives for such a practice are not obvious. In Triad 85, the number 21,000, thrice repeated, is characteristic of three   The matter is also curious, as regards the main principle of what we term Arabic numerals —*(II)*

[k] *Until Ida*—" Usque ad tempus quo Ida filius Eobba regnavit, qui fuit primus rex in Bernicia, id est, Iberneich, de gente Saxonum."— *Nennius*, cap 63 Cambricè y Berneich or Bryneich This is the Inbher Onic of the Irish translator, which, however, he correctly places north of Humber —*(II)* This passage is greatly corrupted in L   co h-ıɒa is transformed

Legion ; the tenth battle at Robruid; in the twelfth battle there were slain, by the hand of Arthur, eight hundred and forty men[j] in one day, and he was victorious in all these battles. And the Saxons sought assistance from Germany, and it was from thence *they brought their kings until the time of* Ida[k], who was the first king that ruled over them at this side of Inbher Onic, that is, to the north of Umbria [*Humber*] Ida was the son of Ebba Enfled, the daughter of Edwin[l], was the first of the Saxons that was baptized in the island of Britain

INCIPIT CONCERNING THE WONDERS OF THE ISLAND OF BRITAIN[m] HERE.

XXV The first wonder of the island of Britain is Loch Lemnon, there are sixty islands and sixty rocks in it, and sixty streams *flow* into it, and one stream out of it, that is the Leamain[n].

The

---

into conao, and uaoaib ifor into uceibe for, which is nonsense For Inber Onic this MS reads Inbeneopao ı abra a cuaıch D. reads Inobıp Onic .ı. for muıp acuaıo U reads In bene poıc ı frı Umbpıa acuaıo, and B has it In benepoc ı. frı Ubpa a cuaıc —(*T*)

[l] *Enfled, daughter of Edwin.*—Her baptism by St. Paulinus is related in Beda, 2, cap 9 The mention of her occurs in the midst of those "Saxonum et aliarum genealogiæ gentium", which Nennius, at the suggestion of Beulan the priest, "noluit scribere," but which Bertram and Mr Stevenson have printed from varying copies. The remarks originally made on the mode in which the Historia was treated explain the force of *scribere* Nennius was dissuaded from including them in his edition The translator Gua-

nach must have been in possession of the Genealogiæ, but imitated Benlan's pupil in the rejection of them, only culling out of them this sentence about Eanfled, because of the religious interest it possessed —(*H.*) The MSS of the Irish version differ here, as in other cases where there are proper names Ioa mac Euba Eanfleɔ ıngen Eouın, U Ioa fılıur Eabba Enfleız fılıa Eouın, D Ioa mac Euba Eanfleo ıngen Eouın, B Ioa mac Eoba Enfleo, no Ecne, ıngean Aeoaın, L Here the copies of this work in the Book of Ballymote and in the Leabhar na h-Uidhri end, at the end of the copy of the Book of Ballymote are the words fınıc oo'n Opeacnocar, "*Britainısm* (ı e the history of Britain) ends "—(*T*)

[m] *Wonders of the island of Britain —* The legend of St Patrick seems to be

In τ-ιngnaδ τanaιρτe, ινδbeaρ ρροτha Τρanon aρ lιnaδ ó bonn ρριa aen τuιnδ, ⁊ τρaιz amuιl [cac] muιρ eιle.

In τρeaρ ιngnaδ, na h-uιρce τeιnδτe.

In ceaτρamaδ ιngnaδ, τobaρ ρalaιnδ ινδτe

In cuιceaδ [ιngnaδ], δa buιlz uaιneιnτe ιnbeρ Sabρaιnδe ; δo zηιδ

scriptum in all the copies, and there is not "aliquod volumen Britanniæ" that contains it not. But it is otherwise with the Genealogiæ, and also with the Mirabilia, which various copies, and the two first editors in print, have not included. Mr. Stevenson has printed them, to the number of thirteen, which is also the number in the Irish. But the sixth and seventh of the Irish translation are made out of the seventh of the Latin, the eleventh is the twelfth, the twelfth and thirteenth do not occur in the Latin, neither do the Latin sixth and thirteenth occur in the translation. The Walhæ Mirabilia, given in verse by Ralph Higden, appear to me to be only twelve in number, but it is uncertain whether one *mirabile* at Basingwerk is intended, or two, in which latter case there are thirteen. There is not above one of them that coincides with Nennius's; but, however varied in the selection of instances, the *mirabilia* seem to have had a fixed and conventional number. That number, 13, I conceive to be the same sacred number, 12, above spoken of, the difference being that of the zodiacal number with or without the sun, and the apostolic number with or without its Head. The British 13 is not quite

unlike the Hebrew 8, being the overflowing of fulness. The thirteen natural *mirabilia* of Britain form a counterpart to its thirteen tlysau, i.e. jewels, toys, or trinkets, being magical talismans of the most portentous virtue, of which a catalogue is printed in the Mabinogi of Kilhwch, p 353-5, and another in Hynavion Cymreig, p 67 Caervyrddin, 1823.—(II)

" *The Leamain.*—Lake Lomond in Scotland is here greatly shorn of its marvels. The Latin places an eagle upon each rock, cap. 67, Stevenson. But Geoffrey adds, that once a year the sixty eagles assembled together, and sang aloud their prophecies of whatever events were about to happen.—Lib ix cap 6. Also in Gervas of Tilbury, *De Regno Britonum*, p 44. The Leamain here, and Lenin or Leun of the Latin, is the river Levin, flowing out of Lomond into the Clyde, by the famous fortress of Alclyde or Dunbarton.—(II) L. reads ᶜoch ᶜoma. D makes the number of islands, rocks and streams xl instead of lx, the transposition of the x is easy, but the number of rocks and streams is written in full, ceachρaca. L reads sixty in each case, and after the sixty rocks adds, ⁊ meδ aρoιlι

The second wonder is the mouth of the stream Trianon°, which is filled from the bottom with one wave, and ebbs like every other sea

The third wonder[p] is the fiery waters.

The fourth wonder is the fountain of salt *which is* there

The fifth wonder, i e two bubbles[q] of froth at the mouth of the Sabiain

in each Laemhain (in the Latin copies Lemn and Leun), the name of the river running out of this lake, is also the name of a river in the Co. Kerry in Ireland, which runs into the Lake of Killarney, and of another in Scotland, from which the district of Lennox, anciently Leamhain, or Magh Leamhna, has its name —(T.)

° *Tranon.*—Trans Hannoni, Thrannom, Stiannom, Trahannom, is Tiaeth Antoni, the astuary of the Anton or Southampton river, Ptolemy's Mouth of the Trisanton, Τρισαντωνος ποταμοῦ εκβολαι—See Gibson's Camden's *Britannia*, p 212, Nennius, cit. ibid. In Italian romance, Bevis of Hampton is Buovo d'Antona The name Tris-Anton comes from *tri*, three, indicating the triple form of the enclosure made by the Isle of Wight, and consisting of the Hampton river and the two channels of Ryde and Yarmouth, as also Claus-entum, for the same waters. signified the Enclosure of Anton. The name Anton itself is simply *free from waves* or *billows*, as all sheltered waters are, to the extent and degree of their shelter This foolish wonder seems only to describe the violence of a spring-tide.—(H) L reads,

inbeaṗ ṗṗoza linaiṗ ṗṗi h-en zuṁo, ⁊ zṗaȝio aṁlaio can muiṗ i. Eiȼhne — (T)

[p] *Third wonder* — This is *in regione Huich* The waters were in a paved bath, and were either hot or cold, according to the bather's wish. The fourth wonder, in the same region, is no wonder at all, but the writer imagined there was no salt in the earth, only in the sea —(H)

[q] *Two bubbles* —D. reads ou builȝ hillam biȼhe, which is plainly corrupt The reading of L has been followed In the Latin, "Duo Rig Habren" which is interpreted, "duo *reges* Sabrinæ" piȝ is a king in Irish, but could duo rig mean the two *rams*, from the Celtic peiȼe, which would be easily confounded with piȝ in sound? The Latin adds 'et bellum faciunt inter se in modum arietum"—(T) The Latin says, "When the sea is poured into the mouth of the Severn *to a full head of water*, ['Ad sissam—in unaquaque sissa" *Sissa* is a known corruption of *assisa*, and I do not clearly know what the assize of water is, but I suppose it to be water brought to a head, as at mill-dams Ducange cites, from a charter of A D 811, "aquas et

ᵹmᴀ ᴄpoιᴅ, ⁊ bpιpeᴀᴅ cᴀch ᴀ ceιle ᴅíb, ⁊ ᴄιᴀᵹᴀιᴄ ɼop culu ᴅo
pιᴄιpe, ocuɼ conᴅpecᴀιᴅ ᴅopᴅιɼe, ιɼ ᴀmlᴀιᴅ [ɼιn] bιᴅ ᴅo ᵹpéᴀɼ

In uιᴄᴅ [ιnᵹnᴀᴅ], ᴸoch heιlιc cen uιpce ιᴅo ná ᴀɼp, ⁊ ceᴀnel
pᴀιn éιpc ᴀnn cᴀchᴀ h-ᴀιɼᴅe, ⁊ nι ɼoιch ᴅo ᴅuιne ᴀcᴄ co ᵹlun, xx
cubᴀᴄ ιnᴀ ɼᴀᴅ, ⁊ 'nᴀ leᴄheᴀᴅ, ⁊ bpuᴀchᴀ ᴀpᴅᴀ[ιme].

In uιι.mᴀᴅ [ιnᵹnᴀᴅ], ublᴀ ɼop uιnᴅpιnᴅ ᴀᵹ ɼpuᴄ Ᵹoᴀιp

In ᴄ-ochᴄmᴀᴅ ιnᵹnᴀᴅ, pochlᴀιᴅ ɼιl ι ᴄíp Ᵹuenᴄ ⁊ ᵹᴀeᴄh ᴄpι
bιᴄ ᴀp

In nomᴀᴅ, ᴀlᴄoιp ɼιl hι ᴸoιnᵹɼᴀιb, ɼuιlnᵹιᴅ é ιn ᴀéɼ comᴀιɼᴅ
cιᴅe ɼιp o ᴄᴀlmᴀιn ɼuᴀɼ.

In ᴅeιchmeᴀᴅ [ιnᵹnᴀᴅ], cloch ɼιl ɼop cᴀpn ιn bocuιlᴄ, ⁊ ᴀ ᴄeᴀl-
ᴄᴀᴅ con Ապᴄuιp ιnᴅᴄe, ⁊ cιᴅ beᴀpᴀp ɼon ᴅomᴀn ɼo ᵹᴄhᴀ ɼop ιn
cᴀpnᴅ cenᴅᴀ

In

---

assisas aquarum."] two heaps of surf are
collected on either hand, and make war
against each other like rams, and each
goes against the other and they collide together, and secede again from each other,
and advance again at each sissa [swell?]"
This seems to be meant for a description
of the phænomenon called the Bore, which
may be seen in some æstuaries, among
others at Bridgewater.—(H)

' *Loch Heilu* —Elec, L.—(T) This
Loch Heilic is called in the Latin Finnann
(or Fountain) of Guur Helic or Guor Helic, and said to be twenty feet (not cubits)
square It was in the region of Cinliplnc,
Cinliplnc, or Cinloipiauc Near it, and
forming but one wonder with it in the
Latin, was the river Guoy (Wye) and the
apple-bearing ash Helic means willow-
trees, and is the ancient name of Ely

There is also a place in Herefordshire
called Rhyd y Helig.—(H)

⁵ *Ash tree* —Mr O'Donovan informs me
that uιnnɼenn is still in use in the north
of Ireland as the name of the ash tree,
in the south and west the common word
is ɼuιnnɼeoᵹ, but the old form is preserved in the name of the river Fuιnn-
pιonn, in Cork, and in that of Աᴄh-Fuιnn-
pιonn, or Ashford in Limerick.—(T)

' *Gwent* - Gwent was chiefly composed
of the modern Monmouthshire The
cave is said to be entitled *Wth Guint*,
that is, Gwyth Gwynt, and to mean *flatio
venti*. *Gwyth* is rage or violence, but
also means a channel or conduit through
which anything is conveyed, and that is
perhaps the sense here.—(H) The word
ɼochlᴀιᴅ (ɼoclae, L), a cave, is now obsolete, but is explained a cave in Cormac's

Sabrain   They encounter and break each other, and move back again, and come in collision again, and thus continue perpetually

The sixth wonder *is* Loch Heilic[r], which has no water *flowing* into it or out of it, and there are different kinds of fishes in it at every side; and it reaches, *in its depth*, only to a man's knee; it is twenty cubits in length and in breadth, and *has* high banks.

The seventh wonder, apples upon the ash tree[s] at the stream of Goas

The eighth wonder, a cave which is in the district of Guent[t], having wind constantly *blowing* out of it

The ninth *wonder*, an altar which is in Loingraib[u] It is supported in the air, although the height of a man above the earth

The tenth wonder, a stone which is upon a cairn in Bocuilt, with the impression *of the paws* of Arthur's dog[v] in it, and though it should be carried away to any part of the world, it would be found on the same carn *again*

The

Glossary, and the corresponding word in the Latin is *fovea* With, the name given to this cave in the Latin, and explained *flatio venti*, seems cognate with the Irish ᵹaeꞇ, a blast of wind —(*T*)

[u] *Loingraib*.—Rach, L —(*T*) The altar of Llwyngarth in Gower, upon the sea shore The story, as told in the Latin, was this St Iltutus beheld a ship approaching, which contained the body of a saint, and an altar suspended in air over it. He buried him under the altar, and built a church over it, but the altar continued suspended in the air. It was but slightly raised, for a regulus or local prince, being doubtful, proved the fact by passing his rod or wand under it. He was punished for his incredulity by a speedy death, and another man, who peeped under it, by blindness —(*H*)

[v] *Arthur's dog*—The impression upon the carn in Buellt is said to have been made by Arthur's dog, Cavall or Caball, during the chase of the porcus Troynt, i e the Twrch Trwyth That famous boar had been a king, but was thus transformed, and one Taredd was his father He was the head and summit of that pile of porcine allusions which are known to form a peculiarity of British superstition. Llywarch Hen says, in a proverbial tone,

"In need, Twrch [himself] will crack pignuts

Marwnad Cynddylan, st 89

Cavall did, indeed, hunt the Twrch

In xi.aꝺ [ingnaꝺ], ꝼil aꝺnacul i ꝼeaꝛann Aꝛgingi, τan uii τꝛaigi, τan .x., in τan .xii., in τan a cuic ꝺeag ina ꝼaꝺ

In ꝺaꝛa [ingnaꝺ] ꝺeag, cloch ꝼoꝛ eaꝛ i m-bꝛebic

In τꝛeaꝛ [ingnaꝺ] ꝺeag, bꝛo ꝼoꝛ bleiτh ꝺo gꝛeaꝛ im Machlinꝺ i Cuil, acτ ꝺia ꝺomnaig, ꝼo τalmain imoꝛꝛo ꝺo cluinτeaꝛ.

Aτa τiꝛꝛa in gꝛain im Meaꝺon, i τiꝛꝛa o ꝼilenn gꝛan can anaꝺ.

[Aτa ꝺno ann τibꝛa ó m-bꝛúchτaꝺ cnaime en ꝺo gꝛéꝛ 'ꝛin τíꝛ chéτna]

Aτaiτ ꝺna eoin ꝺiaiꝛmiꝺe ann in aꝛaile caꝛꝛaig, ⁊ laiτ ꝼo'n muiꝛ amail biꝺ i n-aeꝛ

Aτa ꝺna baiꝛꝛneach ꝼoꝛ caꝛꝛaig inτe, i baiꝛꝛneach oc Ceoil τꝛicha mile cemenn oꝛ muiꝛ

Aτá ꝺno glenn i n-Aenguꝛ, ⁊ eigim cacha h-aiꝺchi luain ann, ⁊ Glenꝺ Ailbe a ainm, ⁊ ni ꝼeaꝛ cia ꝺo gni ꝼuiτ

INGANTA MANANN ANN SO SIS

XXVI i in ceaꝺna, τꝛaig cen muiꝛ

In

Tiwyth, but he was Sevwlch's dog, not Arthur's See the Mabinogi of Kilhwch, p 291. The Carn Cavall is a mountain in Buellt and the publishers of the Mabinogion have given an engraving of a stone with a mark like a dog's paw, conjectured to be the one in question —*Ibid* p 360 —(*II*)

" *Argingi* —In L, Ergneꝺi —(*T*) The land of Aigingi is Figing or Ergengl, called in English Erchenfield or Archenfield, a district of Herefordshire. The sepulchre in question was beside the fountain called Lieat Anir, the last word being the appellation of one of Arthur's knights,

whom Arthur slew and buried at that spot Llygad Annir, the Eye of Anni is the fountain's name and Anni i e Lackland, the man's. The lengths given in the printed Latin are six, nine, and fifteen feet, and the author attests the fact on his own experience, "et ego solus probavi" One copy has "Oculus Annimur," for which we can read "Oculus Annir Mawr "—(*II*) A superstition exactly similar, connected with the Dwarf at Tara, is mentioned by Mr Petrie, in his History and Antiquities of Tara Hill, p 156 —(*T*)

Brebic —Clogh aꝛ aꝛ i bꝛebic, L —

The eleventh *wonder*, a sepulchre which is in the land of Aigingi[w], *which* one time *measures* seven feet, *another* time ten, *another* time twelve, and *another* time fifteen feet in length.

The twelfth wonder is a stone in a cataract in Brebic[x]

The thirteenth is a quern[y] which constantly grinds, except on Sunday, in Machlin in Cul.   It is heard *working* under ground

The well of the grain is in Meadon[z], that is, a well from which grain flows without ceasing

There is in the same district a well from which the bones of birds are constantly thrown up

There are also innumerable birds there on a certain rock, and they dive under the sea as if into the air

There are also limpets on the rocks there, viz, limpets at Ceoil, thirty thousand paces from the sea

There is a valley in Aengus[a], in which shouting is heard every Monday night ; Glen Ailbe is its name, and it is not known who makes the noise

THE WONDERS OF MANANN[b] DOWN HERE

XXVI The first wonder is a strand without a sea

The

This wonder does not occur in the Latin. I cannot explain *Brebic* —(*T*)

[y] *A quern* —No notice of this or the succeeding "wonders," is found in the Latin. Machlin is a town in Ayrshire, a district of Galloway, in the stewartry of Kyle, which latter is here styled Cul and Ceoil. "Eadbertus campum Cyil cum aliis regionibus suo regno addidit." —*Bedæ Epitome*, A. D 750. It is the same word as the Irish Cul.—(*II.*)

[z] *In Meadon*, or " in the middle," im meadon is the reading of L   D reads im megongan, " in Megongan ," but I know not what place is intended. For can anan, L reads do gper, i e always —(*T*.)

[a] *Aengus* —The county of Angus or Forfar in Scotland   The words and clause within brackets, and some other corrections in the text, are from L —(*T*)

[b] *Wonders of Manann;* or the Isle of Man —There are five such in Nennius The fourth is thus stated A stone walks by night in the valley of Cithemn, and

In canaíroi, ach puil pooa o'n muip, ⁊ línaio in can línap muip ⁊ cpáigio in can cpaigip muip

In cpeap, cloch imcigeap a n-aioaib aca ɪ n-Ꝝlino Cinoenn, ⁊ cɪa poceapoap ɪm muip no ɪ n-eap bio pop bpu ɪn ꝝleanoa ceona

oe Cruichneachaio incipic

XXVII. A cip Cpaiaa cpa cangaoap Cpuicniꝝ, ɪ. clanoa Ꝝue-leoɪn mic Epcoil ɪao Aꝝachippɪ a n-anmanoa Seippup bpacap cangaoap coipeac, ɪ Solen, Ulꝼa, Neccan, Opopcan, Aenꝝup Leceno Faca a ciaccana ɪ Policopnup, pɪ Cpaiꝝia, oo pao ꝝpao oa piuip, co po cpiall a bpec ꝝan cocpa Lovap ɪap pɪn cap

once upon a time was thrown into the whirlpool Cereuus, which is in the middle of the sea called Mene, but the next day was undoubtedly found on the shore of the above-named valley.—(*H*) The second wonder, "Mons qui gyratur tribus vicibus in anno," is omitted in both the Irish copies. In the Latin, the third wonder (second in the Irish) is nothing miraculous, 'Vadus quando innundatur mare et ipse innundatur," &c., the Irish translator perceived this, and therefore adds pooa o'n muip, a toad *which is far from the sea* L makes the first and second one thus, Cpaig cen muip, ɪ ach poca o'n muip, &c The section 'De mirabilibus Hiberniæ" is omitted in the Irish copies (*T*)—See Appendix

c *Of the Cruithnians*, i e of the Picts This section, which occurs only in the Books of Leacan and Ballymote, is entitled in the former Oo Chpuichnechaib ano-peo, oo peip na n-eolach, "Of the Cruith-nians here, according to the learned" But what follows is no part of the Britannia of Nennius, and is not found in any Latin copies The Book of Ballymote is adopted as the basis of the text.—(*T*) For a dissertation on the origin and history of the Picts see Additional Notes, No XVII

d *Gueleon, son of Ercal*.—Gelonus, son of Hercules by Echidna, was the ancestor of the Geloni, a people of Scythia, who painted their bodies, and are, therefore, assumed to have been the ancestors of the Picts

"Eoïsque domos Arabum pictosque Gelonos "
Virg Georg ii 115

Some have supposed them to be a people of Thrace, or at least to have settled there in one of their migrations, because Virgil, in another place (*Georg* iii. 461), says of them

———— Acerque Gelonus
Cum fugit in Rhodopen atque in deserta Getarum "

This perhaps, may possibly have been

The second is a ford which is far from the sea, and which fills when the tide flows, and decreases when the tide ebbs

The third is a stone which moves at night in Glenn Cindenn, and though it should be cast into the sea, or into a cataract, it would be found on the margin of the same valley

Of the Cruithnians[c] incipit

XXVII The Cruithnians came from the land of Thracia; they are the race of Gueleon, son of Ercal[d] (*Hercules*). Agathyrsi[e] was their name Six brothers[f] of them came at first, viz, Solen, Ulfa, Nechtan, Drostan, Aengus, Leithenn   The cause of their coming[g] *was this*, viz, Policornus, king of Thrace, fell in love with their sister, and proposed

the origin of the tradition that the Picts were a *Scythian* people (" de Scythia, *ut perhibent*," says Bede, lib 1. c. 1) who came into Ireland from *Thrace*. For ᵹueleoin, (which has been adopted from L), B reads ᵹleoin.—(*T*)

[e] *Agathyrsi.* B reads Aᵹanchippi. The Agathyrsi were a Scythian tribe, said to be descended from Agathyrsus, a son of Hercules   See above, p 49, and note ᵍ They are also called *picti* by Virgil, Æn. iv. 146. See the legend of the birth of Agathyrsus and Gelonus, and the cause of their being sent away from Scythia to emigrate, in Herodotus, lib. iv. c 9, 10. The account given by Herodotus of the Agathyrsi is that their country abounded in gold, but that they were themselves effeminate, and had their women in common. —*Ibid.* c. 104 The story of the Agathyrsi coming first to Ireland, and being sent on

from thence to North Britain, is told by Polydore Virgil and others.   He says, "Quidam hos Agathyrsos esse suspicantur, Pictosque vocitatos, quod sic ora artusque pingerent, ut ablui nequirent, sed Pictos undecunque dictos, satis constat populos Scythiæ fuisse."—(lib. ii. p 38, Edit. Basil. 1555) See also Hector Boethius (Hist. Scotorum, lib 1 fol 4, line 50. Edit. Paris, 1575), and Fordun's Scotichronicon.—(*T*)

[f] *Brothers,*—L. omits the word bpacap. —(*T*)

[g] *Cause of their coming.*—Mr Pinkerton, who has quoted this account of the Picts from the Book of Ballymote, in the Appendix, No 14, to his Enquiry into the History of Scotland, makes the words paca a ciaccana a proper name, and translates this passage " Fiacta-atiactana, *alias* Policronus, King of Thrace," &c.

τap Romanchu co Fpanᵹcu, ⁊ cumτaiᵹiτ piaτ caτaip ann i Pic-
τauip, a picτip i. o n-apmτaiƀ   Ocup oo paτ pi Fpanᵹc ᵹpao oia
piaip.   Looap fop muip iap n-oeᵹ in τ-peipeao bpaτap .i. Leiτino
l cino oa laa iap n-oul fop muip aτbaτh a piup.   Ᵹabpaτ Cpuiτ-
niᵹ inƀep Slaine i n-Uib Ceinopelaiᵹ   Qτbepτ piu Cpemτano
pciaτ-bél, pi Laiᵹen, oo bepao failτi ooib ap oicup Tuaiτe Fioƀa.
                                                         Qobepτ

This is only a specimen of the innumerable ludicrous mistakes which Pinkerton has committed in his translations from the Irish   In the next sentence ᵹan τocpu, signifies not "without settling a dowry *on her*," as Pinkerton renders it, in conformity with modern ideas, but, "without giving a dowry *for* her," to her father or next of kin, according to the practice of the ancients. Policornus, the fabulous King of Thrace, mentioned in this legend, is elsewhere in the Book of Ballymote (tol 23, *a a*) called Pohornus, and in the Book of Lecan (tol 13, *b b.*), Pihornis.— See Addit Notes, No XVIII —(*T.*)

ᵇ *Without . a dower.*—L. reads cen pochpaioe, without forces.—(*T*)

ᶦ *Pictavis.*—The Lemonum of A. Hirtius de B. Gall c. 26, and Augustoritum of Ptolemy, afterwards Pictavia or Pictaviæ, Pictava or Pictavæ, now Poictiers. Ammianus has it Pictavi, from the people, xv. c 11; others Pictavium. Whether the Pictones or Pictavi were so called by the Romans from any usage of painting, or whether it was a native name, is uncertain. Brutus in his voyage from Troy hither visited Poictou, where Goffarius Pictus or

Goffar Picti, was then reigning —Galfrid, Mon. i. c 12 The derivation of this name "from their arms," alludes to the word *pike* in English; pioc, Irish, *puᵍ*, Welsh, *picca*, Italian, *pica* (and see also *pictare*), apud Du Cange.—(*H*)   In the account already given, p. 53, *supra*, the Picts are described as having been first in Orkney, before they went to France and founded Poictiers. The tradition that this city owed its origin to the wandering Agathyrsi was also current in France. Du Chesne says · "Il est certain que Poictiers, ville principale et premiere de toute cette contrée, est tres antique, mais incertain qui en ont esté les premiers fondateurs L'opinion de plusieurs François est que ce peuple est une ancienne Colonie des Scythes dits Agathirses, lesquels, au dire de Pline, Pomponius et Solin, se peignoient les cheveux et le visage, afin de se rendre plus redoutables, et pour ce estoient appellez *Picti*. Que ces Agathirses peints vindrent premierement planter leurs pavillons en la Grande Bretagne, ou estans multipliez se fit encore cette peuplade, laquelle vint bastir la ville de Poictiers, et l'appella *Pictavis* en Latin, comme ce

posed to take her without *giving* a dower[h]. They after this passed across the Roman territory into France and built a city there, viz, Pictavis[i], called à pictis, i. e from their arms. And the king of France fell in love with their sister. They put to sea after the death of the sixth brother[k], viz, Leithinn; and in two days after going on the sea their sister died. The Cruithnians landed at Inbher Slaine, in Hy-Ceinnselagh. Cremhthann Sgiathbhel, King of Leinster, said that he would give them welcome on the expulsion of the Tuatha Fidhbha[l]. Drostan, the Druid of the Cruithnians, ordered that the

qui diroit *force peinte.* Ridicule opinion puis que ce peuple est avoue barbare par tous les anciens Autheurs, et partant ignorant de la lanque Latine, laquelle mesme n'estoit point alors, ou n'estoit en telle splendeur, que les estrangers en recherchassent la connaissance."—*Antiquitez, &c, des Villes de France,* tom. i. p. 535 John of Salisbury, in his Polycraticon, sive de Nugis Curialium, suggests also a Latin derivation (lib i c. 13). "Avis picta urbi Pictavorum contulit nomen, levitatem gentis colore et voce præfigurans." But all these are manifest fables, derived from fanciful analogies of sound; for the inhabitants of Poictou were known by the name of *Pictones* in Cæsar's time, before they had any intercourse with the Latins This objection, however, does not apply to the derivation from *pica,* for that word existed also in the Celtic languages, although it may, perhaps, be as fanciful as the rest —(*T.*)

[k] *Sixth Brother.*—L. reads ᵭn ᴄ-ᵱᵻnnᵱᵻn bᵱaᴄ haᵱ, " the eldest brother." If this

reading be of any authority, it will, therefore follow, that Leithinn, though mentioned last, was the eldest brother. —(*T.*)

[l] *Tuatha Fidhbha.*—Ⴒhuaᴄᵻhᵻ Fᵻ ᴣ ᴆa. L. No mention of this colony has been found except in this legend Yet it is curious that the inhabitants of the barony of Forth were an English or Welsh colony, although they are certainly not in Ireland long enough to have given rise to this story, which is, however, of great antiquity, much less can they be supposed to have been here since A M 2931, the period assigned by O'Flaherty to this Cruithnian invasion. See the Additional Notes, No. XVIII Pinkerton and his Irish assistants, not knowing that Tuatha Fidhbha was a proper name, translate this passage thus "Creamthan Sciathbel, King of Leinster, told them they should be welcome, provided they would free him of the *tribe-widows* " —vol. 1. p. 507. But his version of this tract is full of similar errors, which it would be waste of time to point out individually.—(*T.*)

Aobept Opopran, opim Cpuirneac i. bleagon uii xxc. bo fino vo
vopruz mbaille i ffeappaioi in cach Do ponnao inoí rin, ꝥ vo ponnao in cac voib .i. cach Apoa-leamnacra in Uib Ceinopelaiz. Zac
aen nó zonrír no laízeo ir in leamnacr ni cumzao a neim ni vo
neoc oib. Ro mapbra ona iaprain Tuara Fioba Mapb cearpap
vo Chpuirneacaib iap rin .i. Opopran, Solen, Neacrain, Ulra
Zabair Zub ꝥ a mac .i. Cathluan neapr niór a n-Epinn, zon in-
oapbpavap Epimoin ꝥ zo rapoa mna na feap po bairea immaille
fpi Dono voib .i. mna bperre ꝥ buairre ꝥra.

XXVIII. Anair reiren oib op bpeazmaiz. IS vaioib zach
zeirr, ꝥ zach rén, ꝥ zach rpeóo, ꝥ zora en, ꝥ zac mana. Car-
luan ba h-aipo-pi oppo uili, ꝥ ir é cer pí po zab oib a n-Albain; lxx.
piz oib fop Albain o Charluan zu Conpranrin, ꝥ ir é Cpuirneac
veioeanac pop zab. Oá mac Cathluain i Cathmolovop ꝥ Carino-
lacan; in va cupaio, Im mac Pipn, ꝥ Cino athair Cpuirhne; Cpir
mac Cipiz a milio , Uairneim a filio; Cpuirne a ceapo , Donnall
mac

<hr/>

m *Ard-leamnachta.*—The hill or height
of new milk This name, which perhaps
gave origin to the fable, is now lost. The
description here given of the battle, and
of the advice of the Druid Drostan, is very
obscure, but it is explained by the more
full account of the transaction which will
be found in Note XVIII at the end of the
volume, from which some explanatory
words have been inserted in the translation, to render it intelligible. For vo ponnao in car, L. reads vo pavao in car —(*T*)

n *Solen*—L reads Rolen in this place,
but in enumerating the chiefs of the
Cruithnians above, Solen, as in B —(*T*)

o *Gub*—L reads Zib, Keatinge reads
Gud See Addit Note XVIII —(*T*)

p *Donn.*—See above, pp. 55–57, and note
m, p 56, where the names of the chieftains
drowned with Donn are given in a stanza
cited from a poem by Lochy O'Flynn, a
celebrated historian and bard of the tenth
century —(*T*)

q *Breaghmhagh* —Bregia, the great plain
of Meath, in which Tara is situated.—(*T*.)

r *Sreodh* —For the meaning of this word
see note on the following poem, line 149,
p 144 Pinkerton's version of this passage
is ludicrously absurd· "They were in
want of order and distinction· had neither
spears (for hunting), nets (for fowling),
nor women."—(*T*.)

s *Last Cruithnian that reigned.*—Not true
in fact, but the *Nomina Regum Pictorum*

the milk of seven score white cows should be spilled [*in a pit*] where the *next* battle should be fought. This was done, and the battle was fought by them, viz., the battle of Ard-leamhnachta[m], in Hy-Ceinnselagh Every one *of the Picts* whom they wounded used to lie down in the new milk, *and* the poison *of the weapons of the Tuatha Fidhbha* did not injure any of them The Tuatha Fidhbha were then slain Four of the Cruithnians afterwards died ; namely, Drostan, Solen[n], Nechtain, *and* Ulfa *But* Gub[o], and his son Cathluan, acquired great power in Eri, until Herimon drove them out, and gave them the wives of the men who had been drowned along with Donn[p], namely, the wife of Bres, *the wife* of Buas, &c

XXVIII. Six of them remained *as lords* over Breagh-mhagh[q] From them *are derived* every spell, every charm, every sreodh[r], and *augury by* voices of birds, and every omen. Cathluan was monarch over them all, and he was the first king of them that ruled in Alba Seventy kings of them *ruled* over Alba, from Cathluan to Constantine, who was the last Cruithnian that reigned[s] The two sons of Cathluan were Catinolodar and Catinolachan[t] ; their two champions *were* Im, son of Pern, and Cind, the father of Cruithne[u]; Cras, son of Circch, *was* their hero; Uaisneimh *was* their poet; Cruithne their artificer; Domhnall, son of Ailpin[v], was the first *Gadelian king*, till he was killed

(ap. Innes, App 798), were carried down no further. Five Pictish princes reigned after Constantine during 22 years —(*II*) See what Innes has said on this Irish account of the seventy kings, vol i. p. 102.—(*T*)

[t] *Catinolachan.* — L. reads Da mac Cathluan ro gabrat Cruithentuath i. Catinolodaror ┐ Catinalachan "The two sons of Cathluan took possession of Cruithen-tuath, viz., Catinolodaior and Catinalachan" Pinkerton puts a full stop

at cupaib, and translates in ba cupaib "in great distress."—(*T*)

[u] *Cruithne* —Cuithne, B.—(*T*)

[v] *Ailpin.*—Domnall mac Ailpil ir e cairech ro gob go ro marb britus mnai Iracon, L. There is some sad confusion and omission of words in the text. I have supplied conjecturally in italics in the translation what I suppose to have been the meaning. For Britus, son of Isacon, see above, p. 27.—(*T*)

mac Ailpin iſ é toiſec, ʒo ſo maſb bſicuſ imoſſo mac Iſicon.
Clann Neimiɒ ſo ʒabſac iaſ m-bſicuſ .i. iaſ Ʒlun. Cſuichniʒ ſo
ʒabſac iaſ ſin, iaſ cecc ɒoib a h-Eſinn. Ʒaeɒil imoſſo ſo ʒabſac iaſ ſin .i. meic Eſc mic Eacɒach

[XXIX Do chuaiɒ o macaib Mileɒ Cſuichnechan mac
Locic, mic Inʒi la bſeacnu Foiſcſen ɒo chachuʒuɒ fſi Saxain, ⁊
ſo choſain ciſ ɒoib Cſuichencuaic, ⁊ aſaiſ ſen aco. Ache ni
baɒaſ mna leo, aſ bebaiſ banoſpoche Aban Do luiɒ iaſum
Cſuichnechan ſoſ culu ɒo cum mac Mileɒ, ⁊ ſo ʒab neam, ⁊
calam, ⁊ ʒſian, ⁊ eſca, oſſiche, ⁊ ɒaichi, muiſ, ⁊ ciſ, [coſ] ba ɒo
maichſiu flaich foſſo co bſach ; ⁊ ɒo beſc ɒa mna ɒec foſ-
cſaiɒi baɒaſ oc macaib Mileɒ, aſo bace a fiſ iſ in faiſſʒe ciaſ
aſ aen ſe Donn ; conaɒ ɒo feaſaib h-Eſinɒ flaic foſ Cſuichnib
o ſin ɒoʒneſ.]

XXX CRUICHNIʒh [ciɒ] ɒoſ faſclam,

i n-iac Alban n-ampa,

ʷ *Glun.*—Ʒalu, L.—(*T.*)

ˣ *Sons of Erc,* i e Fergus, Loarn, and
Aengus; see Innes, App. p. 801. Fordun.
iv. c 9 —(*T*)

ʸ *Cruithnechan.* — This section occurs
only in L —(*T.*)

ᶻ *Britons of Fortren* —That is to say, the
Gwyddyl Fichti of North Britain, whose
kingdom was called by the Irish Fortren
Mor. Fodla Fortren was one of the seven
fabulous brothers, sons of Cruthne, who
divided Albany amongst them. But Fort-
tren, perhaps, amounts to powerful or
mighty. Dr O'Conor fancifully makes it
a contraction of Fortraigh Greine, *sunrise,*
i e the east —Script R. H iii. p.55. It is
the name of the whole realm; and has not

been ascertained to have been special to
any part of it It was, I scarcely doubt, the
Gwyddyl Fichti name as well as the Irish
name , for the prefix *For,* which is the
gor of the Welsh, is prevalent in the composition of Pictish names of places.—(*Il.*)

ᵃ *By heaven and earth, &c.*—This is the
ancient Irish oath, by which the various
elements and parts of nature were made
guarantees of the bargain, and enemies to
the forswearer The oaths exacted from
his subjects by Tuathal Teachtmar, and
that given to the Lagenians by King
Loeghaire mac Neill, are memorable instances of it. At an earlier epoch King
Hugony the Great is reported to have se-
cured the crown to his family by the same

killed. *First*, Britus, son of Isacon, *possessed Britain*. The clan Neimhidh obtained it after Britus, that is after Glun[w] The Cruithnians possessed it after them, after they had come out of Eri. The Gaedhil possessed it after that, that is, the sons of Erc[x], son of Eochaidh

XXIX. Cruithnechan[y] son of Lochit, son of Ingi, went over from the sons of Mileadh to the Britons of Foirtren[z], to fight against the Saxons, and he defended the country of Cruithen-tuath for them, and he himself remained with them [i e *with the Britons*]. But they had no women, for the women of Alba had died. And Cruithnechan went back to the sons of Mileadh, and he swore by heaven and earth[a], and the sun and the moon, by the dew and elements, by the sea and the land, that the regal succession among them for ever should be on the mother's side ; and he took away with him twelve women that were superabundant with the sons of Mileadh, for their husbands had been drowned in the western sea along with Donn ; so that the chiefs of the Cruithnians have been of the men of Eri from that time ever since

XXX The Cruithnians[b] who propagated
In the land of noble Alba[c],

With

mode of oath , but it is not said whether he first introduced it.—Ogygia, iii c. 38 See Battle of Magh Rath, p. 2, 3, and the note, ibid See also the verses of the bard Malmura in O'Con. Proleg. ii. p lxxix Perhaps, in terming it the oath per res *creatas* omnes, Mr O'Flaherty may be employing an important phrase of his own theology, not apparent in that of his Pagan ancestors The spirit of the adjuration *per res omnes* has infused itself into the celebrated production, otherwise Christian, called the Feth Fiadha or Lorica

Patricii; apud Petrie on Tara, pp. 57–68, where that incantation is rather indulgently translated, by inserting within brackets such words as tend to remove the invocation, otherwise apparent, of the *res creatus omnes.*—(*H.*).

[b] *The Cruithnians.*—This very ancient poem occurs only in L & B. The text in both is very corrupt, and often unintelligible. B. has been chiefly followed In line 1, cio is inserted from L., in line 3, L. reads belzu for beloa.—(*T.*)

[c] *Alba.*— Alba, genitive Alban, dative

го n-a m-bριζ bιl belυa,
cια τιρ αρ nac ταρζα?

Cια ϝοconn ϝορ ρο ζluαιρ,   5
o cριcαιb ιn coζαιυ?
ϝρι ρnιm τοnυ ταρ ρρεατhαρ,
cια lín lonζ υo louαρ?

Cια ρlonυυ ϝρια τιαcταιn
υo ριαcταιn na ριζε?   10
αρ α n-αιρm ϝαυειn,—
ιρ cια n-αιnm α τιρε?

Τραιcια αιnιn α τιρε
ζο ρίρε α ρέοlτα

ιαρ

Albain (Alban, undeclined, in Welsh), Albany, is a well-known appellation for that part of Britain which the Picts occupied See Mr O'Donovan's Grammar, p 106 Fable refers it to Albanact, brother of Locrine and Camber, and, like the names of Lloegyr and Cymmry, it is utterly unknown to ancient historians and geographers Nay, indeed, the triple division of the island into the Anglo-Roman, Cambro-British, and Scoto-Pictish portions, was a post-Roman circumstance, to which this late nomenclature has adapted itself The name Braid-Alban, Jugum Albaniæ, Collar of Albany, indicates the elevation of that district, while the highest ridge or summit of the Braid-Alban was styled the Drum-Alban, Dorsum Albaniæ It is Adamnan's Dorsum Britanniæ, his mention of it is always as the boundary of Pictland towards the Scots ; and crossing the Dorsum Britanniæ is the conventional phrase for entering the former kingdom from the west See Adamn i 34, ii 32, 43, 47; iii 14 Why one of the three parts should thus be termed *Britannia*, i e the whole, may be explained from that part alone having retained an independence, varying in its limits, as the upper or lower wall was maintained. And the Irish abbot of Iona has therein the support of the ancient Welsh, by whom Alban was also termed Prydyn (an old form) though never Prydain. See Taliesin, p 75, l. 22. Golyddan, p 156, l. 14, p 157, ll 25, 65. Taliesin (or rather some one assuming his person) uses that name triadically, that is, in distinction from Lloegyr and Cymmry, which makes it the precise equivalent of Alban

With glorious illustrious might,
From what region did they come?

What cause also moved them   5
    From the countries of war?
    To traverse the waves[d] over the floods,
    In what number of ships did they embark?

How were they named before they came
    To attain their sovereignty?   10
    (*They were named* from their own[e] weapons) —
    And what was the name of their country?

Thracia[f] *was* the name of their country,
    (Until they spread their sails,

After

saying, of the Serpent of Germany, " she shall conquer *Llocgyr* and *Prydyn*, from the shore of the German Ocean to the Severn, and then shall the Brython lose all their land, *except wild Walha* "— p 94 st. 29–31 The improbable statement in Giraldus and the Brut of Kings, that the Humber was the south limit of Alban, arose from the lower, or Picts, wall, passing through Northumberland, as appears from the oldest of the Welsh copies, where it is said that Alban lay " from the river Humber to the penrhyn of Bladon ," for Cape Blatum was the western terminus of the Severian wall, therefore its eastern terminus in Northumbria should have been said for the Humber Brut Tysilio, p 117 Roberts (interpolating the word *northwards*), p 33, Giraldi Descript Cambriæ, cap. 7, p 886 —(*H*)

[d] *The waves*—Lines 7 and 8 are given thus in B

    Cia lin long ap ceaʒap
    Fpi pnim cono do loðap?

In what number of ships did they embark
And set out to traverse the waves?

The reading of L is preferred, as most in conformity with the metre —(*T*)

[e] *Their own*—For ꝼaðem L reads boðene, a form of the same word, now written ꝼein See O'Donovan's Irish Grammar, p 130.—(*T*)

[f] *Thracia*—According to Tzschucke, the Agathyrsi did not inhabit Thrace, but the Bannat of Temeswar, and part of Transylvania. Tzsch. in Pomp Melam, tom 6, p. 12 The ancients do, however, impute to the Thracians the use of certain blue punctures, as ornaments of nobility, but not

ıaıı na taıpcıul teacta,   15
    a n-aıptıup na h-Eoppa,

Agantıpı a n-anmann
    am pano Epcaıl-ıcbı
    o ceapptapoı a cuctlí
    atbeptap cıo Pıctı.   20

Pıctı ın aıcme at paıb
    poʳ taıtne teact muıp,
    ʒan ʒnım n-oeıpeoıl n-oooɔaıɓ,
    ʳıl n-ʒeleoın mıc Epcoıl

h-uaoıɓ peıpeap bpatap,   25
    fpı latap ʒan lıun,
    oo pepc blao ʒo poao,
    ın peactmao a pıuп

Solen, Ulpa, Nectaın,
    Opoptan oectaın opetell.   30
    a n-anmano a n-aeboup,
    Aenʒup aʒup Leıteno.

                                               Lan

any general painting of the body. See *Notæ Threciæ*, ap. Ciceronem de Off. ii c. 7 Herod Terps cap 6. Their women also wore these marks (some say on the hands and face), and they are represented by Dion Chrysostom as marks of their rank and dignity. Orat. xvii. cit. Wesseling in Herod ii s But poets represent them as a badge of infamy for having slain Orpheus for example Phanocles ap Stobæum, Flor. ii. 478 (Ed. Gaisford),

Ἂς ἀλόχους ἐστίζον, ιν' ἐν χροὶ σήματ' ἔχουσαι
Κυάνεα στυγιροῦ μὴ λελάθοιντο φόνου —
(*H.*)

Ercal-Itbi, i c. perhaps Epcal ın Chebı, or Hercules the Theban. This is the reading of L, for which B, running both words into one, reads Epctbı. In the next line the name Pıctı is derived from tattoeing, although just before (line 11), it was derived from *pikes.*—(*T.*) Agathyrsus and Gelonus were brothers of

After they had resolved to emigrate),   15
In the east of Europe.

Agathyrsi was their name,
In the portion of Ercal-Itbi[s];
From their tattoeing their fair skins
Were they called Picts   20

The Picts, the tribe I speak of,
Understood travelling over the sea,
Without mean, unworthy deeds[h],
The seed of Geleon son of Ercal.

Of them[i] six brothers   25
With alacrity, unflinching,
For glory's sake set out;
The seventh *was* their sister.

Solen, Ulpha, Nechtain,
Drostan the powerful diviner,   30
Were their names *and* their order,
Aengus and Leithenn.

The

Scytha, and sons of Hercules or *Ercul*, called in Welsh *Erculf*. Herod. Melp. cap. 10 Steph. Byzant. in Γελωνὸν. The bard seems to make Gelonus (Geleon) the ancestor, and Agathyrsi the name, of one and the same tribe.—(*H.*)

Unworthy deeds.—L. reads line 23, thus

Ceⱷ ᵹním n-Ⲉрcаіⳑ n-оⱬⱬаіⳑ.
The hundred deeds of mighty Ercal.

And in the next line the same manuscript has Ⲉolchoin for Ᵹeleoin, which seems a manifest mistake of transcription.—(*T.*)

[i] *Of them.*—In B. h-Ua oіⳑ, which I have supposed to be intended for h-uaоіⳑ, and translated accordingly. L. reads h-Uаіⱬір, which may perhaps mean, "Of their country." In line 26, for lіun L. reads lіuⳑ.—(*T.*)

Lan ꞃꞁ Tꞃaꞁʒꞁa tꞃeabta
ꝺo ꝺecꞃa a ꞃuꞁꞃ ꞃocla,
ꞃo bo ꝺamna ꝺeabṫa,
ʒan taꞃba ʒan tocꞃa.   35

Tanʒaꝺaꞃ lea ꞁn ꝺeꞁʒ-ꝼꞁꞃ,
o tꞁꞃꞁꞃ, o tꞃeꝺaꞁꞃ,
luct tꞃꞁ lonʒ co loꞃmuꝺ,
nonbuꞃ aꞃ tꞃí céꝺaꞁꞃ   40

Cꞁnʒꞃet ꞃeac tuꞁnꝺ cꞃꞁchꞁ
Fꞃanʒcu, ꞃꞁacu ꝼaꞁlʒꞁꞃ,
[ʒnꞁꝺ] catꞃaꞁʒ aꞁꞃm aꞁblꞁꞃ
ꝟꞁaꞃ ba aꞁnm Pꞁctabꞁꞃ.

Pꞁctabꞁꞃ a Pꞁctꞁꞃ   45
atbeꞃtíꞃ a catꞃaꞁʒ,
ba ꞃlonnuꝺ ꞃlan ꞃocꞃaꞁꝺ
ꞁaꞃum ꝺaꞃ ꞃꞁn ꞃat-múꞁꞃ.

Rꞁ ꞃo ċaꞃ a ꞃuꞁꞃ,
tꞃé ʒlꞁaꞁꝺ ʒo n-ʒaꞁꞃʒe,   50
ꝺꞁ ꞃoconn a ꝼeꞃʒe,
[a ꝺtoch]ꞃunꝺ ꝼoꞃ ꞃaꞁꞃʒe.

Foꞃ

ʲ *Absolute sovereign* —Literally *full king*, i e *ard righ*, or supreme king over the reguli or toparchs of Thrace —(*H*)

ᵏ *Sought* —L reads ꝺo cheatḣꞃa, admired or fell in love with —(*T.*)

ˡ *Flocks* —The reading of L. is here followed B has tꞃeabaꞁꞃ, "from their houses" In the next verse B has ʒol-lopmuꝺ B has also nꞁe lonʒ, *nine ships*, instead of tꞃꞁ —(*T*)

ᵐ *Three hundred and nine* —It is curious that this number makes 12 also, on the principle explained p 112, *suprà*, note ʲ.—(*T.*)

ⁿ *Sea* —B reads an cꞃꞁcu, "they passed through *the countries*"—(*T.*)

ᵒ *They built.*—ʒnꞁꝺ added from L, as

The absolute sovereign[j] of populous Thrace
   Sought[k] their lovely sister,
   (It was the cause of conflict)
   Without gift, without dowry   35

They came away with her, the good men,
   From *their* lands, from *their* flocks[l],
   A company of three ships in good order,
   Three hundred and nine[m] persons   40

They stepped on land from the surrounding sea[n]
   Of France,—they cut down woods,
   They built[o] a city *with their* many weapons,
   Which was named Pictabis

Pictabis[p] a Pictis   45
   They named their city;
   It remained a good and free name
   Afterwards upon the fortress

The king sought their sister
   By battle fiercely[q],   50
   And in consequence of his anger
   They were driven upon the sea

On

necessary both for the sense and for the metre. This verse is obscure. The words cατραιჳ αιηm αιblιr will admit of being translated "a city in a pleasant [or beautiful] situation" The events alluded to are given above, p. 123.—(*T.*)

[p] *Pictabis*—Pictabis or Pictavia, Poictiers, is here derived from the Picts, contrary to the prose preface, which had derived it from *pikes;* unless the word *pictis* here be taken to mean pikes, and not the name of the people.—(*II.*)

[q] *Fiercely*—B. reads ჳo ncιnჳe In line 52, the first syllable of ხcοτhꝃunხ, which is necessary for the metre, is supplied from L—(*T.*)

Fop tpacc mapa meaodaid
  long lelaig lucc lacaip,
  anaip ap a feipiup   55
  acin peipeao bpacaip

baoap in Piccaue,
  [go] n-gpaine oia n-glenail,
  a n-ainm po bo aeoa,
  aipm ippaba Elaip.   60

Elaio app a céle,
  co n-oene po oiúo,
  cino oa lá gac laccu,
  acbac accu a piup

Seac bpeacnaib 'na peimim,   65
  co h-Epinn na h-aine,
  po cogpac a cinopem
  gobpac inbep Slaine

Slaigpeac pluag [Fea] poglac,
  oia pognam i nemni,   70
  cpia glunou gapga
  i cach Apoa-leamnacc.

                                        Laic

r *With her* —acin, the reading of L,
is a combination of aci, *with her*, and in,
the article. B reads accu in—(*T*).

s *Renowned.*—paoa, L, i e. long, or far-
famed —(*T.*)

t *Elaiɲ*.—" The place where Elaiɲ was;"
that is to say, the see of St. Hilary, bishop
of Poictiers from A. D. 350 or 355 to
368 or 369, and one of the most illustrious fathers of the western church. Venantius Fortunatus, one of his successors
in that see, writes thus in his eulogy
of the pious Queen Radegund, lib. vii.
i. ii.

" Fortunatus ego hinc humili prece, voce, saluto,
    (Italiâ genitum Gallica rura tenent)
Pictavis residens, quâ Sanctus Hilarius olim
    Natus in urbe fuit notus in orbe pater."—(*H*)

On the shore of the sea was shattered,
  A ship, swift sailing, well manned,
  There remained, as we know,   55
  With her[r] the sixth brother.

They were in Pictavia,
  With success attaching to them;
  Their name was renowned[s]
  At the place where Elair[t] was   60

They stole away thence together
  In haste, under sorrow,
  At the end[u] of two tempestuous days,
  Their sister died with them

Passing by Britain in their voyage,   65
  To Eri the delightful
  They directed their course,
  And reached Inbher Slaine[v].

They cut down the plundering host of Fea[w],
  Who were aided by poison[x],   70
  By their fierce deeds,
  In the battle of Ard-leamhnacht.

The

[u] *At the end.* — L. reads cinca la co lochca "From the fault of a stormy day "—(*T*)

[v] *Inbher Slaine* — The mouth of the River Slaney at Wexford. See above, p 123.—(*T.*)

[w] *Fea*, added from L *Fea* signifies " of woods." This was the host of the Tuath Fiadhbhe, or "people of the woods," mentioned in the prose narrative, p 123 —(*T*)

[x] *Poison* —The reading of L has been followed B reads via fognav a noemnacc, and in the next line a n-glungnu See the story, p. 125, above, and in Additional Notes, No XVIII In line 71 B reads opian for cpia, which is given in the text from L, as being probably the more correct reading —(*T.*)

Laic anᵹbaide, aimble,
  fea faidbe fudan,
  ᵹona danaib ᵹo n-decnaib,   75
  do bhreacnaib a bunad.

Ba manb nec no cheiᵹoir
  acc ceilᵹceir a fuile,
  ᵹo bom cru doenne,
  cid cu nó cid dune.   80

Onui Cnuicnec in capdair,
  fuain ic amcir amlaid,
  lemlacc if innalad
  fni camad fon calmain.

Tuccra cainc cneab-clann,   85
  la Cnemcand coin cenn-balc,
  co comlacc an aicmid,
  fon faicci Andlemnacc

Slaiᵹread sluaiᵹ Fea faebnach
  ᵹan cnebad if ᵹan copad,   90

                                              no

<hr>

[1] *Their origin*—See above, p 123 This stanza is thus given in L.

  Laich anᵹbaidi faidbe
    co nᵹainbe ne pudan
    co namib co noecnaib
    do bneacnaib a mbunaid.

  ['] Heroes hard cutting
    With roughness, with hurtfulness,
    With wonderful weapons,
    Of the Britons *was* their origin "—(*T*)

[2] *They struck.*—No cheiᵹoir is the read-

ing of L and is adopted in the text instead of no feccir in B —(*T*)

  [4] *Wasted away*—This line is thus given in L

        Con bo cru de sen e,

  but the meaning is the same —(*T*)

  ['] *Of friendship* —i e a friendly friend, a benefactor. In L. incapdair —(*T*.)

  [c] *Were washed* —analad, L. The word malaim, analaim, or ionnlaim is still in use in Scotland, and in many parts of

The heroes valiant and numerous
    Cut down knotty woods,
    With wonderful arts,
    From the Britons *was* their origin[y]   75

Dead was every one they struck[z],
    If but his blood they shed,
    So that he wasted away[a] on that account,
    Whether *he were* a dog, or whether *he were* a man   80

A Cruithnian Druid, of friendship[b],
    Discovered a cure for those thus wounded,
    New milk in which were washed[c]
    Those who lay *wounded* on the earth

The herds *of cows* of the tribes were brought,   85
    By just Cremhthann the headstrong[d],
    Until the herd was milked
    On the green[e] of Ardleamhnacht

They cut down the troops of Fea, of sharp weapons[f],
    Leaving them without tillage and without produce,   90

                                            By

Ireland. If, however, we read in n-alaib, which may possibly be also the reading of B., the line may be translated "new milk, in the wound." The next line is from L., but B reads an-uramao pop-tamail, which (if the words be so divided) will signify, ' in powerful [or efficacious] bathing "—(*T*)

  [d] *Headstrong* —The word cenn-balc is literally thus rendered, but does not involve the idea of perverse obstinacy im-

plied in the English word *headstrong*. cenn, a head, is often used as a sort of intensitive in composition. It may mean, however, a stout head, i.e. chief or leader. For cenn-balc, L. reads certbalc, and in the next verse, co tomlact a pach nem, which is corrupt.—(*T*)

  [e] *Green* —See above, p 93, note u. The word faiczi is omitted in L.—(*T*)

  [f] *Sharp weapons* —Faebruch is the reading of L. In B. this line is given

po cobṗaṫ ṫia n-ṫiṫh ġliaiṫ,
Cṗemṫaṫṫ ṗciaṫbel ṗcoṗac

Sġuiṗṗiṫ ann in Cṗuiṫniġ
ṗoṗ ṫuiṗṫib ṫṗi maiġe,
comṫaṗ ecla ṗaebaiṗ   95
na Ġaeiṫil ġo n-ġloine

Ġaṗ iaṗ ṗin ġo n-aṗaṫ
ceṫṗuṗ blaṫac bṗaṫaṗ,
Solen, Neachṫan, Ṫṗoṗṫan,
Ċlenġuṗ, ṗoṗṫán ṗaṫac   100

Ṛo ṗaiṫ a n-ṫeaṗ Ulṗa,
iaṗ n-uṗcṗa a caṗaṫ,
in Ṛachṗanṫ i m-bṗeaġaiḃ,
anṫ ṗo mebaiṫ malaiṗṫ

Moṗṫaṗ occa Caṫluain,   105
niṗ bo ṫṗuaġ in ṫ-aiṗe,

                                                       ṫo

<hr>

thus, Sliġṗeaṫ ṗluaġ ṗea ṗebac, while
ṗliġṗeaṫ is an evident mistake for ṗloiġ-
ṗeaṫ, and ṗea ṗebac is probably the
name of the hostile tribe Fea Fidhbhe
See above, line 72   In line 90 the reading of L has been followed   B reads
ġan ṫṗeib iṗ ġan ṫobac —(*T*)

⁸ *Then defeat,* i. e. the defeat of the
Tuath Fidhbhe   ṫia n-ṫiṫh has been
adopted from L   for ṫuaṫ ġliaiṫ, which
is the reading of B —(*T*)

ʰ *The three plains.*—These words seem
to denote some place in the County Wexford   Perhaps ṫṗi maiġe should be taken
as a proper name but it is not now known
as such   It occurs in both copies   In L
lines 93 and 94 are transposed, and the
stanza is read thus

Cuiṗiṫ anṫ ṫṗi maiġi
na Cṗuiṫnich co n-ġaiṗi
cumṫaṗ eaġla ṗaebaiṗ
na Ġaeiġil co n-ġlaine.

" On the three plains planted
    The Cruithneans with prosperity
    Until dread of their arms
    Had seized the noble Gaels "—(*T*)

By their defeat in the battle[g],
Cremhthan Sciathbel of horses was protected

The Cruithnians settled themselves
On the lands of the three plains[h],
Until dread of their arms   95
Had seized the noble Gaels

Soon after that died[i]
Four of the noble brothers,
Solen, Neachtan, Drostan,
Aengus, the prophetic pillar   100

From the south was Ulfa sent
After the decease of his friends;
In Rachrann in Bregia[j]
He was utterly destroyed

Cathluan was elevated[k] by them,   105
(No despicable chieftain),

As

In line 95, B. reads oibil instead of ꝼaebaip, which latter reading has been adopted in the text. The word τuipτib in line 94, which is omitted in L, appears to signify sods, soil, lands —(T)

[i] *Died* —co-nᵹabao, L. In line 98 L reads bpaτhap blaoach, and in line 99, B reads Ulpha instead of Neuchτun, which last name has been substituted in the text from L, as being in accordance with the prose, especially as B. immediately after agrees with L in the account given of Ulfa in the next stanza —(T)

[j] *Rachrann in Bregia* —Rachrann was the ancient name of the rocky island of Lambay, near the Hill of Howth, which is in the territory of Bregia. Lines 103 and 104 are from L. B. reads,

in a cupnn im-ḃpeaᵹaib
ano po meaoaip malapτ.

" In his carn in Bregia
Did he meditate malediction' —(T)

[k] *Elevated.* — L. reads mapbτap, " is killed," which is plainly wrong. In line 106 B reads bo aτpuaᵹaipe, the reading of L. has been preferred —(T.)

T 2

oo ριξ γοραιb uιle
ρια n-oul a τίρ n-aιle.

Αn αρbeρτ γριu Εριmon
aρ ιn Ερinο ρeετaρ,   110
aρ na oeαρna oeαbaιo
ιmmon Ceαmaιρ τeετaιo.

Cρι cét ban oo bρeατa,
ooιb ρορ τeτha τlατaιξ,
cιoeαo ρo bo τuαcaιl,   115
ξac bean ξο n-a bρaτaιρ

bατaρ ρaτa γορρo,
γριo ρenmu γρι oιρe,
comο ροιρe a mάτaρ,
ρuρ ξnaτh ξab ιn ριξι   120

Reρoaιρ aρ ιn Εριnn
ιna ρeιmιm ρaτ-ξlιno,
ξan muρéιρ ξan maρc-luaξ,
ιm Cατluan mac Caιτmιno.

Caτ-moloooρ cnaρ-cρuaιo   125
ιρ Caρmacan ξluaιρ.

                                                      bαoαρ

¹ *Spake.*—Α oubρao ριu L In the next line L reads corruptly ριn n-Εριnοριn n-eιτaιρ; in line 111 oeαρnρao for oeαρna, and in line 112, τeετaιch for τeετaιo —(*T.*)

ᵐ *Teamhair.*—The royal palace of Tara, in the county of Meath. See Mr. Petrie's Essay on the History and Antiquities of Tara Hill (Trans. of the Royal Irish Aca-demy, vol xvii)—(*T.*)

ⁿ *Agreeable.*—This line is given in B. thus ooιb ρo ρceτeu τlατaιξ. The read-ing of L. has been preferred. The true reading was probably ooιb ρορ τeτha τlατaιξ —(*T.*)

º *And her brother.*—lit. " with her bro-ther." The meaning is that the Irish were

As king over them all,
Before they set out to another country.

For to them spake[l] Erimon
    That out of Eri they should go,   110
    Lest they should make battle
    For Teamhair[m], *as* a possession.

Three hundred women were given,
    To them they were agreeable[n],
    But they were most cunning,   115
    Each woman and her brother[o]

There were oaths *imposed* on them,
    By the stars, by the earth,
    That from the nobility of the mother
    Should always be the right to the sovereignty[p]   120

They set out from Eri
    On their oath-bound expedition,
    Without families, without cavalry,
    With Cathluan, son of Caitminn[q]

Catmolodor[r] the hard-knobbed,   125
    And Cathmachan the bright,

                                        Were

---

cunning in obtaining conditions from the Picts, before they gave them women —(*T.*)

[p] *Sovereignty*.—This distich is very corrupt, for ꝓoꝓꝓo, line 117, B reads eꝓꝓu. The text is corrected from L. Line 120 is also adopted from L., instead of ꝓo ᵹnaꞇaiᵹ iꝓꝓiᵹe, the reading of B. L reads oemnu in line 118, for ꝓennu. In line 117, ꝓaꞇa signifies not so much *oaths* as obli-gations guaranteed by oath or otherwise —(*T*)

[q] *Caitminn*.—Caiꞇnio. B.—(*T*)

[r] *Catmolodor*.—This name is now Cadwaladyr. He appears to be called "hard-knobbed," in allusion to the deep scars with which his body was tattooed or ornamented. Lines 125 and 126 are given thus in L.

baoap ʒilli ʒlopoa
oá mac cpóoa Catluain.

Ꭺ copaio cpuaio comnapt
ba tpom balc a taipm ream   130
Cinʒ coceppnn oia ceppn-peom
Im mac Peppnn a n-ainm-peom

h-Uaipem ainm a pilio
no pípeo in peo-ʒin,
po bo pup oia milio   135
Cpup mac Cipiʒ Cetlim

Cpuitne mac coip Cínca
ooib po thincha tochmopc,
co tuc banntpact blat-ʒlan
oap Ꭺthmaʒ, oap Ꭺtʒopt   140

Ꭺnait oib a n-Ꭼalʒa,
ʒo lin cepoa ip cupac,   .

nao

Caonolooop clechtip,
ip Catainlocach cnap puaio

" Cadnolodon, the chief,
  And Catainlocach the red-knobbed "

The word clechtip signifies the person
in a tribe to whom belonged the right of
final appeal In line 127 L. inserts ʒlana
before ʒlopoa.—(*T.*)

s Their trampling.—This line is from L
B reads ba oopnn balc a toip-peom. In
the next line B gives Cind, not Cinʒ, as
the name of the first champion, which
agrees with the prose (see page 125), and
reads Cino co cepo oia cepo-peom,

" Cind skilful in their art ' [i. e. war]
In the next line the scribe has written
.uii mc pipt, " the seven sons of Pirt," for
" Im, son of Pirnn."—(*T.*)

t Huasem, or Uasem, for the H is only
euphonic. L. reads h-Uaipneam This
name sounds not unlike that of Ossian,
which, however, is always written Oipin
in Gaelic In the next line in pet-ʒean,
L—(*T*)

u Cetlim.—Cheitlem. L. I have taken
this word for a proper name, cet lim
might signify, " I acknowledge," " I allow."—(*T.*)

Were glorious youths,
    The two valiant sons of Cathluan

His hardy, puissant champions,
    Heavy, stern, was their trampling[s],   130
    Cing, victorious in his victory,
    Im, son of Perun, *were* their names

Huasem[t] was the name of his poet,
    Who sought out the path of pleasantry
    Ruddy was his hero,   135
    Crus, son of Cirigh Cethin[u]

Cruithne, son of just Cing[v].
    Attended to their courtship,
    So that he brought a company of fair women,
    Over Athmagh, over Athgort   140

There remained of them *behind* in Ealga[w].
    With many artificers and warriors[x],

Who

---

[v] *Cing.*—Cpuichniʒ meic coip Ʒinʒa
L In the remainder of this stanza the
text of L has been followed B reads

    Ro cinca accocmop
    Co cuc banncpacc mblach ʒlan
    Ua pach ʒopc,

which must be corrupt, for it violates the
metre Different duties are assigned to
Cruithne here, and in the prose account,
where he is called a ceapo, their artist
or artificer. The places called Athmagh
and Athgort, line 140, are unknown.—
(T)

[w] *Ealga* —B reads melʒa, which is
perhaps a mistake for in Elʒa Elga or
Ealga was one of the poetical names of
Ireland An cpeap ainm (says Keatinge)
Inip Ealʒa i. oilen uapal Oip ap
ionann inip ꞁ oilen, ꞁ ap ionann ealʒa ꞁ
uapol, ꞁ ap pe linn peap m-Ꝺolʒ pa ʒnac
an c-ainm pin uippe "The third name
(of Ireland) was Inis Ealga, i e noble
island ; for Inis is the same as island,
and Ealga is the same as noble, and this
was its usual name from the time of the
Fir-bolgs."—(T)

[x] *Warriors*—B reads cpuan for which

nau cepeao pop bpeaʒmach
peipeap vemnac vpuav.

Opuiveact ip iolact, maic,   145
in aile min ʒlan mup ʒlan,
bapc vibeipʒi, vuain ʒil,
ip uaioib po munav

Mopav ppev ip mana,   150
paʒa pin, am pona,
ʒocha en vo paipe
caipi ʒac ceol cona

Cnuic ip coipci apcopa
cen cpoʒa cuach caille,

cuapʒaibpec

cupach, the reading of L, has been substituted The next line is also taken from
L B reads na po ceippeav bpeaʒmac,
"they would not leave Breghmagh" The
Diuids are called "demon-like," or "de-
vilish" as being skilled in demoniacal
arts.—(T)

' Druidism —The word maic is so explained in an old glossary in the Library
of Trinity College, Dublin The whole
stanza is thus given in B

Opuivecht 7 iolacht mac mapc
    min balc mup ʒlan ʒlep
    vibav ʒa vuan ʒil
    ip uaioib po munav

which is so corrupt that it is difficult to
translate it, and it is also inconsistent
with the laws of the metre. The text of
L has been followed with one correction

of uaioib po in the last line, for uaib pib
po —(T)

² Sredhs —B reads pleaʒ, a word which
may signify "spears," but the reading of
L is preferred as being in accordance with
the prose See p 125 As the meaning
of the word ppev or ppeov is doubtful, it
has been left untranslated See the poem
attributed to St Columba, Miscell Irish
Arch Soc, vol 1 p 2, and note 31, p 12,
where Mr O'Donovan conjectured it to
be the ancient form of cpcav, a flock or
herd But he has since found another copy
of that poem in a parchment MS in the
Bodleian Library at Oxford, Laud 615,
p 7, where the word is twice written
with an aspiration on the v, thus "ní háʒ
ppeoiv aca mo cuiv; and again, na ha-
ouip vo ʒocaiv ʒepʒ, na ppeov, na pen
ap bic ce ' it is also found written in

Who settled in Breagh-magh,
Six demon-like druids

Necromancy and idolatry, druidism[y],   145
  In a fair and well-walled house,
  Plundering in ships, bright poems,
  By them were taught

The honoring of sredhs[z] and omens,
  Choice of weather[a], lucky times,   150
  The watching the voices of birds,
  They practised without disguise

Hills and rocks *they prepared* for the plough,
  Among their sons were no thieves,

                                        They

MSS indifferently ꞃꞃeꝺ and ꞃꞃeᵹ, from which we may infer that the final letter was always intended to be pronounced with aspiration, therefore the word must be ꞃꞃeꝺ, ꞃꞃiaꝺ, ꞃꞃeꞇ, or ꞃꞃeoꞇ, *a sneezing,* a word still in use, which is also frequently written ꞃꞃoꞇ or ꞃꞃoᵹ It is well known that sneezing, both among the Greeks and Romans, and also in the middle ages, was regarded as ominous, and made use of for the purposes of divination This superstition was prohibited by several enactments of councils and synods, and formed a frequent topic of reprobation from the pulpit As an example we may cite the following passage from a sermon preached by St Eligius or Eloy, who became Bishop of Noyon about the year 640, "Similiter et auguria, vel *sternutationes,* nolite observare, nec in itinere positi aliquas aviculas cantantes attendatis, sed sive iter, sive quodcunque operis arripitis signate vos in nomine Christi, &c "—Vit S Eligii lib ii c 15, apud Dacherii Spicil p 97 See also the "Libellus abbatis Pirminii," published by Mabillon, which he supposes to belong to the year 758 "Noli adorare idola non ad petras, neque ad arbores, non ad angulos, neque ad fontes, ad trivios nolite adorare, nec vota reddere. Precantatores, et sortilegos, karagios, aruspices, divinos, ariolos, magos, maleficos, *sternutus,* et auguria per aviculas, vel alia ingenia mala et diabolica nolite facere et credere "—Vet Anal p 69 These examples will suffice to shew the late continuance of this class of superstitions —See also Grimm's Deutsche Mythologie, p 647 —(*T*)

[a] *Weather.*—This line is from L B reads ꞃoᵹa ꞃean ni ꞃona Line 152 is also

níṗ bo inʒaṗʒ ṫuċtu
co ṗo maṗḃ ḃṗeaṫnu.

ḃa ᴅe ʒaḃṗat Albain,
aṗᴅ-ʒlain ṫalcain ṫlac-mín,   170
co n-imaᴅ amlaeḃ
co Cinaeṫ mac n-Alpin

                                        Aṗ

sibly the Glas-cu of the Strathclyde Britons was Forcu in their vocabulary.—(*H*)

" *Onsets*, i e the fierceness of his onsets
was not relaxed or diminished until, &c
For ṫeċtu, line 166, B. reads ṫṗeḃtu,
and, line 167, ṫuiciu for ṫucṫhu   The
readings of L have been followed in the
text —(*T*)

¹ *Conquer*—L adds Cṗuiċniʒ, "the
Cruithnians seized on Alba," and gives
this stanza thus

        ḃa ᴅe ʒaḃṗaᴅ Cṗuiċniʒ
        Alban ṫuṗṫhiʒ ṫlacc min
        eṗ cloḃ a n-il ael
        co cineaᴅ mac Alpin

    Thus did the Cruithnians acquire
    Alban, the fruitful, the smooth-surfaced,
    After defeating their many rocks [?]
    To Cinaedh Mac Ailpin

or ael may signify sharp weapons   But
B has im for co, in line 172—(*T*)

ⁱ *Many an Amlaff*—Amlaff, Amlaib,
Aulaib, &c, for Olaf, was the prominent
name among those northern vikingar, who
ravaged, and in part conquered, Ireland
and Pictland, during the ninth and tenth
centuries.   See Battle of Magh Rath,

p 290, and the Editor's note.   In 852(3)
Amlaip, king of Lochlin, came into Ire-
land and exacted tribute there —Ann
Ult.   In the spring of 866 he ravaged
Pictland.   Three years later he was slain
by Constantine, king of Picts —Ann Ult
and Chron. Pict.   Among the Danes of
Northumbria and Lothian the name of
Anlaf was popular, and one of their An-
lafs fought on the Scottish side at Brunen-
burg in 937 —Chalmers' Caled. i 337, 338
Amlaib Mᶜ Illuib, son of Indulf (so Dr.
O'Conor), king of Albany, was slain by
Kenneth, son of Malcolm [son of Domhnall, ap Ann Ult , but erroneously], in
976 or 977 —Tig. et Ann Ult in annis.   It
would seem as if king Indulfus had married
some vikingr's daughter, to have an Amlaff
for his son.   The year 979 saw the death of
the son of Amlaff the younger, grandson
of Amlaff the elder, at the battle of Temora   And in 980 Amlaibh Mᶜ Sitriuc,
last Danish king of Dublin, retired to
Iona   It is evident that this popular name
had come to be expressive of the nation
who used it, as those of John, Patrick,
and David have connected themselves with
three sections of our island empire, with

His onsets[h] were not without fierceness,
Until he had slain the Britons

Thus did they conquer[i] Alba,
    Noble, gentle-hilled, smooth-surfaced,   170
    With many an Amlaff[j],
    Down to Cinaeth mac Alpin[k],

                                           For

this further resemblance to the two latter, that Olaf son of Tryggvi, and St. Olaf, were the apostles of religion in Norway

The main error of our bard, if the reading in the text be correct, would consist in the supposition that an intermixture of Northmen with Scots and Picts existed from the beginning, and that "many an Amlaff" had combined with the Cruthnich in their first occupation of Albany. If, however, we were at liberty to make a transposition of two lines, we might thereby restore the truth of history to our bard. That they "seized on Alba, with many an Amlaff, till Kenneth Mac Alpin," would be enormous error, but that they did so "till Kenneth Mac Alpin with many an Amlaff," is the truth. For it was in his (the first Scoto-Pictish) reign, that Danari (the Danes under Amlaiv) vastaverunt Pictaviam for the first time. —Chron Pict in num. 77 —(H)

Perhaps the word amlaeb in the text (if that be the original reading) may not be a proper name, but may be used in the sense of a champion, a hero, from which the proper name is derived, but for this we have no authority, and it is,

therefore, more probable, that the bard had no idea of speaking of "Amlaffs" at all, and that in line 171 there are mistakes of the scribe We should read perhaps a niomao nil ceb, i e "with their many arts" or sciences Ceb is explained ealaoa, arts or sciences, in old glossaries and ml may easily be confounded with nil But as this is only conjecture, no alteration has been made in the text — (T)

[k] *Cinaeth mac Alpin.*—Kenneth Mac Alpin was king of Scots, or of the British Dalriada, called Airer-Gaedhal, i e territory of the Gael, which name of Gael, Gaithel, or Gaedhael was then synonymous to that of Scots The country bearing the *national* appellation of Argyle included, besides the modern Argyle proper, the territory of Loarn or Lorn, and those of Knapdale, Cowel, and Cantire, being bounded to the east by Mount Drum-Alban, Adamnan's Dorsum Britanniæ, and southward by the Firth of Clyde In 843 he wrested the kingdom of Albany out of the hands of its last native ruler, Bruide the Seventh, and the Scots and Picts were never again disunited This is the usual epoch of the

His onsets[h] were not without fierceness,
Until he had slain the Britons

Thus did they conquer[j] Alba,
Noble, gentle-hilled, smooth-surfaced,   170
With many an Amlaff[j],
Down to Cinaeth mac Alpin[k],

For

this further resemblance to the two latter, that Olaf son of Tryggvi, and St. Olaf, were the apostles of religion in Norway

The main error of our bard, if the reading in the text be correct, would consist in the supposition that an intermixture of Northmen with Scots and Picts existed from the beginning, and that "many an Amlaff" had combined with the Cruthnich in their first occupation of Albany. If, however, we were at liberty to make a transposition of two lines, we might thereby restore the truth of history to our bard. That they "seized on Alba, with many an Amlaff, till Kenneth Mac Alpin," would be enormous error, but that they did so "till Kenneth Mac Alpin with many an Amlaff," is the truth. For it was in his (the first Scoto-Pictish) reign, that Danari (the Danes under Amlaiv) vastaverunt Pictaviam for the first time. —Chron Pict in num. 77 —(H)

Perhaps the word amlaeb in the text (if that be the original reading) may not be a proper name, but may be used in the sense of a champion, a hero, from which the proper name is derived, but for this we have no authority, and it is,

therefore, more probable, that the bard had no idea of speaking of "Amlaffs" at all, and that in line 171 there are mistakes of the scribe We should read perhaps a momao nil aeb, i e "with their many arts" or sciences Aeb is explained ealaoa, arts or sciences, in old glossaries and ml may easily be confounded with nil But as this is only conjecture, no alteration has been made in the text — (T)

[k] *Cinaeth mac Alpin.*—Kenneth Mac Alpin was king of Scots, or of the British Dalriada, called Airer-Gaedhal, i e territory of the Gael, which name of Gael, Gaithel, or Gaedhael was then synonymous to that of Scots The country bearing the *national* appellation of Argyle included, besides the modern Argyle proper, the territory of Loarn or Lorn, and those of Knapdale, Cowel, and Cantire, being bounded to the east by Mount Drum-Alban, Adamnan's Dorsum Britanniæ, and southward by the Firth of Clyde In 843 he wrested the kingdom of Albany out of the hands of its last native ruler, Bruide the Seventh, and the Scots and Picts were never again disunited This is the usual epoch of the

níp bo ingapg ruchtu
co po mapb bpeatnu.

ba ve gabrat Albain,
apv-glain talcain tlac-mín,   170
co n-imav amlaeb
co Cinaet mac n-Alpin

Ap

sibly the Glas-cu of the Strathclyde Britons was Forcu in their vocabulary.—(H)

ʰ Onsets, i e the fierceness of his onsets
was not relaxed or diminished until, &c
For techtu, line 166, B. reads tpebtu,
and, line 167, tuiciu for tucchu The
readings of L have been followed in the
text.—(T)

ⁱ Conquer.—L adds Cpuithnig, "the
Cruithmans seized on Alba," and gives
this stanza thus

ba ve gabrav Cpuithnig
Alban tupchig tlact min
ep clov a n-il ael
co cineav mac Ailpin

Thus did the Cruithmans acquire
Alban, the fruitful, the smooth-surfaced,
After defeating their many rocks [?]
To Cinaedh Mac Ailpin

or ael may signify sharp weapons But
B has im for co, in line 172.—(T)

ʲ Many an Amlaff.—Amlaff, Amlaib,
Aulaib, &c, for Olaf, was the prominent
name among those northern vikingar, who
ravaged, and in part conquered, Ireland
and Pictland, during the ninth and tenth
centuries. See Battle of Magh Rath,

p 290, and the Editor's note. In 852(3)
Amlaip, king of Lochlin, came into Ire-
land and exacted tribute there.—Ann
Ult. In the spring of 866 he ravaged
Pictland. Three years later he was slain
by Constantine, king of Picts.—Ann Ult
and Chron. Pict. Among the Danes of
Northumbria and Lothian the name of
Anlaf was popular, and one of their An-
lafs fought on the Scottish side at Brunen-
burg in 937.—Chalmers' Caled. i 337, 338
Amlaib Mᶜ Illuib, son of Indulf (so Dr.
O'Conor), king of Albany, was slain by
Kenneth, son of Malcolm [son of Domhnall, ap Ann Ult, but erroneously], in
976 or 977.—Tig. et Ann Ult in annis. It
would seem as if king Indulfus had married
some vikingr's daughter, to have an Amlaff
for his son. The year 979 saw the death of
the son of Amlaff the younger, grandson
of Amlaff the elder, at the battle of Temora And in 980 Amlaibh Mᶜ Sitriuc,
last Danish king of Dublin, retired to
Iona It is evident that this popular name
had come to be expressive of the nation
who used it, as those of John, Patrick,
and David have connected themselves with
three sections of our island empire, with

tuapzaibpet a tinopem   155
puno a n-inbep bonni.

ba heao looap uainoi
zo-n-zluaipe na zpibe,
ima taiz co tpene
i tip maipeach Ile   160

Ip

from L. B reads chaipe zan cel cona Fon paipe, line 151, B reads aipe.—(*T*)

[b] *Inbher Boinne.*—The mouth of the river Boyne, which runs through the region of Bregia, where the Picts, according to the account here given of them, had their settlement in Ireland. In line 153, L reads coipei, and in line 155, tuapzaibpet oia tinopum, where B. has po tozpat. In line 156, the reading of L is adopted. B reads zabpat inbep m-boinoe, but the text in both copies is probably very corrupt.—(*T*)

[c] *Away.*—L reads ba heaoap oo looap, " by Edar [the hill of Howth] they passed from us." In lines 159, 160, B reads

    imma iat co opene
    i tip iat peach Ile.—(*T*)

[d] *Ile.*—The island of Ilay or Ila, one of the five Ebudæ or Hebrides, anciently Epidium, and long the capital seat of the Lordship of the Isles. It lies outside of the Mull of Cantire or Epidian Foreland, to the inside of which lies Boot or Bute. And I suppose that King Bruide the First, whom I have argued (See Addit. Notes, No XVII.) to be the very first

king of Gwyddyl Fichti in Britain, was called Brudi Bout, from that island. If the first descent was on Ilay, Bute was a snug and likely place to become the royal residence.

This statement is somewhat different from that of Nennius, cap 5, that the Picts *first* occupied the Orkneys, " et *postea ex affinitimis insulis vastaverunt non modicas et multas regiones, occupaveruntque eas in sinistrali parte Britanniæ;*" though even he admits that they did not occupy the mainland from the Orkneys immediately, but from the other islands. Beda says generally, ' *habitare per septentrionales insulæ partes cœperunt,*" and that phrase, which meant no more than Alban or the ultra-mural Britain in general, may possibly have suggested the statement in the Historia Britonum. That they stood over from Cruthenia in as nearly as may be the same course, as in after days their neighbours of the Dalriadha pursued, is the probability, as well as the best authority. When we read that Muredach, son of Angus, was the " primus colonus" of Ilay (Ogygia, p. 470), of course we merely understand

They prepared their expedition
Here at Inbher Boinne[b]

                                          155

They passed away[c] from us
With the splendour of swiftness,
To dwell by valour
In the beautiful land of Ile[d].

                                          160

                                          From

that he was the first Dalriadhan settler.

The termini given by this poet exclude the Orkneys, of which the Irish legend seems to say nothing, and, though Nennius in cap 5 mentions the temporary occupation of them by the Picts, in his first chapter he places them ultra Pictos, which the name of the Pightland Firth doth likewise imply. Yet it is not to be doubted that the Picts did possess those islands before the Norwegians. See Wallace's Orkneys, cap xi p. 67, Ed. 1693, Adamnan, ii. cap. 42. The History of the Picts ascribed to II Maule of Melgund has a legend of Leutha, king of the Picts of Orkney, who subdued and gave his name to the isle of Lewis, p 29, Ed Glasg 1818 The Diploma of Thomas Bishop of Orkney (ap Orkneyinga Saga, p. 549, 550) avers, upon the authority of ancient records, that the Norwegians found two nations in Orkney, the Peti (Picts) and the Papæ, but entirely destroyed them both The former is a known Saxon and Norse softening of the name Pict. "Scotiæ ac *Petiæ* insularumque quas Australes vel Meridianas vocant" Saxo Gramm Hist Dan. ix. p. 171 etc We must

adopt the conclusion, that the Papæ were the Irish fathers of the rule of St Columkille, who repaired to the Orkneys, and obtained possession of Papa Stronsa and Papa Westra, as he had done of Iona, though, perhaps, with this addition, that all the inhabitants of the Papa islands, and not alone the religious, came to be so called. That opinion, I think, is decided by the statement of Ari Froda, that, when Ingulf the Norwegian visited Iceland, he found some Christians there, whom the Northmen call Papæ, who, not choosing to associate with heathens went away, leaving behind them Irish books, bells, and croziers, and from these things it was easily judged they were Irish Arius, cap ii p. 10, Ed 1744 If Iceland be the Thule Insula of Dicuil, who wrote his book De Mensurâ Orbis in 825, he had thirty years before conversed with some clerici who had sojourned upon that island from the 1st of February to the 1st of August, and in the summer could see to catch the lice upon their shirts at midnight —Cap vii s. 2, n. 6 This was seventy-nine years anterior to the voyage of Ingulf. Arngrim Jonas

Iṗ aṗ ɣabṗac Albain,
apo-ɣlain aileṗ coiṗciú,
cen oich lucc la cṗébcu
o cṗich Chac co Ḟoiṗcu.

Roṗ bṗiṗ Cacluan caċu   165
ɣen cacu cen cechcu

níṗ

observed that the small island of Papey, in East Iceland, was probably a seat of the Irish Papæ, and expressed the like opinion (which Mr. Pinkerton has adopted without acknowledgment) of Papa Stronsa and Papa Westra Arngr Island. Primordia, p 375, Ed II. Steph St Cormac the Navigator, called O'Liathain, whose daring coracle visited the Orkneys under letters of safe conduct obtained for him by Columbkille from Bruide, king of Picts, sailed about with the express object of finding for himself an eremus (hermitage) in oceano Adamnan, i cap 6, ii, cap 42 Thus it was that the kings and toparchs of the Peti received the Papæ into the smaller isles. The same Dicuil mentions some little islands, to be reached in two days and the intervening night, in a boat of two benches, from septentrionalibus Britanniæ insulis (Orkneys?), and which I take to be the Feroes, in quibus in centum ferme annis (from 825, making 725) eremitæ ex nostrâ Scottiâ navigantes habitaverunt, but the latrones Nortmanni had driven them away, and the islets were vacuæ anachoretis, but full of sheep and wild fowl —Ibid s 3 —(II) The word gnibe, line 158, has been supposed to signify swiftness. In the

Leabhar Gabhala of the OClerys, p 96, in an historical poem by Eochaidh O'Flynn, we find an apo abair n-imgnib, where the Gloss is lap an uapal cigepna apo ba comluac m-oeabaio no in iopgail, i e " the noble lord who was all *swiftness* in battles and conflicts " And in the ancient metrical Glossary called " Poetry is the Sister of Wisdom," gnib is explained ainm oo luap, "a name for *swiftness* " —(*T*)

e *The people* —Lines 163 and 164 are from L B reads

cen oich clacc la cṗebcu
o chṗicac co ṗoiṗciu,

which is manifestly corrupt —(*T*)

f *Cat* —The region of Cat is the country now called Cathanesia, or Caithness Its derivation from Caith or Cat, one of Cruthne's seven sons, is a patronymical fable Whether derived from the wild cat, like the Clan Chattan, whose territory included Caithness (see Scott's Maid of Perth, in chap 4), or from *cath*, war, battle, the sound of it seems to recur in the names Cathluan, Catnolodar, Catnolachan. That province may have owed celebrity to its position as a northern

From thence they conquered Alba,
    The noble nurse of fruitfulness
    Without destroying the people[e] or their houses,
    From the region of Cat[f] to Forcu[g]

Cathluan gained battles   165
    Without flinching or cowardice,

                                     His

terminus, as Nennius says, " a Totenes usque ad Catenes "

The Tractatus de Situ Albaniæ (composed by an Englishman, at least not by a Scot, soon after 1185, and printed by Innes, ii., 768-72, with a suspicion that Giraldus was its author), divides Albania into the seven portions of seven brothers, of which the seventh was " Cathanesia citra montem et ultra montem, quia mons Mound dividit Cathanesiam per medium," The Mons Mound was Mount Ord, and the Cathanesia cis montem was the Sudurland (southern land) of the Northmen. " Of old, Sutherland was called Cattey, and its inhabitants Catteigh, and so likewise was Caithness and Strathnaver, and, in the Irish, Sutherland to this day is called Catey, and its inhabitants Catigh ; adeo ut Catteyness nihil aliud sit quam promontorium Cattæ seu Sutherlandiæ, quod promontorium a latere orientali montis Ordi prætenditur."—Blaew cit. in Brand's Orkney, cap. xi As Caithness lies not at all north, but fairly east, of Sutherland in its enlarged sense (for Dunnet Head in Caithness is only 58° 35', and Cape Wrath is 58° 34'), it is evident that the Sudurland of the North-

men was only the portion properly so called, and that they did not include therein the Strathnavern But as they divided those parts into the jarldom of Katanes and the Sudurland, we should, I think, infer that Strathnavern was included in the jarldom, while the Sudurland, though infested, and perhaps partly inhabited, by Northmen, was not thus feudally detached from the crown of the Scoto-Picts. Sir Walter Scott mentions, that the territory of the Clann Chattan comprehended Sutherland and Caithness [Cathanesiam citra et ultra], and that the Earl of Sutherlandshire was their paramount chief, with the title of Mohr Ar Chat , and, though he includes Inverness, and even Perth, within the limits of that clan or league of clans, as referrible to the fifteenth century, we may safely esteem that the Chattanaich originally denoted the people of Katanes within and without Ord.—(JT)

  [g] *Forcu* —Of the place here called *Forcu* I can give no account. It must have been on the southern extremity of Fortren Mor For is the favourite Pictish prefix, as in Fortren, their kingdom, Forteviot, their palace, Fordun, Forfar, Forres, &c Pos-

Ap cpeacao n-apo n-aicmo,
    pop aiccib cen uchneim
    ní cellóap in coclaig,   175
    ap óe aóbepap Cpuicmg

Coeca pig cém cpecac,
    map aen óe pil Ecóac,
    o Fepgup po pípíó
    co mac m-bpigac m-bpecach   180

Se piga ap pe óeicib,
    óib ppi peicim puil cpech
    cappac pice puiclech,
    gabpac pige Cpuicneac

                                    Cpuicnig óop popclam
                                                [ÓO

conquest, although three princes of the Pictish line, Kenneth, Bruide, and Drustan, kept up a struggle against the son of Alpin till 846 —(*H*)

[1] *Plundering* —L reads cechnao, and in the next line aicib for aiccib But cen uchneam is adopted from L. instead of cen uch in B In line 175 L reads na cochlao The writer's meaning in this stanza seems to be, that the name of Cruithnian was derived from cpeacao, plundering But the whole passage is very obscure The word apo, line 173, I have taken to signify a place, a point of the compass, a sense in which it is still used, and aiccib I suppose to be the same as paiccib, a word that has already been explained, see above, p 93, note [u] Cpeacao, in line 173, might also signify wounding,

scarring, alluding to the tattooing practised among the Picts, but it will be difficult to make the remainder of the stanza square with this. The translation adopted is therefore, more probably the intended meaning, especially as the word cpecac appears to be used in the same signification in line 177, and see line 182 —(*T*)

[m] *Fifty kings* —That is to say, inclusive For Macbeth, king of Scots and Picts, is the fiftieth in the enumeration of the Scots kings from Loarn Mac Erc, in the Duan Albanach, a contemporary poem, and apud Ogygia, p 488, and the Tables in Pinkerton, u p. 352, 353 In the list of the same, ap Innes App. p 767, he is only the fortieth But without counting the three competitors from 843 to 848 he was numbered ninety-second in the

For plundering¹ known places,
    And greens, without remorse,   175
    For not practising inactivity,
    For this are they called Cruithnians.

Fifty kings[m] of plundering career,
    Every one *of them* of the race of Eochaidh[n],
    From Fergus, most truly,
    To the vigorous Mac Brethach[o].   180

Six kings and six times ten
    Of them who attended to bloody plunder:
    They loved merry forays,
    They possessed the sovereignty of the Cruithnians
           The Cruithnians who propagated[p].

HERE

Pictish catalogue from Cruithne, the seventy-ninth from Brudi Bout, and the fifty-seventh from Drust Mac Erp —(*H*)

[n] *Eochaidh* —This was Eochaidh Muinreamhan, father of Erc, and grandfather of Loarn and Fergus, himself the third in descent from Cairbre Riada, and the fourth from Conary II, king of Erin, whom the princes of the Dal Riada affected for the founder of their race, the " Clanna Chonaire " Duan, ver. 27 —(*H*)

[o] *Mac Brethach*, or perhaps we should read Mac Bethach See Additional Notes, No. XIX. This stanza and the next occur only in the Book of Ballymote. If they are a portion of the original poem the writer must have lived after A. D. 1040, in which year Macbeth began his reign —(*T*).

The sixty-six kings mentioned in the next stanza are evidently the kings of the old Cruithnian race, beginning with Cruithne Mac Cinge, and ending with Drusken Mac Feredach, according to Fordun's list, which contains exactly sixty-six kings, including Keneth Mac Alpin, by whom Drusken was overthrown, and in whose person the Fergusian and Pictish monarchies were united —(*T*) Of these kings thirty-three are Pagan and thirty-three Christian ; a circumstance which looks like contrivance. And we may add that sixty-six (like 309, the number of the original Agathyrsi, see p. 133, line 40), is the bardic expression of 12 —(*H*)

[p] *The Cruithnians who propagated* —This is a repetition of the first line of the poem, a usual custom with Irish scribes, to mark

[oo ɓunɑoɑıɓ nɑ cɾuıċhneċh ɑnoso ɓoɓeɑꞅcɑ]

XXXI. Cɾuıċhne mɑc Cınꞗe ꞅɑꞇɑꞃ pıcꞇoꞃum hɑbıoɑnn ın ɑcɑ ınꞅolɑ .c. ɑnnıꞅ ꞃeneɓɑıꞇ; .uıı. meıc ꞃo ꞇeɑċhꞇ; ɑꞇe ɑnn ꞃo ɑ n-ɑnmɑno ı. Fıb, Fıoɑch, Folꞇlɑıꞗ, Foꞃꞇꞃeno, Cɑıꞇꞇ, Ce, Cıꞃ-cınꞗ.

Cıꞃcın lx ɑnnɑıꞃ ꞃeꞗnɑu.

Fıoɑc xl. ɑnnıꞅ ꞃ.

Foꞃꞇꞃeno .xl ɑnnıꞅ ꞃ

Folꞇlɑıo xxx ɑ ꞃ

Ꞗɑꞇꞇ xıı ɑ ꞃ.

Ce .xu ɑ. ꞃ

Fıoɓɑıo xxııı. ɑ ꞃ

Ꞗeıoe Ollꞗoꞇhɑch lxxx ɑ ꞃ

Oenbeꞗɑn [c] ɑ ꞃ

Ollꞃınɑcꞇɑ .lx ɑ ꞃ.

Ꞗuıueo

that the poem they had copied was concluded, lest the next article to it in their MS might be deemed to be a continuation of it—(T)

⁹ Here follows—This title is added from the Book of Lecan, which contains two copies of sect. xxxı one at the beginning of the work, and the other after the Mirabilia, in what seems to have been intended as a new edition or revision of the work. They shall be denoted, as before, by L¹ and L² In L¹ and B the title prefixed is oo bunɑo Cꞃuıċhnech [ɑnn] ꞅo Pinkerton, in his quotation from the Book of Ballymote, has erroneously made this title a part of the preceding paragraph, vol 1 App. No xıv These several copies of this section differ so widely that they will be given separately in the Additional Notes, No XX The text of all that follows is from D—(T)

ˡ Cruithne, son of Cing—Inꞗe, D and L² Cınꞗe L¹ and B—(T) Cing is mighty, a king a prince E Lluyd's Irish-English Dict. But John of Fordun has it (ıv cap 10), "Cruythne filius kynne judicis," and in 1 cap 35. he says, "Clementis unius judicum filius" This homonomy shews him to have understood kynne, kin, or kind, in the modern sense of the adjective kind, i e. benevolent, a sense which has escaped Dr Jamieson's lexicographical researches—(H)

ˢ Regnabat—The transcriber was evidently utterly ignorant of Latin, and has absurdly perverted these words; and the

HERE FOLLOWS[q] OF THE ORIGIN OF THE CRUITHNIANS

XXXI Cruithne, son of Cing[r], pater Pictorum habitantium in hac insula, c annis regnabat[s] He had seven sons These are their names, viz., Fib, Fidach, Foltlaig, Fortrend, Caitt, Ce, Circing[t]

Circing lx annis regnavit

Fidach xl annis regnavit

Fortrend xl annis regnavit.

Foltlaid xxx. annis regnavit

Gatt [i. e Caitt] xii annis regnavit

Ce xii. annis regnavit

Fidbaid [i e Fib] xxiiii. annis regnavit

Geide Ollgothach lxxx annis regnavit

Oenbegan c. annis regnavit

Ollfinachta lx. annis regnavit

Guidedh

same may be said of almost every scrap of Latin which he had occasion to transcribe, his attempts at *Latin* are here given, however, exactly as they stand in the original MS , although they have been, of course, corrected in the translation —(*T.*)

[t] *Circing* —In B these names are given thus Fib, Fidach, Fonla, Fortreann, Cathach, Cait Ce, Cirig The insertion of Cathach renders it necessary either to make Caitce one name, not two separate names, as the above list, and some other transcribers (no doubt rightly) have done, or else to make Fodla-Fortrean, (i e. Fodla of Fortren) one name, although in the above list they are given as two, for Foltlaid is the same as Foltlaig and Fodla. Cathach is omitted in L[1]. in the list of the sons of Cruithne given above, p. 51, and

also in the Chronicon Pictorum, Innes, vol. ii p 773, App No ii , and Pinkerton vol. i App. Nos x xi. But his name occurs in the verses attributed to Columkille, which immediately follow in this place in B , and are the same as those given above, p. 51, where cetach was understood to signify an hundred The verses might be rendered,

Cait, Ce, Creach Cetach of children [i e the fruitful]
Fib, Fidach Fodla of Fortrenn

or else,

Caitce, Creach Cetach of children,
Fib, Fidach, Fodla Fortren

These seven *fabulous* brothers are symbolical of seven *real* territorial divisions See above, p 51 —(*T.*)

X 2

Ȝuiveȝ Ȝaech bpeatnach .l. a p.

Ȝeapcuipcibont . . . . .xxx. anȝ uaȝ, ⁊ bpuiȝe ba h-ainm ȝo
ȝac aen ꝼeap; ⁊ penauepunc hibepniam ⁊ Alboniam pep .cl. an̄.
uic inuenicup i leabpaib na Cpuichneach.

bpuiȝe Pance ainm in ceȝ bpuiȝe

bpuiȝe Uppance

bpuiȝe Leo.

bpuiȝi Ȝanc.

bpuiȝe Ȝunȝ.

bpuiȝe Upȝann

bpuiȝe Upȝainc.

bpuiȝi Ꝼec.

bpuiȝe Uppexip.

bpuiȝi Ꝼeoip.

bpuiȝi Cal.

bpuiȝi Upcal.

bpuiȝi Cinc.

bpuiȝi Apcinc.

bpuiȝi Ꝼec

bpuiȝi Uppec

bpuiȝi Ru.

bpuiȝi Epu.

bpuiȝi Ȝapc.

bpuiȝi Cinic.   bpuiȝi

---

u *Geascuirtibont.* — There is evidently
some omission or confusion here The
Chronicon Pictorum divides Geascuirtibont into two, Gestgurtich and Brudebout, inserting between them Wurgest
The words are· "Gestgurtich xl Wurgest, xxx. [Innes reads xl] Brudebout
(a quo xxx. Brude regnaverunt Hiberniam et Albaniam, per centum l. annorum spatium) xlviij. annis regnavit"
—Pinkerton, vol 1 p 492. We ought,
therefore, to read, in all probability,
" Geasguirti xxx Bout. xxx. — There
were thirty of them afterwards, and
Brude was the name, &c." If we count
Bout as one of those who were called

Guidedh Gaeth, a Briton, l. annis regnavit.

Geascuirtibont[u] . . . xxx of them thenceforward, and Bruide[x] was the name of every man of them, et regnaverunt Hiberniam et Alboniam per cl. annos, ut invenitur in the books of the Cruithnians.

Bruide Pante was the name of the first Bruide.

Bruide Urpante,

Bruide Leo

Bruide Gant

Bruide Gund.

Bruide Urgann

Bruide Urgaint.

Bruide Fet.

Bruide Urfexir

Bruide Feoir

Bruide Cal

Bruide Urcal

Bruide Cint

Bruide Arcint.

Bruide Fet

Bruide Urfet.

Bruide Ru.

Bruide Eru.

Bruide Gart.

Bruide Cinit   Bruide

Bruide, there will be thirty-two in all, or, omitting him, thirty-one. The Chronicon Pictorum names only twenty-eight (exclusive of Bruide Bout), giving in regular order a name, and then the same name with *ur* [which is perhaps the Gælic ιαη, *after*] prefixed: Pant, Urpant; Leo, Urleo; Gant, Urgant, &c.—(*T.*)

[x] *Bruide.*—It will be observed that in many places the Irish transcriber has written this word ბრuιჳe with *g* instead of *d*, a circumstance of no importance, further than that it proves the *d* to have been aspirated in the pronunciation. Uniformity has been preserved in the translation.—(*T.*)

bruigi Cino

bruigi Uip.

bruigi Uirup

bruigi Gruic.

bruigi Urgrich.

bruigi Munaic.

bruigi Ur

bruigi Giogie.

bruigi Cpim.

bruigi Urcpin

bruige Urmain.

regnauepunc. cl. ann uc oiximmup, ⁊ po bai Alba cen pig ppia pe uile co h-aimpip Guo, cec pig po gab Albain uile cpi comaipli no ap eigin

XXXII Acbepaic apaile comao h-e Cacluan mac Caicming no gabao pige ap eigin i Cpuicheancuaich ⁊ a n-Eipino i lx. bliadain, ⁊ iappin po gab Guo i l.

Capam c. añ regnauic

Morleo a xu. a. re.

Deocillimon xl. añ regnauic

Cimoioo mac Aipccoip .uii. a p

Deopc l a p

bliebltc u. a p

Deococpeic ppacep Cui .xl. a. p

Urconbept xx. a p

Cpucbolc uii. a p.

Deopoiuoip

¹ *Gud.*—The statement that Albany had no king till Gut, and the mention of Gut (unless he be the same as Gilgidi), are absent from the Pict. Chron. In lieu of Cathluan sixty years, and Gud fifty years, it gives Gilgidi 101 years In the list here given Usconbest's reign is reduced from thirty to twenty, and that of Crutbolc

Bruide Cind.

Bruide Uip

Bruide Uirup.

Bruide Gruith.

Bruide Urgrith.

Bruide Munait.

Bruide Ur.

Bruide Gidgie.

Bruide Crin.

Bruide Urcrin.

Bruide Urmain.

regnaverunt cl. ann ut diximus; and Alba was without a king all along until the time of Gud[y], the first king that possessed all Alba by consent or by force.

XXXII. Others say[z] that it was Cathluan, son of Caitming, who *first* possessed the sovereignty by force in Cruithentuath and in Eri, for sixty years, and that after him succeeded Gud for fifty *years*.

Taram c. annis regnavit.

Morleo xv. annis regnavit.

Deocillimon xl annis regnavit.

Cimoiod, son of Arteois, vii. annis regnavit

Deort l. annis regnavit.

Blieblith v. annis regnavit

Deototreic frater Tui xl. annis regnavit.

Usconbest xx. annis regnavit.

Crutbolc vii annis regnavit.

Deordivois

(Belga Pictus) interpolated In other respects it agrees very nearly with the Chron.—(*H.*)

[z] *Others say.*—The second list of kings which begins here appears to have come from the same source as that given by Fordun (Scotichron iv. c. 11), except that he begins with Cruythne, son of Kynne, instead of Cathluan, son of Caitming —(*T.*)

Deopoiuoip xx a pegn

Uipt l annop p

Ru c. añ p.

Zaptnaic .iiii. ix a pe

bpec mac buitheo iiii. a p

Uipo ignauit xxx

Canatulacma .iii annip p

Upaoach uetla .ii a p

Zaptnaic ouipeip lx a p

Colopc mac Aithiuip .lxxu

Dpupt mac Epp c pegnauit, ᚓ c cata po gein Nonooecimo anno peigni eiup Patpiciup panctup epipcopup ao hibepniam pepuenit

Colopc mac Amel iiii a p

Nectan mop bpeac mac Eipip xxxiiii a p Teptio anno pegni

---

[a] *Gartnait.*—M Van Praet's attested copy of the Chronicon Pictorum, published by Pinkerton, gives this passage thus

 gartnaithloc a quo gartnait iiii
 regna vere ix ā reḡ"

Which Mr Pinkerton interprets thus

"29 Gartnaith loc, a quo Gartnait iiij regna
30 Vere ix an reg"

Thus making *vere* the name of a king Innes reads Gartnaithboc, and likewise makes Vere the thirtieth king. But are not the words "vere ix. an reg" an evident correction of "iiii regnavit," intimating that the real length of Gartnaithloc's reign was nine, not four years? The Irish transcriber evidently intended to adopt this correction, but in doing so retained the iiii, expunging the other words Fordun (iv c 11) has "Garnathbolger annis ix." The reign of Canatulacma appears to be fixed at thrice, but may be four years, as in the Chron Pictorum, for iii and iiii are easily confounded, and in this case it is not quite certain which was intended by the scribe Uradach-vetla is assigned two years, which agrees with Innes, but differs from M Van Praet's copy, in Pinkerton, which has iv —(*T*)

[b] *Gartnait-duiper* —Fordun has Garnard *Dives*, from which we may presume that *duiper* signified rich Perhaps the *d* is an expletive derived from the final *t* or *d*

Deordivois xx annis regnavit

Uist l annis regnavit

Ru c annis regnavit

Gartnait[a] iin ix annis regnavit.

Breth, son of Buithed, vii. annis regnavit

Uipo-ignavit xxx.

Canatulacma ini annis regnavit

Uradach-vetla ii annis regnavit

Gartnait-duipeir[b] lx annis regnavit

Tolorc, son of Aithiur, lxxv

Drust. son of Erp, c *annis* regnavit, and gained[c] a hundred battles Nonodecimo anno regni eius Patricius sanctus episcopus ad Hiberniam pervenit

Tolorc, son of Aniel, iin annis regnavit

Nectan-mor-breac[d], son of Enip, xxxiiii. annis regnavit   Tertio anno

of Garnard or Garnait, and if so, *uipeir* is not far from the Irish ṗoιоbιp, rich (the initial ṗ aspirated), which is pronounced very nearly as *uiphir*.—(*T*)

[c] *Gained*—The Latin has " c. bella peregit " ρο ʒein signifies properly, wounded, killed, and hence, won, gained, when applied to battles —(*T*)

[d] *Mor-breac*, for Morbet [as in Pict Chron.] bene The statements which follow are false and out of chronology Pictland and Abernethy were not then Christian nor was St Bridget yet born, nor was Darluchdach yet abbess of Kildare. Very long after the death of both these ladies, and about 608, Nectan II founded the church of Abernethy —Register of St Andr cit Pink i 296, ii 267.—(*H*)

St Darluchdach was the immediate successor of St Bridget, as abbess of Kildare, and died on the anniversary of St Bridget's death, having survived her but one year Colgan Vit S Darlugdachæ ad i Feb There are different dates assigned to St Bridget s death, varying from 510 to 548 Colgan has decided in favour of the year 523 —Trias. Th. p. 619 Fordun (iv c. 11) gives the series after Garnaitduiper thus Hurgust, son of Fergus, twenty-seven years; Thalargen, son of Keother, twenty-five Durst " qui alias vocabatur Nectane filius Irbu annis xlv Hic, ut asseritur

' Centum annis vixit et centum bella peregit '

Quo regnante sanctus Palladius [not Patricius] episcopus a beato Papa Celes-

peꞛmi eiuꞃ Daꞃluꞃoach abbaṫiꞃṫa Cille ꝺaꞃa ꝺe Uꞓeꞃniam aχu-
laṫ ꝓ χꝓō aꝺ ꞓꞃiṫiniam ꝼꞃi anno aꝺuenṫuꞃ ṫui immolaueiṫ Nec-
ṫonꞙuꞃ anno uno Uꝓuꞃꞃiꞃe Deo ⁊ ꞃanċċaꞁe ꞓꞃiꞝṫea ꝓꞃeꞃenṫe
Daꞃluꞃoeach que canṫauiṫ all ꞃuꝓeꞃ iꞃṫam.

Daꞃṫꞃuiṫimoṫ χχχ a ꞃeꞝ

Ꞛalamaꞃꞓiṫh .χu. a. ꞃeꞝ.

Da Dꞃeꞃṫ .ı Dꞃeꞃṫ ꝼı ꞓuꝺꞃoꞃ χu. anniꞃ ꞃeꞝ ūṫuṫ   Deꞃꞃṫ
ꝼı. Ꞛıꞃuim ꞃoluꞃ .u a ꝓ

Ꞛalum cenamlaꞃeh ıııı a ꝓ

Ꞛaꞃṫnaiṫ ꝼı. Ꞛıꞃom uıı a ꝓ

Cailṫaine ꝼı Ꞛıꞃom anno ꝓ

Ṫaloꞃꞝ ꞃ. Muꞃṫolic χı a ꝓ

Dꞃeꞃṫ ꝼı. Manaiṫ uno a ꝓ   Cum ꞓꞃıueno ı anno

ꞓꞃuıꝺe mac Maelcon .χχχ. a ꝓ Mochṫaauuo anno ꞃeꞝmi eiṫ
ꞓaıꞓṫiꞃaṫuꞃ eꞃṫ Eꞃanċṫo Columba

Ꞛaꞃṫnaiṫ

tino missus est ad Scotos docendos, longe tamen ante in Christo credentes." Then follow Talaigar, son of Amyle, two years, Nectane Thaltamoth, ten years In the next chapter he ascribes the foundation of Abernethy to St. Bridget and her seven virgins, but places it in the reign of Gainard Makdompnach, the successor of the Brude in whose time St Columba preached to the Picts, which is of course more probable Pinkerton and Innes are both mistaken in their reading of the Chron Pict in this passage, which is not "abbatissa cillæ Daiadæ, Hibernia exulat proxime ad Britanniam,' but "abbatissa Cille-dara de Hibernia exulat pro Christo ad Britanniam," as may be seen by their own edition of M Van Praet's attested copy What the contracted word ꝼꞃi stands for in the text I do not know. The Chron Pict reads "secundo"—(T)

^c *Two Drests* —If I am right in considering Daoꞃeꞃꞃṫ [read Daoꞃeꞃṫ] as two words, and translating "two Drests," the Irish version has enabled us to correct a mistake which Innes and Pinkerton have both committed in their interpretation of this passage of the Chron. Pictorum, which stands thus in M Van Praet's attested copy

dadrest ı drest fili^o
girom ı drest fili^o wdrost ı
an gregii drest fili^o girom sol^o
ı an reg

From this Innes and Pinkerton have given us *three* kings, viz ı Dadrest, who

anno regni ejus Darlugdach, abbatissa Cille-Dara de Hibernia exulat pro Christo ad Britiniam; [secundo?] anno adventus sui immolavit Nectonius anno uno Apurnighe Deo et sanctæ Brigidæ, præsente Darlugdach, quæ cantavit alleluia super istam [hostiam]

Dartgutimoth xxx. annis regnavit.

Galamarbith xv annis regnavit

Two Drests[c], i. e. Drest, fil Budros, xv annis regnaverunt communiter. Drest, fil Girum, solus v annis regnavit

Galum-cenamlapeh iiii. annis regnavit

Gartnait, fil Girom, vii annis regnavit

Cailtaine, fil Girom, anno regnavit

Talorg, fil. Murtolic, xi annis regnavit

Drest fil Manaith, uno anno regnavit   Cum Brideno[f] i anno

Bruide Mac Maelcon xxx annis regnavit. In octavo[g] anno regni ejus baptizatus est a sancto Columba

Gartnait,

reigned one year, 2. Drest, son of Girom, and 3 Drest, son of Udrost. Drest, son of Gnom, they make to have reigned one year alone, five years jointly with Drest, son of Udrost, and then five years alone I have very little doubt, however, that Dadrest, should be read Da Drest, which words signify *Duo* Drest. If this conjecture be correct it will prove that the Chron Pictorum was translated from a Gaelic original, more ancient than our present Irish transcript, which appears from the mistakes with which it abounds, to have been taken from a Latin copy I would propose to read the passage thus " Duo Drest, i.e. Drest filius Girom et [for the i here either signifies " i e " or is a mistake for *et*] Drest filius Wdrost

v annos conregnaverunt   Drest filius Gnom solus v annos regnavit " Thus the Irish and Latin will agree, except in the length of the joint reign, which the Irish transcriber makes to be fifteen years It is some confirmation of the emendation here proposed, that of the five lists of Pictish kings quoted by Pinkerton, vol i. p 242, and tables at the end of vol 1, Dadrest appears only on the authority of the Chron. Pictorum, as he and Innes have understood it The contraction ucuc is probably intended for " communiter "—(*T*)

[f] *Cum Brideno*—Galumcenamlapeh in the Chron. Pictorum is placed after Drest, son of Munait, and the words ' cum Brideno i anno," apply to him —(*T*)

[g] *In octavo*—The transcriber has here

Ʒaптnaιτ ꝼ Ꝺomnach χι. α п.

Neachтan nepō Uenn χχ. α. п.

Cιnhoιnτ ꝼ. Luιτnιu .χιχ. α. п.

Ʒaптnaιτ mac Uιuꝺ .u. α. п

Τolonc ꝼnaтeп eonum ꝺuoꝺeιcιm α. п.

Τoloncan ꝼ Enꝼпeτ .ıııı.

Ʒaптnaιnτ ꝼ. Ꝺonuel uι. α п ꝛ ꝺeιmιꝺιum annι.

Ꝺnuꝛc ꝼnaтeп eιuꝛ uıı. α п

Ƀпιꝺe ꝼ Ꝼle .χꝛ α п

Τaпan ꝼ. En ꝼιꝺaιꝺ ıııı.

Ƀпeι ꝼ. Ꝺeιnιleι χι α. п.

Nechтan ꝼ. Ꝺeιnιle .χ. α п

Ꝺпeꝛт ꝛ Elпen conneʒanaueιnт u α. п

Onbeп ꝼ. Uпʒuпт .χχχ. α. п

Ƀпeιтe ꝼ. Uuʒuт .χu α. п

Cιnιoꝺ ꝼ. Iuuпeꝺeʒ .χu. α п

Alпιn ꝼ. Uuoιꝺ ııı annıꝛ пeʒnauιт ꝛ ꝺιmιꝺon пeʒnı

Ꝺпeꝛт ꝼ. Τaloncan .ı. α п

Τaloncan ꝼ Ꝺoꝛтan [ıı] uel u. ꝺeʒ

Τalonceन ꝼ Onuꝛт χıı. ꝛ ꝺιmιꝺoιn α п

Canul ꝼ. Τanʒ .u α. п

Cuaꝛтanтιn ꝼ Uuꝛʒuιꝛт χχꝛu.

Uιꝺnuꝛт

made sad work, but the text is printed without correction He mistook m for m, and by confounding the uo of octauo with the no of anno, he has produced the compound Moctaauuo anno, which the Chron. Pictorum enables us to decipher.—(*T.*)

ᵇ *Toloic*—The Chron. Pictorum inserts "Breidei fil. Wid v. an. reg" between

Gartnait mac Uiud or Wid, and this Toloic; and that the omission was a mistake of the Irish transcriber is evident from the word *eorum.*—(*T*)

ⁱ *Conregnaverunt.*—The scribe has strangely blundered this word: he has also written α. п at the end, where the п is redundant.—(*T*)

ᵏ *Dimidium.*—The word пeʒnı added ın

Gartnait, fil Domnach, xi annis regnavit

Neachtain nepos Verp. xx annis regnavit

Cinhoint, fil Lutriu, xix annis regnavit

Gartnait, mac Uuid, v annis regnavit

Tolorc^h frater eorum duodecim annis regnavit

Tolorcan, fil. Enfret, iiii

Gartnairt, fil Donuel, vi annis regnavit et dimidium anni

Drusc frater ejus vii. annis regnavit

Biide, fil Fle, xx annos regnavit.

Taran, fil En-fidaid, iiii

Brei, fil Derilei, xi annis regnavit

Nechtan, fil Derilei, x annis regnavit

Drest et Elpen conregnaverunt[l] v annis

Onbes, fil Urgurt, xxx. annis regnavit

Breite, fil Uugut, xv. annis regnavit

Cinoid, fil Juuredeg, xv annis regnavit

Alpin, fil Uuoid, iii annis regnavit et dimidium[k] anni

Drest, fil. Talorcan, i anno regnavit

Talorcan[l], fil Drostan, [v.] vel xv.

Talorcen, fil Onust, xii. et dimidium annis regnavit

Canul[m], fil Tang̃. v. annis regnavit

Cuastantin, fil Uurguist, xxxv

Uidnust,

the text is an evident mistake for anni, dimioon is of course a blunder for dimi-dium —(T.)

[l] *Talorcan.*—This king is omitted in the Chron Pictorum, but he is given by Fordun The Irish text is corrected from Lynch s copy, Cambrensis Eversus, p 94. The scribe omitted u before uel, and wrote u.oeg for xv —(T)

[m] *Canul*—This king is called fil Tarla in the Chron. Pict. The name of his father is given above Tang̃, with a mark of contraction, which has been retained, as I know not how to write the word in full It may be Tangar or Tangad Lynch gives it " Canul fil Tang," without noticing the contraction.—Cambr Eversus, ib.—(T)

Uioṁuιṗ ṗ Uυιṗᵹυιṗ .χιι αn ṗ

Oροιṗ ṗ Conṗαᴄιn ⁊ Tolopᴄ ṗ Uυᴄḣoιl ιιι α. ṗ. conṗeᵹnaue-
ṗιunᴄ

Unen ṗ Uneιṗᴄ ιιι

Uṗαᴅ ṗ. ḃαṗᵹoιᴄ ιιι α ⁊ ḃροᴅ ι°. α. ṗ

Cιnαeᴅ ṗ Cιlṗιn .χυιι. α ṗ

Oomnall ṗ. Cιlṗιn ιιιι ṗ ⁊ Cυṗᴄαnᴄαn ṗ Cιnαeᴅα .χχ. α ṗ

Ceᴅ ṗ. Cιnαeᴅ .ι°. α ṗ

Ƶιṗιᵹ mαc Ounᵹαιle .χι. uel ιιι. α. ṗ

Oomnαll ṗ Conṗαnᴄιn .χι α ṗ.

Conṗᴄαnᴄιn ṗ. Ceᴅ .χlυ α. ṗ

Maelcolαιm ṗ Oomnαιll .ιχ α ṗ

Cυιleιn ṗ. Ilᴅoιlḃ ṗ. Conṗᴄαnᴅᴄιn .ιιιι α. ṗ

Cιnαeᴅ, uel Ouḃ, ṗ Maιlcolαιm ιιιι α. ṗ

Cυιleιn ι ᴅιmιᴅoιn ṗ

Cιnαeᴅ ṗ Ouιḃ ocḣᴄ α. ṗ

Maelcolαιm mαc Cιnαeᴅα χχχ α ṗeᵹ

Oonᴅcαᴅ uα Maιlcolαιm υιι ṗ

Macḃeαᴄḣαᴅ mαc Ṗιn mιc Lαιᵹ χυι α ṗ

Lulαcḣ u mιṗ.

Maelcolαιm mαc Colαιm mιc Oonncαιᴅ ιαṗ ṗιn

XXXIII

ⁿ *Bargoit* — In the Chron Pictorum, "Wrad filius Bargoit," where the Gaelic genitive *Bargoit* is another proof that this document was copied from an Irish original.—(*T*)

° *Constantin, fil Aedh* — The list given by Lynch (Cambrensis Evers p. 94) omits the three kings between this Constantin and Domhnall fitz Alpin, which is probably a mistake of his transcript, or of the press The Chron. Pietorum gives Eochodius filius Ku, as the successor of Aedh fil Cinaed, instead of Girig mac Dungaile, but adds "Licet Ciricium fil. [Dungaile is probably omitted] alii dicunt hic regnasse, eo quod alumpnus ordinatorque Eochodio fiebat" Innes, vol. ii p 785 Pinkerton, vol i p 495 —(*T*)

ᵖ *Cuilein, fil Ildoilb*, i. e. son of Ildulf, instead of whom the Chron. Pict makes

Uidnust, fil Uurgust, xii. annis regnavit

Drost, fil. Constatin, et Tolorc, fil Uuthoil, iii annis conregnave-runt.

Unen, fil. Unest, iii.

Urad, fil Bargot^a, iii annis [regnavit], et Brod. i. anno regnavit

Cinaed, fil Alpin, xvi. annis regnavit.

Domhnal, fil Alpin, iiii. [annis] regnavit, et Custantan fil Cinaeda xx annis regnavit

Aedh, fil Cinaed, i° anno regnavit.

Girig mac Dungaile xi vel. iii. annis regnavit

Domhnall, fil. Constantini, xi annis regnavit

Constantin, fil Aedh°, xlv annis regnavit

Maelcolaim, fil Domhnall, ix. annis regnavit.

Cuilem, fil Ildoilb^p, fil. Constantini, iiii. annis regnavit

Cinaed, vel Dubh^q, fil Mailcolaim, vii annis regnavit

Cuilem^r i. [et] dimidio [anni] regnavit

Cinead, fil. Dubh, viii annis regnavit

Maelcolaim Mac Cinaeda xxx. annis regnavit.

Donnchad Ua Mailcolaim vii [annis] regnavit

Macbeathad Mac Fin Mic Laig xvi annis regnavit

Lulach v. months.

Maelcolaim Mac Colaim Mic Donnchaid after him.

XXXIII

Indulphus himself the successor of Malcolm See also Ogygia, p 486.—(*T*)

^q *Vel Dubh.* — The words uel oub are written over the name Cineao by a later hand. This is evidently the same king who is called Niger, fil. Maelcolaim, in the Pictish Chronicle, with a reign of five years Lynch's list assigns to this king a reign of 24 years.—(*T.*)

^r *Cuilein* —This king is called Cuilen Rig in the Chron Pict (ap. Innes) Culen Ring (ap. Pinkerton), with a reign of five years. Lynch calls him "Constantin fil Culen uno et dimidio anno." In the Nomina Regum Pictorum (Innes, vol ii. p. 802) he is called Culin Mac Induff, and a reign of four years and a half is assigned to him —(*T.*)

XXXIII bpicinia inpola occiani cui pionoam Olbuan nocpac, ocht c. m. ceimenn ina pao cc ina leichean, ina cimceall imoppo .i u m uii. mozac po h-ocht ceacpaca Ocht cacpaca .xx ic inoci, ┐ u. bepla, .i. Saxain bepla, ┐ bepla bpeacan, ┐ bepla Cpuicneac, ┐ Zaevelz, ┐ Laivean.

Anno .xl. ance naciuicacem Chpipci i. ceacpaca bliavan pia n-zein Cpipc, caniz Zalup [in] inip bpeacan co pazaib a longa ┐ a ploiz in ceo peacht, ┐ co pazaib Labianup cpibpp pucpom poveoiz zialla inopi bpeacan

Cluioy Ceippii in ceachpamao piz iap n-luil caniz a n-inip bpeacan co h-inip Opc.

Ab incapnoacione vomini clui Mapcup Anconup cona Lpachaip i. Luicivo Aupilio Commovo cpeivim inip bpeacan

Aib incapnacioine vomini .clxxx ix. Seuepup Affep Cpipolocanup caniz a n-inip bpeacan Leipip ainm na cacpac ip in Affaic,

iii

ˢ *Britania* —This scrap of Latin, strangely perverted by the ignorance of the scribe, is taken from the opening sentence of Bede's history nocpac I suppose to be an ignorant corruption of the contraction nō epac, and I have rendered it accordingly. Bede's words are "Brittani occani insula, cui quondam Albion nomen fuit, &c . . . quæ per milia passuum octingenta in boream longa, latitudinis habet milia ducenta, exceptis dumtaxat prolixioribus diversorum promontoriorum tractibus, quibus efficitur ut circuitus ejus quadragies octies septuaginta quinque milia compleat" See above, sect ii p 27, where the same statement nearly occurs —(*T*)

ᵗ *Eight times forty* —An attempt to render literally Bede's "quadragies octies septuaginta quinque milia." What follows about the five languages is also founded on a passage in Bede, lib i c 1 —(*T*.)

ᵘ *Galus*, a corruption of Julius i. Julius Cæsar See above, p. 59 —(*T*)

ᵛ *The tribune*.—The word cpibpp is evidently for cpibñp, i e cpibunup See Bede Hist. lib i c 2. "Cæsaris equitatu primo congressu a Brittannis victus, ibique Labienus occisus est"—(*T*.)

ʷ *Clinds Ceasar*, i e Claudius Cæsar. He is called fourth king or emperor after Julius evidently from Bede's words "Claudius imperator, ab Augusto quartus"—c 3 See above, p 63 In the MS

XXXIII Britinia⁵ insola, oceani cui quondam Olbuan nomen erat, *is* eight hundred thousand paces in length, two hundred *thousand* in breadth, and in circumference five thousand seventy and eight times forty'. *There are* in it eight score cities, and five languages, viz the Saxon language, and the British language, and the Cruithnian language, and Gaelic, and Latin

Anno xl^mo ante nativitatem Christi, i e. forty years before the birth of Christ, came Galus^u into the island of Britain ; he lost his ships and his army on his first expedition, and he lost Labienus the tribune^v, *but* at length he took the hostages of the island of Britain

Cluids Ceissir^w, the fourth king after Juil, came into the island of Britain even to the island of Orc

Ab incarnatione Domini clvi. Marcus Antonus^x with his brother, i e Lucidus Aurelius Commodus, devastated the island of Britain

Ab incarnatione^y Domini clxxxix Severus Afer Tripolitanus came into the island of Britain. Leipis was the name of the city in Africa where he was born , he was the seventeenth king after Juil

it

---

the words " Ab incarnatione Domini, clvi " are joined to the preceding paragraph, as if they were the date of the invasion by Claudius , but they are the words with which Bede's fourth chapter begins, and evidently belong to the reign of Marcus Antoninus This correction has, therefore, been made in the text.—(*T*.)

^xAntonus —Read Antoninus. Bede used no word equivalent to devastated. Cnei-óm is explained in the Leabhar Gabhala, p. 37, to signify the breaking down or demolition of ancient boundaries or fast-nesses —(*T*)

ˀ *Ab incarnatione* —Here again in the MS. the date is erroneously joined to the preceding paragraph The authority here is Bede, i. c 5 "Anno ab incarnatione Domini clxxxix. Severus genere Afer, Tri-politanus, ab oppido Lepti, decimus sep-timus ab Augusto imperium adeptus, &c . Itaque Severus magnam fossam, fir-missimumque vallum   . a mari ad mare duxit; ibique apud Evoracum oppi-dum morbo obiit Reliquit duos filios Bassianum et Getam . . Bassianus, Antonini nomine assumpto, regno potitus est."—(*T*.)

in xuiı ꞃíg iaꞃ n-Iuil; iꞃ do do ꞃonad clad Saxan, aubath a caıꞃ Abꞃog Da mac oca baꞃianuꞃ ⁊ Geta ba ꞃeıꞃıo ꞃo gab ın ꞃígı, aınm do Anton

Ab ıncaꞃnatıoıne domını ıaꞃ n-Iuil cc lxxx uı. Dıoclıꞃtan ın tꞃeaꞃ ꞃíg aꞃ tꞃıchad ıaꞃ n-Iuil, ⁊ Maxımın, tanıg ın n-ınıꞃ bꞃeatan Iꞃ na h-aımꞃıꞃ ꞃo gab Caꞃauꞃıuꞃ ꞃígı bꞃeatan uıı. m-blıadna conad ꞃo maꞃb Alectuꞃ, co ꞃo gab ꞃıdeın ꞃígı, tꞃı m-blıadan, conad ꞃo maꞃb Aꞃchıꞃootuꞃ, ⁊ ba ꞃíg ꞃıde ꞃe x m-blıadan Dıoclıꞃten ı n-aıꞃteꞃ ın domaın ac ıngꞃeım na Cꞃıꞃtaıge, ⁊ Maıꞃcımen ına h-ıaꞃtaꞃ

Iꞃ ın ıngꞃım ꞃeo ꞃoꞃ doman Albaın naem ⁊ Aꞃon ⁊ Iuil aıꞃcındeach catꞃach Leıgonum aꞃ an amꞃıꞃ ꞃea aubath

Conꞃtanꞃt ꞃı bꞃeatan athaıꞃ Conꞃtantın mıc Eılıne ı caꞃat baın Conꞃtannoın, ꞃo ꞃcꞃıb Eotꞃobuꞃ conad ann ꞃo gab Conꞃtantın ꞃígı aꞃ tuꞃ a n-ınıꞃ bꞃeatan, daıg ꞃo gab a n-athaıꞃ ꞃlatuꞃ Fꞃanc ⁊ Eꞃꞃaıne ı m-beathaıd Dıoclıꞃteın

Ab ıncaꞃnatıoıne .ccc lx ııı. Gꞃadıanuꞃ cetꞃacha ꞃíg o Iuil. Iꞃ na h-aımꞃıꞃ ꞃıdeın ꞃo gab aꞃaıle Maxım ꞃígı bꞃeatan

Ab

Domini —The words iaꞃ n-Iul are here an evident blunder, and are therefore omitted in the translation The date, as before, is joined in the MS to the preceding paragraph. Bede is the authority, c 6, and see above, p. 65 —(T)

Albain.—Bede, *ubi supr* c. 7. The City Legionum is supposed to be Caerleon, the ancient Isca Silurum, on the river Usk, in Monmouthshire Aaron and Julius are here called *chiefs* (aꞃoeınoeac) of the city, although Bede calls them simply "cives" The word *ardcinneach* or *Erenach*, in later times, was applied almost always to an ecclesiastical officer, although not always one in holy orders, but, as appears from this passage, it properly signified any chief, superior, or person in authority In the Leabhar Breac (tol ııı col 1), SS Peter and Paul are called the *aichinneachs* or chiefs of the Apostles iꞃıac ꞃın oıꞃchınnıg na n-apꞃtal, ı. Petaꞃ ⁊ Pol And again, quoting Eccl. x 16, "Væ tibi terra cujus rex puer est, et cujus principes mane comedunt,"&c. the writer adds Iꞃe ꞃocuınn malaꞃta

it was for him was made the Saxon ditch; he died at Caer Abrog. He had two sons, Basianus and Geta. It was he (*the former*) that succeeded to the kingdom by the name of Anton

Ab incarnatione Domini[z] cclxxxiii Dioclistan, the thirty-third king after Juil, and Maximin, came into the island of Britain It was in their time that Carausius held the sovereignty of Britain seven years, until Alectus killed him, and held the sovereignty himself for three years, until Asclipidotus killed him, and became king himself for ten years. Dioclistan, in the east of the world, was persecuting the Christians, and Maiscimen in the west

It was in that persecution over the world that Saint Albain[a]— and Aron, and Juil, chiefs of the city Leigionum at that time,—died

Constanst[b], king of Britain, *was* the father of Constantine, son of Eiline (*Helena*), the concubine of Constantin Etrobus wrote that it was in the island of Britain that Constantin took sovereignty at first, for his father had exercised dominion over France and Spain in the life-time of Dioclistan

Ab incarnatione ccclxvi[c] Gradianus *was* the fortieth king from Juil It was in his time that a certain Maxim took the sovereignty of Britain

Ab

---

bona tuataib ⁊ bona cellaib ica mbit na pig ⁊ na airciniogh atta uilpi oo craep ⁊ oo raebaioecht in traegail "This is the cause of the destruction of the districts [i. e. chieftainries], and of the churches, whose kings and chiefs [*an chinneachs*] are devoted to gluttony and worldly intemperance."—(*T*)

[b] *Constanst*, i. e. Constantius, (or Constantinus, as Bede calls him) father of Constantine the Great, this paragraph, including the reference to Eutropius, is taken from Bede, i. c. 8 At the word baig the transcriber of the MS began a new paragraph with a large capital letter ornamented with colour, as if beginning a new subject, such was his ignorance.—(*T*)

[c] *Ab incarnatione* ccclxvi.—Read ccclxxvii as in Bede, i c 9 This date is affixed in the MS to the preceding paragraph. The next date is also misplaced in the same way —(*T*.)

Ab incaɼnacione ꝺomini cccc.xc iiii Aɼcacuɼ i ɼiʒi in ꝺomain .i.
Coecaiɼ in cɼeaɼ ɼiʒ cecɼacha iaɼ n-Auʒuɼcuɼ. Pilaciuɼ bɼic ꝺo
ʒabail iɼɼɼi, ⁊ ꝺo coʒail na Cɼiɼcaiꝺe

Ab incaɼnꝺacioine ʒ cccc ui. Cecɼi bliaꝺna cecɼacaꝺ ɼeʒɼin
ꝺe bliaꝺnaib o h-Eolaiɼ ɼiʒ na n-Ʒaech ɼiʒaꝺ Ʒɼaꝺian coɼaiꝺ a
m-bɼeacnaib, ⁊ iaɼꝺain Conɼcanncin iaɼɼɼin ɼi o amain iicoɼa ina
aiɼ o inoɼacuɼ conaꝺ ɼo maɼb Conɼacinuɼ comaeɼ cɼe [f]oɼconɼa
honoɼii Canic Conɼcanɼ a mac a mancainꝺe ɼo ʒab ɼiʒi.

Ro bɼiɼ cɼa Roim iaɼꝺain in miliɼimo .c lx iiĩ. m-bliaꝺan o ɼo
cumcaiceaꝺ; iɼ e ɼin cɼich flachuɼa Roman foɼ iniɼ bɼeacan
iaɼ cccc.lxx. bliaꝺan, o ɼa ʒab n-luil iniɼ bɼeacan, ɼeɼ ꝺibaꝺaɼ
Romanaiʒ imm a milcneach, ⁊ niɼ [f]aɼʒaibɼeac oʒbaiꝺ no aeɼ
eaʒna inoce. ⁊ ɼuʒɼac Romanaiʒ, ⁊ niɼ leʒɼeac uaꝺaib eciɼ

Iɼ aiɼiɼin ꝺo ɼonɼac Ʒaeuil ⁊ Cɼuichniʒ no ꝺa cineꝺ comfoc-
ɼaib iɼen bɼuiꝺ ⁊ cɼeic.

Do cuaɼ o bɼeacnaib co n-ebaiɼc lib co Romancu aɼ ꝺaiʒ
cobaɼca, ⁊ ꝺuɼuchc milnec calma cuccu ꝺaɼ in n-iniɼ ɼuachc
Cɼuicneac

<hr />

d *Arcatus,* i e Aɪcadius foɪ i **Coe-**
caiɼ we should evidently read ɼil oɪ mc.
Ceocaiɼ Bede, ib. c 10 —(*T*)

e *Forty-four yeaɪs* —Foɪ ʒ ɪead ꝺ, i e
Domini. This is all confusion On comparing it with Bede, ib c 11, it will be
seen that the transcribeɪ has given the
date cccevi instead of ccccvii ; that he
has omitted the name Honoɪius, and has
converted Bede's "loco ab Augusto qua-
diagesimo quaɪto" into foɪty-four *yeaɪs* ,
the woɪd **ɼeʒɼin** is unintelligible, and
no attempt has been made to tɪanslate it
Nor has any attempt been made to tɪanslate
what is said about Constantine, which is

rendeɪed unintelligible by the gɪoss igno-
ɪance of the tɪanscɪiber , no sense can
be made of it without extensive conjectu
ɪal emendations. It is evidently intended
to ɪepɪesent the following statement of
Bede, "Hujus [scil Gratiani] loco Constantinus ex infima militia, pɪopter solam
spem nominis, sine meɪito virtutis, eli-
gitur "—(*T*)

f *Rome* —This paɪagraph is made up
fɪom the following passages of Bede, i.
cc 11, 12 "Fracta est autem Roma a
Gothis anno m lx iv. suæ conditionis, ex
quo tempoɪe Romani in Britannia regnare
cessarunt, post annos ferme quadringentos

Ab incarnatione Domini cccxcIV Arcatus[d] was sovereign of the
world [son of] Toetas [*Theodosius*], the forty-third king after Augustus. Pilacius [*Pelagius*] a Briton, adopted heresy, and destroyed the
Christians

Ab incarnatione D cccv Forty-four years[e]   two years
before Eolair [*Alaric*], King of the Gaeth [*Goths*], Gradian the champion is made king of the Britons ; and then Constantine, afterwards
                  . until Constantinus Comes killed him at the
command of Honorius. Constans, his son, came from being a monk,
and took the kingdom

Now Rome[f] was destroyed afterwards in the thousandth one
hundredth and lxiv[th] year from its foundation That was the end
of the Roman dominion over the island of Britain, after cccclxx years
from the time when Juil took the island of Britain. The Romans
extinguished it as to its military power, and there were left in it no
warriors nor men of learning, and the Romans carried them off and
would not suffer them to return

It was then that the Gaedhels and the Cruithnians, two border
tribes, took captives and spoil.

There went *ambassadors* from the Britons with presents[g] along
with them, to the Romans, to seek relief, and there came to them a
valiant army across the island, who attacked the Cruithnians and
                              Gaedhels,

---

septuaginta ex quo Caius Julius Cæsar
eandem insulam adiit ” . “ Exin
Britannia in parte Brittonum omni arma-
to milite, militaribus copiis universis, tota
floridæ juventutis alacritate,” [this seems
to be what the Irish translator has sought
to express by the word miltneach] “ spoliata, quæ tyrannorum temeritate abducta
nusquam ultra domum rediit, prædæ tantum patuit, utpote omnis bellici usus
prorsus ignara, &c ” The Irish is very
corrupt, but with the Latin before us we
cannot miss its meaning —(*T*)

[g] *With presents* —The words co n-
ebairc lib ought evidently to be co n-
epircib, for they represent Bede’s “ legatos Romam cum epistolis mittentes,’
i. c. 12.—(*T.*)

Cɼuṫneac ⁊ Ȝaeḋelu; ⁊ ꝺo cuaḋaɼ ꝺia ꝺiȝ iaɼꝺain. Ꝑo ceꝺoiɼ ꞇanȝaꝺaɼ namaiꝺ ⁊ ɼo ꞇumɼeaꞇaɼ ḃɼeaꞇain amail ȝoɼꞇaḃaiꝺ.

Ꞃo ꝼaiꝺiꞇ na ꞇechꞇaiɼe ꝺo apiɼ ⁊ ꝺo ɼochꞇ leȝon ꝺo coḃaiɼ ḃɼeaꞇan, ⁊ ɼo caiꞇaiȝɼeaꞇ ꝼɼia naiḃoiḃ ḃɼeaꞇan ⁊ ɼo h-aꞇnaiȝiꞇ in claḋ leo ꝺo ɼiȝ [leg. ɼiȝne] in ꝺala Seueɼuɼ; ba ꝺo claḋaiḃ in ꝼecꞇ ɼin i uii. ꞇɼaiȝꞇe na leiꞇe ⁊ .xii. ina aiɼꝺe o muiɼ co muiɼ; a ꝼoꞇim ꝺa ꝼuaiɼ, ⁊ ꝺainȝniuȝiꝺ amail na ꞇiɼoiɼ ꝺoɼiɼ ꝺia coḃaiɼ ⁊ loḋaɼ aɼ.

Oꝺ cualaꝺaɼ Ȝaeḋil ⁊ Cɼuiꞇhniȝ amail cona alꞇa ɼo caiɼoiḃ ꝺo cuaꝺaɼ ꝼuꞇiḃ.

Aḃ incaɼnaiꞇioɼe .cccc xx iii Ꞇeoṫaɼ iunioɼ poɼꞇ honoɼium in ceaꞇhɼamaꝺ ɼiȝ .xl. iaɼ n-Auȝuɼꞇuɼ.

ʰ *Mowed down.*—Bede's words are " et quasi maturam segetem obvia quæque metant, calcant, transeunt ".—*Ib.*—(*T.*)

ⁱ *Stones*—The text reads claꝺaiḃ, which should evidently be clacaiḃ, and is translated accordingly —(*T*)

ᵏ *Wolves.*—" Sicut enim ager a feris, ita miseri cives discerpuntur ab hostibus."—*Bede, ibid.*—(*T*)

ˡ *Theothas.*—" Theodosius junior post Honorium quadragesimus *quintus* ab Augusto," &c.—*Bede,* i. 13 It is curious that the Irish compiler stops short just before Bede's account of Palladius being sent to the Scots by Pope Celestine, probably for the same reason which led to the omission of Nennius's section De Mirabilibus Hiberniæ, because there existed al-

Gaedhels, and they returned to their home then   Immediately the
enemy came, and mowed down[h] the Britons like a ripe corn field

The ambassadors were sent again, and a legion came to the assistance of the Britons, and fought against the enemies of the Britons, and
the ditch which the second Severus made was repaired by them ; it
was of stones[i] this time, i e seven feet broad and twelve high from sea
to sea; of sods they found it, and they fortified it so that they might
not *be required* to come again to assist them, and they departed

When the Gaedhels and the Cruithnians heard *this* they came upon
them (i e *upon the Britons*) as wolves[k] upon sheep

Ab incarnatione cccc.xxii   Theothas[l] junior post Honorium the
forty-fourth king after Augustus.

ready in the Irish language what the writer
regarded as the better and fuller account
of these events. The above abstract of
Bede is of no historical or literary value,
and would be unworthy of publication
except as it forms one of the interpolations introduced into the Irish version
of the Historia, in the manuscript from
which the text of this work has been
principally taken   The many ignorant
blunders made by the scribe in this portion of his work, prove that the persons
employed in making these transcripts
were often possessed of no literary qualifications for such a task, except the art
of penmanship.—(*T*)

APPENDIX.

l

[Oo peαrταιb Cαιrnich ann so.]

αbας Sαρραn ρι̇ι m-bρeταn ιαρταιn, ⁊ ̇ζαbαιρ neαρτ Sαχαn ⁊ Cρυιτneαc ; ⁊ τυ̇ζ oo ρετι̇ζ ιṅζeαn ρι̇ζ αlbαn ι. bαbοnα ιṅζeαn Lοαιρno mιc Eιρe, ⁊ nι h-ί ρο nαιρceo oo αcτ α ρι̇υρ .ι. Eιρc ιṅζeαn Lοαιρno ̇ζοn τρυllα lα Ⅲυιρ̇eoαc mαc Eο̇ζαιn mιc Neιll co h-Eιριno

⁊

<hr />

a *The miracles of Cannech.*—This legend is probably subsequent to A. D. 1092, when the primacy of the see of Lyons was decreed, perhaps also to the synod of Cashel in 1172, which established canons of affinity, since its author accounts it a sin in Muirchertach to marry the widow of his maternal aunt's son. Though possibly the sin of David, killing and then marrying, may be what he complains of —(H.)

b *After this.*—This legend occurs only in the Book of Ballymote, where it is inserted between what I have numbered sections xiv and xv, *suprà* p. 75, i.e. immediately after the account of the complete subjection of the Britons to the Romans. The words "after this," however, must imply some considerable time after the Romans had abandoned Britain,

for if Sarran had dominion, as the story goes on to say, over the Saxons as well as over the Picts, his reign must have been subsequent to the Saxon invasion which is dated A. D. 449, and some time subsequent, for his father-in-law, Loarn, king of Scotland, began his reign A. D. 503. Ogygia, p. 471. The genealogy of Sarran or Suran, the father of St. Cairnech, is thus given by Colgan from the genealogy of the saints in the Book of Lecan Saran, son of Colgan (or Colchuo), son of Tuathal, son of Fedhlim, son of Fiachra Cassan, son of Colla-da-Crioch. Acta SS. p. 783, n. 1, and see also p. 713, c. 4. In another authority quoted ib. n. 2, Fedhlim is made the son of Fechim son of Fiach son of Colla-da-Crioch, but the first is more correct; and as Colla-da-Crioch flourished from the year 297 to

I

OF THE MIRACLES OF CAIRNECH[n] HERE

SARRAN assumed the sovereignty of Britain after this[b], and established his power over the Saxons and Cruithnians. And he took to wife the daughter of the king of Alban, viz, Babona[c], daughter of Loarn, son of Erc[d] And it was not she that was married[e] to him, but her sister, viz, Erc, daughter of Loarn, until she eloped with Muiredhach, son of Eoghan, son of Niall, to Eri and she bore him four

about 350, according to O'Flaherty's Chronology, we may reasonably suppose Saran to have reigned about the year 500, or somewhat later —(T.)

[c] *Babona*—Pompa or Babona, daughter of Loarn Mor Mac Erc, first king of Scots in Lorn called after him, *circa* A D 503 Ogygia, p. 471 Colgan, Acta SS xxviii. Martii, p 782. She bore to Sarran three sons· St Carnech, St Ronan, and St. Brecan or Becan (ibid), of which names the first only occurs in the following list. This Sarran was son of Coelchu, and fifth in descent from Fiachra Cassan, nephew to Colla Huas, 130th king of Erin, and was one of the chiefs of Orgiellia or Oriel in Ulster. Ogygia ibid. and p. 359, 363. —(H)

[d] *Erc*, or *Ercus*, as O'Flaherty and Colgan call him for distinction's sake, for *Erc* occurs in this story as the name both of a man and of a woman —(T)

[e] *Not . . . married*—This contradiction may perhaps be explained by reference to the irregularities prevalent in a much later age of Irish Christianity So late as the time of Malachi of Armagh, contractum conjugiorum . aut ignorabant aut negligebant Bernardi Vita Mal. in tom iv p. 128, Mabillon. But, under his correction, "concubinatus honestat celebritas nuptiarum," p 130 The meaning of this is, probably, well explained by Di Lanigan as of the system of betrothals or *sponsalia de futuro*, not followed up by the *contractus conjugii*, or actual marriage *de*

2 A 2

⁊ co ꞃuc ceiꞇꞃi macu ꝺo ı Muıꞃceaꞃꞇac mac Eꞃca ⁊ Feaꞃaꝺac ⁊ Ꞇıᵹéaꞃnac ⁊ Maıan.

Clanaıꞃ umoꞃꞃo Saꞃꞃan babona co ꞃo ꞇuıꞃmeaꝺ leó u meıc ı Luıꞃıᵹ ⁊ Caıꞃnech ⁊ Eꞃꞅcoꞃ Oallaın ⁊ Caemlac , ⁊ aꞇbaıl ıaꞃ coꞃcuꞃ ⁊ ıaꞃ m-buaıꝺ ı ꞇaıᵹ Maꞃꞇaın.

Luıꞃıᵹ, ımoꞃꞃo, ꞃo ᵹab ıaꞃ ꞅın, ᵹo n eꞃecꞇ a neaꞃꞇ ꞃoꞃ Saxana, ⁊ con n-eꞃa caꞇaıꞃ ꞃoıꞃecneac ı uaıl maınꞃꞇꞃech Caıꞃnıc ı a bꞃaꞇaıꞃ   Muıꞃceaꞃꞇac mac Eꞃca ın ꞇan ꞅın ı uaıl ꞃıᵹ bꞃeaꞇan

⁵

præsenti Irish Eccl. Hist. iv pp 64, 70-72 In the very rude age of Sarran and Babona, we may understand how the latter was taken to wife, but not married although the mother of three or four sons.—(*H*)

ᶠ *Four sons*—Erc, daughter of Loarn Mac Erc, was married to Muredach, son of Eoghan mac Niall Naoighiallach and bore him four sons, Muirchertach, king of Erin, Feradhach, Tighernach, and Maon. And after Muredach's death she was remarried to Fergus, son of Conall Gulban, another grandson of Niall the Great to whom she bore four other sons, Sedna (progenitor of the Gulbanian kings of Erin), Fedhlim (father of St Columkille), Brendan, and Loarn Ogygia and Colgan, *ubi supra* —(*H.*) See Additional Notes, No XXII

ᵍ *Five sons*—Only four are here mentioned In the Naemh Seanchus, or Genealogies of the Saints, preserved in the Book of Lecan, (in the tract which Colgan attributes to Aengus the Culdee, and frequently quotes, under the title of " Libellus de matribus Sanctorum, ') only three sons of Babona and Sarran are mentioned,

perhaps because three only were saints Pompa ınᵹen Loaıꞃn maꞇaıꞃ Chaıꞃnıᵹ. ⁊ Bꞃecaın, meıc Saꞃaın, ⁊ Ronaın ꞃınꝺ mıc Saꞃaın. 'Pompa, daughter of Loarn, was the mother of Cairnech and Brecan sons of Saran, and of Ronan Finn son of Saran "—(*T*) Saint Cairnech was the son of Saran and Pompa, or Babona But of the other three the case is less plain St Dallan, according to Colgan, was the son of Colla (son of Erc, of the line of Colla Huais, king of Erin), by a mother named Forgail, A SS Jan xxix p 203 His real name was Eochaidh, and he was surnamed Dallan, by reason of his blindness. He was lineally descended from Colla Huais, and was cousin-german to St Maidoc of Ferns, their fathers, Colla Mac Erc and Sedna Mac Ere, being brothers See Ogygia, in c 76 Of Caemlach I cannot say anything But the word Luirig, if it were a name at all, would seem only to be a surname, for it is the Latin word *lorica*. Armour was not early worn in Ireland At the battle of Seghais, in Leinster, Tighernach, ann 709, the Britons

four sons[f], viz. Muircheartach Mac Erca, and Fearadhach, and Tigh-earnach, and Maian.

And Sarran had issue by Babona; and there were begotten by them five sons[g], viz, Luirig, and Cairnech, and Bishop Dallain, and Caemlach; and he [i e *Sarran*] died after victory and after triumph in the house of Martin[h]

Luirig then succeeded *to the throne, and* he extended his power over the Saxons, and he forcibly built a fort within the precincts of the monastery of Cairnech his brother   Muircheartach Mac Erca[i] happened

who served on Ceallach's side were remarked for wearing the luirig   But it may be that the appellation is rather obtained by changing the orthography of a real name than in the way of a surname. See below, p. 190, note.—(*H*) Luiach occurs as a proper name in Irish history, but who the Luirig was who is described in the legend before us as a British or Cornish king, I do not know —(*T*)

[h] *Martin* — The house of Martin is Tours in France, which city he appears to have conquered, and bestowed the bishopric on his son, Cairnech.   But neither of those facts appears otherwise than by implication.—(*H.*) Unless we suppose Tech-Martain to be the name of some place where there was a monastery dedicated to St. Martin, if so, Sarran dying with victory and triumph may signify that he died a monk.   There are two places called St. Martin's in Cornwall   But at that time, a little before the Benedictines, all Irish monks were of the Martinist foundation, and every monas-

tery, in a certain sense, a House of Martin. —(*T*)

[i] *Muircheartach Mac Erca.*—This monarch, called Mac Erca, from the name of his mother, Erca, daughter of Loarn, was king of Ireland from 509, according to Tighernach, but, according to the more probable chronology of the Annals of Ulster, from 513 to 534   The account here given of him is not very consistent with his reputation as the first Christian king of Ireland, " a good and pious sovereign" Lanigan, i p 435 We may perhaps, suppose that the murders for which he was banished from Ireland in his youth, and the subsequent parricide of his grandfather, for which he was banished from Scotland, were committed before his conversion to Christianity. But the same excuse cannot be made for other immoralities attributed to him. See Petrie's Essay on Tara Hill, Transactions Royal Irish Academy, vol xviii Antiq p 118, sq. The whole of this strange legend gives a curious picture of the loose

ıſ ꝼoſlaim ſaıꝛcın, ıaꝛ na ꝟıcuꝛ a h-Eꝛınꝺ aꝛ na Cꝛoſꝛana ꝺo
maꝛbaꝺ, ⁊ ıaꝛ na ꝺıcoꝛ ıaꝛcaın a h-Ꙇlbaın aꝛ maꝛbaꝺ a ꝼean-
acaꝛ ı Ꙇoaıꝛnꝺ ꝛıſ Ꙇlban; conaꝛ caꝟla ꝺo coıꝛeaꝛcaꝺ a aıꝛm ın
can ꝛın co Caıꝛnꝺec co mac ꝺeꝛbꝛcacaꝛ a macaꝛ; co n-ebaıꝛc
Caıꝛneċ ꝛıꝛ, boꝺ ꝛıſ Eꝛenn ⁊ bꝛecan cu caıꝺcı, ⁊ ꝺo ſeba neam
ıaꝛꝺaın acc co n-ꝺıcuıꝛea Ꙇuıꝛıſ ꝺo neaꝛc aca ꝼoꝛ ın n-eclaıꝛ
Ꙇnꝺꝛın luıſ mac Eꝛca ſa ꝛıſ ⁊ acbeꝛc a h-aıceaꝛc ıaꝛ ꝛuaccaın
ı. Na cuıꝛıcaıſ ꝺo cacaıꝛ ı uaıl Caıꝛmıc eꝛꝛcoꝛ Ꝺaꝛ mo Ꝺebꝛoc,
aꝛ Ꙇuıꝛıc, aꝛ calma ꝼoꝛꝛıı ın ꝛeaca aıſı allca ꝛıl aıccı anꝺaꝛ
ꝼeın ⁊ ın Coımꝺe ꝺıa n-aꝺaıꝛ Ceıꝺ ınac Eꝛca ꝛꝛıa culu Caıꝛnec
ıaꝛcaın aſuꝛ ꝛloꝛıoıꝛ a h-aıceaꝛc Ꝫabaıꝛ ꝼeaꝛſ moꝛ Caıꝛnec
ꝺocaın ⁊ ꝺıxıc, m'ıccı ꝛoıꝛeoꝛınoıc ꝛom Ꝺıa co ꝛoꝛ ın aꝺbuꝛ na
h-aıſı ꝛın ꝛo ſaba baꝛ ⁊ leaccꝛu a ınıc Eꝛca h-Eꝛaılꝛ Caıꝛneach annꝛın aꝛ mac Eꝛca cecc ꝺo ꝺıcuꝛ a bꝛacaꝛ, ⁊ ſabaıꝛ
ꝺocaın aꝛ aeꝺ coınꝛac, ⁊ ua luıꝺ ꝺı h-eꝛaıl Caıꝛmıc ꝺo ꝺıcuꝛ ın
ꝛıſ. Co n-ꝺeaꝛna Ꝺıa moꝛ mıꝛbuılı aꝛ Caıꝛneach anꝺꝛın ı coꝛ
ꝛaeꝺ aſ n-allaıſ aꝛ ın c-ꝛleıb co h-aeꝛecc ınꝺ ꝛıſ, ſoꝛ ꝺeꝛlaıꝛ ın

ꝛluaſ

notions of morality entertained by its author It is not merely that Sarian is
represented as marrying one sister and
living with another, that St Cairnech is
represented as born in incest, and Muircheartach in adultery, for these things
may have happened in a state of heathen
ism without reproach to the hero of the
story, but St Cannech, a Christian bishop,
is represented as instigating Muircheartach
tach to the murder of Luirig, and exult-
ing over the death of his brother in language very inconsistent with a profession
of the Gospel, and all this without any
apparent consciousness in the writer of
the legend that he was attributing to his
hero anything unbecoming the Christian
character.—(1)

ᴶ Crossans.—These were the cross-bear-
ers in religious processions, who also combined with that occupation, the profession,
if we may so call it, of singing satirical
poems against those who had incurred
Church censure, or were for any other
cause obnoxious In this latter capacity
they often brought upon themselves the
vengeance of the lawless chieftains whom
they lampooned —(T)

ᵏ Judge.—The word Ꝺebꝛoc is explained in the Leabhar Breac, fol 14, a., by the

happened to be at that time with the king of Britain, learning military science, after he was expelled from Ireland for having killed the Crossans[j], and after having been subsequently expelled from Alba, for having killed his grandfather, Loarn, king of Alba. It happened that he was at that time getting his arms consecrated by Cairnech, the son of his mother's sister; then Cairnech said to him, Thou shalt be king of Eri and of Britain for ever, and shalt go to heaven after, provided thou canst but prevent Luirig from exercising his power against the Church Then Mac Erca went to the king, and after he came he told his message, viz.· Build not thy city (*said he*) in the precincts of Cairnech the bishop. As God is my judge[k], says Luirig, I think more of the power of the pet wild fawn he has, than of his own *power*, or *of the power* of the Lord God whom he adores Mac Erca returned to Cairnech, and told him the result[l]. Great wrath suddenly seized Cairnech, et dixit, My prayer to my Lord, to my God, is, that that very fawn may be the cause of his death, and by thy *hand*, O Mac Erca! Cairnech then commanded Mac Erca to go forth and destroy his brother, and he [*Mac Erca*] immediately took upon himself to fight him; and he went forth at the command of Cairnech to destroy the king And God worked a great miracle there for Cairnech. viz he sent a wild fawn[m] out of the mountain into the king's assembly, and

paraphrase ⁊ap mo Ðia mbpaτa, i e. "by my God of judgment" The meaning is· ' I would as soon attribute miraculous powers to the pet fawn that follows him as to Cairnech himself, or the God he worships." The word Coimbe, here translated "Lord God," is the title generally given to Christ.—(*T*.)

' *The result*—Literally his desire, i e, what he had desired to be done in regard to Luirig —(*T*)

[m] *A wild fawn*—Meaning of course *the* wild fawn already spoken of, for otherwise the prayer of St. Cairnech would not have been fulfilled. Fawns and deer occupy a prominent place in Irish hagiography, and were the subjects of many miracles St. Berach. of Cluain Coirphthe, had a deer which was sent to him miraculously to carry his luggage, when he

ſluaʒ na ꝺıaıꝺ ac ın ꝓıʒ ʒona banꝺalaıb, ⁊ ꝺıxıꞇ Mac Eꝑca, maꞇ
cıalla chach a ꞇıʒeaꝑna ꝼꝓıꞇ cleꝑeach ꝺaıʒ buꝺ ꝼullı ʒach aım-
neꝺ lene ın cumꞇacꞇa ꝼꝓı Luıꝓıʒ Anꝺꝓın ꝓuıꝺıꝓ Mac Eꝑca ın
loꝓʒ caꞇa ı ꝓlıꝓ ın ꝓıʒ coꝓ comꞇꝑom ; ⁊ cuꝑꞇaıꝺ ʒa cleꝓıʒ ⁊ cenꝺ
laıꝓ ꝑe comaꝑꞇa, ⁊ ꝺıxıꞇ, cenꝺ ꝺo bꝑaꞇaꝓ ꝺuıꝺ a Caıꝓnıc ; eꞇ
ꝺıxıꞇ Caıꝓneach, leıc ꝺamꝓa an cnaım, ⁊ ꞇomaılꝓıu ın ꝓmıꝓ, ⁊
ꝓoꝓıa ʒac ꞇꝑeaꝓ comaꝓba ꝓunꝺ co bꝑaꞇh ⁊ ın Eꝓınꝺ.

Ꞇecꞇaıꝓ ʒeıll ⁊ neaꝓꞇ ın ꞇıꝓı annꝓın, ⁊ Caıꝓnec, ꝼꝓı ꝓecꞇ
m-blıaꝺna, ım moꝓ ꝓıʒı bꝑeꞇan, ⁊ Caꞇ, ⁊ Oꝓc, ⁊ Saxan

Co n-ꝺeaꝓna Mac Eꝑca ꝼuıllınꝺ ın ꝓeccaıꝺ .ı bean Luıꝓıc ꝺo
ꞇabaıꝓꞇ ıaꝓ caꞇaʒaꝺ ⁊ ıaꝓ comlenʒaıb co moꝓ ꝼꝓı ꝓıʒ Fꝑanʒc, a
coꝓnam a ınʒene ꝼꝓıꝓ, co n-ꝺoꝓćaıꝓ ıc Mac Eꝑca ꝓoꝺeoıꝺ ın ınʒen,

⁊

---

set out in search of a suitable place for the foundation of his monastery. Vit S Berachi, c 12 Colg Acta SS p 342 Deer, at the prayer of St Attracta were made to carry timber to build the castle of the tyrant king of Connaught Vit S Attractæ, c 13, ib p. 280 A fawn, together with other wild animals, lived with St Kieran of Saigher, "man-erunt mitissime apud eum et obediebant ei secundum jussionem viri Dei in omnibus quasi Monachi "—Vit c 6, ib p 458 A wild deer came daily to St. Einania to be milked. Vit S. Fechini, c 41, ib. p 138, a miracle which was also vouchsafed to St Crumtheris Vit. Trip S Patr iii c. 74 The wild deer also obeyed St. Molagga of Teghmolagga Vit c 19, 20, Acta SS. p. 147, 148. A deer brought St. Columbkille his books which he had lost O'Donnell, lib. i. c 3 Trias Thaum

p 407 St Patrick found a deer suckling her fawn in the spot where the northern altar of the cathedral of Armagh now stands, and, taking up the fawn, the deer followed him "velut mitissima ovis." Joechin c 163 Comp also Eleran c. 86, Colg Triad Th p 46. And the same thing happened at Sabhall or Saul. Trip. iii c 71 On another occasion St Patrick and his companions passed through the hostile ambuscade of King Leogaire to Tara, the saint and his followers appearing to their enemies like eight deer, and the boy Benen, like a fawn, carrying a small bundle on his shoulder, which contained the sacred Bible of the saint Vit Trip. i. c. 60. To commemorate this miracle Saint Patrick composed the *Iorica* or *Fedh Fiadha*, first published by Mr Petrie from the Liber Hymnorum. Essay on Tara, p 56, sq —
(*T.*)

and the host all went in pursuit of it except the king himself and
his women. Et dixit Mac Erca, If you had been just, my Lord,
towards your cleric, it is certain that it would give increased happi-
ness to have the royal robe on Luing   Then Mac Erca thrust his
battle staff into the king's side, so that it was balanced[n]. and he
returned to his cleric, and the head *of the king* with him, as a
token ; et dixit, *Lo, here* is thy brother's head for thee, O Cairnech   Et dixit Cairnech, Leave me the bone, and eat thou the
marrow, and every third coarb[o] shall be thine for ever, here[p] and
in Eri.

Then he (*Mac Erca*) took the hostages and the power of the
district *into his own hands, conjointly* with Cairnech, for seven years,
as also the supreme sovereignty of Britain, and Cat[q], and Orc, and
Saxonland

And Mac Erca *then* committed an additional sin, that is, he took
to himself the wife of Luing, after many battles and conflicts with
the king of France, to take his daughter from him, until at last the
daughter

[n] *Balanced.*—That is, it passed through the King's body, so that as much of the spear appeared at one side as at the other. Or it stood balanced in the wound, without falling.—(*T*)

[o] *Coarb*—The comharb or coarb is the successor and representative of the original founder in any prelacy, episcopal or conventual   The word seems here used for the benefice itself That the king was often the impropriator or commendatory of the coarbs, subject to the maintenance of the clergy of the mother church, appears from the Tribes and Customs of Hy-Many, p. 77, note ', Davis cit. ibid   An extensive se-

cularization of that sort is here offered by Cairnech, as a reward to Murchertach for killing his brother.—(*H*) The word coarb, however, was also used to denote a succes-sor in a *civil* office, as a king, chieftain, or judge, and this may possibly be its signi-fication here, although the former is more probable, as the grant in this case comes from the spiritual chief, in return for sup-posed services done to the church.—(*T*)

[p] *Here*, i. e in Britain, for Luing is said to have been a king of or in Britain, and the scene of the legend appears to have been placed there.—(*T*)

[q] *Cat*—Cat is Catanesia or Caithness,

⁊ cu puc ceiṫṛi meic do .i Conſtantin, ⁊ Ᵹaedeal Ƒict, o ṫaat
puiṗiᵹ Ḃṛetan ⁊ ṗiᵹ Ḃṛeaṫan Coṗṅd ; Nellend a quo ᵹeṅṛ Nellan

of which mention has already occurred
See p 148, note ᶠ —(H)

' *The daughter*, i e. the daughter of the
king of France I suppose the meaning
to be, that Luirig's wife was the daughter
of the king of France , that after the
death of her husband she was taken by
Mac Erca, that this led to wars with the
king of France, and that Mac Erca finally
succeeded in retaining her If there be
any history in this, it is difficult to trace
it in such records as are accessible to me
It is probably a pure fiction, like many
other things in this *fabula perquam fu-
tilis, Sᵹel ᵹoiṗṗᵹech ᵹan ṫaċ ṛiṗiṅe*
as it is truly called in a note in the
handwriting of old Charles O'Conor on
the margin of the Book of Ballymote —
(T)

ˢ *Constantine* —It is to be inquired what
Constantine is here named as the son of
Mac Erca The Britons had a great notion
of some royal saint so called, but distinct
from Constantine the Great. Out of the
tyrant Constantinus, who assumed the
purple in Britain, and wore it in Arles,
and his son, Constans the Monk, they have
formed the kings of Britain, Cystennin
Vendigaid, i e Saint Constantine, and his
son, Constant Vanach, or Constans the
Monk They figure in the mythus of
Vortigern, and also in the heroic mythus
that ensues, Cystennin being father, and

Constant Vanach brother, to Emmrys
Wledig and Uthyr Pendragon Next
comes Cystennin ap Cadwr, prince of
Cornwall, who became king of all Britain in 542, and to whom Gildas in 543
or 544 addresses severe reproaches The
Brut of Kings affirms that he was slain
in the third year of his reign, and buried
in the Cor y Cewri, near Salisbury It
is observable that he was nearly the last
king who could have been there buried,
for in 552 Cynric, son of Cerdic, gained
the victory of Searobyrig or Sarum But
others make a Saint Constantine out of
him Mr Ritson, in his Cornish Saints,
annexed to the Life of Arthur, p 165,
gives " Constantine, king, monk, and martyr, 11th March, 556 Domesday Book '
Hector Boece asserts that he stole away
to Ireland secretly, clam suis, received
the tonsure in an Irish monastery, and
suffered martyrdom while preaching to
Pagans in Scotland.—Lib. ix cit Usshei,
Brit Eccles p 281 ed 2 While John
of Tinmouth says, that Constantine, king
of Cornwall, died peaceably in the monastery of St David of Menevia —Cit ibid
p 282 I regard the whole story of his
tonsure as a blundering fiction, having its
origin in the history of Constans Monachus, son of Constantinus The son of Cador,
however, seems to have been the person to
whom the legend of St Constantine, king

187

daughter' fell into Mac Erca's hands, and she bare him four sons,
viz. Constantine', and Gaedhal-Ficht (from whom descend the kings
of Britain, and the kings of Britain-Coriin') ; Nellenn (a quo gens
Nellan

of Britain, and abbot of Rathain Hua Shua-naigh in Westmeath, had reference. See Petrie on the Round Towers, p. 351, etc. Constantinus Rex Britonum regnum abdicavit et peregrinationis causâ venit Ratheniam tempore S Mochuddæ Cathal Maguire, cit ibid 353. This tale obtained such credit, as to have given the adjoining lands the name of Muigh Constantin before the period (perhaps not very recent) when the legend about the bard Rumann which Mr Petrie quotes, was composed Mochuda died in 637, with no reputation of peculiar longevity. —Lanigan, vol ii p 102. It is, therefore, apparent, that Constantine ap Cador could not have known him, much less have been his coarb, as Maguire pretends But the failure of synchronism will rather give fresh impeachment to the story than raise doubts as to the person who is meant, for the day of commemoration is the same (March 11th) at Rathain as it was in Cornwall We may regard the Irish legend as an explanation of what is read in Boece. As to the other story, that Constantine of Rathen was Constantine Mac Fergus, king of Albania or the Cruthent, it is wholly absurd and forged For Constantine Mac Fergus the Pict acceded in 788 or 789, and died king in 819 But he is not found in the text of the ancient Irish Festilogies.

Now of all these persons, it is evident that St Constantine ap Cador, king, martyr, and monk, should be the son fabulously ascribed to king Mac Erca For that son was a Cornubian king , and the date of Muirchertach, who died in 533, squares well with that of a son who (after a short reign) died in retirement in 556 Tighernach, ann 588, mentions the Conversio ad Dominum (tonsure) of one Constantinus, with no further explanation

The name of Gaedhal Ficht is merely that of the nation of Gwyddyl Fichti, or North Picts of Britain, and is far from unimportant, as an Erse recognition of that Welsh appellation The Scotch being also of Mac Erca's family, the whole of Britain, by means of Constantine, or Gaedhal Ficht, and of Loarn, is made, in some sort, to derive itself from Erc, mother of Muirchertach and Loarn But such stuff will not bear a narrow examination.— (II.)

' Britain-Corinn, i. e. Cornwall —(T) The title of the Cornish saint, Iddawg Corn Prydain, is usually rendered Horn of Britain, in a personal sense, like Post Prydain, Pillar of Britain. But this passage confirms my suspicion, that Corn Prydain simply meant de Cornubiâ or Cornubiensis, Corn-Wealh —(H)

2 B 2

lan, ⁊ Scanᴅal in mac ele, a quo ᵹenſ Scanᴅail ı a n-Eſınn ó ᴛáıᴛ
clanna na ᴅeſı ſın

Co n-ᴅeſınaᴅ moſ-ᴛınol cleſec n-Eoſſa co Ꞇoſınıſ Maſᴛan
ı ſecᴛ n-eſſuıc xxx aſ ccc. ma comaſᴅa Peaᴅaıſ, ᴅo ſaıᵹıᴅ
Caıſnıch eſſcoſ Ꞇoſınᴅſı ⁊ Ḃſeᴛan-coſnᴅ, ⁊ na n-uılı Ḃſeaᴛnach,
ᴅo ᴅıcuſ caca h-eıſſı, ⁊ ᴅo ceaſᴛuᵹuᴅ ᵹaca ᴛíſı ımmuſᴛ na
h-ecalſa , ⁊ aᴅſoſaſᴛ conᴅacᴛ maſᴛſa ın beaᴛa ᴅo Chaıſnech
aſ ſob é a ᴛoᵹa beaᴛa maſᴛſa , ⁊ ſuaıſ Caıſnech LLL eſſcoſ ᴅo
ᴛoᵹmaſ maſ maıllı ſe Caıſnᴅech ᴅıa n-cleſſí, ⁊ ᴅo coıᴅ ın Lıen
ᴅa h-eılıᴛſı ı a ᴅualuſ Mıc Eſca ⁊ Muıſeaᴅaıᵹ

Ꝺo luıᴅ Caıſnᴅech ſeımc ᵹo Ḃſeᴛnaıḃ Coſnᴅ no Caſnᴛıceon, ⁊
ſo cuınᴅaıᵹeaᴅ caᴛoıſ ſo ᴛalmaın laıſ aſ ᴅoıᵹ na ſaıcıᴅ ſe ᴛíſ
na ᴛalum na h-eoıſ , coſ ſuılleſᴛaıſ neſᴛ ⁊ ſıᵹı Mıc Eſca ſé
ḃlıaᴅna, ⁊ co ᴛáınıc co n-Eſınᴅ ſeımc, conaᴅ h-é céᴛ eſſcoſ claınᴅı
Neıll ⁊ Ꞇemſach, ⁊ ᵹoſ bé céᴅ maıſᴛíſ ⁊ céᴅ manach Eſenᴅ, ⁊
céᴛna ḃſeᴛeam ſeaſ n-Eſenᴅ ſoſ

Coſ

---

u *Coarb of Peter* —The coarb of Peter
is the Pope What follows is very obscure, but it seems to me to imply that
Cairnech and his clergy, in consideration
of his relationship to the heads of the Hy
Niall, were placed in possession of the
metropolitan see of Lyons, which in the
Council of Clermont, A D 1092, was for-
mally established as the primacy of all
France If so, we have now made him
primate of France, of Armorica at Tours
(taking that construction of the House of
Martin, above, p 180), of Wales and Cornwall, and in effect, of Ireland, of whose
church he assumes the entire disposal

The name Cairnticeon, attached to Cornwall, I believe to mean Carentociawn, the
diocese or jurisdiction of St Carentoc, by

whom that country was converted —
(H.)

There was a council held at Tours, in
the year 566 or 567, on the 17th of November, in the church of St. Martin, in
which Euphronius, bishop of Tours, presided, assisted by eight other prelates
The object of the Council was the refor-
mation of discipline, and its twenty-seven
canons which remain all relate to that
subject They may be found in the printed
editions of the Councils, and there is an
abstract of them in Richard, Analyse des
Conciles, tom 1 p 569, sq 4° Paris, 1772
From this it would seem that there was
here possibly some foundation of fact in
the mind of the writer of this legend. St.
Carnech was originally of Cornwall, and

Nellan), and Scannal, the other son, a quo gens Scannail; i e it is in Eri the descendants of the two last are

Now a great synod of the clergy of Europe was made at Tours of Martin, viz, three hundred and thirty-seven bishops, with the coarb of Peter[u], to meet Cairnech, Bishop of Tours and Britain-Cornn, and of all the British, to cast out every heresy, and to reduce every country to the discipline of the Church And the chieftainship of the martyrs of the world was given to Cairnech, because martyrdom was his own choice. And Cairnech found thrice fifty bishops who made it also their choice to accompany Cairnech in pilgrimage. and that number went to Lien[v] in pilgrimage for the sake of Mac Erca and Muiredhach

Cairnech then set out to the Britons of Cornn or Carniceon, and a city was built by him under ground, in order that he might not see the earth, nor the country, nor the sky, and he increased the strength and sovereignty of Mac Erca for a year, and he (i e Cairnech) came to Eri before him, so that he was the first bishop of the Clann-Niall and of Temhar (*Tara*), and he was the first martyr and the first monk of Eri, and the first Brehon[w] of the men of Eri also.

Now

may have been connected with the Armorican Britons, whose affairs appear to have formed a part of the business of the above-mentioned Council of Tours, for its ninth canon prohibits the consecration of a Roman or Briton to the episcopal office by an Armorican bishop, without the license of the metropolitan (of Tours) or the comprovincial bishops This would seem as if the Armorican bishops were then seeking to exercise an independent jurisdiction, perhaps, in conjunction with the ecclesiastics of Cornwall —(*T*)

[v] *Lien*, probably Lyons —(*T*)

[w] *Brehon*, i. e. judge The author of the legend was determined to concentrate in the person of his hero every ecclesiastical perfection This tale was either unknown to Colgan, or else he did not consider it worthy of any notice He makes no mention of any tradition that Cairnech was a martyr, nor of any of the other particulars here recorded —Vit. Cairnech. ad 28 Mart p 782 —(*T*)

Coṅ caταιοṗεοαρ umoṗṗo Ḟṗαιṅ⁊ε ⁊ Saxαιn οια ειṗ ḟṗι Mac
Eṗca, ⁊ ⁊oṅ τo⁊lao a cṗιch ⁊ a cαταιṗ ṗé cιαn ο'αιmṗιṗ, ⁊ ⁊oṅ
milleao cṗιchαο ⁊ cumacτα nα τιṗι bα ṅeaṗṗα οo ṗe meτε α
cumacτα

* Made war.—The legend speaks only
of the triumphs of Mac Erca, and concludes with his elevation to the sovereignty of Ireland For an account of his
miserable death see Petrie on Tara Hill,
pp 119, 120, and the Four Masters, ad
ann 527 ; also Cossgrave in Vit S Cuth-
berti c 1. ap Colgan, ad 20 Mart p 679,
and the notes, p 690 —(T)

The writer of the legend might have
gone on to say that St Cannech contributed to the cruel fate of King Mac Erca,
by his bitter and not inoperative male-
dictions on him and his house, and was
to him what Saints Ruadan and Columkille were to king Diarmid Mac Ceir-
bhoil —See Cambrensis Eversus, p 74,
Petrie on Tara Hill, p 122

It remains to inquire what is meant by
the legend of Sairan conquering, and his
son Luing governing, Britain, England,
and Pictland? Perhaps nothing. It is,
however, true that, somewhere about those
times, an Irish force conquered the island
of Mona or Anglesey That island was
recovered out of their hands by Caswallawn Lawhir, or the Longhanded, father to Maelgwn Gwynedd, king of Britain who defeated their leader, Serigi or
Sirigi, at the place marked by the Cerrig y Wyddyl or Stones of the Irishmen.
Lhoyd and Powel, Descr. of Wales, p 15,

Warrington 1 p 40 , Camden, 11. p 60,
Rowlands Mona, p. 147, Triads, series 1.
t1 49, ser. 11 tr. 40 But Lhoyd, as well as
D Langhorne, Chro Reg. Angl p 73, errs
in saying that the Gwyddyl Fichti or Picts
were in Mona, instead of the Gwyddyl or
Irish , which is contrary to the Liber
Triadum, misquoted by Langhorne The
latter makes the further mistake of supposing Gwyddyl Fichti to mean Cruthenians from Clanboy The troops of Ganval the Irishman says Triad 8, series 3,
came into N Wales and settled there for
twenty-nine years, until they were driven
into the sea by Caswallawn ap Beli But
it is incredible, that the only two Cas-
wallawns whose acts are recorded should
both have driven the Irish out of North
Wales , or that an Irish inroad of the
fractional duration of twenty-nine years
should be referred to Cæsar's days ; and
I doubt not that the Irish settlers for
twenty-nine years were those whom Caswallawn Lawhir expelled. They had taken
strong hold of Mona For Caswallawn,
after his victory at the Cerrig, slew Sirigi
at his town of Llan y Gwyddyl (Irish
Church), now Holy-Head, which the
Irish had built Rowlands, ibid Oval
and circular trenches continue to be
shewn in Mona as the ground plots of
the Irish habitations, or cyttiau yr Gwyd-

Now, after this the Franks and the Saxons made war[x] against Mac Erca, and he destroyed their country and their cities after a long contest, and the country and the power of the territories adjacent

delodd.—Rowlands, p. 27. If the Irish population were then expelled (and not, as I rather suppose, subjugated), the memory of its having been firmly seated there appears in Golyddan's division of the Irish of Voitigern s day, into those of Ireland, Mona, and North Britain,

"Gwyddyl Iwerddon Mon, a Phrydyn"—Arch Myvyr i 156

But Einion, father of Caswallawn, for whom his son reconquered Mona, was styled Amanus Rex Scotorum, i. e Einion Vrenin o Wyddelodd, king of the Irishmen. See Vaughan, cit Camden, ii 69

Now this Caswallawn is said to have reigned over Gwynedd seventy-four years, from 443 to 517 But that chronology is tainted with the omission of two generations, and the confounding of two different Einions His true pedigree is Cynedda, Einion Urdd. *Ouain Danwyn, Einion Vrenin o Wyddelodd,* Caswallawn Lawhir See Rowlands, p 155. Cambro-Briton, i p 247 The insertion of these generations may bring the date of Sirigi's death into the life-time of Muichertach, for he obtained the crown of Ireland in 513, and reigned over it till 533. Now, it seems possible, that the conquest of Mona by the Irish, may be the conquest of the British island,

so largely exaggerated in this piece, and that the *Luiny* subsequently slain in Britain may be Sirigi, as most writers spell the name Here we read that Mac Erca sinned in taking Luirig's widow for his wife; but in Lynch we read, that he perished by the vengeance of Sin or Sheen (daughter of Sigh), whose father he had put to death. Cambr Evesns, p 74 In the prophecy of St Cairneach it is said,

' Sin is the woman who kills thee O son of Erc, as I see '

and it enumerates her eleven names, but does not give her father's name See Petric on Taia, p 120 Sigh certainly approaches to Sirigh If there be any truth at all in Muirchertach's having sojourned in Britain, it was probably enough among the Irish of Mona, and during the five years of anarchy, 508–13 preceding his accession, when Ireland had no king That Cairnech may have presided over the Irish Church or Llan y Gwyddyl that he may have quarrelled with Sirigi concerning the fortifications of that place, and that both he and Muirchertach were considered instrumental to his destruction, are all possible circumstances But whether their suggestion throws any glimmer of light on this extravagant narration, I leave others to judge.—(*H*)

cumacꞇa ⁊ a neꞃꞇ , ⁊ ꝥo ꞇainic iaꞃ ꞃin a moꞃ loinꝝeaꞃ ꝺo ꝝabail
ꞃiꝝi na h-Eꞃeno , ꝝo ꝺeiꞃiꝺ ic Ꝼán na lonꝝ ꞃoꞃ boino, ꝝoꞃ loiꞃcꞇe
laiꞃ a lonꝝa .i. ꝝonaꝺ uaꝺa Ꝼán[na]lonꝝ, ⁊ ꝝoꞃ maꞃbaꝺ coiꝝeꝺ-
aiꝝ na h-Eꞃeno iaꞃꞇain, ⁊ ꝝo ꞃo ꝝaib a ꞃiꝝi ꝺo ꝺileꞃ co bꞃaꞇ ꝺo
ꞃéiꞀ ⁊ ꝺá cloino Ꝝoꞃ milleaꝺ cumaċꞇa ⁊ neaꞃꞇ bꞃeꞇan ꝺia h-eiꞃi
moꞃin

II

ꝺO INꝝ̇ANꞇAIꝺ EꞂENN ANOSO ꝺA ꞂEꞂ ꞀEꝺAIꞂ ꝝ̇ꝆINꝺ ꝺA-
Ꞁacha.

i Iniꞃ Ꝝ̇luaiꞃ a n-Iꞃꞃuꞃ ꝺoinnann, iꞃe a h-aiꞃꝺi, na cuiꞃꞃ beꞃaꞃ inꞇi ni lobaiꞇ iꞇeꞃ, acꞇ ꞃaꞃaiꞇ a n-inꝝne ⁊ a ꞃuilꞇ ⁊ ꝺo beꞃ ꝝac
aen inꞇi aicni aꞃ a aꞇhaiꞃ ⁊ aꞃ a ꞃenaꞇhaiꞃ co cian iaꞃ n-eꝝaib,
⁊ ni lobann ciꝺ in ꞃeoil aꞃcena cen ꞃailliuꝺ inꞇi

11

 Fan-na-long, i e the drawing up of the
ships   This place is now unknown.—(*T.*)

 Wonders—The following account of
the wonders of Ireland is taken from the
Book of Ballymote, fol. 140, b.   Another
tract on the same subject, but differing
both in the number and order of the
"Wonders" described, is to be found in
the MS Library of Trinity College, Dublin H 3, 17, col 725, the same volume
from which the text of the Irish Nennius
has principally been taken in the present
work   It shall be referred to in these
notes by the letter D. as before

The *Mirabilia Hiberniæ* are described
by Nennius, Giraldus Cambrensis, Ralph
Higden in his Polychronicon, who relies
entirely on Giraldus ; O'Flaherty's Ogygia, part III c 50, p 289 See also Ware's
Antiquities of Ireland, by Harris, chap
xxxiv p 227 —(*T*)

^a *Glen-da-locha*—The Book of Glendal-
loch is not now known to exist The book
which is preserved in the Library of Trinity College, Dublin, and which was
quoted by Mr Petrie, in his Essay on Tara
as the Book of Glendaloch has since been
ascertained by Mr Curry to be the Book
of Leinster.—(*T*)

^b *Inis Gluair*, now Inish-glory an island
about a mile west off the coast of Erris,
County Mayo   See O'Flaherty's West
Connaught, and Mr Hardiman's note,
p 81, also O'Donovan's Hy-Fiachrach,
p 492   O'Flaherty (Ogygia, p 290)
makes this the seventh wonder   In D it
is the sixth, and is thus described· Iniꞃ
Ꝝ̇luaiꞃ bꞃeꞃaino a n-Iꞃꞃoꞃ ꝺomnuno a

cent to him were also destroyed by the greatness of his power and of his strength; and after this he came with a large fleet to take the sovereignty of Eri He landed at Fan-na-long on the Boyne, where he burned his ships, from which *circumstance* comes *the name of* Fan-na-long*[y]*; and he killed the provincial *kings* of Ireland afterwards, and took their sovereignty by right for ever, for himself and for his descendants And then the power and strength of Britain was destroyed after him

II.

OF THE WONDERS[z] OF ERI HERE ACCORDING TO THE BOOK OF GLEN-DA-LOCHA[a].

1 Inis-Gluair[b] in Irrus Domhnann, this is its property, that the corpses that are carried into it do not rot at all, but their nails and hair grow, and every one in it recognises his father and grandfather for a long period after their death Neither does the meat unsalted rot in it

11

Connaccaib na mainb bid inni noco bpencio, ⁊ nocho lobaio, ⁊ faicio a fulcu, ⁊ a n-ingne, ⁊ oo bein cach aichne fon a muinoein fein inci "Inis Gluair of St. Brendann, in Irrus Domhnann in Connacht: the corpses that are in it do not stink or rot, and their hair and nails grow, and every one recognises his own relations in it" The island was sacred to St. Brendan, and still contains the ruins of churches dedicated to that saint. Giraldus mentions this miracle, but gives a wrong name to the island "Est insula quædam in occidentali Conactiæ solo posita, cui nomen *Aren*, a sancto Bren-

dano, ut aiunt, consecrata In hac hominum corpora nec humantur, nec putrescunt; sed sub divo posita et exposita permanent incorrupta. Hic homines avos, atavos, et tritavos, longamque stirpis suæ retro seriem, mirando conspiciunt et cognoscunt"—Top. Hib Dist ii. c. 6. Aran was not dedicated to St. Brendan, but to St. Endeus, see Cambr. Eversus, pp 7, 8. Inish-glory is at present uninhabited; but it contains the ruins of some very ancient dwellings; and leeks and other garden herbs, introduced by the Monks of St. Brendan, are found growing wild in several places on the island.—(*T.*)

ıı Loc n-Echach; ıꞃı a aıꞃoı, cꞃanꝺ cuılınn ꝺo beꞃaꞃ ıno ꞃꞃı ꞃecc m-blıaꝺnaıb ıꞃ cloc a m-bı ꝺe ıꞃ ın ᵹꞃıan, ⁊ ıꞃ ıaꞃann na m-bı ıꞃ ın uıꞃce, cꞃanꝺ umoꞃꞃo na m-be uaꞃꞃu

.ııı. Tıꞃꞃa loca Con ı Connaccaıb; ıꞃı a h-aıꞃoı ꞃꞃı ꞃın loc ꞃıl na comꞃocuꞃ, cuıᵹ tꞃoıᵹıꝺ etuꞃꞃu ꝺo ᵹꞃeꞃ, cıa ꞃoꞃbꞃıo cıa ꞃeꞃᵹaıc ın loc ꞃechıoꞃı he ın cac aıꞃoı ꝺıb ꞃın ꝺo ᵹꞃeꞃ

.ıu. Tıꞃꞃa Ᵹabla lıuın ı n-Aıꞃᵹıallaıb; ıꞃı a aıꞃoı ꞃuılc ꝺaꞃ acabaꞃ h-ıc lıata ꞃo cetoıꞃ

u

'*Loch n-Echach*, i e the lake of Eochach or Eochadh, now Loch Neagh. Ogygia, p 292. It is very generally believed that this lake possesses the property of petrify-ing wood   Harris, in his edit of Ware's Antiquit p 228, quotes Boetius, Hist Lapidum et Gemmarum, for a statement respecting Lough Neagh exactly the same as that of the text, but says that it has been found to be certainly false It is popularly believed, however, to the present day Nennius describes the miracle thus " Est aliud stagnum quod facit ligna durescere in lapides homines autem fingunt ligna, et postquam formaverint projiciant in stagno, et manent in eo usque ad caput anni, et in capite anni lapis reperitur Et vocatur Loch Echach " Comp O'Flaherty, Ogygia, p 290, n 3   In D. this is the second wonder, and is thus described Loch n-Eochach, ꝺo nı ꝺo cꞃunꝺ chuıllıno a cıno uıı m-blıaꝺna conaꝺ ıaꞃann a m-bı ꝺe n talmaın, ⁊ cloc a m-bı a n-uıꞃcı, ⁊ cꞃanꝺ a m-bı oꞃ uıꞃce " Loch n-Eochach makes a holly tree at the end of seven years, so that the part that is in the earth becomes iron, and the part that is in the water becomes stone, and the part that is out of the water remains wood " Cambrensis has not mentioned this wonder although he relates a story about the origin of this lake, which he says was originally a fountain, that was permitted to overflow the country, in consequence of the unnatural crimes of the inhabitants   And this too in Christian times, for he adds " Quod piscatores aquæ illius turres ecclesiasticas, quæ more patriæ arctæ sunt et altæ necnon et rotundæ, sub undis manifeste sereno tempore conspiciunt "—Topogr d 2, c 9 This story bears evident marks of a desire to brand the Irish with odious imputations ; but if we omit the accusation of unnatural crimes, and the insinuation that the event took place in Christian times, the rest of the legend occurs, nearly as it is related by Cambrensis, in that curious collection of Irish historical and bardic traditions, the Dinnseanchus

According to this Irish legend Lough Neagh is said to have broken forth in the

ii Loch n-Echach[c]; its property is: a holly tree that is placed in it for seven years, the part of it that sinks into earth will be stone, the part that remains in the water will be iron, and the part that remains above *water* will be wood

iii. The well of Loch Con[d] in Connaught; its property is, with regard to the lake that is near it, there are five feet *in difference of height* between them at all times Whether the lake swells or shrinks *the well* imitates it in each change continually

iv The well of Gabhal Liuin[e] in Oirghialla; its property is, that *human* hair upon which it is poured will become immediately grey

v

---

reign of Lugadh Sriabh n-dearg, A. D 65-73, Ogyg. p 289. See also Lynch, Cambrensis Eversus, pp. 132, 133—(*T*)

[d] *The well of Loch Con*—This well is now unknown in the vicinity of Loch Con, a lake in the barony of Tirawley, County Mayo There is nothing miraculous in this wonder, which is the ninth in O'Flaherty's list —Ogygia, p 291

Districtu Mayo foris, atque Tiraulæ in oris
Loch Canis ad ripam, spatio remeabilis æquo,
Exundante lacu, vel subsidente, scaturit
Proximus, accessu fugiens, rediensque recessu

D describes the seventh wonder Τιρρα LoϲαϽ [read Loϲα Con, the scribe wrote Ͻ for 9, the contraction for con] a Connaϲϲaib ϲiϽ moɲ a ϲhuile ꞇ ϲiϽ moɲ a ϲaρꞇ biϽ u ꞇɲaiʒϲi aϲaɲɲu Ͻo ʒɲeɲ ' The well of Loch [Con] in Connaught, whether there is a great flood or whether there is a great drought, there are always five feet *difference of height* between them.'' —(*T*)

[e] *Gabhal Luin*—Now Galloon, a parish in the barony of Dartry, in Monaghan, which county was a part of the ancient Oirghialla, or Oriel Giraldus places a well possessing the same wonderful property in Munster, and mentions another having an opposite efficacy in Ulster · "Est fons in Momonia, cujus aqua si quis abluitur statim canus efficitur. Vidi hominem cujus pars barbæ, limphis istis lota, canis incanduerat, altera parte tota in sua natura fusca manente. Est e contra fons in Ultonia, quo si quis abluitur, non canescet amplius. Hunc autem fontem feminæ frequentant, et viri caniciem vitare volentes."—Dist. 2, c. 7 On which Lynch remarks " De his fontibus id universim dico cum nec hodie nec memoria majorum fontes ejusmodi dotibus imbuti esse deprehenduntur, nullam supetere rationem cur affectiones illis a natura insitæ temporis diuturnitate evanescerent. Ac insuper addo, cum indefinite fontium loca de-

.u Τιρρα ρleιbe δlαδma, ιρι α h-αιρδι δια nορ ρeʒα no δια nορ cαιδlea neach m an αeρ ι colαδ ρleochαιδ co n-δencuρ oιρρριonn ⁊ ιυδαρτα αιcce.

uι. Τιρρα Rαcα bocħ ι Τιρ Conαιll, ιρι α αιρδe ρρι ʒac n-δuιne αcορ cι, mαδ ροcα a ραeʒul eρʒιδ anαιρο in α αιʒιδ, ⁊ ρo ʒnι connʒuρ mορ ρριρ Maδ ʒαιριc imoριρο α ρe ρορ leci ριρ δο ρhαc co ʒριαn

.uιι Τιρρα uιρce ρomblαιρ ι cαeb in Conαιnn Ιρι αιρδe in
τοραιρ

siguet, eum in non modicam errous suspi cionem venire."—Cambr Evers .p 8, comp also p. 100. It is evident, however, from the present tract, that similar tales were current among the Irish themselves, and therefore that Cambrensis did not, in this instance at least, draw wholly on his own invention In D. the well of Galloon is thus described, and stands eighth in the list of wonders Τιρρα ʒαbρα luín a n-Οιρʒιαl-lαιb lιαcαιʒ nα ρulcu cuρ a cαbαρcuρ α h-uιρce "The well of Gabai [read Gabhal] Luin, in Oirghialla, it renders grey the hair on which its watei is pouied " O'Flaherty omits this wonder.—(T)

ᶠ Sliabh Bladhma, now Sheve Bloom. The irritable well heie mentioned is the source of the River Bearbha, now the Bar-row, in the barony of Hy Regan, now Tinnahinch, in the north-west of the Queen's County It floods the lower countiy for miles in the rainy seasons, a circumstance which probably gave rise to the legend in the text In D this is the ninth wonder, and the story is told thus Τιρρα ρleιbe δlαδma δin. Do ní ρleδ-

chαδ mορ δια n-αιcceρ h-ι ó δuιne, ní coιρceαno on ρleocαδ co n-δencuρ ιο-bαιρc cuιρρ Cριρc αʒ an cιbραιδ. "The well of Sheve Bladhma then It makes a great flood when it is looked upon by a man ; the flood does not cease until the offering of the Body of Christ is made at the well" Many similar traditions re-specting wells still prevail amongst the peasantry in every part of Ireland Mr O'Donovan, in a communication to the Editor, says "To this day the Irish retain the notion that if a pure spring well, whether consecrated or not be defiled by throwing any nauseous filth into it, or washing soiled clothes in it, it will either diy up or migrate to some other locality, and many examples of such migrations are pointed out in every county in Ireland. The well of Sheve Bladhma appears to have been more deeply vengeful than any of our modern wells, since the glance of a human eye, or the touch of a human hand, was an offence which threatened inunda-tion to the neighbourhood, and could only be expiated by the sacrifice of the Mass

v The well of Sliabh Bladhma[f]: its property is, if any one gazes on it, or touches it, its sky will not cease to pour down rain until mass and sacrifice are made at it

vi. The well of Rath Both[g] in Tir-Conaill: its property to every one who seeks it is, *that* if his life is to be long it rises up against him, and salutes him with a great murmur of waves If his life is to be short it sinks down suddenly to the bottom

vii. A well of sweet water in the side of the Corann[h]; the property

itself" O'Flaherty does not mention this well in his metrical list of wonders; but Cambrensis gives the following version of it, in which, as usual, he greatly improves upon the story. "Est fons in Momonia, qui si tactus ab homine, vel etiam visus fuerit, statim tota Provincia pluviis inundabit quæ non cessabunt donec sacerdos ad hoc deputatus, qui et virgo fuerit a nativitate, tam mente quam corpore, Missæ celebratione in Capella (quæ non procul a fonte ad hoc dignoscitur esse fundata) et aquæ benedictæ, lactisque vaccæ unius coloris aspersione (barbaro satis ritu et ratione carente) fontem reconciliaverit." Top. dist. 2, c. 7, Comp. Cambr Eversus, pp 8, 9—(*T.*)

[g] *Rath-Both*, now Raphoe, in the county of Donegal. This wonder, which is not noticed by Giraldus or O Flaherty, is the tenth in D, and is thus described Tibra Ratha both a crich Conaill mad saeglac inti téid da fegad tibaig tar a bruach amach, mad tru imorro, ni tic tar a hor amach. "The well of Rath-Both, in the Connell country if the person who goes to look at it is long-lived it overflows out over its brink; but if he is withering it does not go forth over its edge" At Acha, or St. John's well, near Kilkenny, it was believed that the holy well overflowed at midnight on St. John's Eve, but no such property as that ascribed to the well in the text seems to be now remembered at Raphoe—(*T*)

[h] *The Corann*, a plain from which rises Sliabh Gamh, near Colooney, in the county of Sligo, on the side of which mountain this well is still pointed out, and the popular belief still attributes to it the property described in the text Giraldus mentions this well, but he places it erroneously on the *top* of the mountain; "Est et in Conactia *fons dulcis aquæ* in vertice montis excelsi, *et procul a mari*, qui die naturali bis undis deficiens, et toties exuberans marinas imitatur instabilitates."—Top Dist 2 c 7. From the expressions marked in italics it would seem that Giraldus had before him a copy of the Irish account of these wonders, or a translation of it. No marvellous story lost any of

topaip pini linab ⁊ tpaʒab po aipbi mapa, ⁊ ipcian o muip cena.

uiii. Capn tpacta Eotaili; noco luʒa it cithep e in tan ip lan ap in tan ip tpaiʒ, ⁊ teb muip tap na caipʒib mopaib na muip-beac impi pan can

ix. Cloc pil i loc na n-Oncon i pleib i pail Ʒlinni bo loca; ip a aipbe, bia m-buailteap i bo plepc tpi mopaibi pleochab ⁊ ʒpian iapum.

x. Ite annpo tpi h-inʒantai Tempa i mac uii m-bliaban bo tupmib

its wonders by passing through his hands, but it is evident that he copied from a native original. In D this is the eleventh wonder, and the story is told thus Tibna puil a taib in Copinb bo ní tuile ⁊ tpa-ʒab pa copmaliup in mapa "There is a well in the side of the Corann, which flows and ebbs after the similitude of the sea" A miracle similar to this has been already given amongst the wonders of Man. See above p 121.—(T)

' The strand of Eothail.—The great carn on Trawohelly strand still remains, but its miraculous property seems to be no more than this, that it is never covered by the sea "Super fluctus mirabiliter eminens," as O'Flaherty says, Ogygia. p 174 It is recorded in the account of the battle of Magh Tuireadh that this cairn was raised over Eochaidh Mac Eirc the last king of the Firbolgs who was killed on the strand of Trawohelly by the Tuatha-de-Dannan, headed by Nuadha of the silver hand, A M 2737, Ogyg part iii c 10. Keating in loc

The miraculous property of the carn of Trawohelly is spoken of in the Libellus de Matribus Sanctorum, as Colgan calls it, and which he attributes to Aengus the Culdee After enumerating the seven daughters of Dallbronach of Dal Conchobhair in the Decies of Bregia, and the long list of saints sprung from them, this document proceeds (Book of Leinster, fol. 239, b. col. 4. MS. Trin Coll. H 2 18) Ocup conb pancatap imacallaim uile na naim peo i capn Tpacta Eoraile, ⁊ co pinʒiet aentaio, ⁊ apbeptatap nech coinpepab i talam a n-oentaio na pic-pab a unim nem, ⁊ na biab a atʒabail i talmain Ocup in capnpa in pa com-paicpem co ti muip oap poe h Piacpach na tiepab taipip. Ocup apbept eppcop Mane.

Nec con pcepa oentaio ap noeb
pec bib cloen bib mep
ni aicpeba talam tino.
ni pia a anim pop nem

"And all these saints met in a synod

perty of that well is, it fills and ebbs like the sea, though it is far from the sea too.

viii The carn of the strand of Eothail[i]. It is not the less seen when the tide is full than when it is at low ebb, and notwithstanding that the tide rises over the large rocks on the beach around it to and fro

ix. A stone in Loch na n-Onchon[j], in a mountain near Glenn-da-Loch, its property is, if it be struck with a wand by way of assault, rain will ensue, and sunshine after.

x These are the three wonders of Teamhar[k], viz a youth of seven

at the Carn of Tragh Eothaile, and they made *a covenant of* union, and they said of whosoever should break that union on earth, his soul shall not reach heaven, and he shall not recover *his station* on earth And as for this carn at which we have met, the sea shall never cover it until it overflows the surface of Hy-Fiachrach And Bishop Mane said,

" Whosoever shall dissolve the union of our saints,
Whether he be degenerate, or whether he be mad,
Shall not inhabit the firm earth,
His soul shall not reach to heaven "

See also the copy of the same tract preserved in the Book of Lecan, fol. 43, and O'Donovan's Hy-Fiachrach, p 117, note ᶜ The carn of Trawohelly is the eighth in O'Flaherty's metrical list of wonders, it is not mentioned in D —(*T*)

ʲ *Loch na n-Onchon,* i e. the Lake of Otters. This is the name of a lake in the hills near Glandaloch, perhaps the same which is now called Loch-na-hanagan There is a stone called the Deer-stone in the Glen itself, on the south side of the lower lake,

of which some similar tales are told; but the original traditions are now so much corrupted by the ignorance of the guides and the folly of visitors to the lakes, that no dependence can be placed on them, as representing ancient thought —(*T*)

ᵏ *Teamhar* —The three wonders of Tara are given separately in D The first is there the nineteenth wonder, and is thus described Mac uii m-bliaoan po bui a Ceampaig, ┐ po cuipim clano pon aimpip pin. "A boy of seven years *old* that was at Tara, and begot children at that age."

The grave of the dwarf is the fifteenth wonder in D , and is spoken of in these words· Lige in abuic a Cempaig, cpi cpoigci innci oo cach ecup beg ┐ mop. " The grave of the dwarf at Teamhar , it is three feet *long* to every one whether great or small " The meaning is, that every one, whether a child or a full-grown man, who attempts to measure it, finds it exactly three of his own feet long O'Flaherty has thus versified this wonder.

τυρμιο cloinne; ⁊ liʒe in abuic .u τραιʒιο do ʒaċ ouine ann cia beoir beca no mora; ⁊ in lia Ƒail i in cloc no ʒerreo ƒa caċ riʒ ap ƒaemƒao ƒlaτa Tempac

χι Linn muilino ƒil i Cluain Ƒerτa Molua; iri a h-airoe na oaine no oor ƒoτραιc inτi oτa braiʒiτ na linne oo ʒnic lumu oib Nemincoiτ eċ imorro, oτa rin ruar

χιι Aonacul Mic Rurταιnʒ i Ruireċ i Cailli Ƒollomain i Mioi

---

which stands first in his list.—Ogygia, pp 290

'Temoria, nam tumulum lapis obtegit, in quo
Vir puer aut infans tres, et non amplius, æquat
Quisque pedes longo, numerum discrimine nullo
Multipheat minutve pedum proportio dispar."

See also Petrie on Tara Hill, p. 156 —(T)

Another form of this idea may be termed the Procrustean; where a grave (Giraldus. Itin. Camb ii. cap 3, Higden, p 189, where read *se conformem* for *deconformem*), or a bed (Sir J. Ware, Ant Ilib. ed Harris, p 63), fits the length of whosoever lies down in it Such was the grave upon Crugmawr or Pen Tychryd Mawr, in the vale of Aeron, in Cardigan

'Which to the form of every
Visitor conforms itself,
Where if armour be left
Entire at nightfall
Certainly at daybreak
You shall find it broken."—*Higd*

The tychryd mawr, great house of shuddering, was the palace of the chief of the giants; and it is well if no atrocity was connected herewith. See as above cited, and Hynavion Cymreig, pp 155, 156

Compare the Ergengl Wonder, No. xi pp 118, 119, above.—(H.)

The Lia Fail is the seventeenth wonder in D. and is thus described Cloch ƒil a Tempaiʒ i lia ƒail, no ʒeirio ƒo coraib caċ oin no ʒabao riʒe n-Erino "There is a stone at Tamhar, i e Lia Fail, which used to roai under the feet of every one that assumed the kingdom of Eri." For an account of this stone see Ware's Antiquities by Harris. pp. 10, 124, and Petrie on Tara Hill, p 138, where the question is discussed whether this famous stone was ever removed from Tara. and whether it is the same which now forms the seat of the ancient coronation chair in Westminster Abbey, as is generally supposed —(T)

' *Cluain-feairta Molua*, now Clonfertmulloe, an old grave-yard, giving name to a parish dedicated to St Molua, at the foot of Slabh Bladhma, in the barony of Upper Ossory, Queen's County "In confinio Lageniensium et Muimoniensium, inter regiones Osraigi et Hele et Laiges," are the words in which the situation of the ancient Church is described in the life of St.

seven years of age begetting children; and the grave of the dwarf, which *measured* five feet for every one, whether small or large; and the Lia Fail, i e. the stone which shouted under every king whom it recognised in the sovereignty of Teamhar

xi There is a mill-pond at Cluain-fearta Molua[l]; its property is, the people who bathe in it at the neck[m] of the pond become lepers· it injures not *if entered* in any other place

xii. The grave of Mac Rustaing at Rus-Ech[n], in Cailli Follamhain,

Molua, and they apply exactly to the site of the present grave-yard Fleming, Collect. p. 374 Ussher, Primord p 943 Lanigan, vol ii p 206 St Molua's day was the 4th of August No trace of the pond. or tradition of its wonderful property, is now to be found in the parish

In D. this is the eighteenth miracle, and is described thus· Ατα lino muilino a Cluain-Pheanta Molua, ⁊ clamaiʒ na oaine τiaʒaio innci acc manaiʒ aenτa-oaca Molua Αcα inao aile irin lino ceona, oa τnaiʒ oeʒ acanpu . . . oenann puoain mao ann rin τiaʒain innci. "There is a millpond at Cluain Fearta-Molua, and the people that bathe in it become lepers, except the monks in communion with Molua There is another place in the same pond, twelve feet distant . . . . and it doth no harm if it is at this place it is entered." The monks evidently put out this story to secure their own bathing-place from public intrusion. —(*T.*)

[m] *Neck.*—The word bnaiʒc denotes the sluice or narrow canal through which the water flows from the linn or pond upon the wheel of the mill Mr O'Donovan informs me that these words are still so used in the County Kilkenny and probably in most other parts of Ireland.—(*T*)

[n] *Rus-Ech.*—The old church of Roseach, now Russagh, is still remaining, near the village of Street, in the north of the county of Westmeath, adjoining the County of Longford, but the grave of Mac Rustaing is no longer pointed out or remembered Mac Rustaing was the maternal brother of St Coemain Brec, and was probably an ecclesiastic, as he is spoken of as one of the eight distinguished scholars of Armagh, about the year 740. See Mac Conglinne's Vision, Leabhar Breac, p. 219. St Coeman Brec, Abbot of Roseach, died 14th September, A. D 615 (Ussher, Primord Ind. Chron), on which day he is mentioned in the Felire of Ængus. At the end of the month of September, in the MS. of the Felire preserved in the Leabhar Breac, there is the following account of the grave of Mac Rustaing Coeman δnecc Mac Nirre .i. o Rorr

Midi ní cumaing ben a fegad cen maidm a delma esti, no ard-gaire m-baet

.xiii Macrad o Chailli Fochlad .i. di ingin, Crebra ⁊ Lessa a n-anmann; ro labraidset a m-brionnaib a maithrec, ⁊ ised asbertsat, tair a naeb Patraic ⁊ slanaig sin

xiv

each hi Caille Folamain hi Mide ata side, ocus Mac Rustaing mar oen fris, ⁊ cland oen mathar eat a n-dis No hi Ross liac ata Coeman Brecc, ut Oengus dicunt [sic], sed nescio ubi est Rossliacc Adnocul din Mic Rustaing i Ross each hi Mide Ni chumaing nach bén a feagad cen maidm a delma esti no cen ardgaire boeth iarum, ut dixit,

Lige Mic Rustaing raide,
Hi Rosseach cen imnaire,
Mat chi cech ben baigid,
Braigid ⁊ bangairid
Critan ainm Mic Rustaing rain,
Garbdaire ainm Mic Samain,
Aindiairr ar Mac Conglinde,
Mor do laidib do rinde

"Coeman Brecc Mac Nisse, i e at Ross Each in Caille Follamain, in Meath, he is, and Mac Rustaing along with him, and they were both the children of one mother Or it is in Ros Liag that Coeman Brecc is, ut Oengus dicunt [dicit], sed nescio ubi est Ros Liag. The grave of Mac Rustaing is in Ross-Each in Meath No woman can look at it without a sudden exclamation, or a loud frantic laugh Ut dixit,

The grave of Mac Rustaing, I say,
In Ros Each, without disgrace,
Every woman who sees shouts,
Shrieks, and loudly laughs.
Critan was the name of fair Mac Rustaing,
Garbdaire was the name of Mac Samain,
Aindiairr was Mac Conglinde,
Many were the poems he made"

Mac Rustaing's grave is the twentieth wonder in D, and is thus spoken of Aon cul mic Rusdaing noco fedann bean afegad gan gaire, no sgort. "The grave of Mac Rusdaing; no woman can look at it without a laugh or scream" —(T)

° *Caille Fochladh*, or the wood of Fochladh. See O'Donovan's Hy-Fiachrach, p 463, where the situation of this celebrated wood is ascertained The story of a voice from the wood of Fochladh is told in the Confessio of St Patrick, the Hymn of St Fiech, and all the Lives except that attributed to Probus The Confessio does not speak of the voice as coming from children, and neither do the second and fourth Lives in Colgan This was, therefore, probably the original story, but Fiech and the Tripartite Life speak of children, macraid Caille Fochlad (Fiech, n. 8), pueri in sylva Fochladensi, (Trip. i c. 30), and the other Lives add to this

in Meath, no woman has power to look at without an involuntary shriek, or a loud, foolish laugh

xiii The children of Cailli Fochladh°, viz, two daughters, Crebra and Lesra were their names, they spoke from the wombs of their mothers, and what they said was, Come, O Saint Patrick! and save us

that they were children yet unborn, "vox infantium ex uteris matrum ex regionibus Connactorum *Hoch aillilo fortaich* [which Colgan interprets, heu, accede huc ter auxilium], (Vit. 3ᵃ c 20), infantuli Hiberni maternis uteris inclusi voce clara clamantes," (Jocelin, cap. 21). The scholiast on the hymn of Fiech gives us the names of these children, telling us moreover their number and their sex he adds, that their voices were heard throughout all Ireland, and even by Pope Celestin at Rome. "Ipse Cœlestinus quando ordinabatur Patricius audiebat vocem infantium eum advocantium Infantes autem, de quibus hic sermo est, vocabantur Crebrea et Lessa, duæ filiæ Glerani filii Nenn, et hodie coluntur ut sanctæ, et ab ipso Patricio erant baptizatæ· et in ecclesia de Forcland juxta Muadium fluvium [the Moy] ad occidentem, requiescunt. Quæ autem tunc in ventre matris existentes dicebant, erant hæc. *Hibernienses omnes clamant ad te* Et hæc sæpius ab eis decantata audiebantur per Hiberniam totam vel usque ad ipsos Romanos" Jocelin (c. 59) mentions the baptism of the daughters of Gleran, and tells us that

they were the same who had called St Patrick out of their mother's womb, and that they afterwards became saints, but he does not give their names The Tripartite Life gives us their names, and although, in the place already cited, the author had called them pueri, and in another place (ii. c. 77) he speaks of *multos* infantes in utero matrum existentes, yet here (ii. c 86), he says: "Ibi vir sanctus baptizavit, Deoque consecravit duas celebratæ sanctitatis virgines Crebream et Lassaram, Gleranno viro nobili Cuminei filio natas Hæ sunt quæ inclusæ in utero materno, in regione de Caille-Fochladh, referuntur dudum ante in persona [i e in the name of, or on behalf of,] infantium Hiberniæ clamasse ad S. Patricium, dum esset in insulis maris Tyrrheni, efflagitando ut seposita mora ad Hibernos convertendos acceleraret earumque sacræ exuviæ ut patronarum loci, in summa veneratione in ecclesia de Killfhorclann juxta Muadium versus occidentem asservantur" See Ussher, Prim. p 832. The children of Caille Fochladh are not mentioned among the wonders of Ireland in D., or by O'Flaherty.—(*T*)

ʃiu Sil in Ƒaelcon ı n-Oʃʃaıʒıḃ aτa.   Aıʃoı ınʒnao acu
Ḋelḃaıτ ıaτ ı conaıḃ alτaıo, ⁊ τıaʒaıτ ıaτ ı conʃecτaıḃ, ⁊ oıa
maʃḃτaʃ ıaτ ⁊ ƒeoıl ına m-belaıḃ ıʃ amlaıo bıo na cuıʃp aʃ a
τıaʒaτ, ⁊ aıτnıτ oıa muınτeʃaıḃ naʃ ʃoʒluaıʃτeʃ na cuıʃp, aıʃ oıa
n-ʒluaıʃτeʃ nı τıcʃaoʃum cucu ʃempeʃ

ʃıu Τoʃann moʃ oo τaıoecτ ı n-aımʃıʃ Ḋonncaıo mıc Ḋomnaıll
                                                    mıc

ᵖ *Descendants of the wolf.*—This story is
given much more fully in D, where it
stands as the twenty-second wonder —
Aτaıτ apoıle oaıne a n-Eıʃıno ı ʃıl
Laıʒne Ƒaelaıo a n-Oʃʃaıʒe, τıaʒaıo a
ʃıcṫaıḃ mac τıʃe, ın τan ıʃ aıl leo, ⁊
maʃḃaıo na h-ınoıle ʃo beʃ na mac
τıʃe, ⁊ ʃaʒḃaıo a cuʃpu ʃeın, ın τan
τıaʒaıo aʃ na conʃachτaıḃ aıchnıʒıo oıa
muınτeʃaıḃ can a coʃpu oo cumʃeuʒuo,
aʃ oıa cumʃcaıoτeʃ nı ʃeʃʃao τeachτ
τaʃıʃ aʃ na coʃpaıḃ , ⁊ oıa cʃechτ-
naıʒτeʃ amuıch beıo na cʃecτa ʃın na
coʃpaıḃ anoʃna τıʒaıḃ ⁊ bıʒ ın ʃeoıl
oeaʃʒ caıτaıo amuıch ana ʃıaclaıḃ
" There are certain people in Eri, viz.
the race of Laighne Faelaidh, in Ossory,
they pass into the forms of wolves whenever they please, and kill cattle according
to the custom of wolves, and they quit
their own bodies, when they go forth in
the wolf-forms, they charge their friends
not to remove their bodies for if they are
moved they will not be able to come
again into their bodies , and if they are
wounded while abroad, the same wounds
will be on their bodies in their houses;
and the raw flesh devoured while abroad

will be in their teeth " Giraldus Cambrensis tells a story of two wolves who had
been a man and woman of the Ossorians,
but were transformed into wolves every
seven years, in virtue of a curse imposed
on their race by Saint Naal or Natalis,
abbot of Cill-na-managh, or Kilmanagh,
in the Co Kilkenny, who flourished in
the sixth century   They had been banished to Meath, where they met a priest
in a wood, a short time before Earl John
came to Ireland in the reign of Henry II ,
and retaining, it seems, the use of language they foretold the conquest of Ireland by the English   The following is a
part of what the wolf said to the priest
" De quodam hominum genere sumus
Ossyriensium, vnde quolibet septennio
per imprecationem sancti cuiusdam Natalis scilicet Abbatis, duo, videlicet, mas
et fœmina, tam à formis, quam finibus
exulare coguntur.   Formam enim huma-
nam prorsus exuentes induunt lupinam.
Completo vero septennii spacio, si forte
superstites fuerint, aliis duobus ipsorum
loco simili conditione subrogatis, ad pri-
tinam redeunt tam patriam quam natu-
ram.' —*Top. Dist.* 2, c 19

xiv The descendants of the wolf[p] are in Ossory. They have a wonderful property They transform themselves into wolves, and go forth in the form of wolves, and if they happen to be killed with flesh in their mouths, it is in the same condition that the bodies out of which they have come will be found; and they command their families not to remove their bodies, because if they were moved, they could never come into them *again*

xv. Great thunder happened in the time of Donogh[q], son of Donall,

Cambrensis, whose credulity was unbounded, gave full credit to this strange tale Not so Fynes Moryson, who holds it up to ridicule, but it appears from what he says, that the tale was currently believed in his time " It is rediculous," (he says), " which some Irish (who will be believed as men of credit) report of men in these parts [Upper Ossory and Ormond] yeerely turned into wolves, except the aboundance of melancholy humour transports them to imagine that they are so transformed "—*Itin* p iii., c 5, p. 157 —(*T.*) For the legends and facts concerning this strange and widely-diffused class of demoniacs or melancholics, consult Herodotus, iv 105, Pliny, viii 22, Olaus Magnus, de Gent Septentr lib xviii. cap 45–7, Gervas Tilbur Otia Imper i. c 15, Marie de France, Lai du Bisclaveret, i. p 178, William and the Werwolf, Lond, 1832, P. Lancre Tableau, etc des Mauvais Anges, pp 259, 309, Hakewill s Apologie, i cap i s. 6, Boguet Discours des Sorciers, cap liii, Verstegan's Restitution, p 237, Life of Nathaniel Pearce,

i pp 287-9, ii p 340 —(*H*)

q Donogh —Donogh, son of Donall, son of Murrough, was king of Ireland from A. D 770 to 797, according to O'Flaherty's chronology, Ogyg, p 433 The Four Masters have placed the great storm, here counted as one of the wonders of Ireland, under the year 799, their words are Ꞇꞔꞃꞁꞌ ᵹꞗeꞇ ꞗꞃꞁ, ꞇꞑꞁꞌeꞗ ꞇemꞩꞇꞃeꞁꞌ ꞁꞃꞃꞁ ꞇꞩ ꞑꞃꞁꞌ ꞗeꞁꞁ Ᵽꞇꞃꞃꞁꞌꞃe ꞁꞗ ꞗꞁꞑꞃꞁꞌ ꞃꞩ, ꞃꞩ ꞁꞃ mꞃꞃꞗꞗꞃꞑ ꞗeꞁꞃꞁeꞗꞗꞗ ꞗꞃ mꞁꞁe ꞗꞁ eꞁꞁꞃ Ꞇꞩꞃꞗꞃꞗꞃꞁꞃꞁꞗ, ꞁꞗ ꞗꞩ ꞑꞃꞁꞗ ꞃꞁ mꞃꞁꞃꞁ ꞩꞁꞇeꞁ Ᵽꞁꞇꞃe ꞁ ꞇꞃꞁ ꞁꞃꞗꞩꞃꞁꞗ. "A violent wind, thunder, and lightning occurred this year on the day before the feast of Patrick, so that a thousand and ten men were killed in the territory of Corco Bhaiscin, and the sea divided the island of Fitae into three parts." The island of Fithi is a small island, now called Mutton Island, on the coast of the county of Clare, opposite Kilmurry Ibrickin The two other parts of the original island are still to be seen near it, they are insignificant islets, or rather lofty masses of rock close to Mut-

mic Mupchaid pig Epenn, gup mapb xup ap mili i epic Copco
baipcind 7 co po pann innpi pici i epi

χιιι. Cpi h-ingunca la Cluain mic noip   Pep cen cend ppi pe
pecc m-bliadan.   Ince bucuc a ainm i Maelcamain   In dall no
ced pon Sinaind co cabpad lep epcung gac ladpa lam 7 cop do.   In
c-adnacul po clap i Cluain beup 7 ni pepp 7 ni clopp do adnacul
ann, 7 po ppic pep mop-ulcac ind, 7 bpaena pola depge caipip,
bappac uip-beici do peuabaib cengal ime.   Cuig cpaigi deg ina
pod, 7 .xxx. cpoiged do calam uapu

.χιιι. Loc Laig i epic Umaill la Connacco do elud piap co
muip nad bai de acc a lacpach

χιιιι.

ton Island   Mr O'Donovan remarks, in
a communication to the Editor, that the
barony of Ibrickin was originally a part
of Corco-Bhaiscin, before the Ui Bracain,
or Mac Gormans, settled in that country
This fact appears from the position of
Mutton Island, which is here, and by the
Four Masters, said to be in Corco-Bhaiscin, and also from the Life of St Senan,
who was the patron of the Corco-Bhaiscin
race —(T.)

ʳ *Clonmacnois.*—The first of these three
wonders is the twenty-third wonder of
Ireland in D   Ro bai duine a Cluain-
mic-noip, iap ceacc a cind de cpe
cpeblaid, 7 po bai uii m-bliadna 'na
beacaig iap pin, cpe na meide, no cuin-
gead biad 7 no caiched   " There was
a man at Clonmacnois, after his head
came off through disease, and he was
seven years afterwards living, through
his trunk he called for food and con-
sumed it " The same story is told by

Tighernach ad an 549, and by Keating
under the reign of Tuathal Maelgarbh
(A D 533–544), who tells us that this
headless wonder lived in that state for
four years among the monks of Clonmacnois, his head having dropped off at the
fair of Tailten, in consequence of his
having sworn falsely on the relic called
the hand of St Kieran   This story is
certainly of great antiquity, and was once
extensively believed, it probably originated in a figurative mode of describing
a loss of memory or reason, or some ecclesiastical or spiritual defect   In a note at
August 4, in the Felire of Aengus, a story
is told of St Molua, who went into a
church with St Comgall, and, to their
astonishment, every one in the church,
including Comgall and Molua themselves,
appeared headless   The following explanation of this appearance is then given
Ip de aca po an Comgall .i. m-anmch-
apapu acbach, 7 a cupa cen cheand, 7

Donall, son of Murrough, king of Ireland, which killed one thousand and ten persons in the territory of Corco Baiscinn, and divided Inis-Fithi into three parts.

xvi. Three wonders at Clonmacnois[r] A man without a head during the space of seven years. Inte Bucuc[s] was his name, i e Maltamain The blind man who used to dive into the Shannon and bring forth an eel in each of the forks of his hands and feet The grave[t] which was dug in Cluain, and it was not known or heard that there was an interment there, and there was a great-bearded man found in it, covered with drops of red blood, and a covering of green birch brooms about him. Fifteen feet long was he, and there were thirty feet of earth over him

xvii. Loch Laigh[u], in the territory of Umaile, in Connaght, ran off into the sea, so that nothing of it remained but its place.

XVIII

a ᴄaᴢhaiᴘ cen chino, aᴨ iᴘ colano cen cheno ᴅuine cen anmcaᴘaiᴄ "The reason of this," said Comgall, "is the death of my spiritual director, and I am without a head, and ye are without heads, because a man without a spiritual director is a man without a head" Comgall then appoints Molua his confessor, and immediately the congregation appears to him with heads as usual —(T)

[s] *Inte Bucuc* —Keating calls him Abacuc, the word *inte* signifies " the man," or " the individual," and is a title used much as we now use "Mr ," or as Dominus was used to monks and the clergy. —(T)

[t] *The grave.*—This and the foregoing wonder are omitted in D The story of the blind fisherman is not told elsewhere,

as far as the Editor knows. The legend of the giant's grave appears to be connected with the adventure of the poet Mac Caisi, which will be found in the note, p 210 —(T.)

[u] *Loch Laigh*, a lake in the territory of Umhaile, the ancient country of the O'Malleys, anglicised " the Owles," a district comprising the barony of Murrisk (called umall uaᴄᴄᴘac, or the upper), and the barony of Burrishoole (called umall ioᴄᴄᴘac, the lower), in the county of Mayo See O'Donovan's Hy-Fiachrach, p 499, and the map The disappearance of Loch Laigh is recorded by the Four Masters at the year 848 Loc Laoiᵹ hi epic Umaill la Connacᴄ ᴅo eluᴅ " Loch Laoigh, in the territory of Umhaill, in Connaught ran off," [or was evaporated].—(T)

xviii Loc Leibind do ruud i fuil fri is de cond rala i rair-tib cro amail scamu cet bruiti

xix. Fros fola do fertain i n-aimsir Aeda mic Neill, co frit a rairte cro fola fors ia muigib in Cianacht oc Dumu in Dessa

xx. In mac becc do labrad i Craeb Laisre dia mis iar na gein coro turica scela imda.

xxi In araili lo ro bui in fili Mac Coisi ic con Boinn como fac-caba

v *Loch Leibhinn*, now Loch Leane, about a mile from Fore, in the north-east of the county of Westmeath The miraculous change of its waters into blood is recorded by the Four Masters at the year 864 Loch Lephind do ruad hí fuil, a tairla cac com bo rairte cro amail scama a imeachtair "Loch Lephinn was converted into blood, so that it appeared as sods of gore, like entrails, all round its edge" Dermot, son of Aodh Slaine, king of Meath, and afterwards (A D 658, Ogyg p 43), in conjunction with Blathmac, king of Ireland, had his residence in an island on this lake, in the time of St. Fechin of Fore Vit S Fechini, c. 23 Colgan, ad 20 Jan p 135—(*T*)

w *Dumha Dessa*, i e the monumental mound or tumulus of Dess, the exact site of which has not been ascertained, but Mr. O'Donovan thinks it is probably situated in Cianachta Breagh, near Duleek, in the county Meath The bloody shower is thus described by the Four Masters at the year 875 Gaeth mor, teinteach, ⁊ toirneach i n-Erind a bliadain si, ⁊ ro fearadh fros fola iarum, gun bo for-feil rairte cro ⁊ fola forsna maighib i Cianachta oc Dumhaindessa "A great wind, lightnings, and thunder, in Ireland this year, and there fell a shower of blood afterwards, and particles of blood and gore were found on the fields in Ciannachta, at Dumhan Dessa"—(*T*.)

x *Craebh Laisre*, i e Arbor Lassaræ, the tree of St Lasair, the name of a monastery near Clonmacnois, of which St Airmeadhach (Ermedus or Hermetius), who died A D 681, was the founder and patron O'Clery's Calend at 1st Jan. Colgan, Trias Thaum, p 172, n 45 Four Masters, at the years 681 and 882 The Annals of Clonmacnois (Mageoghegan's transl.), record the birth of the wonderful child at the year 870, in these words "There was a child borne at Crewelasragh, near Clonvicknose, this year, who was heard to call upon God by distinct words, saying *Good God* in Irish, being but of the age of two months" This event is also recorded in the Annals of Ulster, at the year 883, and by the Four

xviii Loch Leibinn' changed into blood during nine days, so that it became sods of blood like unto parboiled entrails

xix A shower of blood was shed in the time of Hugh, son of Niall, so that sods of blood were found about Cianacht, at Dumha Dessa[w]

xx. The infant boy who spoke at Craebh Lasre[x] in a month after his birth, and who disclosed many tidings

xxi. On a certain day the poet Mac Coisi[y] was at the Boyne, where

Masters at 882 Mac occ do la braocc Craoibh Laippe dia da miop iap na genem. "A young boy spoke at Craoibh Laisre within two months after his birth" —(T)

[y]*Mac Coisi*—This was probably intended for the Erard or Urard Mac Coisi, who was chief poet to Ferghal O'Rourke, king of Connaught, and died at Clonmacnois, in the year 983, according to Mageoghegan's Annals, or in 990, according to Tighernach. There was another poet named Erard Mac Coisi, who died in 1023, according to the Annals of the Four Masters, and was chief poet to king Maelseachlainn (or Malachy) II See O'Reilly's Writers, ad ann 990 and 1023 This is the 24th wonder in D, and is thus given Ro bai in file Map Coipi la ann pop bru na doinde, co pucaib na h-éla pop doino condibnaig h-én dib, in tan do pucaib appeau po bai ann bean, cop i appaig in filio oi cio pobich ann puo; a n-galap tpom ap pí do baoup, 7 ba doig le muintep do cuadup ég copium tucpat demna ipin pictpa. Ruc in filio

leip h-i 7 chug da muintip pein iap pin. "The poet Mac Coisi was once on the bank of the Boyne, when he saw the swans on the Boyne, he shot one of them, and when he took it up he found that it was a woman The poet asked her wherefore she was there. I was in grievous sickness, said she, and it was supposed by my people that I died, but demons put me into this shape. The poet took her with him, and restored her to her own people afterwards" Stories of this kind, in which the agents are supposed to be the fairies, are common to this day in every part of Ireland. A full and very particular account of Mac Coisi s adventure is to be found in a legend transcribed by Mr Eugene Curry, from a MS in the possession of Mr. John Kennedy, of Dublin. The story is too long for insertion here, but it differs very much from that given in the text, if indeed it be not a different adventure of the same poet, it places the event in the reign of Congalach, son of Maelmithigh (see n [a], p 211) Mac Coisi was on the bank of Loch Lebhinn (now Loch Leane,

caba in eltai n-eala co tarlaicc cloic doib, co ro ben dar sceit eala dib, sethir dia gabail lasodain, ⁊ do cer do co ro ba ben, ⁊ coma soacht scela uaidi cid do rala di, ⁊ can imus luaidi; ⁊ adfedsi, do i n-galar ba, olsi, ⁊ do cer do muinntir co n-erbalus, ⁊ ised araidi is deamna rom aircellsat leo; ⁊ ros taodban in fili dia muintir

xxii Da topur filed i n-Airtheraib o Ard Maca sair; marb fo cetoir in tí blaises in dala nai. Dia sillter umorro fo tri for sin topur n-aili atraig con baidi in ti na n-deca, conad air nach lamaid daene a tadall act mines tegmad troich.

xxxiii. Congalac mac Mailmithig bai in aenac Taillten in araili lo, co faccaid in loing iar san aeor, co tarlaic aen dib gai i n-diaid brattain, tarrarair in gae i fiadnaisi in aenaig, co tainic duine ar in luing ina diaid, in tan ro gab a inn anuas is ann rogab in

near Fore, Co. Westmeath), when he saw a beautiful woman, of great size, "beyond that of the women of the time," dressed in green, sitting alone, and weeping bitterly. He approached her, and she told him that her husband had that day been killed at Sidh Chodail, and was buried at Clonmacnois. Mac Coisi mentioned this to king Congalach, who set out to Clonmacnois to test the truth of the story The clergy there could give no account of it; but a monk died that night, and on digging his grave they found fresh blood and leaves, and at length, buried very deep, with his face down, the corpse of a giant twenty-five feet in height They put the body down again, and the next day, on opening the grave, which to all appearance was as they had left it, the corpse was not to be found This legend bears a curious resemblance to some circumstances in Sir Walter Scott's beautiful fiction of the White Lady of Avenel.—(*T*)

[z] *Airthera*.—The district now called Orior, regio orientalium, containing two baronies of the Co. Armagh. The wells here spoken of are now forgotten, and have lost their terrors This is the fourteenth wonder in D., and is somewhat differently described, thus Atait da tibraid a n-Oirrtearaib i o Ard Maca soir, in tí ibeas uisci in dara tibrad bid tru, ⁊ bid saeglach, in ti ibeas araile. ⁊ ni fear nechtar dib sec a ceile, conad aire sin na lamar uisce nectair dib d'ol. "There are two wells in Oirthear, viz, east of Ardmacha, the person that drinks the water of one of the wells will

where he perceived a flock of swans, whereupon he threw a stone at them, and it struck one of the swans on the wing. He quickly ran to catch it, and perceived that it was a woman. He inquired tidings from her, and what had happened unto her, and what it was that sent her thus forth. And she answered him. "In sickness I was," said she, "and it appeared to my friends that I died, but really it was demons that spirited me away with them." And the poet restored her to her people.

xxii. There are two wells in Airthera[z], to the eastward of Ardmacha. He who tastes of the one of them is immediately dead. If the other well is gazed upon three times, it immediately swells, and drowns the person who so gazes. Hence it is that people dare not touch them, except wretches [i. e. *the desperate*] alone.

xxiii. Congalach[a], son of Mailmithigh, was at the fair of Taillten on a certain day, and he perceived a ship in the air. He saw one of them [*the crew*] cast a dart at a salmon. The dart fell down in the presence of the fair, and a man came out of the ship after it. When his head came down it was caught by a man from below.

Upon

be poor, and the person that drinks the other will be rich, and no one knows one of them from the other, and therefore no person dares drink the water of either of them."—(*T.*)

[a] *Congalach.*—He was king of Ireland from A. D. 944 to 956, in which year he was killed by the Danes.—Ogyg. p. 435. The fair, or rather public sports of Taill-tenn, now Telltown, near Navan, in the county of Meath, were celebrated, and continued to be frequented by all ranks, until the reign of Roderic O'Conor, who died A. D. 1198. This unmeaning story is the

twenty-fifth wonder in D, and is thus related ꞯai Conʒalach mac Mailmi-chiʒ co fopmna feap n-Epeano uime la ann a n-aenach, co facaoap in luinʒ apanaep co tapplaiʒ fean aipoe, .i. appin luinʒ, ʒablach a n-oeaʒaiʒ bpaoain, co tappla ann pin n-oipeuctup in piʒ. "Congalach, son of Mailmithigh, with the greater part of the men of Eri around him there, was at the fair, when they saw a ship in the air, and a man out of it, i e, out of the ship, cast a fork against a salmon. There happened to be there an assembly of the king."—(*T*)

in feṙ aṁiṙ.   Co n-veḃeṙc in feṙ anuaṙ, acacaṙ icom baḃuv aṙ
ṙe   Lec uaic vo aṙ Conȝalac, ⁊ lecaiṙ ṙuaṙ ⁊ ceiv uaiviḃ foṙ
ṙnam iaṙcain

ꞃꞃiu Aṙaili ailiciṙ vo Ȝaivelaiḃ vo ṙala vo Coṙṙmiṙ Maṙcain ic ciaccain o Roiin, como ṙacca a macaiṙ ic fovail loma ⁊
ṙeola vo boccaiḃ in coimvev, co call uaivi ṙoṙcle in muivi i m-boi
in loiṙ, ⁊ ṙo bai ica iaṙṙaiv ina ṙiavnaiṙi, ⁊ ni vecaiv in macaiṙ
innonn eceṙ acc a Roṙ ailiciṙ vo ṙiȝni a fovail, ⁊ aṙ onoiṙ Maṙcain vo ṙiȝne, ⁊ ṙi Cainciȝeṙn macaiṙ hui Danȝail mic baecamnaṙ
vo ṙiȝne in fovail, ⁊ ṙo caiṙṙen via macaiṙ in ṙaiṙcle iaṙ m-blia-
vain iaṙ coivecc anall vo, ⁊ cuc ṙi aicni ṙaiṙi, ⁊ ba cuimṙi via
muivi ṙen, coniv ve ṙin aṙ folluṙ ȝac fovail vo ȝniceṙ a n-uaim
Maṙcain co n-ȝeb ȝṙeim i Coṙṙmiṙ Maṙcain.

ꞃꞃu. In lanamain beo ṙṙi Cluain iṙaiṙv anaiṙ   baḃlu ⁊ biḃlu
a n-anmann

ꞃꞃui Cloc ṙil i cill i n-Ullcaiḃ, iṙi a h-aiṙci, via cṙeccaṙ in
cell ṙuil vei ceiṙeṙṙin eṙci cṙi cṙac ṙoimi

.ꞃꞃuii Loc Suivi Ovṙain i ṙleiḃ Ȝuaiṙe vo eluv co n-vechaiv iṙ
in Feḃail

                                                          ꞃꞃuiii

<hr />

[b] *Tours of Martin* i c Tours in France
The uaimh, or Cave of St Martin was
probably Desertmartin, in the county of
Londonderry, where the memory of St
Martin was held in great veneration   Of
Uadangal, son of Baethamhnas, mentioned
in this legend nothing is known   In the
ancient tract on the names of celebrated
Irish women, preserved in the Book of
Lecan (fol. 193–202), three women of the
name Cantighern are mentioned   One was
the wife of Fiachna, son of Baedan, king
of Ulidia, who was killed, according to the
Four Masters, A D 622   Another was

Cantighern daughter of Guaire O'Locht-
nain, and wife or mistress to Flann
O Maelsheachlain Guaire, her father, was
a lector in Clonmacnois, and died, according to the Four Masters, in 1054
The third was Cantighern, a daughter of
Cellach Cualann of Leinster   She died,
according to the Four Masters, in 728 —
(*T*)

[c] *Bablu and Biblu*—Nothing is known
of this couple beyond what is here said
The meaning probably is that they continue still alive, like the tradition about
Nero, Arthur in Avallon, &c —(*T*)

Upon which the man from above said, " I am being drowned," said
he. " Let him go." said Congalach, and he was allowed to come up,
and he went away from them, swimming in the air, afterwards.

xxiv A certain pilgrim of the Gaedhelians happened to arrive
at Torinis of Martin, on his way from Rome   There he saw his
mother distributing milk and flesh meat to the poor of the Lord
He took away from her the cover of the muidh [*vessel*] which contained the milk, and she was looking for it in his presence   And
the mother had not gone thither at all, but it was in Ros Ailither
she made her distribution *at home*.   And it was in honour of Martin
she made it   And it was Cantighern, mother of Ua Dangal, son of
Baethamhnas, that made the distribution   And he shewed the cover
of the vessel to his mother in a year after his coming home, and
she recognised it, and it fitted exactly her own muidh   So that
it is manifest from this that every distribution *of alms* that is made
in Martin's Cave is as effectual as if distributed at Torinis of
Martin[b]

xxv The couple [*man and wife*] who are alive to the east of
Clonard   Bablu and Biblu[c] are their names

xxvi There is a stone[d] in a church in Ulster whose practice
it is to shed blood three days previous to a plunder of the church

xxvii The lake of Suidhe Odhrain[e], in Sliabh Guaire, migrated
and went into the Fabhal

XXVIII

[d] *A stone.*—This is the twenty-seventh
wonder in D, where it is thus given
Ata cloc ana paile ceall a n-Ulltaib,
⁊ tig fuil ar in cloc in tan airgtear in
chill, no re na n-argain.   " There is a
stone in a certain church in Ulster, and
blood comes out of the stone when the
church is plundered, or before it is plun-

dered."—(*T*)

[e] *Suidhe Odhrain* i. e, Sessio Odiam,
now anglicised Syoran or Sceoran, is a
townland in the parish of Knockbride,
barony of Clankee, county Cavan   Sliabh
Guaire, now Slieve Gorey, is the name
still given to a mountainous district in
the same barony   The Fabhal (read Fa-

.ꝛꝛuııı Cꞃoꞃ cloıcı moꞃ baı ꞃoꞃ ꝼaıctı Slaıne ꞁ m-bꞃeȝaıb ꝺo cumȝabaıl ıꞃ ın aeoꞃ, ꞁ a combac ıꞃ ın aeoꞃ, ȝuꞃ ꞃancaꞇoꞃ a buıꞃ ꞁ a bloȝa Caıllꞇın ꞁ Cempaıȝ ꞁ ꝼınꝺabaıꞃ n-aba

ꝛꝛıꝛ. Cıꞃꞃa Maılȝobann ıllaıȝnıb; ın Dec ꝼleꞃcac a h-aınm; oꞃ abaınn Lıꝼı aꞇa; ꞃı a h-aıꞃoı ın ꝼleꞃc uınꝺꞃenꝺ cuꞃꞇaꞃ ınꞇı ꝺo nı ꝼleꞃc cuıll, ꝺı ꝼo ceꞇoıꞃ, maꝺu coll ꝼoceꞃꝺaꞃ ınꞇı ıꞃ uınꝺꞃıunn ꝺo ꞃoaıȝ eꞃꞇı.

ꝛꝛꝛ Cloıcꞇeach ꞇeneaꝺ ꝺo aıcꞃın ıc Ruꞃ Dela ꞃꞃı ꞃe .ıꝛ n-uaꞃ, ꞁ eoın ꝺuba ꝺíaıꞃımꝺe aꞃ, ꞁ aen en moꞃ eꞇuꞃꞃu, ꞁ no ꞇeȝoıꞃ

na

ball, for ꝼebal, in the Irish text,) is the name of a stream tributary to the Boyne. The emigration of this lake is thus re-corded, at the year 1054, by the Four Masters Coch Suıꝺe Oꝺꞃaın hı Sleıb Ȝuaıꞃe a eluꝺ ın ꝺeıꞃıꝺ oıꝺce ꝼeıle Mıcıl con-ꝺeacaıꝺ ıꞃ ın ꝼeabaıll, ȝuꞃ bho hıonȝnaꝺ moꞃ la cach "The lake of Suıdhre Odhraın, ın Sleıbh Guaıre, migrated on the latter part of the night of St Michael's eve, until it came into the Fabhall, which was a great wonder to all" See also the Annals of Ulster at A D. 1054 There is no lake, or tradi-tion of a lake, now in this townland — (T.)

ꝼ Slaine, now Slane, a village on the Boyne, county Meath, in the ancient dis-trict of Bregia —(T)

g Finnabhair-abha, i. e the Bright Field of the River, now Fennor, a townland giving name to a parish in the barony of Duleck, county Meath. Several places in Ireland were called Finnabhair, which

Jocelin, Vit S Patr c. 94, translates, "albus campus,' the place there spoken of, and in the Tripartite Life (part iii., c. 4), was in the diocese of Clogher; but Finnabhair Abha was evidently in Meath, as appears from its being mentioned in the text in connexion with Slane, Telltown, and Tara, and in the following passage from the Calendar of the O'Clerys, it is said to be on the River Boyne 2 Maii Neac-ꞇaın, ꝺeıꞃȝıobaıl Paꝺꞃaıc, o Cıll Uınche ı ȝ-Connaıllıb Muıꞃꞇeımne, ꞁ o ꝼıon-nabuıꞃ aba ꞃoꞃ bꞃu boınne Mac ꝺo Cıamaın ꞃıuꞃ Paꝺꞃaıc e "Mau 2 Neachtain, a disciple of St Patrick, of Cill Uinche in Conaille Muirtheimhne, and of Fionnabhair-abha, on the banks of the Boyne. He was the son of Leamhan, the sister of Patrick." In a gloss on the name of this place in the Felire of Aengus (ad 2 Mau), it is said to be ı m-bꞃea-ȝaıb. "in Bregia," so that Finnabhair-abha is completely identified with the modern Fennor in Meath. See Ordnance

xxviii. A great stone cross which was on the green of Slaine[f], in Bregia, was taken up into the air, and was shattered in the air, so that its shreds and fragments were carried to Tailten, to Tara, and to Finnabhair abha[g].

xxix The well of Maell-Gobhann[h], in Leinster. The Deach-Fleseach [*the wand transformer*] is its name Over the River Liffey it is. Its property is: the ash wand that is put into it is immediately made into a wand of hazle ; and if it be hazle that is thrown into it, it will be ash at coming out of it

xxx A belfry of fire[i] which was seen at Ross Dela, during the space of nine hours, and black birds, without number, coming out and going into it. One great bird *was* among them, and the smaller birds

Map of Meath, sheet 19 —(*T.*)

[h] *Mael-Gobhann* —This well has not been identified, and the name is now obsolete It is the twelfth wonder in D, and is thus described. Ꞇibꞃa ꝼil a ꞃleib Ꞡaiᵹen, ꝼlaꞇ cuill inꞅi, ꝼlaꞇ uinꞃeann ꞇic aiꞃꝺe; no uinnꞃeann innꞅi ⁊ ꝼlaꞇ chuill aiꞃꝺe. "There is a well in a mountain in Leinster, a rod of hazle *put* into it, comes out a rod of ash, or ash *put* in, and a rod of hazle *comes* out of it " —(*T.*)

[i] *A belfry of fire.*—Cloicꞇeac ꞇeneꝺ, i e. a steeple, or belfry of fire, a column of fire: the word cloicꞇeac is the name given to the round towers in every part of Ireland. Roꞅ Dela, the place where the miraculous tower of fire was seen, is now Ross-dalla, a townland in the parish of Durrow, near Kilbeggan, county of Westmeath. The phenomenon is thus described by the Four Masters, at the year 1054. Cloicꞇeach ꞇeneꝺ ꝺo ꝼaiꞅceꞃ-ꞃin iꞃin aeꞃ uaꞅ Roꞅ ꝺeala ꝺia ꝺomnac ꝼeile Ꞡuinᵹi ꝼꞃi ꞃe coiᵹ nuaꞃ eoin ꝺuba ꝺiaiꞃmiꝺe inꝺ ⁊ aꞅꞅ, ⁊ aon en moꞃ inꞅ meꝺon, ⁊ no ꞇeiᵹiꝺ na heoin beᵹa ꝼo aeiꞇib ꞃiꝺe an ꞇan ꞇeiccoiꞅ iꞅ in cloicꞇeach. "A belfry of fire was seen in the air, over Ross-deala, on the Sunday of the feast of St Guirgi [George] for five hours, blackbirds innumerable *passing* into and out of it, and one large bird in the middle of them, and the little birds went under his wings when they went into the belfry "

In the year 1054, the feast of St George was on Saturday, the annalist must, therefore, mean the year 1055, unless we suppose him to speak of the day after as " the Sunday of the feast of St George."—(*T*)

na h-eoin beza po clumaib in ran no cezeb ip in cloicceac, 7 can-
cacap in aenpecc uile amac 7 conup zabpac coin leo na n-inzmib
i n-aipbe, 7 no lecpec pip co calam uaibib, 7 iac maпb   Luiopec
in enlaic ap iapcain, 7 in caill pop pa n-bepibap b'elliz pocu co calam, 7 in baipbpu pop pa n-bepib in c-en mop uc po puc laip cona
ppeinaib a calinain, 7 ni pep cib imluaib

   xxxi Inip loca Cpe i epic Eili; nip lamaic ecaibe boinenba
no animannai boinenna bo mil no bo buine, 7 ni epil pecrac inbi, 7
ni cumacap a bunacul ince

   xxxii Muilenn Cilli Cepp i n-Oppaizib, ni meileab i n-bom-
nac acc na n-oezeb, 7 ni meil nac [pora] i n-zaibi, 7 ni lamaic mna
реacc inb

   .xxxiii Lacain linbi Senbocо Colmain , cia bopapcap in im-
                                                                pope

i *Loch Cre*.—This lake is now dried up,
but the island remains, surrounded by a
bog, and contains the ruins of a church,
which still exhibit a beautiful specimen
of the architecture of the eleventh century The bog is now called, from the
island, Moin na h-inpe, "the Bog of the
Island," and the name is anglicised Mona-
hinsha or Monainsha It is situated in a
townland of the same name, in the parish
of Corbally, barony of Ikerrin, which was
formerly a part of the district of Ele, in the
Co Tipperary, about two miles S E of the
town of Roscrea The church is figured in
Ledwich's Antiquities of Ireland, p 115
(2nd edit), and appears to have been dedicated to St Helan, or Hilary, see the
Calendar of O'Clery, at Sept 7 The
story of the island in which no female
could live is as old as the time of Giraldus

Cambrensis, who mentions also another
island in the same lake called, Insula Viventium (inip na m-beo), in which no
man could die but in the text both pro-
perties appear to be attributed to the
same island " Est lacus" (he says) "in
Momonia Boreali, duas continens insulas,
unam majorem et alteram minorem Major
ecclesiam habet antiquæ religionis Minor
vero capellam cui pauci cœlibes quos Cœ-
licolas vel Cohdeos vocant devote deser-
viunt In majorem nunquam fœmina vel
fœminei sexus aliquod animal intrare potuit, quin statim moritur Probatum
est hoc multoties per canes et catos, alia-
que sexus illius animalia, quæ periculi
causa frequenter advecta statim occubue-
runt, &c In minori vero insula
nemo unquam mortuus fuit, vel morte
naturali mori potuit Unde et *Viventium*

birds used to nestle in his feathers when they went into the belfry
And they all came out together.   And they took up dogs with them
in their talons, and they let them drop down to earth and they dead.
The birds flew away from that place afterwards, and the wood upon
which they perched bent under them to the ground.   And the oak
upon which the said great bird perched was carried by him by the
roots out of the earth, and where they went to is not known.

xxxi The island of Loch Cre', in the territory of Eile.   No
female bird, or female animal, whether beast or man, dare enter
upon it.   And no sinner can die on it, and no power can bury him
on it.

xxxii. The mill of Cille Cess[k] in Osraighibh.   It will not grind
on the Lord's day, except for guests   And it will not grind even
a handfull that has been stolen.   And women dare not come into it.

xxxiii. The ducks of the pond of Seanboth of Colman[l]   Though
they

Insula vocatur."—Dist. 2. e. 4. From the mention of Culdees in the above passage, Ledwich has taken occasion to connect with Monaincha some of the most absurd of his speculations See Lanigan Eccl. Hist vol iv, p 290 —(*T.*)

[k] *Cill Cess.*—This place has been identified by Mr. O'Donovan, who proves that it is the same which is now anglicised Kilkeas, and still called in Irish Cill Céire by the neighbours. It is a parish in the diocese of Ossory, barony of Knocktopher, in the county of Kilkenny. The well is spoken of by Giraldus, who calls it the well of St. Lucherinus. "Apud Ossyriam est molendinum Sancti Lucherini abbatis, quod diebus Dominicis nihil, de furto vero vel rapina nunquam molit."

Dist. 2, e 51. But the peculiarity of excluding women is ascribed by Cambrensis to the mill of St. Fechin, at Fore, in Westmeath Ibid. c 52 The word ꝼoꞇu inserted between brackets in the text, is added by a later hand, and signifies a handful. This is the twenty-first wonder in D, and is thus described· Muilleann Chille Ceire a n-Orraigib nocu meleano oe oomnaig aꞇꞇ cuiꞇ na n-aigeao, ⁊ ní meleann apbup gaioe oo gnep. "The mill of Cill Ceise in Ossory, it does not grind on the Lord's day except the share of the guests, and it will not grind stolen corn at any time" —(*T.*)

[l] *Seanboth of Colman.*—A church dedicated to St. Colman, which Mr. O'Dono-

pořc aıoci maɼaen la h-uıɼce na lınoı ı caıɼı ꝼoɼ cenıo cıa no
loıɼcoıɼ ꝼeoa ın calman ꝼon coıɼı ɼın nı h-auɼcoıcıɜ, ⁊ nı ceɜ ın
uıɼce.

    ꝛꝛꝛıu Nı aıcɼebaıc ono, loıɼcıno no nacɼaca ı n-Eɼınn uılı,
⁊ cıa co beɼcaɼ a h-ınaoaıb eılı ıncı aɼlaıo ꝼo cecoıɼ, ⁊ ıɼeo ɼon
ɼo oeɼbao, acc luc ꝼael ⁊ ɼınnac nı baı ⁊ nı bıa nac n-anna [n-an-
manna] auɼcóıcech ıncı ⁊ ıɼ meɼaıɼ aɼ ceɼ ⁊ aɼ ꝼuacc.   Muıɼ
caıɼɼɼı .uıı m-blıaona ɼe m-bɼach   Fınıc   Amen   Fınıc

                                                       III.

i n-uıɼce ꝼoɼ cenıo cıa ɼo loıɼccheu
ꝼeoa ın oomaın ꝼon coıɼe ní chꝼıɜ ın
uɼce co caɼcaɼ ıaeɼɼom aɼɼ ıɼın lıno
cꝼonaı " Colman O'Fıachrach, i. e. at
Senbotha Fola, ın Hy-Cennselaıgh, ıt ıs
ın hıs church are the ducks, whıch are
not to be touched, for although they are
cast by a mıstake made at nıght, ınto
water on the fire, though the woods of _all_
the world were burned under the pot, the
water would not be heated untıl they are
taken out of ıt and put ınto the same
pond from whıch they were taken '—(_T_)

    ᵐ _Tested_—The popular belief ascrıbes
thıs peculıarıty of Ireland to the prayers
of St Patrıck , an opınıon whıch ıs defended by Dr Davıd Roth, ın hıs Eluci-
datıones ın locelınum, publıshed by Mes-
sıngham, Florıl p 127, sq   But ıt ıs
rejected by Colgan, Append. v. ad Acta
S Patr c 20 (Trıas, p 255), and by Lanıgan (vol ı. p 252, n 108), who maın-
taın that there never were any venomous
reptıles ın Ireland   In D thıs freedom
from venomous creatures ıs also mentıoned last, as the twenty-eıghth wonder

van has shewn to be the same whıch ıs
now called Templeshanbo, ın the dıocese
of Ferns, sıtuated at the foot of the moun-
taın called ın Irısh Suıghe Laıghean,
and ın Englısh, Mount Leınster   The
sıtuatıon of thıs church, whıch was unknown to Archdall and Lanıgan, ıs thus
descrıbed ın the Lıfe of St Maıdhoc, c 26,
publıshed by Colgan (Acta SS p. 211)
" Quodam dıe venıt S Moedoc ad monas-
terıum quod dıcıtur Seanbotha, juxta ra-
dıces montıs quı dıcıtur Scotıce Suıghe
Lagen, ıd est Sessıo Lagınensıum "   The
monastery was founded by St Colman
O'Fıachrach, whose memory was there celebrated on the 27th of October Colgan,
ıbıd p 217, n 26, and p 210, n 46. The
story of St Colman's ducks ıs now forgotten ın the neıghbourhood, but ıt ıs
told by Cambrensıs, Top. Hıb. Dıst, 2,
c 31, ıt occurs also ın the followıng note
on the Felıre Aenguıs, at the 27th of
October Colman ua ꝼıachɼach .ı. hı
ɼꝼnbochaıb ꝼola ı n-Uıb Cꝼnoɼelaıɜ Iɼ
na chıll acauc na lachaın, ⁊ nı lamaıɼ
eac; aɼ cıa ꝼocepcaɼ ı n-ımꝑoll aıoche

they were put by mistake of night, with the water of the pond, into a pot upon a fire, and although *all* the woods of the earth were burned under that pot, they would not be injured, nor would the water become hot.

xxxiv. There live not then, toads nor serpents in all Eri, and even though they be brought from other places unto it they die immediately, and this has been tested[m] Except the mouse, the wolf, and the fox, there has not been, and there shall not be, any noxious animal in it And it is temperate of heat and cold The sea[n] *will come* over it seven years before the *day of* Judgment. Finit. Amen. Finit[o].

III

Ⓐⱃ ⱁⱀⱎⱀⰰⰱ ⱁⱁⱃ ⰰⰱⱃ ⰾⱒ ⰰ ⱀ-ⱇⱃⰱⱀⰱ ⰱ ⰿⰰⱀ naⱅⱒⰰⱁⱃ ⱐ ⰿⰰⱀ ⰾⰽⱁⰿⰰⱀ ⱐ ⰿⰰⱀ ⰾⱁⱃⱂⰽⰰⰿⰱ ⰱⱀⱀⰽⱃ ⱐ ⰿⰰⱀ ⱂⱁⰱⱃⱎ ⱀⰽⱀⱀⱐⰱⰸ ⰰⱌⱅ ⱃⱀⱀⰰⱃⰸ ⱐ ⰿⰱⱌ ⱌⱃⱂⰽ, ⱐ ⰱⰰ ⱅⱒⱏⰸⱅⰰⱀ ⰿⱁⰸⰽ ⰰ ⱅⱃⱂ ⰰⱃⰾⰽ ⱌⰱⰰⰸⰰⰱⱁ ⱐⰸ ⱃⱁ ⱌⱅⱁⰱⱀ ⰿⱁⱌⱃ ⱌⰰⱀ ⱃⱐⰱⱂⰽⰰⱒ; ⱌⱁⱀⰰⰱ ⰱⰰⱌ ⱃⱃⱀ ⱃⱃⱂⰿ ⰿⰸⱐⰰⱀⱅⰰ Ⰹⱃⱂⰽⱀⱀ ⱏⱐⰾⰽ ⱌⱁⱀⱏⱐⰸⰽ ⱃⱃⱀ. "There is another great wonder in Eri, viz, there are no snakes, nor lions, nor toads in it; and there are no venomous beasts except the fox and wolf, and if they are brought into it from another country they die in it immediately without delay These are the principal wonders of all Eri we know."—(*T*)

[n] *The sea*.—Ralph Higden (Polychron. lib. 5, c. 4) has recorded the tradition that St. Patrick obtained for the Irish this privilege, that no Irishman shall be alive during the reign of Antichrist. This serves to explain the expectation that the sea shall cover Ireland seven years before the day of judgment In the Leabhar Breac (fol 14, b) there is an account of St. Patrick's expulsion of the demons from Ireland, and of the seven requests which he obtained of the Lord The first three of these were· Ⱌⱃⱂⰽ ⰱⱁ ⱃⰽⱃⰰⰱ Ⰹⱃⰽⱀⱀ ⰱⱁ ⰸⱀⰽ ⰰⱃⱅⱃⱃⰸⱃ ⱃⰽ ⰿ-ⰱⰰⱃ, ⱌⱃⱁ ⱃⱃⱂ ⱃⰽ ⰽⱀ ⱏⰰⱃⱂⰽ, ⱀⰰ ⱃⱁ ⱒ-ⱃⰰⱅⱅⰰ ⱃⱃⱃⰽⱃⱀⱁ ⱃⰰⱃⱃⱂ ⱂ ⰿ-ⰱⱃⰰⱒ, ⱐ ⱌⱁⱀⰰ ⱃⱁ ⰰⱃⱅⱅⱃⰽ ⰱⰰⱁ ⰽⱌⱅⱃⰰⱃⱀⰱ ⱃⱀ ⰿⱁⱃⱃ; ⱐ ⱌⱁ ⱌⱃ ⰿⱏⱃⱃ ⱌⰰⱃⱃⱃ ⱏⱃⱀ. m-ⰱⰾⱃⰰⰱⱀⰰ ⱃⱃⰰ ⰿ-ⰱⱃⰰⱅ. ' Whosoever of the men of Eri repents before death, even the space of one hour, hell shall not be shut on him at the judgment, and foreigners shall not inhabit the island, and the sea shall come over it seven years before the judgment" It is evident that this last is regarded as a blessing to the Irish, because, by that means, Ireland shall be saved from the persecution of Antichrist.—(*T*)

[o] *Finit*—In D. there occur the following wonders, not mentioned in the fore-

III.

[ᴅuan eiᴚeannach]

Maelmuᴚa Oᴄna cc.

Canam bunaᴅaᴩ na n-ᵹaeᴅel
ᵹaᴩ cloᴄ n-ᵹlíᴠᴠ

Canaᴩ

going list, the numbers prefixed denote the order in which they stand in the twenty-eight wonders of which the list given in D. consists

1 Loch Lein, ceaᴛhᴩa chiᴩcilla uime .i. ciᴩcall ᴩoain, ⁊ chiᴩcall luaiᵹi, ⁊ chiᴩcall iaᴩᴩᴅ, ⁊ ciᴩcall uma "Loch Lein; four circles are round it, viz, a circle of tin, and a circle of lead, and a circle of iron, and a circle of copper" This is the first of the Irish wonders mentioned by Nennius "Est ibi stagnum quod vocatur Loch Lein, quatuor circulis ambitur. Primo circulo gronna stanni ambitur, secundo circulo gronna plumbi ambitur, tertio circulo gronna ferri, quarto circulo gronna æris ambitur, et in eo stagno multæ margaritæ inveniuntur, quas ponunt reges in auribus suis" This is the tenth wonder in O'Flaherty's metrical list, Ogyg p 291 Loch Lein, now the upper lake of Killarney, but anciently both lakes were regarded as one, and called Loch Lein

3 Loch Riach ᴅan Tuaᴩᵹaib ill ᴅaᴛu in ᵹac lo "Loch Riach, [now Lough Reagh, near a town of the same name in Galway] then, it takes many colours every day" This is O'Flaherty's

twelfth wonder.

4. ᴅiᴩna in ᴅaᵹᴅa ᴅon i. cloch ᴅo beᴩaᴩ aᴩ in muiᴩ ᴅo ᴛaeᴛh ᴩo ceᴅoiᴩ co ᴩuib ᴩoᴩ bᴩu in ᴛobaiᴩ ceona "The Dirna of the Dagda, viz, a stone which is taken out of the sea, it returns immediately, and is found at the brink of the same well." This resembles the third wonder of Man See above, p. 121. The word Dirna denotes a stone weight.

5 Iubuiᴩ mic n-Ꙍinᵹciᴩ a n-eaᴩ maiᵹi aᴛ ciᴛheaᴩ a ᴩcaᴛh ᴛiᴩ aᴩ in n-uiᴩci co ᴩolluᴩ ⁊ ni ᴩeᴄᴛaᴩ h-e ᴩein ᴩoᴩ ᴛiᴩ "The yew tree of the son of Ꙍingcis at Eas Maighe; its shadow is seen below in the water, and it is not seen itself on the land" Eas Maighi is the cataract of the river Maigne, at Cahirass, in the county Limerick It does not appear who the son of Ꙍingcis was This is O'Flaherty's eleventh wonder.

13 Tiᴩᴩa ᴩleibe ᵹam; ca lan innᴛi .i. lan ᴅo ᴩal ᵹoiᴩᴛ, ⁊ lan o'ᴩiᴩ uiᴩci "The well of Sheve Gamh, two fulls are in it [i e. it is full of two things], viz, full of salt sea-water, and full of pure water" The well of Sheve Gamh, or the Ox Mountains, county Sligo, is still well known O'Flaherty describes it as his

III.

DUAN EIREANNACH[p]

Mœelmura of Othain[q] cecinit

Let us sing the origin of the Gaedhel,
Of high renown in stiff battles,

Whence

fourth wonder

16. Copp innṙe ʒeıo naċ h aenuıp oí o ꞇopach ṡomaın can chuıpp aıle ꝼapıa. "The crane of Inıs Geıdh has been alone from the beginning of the world, without any other crane with her" Inıs Geıdhe, ı e. Insulæ Sanctæ Gedhıæ, now Inıshkea, oı Inıshgay, ıs an island about thıee mıles off the coast of Errıs See O Donovan's Hy Fıachrach, and Map Very lıttle ıs known of the saınt who has gıven her name to the ısland, but the existence of the lone crane of Inıshkea ıs stıll firmly believed in by the peasantry This ıs O'Flaherty's sıxth wonder.

21 Cıanan ṡaımlıaʒ maınıʒ can lobaıo can bpenao co na ballaıb ocaıb con ꝼap ꝼuılꞇ 7 ınnʒean. "Cıanan of Daımhlıag [Duleek] remaıns without corruption, without stınkıng. with hıs members perfect, and hıs haır and hıs naıls grow" This curıous tradıtıon ıs mentıoned in the notes to the Felıre Aenguıs, at the 24th of November; ıt may, perhaps. be understood as communıcatıng to us the fact that the whole body of the saınt was preserved as a relıc at Duleek. St Cıanan was one of the earlıest Irısh Chrıstıans, to whom St Patııck, accordıng to Tıghernach, gave

hıs own copy of the Gospels· ıp oo ꞇuʒ Paꞇpaıc a ꝼoıpcela He dıed A. D. 489 Tıgern. in anno.—(*T*)

[p] *Duan Eıreannach*—I have gıven the name of Duan Eıreannach to thıs poem, for convenıence sake, as ıt seems of the same natuıe wıth the Duan Albannach, whıch ıs already known by that name to the students of Irısh and Scottısh hıstory Although quoted by O'Flaheıty (Ogyg ııı c 72), and by Keatıng, thıs ancıent poem has neveı been publıshed, and may be saıd to be unknown to au hıstorian. It ıs heıe pıınted from a veıy good copy in the Book of Leınster, in the Lıbıaıy of Trın Coll (II 2 18), compaıed wıth two other copıes, one in the fıagment of the Book of Lecan, whıch ıemaıns in the same Lıbrary (II 2 18) and the other in a paper MS in the handwrıtıng of Tadhg O'Neachtaın, also in the Lıbıary of Trın. Coll (H ı 15, p 27), whıch seems to have been copıed from the Book of Leınster. Mr O'Reılly (Tıans of Gaelıc Socıety. p lvı), speaks of "a very fine copy of ıt", whıch was in hıs own possessıon ; but if he alludes to thıs ıt turns out to be only a transcrıpt in hıs own hand-wrıtıng made from the copy in

canap τapla τonoʒup vilſno
vocum n-ſpſno

Cιτne ιn pſhanv ιn po τpebpaτ   5
τuιppſη pſne
cιv vop puc ι τſpce τípe
vo puιnιuv ʒpéne

Cιappo τucaιτ povop poʒluaιp
pém vo ċapτιul,   10
ιn vo τecev, nó ιn vo cſnac,
no ιnv' ʒapcιuv?

Cιav e ap vιlpιu voιb pop vomun
ιnv a τaevιn
vιa n-anmmιʒuv ιn a n-aτpeb   15
Scuιττ nó Ʒaevιl.

Cιamvιp

H ι ι5, the worst of the three copies from which the text is here printed This transcript is now in the Library of the Royal Irish Academy, but is, of course, of no authority In the following notes the readings of the Book of Lecan will be distinguished by the letter L , and those of O'Naghten's copy by N.—(T)

ᵠ Maelmura of Othain, or of Fathain (the F being aspirated and omitted), now Fahan, near Loch Swilly, in Inishowen, Co Donegal See an account of Maelmura in O'Reilly's Irish Writers (Trans Gaelic Soc. p lvi). See also the Four Masters, at the year 884, and the Leabhar Gabhala of the O'Clerys, in the Library of the Royal Irish Academy, p 207, where, after mention made of the historical poem written by him for Flann Sionna King of Ireland, his death is thus recorded : Maelmupae ſeιpιn an pιle poιpecτe pιneolacſτaιpιve epʒna an beplu Scoιτeccoa vo ecc ιpιn ochτmav bl vo plaιτh Ploιnv τ-Sιonna 884. "The same Maelmura, a learned, truly-intelligent poet, an historian skilled in the Scottic language, died in the eighth year of the reign of Flann Sionna, A D 884." The writer then quotes a poem in praise of Maelmura, which is too long for insertion here —(T)

ʳ Mighty stream —Tonoʒup, compounded of τonv, a wave, and ʒup, powerful

Whence did the mighty stream[r] of ocean
  Waft *them* to Eri?

What was the land[s] in which they *originally* lived,   5
  Lordly men, Fenians[t]?
What brought them, for want of land,
  To the setting of the sun?

What was the cause that sent them forth
  Upon their wanderings?   10
Was it in flight, or for commerce,
  Or from valour[u]?

What is the proper *name*[v] for them,
  As a nation,
By which they were called in their own country   15
  Scuit or Gaedhil?

Why

In the preceding line, ᵹleⱅeno is rendered *battles*, on the authority of O'Clery's Glossary, where ᵹleⱅen is explained ᵹleo [battle], and ᵹleo ⱅeann [stein fight]. For canaⱃ ⱅapla, line 3, L reads can ooⱃ pala —(*T.*)

[s] *What was the land.*—Ceⱃⱃⁱ uⱃⱃano. L. "what was the division."—(*T*)

[t] *Fenians* — Alluding to the story of Fenius Farsaidh, King of Scythia, and the school of learning established by him under the superintendence of Gaedhal, son of Eathor. See Keating (Haliday's Transl. p 225), and O'Donovan's Irish Grammar, p xxviii. sq. ⱅoⱃ is a lord, a chief (in the oblique case ⱅuiⱃ)· ⱅuiⱃ-

ⱃeⱃ (which in the plural would be better written ⱅuiⱃⱃⁱⱃ) will therefore signify noble or lord-like men —(*T.*)

[u] *Valour* —"Did they leave their former habitations in flight from their enemies, or for the sake of commerce, or from a spirit of adventure and love of conquest?" L reads (cⁱaⱃⁱ ⱅuccaⱐⱅ in ⱃo ⱃoᵹluaⱃⁱ), ⱃem ⁱaⱃ ⱅaⱃⱅuil?—(*T*)

[v] *Name.*—The language here is very rude, and perhaps has been corrupted by transcribers L. reads,

  Ce oⁱae aⱃa oiⱃliu oaib
      ⱅinoiu ⱅaioen
  oia n-ammeouᵹ ina n-oaⁱⱃⁱⁱb
      ⱃcuiⱅ no ᵹaeioⁱl —(*T*)

Cıamoıp ṗſıe acteptha
  oo anmano oóıb
acuſ ʒaeoel anoop ʒleıo
  can ooppoıo.   20

bıo nuſ pélſaṗu oamſa
  coṗ ba tıṗech,
oaıʒ ıt eolach ı ſṗeıt ſſncaı a
  mac Mılſo

Mao aıl oo oıa bıo ınnıu ouıt   25
  ní ba máṗach
oṗo ſſncaṗa mac Mıleo
  ſeıb ṗo ṗelao.

Rıʒ-mac Noe náıṗ laṗeṫ
  ıſ uao aṗ cınıuo   30
oo ʒṗecaıb oún conaṗ m-bunuo
  conaṗ n-oлıʒuo.

                                            Oou

---

* Fene —L. reads,

    Cetıſ ſene aſa m-beaṗoaıſ
      ſſıu mbu aınm ooıb
    ocuſ ın ʒaeıoıl ṗuſ ʒleıʒ
      can ooſ ṗooıʒ.—(T.)

× *Ignorant.*—The word tıṗech occurs
again, line 146 In L. the following stanza,
which does not occur in the other copies,
is inserted here.

    Cıone ṗemeno ſoṗṗa ṗoboaṗ
      ṗıuch ſeṗʒach
    no cıa mac oo maccaıb Mıleao
      cuıſ a m-beaṗṗthaṗ.

" What adventure were they upon
   In their angry course,
Or what sons of the sons of Miledh
   Are they to be traced to?"

And then follows:

    buo leıſ noo ṗela oam uıle
      coṗ bo cıcheach
    Aṗ ba ſeaṗṗoa aṗṗeıch ſeancaṗa
      mac Mıleao.

   " It is all clear to me,
     And it is visible,
   For I am excellent in the stream of history
     Of the sons of Miledh "—(T.)

ᵞ *Willing.*—mao coıṗ le Oıa, L. · and

Why was Fene^w said to be
  A name for them ?
And Gaedhil—which is the better,
  Whence was it derived ?   20

Although thou revealest it not to me,
  But leavest *me* ignorant^x,
For thou art learned in the stream of history
  Of the sons of Miledh,

Yet if God be willing^y, thou shalt have to-day,   25
  Not to-morrow,
The order of the history of the sons of Miledh,
  As it happened

The royal son of righteous^z Noah, Japheth,
  From him is our descent,   30
Of the Greeks^a are we, in our origin,
  In our laws.

Of

in line 28, ᚏᚓᚔᚁ ᚐᚑᚏᚐᚂᚐᚑ—(*T.*)

^z *Righteous.*—ᚅᚐᚔᚏ, omitted in L —(*T*)

^a *Greeks.*—The alleged Grecian origin seems to require a descent from Japhet through Javan, whose name was anciently identified with Iaon, the open form of Ion, ἀπο δὲ Ἰωνάνου Ἰωνία καὶ πάντες Ἑλ- ληνες —Josephus, i. vi. i.   But if Fenius Farsaidh was the great-grandson of Japhet by Magog, as Mr. O'Flaherty found it (Ogyg. p. 9, 10), and as the Scythian mythus requires, why are Miledh's sons said to be of the Greeks?—(*II*)   The author of the life of St. Cadroe (Colgan,

Acta SS. p 494) has given a legend of the origin of the Scots, in which they are said to have been a colony from a city called ' Chouscon," situated on the river Pactolus, between the regions of Choria [Caria] and Lydia   The inhabitants of this city having discovered the superior fertility of Thrace, set out, " junctis sibi Pergamis et Lacedæmoniis, ' with their wives and property, to take possession of that country, "ut cupitam terram pos- sessuri peterent."   They were driven. however, by terrific storms, out of their course, through the Straits of Gibraltar,

226

Don τρειb ιρ αιmρυ ρο ξαbρατ
　ρlατιυρ ρυιlεc
ρορ bιτ bροѕnαc; ο τυρcbαιl ξρειnε　　　　35
　co α ρυιnεο

Ϝlαιτειn cροοα ροξαb ιn mbιτ
　n-ξlѕραc n-ξlεξραc;
Nεmbρóτ α αιnm ϝѕρ lαρ ήοѕρnαο
　ιn τορ οѕρmαρ　　　　40

Luιο Ϝѕmιυρ chuιce αρ ιn Scιτια
　ρορ ρluαξαο,
ϝѕρ αιρεξοα εcnαιο εolαc
　bριυτmαρ bαξαch.

bα oѕn bερlα boí ιρ ιn οοmυn　　　　45
　ιn ρο ξαbρατ,
οά héρlα οéc αρ τρι ϝιchτιb
　ταn ρο ρcαρρατ.

Scol

and then up to Ireland (which the author represents as being then inhabited by Picts—gentem Pictanorum reperiunt) They landed under Cruach an eile, now Cruach Patrick, in Clew Bay, Co. Mayo. They proceeded thence to Clonmacnois, then to Armagh, Kildare, Cork, Bangor, and even to Iona, in short, they obtained possession of the whole island (particularly of its ecclesiastical cities, although so long before Christianity), and they called it first Choriscia, from the name of their native town, and then Scotia, from Scotta, daughter of the king of Egypt, and wife of Niul, son of Æneas (i. e Fenius), a Lacedemonian, who was one of their leaders See Colgan's notes, n. 39, 40, ib. 502 The author of the Life of St Cadroe is supposed by Colgan to have written A. D 1040. The common story given by Colgan (note z, ad Vit S. Abbani. 16 Mart. p 621) represents the migrations of the Scotic colony to have been from Egypt to Greece, thence to Spain, and thence to Ireland —(T.)

b *In this world* —Uαρ bιτ bροιnεch, L.
c *Nembroth*, i. e. Nimrod L omits ϝερ in line 39, and writes the name Nεbριoτh.

Of the most illustrious people that *ever* enjoyed
  A bloody sovereignty
In this world[b] of woe ; from the rising of the sun   35
  To its setting

A valiant prince took dominion over the world,
  The wide-spread, noisy *world ;*
Nembroth[c] his name, a man by whom was built
  The very great tower   40

Fenius came unto him[d] out of Scythia,
  Upon an expedition,
A man illustrious, wise, learned,
  Ardent, warlike

There was *but* one language in the world[e]   45
  When they met,
Twelve languages and three score[f]
  When they parted.

A

N has Nempoð.—(*T*)

[d] *Unto him* —Keating, who quotes v 41–52 of this poem, omits chuice, which occurs in all the other copies in L it is written chucai The omission is necessary to the metre In line 42, L reads ꝼor ꞅa ꞅluaꞁꞃeꝺ, and Keating ꝼoꞃꞃ aн ꞅluaꞁaꝺ, which is also required by the metre In line 44, for baꞁach, warlike, L and Keating read buaꝺac, victorious; and N buaꞁac, which is wrong, unless it be intended for buaꝺac Dr Lynch, in his unpublished translation of Keating, a MS. in the possession of Mr O'Donovan,

renders this stanza thus

"Egressum Scythia Fenius numerosa secuta est
  Turba virûm, studiis nimirum addictus, et armis
  Felix ille fuit, necnon vir mente sagaci "—(*T*)

[e] *In the world* —Keating reads, baoi ꞅaн ꝺoнiaн, and in the next line, maꞃ ꝺo ꞁabꞃaꞇ. L reads iнꝺiꝺ ꞁabꞃaꞇ Dr. Lynch has paraphrased this stanza thus

"Ingressis turrim mortalibus, unica lingua
  Nota fuit, digressi septuaginta loquuntur
  Et binas linguas "

In line 43, N and Keating read ꝼiciꝺ for ꝼichꞇib —(*T*)

[f] *Twelve and three score* i. e. 72 The

Scol móp la Faſmiup ic foglaim
 in cec ſpgna,   50
Fſp apo aoina po bío co ampa
 in cec bſplu

bpíſta mac oo Faſmiup Fappaio
 ba oual co bpaτ,
ap cumτac in τuip la τuaiτh τalman   55
 Nél oapogpao

Rancaτap pcela co Fopaino
 la mſτ n-gpiſτa,
Nél mac Faeniupa ica fileτ
 bepla in beτha   60

bpeτa Nél fa oſp in Egipτ
 féin n-guipm n-glſpe,

                                                           oo

number of Noah's sons and their posteri-
ties, as enumerated in Gen x. and 1 Chron 1
is 73 from which arose the number of 72
languages, both among Jews and Christians Philistim being omitted, as having
been introduced parenthetically (Gen x
14. 1 Chron 1 12), not as one of the
original tribes, but in reference to a later
subdivision Peter Comestor, in his Scho-
lastic History, has said, " Texuntur ex eis
72 generationes, 15 de Japhet, 30 de
Chem, et 27 de Sem "—fol xiv But Vin-
cent of Beauvais mentions both reckon-
ings thus . " Fuerunt ex tribus Noe filiis
gentes 73 (vel potius ut ratio declarat 72),
scilicet 15 de Japhet, 31 de Cham, et 27 de

Sem, totidemque linguæ esse cœperunt "
—*Specul. Doctrina*, i c 44 The angels
whom Jacob beheld ascending and de-
scending the ladder were 72 in number,
and they were the angels of the 72 nations Simeon ben Jochai, cited Bartolocci
Bibl Rabbin 1 p. 228-9, Reuchlin de
Verbo Mirifico p 938 This idea is agreeable to the Greek version of Deut xxxii
8 "according to the number of the angels
of God." The Mahometans likewise adopt
the number 72 as that of the nations divided at Babel, and in analogy to that
division they boast of their religion being
divided into 72 sects, while they allow
only 71 to the Christians, and 70 to the

A great school *was founded* by Fenius, to instruct[g]
   In all knowledge,   50
A man deeply learned, who excelled
   In every language

A son was born to Faenius Farsaidh,
   Who separated[h] *from him* for ever,
On the building of the tower by the men of the world, 55
   Nel, whom he loved

News came to Forann[i]
   With great eclat,
Of Nel, son of Fenius, who knew
   All languages of the world   60

Nel was carried southwards to Egypt,
   Heroes[j] of dark blue weapons,

                        The

Jews   See Rycaut's Turkish Empire, p. 118   Compare also Keating, Hist of Ireland, p. 61, and O'Flaherty, Ogyg part ii p 63 —(*II.*)

[g] *To instruct*—L. reads ꝏ ꝼoꝣlaim la Feniup, and gives lines 51 and 52 thus·

  Ꝼéɼ aɼo aɾɼa co mbuaɼꝺ ac cach
          ɼa beɼla

Keating gives them thus·

  Ꝼeaɼ aꝺaɼɼaeaꝣɼuɼꝺeolac [oɼ uɼlmoɼ]
          ɼa ꝣac beaɼla.

Dr. Lynch paraphrases this stanza thus

    " ———— se calentissimus artis
 Cujusvis Fenius, linguæ et cujusvis peritus
 Evasit, multis in lingua quaque Magister —(*T*)

[h] *Separated*—Ꝺual is now obsolete; but seems to signify separated In the next line L. reads ꝺo ꞇuaɼch, grammar would seem to require ꞇuaꞇaɼb, but it would be inconsistent with the metre, ꞇuaɼch is the reading of all the copies, and is used again in the same sense, l. 83 —(*T*)

[i] *Forann*, i. e Pharaoh This stanza is quoted in Haliday's edition of Keating, p 233, and in the manuscript copy by John Torna O'Mulconry, but it does not occur in Lynch's translation For la ver 58, Haliday and O'Mulconry read ꝣo —(*T*)

[j] *Heroes*—Ꝼein, cognate with ꝼenɼɼo, a soldier, a hero, or the word may be the same as ꝼine, a tribe, a nation "A people

vo bρſčh ınʒſn Fhoρaınv
vó vaρ éρe

Ruc Scočča ρcíč mac vo Neól   65
   aρ n-vul ın Aeʒıρč,
ſpρ cſč cača Ʒoevel ʒlaρρ
   fíp flača fſʒelč

Fſnı o Fhaſnıuρ aρ a m-beρčoρ,
   clú cſn vocča,   70
Ʒaevıl o Ʒaevıul ʒlaρ ʒaρča
   Scuıčč o Scočča.

Sív móρ ı m-bačaρ la Fhoρaınv
   la mſič n-uabaıρ ;
ρoρvaρ vuanaıc ı n-válaıb   75
   ρoρvaρ ρluaʒaıʒ.

Sluaʒ čuače De léıcſρ Foρaınv
   uav aρ omun,
ʒebſρ foρ a ρlıcč co vρſmun   80
   co muıρ Romuρ.

                                             báčıρ

or heroes of dark blue weapons" is possibly a description of the Egyptians, but it may perhaps better be taken in apposition with Nel, as descriptive of his followers; his son Gaedhal is by some said to have been called ʒlaρ, or green, from the colour of his armour (Haliday's Keating, p. 237), the weapons of the followers of Nel may therefore be here called ʒuıρm, i e. dark blue or black, for a similar reason ʒleρ denotes weapons, arms; the word is thus explained in a glossary ʒleρa .ı. ʒleρa ı ınvle no aρma —(*T.*)

   [k] *Daughter.*—L inserts her name Scoča and in line 65 the same MS. reads ρuʒ Scoča ınʒen vo Nıul, an error which has been corrected by an ancient hand which has written no mac over the word ınʒen —(*T*)

   [l] *A hundred fights.*—L. reads eρρıč cača,

The daughter[k] of Forann was given
　　Unto him afterwards.

The beauteous Scota bare a son to Nel,　　　　　　65
　　After his arrival in Egypt,
A hero of a hundred fights[l], Gaedhal Glass
　　Endowed with sovereign righteousness

The Feni from Faenius are named,
　　Not small *their* renown[m]　　　　　　　　70
The Gaedhil from Gaedhuil Glass are called,
　　The Scots from Scota

In great peace were they with Forann,
　　And in great pride ;
They recited poems in their assemblies,　　　　75
　　They recited battles[n]

The hosts of the people of God Forann permitted
　　To go forth from him through fear,
He followed in their track fiercely
　　To the sea Romhuir[o].　　　　　　　　80

Forann

a hero of battles , and in the next line ꝼꞃꞃ ꝡꞁꜰꞇꜳ ꝼꞁꜱꞡꜱꞇꜱ.—(*T*)

[m] *Renown*.—L and Keating (Haliday's ed. p 238,) and O'Flaherty (Ogyg p 349,) read ꝟꞃꞁꞡ ꞡꜳn (or cꜳn) ꝺꝋꞇꞇꜳ, which O'Flaherty renders " res manifesta satis " Cꜳn ꝺꝋꞇꞇꜳ is, literally, without difficulty —(*T*.)

[n] *Battles*.—They recited *duans* (historical poems), and tales or histories of bat-

tles, or perhaps we should render lines 75, 76, thus " They were poetical [fond of poetry] in their assemblies , They were warlike [or numerous]" For ꝓꝋꝺꜳꞃ, in lines 75 and 76 L reads nꞁꝺꝋꝋꞃ, which includes a negative ; and in line 73, ꞃꞁꜱꞇ mꜳꞃ ꝓꝋm ꝟꜳꝺꜳꞃ ꞇꜳ ꝼꝋꞃꜳꞃꝋ —(*T*)

[o] *Romhuir*.—mꞣꞁꞃ ꝓꝋmꞣꞁꞃ, a corruption of mare rubrum   L reads ꝺꞔ mꞣꞁꞃ ꝓꝋ-mꞣꞁꞃ instead of ꝵꝋ.   Haliday (p. 245)

báčip Pomaino a lín uili
    aubul caipooe,
čṛna čuač Oe ba číṛ,
    ní poṛ báio ino paipṡṡe.

Ačpaiṡpeč clanna Niúil peṛṡ Popaino,   85
    combčaṛ bṛónaiṡ,
báiṡ nac becačaṛ bon biṡail
    laṛ in copaio

Cio in čan na čṛna Popaino
    bon piao paenach,   90
čuača Eṡṣpč ecla la claino Néoil
    bia n-baepao

Čallṛačaṛ libṣna Popaino
    a číṛ čṛebṛač,
in aiochi uaiṛ baṛ belac   95
    maṛa puaio ṛaipṛeč.

Raiṛeč ṛec Inbé ṛec Aṛṛia,
    aṛ bon pṣṣio,
bon Sciċia, co m-bṛíṡ n-uaṛail,
    ba číṛ pṣṛṛin   100

                          Poṛ

absurdly translates maṛa ṛomuiṛ, "the great sea," and in the same place he also makes the stupid blunder of rendering čuača Oe (line 75), "Dannan's tribe."—(T)

   p *Chariots* —This translation is entirely conjectural. The word caipoe, which has been rendered *chariots*, is now obsolete, and the meaning assigned to it is very doubtful.—(T.)

   q *Reached* —L. reads ṛola.—(T.)

   r *People of Egypt* —Lines 91 and 92 are

Forann was drowned with all his multitude
    Of mighty chariots[p] ;
The people of God reached[q] their own country,
    The sea did not drown them.

The children of Nel raised Foran's ire,   85
    So that they were sorrowful,
Because they joined not in revenge
    Along with the champion

But when Forann returned not
    From his onward journey,   90
The people of Egypt[r] were dreaded by the sons of Nel
    Lest they should enslave them.

They seized the ships[s] of Forann,
    They deserted[t] their country ;
And in the night time over the track   95
    Of the Red Sea they passed[u].

They passed by India, by Asia,
    The way they knew[x] ;
To Scithia, with noble might,
    Their own country.   100

Over

thus given in L. · aᴅpaiᵹpeᴄaᴘ ᴄuaċa
ℇiᵹepᴄ, ᴀp ᴅia n-ᴀepaᴅ, " the people of
Egypt attempted to enslave them "—(*T.*)

  [s] *Ships.*—Ŀibepna, evidently the Latin
Liburna navis, a swift boat, or galley.
—(*T*)

  [t] *Deserted.*—L. reads huaᴄhip peppaᴅ,

and in the next line pop for ᴅap —(*T.*)

  [u] *Passed.*—peppaᴅ, they sailed, L.—(*T.*)

  [x] *They knew.*—L. reads,

    Reppaᴅ pech Inᴅia, pech Aippia,
      apa pepin,
    ᴅochum Sceiᴄhia, com-bpiᵹ uapail,
      ᴄia ᴄip pepin.—(*T*)

Foṗ muincino maṗa Caiṗṗ ᵹaḃṗac
  ceciṗn oiliṗ
ṗaṗacṗac Ɗlaṡṡ in Coṗoniṡ
  aṗ muiṗ Ɫiḃiṗ

Ɫuio Sṗú mac Eṗṗiu iaṗcanaiḃ   105
  ḃa cṡ miṗṗṗu
cimchell acuaio cṗom co oace
  ṗleḃe Riṗṗi.

Ro ᵹaḃ a n-Ɗolᵹaca ᵹaecac
  comol ᵹṗianoa   110

  anaiṗ

ʸ Surface.—Muincinn is explained uaic-
caṗ by O'Cleṡy —(T)

ᶻ Band —L. reads, cachaṗ n oiliṗ,
" they took a desirable fortress." In the
next line, for ṗoṗacṗac, L has ṗo ᵹaḃṗac
—(T)

¹ Coronis, i e they left Glas dead at
Coṗonis In the margin, after the word
Coṗoniṗ, the scribe has written n loci,
i. e. "nomen loci" L. reads Coṗcuiṗ
According to the historical poem of Giolla
Coemhain, preserved in the Leabhar
Gabhala, the descendants of Nel or Niul,
after leaving Egypt, remained in Scythia
for a considerable time, contending for the
sovereignty of the country; but being at
length expelled, they formed a settlement
on the Caspian Sea, where Agnoman, the
seventh in descent from Niul (see Ogygia, page 67) died. After remaining
there a year they set out again, passed
through the Lybian Sea, and Glas, the

son of Agnoman, and brother of Lamhfinn
and Elloth, died at Coronis The poet's
words (Leabhar Gabhala, p 61) are as
follow

  Ranᵹacaṗ muiṗ Ɫiḃiṗ lán
  ṗeolao ṗe ṗamluice ṗlán,
  Ɗlaṡ mac Aᵹnomain naṗoṗ
  an acḃach i Coṗoniṗ

  " They reached the full Lybian Sea,
  They sailed six full summer days
  Glas, son of Agnoman the wise
  Died at Coronis"

The prose account in the Leabhar Gabhala (p 58), states that their settlement
at the Caspian Sea was in an island that
they remained there a year, and on the
death of Agnoman set out through the
Lybian Sea to *an island* called Coronis,
where Glas, son of Agnoman, died, after
they had been there a year Keating calls
this island "Coronia in *the Pontic* Sea"

Over the surface[y] of the Caspian sea they passed,
    A faithful band[z],
They left Glas in Coronis[a],
    On the Sea of Libis

Sru, son of Esru[b], went afterwards,   105
    He was without dejection[c],
Round by the gloomy north rapidly
    To Slieve Riffi.

He settled in fiery Golgatha[d],
    A noble deed[e];   110

                                      There

—Haliday's edit p 251 The Glas here spoken of, therefore, is not Gadhael Glas, but Glas, son of Agnoman, the eighth in descent from him *Coronis* is most probably Cyrene on the Lybian Sea "Ab ea parte quæ Lybico [mari] adjacet," says Pomponius Mela, "proxima est Nilo provincia quam Cyrenas vocant"—*De Situ Orbis*, l. 1 c. 7. And his annotator, Joh. Olivarius, adds, "nunc dicta Corena" —See also Herodotus, l 111. and iv — (*T.*)

[b] *Sru, son of Esru*—Sru, son of Asruth. was the grandson of Gadheal Glas, and the leader of the descendants of Niul in the expedition from Egypt to Scythia. But if the preceding stanza relates to the death of Glas or Lamhglas (as Keating calls him), who was the sixth in descent from Sru, it is evident that there has been some confusion or transposition. The error, however, occurs in all the copies of this poem which are accessible to me —(*T*)

[c] *Without dejection* —N reads cen mirpi, a mistake for cen mirpi or mibpi But L. reads ar in rceiti, "out of Scythia"—(*T*)

[d] *Golgatha* —Golgothain, L Golgaota, N. O'Flaherty calls it Gaecluige, on the authority of the poem of Giolla Coemhan already referred to (Leabhar Gabhala, p 60) The prose account, ib p. 59, gives it the same name, cf v 117 It is very doubtful what place is intended by this appellation; some suggest Gothia (Keating, p 251), others Galatia, but O'Flaherty prefers Getulia (Ogyg pp. 66, 67) This stanza is probably a continuation of the adventures, not of the original expedition under Sru, but of that under Lamhfinn and Elloth, the brothers of Glas, son of Agnoman, who died at Coronis. According to Keating (p 247, Haliday), Sru and his followers went no far-

anaip anꝺ a chlanꝺ cen ꝺiʒna
ꝺá céꞇ m-bliaꝺna

bpaꞇh mac Ꝺeaʒaꞇha ꝩop n-ainich
piʒꝺa ippeꞇa,
apin co h-em eʒpaiꝺ poꞇhuaiꝺ   115
i ꞇuapcepꞇ m-beaꞇha

ba ꝺe ʒabaip iap n-Ʒaeꞇhlaiʒib
co h-inꝺpib
piʒꝺa a loinʒpin ꞇapcnam mapa
Ꞇappian ꞇpillpich   120

Ꝺo Chpſiꞇ ꝺo Shicil pop pſppaꞇ
pop pi ꞇinpſm

          pec

ther than Crete, where he left a colony and died. But the account given in the Leabhar Gabhala makes him pass down the Red Sea, into the Ocean, by the island of Taprabana [Ceylon], the Riphæan mountains, and so to Scythia —(*T*)

Sheve Rith (line 108) is Mount Rhiphæus in Scythia, now called the Ural mountains, which the Irish antiquaries undoubtedly connected with the name of Riphath, grandson of Japhet, Gen x 3 Josephus, however (1 c 6), says, 'Ριφάθης δε 'Ριφαθαιους, τους Παφλαγονους λεγομενους —(*H.*)

e *Deed.*—L reads comaen n-ʒpianꝺa. N has ꝺa ceꞇ ʒpianꝺa, which is an evident mistake Authorities differ as to the number of years that the posterity of

Lamhfinn remained in Gaethluighe The old copies of the poem of Giolla Coemhain read thirty (see Haliday's Keating, p 251; Ogyg. p. 72), but the O'Clerys, in their copy of this poem in the Leabhar Gabhala (p. 62), have 300 Keating, (*loc. cit*), prefers 150, on the ground that Brath, the leader of the expedition from Gaethluighe to Spain, was the ninth in descent from Lamhfinn, who first settled at Gaethluighe. But this would be allowing less than twenty years to a generation Our author assigns 200 years to this interval,—another proof that this stanza describes the adventures of Lamhfinn, not of Sru son of Esru, and that some stanzas are probably lost O'Flaherty adopts the term of 500 years, and

There dwelt his descendants without disgrace
    Two hundred years.

Brath[f], son of Deagath, performed
    A royal journey,
From thence with great speed northwards.   115
    To the north of the world

It was then he passed from Gaethligh[g]
    To the islands;
Royal his fleet, ploughing the sea
    Of sparkling Tarrian[h]   120

By Creid[i], by Sicil, they sailed
    In their course,

                      By

points out the source of the difficulty in the legend, that Niul, or Nel, son of Fenius Farsaidh, was contemporary with Moses, which he could not be without extreme longevity, as the genealogies make him only the fifth in descent from Noah; Ogyg. p 72. O'Flaherty, therefore, places the settlement of Lamhfinn at Getulia, about the year A.M 2245 (i.e. about 200 years before Moses), and the expedition of Brath from Getulia to Spain about A M 2767.—Ogyg p. 82.—(T)

[f] *Brath* —This stanza and the next are added from L They do not occur in the other MSS. Brath, son of Deagath or Deagfath, as Keating calls him (see also line 125), was the leader of the migration from Gaethluighe into Spain, about

the time of the destruction of Troy: Ogyg. p. 82 He was the nineteenth in descent from Fenius The course here assigned to Brath is *northwards*, which is scarcely consistent with any of the opinions on the situation of Gaethlughe with respect to Spain —(T.)

[g] *Gaethligh* —The same place which was called Golgotha, line 109 See above, p 235, note [d].—(T.)

[h] *Tarrian* —Muir Tarrian, or the sea Tarrian, is the Mediterranean.—(T.)

[i] *Creid*, i.e, They sailed by Crete and Sicily, through the Straits of Gibraltar, to Spain Immediately after this stanza the Book of Leinster gives the stanza beginning ꞯa mbꞷenꞇꞧacꞇ ꝺo ꝶala, which it repeats again (lines 137-140) N gives

ρεϲ ϲολομηα hϲϲυιλ αϙϐυιλ
ϙhЄρράιη ιηϙλιϐ.

Ua Ϙεαϲα ρυαιϙ ϙοη ριȝραιϙ   125
    ριȝϙα ιη ϝοραηϙ
ȝεϐϲρ Єρράιη ιη ϝϲρ ϝορολλ
   ιη ϲί ϐρϲȝοηϙ

ϐριȝαηϲια αιηm ηα ϲαϲρας
   ηα ϲέϲ ηαιρεϲh,   130

     ϲορ

it here, but does not repeat it in the second place It is evidently misplaced here and has therefore been omitted.—(*T*)

i Peninsular —The word ιηϙλιϐ is perhaps from ιηϙε, a point And if so, it will signify here "Spain the pointed," that is, running out into a point, peninsular. It might signify also herds of cattle, and then the meaning would be "Spain rich in cattle," which might perhaps allude to the classical fable of Hercules seizing the cattle of Geryon But this latter translation is not so probable as the former —(*T*)

k Deatha.—The father of Biath, who was mentioned before under the name of Deagath, which is only a different spelling See line 113, and note. This passage is very corrupt in all the copies L reads hua ϙεαϲha ϙιη ριȝραιϙ N. has uaϙε αϲα ρυαιϙ ϙοη ριοȝηυιϙ The meaning, however, is evidently what I have given in the translation, although I cannot altogether correct the text —(*T*)

l His companions —Ϝοραηϙ is an ancient form of ϝυιρεηϙ, the crew, attendants, or companions. L., however, reads ριȝϙα ϲρεϐυηϙ, a royal chief, or *tribune ;* and N. reads ριοȝϙα ιη ϝοραɩ̈ιη, "royal the power or force"—(*T*)

m The man —For the meaning of ιη ϲι, see above, p 207, note *s*. Breogan, son of Breath (see above, p 237, note *i*), succeeded his father, as king of the Spanish possessions of the tribe, according to O'Flaherty, in the year of the world 2767. Ogyg p 83 ; Keating (Halliday's Edit), p 255 —(*T*)

n Brigantia —The Flavium Brigantium of antiquity is the port of Betanzos in Spanish Gallicia; and it would have been as completely unknown in Ireland as any other port in Spain, but for a passage in the first Book of Orosius, copied into the third of those geographical epitomes, which usually bear the name of Æthicus Ister "Secundus angulus circium inten-

By the columns of the mighty Hercules,
  To Espain the peninsular[j].

The grandson of the red Deatha[k] of the royal line,   125
  Royal his companions[l],
Took Espain, the very great man,
  The man[m] Breagon

Brigantia[n] *was* the name of the city
  Of an hundred chieftains,   130
                                              The

dit ubi Brigantia Calleciæ civitas sita, altissimum pharum, et inter pauca memorandi operis, ad speculum Britanniæ erigitur "—Oros. p 26, Æthic p 61 Ed Gronovii The farum, or pharos, light-house, is the Tower of Breagon (v. 131), and the words " ad speculum" gave rise to the absurd notion that Ireland was visible from Betanzos. They were probably written when those who did not wish to be burned in their beds kept a sharp look out for vessels from Britain   However, the story hath its foundation in the cited passage of Orosius, and in one subsequent, which mentions Ireland, and is as follows· " Hibernia insula, inter Britanniam et Hispaniam sita, longiore, ab Africo in boream, spatio porrigitur Hujus partes priores intentæ Cantabrico oceano Brigantiam Calleciæ civitatem, ab Africo sibi in circium occurrentem, spatioso intervallo procul *spectant*, ab eo præcipuè promontorio, ubi Scenæ [Shannon] fluminis ostium est, et Velabri Lucenique

consistunt "—p. 28. Havercamp

Observe the progress of falsehood This excellent writer simply says *spectant*, the shores of south-west Ireland *looked* or *faced* in that direction , and states (perhaps falsely, but possibly with truth), that the tower of Betanzos was erected for the purpose of *watching* these islands, " *ad speculum* Britanniæ", and hence, we are told by Malmura, that " Erin was seen from the Tower " Being discovered on a winter's evening, it would seem to have been peculiarly visible in the dark

The Brigantes were, perhaps, the greatest of the tribes or nations inhabiting Britain , and their country reached from shore to shore, from the mouth of the Humber or Trent, to that of the Eden. Therefore, if the names Breagon and Brigant could be shewn identical (which they cannot), it would be sufficiently apparent from whence the former came into Ireland —(*II.*)

tor ṁ-Bregoin assaide in subac
  fossa suidea.

Sairtuaid as tur atcess hErinn [o]
  do iat Luimnig;
fescur gemrid fos fuair Ith
  mac Bregoin buidnig.

Ba m-Bregmtracht do rala,
  co lucht a teglaig,
cetna marb dia cenel ċongbaid
  bebla Slemnaib.

Sairdess bretha Ith in Espáin
  iar na brígaib
tresin dollotar meic mil Mile
  dia digail.

Dond

[o] *Tower of Breogan*—See the story in Keating (Haliday's edit p. 261). This tower, intended as a sort of pharos, or watch-tower, is said by Keating (p. 255) to have been erected in Corunna See Dr Wilde's communication to the Royal Irish Academy on the remains of the Pharos of Corunna.—Proceedings of the Academy, May 13, 1844. In L., line 130, is cetaib aireach, and in the next line, for assaide in subác, we have a suide subach.—(*T.*)

[p] *Was seen.*—rocess, L.—(*T.*)

[q] *Luimnech.*—des h-iar foirind, L. In the next line, for fos L. reads for, and omits buidnig in line 136. The land of Luimnech was the country at the mouth of the Shannon, from the present city of Limerick to the sea.—(*T*).

[r] *Brentracht.*—The plain called Magh Ithe (or the plain of Ith, son of Breogan), through which flows the river Fin; it is the district now called the Laggan, Co. Donegal. Keating calls it brentract mhaige Ite (Haliday's edit.), p. 262. See also the Book of Ballymote, fol. 20, b., and the Leabhar Gabhala of O'Clery, page 69. There is another place called Magh Itha, in Leinster, which, according to another account, was the place at which Ith first landed; and the northern Magh Itha received its name from being

The tower of Breogan°, his delightful seat
   On which he sat.

North-east from the tower was seen[p] Eri,
   As far as the land of Luimnech[q];
On a winter's evening was *it* discovered by Ith,   135
   Son of Breogan, *ruler* of troops

It was at Brentracht[r] he landed
   With the people of his household,
He was the first of his conquering tribe who died,
   He died at Slemnaibh[s]   140

South-eastwards Ith is carried to Spain,
   His strength being gone[t],
With might the sons of brave Miledh returned
   To revenge *him*

                        Donn,

the place where Ith was interred. Keating, p. 267.—(*T*)

[s] *Slemnaibh.*—Keating says, that some historians mention Drumlighean, (now Drumleen, on the Foyle, near Lifford), as the place of Ith's death, but others assert that he died at sea, and that his body was carried to Spain to excite his relatives to revenge Keating, p 267 Leabhar Gabhala, p. 70 This latter account appears to be adopted by our author Where Slemnaibh is I do not know, but the scribe has added, no. loci, i e. nomen loci. L reads ꝼoꞃ ꞃa ꝼenmuꞃ, and in line 138, lim a ᴄeꞃlaich. The following account of Ith's death is given in the Book of Lecan (fol 12): Celebꞃaꞃ hⅠᴄ ꝺoⅠb, ⁊ ᴄꝼⅠᴄ ꝺoᴄum a luⅠnꞃe. ⅠaꞃꞃⅠn ꞃo laꞃeᴄ ꝼoꞃlⅠn na nꝺⅠaⅠꞃ ᴄo ꞃon ꞃonꞃaᴄ a Muⅰꞃ Ⅰᴄha Ro ꞃⅠaᴄᴄ ᴄneꝺach ꝼuⅠlᴄeꞃeꞃꞃnec ꝺo ᴄum a luⅰnꞃe, ⁊ aꝺbaᴄh Ⅰaꞃam ꝼoꞃ muⅰꞃ Ꝺo oꞃᴄaᴄaꞃ ꝺemna ꝼeꞃ ꝺo muⅰnᴄⅰꞃ hlᴄa .ⅰ Ollum a aⅰnm ⅰꞃe céꝺ maꞃb Eꞃⅰnn ꝺo ꞃⅠl Ꞃaⅰoⅰl. "Ith took his leave of them and went to his ship After that they sent a company after them, and they wounded him in Magh Itha He reached, wounded and blood-dropping, his ship. and he died afterwards on the sea. Demons killed a man of Ith's people, Ollum was his name He was the first dead in Eri, of the seed of Gaedhal."—(*T*)

[t] *His strength being gone,* i e being killed or mortally wounded L reads

Ꝺonꝺ Colpꞇa Ꙇmaɪꞃꝣſn ꝣlun ꝣel   145
   Fſꞃ ꞇꞃſn ꞇíꞃec
Ip ꞃcéꝺ Ebſꞃ hſꞃɪmon
   ꞃe meɪc Mɪleꝺ.

Mac Icha Luꝣaɪꝺ caɪn cꞃecac
   coꞃcꞃach cachac   150
Ꝺaꞃ lſꞃ lechan ꝺolluɪꝺ
   ꝺo ꝺɪꝣaɪl a achaꞃ

buɪ bꞃſꝣaɪn bꞃuꞇmaꞃa beoꝺa,
   ꞃeɪb ꞃoꞃ ꞃíme
bloꝺ, Coꞃꞃ, Cualꝣne, Rɪꝣbaꞃꝺ   155
   Cɪꝣſꞃn mac bꞃɪꝣe.

baꞇaꞃ ceꞇhꞃɪ achɪꝣ ꝼɪceꞇ
   nɪꞃ bo uaboꞃ
ɪc ɪꞃꞃaí naꞃꞃɪꝣ cſn baɪꝣul
   ꝼoꞃ ꞃɪn ꞇ-ꞃluaꝣoꝺ.

Sluɪnꝺꞃeꞇꞃa ꝺuɪb uɪlɪ a nanmanꝺ   160
   maꞃ ꝺoꞃ ꞃaeꞃaɪꝣ
ɪaꞃ na n-aꞃɪm boſ ꝺɪaꞃ ꝺɪb
   ɪ ꝼaɪl cec oſnꝼɪꞃ.

                 Ꙇɪꝺne

ɪaꞃ mbaꞃ mbꞃɪꝣaɪch, "after a becoming death;" and in the next two lines, ꝺo loꝺaꞃ meɪc Nɪul mɪc bɪle, ꞃloꝣ ꝺɪa ꝺɪꝣaɪl; "the sons of Niul, the sons of Bile, came, a host, to revenge him." Bile was the father of Milesius, and a descendant of Niul.—(T.)

   ᵘ *Wide-ruling.*—The word ꞇɪꞃec has here evidently the signification of endowed with lands, wide-ruling; in which sense it is applied as a surname to Aongus Tirech, King of Munster, so called because he was fabled to have made extensive conquests in Europe. Book of Munster (MS Royal Irish Academy), p. 32 —(T)

   ᵛ *Descendants.*—The MS. reads buɪ,

Donn, Colptha, Amergin of the white knee,   145
    A hero mighty, wide-ruling[u];
Ir and Eber, Herimon,
    The six sons of Miledh.

The son of Ith, Lugaid, the fair, the plundering,
    Victorious, warlike,   150
Over the wide sea passed
    To avenge his father.

The descendants[v] of Breogan, ardent, vigorous,
    As we enumerated them,
Blod, Corp, Cualgne, Righbhard,   155
    Tighern, son of Brig.

There were *also* four and twenty plebeians[x],
    Who were not proud,
To attend on the chiefs without fail
    In the expedition   160

I shall recite unto you all their names,
    As I have[y] received them,
After their enumeration; there were two of them
    In attendance on each chieftain

                    Aidhne

which is also followed by N., but L reads heu. I have ventured to translate as if the reading was hui, the descendants, grandsons, posterity, a conjectural emendation suggested by Mr. O'Donovan, which seems necessary for the sense. The adjectives bruémara and beoda, being plural, require a plural substantive. For beoda L. reads fir. Bile, the father of Milesius, was the son of Breogan. Ith was also the son of Breogan Therefore, Lugaid was grandson, and all the others mentioned in the text, great-grandsons of Breogan.—(*T.*)

   [x] *Plebeians.*—This quatrain is omitted in L.—(*T.*)

   [y] *As I have* —L. reads ap fond po eing. —(*T.*)

Aione Aile Arral Mitte 165
    Monba Mine
Cuib Cliu Crna Sair Slán Lize
    Life Line

Lizrn Traiz Oollotar Aine
    Nai Orr Aine 170
Fea ronuair mínlec m-brozai
    Frmin Frra.

For oailret clano breozain buionec
    ba zrn mibail,
comtir foznaimthe na trrnfir 175
    oo na rizaib.

Ruc Cruirne mac Cinze a mna uauib
    rorrar n-oirec
inze Tea brn hrrimoin,
    mic Mileo. 180

Mor raethair cérait uili
    for cac m-buaone

                       la

* *Obtained.*—L. reads Feu fo uair min zel in roza. The twenty-four names are very corruptly given in L. They are as follows : Aione, Ai, Aral, Meioi, Monba, Mioi, Cuir, Cliu, Cera, Seir, Slan, Lize, Life, Lizzan, Traiz, Oul, Arao, Aine, Nat, Cer, Ene, Feu, Feimin, Frra. Other variations occur in the list given by Keating, p. 307, who makes the number of chieftains much more than twelve, and says nothing of two servants being assigned to each. Forty-one names are given in the poetical list of the chieftains enumerated in the verses beginning Toirrzh na loinzri tar ler, "The chieftains of the ships over the sea," attributed to Lochy O'Flynn, and preserved in the Leabhar Gabhala of the O'Clerys, p. 71; and O'Flaherty says, "Duces præcipui Hibernicæ expeditionis erant numero quadraginti."—Ogyg iii c. 4, p 182. —(*T.*)

Aidhne, Aile, Assal, Mitte,   165
  Morba, Mide,
Cuib, Cliu, Cera, Sair, Slan, Lighe,
  Life, Line.

Ligean, Traig, Dollotar, Aire,
  Nai, Dess, Aine,   170
Fea, who obtained[z] a fertile territory,
  Femin, Fera.

The sons of the fruitful Breogan decided,
  It was *done* without deceit,
That these stout yeomen[a] should be attendants   175
  Upon the kings

Cruithne, son of Cing, took their women[b] from them,
  It is directly stated,
Except Tea, wife of Herimon,
  Son of Miledh.   180

Great labour[c] did they all undergo
  In every tumult,

With

[a] *Yeomen.*—On the word na is the note in the margin no in, i e. "or in"—(*T.*)

[b] *Took their women.*—The other accounts represent the women as having been given to Cruithne with the consent of Herimon Our author seems to intimate here that they were taken by force Comp lines 215–218. Tea, wife of Herimon was daughter of Lughadh, son of Ith.—(*T.*) I may snatch occasion to note here, what I ought to have said Addit. Notes, line 19, page xli. Old Layamon represents the King of Britain as settling the Scythian Peohtes in Catenes (Caithness) But the Britons scorned to give them wives. So they asked and obtained women from Gilla Caor, King of Ireland.   And

Thurh tha ilke wifmen
That fole gan to spelien
Irlondes speche *v.* 10069

This assumes as notorious the fact, that they *did* speak that language —(*H.*)

[c] *Great labour.*—This is very obscure ,

la mna bpfrre la mná barre
la mna buaigne

banba a pleib Mipp co na pluagaib   185
  pipiuc cuiplec
Pócla in Eblinne apnac
  hEpiu in Uipnpic

Uvocoppat Tuata Oea
  tpia éfpt clitac,   190
o típ tivac vap noi connaib
  von lip letan.

Ro gab hepimon colleit in tpluaig
  iap n-upv tolgvai
timcell atuaiv ba gfn mfpgle   195
  v'inbfp Cholptai

                                             Ro

the meaning seems to be, either that the
Picts had to sustain great labours and
contests in order to obtain their wives,
or that after obtaining them, they had to
endure great labour before they acquired
a permanent settlement See Add Notes,
p lxx, and Keating (Haliday's ed.),
p 317.—(T)

  d *Banba.*—This quatrain is quoted by
Keating, p 288. Banba, Fothla, and Eire,
were the three queens of the Tuatha De
Danaan, wives of the sons of Carmad,
who held the sovereignty of Ireland on
the arrival of the Milesians. Shabh Mis,
which still retains its name, is a mountain south-west of Tralee, in the county of
Kerry Sliabh Ebhline. now Sleibhte
Ebhlinne, is a range of mountains beginning in the barony of Owneybeg and Coo-
nagh, in the county of Limerick, and
extending in the direction of Nenagh and
Cashel, in the county of Tipperary. Uisneach, or Usnagh, is a hill still bearing
the name, about four miles from Ballymore
Lough Sewdy, in the county of Westmeath In line 184. L. reads pepech
cuipleav. N. reads pipiut cuipleac (a
mistake, probably, for cuipleac) and Keating (in Halliday's edit), peitpeac, cuipleac. These differences are merely differences of spelling.—(T)

  e *Sent them,* i. e. sent the Milesians away
In line 188, L. reads tpe chept cpechach,
" with plundering might," i. e. irresisti-

With the wife of Bress, the wife of Bass.
  And the wife of Buaighne

They fought Banba[d] at Sliebh Mis with her hosts,   185
  Faint, wearied,
They fought Fothla at Ebhlinne, murmuring,
  Eire at Uisneach

The Tuatha Dea sent them[e] forth,
  According to the laws of war[f],   190
From the firm land over nine waves
  Of the broad sea

Herimon went[g] forth with half the host
  In proud array,
Round the north (it was without sorrow)   195
  To Inbher Colptha[h].

Donn

ble. In the next line the same MS. has o ᴄhiᴘ ᴄhaiᴄhlech, "from the pleasant land "—(*T*)

[f] *Laws of war* —The story here alluded to is given by Keating, p 291. The Milesians demanded a settlement in the country, or a battle. The Tuatha De Danaan offered to leave the decision of this question to the Milesian judge, Amergin, who was bound to give judgment according to law. He decided against his own brethren; but enjoined that the Milesians should re-embark, and go to sea, *a distance of nine waves*, and that then, if they could effect a landing against the forces of the Tuatha De Danaan, the country

should be their's This was agreed to by both sides. The words in which Amergin is said to have pronounced his judgment are preserved in the Leabhar Gabhala of the O'Clerys, p 72, where they are interpreted by a copious gloss, being in an ancient and nearly obsolete dialect of Irish —(*T*).

[g] *Went.*—L. reads luio and in the next line iaᴘ ᴄuino ᴄolᴄoa, "upon the proud waves." In line 193 the same MS. has ᴄimcheall an ᴄuaio bain can menᴣa.— (*T.*)

[h] *Inbher Colptha* —The bay of Colpa, son of Milesius, who was drowned there Keating, p. 293. This is the name still given

Ro ʒab Ꝺonꝺ ꝺo ꞃin leiꞇ aile
ıaꞃ n-uꝺꝺ ınnaıꞃꞃ
ba maꞃb ıc aꞃcnam cꞅn ċomaıꞃ
ꝺꞅꞃcꞅꞇ h-ıꞃꞃaıꞃ.

Co ꞇuaꞃcbaꝺ coꞃn la lıa a cꞅneoıl
aꞃ lıꞃ leꞇac   200
ꞃꞅn ꞇꞃeb ꞇonꞇec conıꝺ ꞇec Ꝺuınn
ꝺe ꝺon ʒaꞃaꞃ.

ba h-éꞃın a h-eꝺacꞇ aꞃbul
ꝺıa claınꝺ ceꞇaıch
cucum ꝺom ꞇıc ꞇıꞃꞃaıꝺ uılı   205
ıaꞃ baꞃ n-écaıb

Ic ınbıuꞃ Scꞅne ꞃo ꞃauꞃꞃeꞇ
ꞃcél cꞅn ꝺúnaꝺ
ꞃꞃuꞇ ꝺıan ꝺꞅꞃmaꞃ ın ꞃoꞃ ꞃoꞇꞃaıc
Fıal bꞅn Luʒꝺac   210
                                                    Roꞃ

to the mouth of the river Boyne at Drogheda.—(*T.*)

Without strength.—Cen ꞇunʒaıꞃ, L. For the story of Donn's shipwreck see Keating, p 293.—(*T.*)

Irrus.—From this it appears that the south-western promontory of Kerry was anciently called *Irrus,* or the western promontory, for it was there that the shipwreck, according to all tradition, took place.—(*T.*)

Tech Duinn, or the House of Donn. See above, p. 56, note ᵐ. It would be very

desirable to ascertain whether the islands at the mouth of Kenmare river, one of which is now identified by tradition with Tech Duinn, contain carns, or other traces of a pagan burying ground From their inaccessible situation it is not likely that any rude monuments they may contain have been much disturbed The words "stone of his race" probably allude to a custom of later date, when an inscribed stone, marking the name, family, or rank of the deceased, was placed over his grave. For co ꞇuaꞃcbaꝺ, line 199, L. reads aꞃ

Donn went with the other half
   In progressive order,
He died as he was sailing, without strength,
   At the south of Irrus.

There was raised *for him* a cairn with the stone of his race,
   Over the broad sea,   200
An ancient stormy dwelling; and Tech Duinn,
   It is called.

This was his great testament
   To his numerous children,
" To me, to my house, come ye all   205
   After your deaths "

At Inbher Scene they landed,
   The story is not concealed,
The rapid great stream in which bathed
   Fial, wife of Lughadh.   210

They

tocbao, and in line 200, uaiﬂe aﬁ laim-
cheach, also in the next line ﬁoﬁtec, bold,
daring, for tontec, boisterous, wave-bea-
ten.—(*T.*)

This was.—L. reads Combai tﬁacht ao-
bul From this quatrain it appears that the
island called Tech Duinn was believed to
be the burial place of Donn's posterity I
am not aware that it has ever been examined by any competent antiquary, with
a view to test this tradition.—(*T.*)

Inbher Scene, the mouth of the river
Skean, so called from Scene Dulsaine, wife

of Amergin, who was there drowned. See
Keating, p 296; Duald Mac Firbis, Genealogies (Marquis of Drogheda's copy),
p. 45 Inbher Skene was the ancient
name of the mouth of the river Corrane,
in the Co Kerry.—(*T.*)

Fial—The following account of the
death of Fial, who was the daughter of
Milesius and wife of Lughad, son of Ith,
is given in the Leabhar Gabhala, p 74·
Iﬁ in oioche i tanﬃaoaﬁ meic Mileo
in Eﬁinn, tomaoim loch Luiﬃoeach ﬁo
tiﬁ in iaﬁ Mumain. Oia mbaoi Luﬃao

Rop vailptt po h-Epinv opaiz
  map atbpmv
zníptt copa ppi Fipu bolz
  ppi clanv Nemiv

Nip bátap mná poipbe poípe   215
  ce a nozlea
Ap n̊-zait a m-ban zabpat clpmnap
  Tuat Oea

Oo bptt vóib leth cet apba
  co muip meobap,   220
iapp in capvvine coip comoip,
  iapp in clpmnap.

Ro zab hlpimon in tuappptt
  vú via cinivv,
Co na plncup, co na póluv,   225
  co na n-olizuv.

                                              Co

mac locha za potpaiz ipin loch, ꝶ Fial out of the lake Lughaidh came on shore
inzpn Mileo a bean occa potpaiz ipin where the woman was naked, and she
loch. Oo luiv Luzao zup an vu i thought it was another man, and died of
mbaoi an inzpn op e noct ꝶ opo pill paip shame immediately. And from her the
pamlaiv atbail oo naipe po chetoip, ꝶ river and its mouth have their name."
ap vaite anmniztep an abann con a Then follows, in the Leabhar Gabhala, a
mbep. "It was on the night on which poem, said to have been composed by
the Milesians landed in Eri, that Loch Lughaidh on the occasion See Keating
Luighdheach [in Kerry] broke out of (Haliday's Edit) p. 96.—(*T.*)
the earth in West Munster Lughaidh,
son of Ith, was bathing in the lake, and ° *Tuatha Dea.*—According to this ac-
Fial, daughter of Miledh, his wife, was count, the Milesians formed alliances with
with him bathing in the river that runs all the tribes in possession of the country
 This fact, which, if true, would account for

They spread themselves through Eri, to her coasts,
 As is recorded,
They made an alliance with the Firbolg,
 And with the sons of Nemhedh.

There were no charming, noble wives   215
 For their young men;
Their women having been stolen, they made alliance
 With the Tuatha Dea°.

Unto them was given[p] the half of all the land,
 To the boisterous sea,   220
After *this* just and judicious league,
 And after *this* alliance.

Herimon took[q] the north
 As the inheritance of his race,
With their antiquity, with their prosperity,   225
 With their rights,

                 With

the difference of race so manifest in the mere Irish population, is not mentioned by Keating or other popular historians L. reads in v 216, cia ꝑo nᵹlea, and for aꝥ nᵹaic, in the next line, caꝑoᵹaꝥc.—(*T.*)

 [p] *Was given.*—Ꝺoꝑaca, L. For aꝥba the same MS. reads ꝼoꝥba, which is evidently the meaning, and in the next line, meblaꝥ for meꝺbaꝥ. In line 221, iaꝥ ꝑm chaiꝥc michaim chombꝥuꝥ.—(*T.*)

 [q] *Took.*—Ᵹabaiꝥ, L. In the next line L has cona chineaꝺ, "with his race;" and in lines 225, 226, cona ꝑeanchoꝥ,

cona cholach, cona ꝺliᵹeaꝺ. After line 224, there is an omission in N of eighty-eight lines. All the ancient Irish writers agree that Herimon possessed the northern, and Heber the southern parts of Ireland, and yet Giraldus Cambrensis reverses this division in his Topographia Hiber D. III c 6 Camd. p 737 "Procedente vero tempore duo istorum nominatissimi Hibernis scilicet et Herymon duas in partes æquales, regnum inter se diviserunt. Herymoni cessit pars Australis: Hebero quidem Aquilonaris." To this day, however, the people of Munster

Co na n-ꝺúnıb, co na caṫaıb,
   ᵹaıpᵹe pſᵹꞇe,
co na n-ꝺebꞇhaıᵹe ꞇpıa oıbhne,
   co na ceꞇhpe   230

Ro ᵹab Ebſp oſpcſpꞇ ṅhEpenn,
   opꝺ po cınnıup,
co na uꞇmaılle, cona ċommuſ,
   co na bınnıuſ.

Co na buaꝺaıb, co na h-uıle,   235
   co na aeᵹe,
co na ꝺſpaıꝺe ꞇpıa ꝺúpe,
   co na chaıne, co na ꝺene

Ꝺo ċlaınꝺ hſpımoın ꝺo Laᵹnıb
   luaꞇ co cloċꝺa,   240
Leꞇh Cuınꝺ, Connacꞇ, Nıall ꝼappe,
   Nıal ınꝺ pocla.

                Foꞇapꞇ

are called Slıoċꞇ Eıbıp. "Errat autem Giraldus ın dımıdıo Australı trıbuendo Heremonı, &c, cum omnes antıquı uno ore eı trıbuant Borealem, et Hebero Australem." Dr. O'Conor, ın Ann. 4 Mag. p. 10, note 1.—(T.)

ʳ *Fortresses*—Here again ın the text we have cona ꞃꝺunıb, "with their fortresses," whıch ıs ınconsıstent wıth the context, and ought to be con ɑ ꝺunıb. L. reads·

   Con ɑ ꝺıumaſ, con ɑ chɑꝺchaı
      ᵹaıꞃchuꞃ eıᵹnı
   Cona ꞓheıpꞇhıch ꞇpıa opnı
     con ɑ eıꞇꞃı

"With its pride, with its wars,
With its shouts of distress,
With its failures from its rashness,
With its wings."—(*T*)

ˢ *Power*—The MS. here reads cɑn commuſ, but the context shows that the scrıbe ıntended to wrıte cona, and I have altered ıt accordıngly. L. reads cen chomaſ, "wıthout power."—(*T*.)

ᵗ *Harmony.*—Alludıng, perhaps, to the legend, whıch wıll be found ın Keatıng, p. 306, of Cır, son of Cıs, the poet, havıng been allotted to Herımon, and Onee, the harper, to Heber.—(*T*.)

ᵘ *Grandeur*—L. reads cona umlɑ,

With its fortresses[r], with its troops,
    Fierce, active,
With their rash fights,
    With their cattle   230

Eber took the south of Eri,
    The order was *so* agreed on,
With its activity, with its power[s],
    With its harmony[t],

With its victories, with its grandeur[u],   235
    With its hospitality,
With its vivacity *combined* with hardiness,
    With its loveliness, with its purity

Of the race of Herimon are the Lagenians[x],
    Of fame renowned[y],   240
Leth-Cuinn, Conacht, Niall of the south,
    Niall of the North.

The

humility, or submission; and, in the next line, cona ḟeiʒi, in line 237, for τρια δυṗe, L. has cen δuiṗi, "without harshness," and in line 238, cona ḟeile, "with its festivity," omitting cona chaiṗe.—(*T*)

[x] *Lagenians*, i. e. the families of Leinster Ugaine Mor, king of Ireland, whose reign commenced, according to O'Flaherty, A M. 3619, was a lineal descendant of Herimon; and to his son, Laeghaire Lorc, are traced the O'Conors of Offaly, O'Tooles, O'Byrnes, Mac Murroughs, Mac Gillpatricks, and all the great families of Leinster. Ugaine is also the ancestor of Con of the Hundred Battles, and of all the septs called Hy Niall, seated in Meath and Ulster; also of the families of Leath Cuinn, or the northern half of Ireland, with the exception of the Clanna Rudhraighe, and some minor families. The great families of Connaught also, as the O'Conors, O'Flahertys, O'Dowdas, O'Heynes, O'Shaughnessys, &c, who are chiefly of the race of Eochaidh Muighmheadhoin, and therefore belong to the family of Ugaine Mor, and the line of Herimon—(*T.*)

[y] *Renowned*—L. reads luaδ can clothna The word ḟaṗṗe, in the next line, is explained in Cormac's Glossary, .i δeiṗ-

Foṫaꞃṫ, na Ðéꞃɪ, Moᵹ Láma,
   la cuꞃ Cualṅᵹe,
Fɪꞃ Ðalꞃɪaṫaɪ, Coꞃca ꞃɪnne,
   ɪꞅ Coꞃcu ꞃoꞅða   245

Rɪᵹꞃaɪð claɪnne Ecaċ uɪlɪ Ðomblén,
   ṫuɪꞃ ðoṫélaɪb,
Iꞅ ꞃɪᵹꞃað Aɪꞃᵹɪall a buɪcne,
   co loch Febaɪl   250

Fɪꞃ

cɪꞃṫ, ɪ e the south, and has been so translated ; but L. reads here, Nɪall Fɪnn ꞃaɪchle.—(T)

[2] *The Fotharts.*—These were the descendants of Eochaidh Finn Fothart, son of Fedhlimidh Rechtmhar, King of Ireland, A.D. 164. He was banished from Meath, then the seat of the kings, by his nephew, Art Aenan, who began his reign, according to O'Flaherty, A.D. 220.—Ogyg. iii. c. 64. The posterity of Eochaidh Finn Fothart settled in various parts of Leinster, and the baronies of Fothart or Forth, in the counties of Carlow and Wexford, still retain their name. The Deisi were the descendants of Fiacha Suighdhe, son of Fedhlimidh Rechtmhar, and were, therefore, of the senior line of Ugaine Mor. But they were set aside by Con of the Hundred Battles, and afterwards expelled from Meath by Cormac O'Cuinn, his grandson, who began his reign A.D. 254.—Ogyg. iii. c. 69. They settled in the district now called from them Decies, in the County Waterford, and in the barony of

Middlethird, County Tipperary.—(T)

[a] *Mogh Lamha's race.*—Mogh Lamha was the father of Conaire II., King of Ireland, A.D. 212, who married Saraid, daughter of Con of the Hundred Battles, and was the father of the three Cairbres, from one of whom, Cairbre Riada, or Rioghfhada, the Dal-Riada, or race of Riada, are descended. The district of Dalriada, now called the *Rout*, in the county Antrim, takes its name from the race that inhabited it. See Reeves's Eccl. Antiq. of Down, and Connor, and Dromore, note FF p. 318, *et seq.* The genealogy of Mogh Lamha is thus given in the Book of Conquests, p. 147. He was the son of Lughaidh Alladham, King of Munster, son of Coirpre Crimchuin, son of Daire Dornmhair, son of Cairpre Fionnmhor, King of Munster, son of Conaire Mor, King of Ireland.—(T.)

[b] *Cualgne.*—For la cuꞃ Cualᵹne, L. reads la coꞃc ᵹaela. Cualgne is a mountainous district in the north of the county of Louth, now Cooley; the celebrated Cuchullin, of the race of Heri-

The Fotharts[z], the Deisi, Mogh Lamha's[a] *race*,
    With the warrior of Cualgne[b],
The men of Dalriada, Corco-Rinne[c],   245
    And Corco-Roeda[d].

The kings of the race of Eochaidh Doimhlen[e],
    The pillars of his houses,
And the kings of Argiall[f], from Buichne
    To Loch Febhail[g].   250

Fir

mon, was the champion of Cualgne, and perhaps he is here particularly alluded to. Corc Gaela, mentioned in the reading of L., was king of the country now called Eile, or Ely, in Ormond. He was married to Ele, daughter of Eochaidh Mac Luchta, and his descendants were the Corco Gaela. The three Fotharts were his chief representatives, through their mother Finche.—(*T.*)

[c] *Corco-Rinne.*—L. reads copco chupano, but I know not who were the Corco Rinne, or Corco Churann. There is propably some corruption of the text in all the copies —(*T*)

[d] *Corco-Raeda.*—These were the descendants of Fiacha Raide, son of Fiacha Suighdhe, already mentioned as the ancestor of the Deisi. The Corcoraidians occupied the barony of Corcaree in the county of Westmeath —Ogyg. iii. c. 69.—(*T*)

[e] *Eochadh Doimhlen*—He was the son of Cairbre Liffeachar, King of Ireland, and father of Colla Huais, King of Ireland.—Ogyg. iii. c. 75 L omits uili in line 247,

which is evidently redundant· and in the next line the same manuscript reads cuip oia chelaib. He is called "a pillar of his houses," i. e. of the houses or families descended from him, because he was the common ancestor of the O'Kellys of Hy-Many, Maguires, Mac Mahons of Oriel, O'Hanlons, &c.—(*T.*)

[f] *Kings of Argiall*—L has simply na h-Aingialla, the Argialla. They were the descendants of the three Collas, the sons of Eochaidh Doimhlen —Ogyg. iii. c. 76.—(*T.*)

From Buichne to Loch Febhail.—L reads ocha buaibnich. The meaning is, that the authority of the Argialla extended over the district, from the River Buichne to Loch Febhail or Foyle. In St Patrick's time the Argialla had possession of all the country about Loch Foyle and the now counties of Monaghan, Armagh, a great part of Tyrone, and of the barony of Slane in Meath. Where the Buichne is I do not know, but it appears to be the name of a river.—(*T.*)

Fin Oazial o Zréin co Conaio
      cfn nac noímfyy,
oez meic Maine bnfyail Fiacnaiz Oallán,
      acuy Oomlen oilfy

Oubne ooluy cfmen [pooub]   255
      Fochuo aipznec,
Qenoia Cnennia,
      Cofnnia caippoec.

Copppe Qpao, Qpao Cipe,
      Qpao Cliacac,   260
Lacapn bfnncpaize Inmanaiz,
      Oal Fino Fiacac

                                        Foola

ʰ *Coraid.*—Fer da Ghiall, ı e Eochaidh
Ferdaghiall, the ancestor of the Hy-Many,
ın Connaught, whose territory extended
from Grian to Coraidh See O'Donovan's
Genealogies, Tribes, &c , of Hy-Many,
pp. 7, 10. 25, 66, 130, 134 For copaio,
ın lıne 251, L reads copaich, and ın
the next lıne cenoach nımeuy In lıne
253 the words oez meic are omitted —
(*T.*)

ı *Greyness.*—The word pooub ıs ınserted from L and ıs necessary to complete the metre, ıt sıgnıfies, lıterally, *half
black* —(*T*)

ᵏ *Fothads* —The three Fothads were the
sons of Lugadh Mac Con, Kıng of Ireland
A.D 250, according to O'Flaherty's dates
They were called Fothad Aırgtheach, Fothad Caırptheach, and Fothad Canann.—

Ogyg. p 329 The names Aendia, Tren-
nıa, and Coennıa, lınes 257, 258, are
other names gıven to the three Fothads,
Aırgtheach, Caırptheach, and Canann.—
—(*T*)

ˡ *Coıpre Aıad* —In the margın another
readıng ıs gıven thus · no Copppe clıac,
lıacaın, fıozenıo, fono mbıacac , and
the same readıng occurs also ın L, both
readıngs beıng ınserted together, so as to
gıve thıs stanza the appearance of contaın-
ıng sıx lınes

Caıpbpı cach Lıacan, Fıozenıo,
      fono mbıacach,
Caıpppı Qpao, Qpao Chıpı,
      Qpao Clıach,
Lachaıpnı, beanncpaızı Inmanaıchı,
      Oal Fıno Fıacach.

Fir da Ghiall, *who duell* from Grian to Coradh[h],
  Without contempt,
The good sons of Maine, Breasail, Fiachra, Dallan,
  And Domhlen the faithful.

Blackness, darkness, dimness, greyness[i],   255
  The Fothads[k], the plunderers
Aendia, Trennia,
  Coennia of chariots

Corpre Arad[l], Arad Tire,
  Arad Chathach,   260
Latharn[m], Benntraighe, Ionmanaich,
  Dal Finn Fiatach[n]

The

Cairbri, Cach [*read* Chach], Liathan, Fidhgeimdh,
  Of the fertile soil,
Cairpri, Arad, Arad Thiri,
  Arad Chach,
Lathairn, Beanntraighe the beloved,
  Dal Finn Fiatach

Cairpri Arad, Arad Thire, and Arad Chach or Chathach, are the tribes settled in Duharra, and the adjacent territory in Tipperary.—See O'Donovan's Book of Rights, published by the Celtic Society, p 46, *n*.—(*T.*)

[m] *Latharn*.—The district of Larne, Co. Antrim, in the ancient territory of Dalaradia, which derives its name from Lathair, one of the sons of Ugaine Mor. The Benntraighe are the descendants of Beann, son of Connor Mac Nessa, according to some accounts, or of Conganeins, of the Er-

neans of Munster, according to others See M'Firbis, pp. 381, 503 They were settled at Bantry Bay in the county Cork, and also at Bantry, on the borders of the counties of Wicklow and Wexford. The Ionmanaich were descended from Colla Meann in Mughdhorne.—Book of Leacan, fol 88, *b, b*.—(*T.*)

[n] *Dal Finn Fiatach*.—The descendants of Fiatach Finn, who, according to Tighernach, began to reign in Emania, as King of Uladh or Ulidia, in the year A D 108, and in 116, according to O'Flaherty's Chronology, became king of Ireland.—Ogyg p. 142, and p. 301 He was of the race of Herimon, of the family of the Ernai, or descendants of Oilioll Aroun, who settled in Ulster.—Ogyg p 266.—(*T*)

Foula Conppe rceo Tpatpaize
ba coipm típech,

rluaz balc buaoac, muncip hfpimoin,   265
mic Mileo

Maicene Ebip Eozanacta,
uili apoaic,

Ani, loc Léim, Capel, Zlenoamain,
Rorr n-Apzaic.   270

Eocu Rairlinne cfn oponzao
cáin culao,

Eozanacc cec oú i tác,
la bpizu Muman.

Mate Oál Chaipr Oal Cein cecaiz,   275
co nzail ipznai,

                                                   Oal

° *Corpraighe.*—Over the word Conppe
in the text the MS has the correction
no Conppaize in a later hand, and over
Tpatpaize, the correction no Oapcpaize,
which have been adopted in the translation L reads foula Conbpaioi rceo
Oapcpaioi, and in the next line copno
oipeoch The Corpiaighe are the descendants of Carbie Lifteachar, son of
Cormac Mac Art King of Ireland, A D
279 —Ogyg p. 341 The Dartraighe were
a tribe situated near Loch Gill, in the
barony of Carbeiy, Co Sligo, descended
from Lugad Cal, of the family of Ith
Ogyg p. 329.—(*T*)

ᵖ *In every place*· i.e in every place

where the Eoghanachts are to be found,
of which the poet proceeds to enumerate
the principal The Eoghanachts were the
descendants of Eoghan, son of Oilioll
Olum, King of Munster, A D. 237.—Ogyg
p 326. There were various septs of them
in the south of Ireland, as the Eoghanacht Ani or O'Ciermeics, at Ani, now
Knockany, in the Co Limerick, the Eoghanacht Locha Lein, or O'Donohues, at
Loch Lein, now the Lake of Killarney,
barony of Magunnihy, Co. Kerry, the
Eoghanacht Caisil, or Mac Carthys, of
Cashel, the Eoghanacht Ruis-airgid, near
the river Nore in Ossory; Eoghanacht
Rathlenn, or O'Mahonys, in the barony

The families of Corpraighe° and of Dartruighe,
    Fertile is *their* territory,
A mighty host, victorious, the race of Herimon,   265
    Son of Miledh

The descendants of Eber *are* the Eoghanachts
    In every place[p],
At Ani, Loch Lein, Caisel, Glendamain,
    And Ros-argaid   270

Eochaidh of Raithlinne[q], without oppression,
    Magnificent *their* apparel,
The Eoghanachts wherever they are *found*
    In the lands of Mumhan[r]

The nobles of Dal Cais[s], Dal Cein the numerous,   275
    Of illustrious valour,

                    Dal

of Kinelmbeaky, Co Cork, the Eoghanachts of Glendamnach, or O'Keeffe's country, in the Co Cork, the Eoghanachts of the island of Arann, in the bay of Galway, and other branches which settled in Scotland.—Ogyg. p 328. The MS reads cloenoabain in line 269, for which the reading of L. has been adopted in the text, as being more correct.—(*T.*)

[q] *Eochaidh of Raithlinne*. i. e the Eoghanachts of Rathlenn, or O'Mahonys. See last note.—(*T.*)

[r] *Mumhan* i e in the lands, or farms (bruig), i. e. settlements of Munster. In line 271 L. reads Eochu Roichlino apu cen oponga, and in line 273, cach chin

icaic.—(*T.*)

[s] *Dal Cais.*—The posterity of Cais, son of Conall Eachluadh, King of Munster, in the fourth century.—Ogyg p. 386 The title of Dal Cais was given to the inhabitants of Thomond, including the great families of O'Brien, Mac Namara, Mac Mahon, O'Curry, &c. The *Dal Cein* or Cianachts, are the posterity of Cian, son of Oiholl Olum (Ogyg p 328), including the families now known by the sirnames of O'Carroll (of Ely), O'Meagher (of Ikerrin, Tipperary), O'Conor (of Glengiven, Co. Londonderry), O'Hara and O'Gara, in the diocese of Achonry, Mac Cormac of Bregia, &c. For oal cein L. reads cen-

Dal Moga, Dal Cuipc, Dal Ceaca,
Ꙃalenꙃa, Delbna.

Tpaṫpaiꙃi cech ꝺu icac,
Luꙃni im ꝺualaic,   280
Luꙃaiꝺ Láꙃe, Luꙃuipne,
acup Moꙃo Nuaꝺaic.

Nuall claınne Luꙃꝺac mic Ica,
Oll conꝺ puꝺpaꙃ,

                                                    €pne

ꝺach, and ın lıne 277 ꝺal mancha, ꝺal cuıpc, ꝺal ecca cıanachca —(*T.*)

Dal Mogha.—The race of Mogh Nuadhat, or Eogan More, father of Oilioll Olum The Dal Ceata are unknown, but the Dal Corc are probably the descendants of Corc mac Lughach, Prince of Munster, the reputed ancestor of the Stewards of Scotland, of the Eoganacht of Loch Lein, and of the Cuirene, ın Westmeath — Mac Fırbıs, p 165 —(*T*)

Galengs —The Galengs were a branch of the Dal Cein (Ogyg. p 328), comprising the O'llaras, O'Gaıas, O'Cathesıs, and O'Henessys, ın Connaught and Meath They were descended from Cormac Galengach, great-grandson of Oilioll Olum, King of Munster The MS reads ın lıne 278 Ꙃalınꙃ Delnai, but the reading of L has been substituted as more correct The Delbhna were a branch of the Dal-Cais, descended from Lugadh Dealbhaodh, son of Cas. To thıs tribe belong the familıes of Coghlan of Garrycastle, King's County,

Mac Conry (anglicized King) of Connemara, O'Finnellan of Delvin, ın Westmeath, &c. From the different branches of thıs tribe seven different dıstricts or baronies take the name of Delvin.—Ogyg. p 327.—(*T*)

Tratrayhe —L. reads Ꝺapcpaıꝺı The Tratıaıghe were seated ın the rural deanery of Tradıy, ın the barony of Bunratty, Co Clare. They were of the Fırbolg, but the terrıtory became the ınheritance of Lugaidh Dealbaith, who was driven out of ıt by the ıntrigues of hıs daughter, and forced to fly ınto Meath. It ıs also stated that *Trad* was the name of hıs daughter's husband, and hence *Tradrayhe* —M'Fırbıs, pp. 59, 654.—(*T.*)

The Lughni.—These were a branch of the Gailenga (Ogyg p 328), and gave their name to the barony of Luıghne (Leyny), ın the Co Slıgo, and to the barony of Luıghne (Lune), ın the Co Meath.—(*T.*)

Lugaid Lage —The brother of Oilioll

Dal Mogha[t], Dal Corc, Dal Ceata,
　　The Galengs[u], the Delbhna.

The Tratraighe[x] wherever they are *found*,
　　The Luighni[y] are of the same race,　　　　　　　280
Lugaid-Lage[z], Liguirne,
　　And Mogh-Nuadhait[a].

The fame of the race of Lugaidh son of Ith[b],
　　As a great straight *rolling* wave[c],

　　　　　　　　　　　　　　　　　　　　　　　　The

Olum, who slew Art, monarch of Ireland, after the battle of Magh Mucroimhe, near Athenry, Co Galway. A. D 270　Ligh-urn, the grandson of Eochy Finn Fothart, was the companion of Lugaid Lage in the battle, and joined him in the slaughter of King Art.—Ogyg p 328.

[a] *Mogh Nuadhat*—The father of Oilioll Olum, and head of all the race of Heber. He compelled Con of the Hundred Battles to divide Ireland with him, from which the southern half of Ireland was called Leath Mogha, or Mogha's half.—Ogyg. p 315.—(*T*)

[b] *Lugaid son of Ith.*—Our author having mentioned the principal septs descended from Herimon and Heber, the sons of Milesius, now proceeds to celebrate the race of Lugaid, son of Ith, who was the leader and instigator of the Milesian in-vasion. His posterity were settled in the diocese of Ross, south-west of the county Cork, but the principal family of the race now extant is that known by the name of

O'Hedersceol or O'Driscoll　O'Flaherty says that the family of Mac Cathlin, now Campbell, of Argyle, in Scotland, is of this race, being descended from Fothadh Conann, son of Lughadh Mac Con, King of Ireland.—Ogyg pp. 329, 330.　There is a curious historical tract on the history of the race of Lughaidh Mac Ith, in the Book of Leacan, fol. 122, which is well worthy of publication, for the valuable light it throws on the topography and history of a part of Ireland hitherto very little known.　The word nuall, line 283, has been translated *fame*, it signifies lite-rally *a shout*, and metaphorically may be taken to denote fame or celebrity　In the Feilire Aenguis (1 Feb), St. Bridget is called Ḃrigid ban balcc nuallan, " Brid-get, a woman of great shouting," and the gloss says. ı nuall ann, no nuall an, no uapal, no nuall an ı. ıf mop, ⁊ ıf an nuall caıch ocuınchıo ıcze fop Ḃrigic No ıf mop nuall celebapcha oc Ḃrigic, ⁊c; ı e. "nuall ann, a shout there ; or

Eppne Aptbpaige Mupca bapcan,   285
   meic Luzvach

Luzaiv Opcte Luzaiv Zala,
   Ofpza Ofn aible,
pí Dúin Chfpmna beppe,
   Lugaiv Laizve   290

Lán in hEpin vo claino Ip,
   mic Mileo,
Mivip Ruvpaize pí Factna Fatac,
   cona ciniuv baive.

Ciap a ceithfin Conmac cona   295
   maine muach,

                                      conpcu

nuall an, a noble [shout] ; or nuall an, i. e great and noble is the shout of the people asking requests of Bridget, or great is the shout of celebration with Bridget" [i. e. celebration of her festival], &c — (T.)

c *Wave* —L reads oill tuino tupaio, puopaz means straight, direct —(T.)

d *Bascan* — The Ernai, Arbhraighe, [Orbhraigh or Orrery Co Cork], Musca (Muscraighe), and Bascan, are tribes of the race of Herimon, according to the common account. But the Book of Lecan states that by some they are deduced from Ir, son of Ith, fol. 112, b L reads in the next line na tpi luzaio. At line 286 the copy in the book of Leacan ends, but a column was left blank for the continuation, which is now filled with other matter in a later hand —(T)

e *Lugaidh Oirethe* — Lughaid Oirethe, from whom descended the Corco Oirethe, Lughaid Cal, from whom the inhabitants of the district of Calry, of Loch Gill, barony of Carbery, Co. Sligo, and Lugaidh Laighde, the grandfather of Lughaid Mac Con, King of Ireland (from whom came the Corco Laighde, in the west of the Co. Cork), were all sons of Daire, of the race of Ith —Ogyg p 329 —(T)

f *Derga.*—Not known.—(T.)

g *Oen-Aibhle.*—Unknown —(T)

h *Dun-Kirmna* —A fortress at the foot of the Old Head of Kinsale, called in the 17th century, Dun Patrick, from one of the De Courcys, to whom the district belonged —Ogyg p 205, Keating, in the reign of Cearmna. It had its old name

The Ernai, Arbhraighe, Musca, Bascan[d], 285
    Are the sons of Lugaidh.

Lughaid-Orethe[e], Lughaid Gala,
    Derga[f], Oen-aibhle[g]
The King of Dun-Kermna[h], Berre[i],
    Lughaid Laighde 290

Eri is full of the race of Ir,
    Son of Miledh,
Midir[k], Rudhraighe, King Fachtna Fathach,
    With their warlike kinsmen

Ciar with his foot-soldiers[l], Conmac with his . 295
    Of great wealth,

                                    The

of Dun Kermna, from Cearmna, king of the southern half of Ireland, who began to reign conjointly with Sobhairee, both of the race of Ir, in the year A M. 3045, according to O'Flaherty Our author differs from the best authorities, if we are to understand him as deducing these families from Lughad, son of Ith. For the Ernai of middle Munster were descended from Cathaoir, son of Edirscol, King of Ireland , and the Ernai of Dun-Kermna, in South Munster, from Duibhne, son of the same Cathaoir, from whom their posterity were called Corco-Duibhni They were, therefore, of the race of Herimon —Ogyg. p. 271.—(*T.*)

   [i] *Berre*—Now Bearhaven, Co Cork—(*T*)

   [k] *Midir*—There is probably some mistake of transcription in this name, for it does not occur in the genealogies of the race of Ir. Rudhraighe, ancestor of the Clanna Rudraighe, of the race of Ir, was King of Ireland, according to O'Flaherty, A. M. 3845 (Ogyg. p 265), and Fachtna Fathach, or the Provident, son of Cas, and grandson of Rudhraighe, succeeded to the throne, A M., 3899 (ib. p 266) — (*T.*)

   [l] *Foot-soldiers*, or kernes.—For Cup a ceithepn, we should probably read Cup conα ceithepn The last word of this line ought, perhaps, to be cope, for Ciar, Corc, and Conmac, were the illegitimate sons of Fergus Mac Roigh, ex-King of Ulster, of the race of Ir, by Meadhbh, Queen of Connaught (Ogyg iii c. 46). Ciar was ancestor of all the tribes called Ciar-

Copcu Dallan, Copcu Eoluim
Copcompuad

Dál mbuain Conpino comil rípgín,
rírb ngorpa   300
Mog Roich pírra cimiud Pengupa
mic Ropra

Ríge o Pactnu Dál nApaide
epcoa dogaip
rect Laigre Lagín co pebail,   305
na píct Sogaim,

Sil

raighe, in Connaught, viz., Ciarraighe Lu-
achra (comprising the greater part of the
present county of Kerry), the patrimony
of O'Conor Kerry; Ciarraighe Ai, now
Clann Kethern in Roscommon, and Ciarraighe Locha n-Airneadh, in the county
Mayo, comprising that portion of the barony of Costello belonging to the diocese
of Tuam See O'Donovan's Hy Fiachrach,
p 484, and map Conmac was the ancestor of the people called Conmaicne as
the Conmaicne of Moyrein, in the counties of Longford and Leitrim, of whom the
O'Farrells and Mac Rannalls are the principal remaining families; the Conmaicne of
Kinel Dubhan, or Dunmore, Co. Galway;
Conmacne Mara, now Connemara, and
Conmaicne Tola, barony of Kilmaine, Co
Mayo.—O'Flaherty's West Connaught,
pp. 92-94. The third son, Corc, was the
ancestor of the Corco-modhruadh, or Cor-
cumiuaidh, mentioned line 298, in the
barony of Corcomroe, which was origi-

nally co-extensive with the diocese of Kil-
fenora, Co Clare The O'Loghlins of Bui-
ren, and the O'Conor Corcomroe, are the
principal families of this race now remaining —Ogyg pp 275, 276.—(T.)

ⁿ Corca Dallan.—The posterity of Dallan, son of Fergus Mac Roigh, ex-King
of Ulster. The Corca-Eoluim, or Corca-
Auluim, were the descendants of Aulam,
or Corb-Aulam, twin brother of Conri,
son of Fergus Mac Roigh.—Ogyg. p 274.
—(T)

º Dal m-Buain, or Dal m-Buinne, were
the descendants of Buain, son of Fergus
Mac Roigh Their territory comprised
the barony of Upper Massareene, Co Antrim, with the parishes of Kilwarlin and
Drumbo Reeves's Eccl Antiq. p 233,
note', p 364 Ogyg 274 Dal Confinn
were the descendants of Aongus Finn, son
of Fergus mac Roigh, they were the inhabitants of Coolavin, in the county of Sligo.
Ogyg p 275.—(T)

The Corca-Dallan[m], the Corca-Eoluim,
  The Corcumruaidh

Dal mBuain[n], Confinn, of powerful deeds,
  Of fierce valour,   300
Mogh Roith[o], the protector, *are all* of the race of Fergus,
  The son of Ross.

The kings *of the race of* Fachtna[p], the Dal n-Araidhe,
  Warlike, fierce,
The seven Laigse[q] of Leinster the wealthy,   305
  The seven Soghans[r]

                                       The

[o] *Mogh Roith*.—A celebrated Druid of the race of the Ciarraighe His posterity obtained the territory of Fermoy, Co. Cork; from him were descended the families of O'Dubhagain or O'Duggan, and O'Coscraigh, also the saints Mochuille and Molagga, and Cuanna MacCailchinne, chief of Fermoy, celebrated for his hospitality who flourished in the seventh century See Keating, in the reign of Conall Caol and Cellach, Colgan, in Vit S Molaggæ, ad 20 Jan All the foregoing tribes and personages (mentioned lines 295 to 301) are here said to be of the race of Fergus Mac Roigh [so called from his mother's name], who was the son of Ross Ruadh, son of Rudhruighe, King of Ireland, A M. 3845.—Ogyg. p. 265 Mogh Roith is called *protector* from his having, by his magic, assisted the Munster men to defeat Cormac Mac Art, at the battle of Damhdhaire, in the second century. Dudley Mac Firbis translates the name of Mogh Roth, *Magus Rotæ*, and says that he assisted Simon Magus, to make the Roth-ramhach, a magical wheel, by means of which Simon was enabled to ascend into the air, and which is to overwhelm all Europe in some fatal calamity before the day of judgment See this strange legend in D Mac Firbis, p 535 (MS in the Library of the Royal Irish Academy), and Book of Leacan, fol 133 —(*T*)

[p] *Fachtna*·i e the race of Fachtna Fathach, King of Ireland The Dal-Aradians were of the race of Fiacha Araidhe, of the family of Rudhruighe, and race of Ir, King of Ulster, A D 236 —Tighernach, Annal in an , Ogyg iii c. 66; Reeves's Ecclesiastical Antiq., Appendix GG , p 334 —(*T*)

[q] *Laighse*, or *Leix*.—Districts inhabited by the descendants of Laoighseach Ceannmhor, son of Conall Cearnach, of the race of Ir. See Addit Notes, p lxxii, note [s] —(*T.*)

[r] *Soghans* — The posterity of Sodhan

266

Sil Conaill Ʒlaiɼɼ míc Eich
  ba eɼcvaiv oʒɼa
Do Maiʒ Fochaiv vo Maiʒ Uiɼniʒ
  vo Maiʒ Moʒna,   310

Do Maiʒ Sulive vo Fɼɼnmaiʒ
  vo Maiʒ Mace
v'Inbiuɼ buaɼɼe bɼuccaic ɼɼoca
  vo iac Cice

Eoco Maiɼeva in inaicɼe iniav   315
  noɼvv ninʒnav
viam boɼb a Linvmuine laenviɼec
  uaɼ loc linvʒlan.

Laecɼav ɼil Ríʒbaiɼiv mic bɼiʒe
  baiʒ cɼn ʒainne   320
                                Coɼc

Salbhuidhe, son of Fiacha Araidhe. Six of the seven districts inhabited by them were in Hy Many, and one in Meath See O'Donovan's Hy Many, pp. 72, 159, 188 —(*T*)

^s *Conal Glas* —This was Couall Anglonnach, son of Feich, and founder of the families of Conaille Muinthemhne, county Louth Magh Uisnich was the plain round the hill of Uisnech, in the Co Westmeath The other plains here mentioned are unknown —(*T*)

^t *Magh Suidhe.*—The plain about the river Swilly, in the Co Donegal —(*T*)

^u *Fennmaigh* i e the Alder-tree Plain, now Farney, a barony in the county of Monaghan, of which a valuable historical and topographical memoir has recently been published by Evelyn Philip Shirley, Esq *Magh Macha*, mentioned in the next line, is the plain round Armagh, it is generally called by the Four Masters *Machaire Arda Macha*, or the plain of Armagh —(*T*.)

^x *Inhher Buais* —The mouth of the river Buais, now Bush, near the present town of Bushmills, in the north of Dalriada, Co Antrim See Reeves's Eccl Antiq. of Down and Connor What is meant by Iath Aiche, or the land of Aiche, in the next line, I do not know —(*T*)

^y *Eocho Mairedha* —He was drowned

The race of Conall Glas', son of Ech,
    Spread themselves listlessly
To Magh Fothaid, to Magh Uisnigh,
    To Magh Moghna,   310

To Magh Suidhe', to Fernmaigh",
    To Magh Macha,
To Inbher Buais*, of bursting torrents,
    To the land of Aiche.

Eocho Mairedha', the rebellious son,   315
    Of wonderful adventure,
Who was overwhelmed in lucid Linnmhuine,
    With the clear lake over him

The heroes of the race of Righbard, son of Brige*,
    Of valour undaunted,   320

                                     Corc

about A. D 90, by the eruption of the lake, now called from his name, Loch n-Eochadh, or Loch Neagh, which overspread the plain before called Liathmhuine The ancient name of Lough Neagh was Linnmhuine. He is called "the rebellious son" because he eloped with his step-mother There is some confusion in lines 317 and 318; perhaps we should read,

ⴅⴈⴀ mbopb ⴀ linomuine linoʒlⴀn,
    uⴀʃ liⴀꞇmuine lⴀoinopeⴀ

Who was overwhelmed in clear Linnmhuine,
    Above the wide Liathmhuine

N is all confusion, reading the stanza thus

ⴅeⴅ ⴅⴀ mⴀipe ⴅⴀ in mⴀiꞇpe miⴀⴅ
    nopo ninʒnⴀⴅ
Ⴅⴈⴀ m-bopb ⴀ linn muine Ⴅennpeⴅ,
    uⴀʃ loⴅ linnʒlⴀnn

For the legend of the eruption of Loch Neagh, see the Dinnseanchus, and the Leabhar n-Uidhri, fol. 36 — (T)

Righbard, son of Brige — Who this was I do not know The Corc-Oiche were the descendants of Dubhthach Daeltengaidh (i e of the black tongue), and are said to have occupied the land now covered by Lough Neagh, until they were dispossessed and dispersed into Meath, Munster, &c, by Eochaidh Mac Mairedha, a Munster chieftain, in the first century,

Copc oice cloc cloc cṡn timine
     oál ṛaeṛ ṛelle

Se cinṡoa nac oo munciṛ Oṛṡзoin
     ciaṛṛa maзṡn,
Зaḃṛaiзe Succa, Uí Ⲧhaiṗṛiз   325
     Зaleoin Laзṡn

Léiṛ ṛo ⲧhuiṛmiṛṡmaṛ aṛ cṛónic
     cia no nзlṡo?
Inci meoon acuṛ coṛṛach
     acuṛ oeao.   330

Oṡḃ lṡam cipé ṛoooṛ ṛíme
     o ṛo зaḃao hЄṗiu

                                    cona

who was contemporary with the eruption
of the lake —Book of Leacan, fol 134,
Ogyg p 329   The Dal Selle, mentioned
line 322, were descended from Eochaidh,
who gave his name to Loch Neagh —(T)

  ' Six tribes —The MSS read Seomuiz
moue oo muincin Oṛeзoin, and in line
325, Зaḃṛaiзe ṛicca [N ṛioзu]   The
readings adopted are taken from a quotation of this stanza which occurs in a short
account of the death of Finn M'Cumhal,
contained in a miscellaneous MS volume
of the 15th century, in the possession of
Henry J. Monck Mason, Esq., LL D   The
volume is lettered on the back, " Amradh
Coluim-Cille seeo scribenn aile " [Poem
on Columbkille and other writings]   The
whole passage, for which I am indebted to
Mr E Curry, is as follows. Uoḃeṛaio

aṛaile, ⁊ iṛ ḟiṛ ṛin, comao oo iḃ caiṗ-
ṛiз hua ḟailзi oo, ⁊ зo mao oo aiⲧec-
ⲧuaⲧhaiḃ iaoṛioe Umail uⲧḃeṛⲧ Mael-
muṛa iṛin cṛónic

    Se cinṡoa nac oo muincin Oṛeoзain
       зeḃuṛ maiзin
    Зaṛḃṛaiзe Shucca, hui Ⲧaiṗṛiз
       Зaleon Laiзin.

" Others say, and it is true, that he
[Finn] was of the Ui Tairisigh of Ui
Failghe, and that they were of the Aith-
echtuath [or insurgent plebeians], as
Maelmura says in the Chronicle, Six
Tribes," &c.

  This passage is worthy of insertion
here, not only as preserving the true
reading of the stanza before us, but also
because we learn from it incidentally

Corc-Oiche, humblers of the proud, without fear,
   The noble Dal Selle

Six tribes[a] *who are* not of Breoghan's people.
   Who hold lands.
The Gabraighe Succa, Ui Tairsigh,   325
   Galeons of Leinster.

Fully have we made our Chronicle,
   Who will criticise it ?
It has its middle, and its beginning,   330
   And its end

It is certain to me that whatsoever I have related,
   Since the *first* invasion of Eri,

There

that the present poem was known by the name of *The Chronicle of Maelmura.* comp line 327. It would seem, however, that, instead of Se, we should read ꞇꞃꞓ cinꞇꞃa, "*three* tribes," &c , in line 323; for three only are mentioned, and Keating speaks of three only, enumerating the very same three that are here given, all of whom he says were of the race of the Firbolgs Cl ꝺeꞁꞃꞃ ꝺꞃonꝝ ꞃe Seancuꞃ ꝝuꞃab ꝺꞃob na ꞇꞃꞃ h-aꞃcmeaꝺa ꞃo ꝼꞁl a n-Eꞃꞃꞃn, nac ꝺo ꝝaoꞃꝺꞃoluꞃb .ꞃ. Ꝝabꞃuꞃꝺe Shuca a ꝝ-Connacꞇaꞃb, Uꞃ Caꞃꞃꞃꝝ a ꝝꞃꞃꞃꞃ o bꝼaꞃꞁꝝe, ꞁ Ꝝaꞁꞃum Caꞃꝝꞃon "Some antiquaries say that it is of them [viz. of the Firbolgs] are descended the three families that are in Ireland who are not of the Gadelians, viz., the Gabraidhe of [the river] Suck in Conacht, the Ui Tairsigh, in the country of Offaly, and the Gaileons of Leinster "—Quoted from Dudley Mac Firbis's MS Comp Haliday's ed. p 195; O'Flaherty, Ogyg p 175; O'Donovan's Hy-Many, pp. 85, 86, 90 The hint thrown out in the passage quoted from Mr Mason's MS., that the three non-Gadelian families were of the Athachtuaidh, and therefore joined with the insurgents who murdered the nobles of the Gadelian race, and set up a new line of popularly elected kings, is curious See Ogyg ni c. 54, and Keating, at the reign of Tuathal Teachtmar Breoghan being the common ancestor of all the Gadelian leaders, to say that the tribes enumerated were not of the race of Breoghan is equivalent to saying that they were not Gadelian —(*T.*)

cona paiʒbe ní ba fípiu
na bap lṡpiu.

Leop leno lenmaiɔ a panaip ipp   335
    po pṡp ɔulaɔ
munɔip bhpṡʒoin feib aɔbṡpap
    can a mbunaɔ   C.

IV

[ɒuaN alɓaNach]

Ɒal Riaɒa, umoppo, ɔap labpamap ʒo léʒ óp iaɒ nac ffuil
amopup aʒainn ipin m-beaʒan ɔa m-bunaɔup, ⁊ cpaobpʒaoileaɔ
ɔa lampam pan leabappa   Cuipeam pean ɔuain Seancapa a píoʒ
ap Qlbain annpo piop

Mappo aɔep ʒe eapbaɔac í iap píom na píoʒ na pann ɔepe-
anac, ⁊ fop iap pleccaib ele

A eolcha

[b] *Their origin*—Mr Curry has suggested that the first line of this poem ought
to be written Can a mbunaɔup na nʒae-
oil, "Whence their origin [viz *the origin*] of the Gadelians?" which would
make a good sense, and would coincide
with the last line, as is usual in bardic
compositions of this nature, and although
there is a seeming grammatical irregula-
rity in repeating the possessive pronoun
along with the noun to which it refers,
yet instances are not uncommon in Irish
of this sort of redundancy   In the last line
of the poem it is quite impossible to take
canam as a verb, for it would be the future tense, and would make no sense But
O Flaherty, Lynch, Keating, and others,
the best scholars of the seventeenth century, have taken it as a verb in the first
line Still Mr Curry's conjecture is very
ingenious, and may probably be true—
(*T*)

[c] *Duan Albanach*—The author of the
following poem is unknown, but it appears
from internal evidence to have been written about A D. 1057. It is acknowledged
on all hands to be of the utmost value, as
the connecting link in the history of the
Gaels of Ireland and Scotland Colgan says
of it, "quo ego non legi, nec Scoto-Britanni

There will be found to be nothing more true
  Or more plain.

Sufficiently have we followed their true history,   335
  Much more do we know.
The race of Bregon, as it is handed down,
  From whence is their origin[b]

IV.

DUAN ALBANACH[c].

OF the Dalriadans, of whom we have lately spoken[d], we have no doubt *of the truth* of the little we have attempted of their origin and genealogy in this book   We set down, however, here an ancient poem of the history of the Kings of Scotland.

Thus it speaks, although it is defective[e] in counting the kings in the last quatrain, and according to other accounts :

O all

producunt, ullum Regum Scotorum vetustiorem Scriptorem." O'Flaherty says the same thing, Ogyg p 466, and Pinkerton calls it, " beyond question the most ancient monument of Dalriadic history extant" See the testimonies collected by Dr. O'Conor, Rer Hib Script, tom. 1. Proleg. p cxxii.

It is here edited from the MS of Dudley Mac Firbis, in the Library of the Royal Irish Academy, copied by Mr. Curry from the original in the possession of the Earl of Roden Dr. O'Conor has edited it from two MSS in the Library of the Duke of Buckingham, at Stowe Mr. Pinkerton

has also printed it, with a very erroneous version, by the elder Charles O'Conor. As Dr O'Conor's version is also full of errors, it has been thought necessary to add a more correct translation of so important a document to the present work.— (*T*)

[d] *Lately spoken* i.e. Dudley Mac Firbis, in his genealogical work, from which this poem is taken, had lately spoken of the families of Dal-Riada See Reeves's Eccl. Antiq of Down and Connor, p 318 —(*T*.)

[e] *Defective.*—Hence it appears that the defects of this poem are of ancient date They are also noted by O'Flaherty, who

A eolcha Alban uile,
  a ſluaᵹ ſeuta ſoltbuiᵭe,
  cia ceuᵭ ᵹabáil, an eól ᵭuíb,
  ſo ᵹabaᵭaiſ Albanſuiᵹ?

Albanuſ ſo ᵹab, lia a ſlóᵹ,   5
  mac ſen oiſᵭéſc Iſicon,
  bſacaiſ iſ bſiutuſ ᵹan bſat,
  ó ſaiteaſ Alba eatſac

Ro ionnaſb a bſacaiſ bſaſ
  bſiotuſ taſ muiſ n-lét n-amnaſ,   10
  ſo ᵹab bſiotuſ Albain áin,
  ᵹo ſinn ſiaᵭnac ſotuᵭáin

ſoᵭa iaſ m-bſiotuſ m-bláit, m-bil,
  ſo ᵹabſaᵭ clanna Nemiᵭ.

eſᵹlan

says " Verum aliquot desideratis disti-
chis, integrum apographum reperire non
contigit "—Ogyg p 467. The defect,
our author says, is manifest from the
number of kings (fifty-two) mentioned
in the last stanza, which does not agree
with the number given in the poem, or
with that given by other authorities.—
(T)

ᵉ The land of Alba—Albanſuiᵹ may,
perhaps, be for Albanſiᵹe, the kingdom of Alba. Pinkerton and Dr O'Conor
read Albanbſuiᵹ, the land of Alban,
which is perhaps correct, or ſuiᵹ may be
the gen. of ſuᵭ, a wood or forest. In the
first verse Dr. O'Conor takes uile as agreeing with Alban, 'vos docti Albaniæ totius," but he ought to have rendered it,
"vos docti Albaniæ omnes" In verse 3 he is
also entirely wrong; he translates it, " Qui
primi didicerunt scientiam e vestris," but
ᵹabáil is a substantive, not a verb. Mr
Skene, in his English version of this poem
(Collectanea de rebus Albanicis, edited by
the Iona Club, p 70), is still further from
the original, for he renders ver 3. " Learn
who first "—(T.)

ᶠ Numerous.—Dr O'Conor reads ſia,
which may mean with, and lia, as Pinkerton
and the original MS read, may be for le,

O all ye learned of Alba !
 Ye well skilled host of yellow hair !
 What was the first invasion—is it known to you ?
 Which took the land of Alba[f] ?

Albanus possessed it, numerous[g] his hosts ;   5
 He *was* the illustrious son of Isacon,
 He and Briutus were brothers without deceit,
 From him Alba of ships has its name.

Briutus banished his active[h] brother
 Across the stormy sea of Icht.   10
 Briutus possessed the noble Alba,
 As far as the conspicuous promontory of Fothudan[i]

Long after Briutus the prosperous, the good,
 The race of Nemhidh took *it*,

Erglan

with, but it may also signify *numerous* Mr Skene renders ꞃloᵹ, *race*, which is wrong Dr O'Conor might have taught him the true meaning. In the next line Dr. O'Conor renders mac ꞃein " filius istius," which ought to be " filius ille fuit." For ιꞃ, in line 7, Dr O'Conor and Pinkerton read oo. For the fancied descent of Albanus and Brutus or Britus from Isicon or Isacon, and Japheth, see above, p 33.—(*T.*)

 [h] *Active*—Pinkerton and Dr O'Conor take bꞃaꞃ as a proper name, and translate, " His brother Bras," but this is nonsense, for the expelled brother was evidently Albanus; and we have no no-

tice in any of the other accounts of a brother called Bras. Ճꞃaꞃ means active, energetic, restless. For the sea of Icht, see p. 31, note ¹, Dr O'Conor and Mr Skene have mistaken the meaning of the epithet n-amnaꞃ, not perceiving that the n was merely euphonic —(*T.*)

 [i] *Fothudan.*—I am not able to identify this promontory with its modern name It appears to be here spoken of as the extreme northern point of Scotland Old Charles O'Conor (in Pinkerton) and Dr. O'Conor, make Fothudan the name of a man, the former translates this line " to the plains of the hunter Fothudan," and the latter, " usque ad fines venatoris Fo-

Enzlan iap cceacc ap a loing,   15
do aicle cozla cuip Conuing.

Cpuicmiz pop zabpad iapccain,
iap cciaccain a h-Epeann-muiz,
r piz cpi picic piz pán
zabpad díob an Cpuicean-clap.   20

Cacluan an céd piz diob-poin,
aipneopead daoib zo cumaip,
pob é an piz dézeanac dib
an cup calma Cupaincin

Clanna Eacac ina n-diaiz,   25
zabpad Albain iap n-áipozliaid,
clanna Conaipe an caoimpip,
cozaide na cpeun-Zhaoidil

Cpi

---

thudaui " But pinn is certainly a promontory —(T')

k *Erylan* — Dr. O'Conor renders the word
Enzlan as an adjective, *clamantes*, confounding it with apozlopac Mr Skene
makes it the name of a country. " The
race of Neimhidh," he says, " acquired
Earglan," but he does not tell us where
" Earglan " was   Old Charles O'Conor
(see Pinkerton, vol ii p 107) made it
the name of a man, one of the leaders
of the Nemedians, and for this he has
the authority of the Book of Leacan (fol.
276, a), where we have the following
account of the Nemedian chieftains who
survived the battle in which Conaing's
tower was destroyed. Do lodap pin pop

pcail Epind pop ceicfd a n-zalaip 7
in chipa. Mapb beochach do cham 1
n-Epind. A deich mna dia eip pp ne
cpi pichic bliadan Luid Ebac 7 a mac
.1. baath a cuaipceipc in domuin. Luid
Macan 7 Eapzlan, 7 iapcacc .1. cpi meic
beoain mic Sdaipn co Dobap, 7 co h-Ipp-
dobap a cuaipceipc Alban.   " They
passed under the shadow of Eri, retreat-
ing from their distempers and tributes
Beothach died of a plague in Eri. His
ten wives survived him three-score years
Ebath and his son, i. e. Baath, passed
into the north of the world   Matan and
Erglan and Iarthacht, i. e. the three sons
of Beoan, son of Sdarn, with Dobar and
Irrdobar, to the north of Albain "—(T')

Erglan[k], after having disembarked from his ships,⠀⠀⠀⠀⠀15
⠀⠀After the destruction of Conaing's tower[l].

The Cruithnians seized it afterwards[m],
⠀⠀After they had come from the plain[n] of Eri,
⠀⠀Seventy noble kings of them
⠀⠀Possessed the Cruithnian plain⠀⠀⠀⠀⠀20

Cathluan[o] *was* the first king of them,
⠀⠀(I tell unto you briefly),
⠀⠀The last king of them was
⠀⠀The brave hero Cusaintin

The children of Eochadh[p] after them⠀⠀⠀⠀⠀25
⠀⠀Seized upon Alba, after great wars;
⠀⠀The children of Conaire, the comely man,
⠀⠀Chosen *men were* the mighty Gaedhil

The

[l] *Conaing's tower* — See above, p. 48, note [d]. This tower is supposed to have been on Tory island, Co Donegal See O'Donovan's Four Masters, at A. M 3066.—(*T.*)

[m] *Afterwards.* — Mr Skene translates, "The Cruithne acquired the western region" Dr O'Conor has rendered it correctly—(*T*)

[n] *Plain.*—Meaning, perhaps, mαᵹ �, or Bregia. See above, p. 125. Comp. also pp. 139, 145. Old Charles O'Conor, in Pinkerton, and Dr O'Conor, render *plains* in the plural, which is wrong Mr Skene falls into the same error, but he has corrected Dr. O'Conor's " *in Hiberniæ campos* " In line 20 he is also right in rendering clαp *plains* (although wrong

in making it plural), instead of O'Conor's " Cruthniam *illustrem* "—(*T.*)

[o] *Cathluan*—See above, pp 125, 139, 159 In line 22, ᵹo cumαip does not signify *veraciter*, as Dr. O'Conor renders it, nor *explicitly*, as Mr Skene has it Pinkerton reads ᵹo beimin, *verily.*—(*T*)

[p] *Eochadh*, i e. Eochadh Muinreamhar, of the race of Conaire II, King of Ireland, the ancestor of the Dalriadan kings of Ireland and Scotland. See Reeves's Ecc Antiq p 320 King Conaire was called Caomh, or the beautiful (as in line 27), to distinguish him from Conaire I, who was called Conaire Mor, or the Great In line 27, O'Conor and Skene read nα cαiom fip, which would be plural, and is evidently wrong.—(*T.*)

Τρι mec Ερc mec Εαcδαc αιτ,
   τριαρ ϝυαιρ beannαcταιρ Ράτραιcc,   30
   ζαbραδ Clbαιn, αρδ α n-ζυρ,
   Loαpn, Ϝεαρζυρ ιρ Conζυρ.

Dec m-bliαδnα Loαpn, léρ blαδ,
   ι ϝϝlαιτεαρ οιριρ Clbαn,
   ταρ ερ Loαpn ϝél ζο n-ζυρ,   35
   ρεαcτ m-bliαδnα ριćεατ Ϝεαρζυρ

Domαnζαρτ mαc ο'Ϝεαρζυρ αρδ,
   αιρεαm ćúιζ m-bliαδαn m-biοτζαρζ,
   α .χχιιι. ζαn τροιδ,
   δο Comζαll, mαc Domαnζοιρτ   40

Dα bliαδαn Conαιnζ ζαn τάιρ,
   ταρ éρ Comζαιll δο Ζοbρán,
   τρι bliαδnα ϝο cυιζ ζαn ροιnn,
   bα ρι Conαll, mαc Comζοιll

                                             Cετρε

^q *Valiant.*—The word αιτ is rendered *strenuus* by Colgan, Trias Thaum, p. 115, col 1, where he quotes lines 25–40 In line 31 he renders αρδ α nζυρ, "elato animo" Ζυρ signifies mind, courage, spirit, see line 35. Dr O'Conor and Mr Skene read αρδ nζυρ, which is evidently a mistake.—(*T*)

^r *Patrick.*—See Jocelyn, Vit S Patr. c 137, where this blessing is described as given to Fergus only; "Sanctus vero Patricius prædictum benedixit Fergusium" [scil Fergus Muinreamhar, son of Erc,

prince of Dalaradia]. "et voce propheticâ dixit ad illum; Licet hodie videaris humilis, et despectus in conspectu fratrum tuorum, eris in brevi princeps illorum omnium De te enim optimi reges egredientur, qui non solum in terra propria, sed etiam in regione longinqua et peregrina principabuntur;" and see Colgan's note on this passage, Tr. Thaum, p. 114 —(*T*)

^s *Bounds.*—Colgan (*ubi supr*) renders this line "in principatu finium Albaniæ" The poet wishes to intimate that Loarn's

The three sons of Erc, son of Eochadh the valiant[q],
  Three who obtained the blessing of Patrick[r],   30
  Seized upon Alba, exalted *was* their courage,
  Loarn, Feargus, and Aongus

Ten years *was* Loarn (it is known to fame)
  In the government of the bounds[s] of Alba,
  After the generous, courageous[t] Loarn,   35
  Seven and twenty years *reigned* Fergus

Domhangart, the son of noble Fergus,
  Numbered for five turbulent years;
  Twenty-four without a battle
  Are assigned to Comhghall, son of Domhangart.   40

Two prosperous years without contempt,
  After Comhghall, *are assigned* to Gabhran,
  Three years five times[u] without interruption,
  Was Conall, son of Comhghall, king.

Four

sovereignty extended to the very extremities of Alban Pinkerton reads ιαρ-chaιρ Alban, "of western Alban," which is a mistake. Dr. O'Conor has the right reading, but translates it *illustrious* , and Mr. Skene, not satisfied with this, makes it a proper name, "Oιrι Alban," but without explaining what he supposed to be meant For the genealogy of Loarn see Ogyg. p 470—(*T*)

[r] *Courageous*.—Colgan reads, ρeιl ζu nζuρ , O'Conor, ρζel ζo nζuρ, which he renders "historia est nota" Pinkerton has ρhel ζo nζuρ, and translates absurdly, "a space likewise" Mr Skene follows O'Conor's reading, which he renders, not very intelligibly, "keenly the tale." See line 31. Fergus was surnamed the Great, and was called Mac Mιse, from the name of his mother O'Flaherty assigns only sixteen years to his reign, which he says commenced A.D. 513.—Ogyg. p 472 —(*T*.)

[u] *Three years five times* i. e. 15 Mr. Skene renders this, erroneously, "three years and five," although Dr O'Conor's

Cetpe bliaona piceat tall   45
  ba Rí Aobán na n-iol-pann,
  bec m-bliaona po peact, peól n-glé,
  i pplaiteap Eatac buibé

Conncab Ceapp páite, pel blab,
  a xui bia mac Feapchap   50
  tap ép Feapcaip, peagaib painn,
  .xiii bliaona Domnaill.

Tap ép Domnaill bpic na m-bla,
  Conall, Dungal x m-bliaona,
  xiii bliaona Domnuill Duinn,   55
  tap ép Dungail ip Chonuill

Maolbuin mac Conaill na ccpeac
  a xui bó go bligteac,

                    Feapcaip

version is correct In line 41 Pinkerton reads, chonnail gan tap, Dr. O'Conor, conaing gan tap. A note in the margin of Mac Firbis's MS makes Conaing the name of a king, who reigned conjointly with Gobhran, but this must be a mistake.—(T.)

* Provinces lit "of many divisions." Dr. O'Conor and Mr Skene translate, "of golden swords," reading na n-oplann But Dr O'Conor mentions the other reading, p cxxxvii. Pinkerton reads, na molpann, "of extended plains." Tall, in line 45, signifies within, i. e. in possession,—an ancient brehon law term.—(T.)

† Ten years seven times i e seventy years This has been translated by old Charles O'Conor, who furnished Pinkerton with his version of this poem, "ten years by seven," which certainly meant 70, although Pinkerton understood it 17. And it has been rendered 17 by Dr. O'Conor and Mr Skene But let the authority of the Duan suffer as it may, bec m-bliaona po peacht must mean seventy years O'Flaherty assigns to Aidan a reign of thirty-two years, and to Eochaidh Buidhe twenty-three, following the authority of Tighernach. In line 47, peol is literally sailing, and signifies his lifetime, career,

Four years *and* twenty in possession,   45
    Was Aodhan, king of many provinces[x];
    Ten years seven times[y], a glorious career,
    Was the sovereignty of Eochadh Buidhe,

Connchad Cearr *reigned* a quarter, renowned in fame,
    Sixteen *years* his son Fearchar,   50
    After Fearchar (inspect the poems[z]),
    The fourteen years of Domhnall

After Domhnall Breac, of the towns[a],
    Conall *and* Dungall, ten years,
    The thirteen years of Domhnall Dunn,   55
    After Dungall and Conall.

Maeldun, son of Conall, of forays,
    Reigned seventeen years legitimately,

                         Fearchain

reign —(*T*)

[z] *The poems.* i. e. the historical poems, which were the bardic historians' authorities, or which constituted the title deeds of the kings named. See the Brehon law tract (H. 3. 18, p 22) in the Library of Trin Coll Dublin Mr Skene renders these words, "by dominion of swords," confounding ꝑɑɩɴɴ with ꝑɩɴɴ; but Dr O'Conor's version is correct. The reigns assigned to Fearchar and Domhnall in this stanza are too long See Ogyg. p 477; and Pinkerton, vol ii p. 117. This was the Domhnall who was defeated at the Battle of Magh Rath, which gives the date of

his reign —See Tighernach, ad an 637, and O'Donovan's Battle of Magh Rath, pp. 48, 49.—(*T*)

[a] *Of the towns.*—Dr O'Conor renders this "celebrem famâ," confounding bla with blav, *fame*, a totally different word, which occurred a little before, line 49, where he renders ꝑel blav, very absurdly, "regno legitimo inclyto," and Mr. Skene, still more strangely, "a shooting star" In the Brehon laws, bla is put for baile, a town or townland The two Domhnalls or Donnells are distinguished by the surnames of Breac, speckled, and Dunn, brown —(*T*)

 Feancain Fova, feaʒa leac,
vo caiċ bliavain an .ɣɣ.   60

Oa bliavain Eaċvac na-n-eac,
ɲo ba calma an ɲí ɲiʒceac,
aoin bliavain ba flaic iapccain,
Ainceallaċ maic mac Feancaiɲ.

Seacc m-bliavna Ounʒail véin,   65
acuɲ a ceacaiɲ vo Ailpén,
cɲi bliavna Muiɲeavoiʒ maic,
.ɣɣɣ vo Aov na áɲoflaic.

A ceacaiɲ fiċeac, níɲ fann,
vo ḃliavnaib vo caic Oomnall,   70
va ḃliavain Conaill, cém n-ʒlé,
iɲ a ceacaiɲ Chonaill ele.

Naoi m-bliavna Cuɲaincin cain,
a naoi Aonʒuɲa aɲ Albain,

ceɲie

---

^b *Behold thou.*—Dr O'Conor's copy reads, leʒa leac, "read by thyself." The phrase, "look you!" is still in use; see above, line 51 For fova, long, the appellation here given to Fearchair, Dr. O'Conor reads foʒa, which is a mistake. See O'Flaherty, p. 479—(*T*)

^c *Mansions*—The word piʒceac seems to be a compound of ɲiʒ, a king, and ceac, a house; or ceac may be merely the adjective termination, in which case the word will signify royal, as Mr. Skene renders it, perhaps correctly—(*T.*)

^d *Afterwards.*—Mr. Skene renders iaɲ ccain, "of the western regions," not knowing that Irish scribes write cc for v. The death of Ainchellach is given by Tighernach under the year 719 After Ainchellach the Annals mention two kings: Selbhach, son of Ferchair, and brother of Ainchellach, and Eochadh III., son of Eochadh II, who is mentioned line 61. O'Flaherty assigns to these two reigns a period of fourteen years, from A. D. 719 to 733, in which

Fearchair the Long, behold thou[b]
Passed one year over twenty.   60

The two years of Eochadh of steeds,
  He was the brave king of royal mansions[c];
  For one year was king afterwards[d]
  Aincheallach the Good, son of Fearchair.

The seven years of Dungal[e] the impetuous,   65
  And four to Alpin,
  The three years of Muireadhach the good,
  Thirty to Aodh, as supreme king

Four *and* a score, not imbecile,
  Of years Domhnall spent,   70
  The two years of Conall of glorious career,
  And the four of another Conall.

The nine years of Cusaintin the fair;
  The nine of Aongus over Alban;

The

last year the death of Eochadh mac Eochach is recorded by Tighernach. Pinkerton gives Selbhach a reign of twenty years, and to Eochaidh "about ten" The Duan is therefore here corrupted. A stanza appears to have been omitted, and the two lines 65 and 66, as Dr O'Conor suggests, were probably transposed to fill up the gap; but they contain the wrong names There was probably some confusion made by an early copyist in the Eochaidhs, for it is remarkable that the defects in the Duan all occur in connexion with a king of this name. Thus, for Sealbhach and Eochaidh III., the Duan substitutes Dungal and Alpin; it omits Dungal and Eochaidh IV., who ought to come in between Muiredach (line 67) and Aodh (line 68), and it also omits Eochaidh V and Alpin, who ought to come in between Eoganan (line 76) and Cionaeth or Kenneth Mac Alpin (line 77) It is further remarkable that these errors are in each case double, arising from the original

cerpe bliaona Cloba áin,   75
ipa cpi véuz Eoʒanáin

Cpíoca bliaoain Cionaoic cpuaio,
a ceacaip Domnall opecpuaio,
xxx. bliaoain co na bpíʒ,
oon cupao oo Cupaincin.   80

Oá bliaoain, ba oaop a oac,
oa bpacaip oo Cloo pionnpcocac,
Domnall, mac Cupaincin caín,
pó caic bliaoain pa ceacaip

Cupaincin ba calma a ʒleac,   85
po caic a pé ip oá piceac,
Maolcoluim cerpe bliaona,
lonoolb a h-occ aipopuaʒla

Seacc

omission of two kings, and the subsequent
attempt to mend the defect by transposition. The list, as given by O'Flaherty,
with the duration of each reign, is as
follows Muiredach, three years, Dungal II, seven; Eochadh IV., five; Aodh
Fionn, or Aodh I, thirty; Domhnall III,
twenty-four; Conall III, two, Conall IV.,
four, Constantine, nine, Aongus, nine,
Aodh II, four, Eoganan, thirteen,
Eochadh V., part of one, Alpin, four;
Kenneth Mac Alpin, thirty; Domhnal
Mac Alpin, four; Constantine II, Mac
Cinaodha (i e son of Kenneth), fourteen, Aodh Mac Cionaodha, two.—(T.)

' Eoghanan —Here a stanza seems to be
omitted, of which lines 65 and 66 probably formed part, except that for Dungal,
in line 65, we should read Eochadh. See
last note. From the next king, Cionaith
or Kenneth Mac Alpin, the list of kings
here given agrees, or originally did agree,
with the Chronicon Pictorum, see above,
p. 167, where a reign of sixteen years
only is assigned to Cionaith —(T)

' White flowers.—The word pionnpcocac signifies white or fair flowers Old
Charles O'Conor renders it "the fair
haired," which is only an attempt to explain white flowers. Dr. O'Conor and

The four years of Aodh the noble;   75
And the thirteen of Eoghanan[e].

The thirty years of Cionaoith the hardy,
  Four Domhnall of the ruddy countenance,
  Thirty years, with his vigour,
  To the hero, to Cusaintin.   80

Two years (hard was his complexion)
  To his brother, to Aodh, of the white flowers[f],
  Domhnal, son of Cusaintin the fair,
  Reigned a year four times[g].

Cusaintin, brave was his combat[h],   85
  Reigned six and two score *years*;
  Maolcoluim four years;
  Indolph eight, of supreme sovereignty

The

Mr. Skene translate it "white shielded," taking ꝛcoꞇac for ꝛciaꞇać. Constantine (line 80) and this Aodh Fionnscothach were the sons of Kenneth Mac Alpin Girig (or Gregory) Mac Dungail is inserted between Aodh and Domhnall, son of Constantine, both in O'Flaherty's list and in the Chron Pictorum. See above, p 167 But he is omitted by the Duan, perhaps designedly —(*T*)

[g] *A year four times*: i. e. four years The reader will observe that this is the same form of expression which has been already misunderstood by former translators; see lines 43 and 47 Even O'Fla-herty was misled by it here, and assigns to Domhnal, son of Constantine, a reign of *five* years Dr. O'Conor renders it "annum cum quatuor (annis)" The author adopted the unusual mode of saying four, only for the sake of his metre. Ro caiꞇ (line 84) signifies spent or passed (on the throne), i. e. lived or reigned, see lines 60 and 70.—(*T.*)

[h] *Combat* i. e., probably, his contest for the throne, Ᵹleac is a fight, a battle, not "impetus in prælns," as Dr O Conor renders it. This Constantine was the son of Aodh, who was the son of Kenneth Mac Alpin, see line 82.—(*T*)

Seacc m-bliaðna Ðuboða ðén,
    acup aceacaip Cuilén,
    a ·xxuii. óp ᵹaċ cloinn,
    ðo Cionaoċ, mac Maoilcoluim.

Seacc m-bliaðna Cupaincin cluin,
    acup a ceacaip Macðuiḃ,
    cpiocað bliaðain, bpeacaið painn,
    ba pí Monaið Maolcolaim

Se bliaðna Ðonncaið ᵹlain ᵹaoic
    .xuii bliaðna mac Pionnlaoic,
    cap ép Mec beaċaið ᵹo m-blaið,
    .uii. míp i ffplaicíop Luᵹlaiᵹ

Maolcoluim anopa ap pí,
    mac Ðonncaið ðaca ðpecbi,
    a pé noca n-piðip neaċ,
    acc an c-eólaċ ap éolac.   Ḋ eolca

90

95

100

Ðá

¹ *Dubhoda* —This is the king who is called Cinaed, vel Dubh, in the list given above, p. 167. He is also called Duffus by some writers See Ogyg. p. 487, where O'Flaherty translates his name "Odo niger"—(*T*)

ᵏ *Mac Duibh*, or *Macduff*· i e the son of Dubhoda, line 39. O'Flaherty says "Grimus, Scoticè Macduibh, hoc est Duffi seu Dubhodonis filius, quem proprio nomine Kenneth dictum invenio. Rex Pictorum octennio —Cambr Ever page 94. Quippe 7 annis ab anno 997 et

parte octavi ad annum 1004 "—Ogyg. p. 488. There is evidently some confusion in these names in the Irish version of the Chronicon Pictorum, which was Lynch's authority in the place referred to of Cambr. Eversus; but still it is probable that "Cinead fil Dubh" there mentioned (see p 167, *supra*), was the same who is here called Mac Duibh or Macduff.--(*T*)

¹ *Verses mark* —The word bpeacaið is not very intelligible; if it were bpeaccaið, it would mean as verses embellish, celebrate, adorn. Dr. O'Conor's ver-

The seven years of Dubhoda[i] the vehement,
 And four of Cuilen,   90
 Twenty-seven over every clan,
 To Cionoath, son of Maoilcholuim.

Seven years to Cusaintin, listen [j]
 And four to Mac Duibh[k],
 Thirty years (*as* verses mark[l])   95
 Was Maelcolaim king of Monaidh[m].

The six years of Donnchad the wise,
 Seventeen years the son of Fionnlaoich[n],
 After Mac Beathaidh, the renowned,
 Seven months *uas* Lughlaigh in the sovereignty 100

Maelcoluim is now the king[o],
 Son of Donnchad the florid, of lively visage,
 His duration knoweth no man
 But the Wise One, the Most Wise. O ye learned[p]

                Two

sion, which Mr Skene translates, " of che- quered portions," can only be regarded as a guess —(*T.*)

 [m] *Monaidh.* i. e Dun Monaidh in Lorne, in Scotland, the well-known fortress or palace of the Dalriadic kings of Scotland now Dunstaffnage. See Battle of Magh Rath, p. 46, n. [a]. Dr O'Conor makes the absurd blunder of translating ꝓi ℧onaıɓ, " rex montium," and in this he is fol- lowed by Mr Skene.—(*T.*)

 [n] *Son of Fionnlaoich:* i. e. Mac Bea- thaidh, or Macbeth, so called from his mothers's name. See above, p 167 —(*T.*)

 [o] *Is now the king* —Malcolm, son of Donnchad, slew his predecessor Lulach, on the 1st of January, A D 1058, accord- ing to Tighernach, and was himself killed in 1093 This determines the age of the poem, and also of the list of kings before given, which also terminates with Mal- colm, and was therefore, probably, written in his reign. See above, p 167 —(*T*)

 [p] *O ye learned.*—Ⱥ eolca The first words of the poem are written here in the mar- gin, according to a custom of ancient Irish

Dá ríg fóp caogad, cluine,
  go mac Donncaid dpfc puipe,
  dp piol Epc apdglain anoip,
  gabpad Albain a eólaig

scribes, who used to write in the margin the initial word of the poem, whenever the same word occurred at the end of a line. Colgan quotes this stanza, Trias Thaum., p. 115, and translates it thus

" Malcolmus nunc est Rex,
    Filius Donnchadi speciosi et vividi vultus
  I jus annos non novit ullus
  Præter illum scientem, qui omnia novit "

¹ *Kings.*—Only forty-seven kings are enumerated in the present text of the poem. But O'Flaherty has made up the number of fifty-two from the Annals and other sources

The comparison of his list with the poem shews that in the latter two kings have been transposed, and five omitted. The transposed kings are Dungal, changed

Two kings[q] over fifty, listen !   105
    To the son of Donnchadh of royal countenance,
    Of the race of Erc, the noble, in the east[r],
    Obtained Alba, O ye learned.

from the twenty-second to the nineteenth place, and Alpin, changed from the thirty-third to the twentieth. The omitted kings are No. 19, Selvach; the three Eochaidhs (viz No. 20, Eochaidh Mac Eochaidh; 23, Eochaidh Angbhuidh; 32, Eochaidh Mac Aodha finn); and 38, Gairig, or Gregory Mac Dungail.—(*T.*)

[r] *The east* i e. east of Ireland. Scotland is frequently called " the East" by Irish writers. This proves that the poem, or at least this stanza, was written in Ireland, and not in Scotland. For ꞇ, Dr. O'Conor and Mr. Skene read ꞇ, " of the gold," which is wrong, and makes no sense.—(*T.*)

ADDITIONAL NOTES.

a

ADDITIONAL NOTES.

No I. *See page* 29.

THE following table exhibits a comparative view of the names of the cities in the Irish and Latin copies, with the supposed modern names.

IRISH COPIES.	LATIN COPIES.	EXPLANATIONS
Caer Gortigern	Caer Gurthigirn.	Gwrthernion in Radnorshire. Caer Gwerthrynyawn ar llan Gwy. Triad. vi. s. 2.
C. Grutus [Gutais L. B.]	C. Graunth.	Cambridge or Grantchester
C. Mencest[a]	C. Mencipit or Municip. . .	Verulam, at or near St Alban's.
C. Leuill	C Luadnt or Luilid. .	Carlisle
C. Medguid [Meguaid, L. B.]	C. Meguid	Meivod in Montgomeryshire.
C. Colin.	C. Colun	Colnchester in Essex
C. Gusdirt [Gustint. L. B.]	C. Custeint.	Caernarvon.
C. Abrog	C. Ebrauc or Eborauc . .	York.
C. Caradog.	C. Caratauc	Old Sarum. Also a fortress in Shropshire
C. Brut [Graat. L. B.] . .	C. Britton.	Bristow? or Dunbarton?
C Machod.	C. Mauchguid.	Mancester in Warwickshire? or Manchester?
C. Lunaind [Lugain. L. Ludain. B.]	C. Lunden	London.

IRISH

[a] I believe I have correctly allotted the equivalents, in the Irish and Brito-Latin lists. Though the translator had probably an eye to one of the Manchesters when he wrote Mencest.

IRISH COPIES	LATIN COPIES.	EXPLANATIONS
C Oen [Cose L Caisi. B]	C. Gwent . .	Chepstow[b]
C Irangin [Girangon, L. Giraigon, B]	C. Guoirangon .	Worcester
C. Pheus.	C Peris .	Portchester in Hampshire
C. Don [Minchip. L B.]	C Dann. . .	Doncaster
C Lonnoperuisc [Leo anaird puisc L Leoinarphuisc. B] . . .	C. Legion Guarusik	Caerleon-upon-Usk
C. Grugan . . .	C. Gorieon or Guorcon	Warwick[c]?
C. Sant.	C Segeint. .	Silchester in Hampshire.
C Legun [Legion L B]	C Ligion . .	{ Caerleon-upon-Dee, i e Chester.
C. Guidhud [Guhent L Guent B] . .	C Guinting	{ Norwich, or Winchester, or Winwick in Lancashire
C Breatan. . .	C Britton . .	{ Bristow, or rather Dunbreatan, Dunbritton, or Dunbarton
C. Lenidoin [Lergun. L Lerion B.] .	C Lirion	Leicester
C Pendsa	C Pensavelcoit[d] . .	{ Exeter, or Lostwithiel, or Ilchester, or Pevensey
C. Diuithgolgod [Diuithecolcoit. L. Gluteolcoit B] . .	C Droithon .	Drayton in Shropshire.
C Luiticoit . . .	C Luitcoit . .	{ Vulgò Lincoln, but rather Leeds Thoresby Ducatus, p 9
C Urnacht [Urtocht L Uitach, B] .	C Urnach .	Wroxeter in Shropshire
C. Eilimon [Ceilimon L Ceilimeno. B] . .	C Celemion	Camalet in Somersetshire[e].

The

[h] See Llwyd's Brit Descript Commentariolum According to him Chepstow is Caer Went, p 102, and Winchester is Caer Wynt, City of Wind, p 21, Triad iv series 1

[c] Caer Gwair, ap Llwyd. p 33
[d] Pen-savle-coed, statio capitalis in sylâ
[e] The conjecture of Camden, i 175, ed Gibson

The root of these lists of the twenty-eight cities is in the commencement of the Liber Querulus of Gildas, who describes Britannia as being "*bis denis bisque quaternis* civitatibus, ac nonnullis castellis, &c. decorata," and seems as if he were quoting part of his words from some poet, cap. 1, and Beda, 1. cap 1. The general tradition is, that they were the sees of the twenty-five bishops and three archbishops of the British Church, as may be seen at large in Ussher's Primordia, cap. 5 The three archbishoprics were London, York, and Caerleon-upon-Usk The allusion to the words of Gildas and Beda in those of the Historia is so apparent, that we cannot doubt but the original number in Marcus was xxviii., and that the scribe of 946 altered it, by the introduction of other names he had collected, and expunged (as false and exaggerated) those remarkable words in which the author seems to pay a compliment to Fernmael Lord of Guortigernmawn, and perhaps to his own native place, "prima civitas Britanniæ est quæ vocatur Caer Gurthigirn" Of his thirty-three cities the copier places York and Canterbury, the two palls or archiepiscopates of England, first and second; thereby shewing that his repeated dates of "quintus Eadmundi regis" correctly point out his nation, and probably his subjection to the northern primate, the unknown Caer Gurcoc, third, while Caer-Guorthigern has the fourth place. A Welch MS of Genealogies of the same century, viz the tenth, gives the list of twenty-eight cities nearly as it is in Nennius, ap Cambrian Quart Mag vol. iv.

It is a remarkable fact, that Mr. C. Bertram has printed in his Ricardus Corinæus, that of ninety-two British towns *thirty-three* were chief; viz the two free cities or municipia of Verulam and York, nine Roman coloniæ, ten governed by Latin law under the Lex Julia, and twelve inferior and merely tributary. This list is essentially different in names from the Nennian twenty-eight and the five others making the Petavian thirty-three, and is fundamentally distinct in its basis, being civil, not ecclesiastical Yet it exhibits that very number (thirty-three), which the Petavian MS of 946 has effected by adding five names to the twenty-eight. But Mr. Bertram surely never saw that MS What, then, shall we say? That he found the number thirty-three in some other copy, and worked upon it? I regard the enumeration as part of his figments, and no ancient fragment, for if it were true that Eboracum was also governed *suo jure*, Verulam should not have been called Caer Municip, nor would his surname of Municeps have explained whence the tyrant Gratianus came. *Vide* Ric. Corin p 36, Havniæ 1757, p. 111, ap. Johnstone Ant Celto-Norman *ibid.* 1786. (H)

No II *See page* 29

Lluyd, in his Archæologia, tit. 1. p 20, col. 3, supposes Cpuizneac to be a corruption of ὁpizneac, *pictus, variegatus*, see also O'Brien, Dict. in *voce*. But this is scarcely
credible;

credible, Duald Mac Firbis gives the following explanation of this word· Cꞃuiꞇneach (Pictus) neac ꝺo ᵹabaꝺ cꞃoꞇa no ꝺealba anmann, eun, aᵹuꞃ iaꞃᵹ, aꞃ a eineac, .i aꞃ a aiᵹiꝺ aᵹuꞃ ᵹiꝺ ni uiꝑꝑe amain acc aꞃ a coꞃꝑ uile. Ꝺoiꝑio Seꞃaꞃ Cꞃuiꞇniᵹ .i picꞇi, ꝺo bꞃiꞇnaib ꝺo cuiꞃeaꝺ aiᵹiꝺ ꝝeꝺil ꝺo ꝼóꝺ 7 ꝺo baꝺaꞃ oꞃꞃa ionꝺaꞃ ᵹemoiꞃ uaꞇmaꞃa ne a namuiꝺ. "Cruithneach (Pictus), one who paints the *cruths* (forms) of beasts, birds, and fishes on his *eineach* (face), and not on his face only, but on his whole body Cæsar calls the Britons Cruithnigh, i e Picti, because they used to stain their faces with woad, in order that they might appear terrible to their enemies."—*Genealogies.* Marq of Drogheda's copy, p 162. For this quotation I am indebted to Mr O'Donovan Cæsar's words are "Omnes vero se Britanni vitro inficiunt, quod cœruleum efficit colorem Atque hoc horridiori sunt in pugna aspectu , capilloque sunt premisso atque omni parte corporis rasâ, præter caput et labrum superius."—*De Bello Gall* lib v. c. 14.—(*T.*)

No III *See page 29*

Abonia—Eubonia or Manaw is the Isle of Man The Romans considered it as having the same name with Anglesea, viz Mon , and probably with reason, for Mon is a cow, and that idea is preserved in the islet called the Calf of Man But synonymes required a mark of distinction, which is found in the Mona-œda of Ptolemy, the Mon-apia of Pliny, the Eu-bonia of Nennius, and the Eu-monia or Eu-mania of some MSS of Orosius, as well as the Men-avia clearly meant in those which have Mevania. The word united to the primary one is probably that very *aw*, which now forms Manaw, the Welch for Man, and which Beda extended to both in his Menaviæ[f] Insulæ, Hist i cap 9 It meant[g] to blow, both naturally, and in the metaphors of spirit, inspiration, afflatus, &c. This would give us Monavia, and Aumonia or Eumonia (all as one, in ancient spelling), and with the mutation, Auvonia or Euvonia, for the Mona of Winds. In an ancient MS (Harl 3859, ap Cambr Qu Mag. iv p 23), Man is called Manau Guodotin, and in a supplement of Nennius (Nenn cap. 66, ex MS. Cotton, ap Gale, p 116), "regio quæ vocatur Manaw Guotadin." Though not the same place, it is perhaps the same word

[f] So corrected by Mr Sharon Turner, Hist Anglo-Sax i 347, ed iv But in his text, as in Orosius, Mevania

[g] It does not exist as a verb like *aw*, but as a root, in *awel*, a blast of wind, *awelu*, to blow, *awen*, inspiration, &c. And (with a restrictive sense in the prefix *ta*) *taw*, stillness, silence , *tawel*, calm, serene , *tawelu*, to make or become calm See Edw Llwyd, Comp Vocab Owen Dict *Ta* is *superior*, as Dr Owen shews by an instance (a point essential to the legitimate citation of his Dictionary), and ascendancy over wind, or breath, makes a calm, or silence

word as Aneurin's Gododin. Rejecting the *din* (meaning an enclosed or defensible place) we may possibly obtain from the Guodo or Guota the Μονα—Οιδα, or Mona-œda of Ptolemy, for the G disappears in composition But Mona seems to be the foundation of all the names

While the Romans were still ruling in Britain, Man was an Irish Island, "æquè (with Hibernia) a Scotorum gentibus habitata "—Orosius, i cap 2 But whether this had been always so, or became so by the ruin of the Britons, no man now can say The first occupation of Man by the Irish was probably not *later* than A D 254, in which year there is a tradition that King Cormac McArt drove some of the rebellious Ultonians into that island —Tigernach, in anno 254 Nevertheless it may have been *earlier*

The earliest accounts of it, however, are much too early, belonging to the fabulous epoch and legends of the Tuatha De Danann The following statement is extracted from the ancient MS Glossary of Cormac M·Cuillenan[h]. "Manannan Mac Lir was a famous merchant, that lived in the island of Manann He was the best navigator that was in the sea in the west of the world He used to ascertain by heaven-study that is, observation of the heavens, the duration of calm and storm, and the time when either of these two periods would change   " Inde Scoti et Britones eum dominum maris vocaverunt, inde filium maris esse dixerunt, i. e Mac Lir, et de nomine Manannain insola Manainn dicta est[i]." But other authorities tell us, if we are to trust O'Flaherty, that the name of this merchant was Oirbsion or Orbsen, son of Allad, son of Alathan, and nephew of the Daghda, and that he was called Manannan, because of his intercourse with the Isle of Man Orbsen Manannan was slain in battle by Ullinn, son of Tadhg, son of Nuada the Silver-handed, at the place therefore called Magh-Ullinn or Moycullin, in Galway. Some say, that Loch Oirbsion or Orbsen broke out while his grave was being dug See the Ogygia, part iii cap. 14, p. 179; and Keating That the Britons knew this legend of Man, may be supposed from the surname M'Llyr, son of the water or of the sea[k] Bran ap Llyr is the fabulous father of

---

[h] This author died in 908, according to O'Flaherty

[i] Bodleian MS Laud. 610, fol. 83, col a, l 13

[j] In the copy of Cormac's Glossary in the Library of Trin Coll Dub (H 2, 15) there is the following note on the above quoted passage, in the hand-writing of Duald Mac Firbis No o

Inir Manann a ðenar Manannan pir " Or he was called Manannan from the Isle of Manann "—(T)

[k] Cen or Cean, the sea, (*genitive* Cin) is still a living word in Irish.—(Γ) In H A Bullock's History of the Isle of Man, the tradition of Manannan is thus spoken of "Mananan Mac Lyr (the first man who held Man, was ruler thereof, and af-

of the elder Caradoc, and Bran ap Llyr Marini that of Caradoc Vreichbras The conversion of Man to Christianity is ascribed to one Germanus, an emissary of St. Patrick, who was succeeded by two others named Conidrius and Romulus Jocelyn. Vita Patric cap 92, 152, Vita Quarta, cap. 81

By Orck are denoted the Orcades or Orkneys, Orcania of Nennius. Orc in Gaelic is a whale or other large fish, and possibly may have had the same sense in ancient Gaulish and British; as it had also in Latin, "orca genus marinæ belluæ maximum dicitur" (Pomp Festus), whence the *orca* of the Italian romantic poets, and in French *orque*

> " Then shall this mount
> Of Paradise by might of waves be moved
> Out of his place, push'd by the horned flood,
> With all his verdure spoiled and trees adrift,
> Down the great river to the opening gulf,
> And there take root, an island salt and bare,
> The haunt of seals and *orcs* and seamews' clang."—*Paradise Lost*, xi 829-37

Orcades, or Orc Ynys, the islands of whales. See Armstrong's Gaelic Dictionary in *Orc* Other etymologies, from the Teutonic, may be seen in Wallace and Torfæus, but they appear to me false and trivial. The Ορκας Ακρα of Ptolemy was Dunnet Head in Caithness, over against the islands

The Irish translator has omitted a good passage of Marcus and Nennius "So in an old proverb it is said, when speaking of judges and kings, *He judged Britain with the three islands* "—(*II.*)

No IV. *See page* 42

The first man —The two first paragraphs of Irish history are borrowed, with corrections, from Nennius, cap 6; at p 50 of Marcus The Latin has Bartholomæus, Partholomæus, Partholomus, and, as it seems acknowledged that Partholan's name means Bartholomew, we must admire the credulity which could believe that apostolic name to have been known in Ireland 311 years after the flood. Ogygia, ii p 65 The same remark applies to *Simon* Brec. It is very remarkable that Partholan, first King of Ireland, and Brutus, first King of Britain, were both abhorred for having killed

ter whom the land was named) reigned many years, and was a paynim He kept land under mists by his necromancy If he dreaded an enemy, he would of one man cause to seem one hundred, and that by art magic."—*Old Statute Book*, cit

p 3. The natives "pretend he was son to a king of Ulster, and brother to Fergus II who restored the monarchical government of Scotland, 422 "—*Ibid*—(*II*)

killed father and mother See Keating, p 25. By "Nemech quidam filius agnominis,"
the copyists probably understood son of his own cognominis or namesake The transcriber of Marcus has left it blank, in doubt of its meaning, and he did wisely. For
the original reading is "filius Agnomain", or Agnamhain See Ogygia, ii p 65, Wood's
Primitive Inhabitants of Ireland, p. 13, Keating's Genealogy, p. 30. The same name,
Agnoman, occurs very early in the voyages of the Gaidhelians. Gildas Coem ap.
Ogygia, ii p. 67 Our translator corrects the Historia, which had represented Nemed
himself as sailing away again, whereas it was his posterity, after a sojourn of 216
years.—(H)

No V   See page 44.

Viri Bullorum, &c—The Firbolg, Firdomnan, and Firgalian, are inserted by
the translator The name Firbolg is also a general one, and comprehensive of all the
three Mr. O Flaherty does not doubt but they were colonies from Great Britain, of
the Belgæ, Damnonii, and another tribe. Ogygia, i pp 14, 15, Keating, p 39 The
account of the Tuatha De Danann is also inserted They are said to have come from
the northern parts of Europe, and their name may be rendered *The Tribe of Gods from
Denmark.* Danann for Dania, as Manann for Mannia The first mention of the Dani
is in Servius, " Dahæ . . . unde Dani dicti," in Æneid viii 728, and the second,
in Venantius Fortunatus de Lupo Duce, vi. 7, 49

> " Quam tibi sis firmus cum prosperitate supernâ,
> Saxonis et Dani gens citò victa probat "

The three tribes of Tuatha De Danann were descended from the three sons of Danann,
called Gods (and esteemed such) for their skill in magic; whence perhaps the phrase
Plebes Deorum They first came (it is fabled) into the north of Britain, where
they inhabited places called Dobar and Ir-dobar (quere Tir?) and whence they removed to the north of Ireland, and their title of De has been accounted for by the
name of the River Dee O'Flaherty, Ogygia, i p 12 But their story shews, that they
were a race endowed with such arts and powers, as might obtain them credit for a
divine origin. And there is no reason for supposing that Dobar was near the River
Dee. The interpretation of the name of this colony is quite independent of the question of its having ever existed, of which there is neither proof, nor much probability.
Their legend represents them to have spoken a German, not a British, dialect, which
is accordant to the notion of their being Danes, but is by no means accordant to the
catalogue of their names, and so far their story belies itself The letters of which
the invention is ascribed to the Danannian Ogma, brother of the Daghda, are not that
modification of the Latin alphabet used in Irish and Anglo-Saxon writings, but the

cyphers called ogham, the superior antiquity of which seems to me to involve this difficulty, that they almost imply and presuppose the existence of ordinary alphabetic writing —(*II.*)

No VI   *See page* 54

Out of the kingdom of Scythia, &c —There is no probability, and a want of distinct testimony, even legendary, that Ireland ever received any considerable body of settlers, but direct from Britain   Ireland, in effect, received but three classes of colonists. For the Nemedians were Bartholomæans, and the Firbolg and Tuatha De Danann were both Nemedians   Besides this class there were the Gaidhil or Scoti, into which prevalent colony the whole nation resolved itself; and thirdly, the Cruithnich or Pictish settlement   But the Firbolg and Danann were both direct from Britain, the former manifestly, and the latter avowedly. And the Scots, after various peregrinations, went from Pictland or Albany in North Britain to Spain, and thence over to Ireland   The whole mention of Spain in that legend is etymological, and was meant to unite the two names, so slightly dissimilar, and sometimes (as Mr O'Flaherty observes) confounded, of Iberus and Ibernus, as the mention of Scythia is also an etymologism for Scot   The three (or rather two) classes of colonists seem to have been the South Britons, of Belgic origin, the North Britons, of Celtic origin; and certain Britons, who must have belonged either to the one or other division, and were distinguished by retaining in Ireland their custom of staining the skin, at a time when no others did

The name Scoti is identified by Nennius and by Irish bardic antiquaries with Scythæ, and that verbal resemblance is the sole foundation of their travels from Scythia   No Roman, meaning to say Scytha, could express it Scotus, and no savage of Hibernia could think of applying to himself the eastern and generic title of Scythian. Words are almost a waste on such topics.   The name of Scoti is said to be first used by Porphyry, about A D 277[j]   But this must be doubtful in the extreme, as St Jerome[k], quoting Porphyry, would put "Scoticæ gentes" according to his own custom and that of his day, where Porphyry had put τὰ τῶν Ἰουεϱνων ἔθνη   If so, Ammianus will be the earliest who names them, at the close of the fourth century   Before these authors no Greek or Roman had heard of a Scot, and the name Scot was very probably unknown in Hibernia   If it be the same as *scuite*, a wanderer or rover, it is unintentionally explained by Ammianus in his "Scoti per diversa vagantes"   Its origin should date from the time when they devoted themselves to piracy; from

after

---

[j] That is the year to which Schoell, in his   flourishing
Table Chronologique, gives Porphyry's name, as   [k] Epist. ad Ctesiphontem.

after which time, as Ammianus is the first ascertained authority, its *known* origin does in point of *fact* date. And we may suppose that it was not prevalent, until the sea-kings of Erin became troublesome to the neighbouring shores, which was scarcely in the third century, or perhaps after the middle of it, when Cormac Mac Art obtained celebrity in various ways. Achy Mogmedon, father of Niall the Great, seems first to have become formidable in that shape. This supposition squares admirably with the observation in Ogygia iii 72, that although the Irish called their Gaidhelian people Scots, no such territorial epithet as Scotia or Scotland was known in their language, for they had not that name in regard of their land, but of renouncing the land, and making their home upon the deep, and among the creeks and coves of every defenceless shore. The ancient word *scud*, a boat or ship, plural, *scuid*, hath a close agreement with *scuite*, a wanderer, and *Scut*, a Scot, and it may be doubted, whether this obsolete Gaelic word did not primarily signify roving in coracles. Sallee existed before there were Sallee rovers; and so did Ireland, long before she had her scots or rovers. Bardic fable so far says true, that it was the latest denomination of the pagan kings of Erin, and the protracted rovings or wanderings of Eibhear Scot and his family through almost all lands and seas seem like a vast romantic gloss upon the appellation. For they were, indeed, a race of *Errones*, and that is the characteristic feature of their story.—(*II*)

No VII. *See page 60.*

Seeds of battle.—Cæsar speaks of the spikes which Cassibellanus placed in the Thames, as large stakes, not caltrops. "ripa autem erat acutis sudibus præfixis munita, ejusdemque generis sub aqua defixæ sudes flumine tegebantur," (De Bello Gall. v 18), and Bede says, that these stakes remained to his time, "quarum vestigia sudium ibidem usque hodie visuntur, et videtur inspectantibus quod singulæ earum ad modum humani femoris grossæ, et circumfusæ plumbo immobiliter erant in profundum fluminis infixæ'—Hist Eccl i 2. But we can hardly suppose such solid stakes to have been described under the name of "*semen* bellicosum."

I am indebted to Mr Eugene Curry for the following illustrations of the words Ᵹᴘᴀɴᴀ ᴄᴀᴛʜᴀ, which I have translated *seeds of battle*

In a MS glossary on paper, written in the seventeenth century, and now preserved in the Library of Trinity College, Dublin (H. 2 15. p. 126,) the words are thus explained·

Ᵹᴘᴀɪɴ ᴄᴀᴛᴀ .ɪ. ʙᴇᴀᴘᴀ, ᴜᴛ ᴇᴘᴛ, "ᴘɪʟ ᴄᴀᴛᴀ ᴢᴏɪᴘᴛ ᴄᴜɪᴘᴛᴇᴘ ᴘᴏᴄᴇᴘᴛᴇᴘ ᴘᴘɪ ʙᴇʟᴀ- GRAIN CATHA, i. e. spikes; as "SIL CATHA GOIRT [seeds of battle-field] which

are

ɑ cᴘιɕι ɑcɑ eιᴘlιnꝺe," .ι. beɑᴘɑ no ɱ cuιᴘcheᴘ ɑmɑιl ᴘιl ι n-ʒoᴘc ι m-belɑιb uɑcɑιb nɑ cᴘιce. Iᴘe ᴘιn uιl ɑnn ι ιn ʒᴘɑn cɑcɑ.

are put or set in the entrance fords of an unfortified[1] country:" i e. spikes or things that are sown like seed in a field, in the solitary passes of the country. This is what is *meant by* GRAN CATHA [seeds of battle].

The words in inverted commas are evidently quoted from some more ancient tract or glossary.

In the Felire Beg, or little Festilogium, an ancient Calendar, preserved in the library of the Royal Irish Academy, in a MS which is at least as old as the fourteenth century, the following is given (p 23) as the first of three great qualifications of a distinguished champion.

Cᴘeιꝺι ɑᴘɑ neɑmceɑnɑcɑᴘ luech, cuchcleᴘ cu ᴘoceɑᴘꝺɑιb, .ι. Ʒᴘɑιn cu- chɑ, cu ceɑᴘcɑιb ᴘoιche ιn ʒɑe bulʒɑ

Three things that constitute a champion Battle skill with subordinate arts, viz. GRAIN CATHA, with the skilful setting the GAE BULGA [belly spear]

The *gae bulga*, or belly spear, was a short spear which was used by the combatant to strike from beneath, and pierce the belly of his opponent under his shield In the curious ancient romance called Tain bo Cualgne, or "The Plunder of the Cualgnian Cows," the hero Cuchulann, the champion of Ulster, is introduced making use of the *gae bulga*, in his combat with Ferdiadh, the champion of Connaught, at Ath-Fidiadh, the ford of Fidiadh (so called from the name of the hero), now Ardee It appears from this narrative that the weapon was thrown from the foot, and the art seems to have consisted in keeping the adversary busy in protecting his head and body, whilst the *gae bulga* was suddenly seized between the toes, and struck under his shield into his belly. It is described as a barbed dart, which after entering the body threw out thirty blades that sprang loose and inflicted an incurable and deadly wound within

It is not necessary to our present purpose to enter into any more particular account of this probably fabulous weapon, or to collect together the notices of it which occur in Irish MSS It must suffice to observe that both the *gae bulga*, or belly-spear, and the *grain catha*, or battle seed, seem to have been used chiefly, if not always, in fords of rivers, the water serving to conceal the weapon, or the caltrops, from the enemy

[1] *Unfortified*—"Eιᴘlιn.ι eιᴘιnnιl no eꝺɑιnʒſn Eislinn, i. e. unfortified or un fast "—O'Clery's Glossary.

enemy In the case of the battle, or rather the single combat, at the ford of Ardee (described in the romance of the Tain bo Cuailgne), the attendant or esquire of Cuchulann is represented as sending the gae bulga to his master *through the water*, floated probably by some contrivance so as to escape the notice of the enemy, and it was then caught by Cuchulann between his toes, under the water, and driven instantly into the belly of his assailant —(*T*)

No VIII *See page 63.*

The King was baptized —The famous legend of King Lucius (from Nennius, cap 18) has its earliest voucher in Beda, whose accounts of its date are both erroneous and and discrepant[m] Annalists have varied from 138 to 199 in assigning its epoch. But that would not affect the fact itself, were it otherwise authentic There were then in Caledonia and in Cornwall, if not elsewhere, some independent princes or chieftains, of whom this Lucius may have been one. But it has much the appearance of a fable, forming part of the romance of the kings of Britain. Mr Carte has forcibly observed, that Gildas's design led him to speak of it, and yet he doth not mention so much as the name of Lucius, i p 133. The real question is, whether Beda took his brief statement out of Roman or ecclesiastical history, or from a Celtic legend Such a legend might well grow out of a statement, that Christianity was planted in Britain "Marco Aurelio et *Lucio* regnantibus," for the Emperor Lucius (as L Verus[n] was commonly termed) figures in the inconsistent dates of this transaction, both of which are in his life, and intended to be in his reign; and the latter is in his reign "M Antoninus Verus cum fratre Aur. *Lucio* Commodo .. quorum temporibus .. misit *Lucius* Brittannorum rex," &c. Hen. Hunt. 1, p. 304

Nothing can be more confused than the accounts given of this name For in British it is written Lles (whether in speaking of this man, or of any other Lucius[o]), meaning gain or profit; of which Lucius is no translation, though it may very remotely imitate the

---

[m] "Anno ab incarn Domini centesimo quinquagesimo sexto Marcus Antoninus Verus, decimius quartus ab Augusto, regnum cum Aurelio Commodo fratre suscepit, quorum temporibus cum Eleutherius vir sanctus pontificatui Romanæ ecclesiæ præesset, misit ad eum Lucius Britannorum rex epistolam," &c —Hist i c 4. Eleutherius was not Pope until 177, when Verus was dead , and their accession was in 161 "Anno ab incarn D. 167, Eleutherius Romæ

præsul factus 15 annos ecclesiam gloriosissimê rexit, cui litteras rex Britanniæ Lucius mittens ' &c —Epitome, p. 278 Here we get into the reign of the emperors, but are still ten years short of the pontificate of Eleutherius

[n] Julius Capitolinus, pp 179, 183-4, Lugd Bat 1661, Fronto Epist ad Verum, lib ii ep 1, Dion Cassius, pp 1177-8, Aur Vict de Cæsaribus, cap. 16.

[o] *Vide* Triad vi series 2, Brut, p 351, &c

the sound. But they surname him Lleuver, i e. bright or luminous, which is evidently meant to express the etymon of Lucius. Thus inconsistent is fiction Some copies of Nennius have these words· "Lucius agnomine Lever Maur, id est, Magni Splendoris, propter fidem quæ in ejus tempore venit" The author of the Cambreis[p] gave the same rationale of the name Lucius,

> "———— Coilo succedit *Lucius*, orto
> *Lucifero pralucidior*, nam *lucet* in ejus
> Tempore vera fides"

It is furthermore pretended that his real name was Lleirwg, Lleuver Mawr (and consequently Lucius) being merely a title of honour. Neither in the Liber Landavensis, nor in Mr J Williams's Eccles. Antiq of the Cymry, pp. 66–7, nor elsewhere, can I discover any thing that deserves to be called an historical corroboration of Beda. The Welch hagiography applicable to this name is vain and fictitious The family of Bran ap Llyr is described as one of the holy or saintly families of Britain[q], and it is pretended he was the father of Caractacus, who, being taken prisoner with his son, learned Christianity at Rome. But it is well known, that Caractacus was one of the sons of Cynobeline, whose death preceded the war between his children and the Romans. Dion Cassius lx cap 20 This Bran ap Llyr was a sorcerer, whose whole legend is magic. See the Mabinogi of Branwen His grandson, son of Caractacus, is said to have been St Cyllin; but it is tolerably certain, that Caractacus had no son whom the Romans took. Cyllin is fancifully supposed (see Taylor's Calmet v p 259; Triad xlii series i[r]) to have been Linus, first Bishop of Rome after St Peter It is not very likely, that Linus should be written for Cyllinus, which must either change the *quantity*, or reject the *accented* syllable Nor is it likely that the name Linus, as old as mythology[s] itself, and common at Rome, where Martial ridicules[t] at least two persons of that name, should be the mutilated name of a British Celt. Whether a converted barbarian, elegantly tattoed with woad, is likely to have been elected to the apostolical chair of St Peter, forms another question,

---

[p] Pseudo-Gildas in Cambreide, ap Ussher.

[q] Triad xviii This absurd production is full of ignorance, even of that little which we do know Boadicea is confounded with Cartismandua

[r] The general idea was, no doubt, in the mind of the writer of this Triad, which runs thus "Three Saints, *Linus* of the Isle of Britain, Linus Bran ap Llyr, Linus Cynedda Wledig, and Linus Brychan of Brecknock" Here the heads of the three Holy Families (see series 3, Triad xviii) each receive the name *Linus*, with its Latin termination!

[s] Orphei Calliopeia, Lino formosus Apollo

[t] Epigr i 76, ii 38, 54, iv. 66, v 12, vii. 94, xi. 26, xii 49

tion, of which the affirmative decision holds out fair hopes of Lambeth to our New Zealand neophytes. But we may infer, that there was never such a man as this Cyllin. That name is formed of *cy* and *llin*, and means "united by a chord or string," or else "being of a common lineage." Λίνον in Greek is flax; and thence, a chord or string. *Linum* in Latin keeps both those meanings; and *linea* has the further meaning of series or lineage. The British and Gaelic *llin* have *all the three meanings ;* which circumstance leaves reasonable inference, that it is one of the words introduced from the Latin. Neither does the flax culture belong to the savage state, peltries clothe the savage, the nomadic tribes proceed to the use of woollens, and flax and hemp come last. There probably existed no such name as Cy-llin for Caractacus to affix to his son, and it was invented long after the supremacy of the Romans had been established, and perhaps after its subversion.

Lleirwg Lleuver Mawr was grandson of Cyllin, and son of Coel, whom, however, the Chronicle of Kings makes son of Meiric, not of Cyllin. Coel (called a bard in Triad xci.) reigned over Britain, paying tribute to Claudius; and his son Lles succeeded him, whom others call Llenwg Lleuver, and the Latin writers Lucius. This is all a romance. The house of Cynobeline (if there was any remnant of it) did not recover its authority over Britain, as tributaries or otherwise, but the country was gradually reduced into a Roman province. As there was no Cyllin, there probably was, for similar reasons, no Coel; and the true Coels are of much later date. For the Welch word *coel* (not in Gaelic), an omen or presage, charm or enchantment, or other object of superstitious veneration, seems to be formed from the Latin word *coelum* or *cœlum*, what is hollow or concave, and, in the second intention, *heaven*. *De cælo servare*, is to observe omens and auguries; *divinare* is to observe things divine.

It is a reasonable supposition, that the one historical notice of Lucius, Beda's given in a form discreditable to the learning of its venerable author, is not really historical, and that the tale was made up in Britain by somebody, who took the imperial brothers Marcus and Lucius to be the Roman emperor and the British king.—(*II*.)

No IX. *See page 66.*

Geoffrey of Monmouth only miscalls Maximus by the name of Maximian, but the Historia Britonum has made two emperors, Maximus and Maximian, out of that one man.

The remarkable assertion, that Consuls instead of Cæsars now began to reign, can only be explained as of Tyranni in lieu of more regular emperors. For such were Maximus himself, Marcus, Gratianus Municeps, and Constantine III., who all assumed the tyrannic purple in Britain. That accounts for the idea of a derogation; but the

author

author of the Historia, consistently with his general statement, proceeds to speak of Valentinian and Theodosius as consuls.

The epoch of Maximus was very famous in the legends of Britain. In them he is called Maxen or Maxim *Wledig*, i e the *sovereign of the land.* Gwledig is litterally terrenus, from *gwlad*, terra, and the title claims him for a native, as well as a Roman, sovereign. The Chronicle of the Kings describes him as being nephew to Helen, mother of Constantine, and son to her brother Llewelyn, and as being husband to another Helen, daughter of Eudav, a potent British chieftain. See Galfrid v cap. 8–9, Roberts's Tysilio, p. 98 Thus he was a Briton, though a senator of Rome. He is indebted for these legends to the important events of his reign For then it was, that the foundations of Armorican Britanny were laid by the Celtic forces who accompanied him, on his expedition to Gaul, under the command (as a general tradition saith) of one Conan of Meriadawg in Denbigh. Then also the affair of the 11,000 virgins occurred, of which the death of some young women, going to join the Armorican *colony* (Colonia), seems to have been the truth.

There is a curious tale or mabinogi called Breuddwyd Maxen, the Dream of Maximus. He was emperor of Rome, the handsomest and wisest that ever reigned. Under him were thirty-two crowned kings, with whom he went a hunting Being heated, he fell asleep, while they raised their shields for a fence around him, and a golden shield over his head He dreamt that he visited a country, which he traversed, and reached a rough and barren district, beyond which he found a fine city, and in it a hall or palace of great splendour, and in the hall were two bay-haired youths, playing chess on a chess-board of silver, with chessmen of gold They were dressed in black, with frontlets of red gold on their hair, and precious stones therein At the foot of the column supporting the hall sat a gray-haired man on an ivory throne, with golden bracelets, chain, and frontlet, and with a golden chess-board on his breast, and in his hand a golden wand and a steel saw, and he was carving chessmen A maiden sat opposite to him on a golden chair, arrayed in white silk and jewels Maximus sat down in the chair beside her and threw his arms round her neck, and, at that moment of his dream, awoke He sent ambassadors in all directions in quest of her And, at last, three of them found out the country, which was Britain, and the rough district, which was Snowdon, and the city, which was Aber Sain in Arvon, where they found the youths playing chess, the old man making chess-men, and the maiden in the chair of gold They opened to her the suit of Maxen, and she said, that if the emperor loved her, he must come for her. So he came, and conquered the island, and went to Aber Sain, where he found Conan, and Adeon, sons of Eudav, playing at chess, and Eudav son of Caradoc in the ivory throne, making chess-men,

and

and his daughter Helen seated. And he threw his arms round her neck And that
night they slept together. Next morning he asked her to name her dower, and she
demanded Britannia from the British to the Irish sea, and the three adjacent islands
[see above, cap iii], to hold under him, and three cities to be built for her, which
were Caer yn Arvon, Caer Llion, and Caer Vyrddin Helen caused roads to be made
across the island from each city, and they were called *the Roads of Helen the Armipo-
tent* Maxen stayed seven years in Britain, and thereby (by Roman law) he forfeited
the crown imperial, and they chose another emperor in his place. But he went
and besieged Rome, and took it by the valour of Conan and Adeon and their Britons
Then Maxen gave them his army, to conquer territories, and they conquered and
ravaged many provinces. But Conan would not return to his native country, and
remained in Britanny, which is called Llydau Brytaen, and, since many flocked over
thither from Britain, the British language yet remains there"—See the Greal sev
Cynnulliad o Orchestion, &c pp 289–297, London, 1805. Maximus is said to have
had three sons, Cystennin or Constantine, Peblic or Publicus, and Owain or Eugenius
surnamed Minddu or the Blacklipped—Y Greal, &c p 18 This Owain ap Maxen
Wledig is reported to have been the first of those British kings who, after the resigna-
tion of the island by Honorius, ruled it independently of the Roman or Cæsarean system.
See Triads, xvi xxxiv xli lii This name and tradition comes out of Bardism,
and was not accepted by that other school of authors who framed the Trojan dynasty
of kings King Owain, son of Maximus, has been termed a saint, but he seems to
have been more of a magician He buried the head of Bian ap Llyr in the Tower
Hill of London, for a talisman of defence to this island, but king Arthur indiscreetly
revealed it. He was himself buried, both his head and his body at Nanhwynyn, in
the Forest of the Faraon (demons or spirits), and the said Owain slew Eurnach
Gawr, and in the self-same forest Eurnach slew him—Greal, p 18. The mabinogi
or legend of this obscure business seems not to be extant —(II)

No. X. *See page 67.*

From the place, &c —This curious sentence on the limits of Britanny has been, in
the indication of the points of the compass, either taken from a better MS than the
printed copies, or more clearly enounced by the translator. The author describes
Britanny as a triangle with its vertex due W, and the angles of its base N E. and
S E The Cruc Ochident or Tumulus Occidentalis is beyond doubt (as Bertram had
surmised) the precipitous rock of Ushant, notoriously the due W extremity of
Britanny. Its modern name, Ouessant, though ultimately derived from Uxantus,
sounds and perhaps is intended to sound like Ouest, West.

The N E angle is the stagnum, or bay of the sea, above (that is, north of) the Mons Jovis   The super verticem Montis for super Montem was either a mistake of Marcus himself, or of all his transcribers   The Mons Jovis is an extraordinary rock in the Avranchin, otherwise called Mons Sancti Michaelis in Periculo Maris, in French le Mont Jou   See Blondel, Notice du Mont St Michel, p 10 Avranches, 1816. There are two rocks, the Tumbelenia, or Tombelaine, explained by some Tumba Helenæ, but more correctly Tumba Beleni, i.e Hill of Belenus, the Celtic sun-god, and the loftier one, called simply Tumba, as well as Mons Jovis.   The monastery or hermitage there was called Monasterium ad Duas Tumbas in Periculo Maris.   Blondel, ibid pp. 11–119   The Mont Jou received its appellation of Mont Saint Michel, from an apparition of St. Michael Archangel, which was seen there in A D. 708   See Gallia Christiana, xi. p 472, Ogeè Dict de la Bretagne, 1 p 98, Nantes, 1778.   In that year an inroad of the sea swept away, and changed *in arenæ suæ formam*, the forest in which the mount used to stand, and made it an island at high water, and St. Aubert, Bishop of Avranches, built a chapel there by command of the Archangel, which was dedicated in 709   See Blondel, ibid p 14, Gallia Christ. ibid.   Apparitio S Michael. ap Mabillon, A SS Ben sæc 3 part 1. p. 86.   The Avranchin continued to be a part of the County of Brittany until the year 936, in which Alan IV is said to have made over that district to William Long-Sword, Duke of Normandy, and to that province it hath ever since appertained   Recherches sur la Bretagne per Felix De-laporte, 1 p 95–6, Rennes, 1819   Therefore Dom Mabillon antedates the Apparitio Sancti Michaelis, when he states that narrative to have been written "ante sæculum decimum," for its author does not consider the Mount to be in Brittany.

It remains for us to find the S E angle of Brittany at Cantguic[u]   The Armorican meaning of the words *cant guic* is the hundred villages, *centum vici*   And I have no doubt, but the civitas Cantguic or Centumvici, is that of Condivicum, properly Con-divicnum, of the Namnetes   Whether the ancient Gaulish name Condivicnum[v] sig-nified *centum vici*, or did not, that etymology seems to have been attached to it; and may have contributed to introduce the spelling Condivicum   With Ushant for your vertex, and Mont St. Michel and Nantes at the base, you have the Brittany of the Historia Britonum   If Dom Morice has taken any notice of this passage, or the mat-ters to which it relates, in his voluminous work, it has escaped my observation

Mr O'Donovan has justly remarked, that the translator mistakes *crug*, a hill or
mound,

---

[u] Rectè sic ap MSS Petav et Cotton Minus rectè Tanguic, etc.

[v] Adrien Valois supposes, upon uncertain grounds, that it referred to a confluence of streams —Notitia Galliarum, p 367

mound (*tumulus* of Marcus, and *cumulus* of Nennius), for *ciur*, a cross.—Notes on the Hy Fiachrach, p 413.—(H)

No XI. *See page* 68.

The Britons of Letha, &c—Britanny was called, by the Celts of Great Britain, Llydaw, and in Irish Letha, or Leatha, which words are expressed in Latin Letavia. Its derivation is from the Latin *littus*, and is equivalent in sense to the word Armorica, or, with the mutation, Arvorica, whence Procopius took his Ἀρβορυχοι, de Bello Goth I 12. *Lez*, in Armorican, is *shore;* and *Lez ar mor*, or *ar vor*, is *shore of the sea;* sometimes redundantly expressed lez *en ar* vor, which arises from making one word of ar mor, or arvor, littus *m* maritimis Hence the noble family of Lez'narvor See Rostrenen, Dict François-Breton in *Bord de la mer* , Bullet Dict Celtique in *Letav* and *Llydaw* Others have improperly derived the word Letavia from the Laeti, a sort of auxiliary militia, holding lands under the lower emperors of the West

Nennius has a much stranger story, which our translator (if he found it in his copies) has done wisely to reject He says that the British colonists, who married Gaulish wives, cut out the tongues of their wives, that the children might not learn Latin, and that, on that account, the people were called Lled-tewig, pl Lled-tewigion, i e. Semi-tacentes. A similar account is given in the Breuddwyd Maxen, but with less care in adapting the name to its etymon "because of the women and their language being reduced to silence, the people were called the men of Llydaw Brytaen'— Y Greal, p. 297 That notion must have obtained some vogue, for we find Æneas of Britanny, the father of Lmyr Llydaw, called Æneas Lledewig o Llydaw, i e Æneas Semitacens Letaviensis.—Bonedd y Saint, p 30, 31

Leatha was certainly used two ways in Irish, sometimes for Letavia and sometimes for Latium, from which some doubt and confusion hath arisen. See Mr O'Donovan on the Hy Fiachrach, p 410. In the Scholia upon the poet Fiech, in Colgan's Trias, probably by more scholiasts than one, it is explained both ways. That is the origin of the ridiculous fable of king Faradhach Dathi, nephew and successor to Niall of the Nine Hostages, having carried his arms into the Alps and been there slain Like his uncle he attacked Leatha, and like him, met his death there, and his descents upon Letavia, when construed into an invasion of Latium, i. e Italy, bring him, in due course, to the Alps. He was, by some accounts, shot with an arrow, and "the learned say that it was with the same arrow with which Niall of the Nine Hostages was slain"— *Hy Fiachr*, p. 23 Strange indeed! if the arrow which slew Niall upon the coast of Britanny, had found its way to the Alps. But, if they were killed in the same country, it might possibly be the same arrow There the truth of the matter tran-

spires

spues, and it is not a little confirmed by the existence of Dathi's tomb at Rath Crogan, in Connaught. In the Battle of Magh Rath, or Moira, pp. 4, 5, it is mentioned, that Ugaine Mor (King of Erin, anterior to authentic history) took hostages of Erin and Albany, and eastwards to Leatha. And if we understand these words as inclusive of Great and Little Britain rather than of Italy, we shall give compactness to the story, and mitigate its improbabilities.—(II)

No XII   See page 71

Severus the Second, &c—All the Latin copies, after briefly introducing Severus the Second and Constantinus, say, "now we must resume the history of Maximian the tyrant," i e Maximus, and so give the upshot of his attempts. But the translator has thrown Maximus' history into one piece. The ninth emperor is the tyrant Constantinus, who reigned at Arles in Provence. But it is less easy to say who is the second Severus, for Libius Severus of Lucania, Count Riemer's puppet in 461, is clean out of the question.

In the enumeration prefixed to Marcus, he is called "alius Severus Æquantius," p 46, and the text of Marcus twice (pp 62, 80) mentions Gratianus Æquantius as the Roman consul at the time when the Saxons came over, which, any way, is an anachronism, but must relate to Gratianus Municeps and not to the elder Gratian. Nennius has it *Gratianus* (otherwise Martianus[w]) *Secundus*, cap 28. What can this word *æquantius* mean? It is said in the Chronicle of Kings that Gratianus Municeps, with two legions, drove the Scots out of Britain.—Galfrid 5 cap 16. The headings of chapters to Nennius state (cap 24), that "Severus II directed another wall, of the customary structure, to be built from Tinmouth to Rouvenes against the Picts and Scots." Now if Gratianus Municeps caused the Severian or Tinmouth wall to be repaired, he might, for that service, be called "ail Severys," which word *ail* gives the double sense of *another*, or *a second*, and of being *similar* or *equivalent* to the first, or, in the words of the preface to Marcus, "alius Severus æquantius." Certainly, the application of this word both to Gratianus, and to an unknown Severus *occupying Gratian's right place in a series that omits him*, strongly suggests their identity. Geoffrey's Latin steers clear of this Severus, but the Welsh copies marked Tysilio and Basingwerk, introduce him upon the death of Gratianus Municeps (not as king or as emperor, but as commander

der

---

[w] There was a Marcianus in the East three years later than the date in question, viz, 449, assigned, however, to that very year by Beda, i cap 15, and in his Epitome, but there never was a Marcian the Second. Mr Stevenson prints (in his cap 31) Gratiano secundo Equantio, but whether from a text, or by combining together two different texts, does not clearly appear. Gale's readings know nothing at all of Æquantius

der of an auxiliary legion), and set him to work upon *the wall of Severus.* Brut., p. 225, Roberts, p. 103. The interval between Gratianus and Gallio Ravennas (from thirteen to nineteen years), is sufficient to admit of both having laboured upon the wall, the former on the old Severian model, and the latter in solid masonry I take Gratianus Municeps to mean Gratian of Municipium, or Caer Municip, that is, of Verulamium See above, add. notes, No I, p v.

All that follows (briefly here, but more fully in the Latin) concerning the Roman expeditions to reconquer Britain, and their depredations, is false, and not easy to account for The auxiliary legion sent by Honorius, and that afterwards led over by Gallion of Ravenna, to assist the Britons, form their sole historical basis —(H)

No. XIII   *See page* 79

The miracle of Germanus is thus recorded by Hericus Autisiodorensis from his recollection of the oral communications of Marcus Anachoreta, the original compiler of these British histories, with whom he had been personally acquainted. 'The shores of Gaul would be the end of the world, did not the isle of Britain, by its singular magnitude almost deserve the name of another world This island, peculiarly devoted to St German, acknowledges herself indebted to his sanctity for many benefits, being illuminated by his teaching, more than once purified by him from the taint of heresies; and, lastly, adorned with the lustre of many miracles which need not to be repeated, since they have been committed to writing by the study of noble doctors One of them is especially famous, of which the knowledge hath come down to us through the holy old man, Marcus, a bishop of the same nation, who was by birth a Briton, but was educated in Ireland, and, after a long exercise of episcopal sanctity, imposed upon himself a voluntary pilgrimage, and being invited by the munificence of the pious king Charles, spent an anachoretic life at the Convent of Saints Medard and Sebastian, a remarkable philosopher in our days, and of peculiar sanctity. He was wont to relate before many, that German, the holy apostle (to use his own words) of his nation, when he was traversing the Britannias, entered the king's palace with his disciples. It was then severe winter, and very inclement not only to men, but even to cattle. Therefore he sent a message to the king to ask shelter for the approaching night The king refused, and, being a barbarian both by nation and character, made light of the matter Meanwhile German, with his disciples, remaining in the open air, stoutly endured the inclemency of the weather And now, as the evening had closed in, the king's swineherd, having returned from the pastures, was carrying home to his own cottage his daily wages which he had received at the palace. When he saw the blessed German and his disciples starved with the wintry cold,

cold, he drew near, and humbly asked him to state who he was, and why he staid there in the severe frost? Having collected nothing certain from his answer, but being moved by the dignity of his person, he said, I beseech you, my Lord, whoever you are, to consider your body, and enter the lodging of your servant, and to accept such good offices as my poverty permits. for I see that it is of no small importance to mitigate the inclemency of the approaching night even in the meanest dwelling. Not despising the quality of the person, he entered the dwelling, and gladly received the services offered him by the poor man. He possessed only a cow and a calf, and turning to his wife he said, 'Eh? do you not perceive how great a guest you have received? look sharp, then, and kill our only calf, and serve it up for those who are about to sup.' She presently obeyed the order, and cooked the calf, and set it on the table. The bishop, abstinent as usual, desired the others to eat. Supper being finished, German called the woman to collect carefully the bones of the calf, and lay them upon its skin and place them before its mother in the cow-house. This being done (strange to say) the calf presently arose, and, standing by its mother, began to feed. Then, turning to them both, the prelate said 'Receive this benefit by way of compensation for your hospitality, but without prejudice to the reward of your charity.' All extolled the wonderful issue of the event with united praises. Next day the bishop went to the palace, and waited for the king's coming forth into public. German received him as he came out from the interior, and, as soon as he was accessible to verbal reproof, severely asked him why he had denied him hospitality the previous day. The king was stupified and, being astonished at the man's firmness, refrained from answering. Then Germanus with wonderful authority said, 'Go forth, and resign the sceptre of the kingdom to a better.' And he hesitated. German immediately thrust him with his staff, and said, 'Thou shalt go forth, and, as the Lord hath certainly decreed, shalt never again abuse the kingly power.' The barbarian, awed by the divine power in the prelate, immediately went out of the gates of the palace with his wife and children, and made no further attempt to retain it. Then German sent one of his disciples to call forth the swineherd and his wife, and to the astonishment of the whole palace, placed him on the summit of royalty, from which time until now kings proceeded from the race of the swineherd, God wonderfully regulating human affairs through St German. The aforesaid bishop, whose probity whosoever hath experienced, will by no means hesitate to believe his words, assured me, with the addition of an oath, that these things were contained in catholic letters in Britain "—*Herui de Miraculis S. Germ.* i. cap. 55; apud Ph. Labbe Novæ Biblioth MSS tom i. p. 554-5. Compare Marcus, pp. 62-5, Nennius, cap. 30

It is observable that all proper names of men and places are omitted here, Heric being, no doubt, unable to retain them in his memory; consequently Britannia and her

king

king are mentioned generally in lieu of Powys and its local dynasts Germanus visited Britain in company with St Lupus in 429, and again in 447, accompanied by Severus. But all the accounts of his transactions with Vortigern have the character of fable He died on the 31st of July, 448, being an early period of that ill-fated, but long-lived, monarch's career

The Behinus of Marcus, and Benli of Nennius, is Benlli, surnamed Gawr, or the Giant, lord of Ial, a mountainous district of Denbigh —Llwyd Commentariolum, p 91 That Gawr is used properly for giant, and not for a mighty man, seems from Gwilym Rhyvel's mention of the gwrhyd (length or stature) of Benlli Gawr.—Englynion y Davydd ap Owain, v 25 Nothing is known of him besides the fable in Nennius But the grave of his son, Beli ap Benlli Gawr, a fierce warrior, is mentioned in the Beddau Milwyr, or Graves of Warriors, stanza 73 ·

> " Whose the grave upon the Maes Mawr ?
> Proud his hand upon the long-bladed spear,
> The grave of Beli ap Benlli Gawr "

And some account of that grave is given in a prose narrative, printed in Y Greal, p. 239 The late Dr. Owen Pughe imputed to this son of Benlli a modification of the laws of Bardism —Preface to Llywarch Hên , p lx Welsh Diet in *Beli* But for this he has adduced no authority beyond his own assertions Ralph Higden, in Polychronicon (p 223), says. " In Legenda S Germani [i e. in Heric's book] habetur quod dum *Vortigernus* hospitium S Germano denegaret," &c , stating the affair precisely as in Heric, except that where Heric names the king generally, he puts in the name of Vortigern Both alike derive the kings of all Britain, not of Powys, from the swineherd. It is remarkable that this Cadell Dwrnluc was the founder of a line of Powysian princes, and that Cadell, second son of Rodri Mawr, and father to the law-giver, Howel the Good, obtained Powys in the famous division of Wales by Rodri Mawr.   Yet this doth not arise from any confusion of the two men, for Cadell ap Rodri Mawr had not been dead forty years in 946, when the last edition of the Historia is dated; nor was he yet born, " quarto Mervini regis," when the first was compiled For a sample of the ancient genealogies in the Cambrian Biography, Cadell reigned about the close of the fifth century (p. 31), Vortigern died in 481 (p 168), yet Cadell was son of Pasgen, son of Rheiddwy, son of Rhuddvedel, son of Cyndeyrn or Catigern, son of Vortigern! The age of puberty must have been early in those days.   Other genealogies, contained in a MS of the tenth century, make Cadell Dwrnluc father of Categirn, and grandfather of Pasgen, and son to one Selemiawn But Categirn and Pasgen are now universally regarded as two sons of Vortigern So little consistency do the boasted Cambrian genealogies possess. See Cambr Quart Mag. iv. pp 17, 21.

The

The miracle of the calf is one of a class well-known in the hagiography of these islands. St Patrick brought to life five cows that were evisceratæ.—Jocelyn, cap 9 Having banqueted with his disciples upon Bishop Trian's cow and calf, he brought them both to life again, lest the bishop should be in want of milk —Vita Tertia, cap 63 A visitor to St Columba ate a whole sheep for his dinner, but Columba collected the bones and blessed them, and so completely restored the sheep, that a large party made a second dinner of it.—O'Donnell Vita Columbæ, ii. cap 16 A poor woman slaughtered and roasted her only calf for St Bridget's supper, but she restored it to life —Cogitosus, cap. 27. St Finnian of Clonard restored a calf on which he and his followers had supped, and St Abban one which the wolves had devoured —Colgan, A SS xxii Febr p 396, xvi Mart p 611 St Fingar and his 777 companions feasted on a poor Cornish woman's cow, and then he resuscitated the skin and bones —Febr xxiii p 389 —(ll)

No XIV. *See page* 93

Let his blood be sprinkled, &c —The practice of auspicating the foundation of cities, temples, or other solemn structures, by human sacrifice, is not known to me as of any remote antiquity Johannes Malala, a compiler of the ninth century, gives this legend of the foundation of Antioch by Seleucus Nicator "In the plain opposite to the Silpian mountain   he dug the foundations of the wall, and sacrificed by the hands of Amphion, his high-priest and mystagogue (τελεστοῦ), a virgin named Æmathe, between the city and the river, on the 22nd day of the Artemisian month, which is also May, at the first hour of the day, about sunrise, calling αυτην [HER, or IT?] Antiocheia, after the name of his own son, Antiochus Soter Presently he built a temple, which he dedicated to Jupiter Bottius, and diligently erected formidable walls, Xenæus being his architect He also erected upon the banks of the river a brazen pedestal and statue of the sacrificed virgin, as the Fortune of the city, and offered sacrifice to her as the Fortune "—p 256 Subsequently the same Nicator laid the foundation of Laodicea in Syria Having slain a wild boar, he dragged its body round a certain space of ground, and dug the walls according to the track of its blood, "having also sacrificed a pure virgin, by name Agave, and erected to her a brazen statue, as the Fortune of the city "—p 259 Of these statements a certain Pausanias Chronographus appears to be the authority, and no reasonable doubt can be entertained, that they were fabulous, and founded upon the magical doctrines to which that lost and unknown writer seems to have been much addicted From this we collect, that the human victim immolated upon such occasions was rewarded with deification and worship, and accounted a sort of tutelary deity of the place. Merlin was to have been the Τύχη of Vortigern's edifice. But the narrative in Nennius has this distinction, that repeated

failures

failures had shewn the necessity of some piacular rite, wherein it more nearly agrees with the legend of St. Oran of Iona. "The chapel of St Oran stands in this space, which legend attests to have been the first building attempted by St. Columba By the working of evil spirits, the walls fell down as soon as they were built up After some consultation it was pronounced, that they never could be permanent till a human victim was buried alive Oran, a companion of the saint, generously offered himself, and was interred accordingly At the end of three days St. Columba had the curiosity to take a farewell look at his old friend, and caused the earth to be removed To the surprise of all beholders Oran stood up, and began to reveal the secrets of the prison-house, and particularly declared that all that was said of hell was a mere joke This dangerous impiety so shocked Columba that, with great policy, he instantly ordered the earth to be flung in again. Poor Oran was overwhelmed, and an end for ever put to his prating His grave is near the door, distinguished only by a plain red stone" Pennant's Second Tour in Scotland, ap Pinkerton's Voyages, tom iii p 298 We may learn how deeply-rooted this idea was in the islands, by finding it in both the nations and languages, and ascribed to such different persons As to St Odhian or Oran, that he died naturally or by visitation of God, appears in Colgan's Latin excerpta from the unprinted Irish work of Magnus O Donnell, lib ii. c 12 Some account of that saint is also known to exist in the Leabhar Breac, fol. 17.—(H)

No. XV *See page 93.*

Magh Ellite—The Campus Electi in the region of Glewysing, which region is otherwise the hundred of Gwynllwg, in Monmouthshire In the sixth century one Einion was king of Glewysing See Liber Landavensis, pp 129, 379 In the reign of Alfred it was governed by Hoel ap Rhys, and considered distinct from Gwent Asser Vita Alfredi p 15 It is supposed to be named after Glywys, the father of St Gwynnllyw the Warrior, and grandfather to St Catwg the Wise, and to St. Glywys Cerniw, who founded the church of Coed Cerniw[x] in Glewysing See Rice Rees on the Welsh Saints. p 170. The place called Bassaleg is said by Mr Roberts to be written in Welsh Maes-aleg, i e Plain of Aleg, which he conjectures to be the Campus Electi. His conjecture has the more force, from his seeming quite ignorant where Glewysing was, and that Bassaleg was in the heart of that district Roberts s Ant p 58, and apud Gunn's Nennius, p 166

This is very well, yet I have some misgivings as to the prime source of all this The Cor Emmrys was immeasurably more famous than the Dinas Emmrys, and it,

oi

---

[x] Vulgarly Coedkerne

or the little hill which it crowns, was called the Mount of Election, possibly from the inauguration of kings As it is said, in the Graves of Warriors, that Merlin Ambrose (surnamed Ann ap Lleian) lies buried in the Mynydd Dewis, or Mount of Election. —Beddau Milwyr, st 14 But he was notoriously buried in the Cor Emmrys Now, if the mount was that of an election, so also was the plain, and in that sense the Maes Mawr was Maes Elect. That plain was not indeed *in regione Glewysing*, but it was in the *regio Gewisseorum* or in *Gewissing*, the territory of the West Saxon kings, descended from Gewiss. Geoffrey of Monmouth calls Vortigern himself " the consul of the Gewisseans," i e the ruler, by prolepsis, of what afterwards was Wessex — Lib vi cap 6 And when Aurelius Ambrosius desired Merlin's aid (for the Chronicle makes two people of them), upon occasion of erecting the Stonehenge, he sent, precisely as Vortigern had done, messengers in all directions to find him, and they found him " in natione Gewisseorum, ad fontem Galabes," viii cap 10. The writer was Archdeacon of Monmouth, in which county Glewysing is situate, but has in neither place any allusion to Glewysing On the other hand the Welsh seem so baffled with this Saxon name, that the copy entitled of Tysilio entirely suppresses it, and the other copies translate it in the first instance Erging and Lwias, and in the second simply Ewias —Brut Tysilio, pp. 236, 276 Lastly, where Geoffrey saith that Cadwallader's West-Saxon mother was " ex nobili genere Gewisseorum" (xii cap 14), the Welsh translators all say, that she was descended from the nobles of Erging and Ewias —Brut p 384 But Erging and Ewias are in Herefordshire, and have no more to do with Glewysing than they have with the Gewisseans Hence I am inclined to attribute the transfer of this conspicuous fable into the obscure district of Gwynllwg and village of Bassaleg, to an inability to construe the geography of the *Campus Elect in Gewisseis*, the great scene of Merlin's and Ambrose's fame Indeed, the romance of Merlin plainly says, that Vortigern's edifice was upon an eminence in Salisbury Plain —Ellis Metrical Rom iii p 213

The red and white dragon of Dinas Emmrys were the hidden fates or talismans of Britain, originating with king Lludd, son of Beli Mawr, and his brother the enchanter Llevelys It is scarce likely that a country with such great and central sanctuaries should have its fates deposited in so remote and obscure a place In fact, it was not their primary seat For Lludd, being distressed by horrid shrieks on every Mayday night, and learning that the battle of the dragons produced them, measured Britain, and found Rhydychan or Oxenford to be its centre, and there placed a cask of mead, and covered it with a cloth, over which the dragons fought, and fell into the cask and were intoxicated, and then he folded them both in the cloth, and buried them deep in Dinas Emmrys in Eryri —Y Tair Gormes, in Y Greal, p 244, Brut
Tysilio,

Tysilio, p 169, Triad ii 53. Therefore, the dragons originally belonged to *some* place accounted central. But this allegory cannot be mistaken. The night of the Calan-Mai was that very night on which Hengist and the Saxons slaughtered the British convention; the shrieks of the British dragon were those occasioned by that massacre, and the mead-cask over which the dragons fought and got drunk is the banquet, amidst the convivial orgies whereof so much blood was shed. But that was the twyll Caer-Sallawg, or plot of Sarum, of which the Cor Emmrys, or Stonehenge, was notoriously the scene. It is therefore at that place (as I judge) that the hidden dragons of Lludd ap Beli were deposited.

There is another aspect to the prophecy of the dragons, which is perhaps the more esoterical and bardic of the two. By that, both the contending dragons are British. The white dragon (says the Roman de Merlin) slew the red one, but only survived three days. The red dragon was Vortigern, and the white represented his opponents, Ambrosius and Pendragon, who wrested the crown from him.—Roman de Merlin fol xxiv, xxv. Here two British parties are the dragons, and the Saxons not directly concerned; here also the colours are interchanged, the white or prevailing one being the bardic, and the red being that which the bardic party reviled. This theory seems to be in harmony with the eleventh Triad, in which the gormes or oppression of *the kalends of May* is distinguished from that of *the Dragon of Britain,* and the former expressly said to have been inflicted by foreigners from over sea, but the latter by the tyranny of princes and rage of the people.—(II)

No XVI   *See page* 107

Gortigern, son of Guatal, &c—Gortigern, son of Guitaul, son of Guitolin, son of Gloui. It is not known from what parents, family, or province this celebrated person came, though he reigned so long and so eventfully. A pedigree printed in the Cambrian Quart Mag i p, 486 departs entirely from this one, and makes him son of Rhydeyrn, of Deheuvraint, of Edigent, of Edeyrn, of Enid, of Ednos of Enddolaw, of Avnllach, of Avloch, of Beli Mawr. The truth has been hidden deep, and does not appear to me to transpire in either of these Welsh pedigrees. The Welsh call him Gwr-theyrn, from *gwr*, a man (and in second intention, a mighty man), and *teyrn*, a prince. Had this name signified Virilis Rex, the praedicate preceding the subject would have made it Gwrdeyrn, as in Cyndeyrn, Mechdeyrn, Aerdeyrn, and all compounds of which the first word does not end in *d* or *t*, like *matteyrn*, from *mad* or *mat*, good. Therefore Vir Regalis must have been the sense of Gwitheyrn.

A curious variation occurs in the spelling of this person's name, of which the causes are not clearly apparent. Some, as Gildas, Marcus, and Nennius, put Gurthegirn,

Guorthegirn,

Guorthegirn, or Gorthegirn, which seems to combine the British spelling of *gur* with the more ancient and Erse orthography of *tighearn* a prince, while Geoffrey and most of the Anglo-Normans use the now received form of Vortigern, which is hard to come at any way. These difficulties are complicated in one of his alleged sons, whom the Welsh revered under the name of Gwrthevyr, a word of no facile etymology in their tongue. He, in like manner, is Guortimer or Gortimer in the Historia Britonum, and Vortimer with the others. This *guor*, turning into *vor*, seems to indicate that in his name, as in the former, *gur* is the first element and not *guith*. But *teryr* and *timer* are not easy to deal with. Again, the other son, whose name Catigern in Latin should be represented by Catteyrn (Battle-prince) in Welsh, is Cyndeyrn (Head-prince), being the same that they give to St Kentigern of Strathclyde and the exact equivalent of his. There is an obvious uncertainty in these names, such as doth not usually (if indeed elsewhere) occur in British names. This consideration, perhaps, weighed with Gale in thinking Vortigern was of a Pictish family. But, since he was of Gwynedd he is most likely to have been born of an Irish mother, in the days when that people (under their own Ganval and Sirigi, and the Briton Einion Vrenhin) occupied the famous island of Mona. (*Vide infrà* the notes on the Legend of St Cannech). He was accused of his friendship with, and support by, the Irish, as well as the Saxons, though the important upshot of the Saxon affairs has cast the others into shade. An ancient bard says (alluding to the massacre by Hengist, at the feast of the Kalends of May, and boasting that those national festivities had not thereby been crushed and abolished), ' the knife-bearer shall not stab the sword-bearers of May-day, that is not [effected?] which was desired by the foolishly compliant master of the house, and the men of his affection, men of blood, Cymmry, Angles, Irishmen and North Britons"—*Guawd Lludd* v 76. The bard Golyddan mentions him to have been confederated with " the Irish of Ireland, those of Mona, and those of North-Britain "—*Armes Prydain*, v 10. His son Pascent is said to have contended for the crown at the head of an army of Irish from Ireland, and to have lost his life in that conflict —*Galfr Monum* viii cap 16. This does not agree with the account of Nennius, cap 52. that the destroyers of his father permitted him to reign *in duabus regionibus*, viz, Buelt and Guortigernawn, unless we suppose, that he first made that compromise, afterwards contended, with Irish aid, for the insular crown, and, perishing in the attempt, transmitted those lands to his family. For Celtic clanship did not admit of forfeiture, as feodality did.

Whatsoever Vortigern was, it is evident that he was a Briton of such power and influence throughout the island as no other man on record possessed. and maintained a struggle of the most protracted duration against the elements of foreign and domes-

tic

tic anarchy Though it never appears in any Latin shape, the epithet *gurth-enau*, perverse of lips or mouth, became habitually and thoroughly united to his name by his countrymen, owing to his issuing impolitic commands, or (as the Triads say) disclosing secrets.—See Beddau Milwyr, st 40 Triad 45, series i. 10, series ii. 21, 53, series iii Brut y Saeson, p 468 Æræ Cambro-Brit ap Llwyd Commentariolum, p. 141 It deserves to be remarked, that Marcus, the author of the Historia, though setting forth the descent of Fernmael from Vortigern, and fondly magnifying the fastness of Caer-Guortigern, nevertheless writes with all his country's prepossessions against that ruler, and appears, from the unanimity of the copies, to have introduced that nickname into his pedigree.—(II)

NOTE XVII See page 120

Those who have handled the history of the Picts have not produced a satisfactory result. Father Innes, seeing that the name of Picti first appeared to the north of the Roman frontier, after the establishment of Roman civility in South Britain had converted the staining of the skin into a distinctive peculiarity and a conspicuous badge of independence, built upon that palpable origin of the name the too hasty conclusion, that both the divisions of the Picts were indigenous Britons Herein he is followed by Mr Chalmers, the meritorious author of *Caledonia* Mr Pinkerton, on the other hand, swayed by violent prejudices, has denied not only the British, but the Celtic, character of all the Picts He wrote under a Teutonic mania, so extreme, that in one of its paroxysms he maintained the name of Scotland not to be taken from the Scots The same critic framed a wild romance about some Teutonic Peukini, otherwise Piki, who travelled from an Isle of Peuke, in the Black Sea, to Norway, where they gave the name of Vika to a part of that country (now Aggerhuys), and thence came over to Britain as Piks, not Picts

On the strength of this modern mythus, Pinkerton and his followers coolly term the Picts *the Piks*, and the language *the Pikish*, just as if there really were such names in the world It is easy to fly half round Europe with a P and a K, to change P into V in Norway; and change it back into P when you reach the Orkneys But it is less easy to get rid of the T For every Teutonic form of the name Pict, that he is able to cite (Enquiry, etc. i 367, 369, 370) and every Celtic form but one (the Piccardach of Tighernach) has a T, and those Teutonic forms which soften down the name at all, only do so by dropping that very C or K by aid of which the Peukini and pretended Piks became Viks.

But Vik itself is a mare's nest of his finding, and Norway had no such people as
the

the Vik. The noun *vik* is *sinus*, a bay or inlet of sea, occurring also in numerous compounds. Vikr or Vik, in the oblique cases Vikina and Vikinni, was that bay between Sweden and Norway, stretching east and west from Sotannes to Otursnes, on which the ancient city of Tonsburg stood and stands, and at the head of which the Christiania-Fiord runs up to the modern Christiania. It is the Sinus, by way of excellence, sometimes distinguished as Eastern, Vik Austr. Schoning's maps to the Heimskringla give no such land or province at all, but write Vikina across the bay as above described. Though this noun[x] and its cases be certainly used, on many occasions, for the countries lying round the Vik, its true meaning is the bay itself, as any one may see, ex. gr. in Olaf Helga's Saga, chapters xlv. li lxxxii. Nay, so much is distinctly signified by Torfæus himself, Mr Pinkerton's authority, for his words are "The southern coast sloping towards the Western Ocean, between that extremity of Danholm island which looks south-east, and Cape Lindisnes which looks south-west (forty-one miles distant from east to west), being excavated by a recess of the great sea, admits that huge bay called the Oslofiord, which runs up from thence to Oslo [now Christiania], 'and was anciently called Vik, and is now called by the Dutch sailors the Sack of Norway, and the great tract of land adjacent to this bay was also anciently called Vik, a name derived from it [*ab illo sortitus nomen*], which name was subsequently attached to the district of Bahus, which is called Vik or Vik-sidi.'"—Torf. Hist. Norweg. ii cap i p 28. Elsewhere he says, that Dal vik was a province of three districts, surrounding the inner part of that bay of Oslo, which was called Vik, and its neighbours, the Vikenses.—Ibid. cap ii. p 31. Mr Pinkerton but once ventured to refer to page or chapter, alledging *Torfæus*, ii 18, in vol i p 175, which happened to be a perfectly immaterial and safe passage. And no moral considerations deterred him from saying, "the whole northern writers call this country as often Vichia' as Vika, and *have never dropt a single hint* that this name was from vik."—i p 179

From *vik*, bay, gulph or creek, comes *vikingar*, men of inlets, or pirates, "qui in eundem sinum vel portum (somu vik) unde primum solverunt populatum redeunt."—Lex Antiqua[a] Gulathingensis cit. Gunnlaug's Saga p 303. See also Olai Wormii

Mon

"Arius Frodi in his I-landia, speaks of one Koll as bishop "i Vik Austr." whom the Kristni-Saga calls "Vikveria biskup."—Arius, cap ii p 10, Krist cap xii p 108

[y] Regio *Id-sinus-latus*, a name in itself sufficiently convincing

[z] This seems to be merely a cavil on the *Latin orthography* of modern authors in that language, even if it be a true statement

[a] The Gulathings-laug, or Code of Guley in Hordaland, was enacted in the tenth century by Hako the Good, and the western part of Nor-

Mon. Dan. p. 269, and Haldorson's Lexicon in *Vikingr*. Opposite surmises are confuted by the names of the people from places ending in *vik*, as from Sandvik the Sandvikingar, or from Krossavik the Krossavikingar[b]. But a man "or Vikinni," from the great eastern Vik, could not be styled a Vikingr, both because that name was general for all pirates, and because he might not be a pirate. And hence their compound name Vik-veriar, Sinûs-accolæ. Thus we see that there never were any Viks at all, and that Vik-men were only the men[c] who dwelt on that particular bay.

As Innes made all the Picts of one race, so did he; and, with that view, he resorted to such phrases as "the Caledonians and Piks were all one," disguising in some places, what he puts forward in others, that the Caledonians were only one portion of the Picti. Mr. Pinkerton also constantly assumed, that the Caledonians were the northern, and the Vecturiones the southern division; upon no better authority than the pages printed by Mr. Charles Bertram, under the assumed name[d] of Ricardus Corinæus. The following passage, " Dicaledones and Vecturiones, the former certainly the *Northern* Picts bordering on the *Deucaledonian sea*," instances his want of ingenuousness; for Ptolemy's Deucaledonian commenced as far south as the Chersonese of the Novautes, which Solinus calls the Promontory of Caledonia, and we the Mull of Galloway. The fact appears to me to have been the converse. Since the Ptolemaic limits of the Caledonians were from the Murray Firth down to Loch Lomond, their relative position in the Theodosian age can never be inferred, either way, from Ptolemy; those are the tricks of history-making, subservient to system and self, rather than to external and objective truth.

Another main point with this systematist was to assume, against all historical inference, that the Belgæ of Gaul and Britain were not Gauls and Britons in language and nation, because the former had come out of a German stock; and that they were not of the Druidic religion, in the teeth of Strabo's clear and ample statements. Geogr. vol. iv. p. 275–6. Whatever had been, or was even conjectured to have been, of

a German

way, in which that law prevailed, was itself thence called Gulathingslaug. See Hakonar Goda Saga, cap. xi., and Schöning's Heimskr. iii. p. 193.

[b] The case of Jomsvikingar is different. That is contracted from Jomsborg-vikingar, and expresses the pirates, not the people, of Jomsborg; with no analogy to the places that are compounded with *vik*.

[c] In his Modern Geography, grown bolder, Mr. Pinkerton gives us Pik, not Vik, for part of Norway! " This new name," speaking of Picti, " seems to have been native, Piks, or Pehts; and to have originated from a country *so styled* in the south of Norway, whence this colony had arrived."—vol. i. p. 146.

[d] If any one has yet a lingering faith in this forgery, he may divest himself of it by consulting the Speculum Historiale de Gestis Regum Angliæ per Fratrem Ricardum de Cirencestria, in Cambridge library, FF. 1. 28.

a German original, is presumed to have retained the German tongue and institutes, which if true must be equally true of the Irish Belgæ. But it is untrue, "Firboli enim dicuntur Britannicè, et Danannæ Germanicè locuti," the former half of which two-fold tradition, relating to an undoubted and never extirpated people, is not invalidated by the dubious[e] character of the latter —Ogygia, p 10

The Picti or painted folk, beyond the Latin pale, were not all of one sort. Constantine's panegyrist, who first names the five tribes after that peculiarity, mentions the Di-Caledonum (or[f] Caledonum) "*dimumque* Pictorum sylvas et paludes."—*Eumenius*, cap vii. And Ammianus says that, in the time of Count Theodosius, the Picti were *in duas gentes divisi*, namely, Dicalidones et Vecturiones —xxvii cap 8. The Calidones or Caledones were an ancient British tribe ("Quinte Caledonios Ovidi visure Britannos") whose language was the British, for their name is such, and signifies inhabitants of forests, whether the great forest of the North be spoken of, or those Calidoniæ Sylvæ near the Thames, into which Cæsar pursued Cassivellaun —Florus, iii c xi. Moreover we read that of the People of Britain the "habitus corporum" were "varii, atque ex eo argumenta, namque rutilæ Caledoniam habitantium comæ, magni artus Germanicam originem asserunt'—Tacitus Agric. cap xi. But if they were then of a different tongue and nation, the argumenta or conjectures from stature and colour of hair would be superfluous. nor would the question have been merely one of *origin*

When Severus made war, it was against the two greatest British nations then retaining independence, the Maiatæ near Hadrian's wall, and the Caledonian farther north. Both were naked, with their bodies painted in various devices, and still made use of war chariots drawn by small horses.—Herodian, iii p 83 ed H Steph Xiphilin, Epit Dionis lxxv p 1280-1 1283 Reimar. These two denominations are probably equivalent to Campestres and Sylvestres, concerning the latter there is not much doubt, and *mai pl meian* a plain, furnishes an etymon for *Maiate* Thus the two names express the two modes of living ascribed to them by Dion, in the paragraph where he names them, viz, the nomadic and venatic, ἐκ νομῆς καὶ θήρας, and their two habitations, viz, rugged mountains and uncultivated plains, ὅρη ἄγρια . και πεδία ἔρημα —lxxvi cap 12 In Severus's time two tribes were noticed as *being* picti; but, until a century

or

---

[e] Which, moreover, was denied by Keating, according to whom Scot-bhearla was the language of all the colonies that ever came into Ireland till the English conquest. See L Lhuyd in *Scotbhearla* The conquests of the Ostmen are not regarded as colonies

[f] Some copies have "non Dicaledonum," and others "non dico Caledonum" which latter is not bad in point of context, though extrinsic reasons give a countenance to the former reading

or more had elapsed, no tribe is known to have been *named* the Picti   At that later time the name of the Maiate tribe or Mæatæ, living in Galloway and part of Northumbria, had disappeared from the list of free and painted tribes   Yet, for all that, the South-Pictish territory does not seem to have been curtailed on the south, for Candida Casa, the first South-Pictish church, was on Maiate ground, and near the Severian wall.   Meanwhile the other class of Picti Vecturiones was coming into importance, and cutting short the northern bounds of the Calidones, which in Ptolemy's day, seventy years before the war of Severus extended from the Lælamnonius or Lemaanonius Sinus (Lomond) to the Varar æstuary or Firth of Moray

Now it might be that Di-Calidones and Vecturiones were merely two sections of painted Britons, being of one race, as had been the case of the same Calidones and their Maiate allies   For the phrase, "in duas gentes divisi," readily admits of it   Yet it is probable, at first sight, that the Southern and Northern Picts were of different kinds   For the Southern Picts embraced Christianity at the preaching of a Briton, *circa* A.D 412, and just at the expiration of the Roman power   But the contiguous nation of Northern Picts did not receive it until after A.D 563, and then at the hands of Irishmen from Tir-Connell   The interval of 150 years between the conversions of contiguous states, with the distinct sources of conversion, strongly argues diversity of speech and blood.   But we have a little more than conjecture   as both are known to us, in fact, but faintly

In the Northumbrian age, or Beda's, we find much of the diocese or province of St Ninia in the hands of those Irish who came afterwards to be termed Galwegians, which perplexes the matter   But in Ninia's time, for aught that appears, the North Cymmry country (regnum Cambrense and Cumbrense) was extended from Cumbria of Carlisle to Cumbria of Dunbreatan or the Strathclyde Wealhas, with no permanent interruption; and from its first mother church of Candida Casa or Whithern, to St Kentigern's see of Glascu   We have vestiges of the Calidon Picts, whose country bordered upon the Strathclyde principality, sufficient to be recognised, and arising out of disputes too hot and violent to be considered fictions   From and after the middle of the sixth century, Maelgwn Gwynedd was reigning over the whole Cymmraeg tongue and nation, both titularly, and with rather more of authority than most of his race were able to exercise   He was engaged in disputes of which the nature is obscure and mysterious, and beside our present purpose, with the Caledonians or men of the great northern forests   which then (as we know) were called Celyddon   These debates, which ended in the war of Ardeiydd, fatal to the Caledonians, were more immediately carried on by Rhydderch Hael, son of Tudwal, son of Cedig, son of Dyvnwal, Lord of Alclyde or Dunbreatan, and Prince of the Strathclyde Britons

The people of the Celyddon were under the rule of a certain Gwenddoleu ap Ceidiaw, a Cymmry by name, and himself a bard, of whose poetry a minute fragment survives His principal bard was Merddin son of Morvryn, commonly called Merlin the Caledonian,

> "———— de Albania | Sylvestris Calidonius
> Merlinus, quæ nunc Scotia, | A sylvâ Calidoniâ "
> Repertus est binomius, | *Ranulph Polichron* 189

Though some people said he was a native of Demetia or Dyved in South Wales But that was merely a confusion between Merlin Ambrose (who was supposed, through an etymological error, putting Merddin for Myrddin, to have been born at Caermarthen,

> " Ad Kaermerthyn Demecie
> Sub Vortegirni tempore")

and the Caledonian Merlin This confusion of the two men probably originated with Geoffrey of Monmouth, whose Vita Merlini is pervaded with it, and who is thereby compelled to make his Caledonian vastly aged, having lived under a succession of kings,

> " Ergò peragratis sub multis regibus annis[g]
> Clarus habebatur Merlinus in orbe Britannus
> Rex erat et vates, *Demetarumque* superbis
> Jura dabat populis, ducibusque futura canebat '

There

---

[g] Merlinus, p 4, vv 19–22, Londini, 1830, for Roxburgh Club, and ap Gfrœrer Pseudoprophetæ, p 365 The grounds upon which the Paris editors, Messrs Michel and Wright, abjudicate this poem from Geoffrey, as given in Gfrœrer's preface, entirely fail to persuade me I have observed, indeed, that the cæsura of the short vowel in

'Laurea serta *date* Gaufrido de Monume'â'

occurs in but one other instance, the word *media* in v 749 But if this metrical colophon be an addition, it still is testimony of A. D. 1285 That Robert Bishop of Lincoln is complimented at the expense of his immediate predecessor Alexander, whom Geoffrey had extolled when living, and to whom he had inscribed his prose prophecy of Merlin, may either resolve itself into the nature of worldly gratitude, "a sense of benefits to come," or Alexander may have earned such praise by fair promises, and forfeited them by non-performance I see nothing more about conquering Ireland in

> " Sextus Hibernenses et eorum nomina vertet,
> Qui pius et prudens populos renovabit et urbes, '
>   (vv 679, 680)

than had been said in the prose, "sextus Hibernia mœnia subvertet, et nemora in planitiem mutabit, diversas portiones in unum reducet, et capite leonis coronabitur" Neither can I discover a syllable about Henry the Second in either of them Alan, Bishop of Auxerre, writing no later than circa A D 1171, tortured this prophecy into an allusion to him, by interpreting *sextus* to mean either Henry's sixth and bastard son, or some

There are no good reasons for supposing that the son of Morvryn was born very far from the scene of his adventures His sister Gwendydd was the wife of Rhydderch Hael, against whom he nevertheless fought in the war of Arderydd, and after the defeat and death of Gwenddoleu, he fled into the depths of the Caledonian forest, and from his wild and woodland life was called Merddyn Wyllt The contest was connected with the highest points of bardic theosophy, and waged between Gwenddoleu, the patron of Merddin, and Rhydderch Hael, the patron of Kentigern and friend of Columkille, for these transactions nearly synchronize with the conversion of the North Picts by that missionary Taliesin Ben Beirdd at the court of Maelgwn, and others of that order of poets and philosophers, vehemently supported the Caledonians against Rhydderch Hael and King Maelgwn. That these Caledonians were a remnant of the Picts of St Ninia's mission, and South Picts of Beda's history, appears not only from the ancient use of that name in Eumenius and Ammianus, but more immediately. For Merddyn Wyllt, in his interpolated Hoianau, says at stanza 19

" And I will prophesy, before my ending,
The Britons over the Saxons by the energy of the Painted-Men,
Brython dros Saeson Brithwyr a'i medd "

His friend Taliesin, in a poem where he speaks of his bardic sanctuary or conventicle,

other son yet to be born, but without the slightest allusion to the proceedings of Richard Strongbow, just commenced in 1169 Alanus in Merlinum, lib iii p 102, ed 1608 To make Henry himself the sixth Norman king, by counting in both Matilda and Stephen, would be less absurd. But the prophecy was both composed and translated into prose several years before his accession In my humble conjecture, it received its present form in the Conqueror's reign, he being the sixth from Canute the Great inclusively, and the conquest of Ireland is a false prophecy, as others concerning the sixth king are

But this poem is mainly from sources in the British tongue, and composed by a proficient therein. The names of Rodarchus Largus, Ganieda, and Peredur, the intimacy and fellowship of Telgesin with Merlin, the unique and otherwise lost records of Merlin's friend, Maeldin of Arwysth, and of Arthur's pilot Barinthus (Braint),

not to say the whole action of the poem, is from such sources Merlin's exordium, Celi Christe Deus ! is in the pure British of his mystical sect, Crist, Duw Celi ! or Crist Celi, Duw ! For in the whole manuscript there is but one instance of a diphthong in common use (which in femina it neither was nor is) being omitted, viz, lyri for lyræ, v 104 and cœlum occurs seven times But were there not other fine Latinists in Wales ? Vel duo, vel nemo Giraldus could have furnished the Latin, and perhaps could have got up the matter But this is not the mere case of another Welshman, but of another figuring in eastern England, of another at LINCOLN, and patronised by two successive bishops of that see The dedications to the two bishops of Lincoln, and the twofold allusions to one of them, which are alleged for disproof, are, to my mind, as coupled with the rare and peculiar qualifications of the author, a cogent proof

ticle, the addvwyn caer, as a ship on the sea preparing to sail away from danger and persecution, intimates an intention of removing it to the Picts:

> " Usual is the rising surge of the bards over their mead vessels,
> There shall be an impulse unto it in very sudden haste,
> The promise unto them of the green sward of the blue [or woad-painted] Picts
> Addaw hwynt y werlas o Glas-Ficha "—*Mic Dinbych*[h], st 1

The gwerlas of the Glas-Fichti is the orchard of Merlin's 147 apple-trees, concealed in a deep and sweet glade of the Celyddon After the restoration of the Celtic monarchy, the Briton Picts, or Caledones, again became fellow-subjects of the Britons, and were influential by their hatred of the Romans, and attachment to the superstitions they had nominally abjured   And these same were, as I lean to think, the Picts to whose support Vortigern is said to have been much beholden   However that may be, they were those of whom the existence was obscurely recorded in the Arthurian mythus Therein a certain Loth Lot or Leo, was King of the Picts of Lothian (Lodoneis) husband to Arthur's sister, Anna, and father of Medrawd or Modred.—Ussher Brit Eccl p 357, Brut G ap Arthur, p 311   This Leo king of Picts was Llew son to Cynvarch, son of Meirchion, and brother to Urien Reged and Arawn   Arthur gave Lothian and other lands thereabouts to Llew, to Arawn he gave Scotland, and to Urien he gave Reged   This unknown district (absurdly stated by Dr Owen Pughe[i] to have been in Glamorgan) was certainly in the north   It was (saith Brut G ap. A), " Mureif the land otherwise named Rheged ," and so Geoffrey, sceptro Murefensium insignitur, ix cap 9, which phrases seem to express Mureve, Morave, or Moray But the Brut marked B has it parth a mur yr Eifft, " in the direction of the wall of the Egyptians," i e of the Gaidheal from Scota and Pharaoh, but vulgarly the Pict's Wall; and the grant of[k] Scotland to Arawn, and still more the proximity of Loch Lomond to Mureif, seem to prove that *mur*, wall, and not Moravia was the original idea   Leo, King of Picts, was reputed the maternal grandfather of St Cyndeyrn *Garthwys*, that is St Kentigern of *the Region of the Vallum* or *Rampart*, Bishop of Penrhyn Rhionydd (Promontory of the *Rhions*, whatever[l] they may be) otherwise called Glas-gu, which admits of the interpretation *Beloved of the Blue*, i e of the Glas-Fichti.

The

[h] The line quoted in Chalmers's Caledonia, 1 p 204, does not exist

[i] Cambr Biogr in *Urien*

[k] For these writers name it, I conceive, in a more modern way, not as speaking of the true Dalriadha

[l] The Lexicographer Owen Pughe in his second edition, inserts the gloss, *rhion pl ydd a sire*, but offers no sort of authority, nor explains what he means by a sire   I guess the word *rhionydd* to be a northern form of *rhianedd*, ladies as in the place called Morva Rhianedd

The *requiescence* of the North Picts after the final departure of the Roman legions
(' Picti in extremâ insulæ parte tunc primum et deinceps requeverunt, prædas et con-
tritiones nonnunquam facientes") is not attributable to change of character, being still
savage heathen marauders, nor to decline of their power, which was growing, but to
the dissolution of their league with the Di-Calidones, and re-union of the latter to
the other tribes of Britons, by which means the Vecturiones were separated from the
old Roman frontier, and the territory of their former allies to the south of the Grampians became the object of their conquest.—See Gildas, Hist cap xix   The Caledonians and Mæatians came to an end, having gradually lost their territory   The
establishment of that other Pictish people, who in the eleventh and twelfth centuries
were called the Galwegians or Gallovidians, in the heart of Cumbria or the North-
west Wales, must have been a serious blow to the people of the southern Pictavia
The Irish annals mention desultory invasions of St Ninias country by the Cruithne
of Ulster in 682 and 702, and their establishment there towards the end of the eighth
century.—Cit Chalmers, i 358   When Maelgwn of Britain, Rhydderch of Strathclyde, and Aidan M'Gabhian, King of the Scots, were fighting against the Calidonians at
Arderydd, that tribe retained but a remnant of territory between the Clyde and the
mountains of Argyle to the north of Loch Lomond, and we may suppose that the war
of Arderydd was the finishing[m] of them   Though Beda speaks of the Grampian hills
as dividing the country of the Northern from that of the Southern Picts, it is obvious
that he speaks retrospectively, and in reference to the period when the Calidones,
driven from the Varar (the ancient Ptolemaic boundary of the vast Sylva Calidonia),
yet held the Grampian barrier against the Vecturiones; and that only one kingdom of
Picts was existing in his time

We must pronounce against Father Innes, that the Vecturiones or North Picts
were another race   His whole argument, reinforced by Mr. Chalmers' researches,
from the frequency of British names or roots in North-Pictish topography, is to be
answered by the ancient reign of the Calidones from the Varar to the upper wall
For conquerors never fully obliterate the names of places   But, as the Calidonians
were certainly indigenæ within all records of history, their hair and stature alone
raising the suspicion of diverse origin, so the Picts of the most famous Pictish state
are pronounced by all with one voice to have been, like the Scoti in Albany, "trans-
marinæ

[m] The biographers of St Feehin of Fore mention, about the close of the year 664, a certain
Moehoemoch, "Cruthneeh sive Camber," and
though he bore the Irish saint-title of Mochoe-
moch, the tenor of St Feehin's remarks shews he
was a Cambrian Colgan, Jan 20, p 139 I cannot say whether this man were from the remnants
of the Calidonian tribe

marina gens."—See Beda, i 12 , Nennius, cap. v , Galfrid. Monum. iv 17 ; Psalter of Cashel, cit Ogygia, iii. 18 , and the Irish *tot quot* Mr Pinkerton inconsistently maintained that the word Vecturion represented Vikveriar, i e the men of his Vika in Norway. While he was describing the Viks of Vika as constituting the entire of the Picts, and their name as being his very word Pik, he yet well knew that the Vecturiones were only one of the two Pict gentes opposed to Theodosius. But that appellation cannot be shewn to have been other than a Latin one, and their trans-marine origin, and *vectura*, or freightage in vessels, as opposed to the *indigenae*, is probably expressed in it Britanniam qui mortales initio coluerint, *indigenae* an *advecti*, ut inter barbaros, parum compertum —Tacit Agric cap xi If so, then arrival should have been so far recent in Theodosius' time, as to keep alive the tradition of their *vectura*, and also to account for their being unknown or obscure in that of Severus. That they came directly from Ireland seems agreed.—Beda, i cap i., Chron. Sax. p i , Poem in Irish Nennius, Psalter of Cashel, &c They were a tribe of Irish dialect (or language) and nation That is in the nature of fact *Gwyddel* is the Welsh word for *Irish,* and it is an adaptation to Welsh analogies of the name Gaidheal, the Gadche or Gathelic That word means *Irish,* and I have not learned that it means anything else But the Picts of the kingdom of Fortren Mor (as was its Irish appellation) were the Gwyddyl Fichti, or Gaelic Picts The Brito-Irish legend of St Cannech adopts the name, with confirmation of its meaning, in that of Gaidheal Ficht, the fabulous son of Murchertach Mr Pinkerton and Dr C O'Conor were erroneously led to suppose that the Cruthenians of the Dal n-Araidhe in Ulster were meant by the Gwyddyl Fichti —Inquiry, &c i 338, O'C. Proleg. cxxvi., Il Lhuid in Angheâ suâ Walliæ Descript. pp 14, 15, cit. ibid But those were called. both at home and abroad, in Latin and in Erse, Cruthenii, not Picti In fact (and fact is what we want) the Gwyddyl Fichti were the Picts of Albany or North Britain, by whom Madoc ap Me-dion was detained prisoner in that country, "gan y Gwyddyl Fichti yn yr Alban "— Triad lxi p. 68. They were distinguishable from the Gwyddyl Coch, Red Gael, i e having[n] rosy cheeks, not blue tattooed cheeks . *human* cheeks, according to my deri-vation of ἀνθρωποι or ἀνθερωποι, *animal erubescens* or *vultu florido* The Gwyddyl Coch o'r Werddon a daethant i'i Alban, " the red Irish from Erin who came to Albany," were the Dalriadhans under Loarn and Fergus —Triad. ix. They were a refuge-seeking, not a conquering tribe; but proved treacherous to those who admitted them

[1] Nor is the idea confined to the cheeks, for we read,

Cum tu Lydia Telephi
Cervicem roseam ——

them—Triad. vii   On the contrary, the Gwyddyl Fichti, painted or dark-blue
Gaidheal, were an invading tribe who came into Britain by force—Triad vii   It was
against the Gwyddyl Fichti that Vortigern was obliged to hire Saxon aid—Triad
xiv 53   That they were *Milesians*, which is the equivalent of Gaidheal, appears
in the legend of Mileadh Cruthnechan, Milesius Pictus; who went over from Ireland to the Britons of Fortren, to fight against the Saxons, and defend Cruithen-
tuath or Pictland   The *Britons* of Fortren are the Cruthnich in Britain, as opposed
to those in Ireland, and, if the former continued to receive succours in emergency
from the latter, we may the more easily understand that their *vectura* was fresh
in remembrance   That both the peoples, that in Ulster and that in Fortren, had in
Irish but the one common name of Cruthneach, and long after the usage which gave
the name was abandoned, is a fact most opposite to the theory of their distinct origin
All this is old fact, not modern etymologizing. They were Gwyddyl Fichti, of a fabled
connexion with one Gaidheal Ficht, the plain upshot of which is, that they spoke
the Gwyddeleg, and not either the Cymmraeg or the Saxon

Nor is this deficient in verbal harmony with the common legend that they came
from *Scythia* i e from the land of the Scuit, for Scuit Fichti, Mileadh Fichti, and Gwyddyl Fichti, would all be synonymous; and the story of the Cruthnich from Scythia
is just such another frigid etymologism, as that of the Scuit from Scythia   There is
no good standing place, even for credulity, to set up a primæval tradition from the
true Scythia of the East.   Because the tenor of their legend, that they were Agathyrsi descended from Geleon son of Hercules, betrays the derivation of the whole
story from Virgil's lines,

>   " Cretesque Dryopesque fremunt *pictique* Agathyrsi,"

and

>   " Eoasque domos Arabum *pictosque* Gelonos ,"

mixing ignorance with their learning, and bending two tribes into one.   Whatever
the word *pictus* meant of the one it meant of the others also, for Geloni and Agathyrsi were half-tribes (as it were) tracing their origin from two brothers, sons of
Hercules   It was anciently interpreted three ways   wearing painted cloaks, having
the hair only died blue, or having both the hair and body stained. The second is the
sentiment of Pliny   It is not a certain fact that these Scythian tribes ever wore a
stained or stigmatized skin.   See Servius in Æneid iv. 146, and Salmasius in So-
linum, p 133.

When Beda was writing, five tongues were spoken in Britain, English, British
Scottish, Pictish, and Latin, therefore the Gwyddeleg or Gaelic, and the Gwyddeleg
Ficht were not the same. But that is consistent with a modification of dialect from long
separation.

separation, admixture with Britons, and other causes. Without reverting to that remote truth, quite unconnected with Beda's thoughts, of the primitive identity of British and Scottish, it is otherwise manifest, that Beda included, as languages, such changes of dialect as sufficed to impede communication. For if Pictish were Teutonic, then English and Pictish were but two dialects; and if it were Cymmraeg, then British and Pictish, so that, *quácunque viá datá*, two of Beda's tongues were nearly related. In the biographies of St Columkille, the converter of the Picts, a solitary allusion is found to the diversity of Gaelic and Pictish, where it is said that a certain *plebeian* family of Picts, hearing him through an interpreter, believed.—Adamnan, ii cap 32.—*Vide contra*, iii cap 14

Pinkerton, and his follower, Dr Jamieson, relied upon the list of kings as a source for Teutonic etymologies.—Inquiry, &c., i 287-312, Etym Dict i p 35-41. By raking together Teutonic syllables, choosing such various readings of names as suit best, and assuming common etymologies from either source to be from that of their choice, a show of etymological history is set up against real and traditional history. But quite enough appears in this catalogue of kings to confirm, if not to demonstrate, the premised facts. What can we think of one who will contend, that Kenod or Cinedh, in the Latin Kenethus, Elpin, in Latin Alpinus, Wurgest or Vergust, in Latin Fergus and Fergusa, Ungust or Hungus, in Latin Oengus or Aongus, Canul or Conal, Uven, Eoganan, Eoghane or Owen, Vered, Ferat, Ferach or Feredech (Phe-radach, in the signatures of the Pictish princes to King Ungust's Charter of Kihe-mont), Donell, Donnell, Domnal, in Latin Donaldus, Neetan or Neactan, Fidach, Fodla, as well as Cruthen or Cruthne, the first name on the list, are not from the Irish nomenclature? The seventy-fourth king of Picts is Uven, *alias* Eoganan, but Adamnan mentions Iogenanus presbyter genere *Pictus*, ii cap ix, and afterwards, iii cap v, Eogenanus nephew to Aidan, king of *Scots*. Phachan, from Fiach, and Duptaleich, seemingly allied to Dubhtach or Dubbdaleth, and Glunmerath to Glun-mar, one of the various names formed upon *glun*, a knee, occur, together with

Angus

---

¹ The same author, with some ingenuity, pretended that Ungust, son of Vergust, when he overran the petty kingdom of Aregaithel or Scots, made an end of the Dalriadha dynasties of Loarn and Fergus, and set Pictish princes over it. But he drew down upon himself the absurdity of contending, that the Erse names of all the Scots kings after 743 were those of German Piks and Viks, e\. gr Aodh, Donal, Fergus, Conal, Angus, Fogman, Alpin, Kenneth, Domhnal Maolcholuim, Macdubh, Donnchad, and Macbeth! Nay, Mr Pinkerton, after deriving Malcolm (the well-known contraction, if not rather nominative formation, of Maolcholuim) from *mal*, speech, and *kom*, a man, coolly proceeds to spell it upon all occasions Malcom, finding Teutonic etymologies for words of his own making.

Angus, Nectan, and Bolge, among the royal witnesses to the charter of Kilremont About the year 414 the name of Drust or Drost, Drustan or Drostan, came into use among the Pictish princes Under the first of the nine Drusts, Ninia and Patricius are said to have converted British Pictland and Ireland   Whatever the name means, it is the same as the Cruthnechan Trosdan[p] of the Psalter of Cashel. O'Conor's Keating, p 121. Upon the whole I account it clear from their names, that they were Gwyddyl, or an Erse people. And where we find Feradach changing into Vered, Fergus into Wurgest, and Eoghan into Uven, we need not wonder that St. Columkille and the other emigrant monks of the Kinel-Conaill, who seem to have met no impediment of discourse at the Pictish court, should have failed in making themselves understood to ' the plebeians" of some districts without interpretation   The reader need only compare the opposite columns of Welsh and Cornish in Lhuyd's Archæologia, pp 251–3, to appreciate the impediments arising from dialects, even in languages of the most undisputed identity   The Gwyddyl Fichti formed the main body of the ancient Albannaich, or people of the kingdom of Albany, of whom the Highlanders are the remnant, the whole of that body, except so many clans as lay west of the Drumalban hills, in Argyle, Lorn, Knapdale, Cowel, and Cantire. And when those hills divided two hostile states (now united 1000 years) the difference of dialect was more perceptible.

The following historical fragment, in the form of a bardic prophecy, is now inexplicable, but seems to belong to the ninth century, when the Northmen, or men of Norway and Denmark, had obtained a footing in these islands   It is one of the few documents of a forgotten dynasty, and is worth placing on record, for the chances of future illustration —

Pump pennaeth dymbi	Five chieftains there shall be
O Wyddyl Fichti,	Of the Gwyddelian Picts,
O bechadur cadeithi,	Of the character of evil-doers,
O genedyl ysgi	Of a murderous generation
Pump eraill dymbi	Five others there shall be
O Norddmyn mandy	From the habitation of the Northmen
Wheched rhyfeddri	The sixth a wonderful prince,
O heu hyd vedi	From the sowing[q] to the reaping
Seithved o hem	The seventh [sent] by old age

I weryd

[p] Macfarland's Vocabulary, and Armstrong's Dictionary, give Trosdan, a pace, a foot, a sup- port, a prop, a crutch

[q] From his birth to his death

f

I weryd dros h.	To the green-swaid beyond[r] the flood.
Wythved lin o Ddyvi	The eighth, of the line of Tyvy[s],
Nid llwydded escori,	Shall not be estranged from prosperity,
Gynt gwaedd Venni	Till [in] the outcry of Menni
Galwawr Eryii,	Snowdon shall be invoked,
Anhawdd y Dyvi.	Disaster [unto] Tyvy —*Arch Myvyr* i. 73

Everything here is completely obscure, especially the number *five* being repeated Whether the sixth, seventh, and eighth join on to the five Gwyddyl Fichti or the five Norddmyn, depends on whether or not lines 5 and 6 be parenthetical Some combination of the affairs of three nations, Picts, Northmen, and Welsh, is here indicated

It is extreme fancifulness to dispute the meaning of the plain word Pictus, expressive of a notorious fact That crotchet is as old as Verstegan, who says the Picts were not called of painting their skins, as some have supposed, but upon mistaking their true name, which was phichtian or fighters.— Restitution, &c p 124. This was Teutomania But Dr Owen Pughe, under strong Celtomania, invented in his dictionary the gloss, " Peithi, the Picts," and explained it " people of the open plain," &c, and this invention Mr Chalmers has chosen to adopt —i. 204. They were, he says, " called *Peithi*, or Picti Thus a Welsh poet of the seventh century says Glas Phichti " They were called one thing, and *thus* they are called another ! But our concern is with genuine, not coined words The real meaning is shewn directly in Taliesin's *Glas* Fichti, and antithetically in the Gwyddyl *Coch* Claudian, the courtier of Stilicho, had access to all information concerning the tribes, against whom his patron had a frontier to defend

But indeed there were few phrases that could be used in that sense, and were not so applied. The Calidones were called by Ammian Di-Calidones, and the neighbouring ocean by Ptolemy Δουηκαληδονιος, and by Marcianus Heracleota Δουκαληδονιος, the Du-caledonian, of which the former, *Di*, expressed the pronunciation, and the latter the spelling, of *Duʿ*, black *Brith* in British and *Brit*, in Irish, spotted, variegated, party-coloured

[r] To the royal cemetery in the island of Icolm-kill?

[s] Here (as printed) Dyvi, but in the concluding line Tyvi, as appears from the mutations, Dd and D The Tyvy is the large stream dividing Caermarthen from Cardigan

[t] The Finlanders who invaded Ireland were called the Fin-gall and Fin-gent, which name the Irish interpreted *white* strangers, or *white* Pagans, from their own word *finn*, white By mere antithesis to those names, and not upon real grounds of colour, the Danes and Norwegians came to be called the Dubhgent, Black Pagans, and Dubhlochlonaich, Black Pirates —

coloured, is the probable etymon of *Britain*, and hence brith-wi, a spotted man, a Pict, to which in the Horanau is added the other epithet, *black*, brithwyr du   Equivalent to this was Brych or Brech in British, Brec and Breac in Erse, speckled, party-coloured   I have intimated above (p 111, n), that Agned Bregion, i.e Brechion, plural of Brech, was meant by the Britons for Agnetum Pictorum, and Brechin, an episcopal city of the Picts, civitas Brechne of the Pict Chron, is from the same root   So also is the name of Brychan or Brecanus, the legendary founder of Brechinia, Brecheinawg, or Brecknock, whether in the like sense or not   The Manks were not only an Irish people, but probably were Cruthem, or Ulster Picts   For the rebellion of the Ultonians against Cormac Mac Art, in 236, was chiefly of the Cruithnu under Fiach Araidhe; and in 254 he expelled a portion of the Ultonians, and gave their territory to his son, Cairbre Riadha, from whom the Dal-Riadan, Dalreudin, or Rout district (the cradle of Scotland) took name   From this act he was surnamed Ulfada or Banisher of the Ultonians, and they settled themselves in Manand or the Isle of Man   Tighern *in annis*   That island, of whose early and Celtic history scarce another vestige remains (see above, No III p vii), may be regarded as having been a colony of Cruithenians, driven out of North Ulster by the Riadans   Mervyn, King of Man, whom Welsh pedigrees have derived in the female line from the princes of Powys, and who married Essyllt[u], heiress of Conan Tindaethwy, King of Wales, is called in the interpolated Horanau, st. 36, Mervyn *Vrych* o dir Manau   not by reason of freckles on his skin, but as claiming a descent from, or reigning over, Picts, for the Gwasgargerdd, equally ascribed to Merlin the Caledonian, speaks of the " brithwyr du o Manau," black spotted men of the Isle of Man   Man hath scarce any history until the ascendancy of the northern vikingar   But a great annalist speaks of Picts in that country, in 711, more than 100 years before Mervyn Vrych   Striages Pictorum in[v] *campo* Manand[w], ubi Findgaine Mac Deleroith immatura morte jacuit —*Tig* in 711, p 225,

O'Con

Ogygia, p 303   The years 850, 851, witnessed bloody battles in Leinster between the Finngent and Dubhgent, of which the last was continued for three days and nights —Ann. Ulton The Danes who afterwards ravaged Stathclyde and North Wales were called by the Britons the gwyr duon and paganaid duon, although their language has not the word finn   Brut y Saeson, Tywysogion, &c, A. D 870-900, pp 479-484 But they took the phrase from Ireland, whose Ostman kings of Dublin probably sent forth these pirates

[u] In whose right he ruled Wales, A D 818-843, but when, and through what inheritance, he became king of Man, is not apparent   His pedigree in the male line from Beli Mawr may be a sheer fable.   See Powel's and Lloyd's Cambria, p 22

[v] Campaign or battle, vide Ducange, in *campus*, num 5, 6, 7

[w] The Ulster Annals, at 781, speak of Drust the Eighth as " rex Pictorum *citra* Monot,"

O'Con   In the Pictish catalogue, (see above, sect. xxxi) we read, ' Guidid Gaeth *Breatnach*," a Briton, but the Pictish Chronicle gives Guidid Gaed *Brecah*, which variations do all resolve themselves, one way or another, into Pictus.   Nectan the First has several surnames, such as Kellemot and Thalthamoth, but most usually, and in the Pictish Chronicle, Morbet   In this Irish document that unknown word is altered, and, I believe, corrected, thus, Neactan *Mor Breac*[x], the Great Pict   The case of Domhnall styled Breac, Brec, Bric (Dovenald Varius of Cron Reg Scot Innes, n. 789), prince of the Dalriads or Scots, and son of Achy, is full of obscurity. He bore the surname whilst living; as Adamnan says, " temporibus nostris   Domnallo Brecco" &c iii. cap v   At his father's death in 622 he was adult, and fell in the battle of Strath-Cawn or Ceirinn, fought against Hoan king of the [Strathclyde] Britons, in December 642 — Tighern. *in anno*   Yet Ulster Annals, after stating the death of plain Domhnall (not D Brece as in Tig) at A D 642, say, at A D. 685, " Talorg Mac Arethaen et Domhnall *Brecc Mac Eachadh* mortui sunt." The name Talorg is exclusively Pictish, and the author seems as if he considered D Brec, son of Achy, to be such also. How he recovered the crown of his father (which had passed into another family after the overthrow of his brother by the Irish Cruithnich), and what connexions, either Pictish or Cruthenian, he may have had in the female line, is matter buried in the darkness of those times and countries   But he fought at Moira in conjunction with Suibne, prince of the Cruthen, and had fought in 621 conjointly with Conall, son of Suibne If any credit be given to his longevity, and his dying together with this Talorg, his crown must have passed into the hands of the *extranei* of Adamnan (iii 5), i e strangers to the lineage of Aidan M'Gabhran, at or about the time of his defeat in 642, by abdication and flight into Pictland, not by death'   Broienc, broice, broicean, are words of the same sense as breac or brec, and may explain the appellation of Broichan, the magus of the Picts   Adamn ii 33.   The Cruithnich or Cruthenn, who occupied the southern[z] portion of the Dalriandhe in Ulster, and those

others

which obscure phrase may signify " king of Pictland, Man excepted," putting Monot for Monada Sed quære

[x] The other form, Morbet should, perhaps, be spelt Mor-bret, Mor-breat, as in the preceding homonymes of Brecah and Breatnach

[y] As to the two lines of the Gododin, vv 743 872,

" A phen Dyvnwal *a breich* brein a renoyn
A phen Dyvnwal *rrych* brein a renoyn,

although *rrych* may, perhaps be the true reading of them, I cannot discover in those extremely remarkable passages of Aneurin any allusion to the battle of Strath-cawn and death of Dovenaldus Varius, king of Scots There also are difficulties in supposing the author to have composed them so late as 641 The connexion of the names Dyvnwal and Domhnall is also unascertained

[z] Said to have included Down and the southern parts of Antrim —See Dr O'Conor in Tighernach,

others who were in Meath and Connaught, as well as those of Fortren Mor in Britain, are called from[a] *cruth*, form, aspect, countenance, colour, complexion, and so the phrase would resemble our *men of colour*, or may signify *men adorned with figures*. Among the Dalaradian Cruthnich we hear of king Eochaid Laeb or Laib, which Colgan renders *Maculatus;* of king Aodh Brec, who was slain in 563, with the seven Cruthenian clan-kings, by the Hy-Niall of Ulster, "vii righ Cruithneach in Ard mbrecc," Cenfaelad cit Tigh, and of Aodh cognomento Niger, likewise we read of Congal M'Mealeanfaith *Brecc Fortren*, Ann Ult 724, which were not improbably tribule, rather than personal, appellations, and analogous to Nectan Mor Breac. Of these and other such epithets more will be said in treating of this practice, as a superstition cherished in the ages subsequent to its desuetude.

But above all the name of Bruide or Brudi, borne by so many kings of the Gwyddyl Fichti, deserves observation, because it once was official or titular, and common to all, like Pharaoh or Augustus. The Pictish Chronicle says, upon the name of Brudi the First, "a quo triginta Bruide regnaverunt Hiberniam et Albaniam per 150 annorum spatium." and adds their private or personal names. Now that national name, spelt in this and other Irish works Bruide, elsewhere Brudi, Brudi, Bridius, &c., is but the Irish word, *bruid*, spina, quodvis cuspidatum, *bruad*, confodere, *bruid*, vulnus gladio vel cultro factum. What Isidorus Hispalensis questionably says of the name *Scoti* may be truly said of this name. "propriâ linguâ nomen habent a picto corpore, eò quòd aculeis ferreis cum atramento, variarum figurarum stigmate annotantur." This was expressed in the title Bruide, Acu-punctus, the Pict, a name common to a long series of kings, and never wholly disused. If these thirty kings reigned over Albania, there will then be a double list of the kings of Fortren, which absurdity has induced me to analyse these statements. Bruide the First is the fifteenth king, and in thirty kings, counted from him, *there occurs not one Bruide*. But counting again from

Taloic

---

p 96, n 7, Mr O'Donovan in Magh Rath, p 39, note

[a] See Dr Todd's note above, No II, pp v vi Yet a modern author has been found to imagine, that the name is for *crutineach*, hump-backed To meet the absurdity of a nation of hump-backs, it is supposed that Daln'araidhe was a sort of hospital, whither the Picts sent " the infirm and deformed inhabitants of Argyle, to make room for the efficient Irish troops "—*T Woods Primitive*

Inhabitants, p 139 An elegant colony, and a probable theory But unluckily the senders, i e the Picts of Fortren Mor, were Cruithnigh as well as the others, and, therefore, must also have been "crump-shouldered or humpy people!" The essay here cited contains many judicious remarks But its author, like others, has missed the fundamental fact, that the Irish, being a British people, were, as such, a Pict people

Talore III. the forty-sixth king, the third is Bruide, from him the fifth is Bruide, from him again, the fifth, from him the second, from him, the fourth, and lastly, from him, the eleventh. Thus, when it was merely a man's name, we find it recurring occasionally, but when it was titular to all alike, we find it entirely absent. Which evinces that the words, "Hiberniam   spatium" are superfluous and false, as well as the thirty[b] private names, and that these thirty Bruides are simply the kings of Pictland from Brudi Bout to Talore III. For it is obvious that men must be enumerated by their names, but need not be, and frequently are not, by additions of course; as we must say Trajanus, Hadrianus, &c., but need seldom add Augustus. The thirty Bruides end just fourteen years before the accession of Bruide II, that is to say, of the first king by name, and not by title, so called, and he was their first Christian king, baptized by St Columkille. We may therefore suppose that it ceased to be the regal appellation when the increase of civility and approaches of Christianity had caused the actual practice upon which it was founded to fall into desuetude, and may accordingly conjecture, that Cealtraim Bruide, who died in 543, and was the last of the thirty, was also in fact the latest rex seu punctus. In almost all moral concerns the real beginnings precede the historical commencement, and as Palladius himself went *ad Scotos in Christum credentes*[c], so must Columkille *ad Pictos*. For even if he could have wrought what he did upon matter unpredisposed, date and situation shew the probability that Christian influences must have oozed into Pictland from Caledonia and Strathclyde, from Argathelia, and from Dalaradia in Ulster.

We now come to a brief but important corollary. The record of thirty-six kings anterior

[b] These consisted of fifteen names, two of which seem to be lost, each followed by a repetition of the same with Ur prefixed, as Pant, Ur-pant, Leo, Ur-leo. Ur in Gaelic and Erse is *neu, fresh, young, again, a second time*, allied to ıap, *after, succeeding.* Riʒ up, a new king.—Stewart's Exodus cit Armstrong. It is obvious to conjecture that Ur-pant was the Tanist of Pant, and so Ur-bruide of his Bruide. As *tanist* was used without limitation in the sense of *second*, the tanistic battle or tanistic captivity, for the second battle or captivity (see Tighern in 493 and 980), so, conversely, the secondary king was the tanist of the primary, his actual coadjutor, and successor designate. This curiously formed list

may hint to us another circumstance, viz., that (in the days of the thirty Bruides, or painted Piets) the Ur-bruide, during the life of his principal, bore his name, with the tanistic prefix, instead of his own, when he assumed the primary crown. The fictitious character of these names appears, not only from the external history, but from the two first of them, one of which is the Anglo-Saxon name Penda (see Tighern in 631, 639, 650), and the other is the British name Llew.

[c] It was the same in the north of Europe, and the accounts of those *qui ante religionem lege receptam in rerum Deum crediderunt*, may be read in Olaf Triggvason, cap. cxx *et seq.*

anterior to Drust M·Erp, in 414, is of slender authority, and tinctured with manifest fable, and the historical æra is there, upon solid grounds, considered to begin But the first king in that series is Cruthne or Cruidne, which is equivalent to Bruide, and conveys the idea of *tinctus* or *pictus*, as the other of *punctus* Therefore King Cruthne and the first titular Bruide are identical, and if there were thirty-one such Bruides, that is thirty after the Bruide called Bout, it is rather identity of proposition than an inference to say, that there were thirty-one Cruthnes. Mr Pinkerton's just reduction of the Bardic Pictish reigns to the standard of the Irish, Northumbrian, and historical Pictish reigns, yields the dates (approximately correct) of A D 28 for Cruthne, and A D 208 for Brudi Bout. Consequently either Bruide 1 must go up to Cruthne in A D 28, or Cruthne must come down to him in 208, and, as bardic myth exalt antiquity, we shall choose the latter Therefore it seems, that all the kings anterior to Brudi Bout are additions , that he was the planter of the Gwyddyl Fichti or Vecturiones in Albany, and that Cealtraim, the last *ex officio* Bruide, was only the thirty-first Vecturion king. That places the transit of the Cruithnechan or Gwyddyl Ficht colony from Ireland *circa* A. D 208, in the reign of Con of the Hundred Battles, and nearly half a century before Cormac Ulfada drove the Cruthenians out of North Ulster *in Manniam insulam et Hebrides.*—Ogygia p 335 It is sixty-seven years (or some trifle less) after Claudius Ptolemy described the Caledonians of the Du-Caledon sea as stretching from Lake Lomond to the Firth of Moray, the identical year in which the war of Severus against the painted Mæatæ and Caledones began , and 159 years before the war of Count Theodosius against the Du-Caledons and Vecturions By this reckoning, the Cruthnich of the Dalh'araidhe will have crossed over to North Britain some 290 years before their next neighbours of the Dalriadha, or Routs of Antrim and Coleraine (being the Gwyddyl Coch of the Welsh), followed their track and planted their settlement of Argathelia (Airer-Gaedhal) or Scots —See Cambrensis Eversus, ix p 74 This accords with the order of events, as laid down in the Duan Albanach," and in this book " Of the Cruithnigh," by which Britain was first held by Britus (i e the Britons), then by Clanna Nemidh (the Belgians?), and " the Cruithnigh possessed it after them, having come from Ireland, [and] the Gaedil after that, that is, the sons of Ene son of Eochaidh " See above, p 127

The advent and departure of the Cruthnich in the days of Herimon, son of Milesius, 1000 years B C, which is a legend as ancient as Cormac Mac Cuillenan in the ninth century, is a pure mythology, and has made improper use of Pictish materials by bringing into the remotest origins those names of Drostan and Nectan, which did not come up among the Piets before the æra of Ninia and Patrick The fact, that the Piets of Albany came over from Ireland is about the only one it yields us But
their

their migration was evidently from the opposite and near coast of Ulster, where they had their abode This is not only matter of reason, but of tradition   The text of the Colbertine Chronicle of Picts asserts, that the thirty Brudes ruled Hibernia and Albania, but that means the kingdom of Ulster, not all Ireland ; and for evidence thereof we read, in Lib Ballimote, that Brude Cint (who was thirteenth of the thirty) was King of Ulster.—Ap Pinkerton, i. 502-504 Nor are we in the position to affirm, that the Cruithne kingdoms of Daln'araidhe and Fortren Mor did not thus long continue to be one, after the fashion in which Celtic monarchies had unity. Since in 590, at the Synod of Dromceat, we find Aodh, the son of Ainmire, asserting, and then waiving at St. Columkille's intercession, the sovereignty of the kings of Erin over the Dalriads of Britain 'The Irish authorities," says Mr Petrie, " make Gede also *King of the Irish and Scottish* [North British] *Picts,*" and, though they absurdly make him son to King Ollamh Fodla, their tradition supposes the two Cruthenias to have once been one kingdom —On Tara Hill, pp 153, 154 We read in the present work that one Cruithnechan M Lochit from Erin, meaning of course the chief of the Irish Cruthem (see p 127), flew to the succour of those of Fortren against the Saxons (sœe 5 vel infra), which (not to mention its agreeing well with their allegiance to one Brude or Cruthne) argues them to be the same people Subsequent history shews them engaged in bloody wars against Argathelia, under its kings Eochaidh Buidhe and Kenneth Cear, but not against Fortren It is obscurely intimated that Cormac Mac Art, having in 254 expelled the Cruthem from the Routs of Antrim into Man and the Hebrides, did in 258 pursue the war into Albany and exact an acknowledgment of his authority —Ogygia in cap lxix , Ogygia Vindicated, pp 162, 163 If this were so it would increase the probabilities that the Cruthenian kingdom of Fiach Araidhe, slain by Cormac, and the infant colony of Fortren or Pictish Albany, were not reputed nationally distinct

One of the paradoxes once accredited was, that the Cruithne or Cruthnich, descendants[d] of Hir the Milesian through Fiach Araidhe, King of Ulster in A D 240[e] were at no time, in fact, any Cruithne at all , but were so called because the said Fiach was remotely descended from Loncada, wife of Conall Kearnach *circa* B C 12, and daughter to one Eochaid Eachbheoil a Pict of North Britain or of Man — Ogygia, iii pp 190, 278-279 It may be remarked that those Dalaradians, or men of Araidhe, who were not Cruthenians (see Tertia Vita Patricii, cap 58, C. O'Conor in Tighern p 96, Lanigan, Eccl. Hist. vol i. p 218), should seem equally connected through Fiach with this Eochaid. But if the historian of the Ogygia could believe that

a

[d] That is, *quoad* their princes or chieftains
[e] So O'Flaherty Tighernach places his death in 236

a nation could be called *Men of Colour*, or *Men of Figures and Devices* (Picts) during a matter of 600 years, for no other reason than because the chieftain, said to have founded their community, traced his origin, and that *at an interval of two centuries and a half*, from the daughter of a Pictish subject, he must have been a logician callous to the non causa pro causâ. Were the founders of the Connaught Cruthemans[f], and of divers others, also descended in the eighth generation from a Pictish lady? This is but a sample of that bulk of lies with which Fintan and other bards of the sixth century fed the awakened curiosity, rising pride, and unbounded credulity of their countrymen. It is so far germane to the legend of Heremon and the Cruthnich, that it dissembles the condition of the ancient Irish, and assumes that people not to have themselves been painted, neither all nor some. But such is neither the reason, nor is it the fact of the case.

Ireland was peopled mainly, if it was not exclusively, from Britain, in the times before history. But the woad-staining was general in Britannia, throughout all Britain (omnes Britanni) in Cæsar's time, and throughout all free Britain in Severus's time. Therefore it is apparent, that Ireland should have been colonized and possessed by tribes delighting in such adornment. So that Dr Lanigan, when he said "how any of those Crutheni or Picts came to be settled in Ireland is not easy to discover," should rather have set himself to discover how any others but Crutheni could have come thither. Ancient writers neither say that the Irish were painted, nor that they were not, until we come to the days of Valentinian the First, or rather of Julian where the mention of Scoti et Picti may be thought by some to insinuate that the former were not so. But Julius Agricola did report thus much of the Hiberni, that "ingenia *cultusque* hominum non multum a Britanniâ differunt."—Tacit Agric cap xxiv. And the usage in question was so far the most conspicuous *cultus*, of any that the Britons used, as to make these oblique words little different from direct averment. But when the dry tale of Ireland's colonization in British coracles was replaced by the romantic and manifold impostures of Fintan the immortal, and all that school, its inseparable adjuncts of course perished with it.

Though we must infer the existence of this practice, the chronology of its gradual disuse is lost; as indeed are nearly all such real facts, ill compensated with tales of Ogygian date and Herculean audacity. Various causes of desuetude may easily be imagined:—I. The example of such desuetude, and of civility, offered by all Britain south

---

[f] It should be remembered that the pretended Lonncada, that woad-stained Helen of rape and war, flourished some two centuries before the real beginnings assignable to the Gaedhil Picts in Alban, viz, *circiter* A D 208, and yet longer before those of the Manks Cruithne, viz, 254.

1

south of the walls. II That knowledge of other nations and manners, in which the Irish of the piratical age must have exceeded their stationary progenitors III The gradual change wrought by the proximity of a fresh moral power, working a doubt or disregard of old things before the adoption of the new ones, as we see Brahminism shaken, though not abolished, and its suttees dying away In these ways, or in some of them, it came about that the Niallian marauders were distinct in appearance from the Ducalidon Cymmry, and Victurion Gwyddyl, while the self-same cause (viz the desuetude elsewhere) which dubbed the Caledonians *Picti*, had dubbed those Dalaradians and some other tribes *Crutheni*. The conquest of Ulster by Cormac O'Cuin, son of Art, may be regarded as an epoch in the decline of that custom, as his reign forms an epoch in the general civilization of his country

Irish history and mythology, when analyzed, are not really in any other story Ireland peopled Fortren with Cruthenians Last Ulster was always in part occupied by them, "the Cruthenians in Uladh and Moy-Cobha"—Ancient Topogr. from Books of Glendalough and Lecan by C. O'Conor, Sen, in Coll Hib in 672 And there were others, less known, in the parts of Connaught near Boyle "Conaght, first called Olnemacht . . . the Cruthenians, or painted men, in Moy Hai, extending from Loch Ke to Briuol, and to the Shannon."—*Ibid* The royal province of Meath also contained a real toparchy of Cruthem, for it is said in Tigh. A D 666, "Eochaidh Iarlaith ri Cruthne Midhi mortuus est" Again, other Cruthem held a portion of the diocese of Derry, where the district of Dun-Cruthumia, since called Ardmagilligan, and St. Beoadh's ancient episcopal church of Dun-Cruthen, or Dun-Cruthne, now Duncrun, were situate See Vita Septima Patricii in Trias Thaum p 146, O'Donell, Vita Colum i c 99; and Colgan in eund pp 451, 494. Martyrol Dungall cit ibid, S Beatus in A SS Hib viii Mart. p. 562. Which makes several[e] recorded Pictlands in Erin, besides any others of which the record may have perished and independently of the mythus of the Temorian Picts

That mythus is of a large import It professedly belongs to the first origins of the existing Irish people It shews you the Cruthinch powerful in Erin in Hermion's own days, winning his battles, and preserving him from his enemies, and afterwards made to evacuate Ireland under an agreement, in order that they might not obtain the sovereignty of the island, "that they might not make battle for Teamhair" Yet then six chiefs[h], under Drostan or Trosdan the Druid, remained, and received

grants

---

[g] Any of which, perhaps the last-mentioned, may have given birth to Churitinus, surnamed Cruthnechanus, who baptized St. Columba at Tulich Dubhglas in Urconnell

[h] So Keating, from Psalter of Cashel This work says, "six of them remained" See p 125

giants of land in the Campus Bregensis[i], Moigh Breagha, or Breag-mhuigh, whereon
Tara was situated. Strange, that they were banished lest they should possess the
Hill of Tara, and yet were left in possession of the Plain of Tara. It appears through
clouds of fable, that Tara was once their's, Temora or Teamhair Breagh a seat of
painted Druids, and Erin a kingdom of Picts. Make battle for Tara! Why, the
Breagh was their own, and Teamhair was the work of their hands, for they taught to
construct the "fair and well-walled house." Pharmacy and surgery, navigation and
agriculture, were from them. But for them there was neither idolatry, necromancy,
nor divination, and Druidism, it is said, was of the Picti. But for them, no composition
of "bright poems," and bardism was of the Picti.—See p 144. By another tale the Mur
Ollamhan of Tara, and all its arts and sciences, were ascribed to Achy Mac Fiach,
styled the Ollave of Ireland, or Ollamh Fodla. And this king, and his six sons and
grandsons, were called the "seven Cruithnech kings that ruled over Erin."—See the
entry in Tigh A. D 172. The original Cruthenians of Temora were the authors of
every art whereof Milesian Erin could boast the rudiments. We read that the first royal
adultery in Ireland was committed by Tea (daughter of Lughaidh, and wife of Heremon) from whom the name Temora is mythically derived. with Gede Olguthach the
Pict.—Ameirgin on Tara, cit Petrie on Tara, p 130. Thus far the Milesians and Cruthenians are kept distinct. But Heremon and Gede, husbands of one wife, were also
fathers of the same three children; whence Mr Petrie infers their identity.—*Ibid.*
p 153. Now this Gede Olguthach is the second king of Picts, Cruthne's successor,
in the Nomina Reg. Pict., Innes, ii 798; and also[k] in the Pictish Chronicle. Therefore
Heremon seems to identify himself with the second king of Cruthen-tuath; and,
Cruthne's name being taken as merely typical, like Britain, first king of Britain,
Francis of France, Dan of Denmark, &c, then with the first. These mythical equivalents resolve themselves into natural equivalents, for whatever represents *original*
Ireland must (if but a corner of the bardic veil be lifted) disclose to us *painted* Ire-
land. The exposure of the Cruthenian myth may be completed, by adding that the
Ollamh

---

[i] Breagha, son of Breogan, from Brigantium
or Betanzos in Spain (Tor Breogan of Keating,
and Bregatea of Cuan O'Lochain), gave his name
to the Moigh Breagha, where Temora stood,
upon Tara Hill. This is of a piece with all
the rest. That it was the name of Temora's
original possessors is implied in the question
which the bard Fintan asks, but omits to answer,

Teamhair Breag whence is it, tell O ye learned
 [Ollaves]!
When did it separate from *the Brugh?*—
                                    See *Petrie's Tara,* p 131

[k] For, although there he seems to stand ninth,
the intervening seven are the seven brothers from
whom the seven provinces were called, who could
neither in nature all succeed each other, nor could
any of them by Pictish law succeed Cruthne,
being his sons

Ollamh Fodla and his race were styled the Cruithnech kings, *because* he was son to that same Lonneada, daughter of Achy Eachbheoil, who also stands godmother to the Dalaradians, five, if not seven, centuries later! And, that Gede Ollguthach, the father of Heremon's children, was the third son of the Ollamh, who lived ages after Heremon! Tuathal, in A D 130, is feigned to have been son to Ethne, daughter of Imgheal, king of Picts, to have been educated in Pictland, and to have recovered his crown by aid of Pictish arms.—Ogyg in cap. lxvi., Keating, p 213, Cambrensis Eversus, pp 67, 68 Though some pretended that Temora was a seat of monarchy 1200, if not 1500 years before him, he was the earliest founder of Temora! within the purlieus of history, and I suspect he was once known as the builder thereof It gives colour to that suspicion that, in the proverbial names[m] of Erin, in respect of her principal kings, she was called the Teach (House) of Tuathal With deference to Tigernach and others, I would prefer to say that historical tradition has its dawn in Tuathal, A D 130, than in Cunbaoth, B C 305 The long previous anarchy of the Plebeians or Rustics, Aiteachtuatha, after which the restored Tuathal is said to have consolidated the Pentarchal Monarchy, may be no other than that savage disunion out of which the first king of Temora (a Harald Harfagr to Erin) called the Gaelic tribes; a restoration put mythically for a foundation, in order to support the superstructure of fabulous chronology. Whatever he was, he was of Cruithnechan blood and education In the Book of Lecan, fol 14, imperfectly cited by Vallancey, Coll iv 2 p. 2, after stating how Fintan of portentous longevity had preserved the Irish history, it is added, that Tuan of Ulster "preserved it till Patrick's time, and Columcille, and Comgall, and Finnen, when it was written on their knees, and on their thighs, and on the palms of their hands, and it continues in the hands of sages, of doctors, and historians, and it is on the altars of saints and righteous men from that time down' This curious statement exhibits the transition of the stigmatical painting from barbarous adornment to other uses[n], before

its

---

[l] It was a question, as early as the sixth century, when and where Teamhair or Teamhun obtained its name

When was Teamhair [called] Teamhair?
Is it with Partholan or battles? Or,' &c &c

It was agreed among the ollaves, that the name was Milesian or Scot (for other appellations were provided for the ages of the Tuatha De Danann and their predecessors), and so the fable of Heremon and Tea was delivered to the world

[m] The others mostly express natural objects, not works as *fonn*, land, *rath*, land, *crioch*, country, *achadh*, field Clar Chormaic, the table of Cormac, may allude to the introduction of domestic and sedentary arts, while the Cro of Con is of an ambiguous signification.—O Flaherty, Ogygia, part 1 p 19, Hugh O Donnell, cit ibid

[n] To which the Oghams might be conveniently applied Etruscan figures with inscriptions written upon the thighs may be seen in Montfaucon, iii. part 1, p 72, part 2, p 268

its final abandonment, and in the persons of the early Christians; and, even it incorrect as to date and persons, it cannot have proceeded from an author who doubted the existence of acupuncture among the ancient Irish

There may be another, though an oblique, way of tracing this British costume in the colony of Erin. A continual recurrence of surnames of colour, either unnatural, morbid, and disgusting, like *glas, liath, uaine, laib, buidhe,* or strange and grotesque ones, may be accounted for in tribes that had originally been coloured unnaturally, and prided themselves therein; while rarely used by others But such a solution is almost necessary to account for such squalid epithets, when applied to the great primitive heroes, and even the actual founders, of the nations, creatures of a proud fiction, and names not individual, but typical. What origins ever boasted of an Æneas Lividus, or Romulus Discolor, Cadmus the Dingy, or Inachus the Speckled? But the Gaidheal derive themselves from Gaodhal or Gaidheal, son of Nial and Scota. He was constantly called Gaidheal Glas, because his flesh was spotted of that colour (greenish, or blueish, or livid) by a serpent's sting —Keating, p 67 See Malmura of Fahan, in App., Gilda Coemham, &c Here, besides the vile epithet is the very substance of the fact in an altered form the natural man turned to woad-colour by puncture[o] Compare the man Gaidheal *Glas*, with the man Gaidheal *Ficht* in the Cairnech Legend, p 187 The captain of the Nemedians of whom came the Firbolg, was Simon Breac, Maculis Distinctus, or as some have it, Simon Varius Britan the founder of Britain, derives his name (and rightly, I imagine[p]) from *brit,* diversicolor, and he was son to Feargus Leathdearg, Half-red, son of Nemedius, in whom the redness of half his body may have been its natural floridity, as we have observed in the Alban Scots, or Gwyddyl Coch So, again, taking the red colour for the natural, we may form an idea of king Lugadh Riabhdearg, or Red-streak, who was marked with red circles round his body A Dananman hero, son to the great Daghda himself, was Fraoch Uaine A primitive Scoto-Scythian chief, Heber Glunfinn, or *White-knee,* was celebrated as grandfather to Faobhar *Glas* —Ogygia, ii p. 67 See Keating, p. 132 Some causes had introduced into Irish use the strange name Dubhdaleth,

---

[o] That a Druid, officiating mystically, was a serpent, appears clearly enough in Cæsar's account of the *ovum anguinum*

[p] That the bards had in their *Anant,* or old ritual songs, the name Brithan, Britannia (distinct from the fictitious name Prydyn or Prydain, i e Pulcheria), and derived it from *brith,* painted, I infer from the Gwawdd Lludd y Mawr, v 20, and vv 18, 49, confirmed by various considerations And, since *desuetude elsewhere* was the cause of such appellations, that name, Britain or Brithan, should have originated subsequently to the cessation of nudity among the Gauls, excepting (probably) the Lemonian Gauls called Pictones

Dubhdaleth, Both-halves-black. In days anterior to armour[q], I have no notion what a white knee is, except in contrast to a coloured one ; nor can I conceive, otherwise, of a man with *one half* dark, which condition the contrary name Dubhdaleth implies. Jocelyn of Furness tells us of two places in the Crutheman Ardes of Ulster, to both of which belongs the very strange name of Dundalethglas, namely, Downpatrick, well known by that name, and another hill-fort in a marsh not far distant.—Vita Patric c. 38. He interprets the name, *two halves* of a glas, i. e. *a fetter*, from the broken bonds of some prisoners, whom an angel set free, and conveyed to these two Duns. But, comparing it with analogous names of colour, and especially with Leathdearg, and Dubhdaleth, I rather interpret *Dun Dalethglas*, Fort of the Entirely Painted, the Dubhdaleths, the Crutheni of Dalaradia, thus making its sense equivalent in effect to that of the *Dun-Cruithne* in Derry. Besides those analogies, its occurring *twice* in ancient Cruthenia favours the descriptive sense, rather than any historic allusion. The first man, say the verses ascribed to Fintan himself, who cleared Tara Hill of wood, was Liath, Glaucus or Pallidus, son of Laigni Leathan-glas. The meaning of the surname, Broad-stain[r], probably denotes belts of colour like those of king Riabhdearg, but broad ones. It is easy but unnecessary to multiply examples. The dingy colours expressed in those various terms of *glas, dubh, uaine*, &c., were the various tints imparted by the woad, the cœrulens color of Cæsar, the Ethiopian tint of Pliny, and the virides Britanni of Ovid. The tinted knee will be best appreciated from the above-cited statement in the Book of Lecan, that the Irish, both in and after St. Patrick's days, had records of facts "written on their knees." The prevailing idea of such names as I have cited is as old as any memorial we have of the Picts. For of those Caledonians who fought against Severus, entirely naked, and tattooed with figures of animals &c., the only chieftain whose name has come down to us is Argento-Coxus or Silver-hip, evidently so called by the Romans, because he affected to leave his hips unstained.—Dion Cassius lib. lxxvi p. 1285. And the comparison of some analogous names among the hero-deities of the British bards, will add to their force.

Some observations are due to the tradition, that the Pictish rule of succession to
the

---

[q] The modern armorial surnames, Glunduibh or Genumger, Gluniarn or Genuferreus, Gluntradhna or Genucorvi, &c., are quite beside the question.—*Vide* O'Conor, in Quat. Mag. A. D. 978.

[r] *Leathan* and *glas* seem to be both adjectives in the Irish dialect of Gælic, (though, in Highland or Scottish Gælic, *glas* is also a substantive, a green or blue surface), and I know not if any objection thus arises. Where intensity, not extent, of colour is to be measured, there does not, as in *dubhglas* and *liathglas*. Changing *broad* into *long*, the Welsh *Hirlas* exactly corresponds.

the crown arose out of a treaty of marriage with ladies of the blood royal of Erin.—Beda, i. cap. l., and the Irish documents. See also Polydore Virgil. That rule was, that in all cases of doubt they should choose a king in the female line of descent, not in the male. It seems to have been acted upon from the beginning till[*] 783, in the latter years of the kingdom, to such an extent that no son stands recorded to have succeeded his father, either immediately, or with intermediates. The sixty-ninth catalogued king, and the twenty-first Christian, was son to his fifth predecessor. But the tradition of such a treaty is not to be received without much hesitation.

The line male can only be legal, where nuptiæ patrem demonstrant, and can only be real where marriages are held sacred. In Cæsar's time a British woman had sometimes ten or a dozen husbands (as she called them), usually men of the same family; and he who had known her as a virgin was accounted father of all her offspring.—De Bello Gall. i. cap. 14. Strabo had collected from report that it was no better in Ireland, or rather that there was no rule at all.—iv. p. 282. St. Jerome, who had resided in Gaul, and had a slight knowledge of what he said, affirms it without limitation: "Scotorum natio uxores proprias non habet ... Nulla apud eos conjux propria est, sed ut cuique libitum fuerit pecudum more lasciviunt."—Adv. Jovin. lib. ii. tom. ii. p. 335. Verona, 1735. He repeats the same thing, with inclusion of those Britons who were called Atticotti. "Scotorum et Atticottorum ritu, ac de Republica Platonis, promiscuas uxores, communes liberos, habent."—Epist. 69. ad Oceanum, tom. i. p. 413. These reports may be understood as limiting marriage to a possessory right, loosely observed and frequently dissolved. But nations, of which even rhetoric could draw such pictures, must have been incapable of transmitting paternal inheritances, and must have lived under a pure tanistry, until the improvement of manners began to furnish stronger presumptions of parentage. The positive allegations of sonship, contained in the dynasties of the Antiquaries and Bards, may be language[']' of Christian adaptation, even after the names have ceased to be sheer inventions. The mother is the wet nurse; any other economy belongs to art and refinement; and the vehement attachment of the Celtic tribes to their foster brothers

was,

---

[*] Mr. Pinkerton says till 833, but it does not so appear from the lists.

['] Of such adaptation there seems a flagrant instance in the two daughters of Tuathal Teachtmar. The king of Leinster married Dairine, and afterwards became desirous of the other sister, Fither. So he went to Temora and said that Dairine was dead, and that nothing could console him but marriage with Fither, whom Tuathal bestowed upon him. When this fraud was detected, Dairine died of vexation at his misconduct, and Fither of shame at the error into which she had been deceived. Rare sentimentality and tender nerves for A. D. 136–160.

was, *in its origin*, simply fraternal affection. The foster-brother was the only brother, and the common breast the only sure tie between them. In the Mabinogion we remark the paucity of allusions to marriage, considered in any other view than as the fact of occupancy. The Triads of Arthur are very peculiar on this head, for Triad 109 gives "the three wives of Arthur, *who were his three chief ladies*," and 110 proceeds to give his three chief concubines, so that the authors of those Triads saw reason to explain, and explain away, what a wife meant. See also the preface to Davydd ap Gwilym, p 16. But the most singular passage is that of Solinus on the Hebrides "As you go from the foreland of Caledonia (the Mull of Galloway) towards Thyle, in two days' sail you reach the islands of Hebudes, five in number, of which the inhabitants are unacquainted with grain, and subsist on fish and milk. They all have but one king, for they are divided by narrow waters from each other. The king has nothing of his own, all things belong to all. Fixed laws compel him to equity, and, lest avarice should pervert him from truth, he learns justice from poverty, as having no private possessions. But he is maintained at the public expense. No wife is given to him for his own, but he takes for his use, by turns, whatsoever women he is inclined to, *by which means he is debarred from the wish and hope of having sons*" —Solinus, cap 22. This account is most important, as a description, not of barbarism merely, but of its polity. To prevent the evils of a disputed male succession, one purely and necessarily female was provided. The polity therefrom resulting was precisely the Pictish, there no son could stand in his father's place, and in Pictland (nearly to the last) no son ever did. Of the Hebudes, spoken of here as *five*, as well as by Ptolemy, Marcianus, and Stephanus in Ἀβουδαι, viz Ebuda 1, Ebuda 11, Rhicina, Maleos, and Epidium, the last two are undoubtedly Mull and Ilay. But Ilay, by Irish tradition, was the first seat of the Picts when they left Erin, and the cradle of the kings of Fortren Mor. No man can affirm from internal documents how far the Irish of A D 208 were proficients in the art of matrimony, and their external reputation for it was very low. If the ancient laws ascribed to Con and Cormac were satisfactory on these points, it would remain to shew them authentic and uninterpolated. But the contrary may be inferred from the entire silence of Lynch, when he boasts of those legislators, in pp 157–8, and from his slight and general answer to Giraldus,

"As the beautiful edition of them is from a lady's hands, occasional reference to the *original text* is to be recommended

The first series, Tr 59, merely says, "the three chief ladies of Arthur," where the third and greatest series has "wives," but the well-known name of Gwenhwyvar or Guenever, ascribed to all three of them, supplies the want of the word *wife*, besides which the next triad, as in series 3, gives the three *concubines*.

iii. 19, as touching Pagan times, in p. 155 of the C. Eversus The ill-fated Gynæceum of Cormac M'Art was, probably, connected with some desire on the part of that able man, to ennoble and purify the female character   Anecdote speaks truer than general declamation, therefore let us hear the wife of Argentocoxus, or Silver-hip, the Pict. The empress Julia Domna reproached her, that they (the Caledonian women), after marriage, cohabited promiscuously with men But she replied " We satisfy the wants of nature much better than you Romans. For we openly cohabit with the bravest of men, and you commit secret adultery with the vilest." While we subscribe to her estimate of the merits of the case, we cannot doubt the facts of it. Whosoever would too sanguinely argue from ancient tales of marriages, wives, and queens, from Banba and Scota downwards, should bear in mind that Silver-hip had a sort of wife. We know that he had a lady so called, but we also know what sort of wife she was,—not by her personal fault, but by avowed usage of her nation, and how far, or whether at all, her nuptials demonstrated the father   The same Dion who related this had lately said of the Mæatæ and Caledonii collectively, γυναιξὶν ἐπικοίνοις χρώμενοι When the increasing civility of dress and manners had fixed upon the adherents to old fashions of nudity the title of Cruthneans, the latter, no doubt, continued also more barbarous in sexual and social rules. Their removal also was into islands where those rites which ascertain father and son were systematically excluded from the court   There is, therefore, no such mystery in the Pictish prosapia fœminea, or uterine tanistry, as should lead us to take up with that bardic romance of the Cruthnich husbands, bound by a solemn treaty to the unpetticoated government of their Milesian wives Christian or semi-Christian bardism put on dissimulation in dealing with the dark annals of the past; and as it coined fables to dissemble the paintedness of previous generations, so did it others to keep out of sight their γάμον ἀγαμον.

The colour of the Britons, Picts, and Cruthem is not uniformly stated. Cæsar terms it cœrulean, Ovid speaks of the virides Britanni (Amores ii 16, 39), and Pliny says they imitated the colour of Ethiopians, xxii cap. 1 But they used the herb isatis or glastum, called woad, which by preparation will yield blue, green, and black. The use of more than one tint appears grammatically as well as historically. For *glastum* in Latin, *glas-lys* in British, is woad. But *glas*, in British and in Gaelic, means indifferently blue and green It is surprising that even the simplest of men should have called the firmament on high and the grass under foot by one name of colour But in truth the phrase is from the dyer's shop, and not from nature, meaning *glasticolor*, woad-coloured. Of that there is confirmation, in the Gaelic

words* *gorm, guirni, guirme, guirmead,* meaning alike blue and green, blueness and greenness, to stain blue and green, and *guirmean, goirmin,* the *herb woad* Whereas the words not having such double sense, *llasar,* blue, *neillu,* sky-blue, *gwyrdd, u, uaithne,* green (as well as the determining compounds, like *ir-las,* green, *liath-gorm,* azure), do not signify that herb All names for woad seem to be indifferent as to the two colours, and all words thus indifferent to be names of woad. Therefore tradition and etymology combine to recommend the opinion, that Celtic tribes diversified their skins with several tints and colours, as in Christian times they have distinguished themselves by the colour of their plaids

In those districts to which the Roman laws against Druidism did not extend, and where the practice had not, as in most parts of Ireland, come to a natural end, Christianity was, no doubt, its destroying power Besides any connexion it may have had with Pagan creeds, its very nature and object implied the nudity of the greater part of the body, which the Christian decorum has always condemned But it is probable that the formal conversions by Ninia, Palladius Columkille, &c, may have found the custom fast dying away under the approaches of the dawning light Pictland, I have studied to shew, had recently ceased to be governed by a dynasty of Brudes, when Columkille went thither Yet the memory of that ancient usage,—nay, in some sort, the usage itself,—was superstitiously cherished by those who regretted and secretly retained Druidism It was so in Roman Britain it that very time, and among the Northern Picts and their neighbours still later Beli Mawr, to whom every thing British was referred, was son of Manogan, i. e the Spotted-man a name formed upon *manog,* in modern spelling *manaug,* spotted or party-coloured They were joint patrons or tutelaries of the island "Skilfully will I praise thee, victorious Beli! and King Manogan! thou shalt uphold the privileges of Beli's isle of honey "—*Marunad Uthyr,* p 73 The same root, *manaw, macula,* yields the name of another titulary hero-god, *Manawyd,* synonymous with that of Manogan; he was a perpetual guardian of the Cauldron of Britain —*Mab Llyr* v 48

The poem called the Praise of Lludd contains that famous and obscure canticle of the Britons, said to be quoted o'r anant, "out of the hymns," invoking one Brith or Diversicolor, "Brith i Brithan' hail" &c, and describing the sacrifice of a cow that is *vraith* (feminine of brith) or party-coloured —pp 74, 75 Elsewhere it is said· "They
the

(the multitude) do not know the ych brych spotted or variegated ox, with the massive head-band."—p. 45 The bard Avaon says,

> " I have been a cat *with a spotted* head on the triple tree,
> Bum cath *ben-vrith* ar driphren "—p 44

And Meigant says of his order, the bards, " let *the spotted-headed* host from the cow-pen of Cadvan be invited on the day of ample allowance, *byddin* . . *pen-vrith* o vuaith Cadvan."—p 161. In the sorceries of Tintagel tower, when Pendragon put on the similitude of Gorlais, his accomplice, Merlin Ambrose, took the form of *Brith-vael*, that is to say, useful or effectual by variegation, *picturipotens* —Brut G ap. Arthur, p 292 Geoffrey seems to have read *brych* instead of its equivalent *brith*, ' Merlinus in Bricclem."—viii. 19. Avan Red-Spear, the favourite bard of the redoubted king Cadwallon ap Cadvan, praises him in this peculiar phrase

> Mad ganed, mab brith, cythmor radlawn,
> Well-born is he, *son of the painted one*, gracious sea-divider
> Axle of our privilege, he went [against] the leagued valour of the unjust
> Silent were the crowd of kings before the harmonious ones
> Verdure vegetated when the man was born a blessing
> To Cymmry, when Christ created Cadwallawn —p 180, vide *Evan's* spec p 49

Though *mab brith* might signify *pictus*, not *filius picti*, as *mab sant* is *sanctus*, not *filius sancti*, the words *mad ganed* imply the latter sense A certain Brith or Manogan seems to have been honoured as a person typical of Celtic antiquity, which idea would make it "son of Brith" This superstition fell under ecclesiastical censure in the canons of the Synod of Calcuth, in A D 785. Those canons were decreed in Nor-thumberland, with the sanction and signature of Aelfward king of Trans-Humbria, his bishops, and abbots, and were adopted and decreed in like manner by the clergy of King Offa, at Calcuth in Mercia But the following canon evidently originated in the kingdom of Northumberland, which bordered upon that of the Picts, with some intermixture of population "The Pagans, by inspiration of the devil, intro-duced most unseemly scars, agreeably to what Prudentius says in his Enchiridion,

> ' Tinxit et innocuum maculis sordentibus Adam '

Verily, if any one for God's sake were to undergo this blemish of staining, he would therefore receive great reward; but whoever does it from the superstition of the Gen-tiles

[1] If these allusions are to painting upon the shaven crown of the head, they may explain the surname of Maol, Bald, given to Britan, son of Fergus Redside, and founder of Britain

tiles, it does not avail him to salvation "—*Concil. Chalcutense*, ap Wilkins, 1. p. 150. This is a full mild censure, which may, perhaps, imply that the offenders were neither few nor unpopular. Rhydderch Hael, prince of Strathclyde, the opponent of bardism, and more especially of Gwenddoleu the Caledonian and Merddin, invited St. Kentigern or Mungo to Glasgu to restore the Christian religion, which was almost destroyed (penè delcta) in those parts. Kentigern assembled the people, and said· " Whoever begrudge men their salvation, and oppose God's word, by virtue of God's word I warn them to depart, that they may offer no impediment to believers. Quo dicto ingens larvatorum multitudo staturâ et visu horribilis a cœtu illo exiens omnibus videntibus aufugit."—*Jocelyn, Vita Kentig* cap 32, *Pink Vitæ Sanctorum Scotiæ.* Though this is so retailed by Jocelyn, as to give the idea of demons, not men, yet the very word *larvati*, in its ancient sense of *haunted*, larvis exterriti, is contrary to that idea, and in its mediæval sense of larvâ indutus, wearing a hideous mask, it gives what I conceive the truth of this affair, that the Du-Calidons, and other " brithwyr ddu," such as Merddin ap Morvryn and his disciples, removed from the congregation those ugly masks which they had substituted for human faces. But the most signal evidence of the systematic character of that superstition, which the Trans-Humbrian prelates pronounced " unavailing to salvation," is furnished by an ancient bard, who thus describes the three *llu*, i.e troops or courses, into which his order, or certain functionaries connected with it, distributed themselves

[By the] customs of the kingdom	Teyrnas arveieu
The three troops shall be conducted	Dygettawr y trillu
Before the potent visage of Jesus,	Rhag drech drem Iesu,
The troop pure and innocent,	Llu gwirin gwirion
Of the appearance of angels,	Eiliw engylion,
Another troop of men variegated	*Llu arall bruthion*
After the fashion of natives[a] ,	*Eiliw brodorion,*
The third troop, [of men] unbaptized,	Tridedd llu divedydd,
Stubborn co-operators in death,	Syth llaith cyweithydd,
Drive the gluttons into the lot of Devils,	Hwyliant y glythwyr yn parthred Dieivyl,
United among the good ones,	Yn un yn daon
[Though] with the appearance of the un- righteous	Gan dull anghyviawn.—p. 184

The

The two last lines relate (in my conjecture) to *the third llu*, and not to their victims, the *glythwyr,* though it is a matter of inference[b], not of syntax

Now the question arises, were these persons whom the bards applaud, and the synod censures, aculeis ferreis[c] cum atramento, &c, annotati? I cannot quite think it; but prefer the supposition, that they were, upon occasions, simply *painted* in a superficial and removable manner; and not *stigmatized,* as the Du-Calidonian Britons were before St. Ninia, and the Gwyddyl Fichti before St. Columba; without prejudice, however, to their having certain marks partially, and secretly perhaps, imprinted on the body, both for superstition, and as the sign of initiation, and of being a " mab brith."

This entire topic was deprived of much of its chances of elucidation by the destruction of Irish Ulster in the sixteenth and seventeenth centuries; for that kingdom was both the favourite seat of ancient bardism, and the principal residence of the Cruthem or Picts of Erin. But, even as it is, these pages would have contained more illustration had they been written ten years hence.

Postscript.—My attention has been directed to a work manifesting much acquaintance with the history of the clans, entitled, " The Highlanders of Scotland," &c, by W F. Skene, F S. A Scot, Edinb 1837 Its coincidence with several of the main arguments and conclusions above offered obliges me to disclaim the suspicion of having purloined any of them from those pages, the existence of which has only now been made known to me, many months after the whole of my notes have been at Dublin. I specially allude to the doctrine, that the kingdom of Picts, to which the Pictish Chronicle relates, was Gaelic, and that its inhabitants were those people whom we call Highlanders It was entirely unknown to me that such an opinion had ever appeared in print That the Gael Picts were the whole body of the Albannaich, those excepted who dwelt west of Drumalban, was a conclusion that implied the falsehood of the clan pedigrees, exhibited since the fable of the Pictish extirpation became prevalent But

it

---

[b] In the twelfth century Cynddelw inverted this ancient order of the three troops, and arranged it 2, 3, 1, the inference is supported by his words

" Three clamours resort to the one cauldron,
The concourse of tribes, and my preparation,
The troop of variegated pugnacious natives,
Secondly, the troop of wrath, blackish, and roaring aloud,
Thirdly, the cheerful troop, soothing down opposition,
The troop of blessed ones, whom the beautiful loveth

Rygyrchant unpeir teir trydar,
Cynnadlcdd cenedleodd, a'm par,
Llu brithion brodorion bru ydyrgar,
Fil gwythlu gorddu gorddyar,

Trydydd llu nyw, lludd cyvarwar,

Llu gwynion, gwynoydig a gar —
Canu i Ddur p 249

[c] Isidorus Hispalensis

it was out of my power to work out that portion of the subject; and I am glad to see it is there so effectually done.

But there are also points which I am unable to concede   In this work is a third attempt to unite the Vecturions and Caledons, making them all Gaels, whom Innes made all Britons, and Pinkerton all Teutons, and I do not see that it is well sup ported by fact or reasons   Having no space for stating and refuting the arguments upon them, I must go straight to the points   It is not fact, that Ptolemy mentions fourteen tribes of Caledonians, or any tribes of them at all; but the thirteen other names are by him clearly distinguished from the Caledonians   This is writing Ptolemy, not quoting him   I do not believe the list of Bruides consisted originally but of 28. Copies agree in stating they were thirty, and it is as likely, at least, for two names to be lost, as that miscalculation committed   The number 150 was a multiple of 30, not of 28, allotting five years to each king   Nor, if they were 28, could we reduce that number to 14, by retaining the Bruides and rejecting the Ur-Bruides.   For nothing can be surer than that the Ur-Bruides meant something and what they did mean I have already offered a surmise, above, p. xlvi n   The purpose for which these fourteen Bruides are sought, requires them to be all living and reigning at the same time   Consequently we are told, vol. i p 251, that "Bruide is here *stated* to have thirty sons." Let us hear the *statement* 'Bruide Bout (a quo xxx. Bruide regnaverunt per centum quinquaquinta annorum spacium) xlviii annis regnavit"   A series of kings, succeeding B Bout during 150 years, are converted into a family of brothers Lastly, I am far from persuaded, that the Situs Albaniæ did by its "septem reges . septem regulos sub se habentes," mean to express fourteen persons, not fifty-six persons. The latter scheme would extend the type of the Pictish constitution from the kingdom of the Ardrigh to each Maormor kingdom   We know that type existed in the Cruithne of Daln'araidhe. Centaclad, cit Tigh in A D 563

The idea of a subsisting bifarious division of Pictland in the eighth century, Cruithne being the northern and Piccardach the southern, seems to me an illusion built on verbal trifles   The form Piccardach exhibits the only Irish name, founded on Pictus, that Tighernach employs   It is a general term, or used, if with any antithesis, in contrast to those of Ireland.   Its combination with *ard* or *ardach* seems to imply Picts of the mountains; in which case, it is with infelicity restricted to the lowlands   Mr Skene alleges that "whenever Tighernach has the word Piccardach, the Annals of Ulster use the word Pictores, in Latin, instead of Pieti, usually applied by them to the Picts"—i p 36   In fact, Tighernach has the word Piccardach in 728, 729, 734 and 750, and Pictones in 669, 750, and 752   Ulster Annals have Pictores thrice, in 668, 675, and 727; Picti (so far as I observe) not *usually*, but

but twice, in 697, and 787; and the common genitive, Pictorum, eleven times, in 630, 652, 656, 728, 733, 735, 861, 864, 870, 874, and in 877, where they last mention that nation by name, saying afterwards only Fir Albain. The 728 of Tighernach is Pictores in 727, Uit. His 729 and 734 are the genitive Pictorum in 728, 733, Ult. But the Pictones and Piccardach, both applied by Tighernach to the same people in 750, are reduced by the Ulster Annals to the one word, Pictores. Tighernach thought fit to borrow the name of the Pictones, or Gauls of Pictavia. So Hermannus Contractus, an historian of his age, says at A.D. 446, "contra Scotos et Pictavos." It is evident that his learning was wasted upon the Ultonian annalist, who converted it into *Pictores*, Painters. This phrase of Pictores has no relation whatever to Piccardach, only to Pictones. If the common genitive is to be fetched from Pictores, that rule must extend to all the eleven instances, including five subsequent to the fall of the Pictish dynasty. Talorcan M'Congusa was, it is said, a Pict of the north; and, as he delivered[d] up his own brother into the hands of the Piccardach, there must be "a complete distinction" between the latter and the Picts. But surely a fugitive and outlawed *Pict* (see Tigh. A.D. 731) can make his peace with *the Picts* by giving up his brother to them, without our using the word Pict in two senses. Hungust, it is said, receives the title of ri na Piccardach two years before he became king of Pictland; therefore Piccardach was another sovereignty. But *ri*, a king, does not always mean *ardri*, the king; and it is a term applied to maormors of Albany, and Irish toparchs, governing provinces under the ardrigh. Thus the maormor Finleg is styled Ri Albain, Tigh. 1020; and in Ult. 1085, Ceannmor reigning, one Domhnall M'Maelcholuim is also Ri Albain. When the general name is improperly added to *ri*, instead of the name of the toparchy, it only shews the details to be unknown or praetermitted by the writer. I know not whether all Pict princes of the royal blood and succession were *personally* so styled, perhaps not; but we read concerning the Irish Picts at 629 Tigh., Dicuil *ri cenedyl* Cruithne cecidit. Any dynastic theory built upon the mere use of the word *ri* is vain and unfounded. Feebler yet is the suggestion that the northern Picts "were a distinct body under their peculiar appellation of Cruithne." Since the Piccardachs were the southern Picts (we are told), "*consequently* the name of Cruithne, although occasionally applied to all the Picts, would in its more restricted sense belong to the Dicaledones or North Picts."—pp. 36, 37. Whatever it *would* do under certain conditions, it never did so in fact. Its more restricted sense, that is, its more frequent sense, to which its Latin (Crutheni) seems really restricted, was the Picts of Erin. The

only

---

[d] Mr. Skene adopts *the converse statement* from Ult., viz., that his brother surrendered him, while retaining *the year* of Tighernach. Why this is done, I know not.

only prop to this manifest fiction is another equally novel, viz, the interpreting *Cruithen-Tuath*, Picts of the North, p 63, whereas the word *tuath* in that, as in many analogous combinations, is never rendered *the north*, but the *people* or *nation* Cruitentuath is actually applied by the Masters to the Picts inhabiting Ireland — Quat Mag p 29; and see above, pp 126, 158

I have a word to add on the theory that the Cruithnich came from Albany to Erin, instead of the reverse. If strong arguments combine to confute the declarations of all our earliest authors let them stand confuted, but not otherwise The system of Mr Skene requires the Cruithnich or Gaelic Picts to have always held their territory, even from the earliest Roman records, and therefore he is led, systematically, to maintain the above theory. The argument for it runs thus " In all the Irish annals the name given *to the earliest* inhabitants of Scotland is Cruithne "—p 209 For which read, " given *to some* inhabitants of Scotland, by me regarded as the earliest," for more than that is incorrect   " And this appellation is always applied by them to the inhabitants of Scotland, in contradistinction to the Scots or inhabitants of Ireland " Of the instances (certainly rare) in which Tighernach carries that name out of Ireland, I have only noted three or four, in every one of which it is otherwise. In 505 and 663 there is no contradistinction to anything ; and in 560 Cruithnechaibh is contrasted with Albanchaibh, meaning the Scots of Britain It is the same in 731, where Cruithne are opposed to Dalriadhe, unless that whole passage relates to Ulster. The inference follows ' [In the first[e] place,] therefore, it can be proved from Tighernach that the Ultonians or inhabitants of the north of Ireland were Cruithne, and therefore must have come from Scotland " It can be proved from him and from others, that a very limited portion of the Ultonians were Cruithne. We are only carried thus far, that the name Cruithne was applied to a portion of each island; and thence we are to deduce, that Ireland received it from Albany By the same process, *mutatis nominibus*, and with a like disregard of all tradition, we may prove that Ireland was peopled from Argyle and Lorn, and Saxony from England — (*II*)

NOTE

[e] What follows, in the second place, is a desperate allegation that Cruthnia was all Ulster, when it is well known to have not even included all Down and Antrim The plea is, that Fiach Araidh reigned at Emania, and that Cormac fought " against Fiach and the Cruithne " *Ergo* the kingdom of Emania is identical with that of the Cruithne But even these verbal dialectics break down, for the text runs, " against Cruithnia and against Fiach Araidh " Two *againsts*, because two powers, viz, the tribe of which he was *ri* or chieftain, and the kingdom of which he was *ardri* or pentarch See Tigh in 236

No. XVIII. *See pages* 122-124.

The legendary history of the Picts or Cruithnians, as given in the foregoing additions to the Historia of Nennius, will be found in a somewhat more detailed shape in the following documents, which seem worthy of preservation here, as tending to illustrate and complete the subject.

I. The first is a tract on the History of the Picts, which is preserved in the Book of Lecan, fol 286, *b*, col 2, and is evidently compiled from the same traditions which formed the basis of the narrative given in the text, and in the historical poem on the history of the Cruithnean colony, which has been printed, pp 126-153

Iap manbaд Ebip la h-Epemon in Cιпξ[cnoρ ро ξob ρ[n ριξι n-Epenn co c[no cuιc m-bliaдan дec, acc nι baι bliaдaιn Ebip ιр an aιρ[m ριn Ro claρa oι ριξ ραιch leρ ι ραιch Cинoιnд ι cριch Cualanд, η ραιch бeochaιξ uaρ бeoιρ. Do ριnoι ιmoρρo coιcfoaιch an Eριnд ιaρταιn ι дo ρaд ριξι coιcιд Ξaι-leoιn дo Chρeamchunд Scιачbel дo Domnannchaιb, η дo ρaд ριξι Muman дo cheιchρι macaιb Ebιр ι Eρ, Oρba, F[ρon, Feaρξna. Do ρaд ριξι coιcιд Chonдacc дo Un mac Uιcι, η дo Eατan mac Uιcι. Do ρaд ριξι coιcιд Ulaд дo Ebeρ mac Iρ a quo Ulaιд Eamιna

After Eber had been killed by Eremon in [the battle of] Aιgeatιos, he (*Eremon*) reigned over Eri fifteen years; but Eber's year was not in that computation He built two royal forts, viz, Rath Aιnnιn in the country of Cualann[f], and Rath Beothaigh[g] over the Nore He then made provincial kings of Eri, viz, he gave the sovereignty of the Gaileon province to Creamthann Sciathbel, of the Domnann race; and he gave the sovereignty of Munster to the four sons of Eber, viz, Er, Orba, Fearon, Feargna He gave the sovereignty of Connaught province to Un, son of Uιcι, and to Eatan, son of Uιcι He gave the sovereignty of the province of Uladh to Eber, son of Ir a quo the Ulto-nians of Emama.

Iρ ρe lιnд дo ριnдeaд na ξnιma ρa ι. cach Chuιle Caιchιρ la h-Cιmιρξιn n-ξluιn-ξel, ιc[nд bliaдna ιaρριn дo cheaρ Cιmιρξιn ι cach бιle Chιneaд ι Culaιb бρeξ

It was in his time the following deeds were done, viz the battle of Cuιl Caιtheaι was fought by Aιmergin the White-kneed In a year after Aιmergin was slain in the battle

---

f *Country of Cualann* —Cualann originally com-prised a considerable portion of the present county of Wicklow; but in the latter ages it was con-sidered as co-extensive with the half barony of

IRISH ARCH SOC NO 16.

Rathdown, in the north of that county See In-quisition, 21st April, 1636, and Ussh Pιrmoιdia, p 346.

g *Rath Beothaigh*, now Rathveagh

Breg re h-Eremon. Isin bliadain chetna ro meabadar fo thir ix. m-Brosnacha Ele, ⁊ tri h-Uindsinda Ua n-Aililla, ⁊ .ix. Rigi Laigsn

battle of Bile Tineadh, in Culaibh Breagh, by Eremon It was in that same year the nine *rivers* Brosnach of Eile broke over the country; and the three *rivers* Uinnsinn of Ui Ailillа, and the nine *rivers* Righ [Rye] of Leinster.

Isin bliadain chetna sin tancadar Cruithnich a tir Thraigia .i. clanda Geloin mic Ercail iad, Icathirsi an-anmanda Cruithnig mac Inge mic Luchta mic Parrthaloin mic Agnoin mic Buain, mic Mair, mic Faithfeacht mic Iafed mic Naei. Is e athair Cruithneach, ⁊ cét bliadain do i rige. Seacht meic Cruithnic andso .i. Fibra, Fidach, Fotla, Foirtrenn, Caitche, Airig, Cetach, ⁊ a seacht randaib do randsad a fearanna, amail adfed in file·

It was in that same year the Cruithnians came out of the country of Thracia, i e they were the descendants of Gelon, son of Ercal. Icathirsi was their name. Cruithnigh was the son of Inge, son of Luchta, son of Parrtholon, son of Agnon, son of Buan, son of Mas, son of Faithfeacht, son of Jafead, son of Noah[h]. He was the father of the Cruithnians, and he reigned an hundred years The seven sons of Cruithnigh were these, viz · Fibra, Fidach, Fotla, Foirtreann, Caitche, Airig, Cetach And it was into seven divisions they divided their territories, as the poet relates

Moirfesser mac Cruithnech ann
randsad ar seacht a fearand
Caitche, Airig, Cetach cland
Fib Fidach Fotla Foirtrend

Acus is e ainm cach fir dib fuil for a fearand

Fib, imorro, bliadain ar fichit do a rigi

Fidach xl. bliadain.

Foirtrend

Seven sons that Cruithnech had;
They divided by seven their territory
Caitche, Airig, Cetach the fruitful[i],
Fib, Fidach, Fotla, Foirtreann.

And each of them gave his name to his own territory[j].

Fib, therefore, one year and twenty was his reign.

Fidach, xl. years.

Foirtreann,

---

[h] See above, p 51, and note [k].

[i] *Cetach the fruitful* lit Cetach of children. Cetach is here made a proper name, but in the copy of these verses given above, p 50, cetach cland was given as the cognomen or surname of one of the seven sons, and instead of Caitche and Airig, we had Cait, Ce, and Cireach See p 155, n

[j] *Territory* —See p. 50, note [l].

Foirtrſno .lxx. bliaoain
Urpanncaiz oa bliaoain ap fichic.
Urloici oa .x. bliaoain
Uileo Cipic .lxxx. bliaoain.
Gantaen becan, imoppo, bliaoain.
Urgant Caiz tricha bliaoain.
Gniz Finoechta .lx. bliaoain.
Burgniuth Guioit Gaobpe, bliaoain.
Feezgſ bliaoain.
Uippechtaip Gſiz Guipio xl. bliaoain
Caluipgſiz tricha bliaoain
Urchal bruioi pont tri'a bliaoain
  piz Ulao oe aobapta bruioi fpia
  cach feap oib η panna na feap.

Bruioi Cino bliaoain.
Uipchino bliaoain.
Fſz bliaoain.
Uippeaz bliaoain.
Ruaile.
Ro gobrao caeca ap oa chéo bliaoain,
uz epc illebpaib na Cpuicnech bruioe-
Epo, bruioe-Gapz, bruioe-Apgapz,
bruioe-Cino, bruioe-Upcino, bruioe-
Uip, bruioi-Upuip, bruioi-Gpich,
bruioi-Upgpié, bruioi-Muin, bruioi-
Upmuin. Oo pizaib Cpuicneac annpin.

  Seipeap taipeach tanzaoap co h-fpinn
.i. rſeap oeapbpaithpi i Soilen, Ulpa,
Neachtain, Tpoptan, Aengup, Uficino.

  Fath a tiachta a n-Epinn, imoppo,
Polopnur pi Tpaicia oo pao gpao oia
piaip co po tpiall a bpeith can tochpa.
                      Lotap

Foirtreann, lxx. years.
Urpanneait, two years and twenty.
Urloiei, two years and ten.
Uileo Ciric, lxxx years.
Gantaen Becan, one year.
Urgant Cait, thirty years.
Gnith Findechta, lx. years.
Burgnith Guidit Gadbre, one year
Fethges, one year
Uirfechtair Gest Gurid, xl. years
Caluirgset, thirty years.
Urehal Bruidi-pont, thirty years, king of
Uladh[k], from him the name of Bruide
is given to every man of them, and to
the divisions (*territorial*) of the men
Bruidi Cinn, one year
Uirchinn, one year.
Feat, one year
Uirfeat, one year.
Rnaile.
They reigned fifty and two hundred
years, ut est in the books of the Cruith-
nians Bruide-Ero, Bruide-Gait, Bruide-
Argart, Bruide-Cinn, Bruide-Uirinn,
Bruide-Iup, Bruide-Uriup, Bruidi-Grith,
Bruidi-Urgrith, Bruidi-Muin, Bruidi-Ui-
muin. Of the Cruithman kings so far.

  Six leaders came to Eri, viz, six
brothers, viz, Solen, Ulpa, Neachtain,
Trostan, Aengus, Leitinn Now the
cause of their coming to Eri was, Poloi-
nus, King of Thracia, fell in love with
their sister, and he attempted to get
                    her

---

k *Uladh* —In the words piz ulao oe, a cor-
rector has marked the letters piz with dots, to be
erased, but he, probably, omitted to substitute the
correct reading, which in another copy is given
ippize nUlao. If oe, &c Book of Leacan,
fol 13, b, col 2

Lotaṁ iaṁṁin co ṁo tṁiallṁaṁ taṁ Ro-
manċu co Fṁanʒcu, ⁊ ṁo cumṁaiʒṁeaṁ
caṫaiṁ anṁ i Pictaiṁiṁ a pictuṁ a
h-ainm i o na ṁeanṁaib, ⁊ ṁo ṁaṁ ṁiʒ
Fṁanʒc ʒṁaṁ ṁia ṁiaiṁ Lotaṁ ṁoṁ
muiṁ iaṁ n-fʒ in ċuiceṁ bṁaṫaṁ .i. Lai-
tṁn I cino ṁa la iaṁ n-ṁul aṁ muiṁ
aṁbaṫ a ṁiuṁ. Ʒabṁaṁ Cṁuiṫniʒ a n-
inṁbeṁ claine [ṁead t-Slaine] a n-ib
Cṁoṁealaiʒ.

Atbeaṁt ṁṁiu Cṁemṫianṁ Sciaṫbel
ṁiʒ Laiʒín ṁo beṁaṁ ṁailti ṁoib aṁ
ṁiċuṁ Ṫuaiṫi Fiṁʒa ṁoib Aṁbeaṁt
ṫṁa Tṁoṫtan oṁai Cṁuiṫneċ ṁiu, co
ṁoiṁṁeaṁ iaṁ aṁ loʒ ṁ'ṁaʒbail, ⁊ iṁe
lṁiʒṁṁ .i. bleoʒan uii. ṁiċit ṁo mael
ṁinn ṁo ṁoṁtaṁ i ṁail a ṁeaṁṁaiṁea in
caċ ṁoib i. caċ Aṁṁa Leamnaċta a
n-ib Cṁoṁealaiċ ṁe tuaṫaib Fiʒṁa
.i. tuaṫ ṁo Ḃṁeatnaib ṁo baṁ i Foṫ-
aṁtaib ⁊ nṁm aṁ a n-aṁmaib. Maṁb
caċ aenṁṁṁ aṁ a n-ṁeaṁʒṁaiṁ ⁊ ni
ʒeṁṁiṁ act iaṁnaiṁi nṁmi umṁu Caċ
uen ṁo ʒoṁta ṁo Laiʒnib iṁin ċaċ ni
oṁṁaiṁ act laiʒi ṁin leumnaċṁ ⁊ ni
cumʒiṁ nṁm ni ṁoib. Ro maṁbta iaṁṁin
Tuaċ Fhiṁʒa.

Maṁb ceaṫṁaṁ iaṁṁin ṁo ċṁuiṫ-
neaċaib .i Tṁoṫtan, Solen, Neaċ-
tain,

her without *paying* a dowry. They then
set out and passed through the Romans
into France, where they built a city, viz,
Pietairis, a pictis, was its name, i e
from the points (*pikes*). And the King
of France fell in love with their sister.
They set out upon the sea, after the death
of the fifth brother, viz, Laitenn. In two
days after they had gone to sea their
sister died. The Cruithneans landed at
Inbhear Slaine in Ui Cennsealaigh.

Cremthann Sciathbel, the King of
Leinster, told them that they should have
welcome from him, on condition that they
should destroy the Tuath Fidga Now
Trostan, the Cruithnean Druid, said to
them, that he would help them if he were
rewarded. And this was the cure *he gave
them*, viz, to spill the milk of seven score
hornless white cows near the place where
the battle was to be fought, viz. the
battle of Ard Leamhnachta in Ui Cennsealaigh, against the Tuatha Fidga, viz,
a tribe of Britons, who were in the Fotharts[1], with poison on their weapons. Any
man wounded by them died, and they
carried nothing about them but poisoned
iron. Every one of the Leinstermen
who was pierced in the battle had nothing more to do than lie in the new
milk, and then the poison affected him
not. The Tuath Fidga were all killed
afterwards

Four of the Cruithnians died after,
viz, Trostan, Solen, Neachtain, Ulptha,
after

---

[1] *The Fotharts*, now the barony of Forth, in the County Wexford. See above p 123, note [1]

ταιn, Ulpτα, ιαṗ n-ὄιcһαṗ ιn cһατα,
conaὄ ὄοιbṗιn ṗο cһαn ιn ṗṫncһαιὄ ṗο.

after the battle had been gained, and it
was for them the poet sang this

Aṗο leamnacһτα ιṗ τιṗṗeu τһeuṗ
ṗιnὄαὄ cacһ an cacһ eᵹṫṗ
cṗαeὄ ὄαṗ leαn ιn τ-αιnm ιṗloιno
ṗοṗ ᵹοb o αιmṗιṗ Cṗιmτοιno?

Ard Leamhnachta in this southern
country,—
Each noble and each poet may ask,
Why it is called by this distinctive name,
Which it bears since the time of Crim-
thann ?

Cṗιmcһαnὄ Scιατһbel һ-e ṗο ᵹοb,
ὄο ταṗαιὄ aṗ caτ cuṗαὄ,
cen ὄιn αṗ nṫmιb na n-αṗm
na n-ατһacһ n-uατmaṗ n-aᵹaṗb.

Crimthann Sciathbel it was that en-
gaged them ,
To free him of the battle of heroes,
When defenceless against the poisoned
arms
Of the hateful horrid giants

Seιṗṫ Cṗuιτhneacһ ṗο cһιnὄ Ὄια
ταnᵹαὄαṗ ι τιṗ Cṗαᵹια
Solen, Ulpα, Necһταιn naṗ,
Aenᵹuṗ, Leιτhcṫnὄ, ιṗ Cṗoṗταn.

Six Cruithnians—so God ordained—
Came out of the country of Thragia.
Solen, Ulpa, Neachtain the heroic,
Aengus, Leithceun, and Tiostan

Ro cһιolaιc Ὄια ὄοιb, cṗe τluṗ,
ὄια n-ὄιl ιṗ ὄια n-ὄuτuṗuṗ,
ὄια n-ὄιn aṗ nṫmιb a n-αṗm
na n-αιτhecһ n-ṫιτιᵹ n-aᵹaṗb.

God vouchsafed unto them, in muni-
ficence,
For their faithfulness—for their reward—
To protect them from the poisoned arms
Of the repulsive horrid giants.

Iṗ e eoluṗ ὄo ṗuaιṗ ὄοιb
ὄṗαι na Cṗuιτhnecһ ṗο ceὄoιṗ
τṗι l. bo mael ὄon muιᵹ
ὄo blaeᵹan ὄo a n-aen ċuιτιᵹ.

The discovery which was made for
them
By the Cruithnian Druid was this,
Thrice fifty cows of the plains
To be milked by him into one pit.

Ro cuιṗeaὄ ιn caτ co caτ
mon cuιτιᵹ a m-baι ιn lemnaċτ
Ro maιὄ ιn caċ co calma
Ṗoṗ αταcαιb aṗὄ ὄanba   a.

The battle was closely fought
Near the pit in which was the milk,
The battle was bravely won
Against the giants of noble Banba

Iṗ ι n-αιmṗιṗ h-Eṗeamon ṗo ᵹοbuṗ-
ταιṗ Ᵹuba ꞇ a mac .ι. Cατһluan mac
Ᵹuba ι. ṗι Cṗuιτhneacһ neaṗτ moṗ
    ṗοṗ

It was in Eremon's time that Guba
and his son, viz., Cathluan mac Guba,
King of the Cruithnians, acquired great
    power

ꝓoꝛ Eꝑino. Ho co ꝓuꝛ inꝺaꝛɓ Eꝛ-
ꝼmon a h-Eꝑino ꞁ co n-ꝺeaꝑnꝼaꝺ ꝛio
iaꝓꝛiu

Ho iꝛ o macaiɓ Mileaꝺ ꝼꝼn ꝺo chuaiꝺ
Cꝛuithneachan mac Inꝡi la Ƀꝛeatnu
Ƒoiꝛtꝛeano ꝺo chathuꝡaꝺ ꝛe Saxanchu,
ꞁ ꝓoꝛellaꝺ a clann ꞁ a claiꝺeam-thiꝑ
ꝺoiɓ .i. Cꝛuitheantuath iꝛeaꝺ ni ꝑo ba-
ꝺaꝑ [mna] accu aꝑ aꝺɓath banꝺꝛꝓocht
Alɓan ꝺo ꝡallꝓoiɓ. Ꝺo luiꝺ ꝺno, aꝑ
u cul ꝺo chum meic Mileaꝺ ꞁ ꝑo ꝡaɓaꝺ
nꝼm ꞁ talam ꝡꝑian ꞁ eꝛca, muiꝑ ꞁ tiꝑ
ɓeith ꝺo maith ꝑiu ꝓlaith ꝼoꝓꝑo co
ɓꝛath, ꞁ aꝺɓeꝓt ꝺí mnai ꝺec ꝼoꝛcꝛaiꝺ
ꝺo ɓaꝺaꝑ la taꝛcaꝑ Mac Mileaꝺ i n-
Eꝑinn, uaiꝑ ꝑo ɓaitea a ꝼiꝑ iꝛa n-aiꝓꝛꝡi
t-ꝛiaꝑ maꝛaen ꝛe Ꝺonn; conaꝺ o ꝼꝼꝛaiɓ
Eꝛꝼnn ꝓlaith ꝼoꝑ Cꝛuithentuaith ꝺo
ꝡꝛeꝼ iaꝑ ꝼoiꝑino. Mna Ƀꝛꝼꝛi, imoꝑꝓo,
ꞁ Ƀuaiꝺne ꞁ Ƀuaiꝛi ꞁ na taiꝑꝼc ꝑo ɓaitea
uile. Ocuꝛ anaiꝑ ꝛꝼꝑꝼ ꝺiɓ oꝛ Ƀꝛꝼꝡ muiꝡ,
ꞁ iꝛ uaithiɓ cach ꝡꝼꝛ ꞁ cach ꝛꝼn ꞁ cach
ꝛꝑꝼ ꞁ ꝡota ꝼn ꞁ cach mana ꞁ cach oɓaiꝑ
ꝺo ꝡnitheaꝑ

Cathluan iꝛ e ɓa ꝑiꝡ oꝑꝑtha uile ꞁ iꝛ e
cꝼt ꝑiꝡ ꝑo ꝡoɓ Alɓam ꝺiɓ. Lxx ꝑiꝡ
ꝼoꝑ

---

power in Eri; until Eremon banished
them out of Eri, after which they made
peace.

Or, it was[m] the sons of Mileadh themselves that sent Cruithneachan mac Inge
to assist the Britons of Foirtrenn to war
against the Saxons , and they (*the Cruithneans*) made their children and their
swordland, i e. Cruithean-Tuaith, subject to them. And they had not wives,
because all the women of Alban died of
diseases They, therefore, came back to
the sons of Mileadh, who bound them, as
they expected the heaven and earth, the sun
and the moon, the sea and the land, to
be propitious to them, that they would
submit to them as kings over them for
ever And they took twelve supernu-
merary women, who belonged to the Milesian expedition to Eri, whose husbands
were drowned in the western sea along
with Donn. And hence sovereignty over
Cruithentuath belongeth to the men of
Eri, according to some *authorities*. And
they were the wives of Breas, and of Buaidne,
and of Buas, and of the *other* leaders, who
were all drowned And six of them remained in possession of Breagh-Mhagh ;
and from them are derived every spell and
every charm, and every *divination by* sneezing, and *by* the voices of birds; and all
omens, and all talismans[n] that are made

Cathluan was then king of them all,
and he was the first king of them that
reigned

---

[m] *Or, it was*—Here the writer gives another
account, from some other authority.

[n] *Talismans*—For oɓaiꝑ read uꝓaiꝺ. See
p 125, *supra*, and note ᵗ, p 144

ꝼoꞃ Cllbaın ᴅıb o Chaꞇluaın ꞇo Conꞃanꞇın, ıꞃ e Cꞃuıꞇhnech ᴅeıꞃꞁınach ꝼoꞃ ꞁob ᴅıb.

reigned over Alba. There were seventy kings of them over Alba, from Cathluan to Constantine, who was the last of them that reigned.

Ꝺa mac Caꞇluaın ı. Coꞇanoloꞇaꞃ ꞁ Caꞇalachac. Cl ᴅa cuꞃaıᴅ, ım. Pıꞃn ꞁ Cınꞁ aꞇhaıꞃ Cꞃuıꞇhnıch. Cl ᴅa ꞃꞃuıꞇh ı. Cꞃuꞃ ꞁ Cıꞃıc. Cl ᴅa mıleaᴅ .ı. Uaꞃnꞁm a ꝼılıꞁ ꞁ Cꞃuıꞇhne a cꞃꞃo Ꝺomnall mac Clılpın ıꞃe a ꞇaıꞃec

Cathluan's two sons were Cotanolotar and Catalachach. His two champions .. ... Pirn, and Cing the father of Cruithnich. His two wise men were Crus and Cuic. His two heroes ... Uasneam his poet, and Cruithne his worker in metals[o]. Donall mac Ailpin was their leader.

Ocuꞃ ıꞃeaᴅ aᴅbeꞃaıᴅ aꞃoıle cumaᴅ h-e Cꞃuıꞇhıne mac Loıch mıc Inꞁe ꝼꞃn ꞇıꞃaᴅ ᴅo chuınoꞁıᴅ ban ꝼoꞃ Eꞃemon ꞁ comaᴅ ᴅó ᴅo beꞃeaᴅ Eꞃemon mna na ꝼꞃꞃ ᴅo baıꞇea maılle ꞃe Ꝺonn.

And others say, that it was Cruithne mac Loich mac Inge himself, that came to ask the women from Eremon, and that it was to him Eremon gave the wives of the men who were drowned along with Donn.

II. In another part of the Book of Lecan (fol. 141, a, col. 1), the story of the wives given to the Cruithnians is repeated in a somewhat different form. This document mentions the name of the place where this remarkable treaty between the two nations was said to have been agreed on, and contains also a list of the seven Chruithnean kings of Ireland:

Ꝺa n-ocꞇ ᴅéc mıleaᴅ ᴅo ꞇhuaꞇhaıb Tꞃaıcıa ᴅo loꞇaꞃ aꞃ ceaᴅ loınꞁꞃe meıc Mıleaᴅ Eꞃꞃaıne ᴅo Ꞡꞃꞃmaın, ᴅoꞃ beꞃꞇaᴅaꞃ leo co m-baᴅaꞃ a mılıꞇachꞇ. Nı ꞇalꞇaꞇaꞃ mna leo ꞃꞇaꞇım, conaᴅ ᴅo ꞃıl meıc Mıleaᴅ aꞃꞃo ꝼaeꞇaꞃ mna ıaꞃꞃın. Ꝺo bꞃeıꞇh ınꞁꞃna oıꞁꞇhıꞁꞃꞃnna ᴅaaıb o ꝼlaıꞇhnıa Eꞃınᴅ, ꞁ aꞃꞃ n-ꞁlanaᴅ a claıᴅeam-ꞇıꞃ ᴅoıb allae ıꞇıꞃ ᴅꞃeaꞇnaıb .ı. Maꞁ ꝼoꞃꞇꞃꞃnn ꞃꞃımo, ꞁ Maꞁ Cıꞃꞁın ı. ꞃoꞃꞇea, conaᴅ ıaꞃ maꞇꞃa ꞁabaıꞇ ꝼlaıꞇh ꞁ cach comaꞃbuꞃ olcheana ıaꞃ na naꞃꞇaᴅ ꝼoꞃꞃu o ꝼeaꞃaıb Eꞃınᴅ .ı. ꞇꞃı

Twice eighteen soldiers of the tribes of Thracia went to the fleet of the sons of Mileadh of Spain, to Germany, and they took them away with them and kept them as soldiers. They had brought no wives with them at that time. And it was of the Milesian race they took wives afterwards. They received the daughters of chieftains from the sovereign-champion of Eri, and when they had cleared their sword-land yonder among the Britons, viz., Magh Fortrienn, primo, and Magh Cirgin, postea, so that it is in right of mothers they succeed to

---

[o] There is some confusion in this passage, as the reader will perceive by comparing it with p. 124. The scribe appears to have taken the proper name Iın for ımoꞃꞃo.

tpi chaeca ingean po ucpat a h-Epe to maithpib mac, inte Alt na n-ingín a cpich Dal n-Apaiti ipeat atlotap leo

to sovereignty and all other successions, to which they were bound by the men of Eri They took with them from Eri thrice fifty maidens, to become mothers of sons, whence Alt-na-n-Inghean[p], in the territory of Dal Araidhe, from which *place* they departed with them.

Tpicha piẓ to Chpuithnib pon Epint ⁊ Alban i to Chpuithnib Alban ⁊ to Chpuithnib Epenn .i, to Dail Apaiti. Ota tin, Ollumain tia ta mup n-ollaman i teamaip conẓe Fiacna mac Daetain; po naipe pite ẓiallu Epenn ⁊ Alban.

There were thirty kings of the Cruthnians over Eri and Alba, viz , of the Cruithnians of Alba and of the Cruithnians of Eri, i e. of the Dal Araidhe They were from Ollamhan, from whom comes *the name of* Mur Ollamhan at Teamhair, to Fiachna mac Beadain, who fettered the hostages of Eri and Alba

Sect piẓ tin to Chpuithnib Alban po pallnuptaip Epinn i teamaip, Ollam ainm in chetna piẓ po ẓob Epint a Teamaip ⁊ a Cpuachnaib, tpica bliatan ant Ip te ata Mup n-Ollaman i Teamaip, ip leip cetna tepnat peip Teampach.

There were seven kings of the Cruithmans of Alba that governed Eri in Teamhair Ollamh *was* the name of the first king that governed Eri at Teamhair, and in Cruachan, thirty years were his annals[q]. It is from him Mur Ollamhan at Teamhair is *named* by him was the feast of Teamhair first instituted.

Ailill Ollpintacta tape ip in Ollaman a piẓ pop Epinn uili a Teamaip tpica ant. Ip ina plaith pite peapaip inpneachta pina co n-temetha pep ipin ẓaimpiuth.

Aillill Ollfhindachta *came* after Ollamh in sovereignty over all Eri at Teamhair, *for* thirty years It was in his reign the wine snow fell which covered the grass in winter

Fintoll Cipipne taipeip in Aililla tpica annip a Teamaip ⁊ i ceant [*read* ceanantup]. Nach n-aẓ po ẓenaip ina plaithpite

Findoll Cisirne succeeded Aihll thirty years at Teamhar and at Ceanannus [Kells]. Every cow that was calved in his

---

[p] *Alt-na-n-inghean* —This place is not now known The name signifies "height or mount of the maidens" It will be observed, that this version of the story represents the women who were given as maidens, not widows See Reeves's

Eccl Antiq of Down and Connor, p 337
[q] *His annals* that is, the length of his reign This was the celebrated Ollamh Fodhla. See Petrie on Tara, p 29, *et seq* , Keating, p 329, (Halliday's edit), O'Flaherty, Ogyg.

flaithside ro bo chfinnda, isde ita Ceanannus ina lochte

his reign was white-headed and it is from him that the name of Ceanannus *is given* to his places *of residence*

Geide Ollgothach ina diaid side i Teamair ⁊ for Fain-laibe a tirib Mugdorna, ro follnustair tricha ano Is na flaith side ba binnithir la cach a laile amail bid chroit ar meit in cain-chompaic bai ina flaith

Geide Ollgothach after him at Teamhair, and over Fain-Laibe, in the country of Mughdorn [Mourne], he ruled for thirty years. In his reign the voices of all sounded as the music of the harp to each other, so great was the peace in his reign

Slanoll tareisi n-Geiti is ina flaith side ni raibe galar for duine i n-Eire, ro follnustair a Teamair ⁊ slan for Eire tricha ann

Slanoll after Geide. In his reign no person in Eri was diseased. He governed at Teamhair and health was over Eri thirty years.

Bagag Ollfiacha tareis Slanuill, ro follnustair for Eiri a Teamair tricha ann, is ina flaith side tindscanta coicti in Eire

Bagag Ollfhiacha after Slanoll He governed Eri at Teamhair thirty years. It was in his reign that wars were first begun in Eri

Bearngal tareis in Bagaig, ro follnustair for Eiri a Teamair tricha ano is ina flaith side ar rochuir ith a h-Eiri act miach ar mead in choicthe in Eire ⁊ ara lin.

Bearngal after Bagag He governed Eri at Teamhair thirty years It was in his reign that all the corn of Eri, except one sack, was destroyed, on account of the wars in Eri, and for their frequency

Ise sin tra nui uii rig ro gabsat Erinn do Chruithnib Alban

These, then, are the seven kings that ruled over Eri of the Cruithnians of Alba

Do Chruithnib Erein din, di Dal Araidi .i. na seact Laigsi Laigen ⁊ uii Sogain, ⁊ cac C[on]ailli fil i nErinn.

Of the Cruithnians of Eri, i e of Dal Araidhe[r], are the seven Laighsi[s] [Leix] of Leinster, and the seven Soghains and all the Cailli[t] that are in Eri

III The following brief account of the battle of Ardleamhnachta is taken from the

[r] *Dal-Araidhe.* These were Cruithnigh by the mother's side only See Ogygia, part III c xviii.

[s] *The seven Laighsi,* i e. the seven septs of Leix According to the tradition in the country these, after the establishment of surnames, were the O'Mores, O Kellys, O'Lalors, O'Devoys or Deevys, Macavoys, O'Dorans, and O'Dowlings, who are still numerous in the Queen's County

[t] *Cailli* This is a mistake for Conailli, as appears from Duald Mac Firbis's copy of the genealogy of Dal Araidhe, in which it is stated

luzoach abbaτιρρα Cille Oaρa oe hiбeρηια eχιlaτ pρo χρo ao Бριταηιαm, ρ̊. ħ
anno aoueηιτυρ τυι [*read* ρυι] immolauιτ Νeϲτοηιυρ anno uno Αρυρηιɀe Oeo ⁊
ρanϲταe Бριɀτe pρeϲeητe [*sic*] Oaρluɀoach, que ϲanταυιτ all. ρυρeη ιρταm

   Oρeρτ Бυρτhιmoτ χχχ. a. ρ

   Ɀalaηαριlιϲh χυ a. ρ

   Ouoρeρτᶻ .ι. Oρeρτ ϝιl Ɀιριοη ⁊ Oρeρτ ϝιη Бυoρορ χυ. aηηιρ ρeɀηαūūτ Oρeρτ ϝιη Ɀιριοη ρolυρ .υ. a. ρ.

   Ɀaρτηαιτᵃ ϝιη Ɀιριοη υιιι a. ρ

   Caιlτ uρηι ϝιη Ɀιριοιη uno anno ρeɀηαυιτ

   Ϲαlοηɀ ϝ. Μuρτοloιϲ χι. a ρ

   Oρeρτ ϝ. Μuηαιϲh uno a. ρ

   Ɀαlam ϲ{n}ηαleph .ιιιι a. ρ   Cum Бριoιιιo ι°. anno ρſɀηαυιτ.

Бρυιoe mac Μelϲοη χχχ a ρ In οϲταυο anno ρſɀηι eιυρ Бαρτιɀατυρ eρτ α ρanϲτο Columбa.

   Ɀaρτηαιτ ϝ. Oomſϲh χι α ρ

   Νeϲταη ηſp̄ō Ueρб χχ α ρ

   Cιηιαϲh ρ Cuτριη .χιχ α ρ

   Ɀaρτηαιτ mac Uuιo ιι α ρ

   Ϲαlοηϲ ϝρατeη eoρυm ouooeϲιm α ρ

   Ϲαlοηϲαη ϝ Θηϝρſϲh ιιιι α ρeɀ

   Ɀaρτηαιτ ϝ. Oonuel uι α ρ ⁊ oſmeoιum anηι

   Oρυρτ ϝρατeη eιuρ υιι. anηιρ ρ

   Бρυιoe ϝ. Ϝιle χχι α ρ

   Ϲαραη ϝ Θηϝιoαιɀ ιιιι α ρ

   Oρeι ϝ Oeρeleι χι. α

   Νeϲhταη ϝ Oeριleι χ α ρ

   Oρeρτ ⁊ Θlριη ϲοηρſɀηαūūτ υ α

   Onuιρ ϝ. Uρɀuιρτ .χχχ ρ.

Бρeτe

ʸ These contractions probably stand for "secundo autem" See above, p 163, and note

ᶻ The reading here given strongly confirms the
conjectural emendation of the passage suggested
note ᵉ, p 162 The word ϝιη is an evident
mistake of the transcriber for ϝιl. or *filius*,
arising from his not understanding the contraction
ϝῑ, which he has himself sometimes retained

It appears also that the contraction ūτūτ, p 162,
which I there supposed to be intended for "communiter," is really a corruption of the termination *verunt*, of the word "regnaverunt"

ᵃ Here one of the kings, viz, Galum-cenamlapeh, is omitted, but he is placed after Drest,
son of Manaith, as in the Chron Pictorum See
p 163, note ᶠ

Brete fi Uurgut .xu. a. r.
Oimod f. Uurſbeg .xii. a. r.
Elpin f. Uuroid .ui. a. ⁊ dimſdio regni[b]
Drest f. Talorcan i°. a. r.
Talorgſn f. Druistſn .iiii. uel .u. a. r.
Talorcſn f. Omuist .xii. ⁊ dimſdio a. r.
Canaul f. Tan̄g .u. a r.
Caustantin f. Uurguist .xxx. u. a. r.
Uionuist f. Uurguist .xii. a. r.
Drest f. Constantin ⁊ Talorc f. Uuthoil .iii. a conregnaūunt.
Unſn f. Unuist .iii. a. r.
Uurad f Bargoit .iii. a. r. ⁊ Bred i°. a. r.
Cinaed f. Alpin .xui. a. r.
Domnall f Alpin .iiii. a. r. ⁊ Custantin f. Cinaeda .xx. a. r.
Aed f. Cinaeda .ii. a. r.
Giric mac Dungaile .xi. uel .iii. a. r.
Domnull f. Constantin .xi. a r.
Custantin f. Aeda .xl. a. r.
Maelcolaim f. Domnaill .ix. a. r.
Culſn f. Ildoilb f. Constantin iii. a. r.
Cinaed [uel Dub][c] f. Maelcolaim .uiii. a. r.
Culſn f. Ildoilb .iiii. a. r.
Cinaed f. Cot. .xx iiii. a. r.
Custantin f. Culeain i°. ⁊ dimſdio a. r.
Cinaed f. Duib .uiii. a. r.
Maelcoluim f. Cinaeda xxx. a. r
Donnchad hua Mailcolaim .ui. a. r.
Mac Bſthad mac Fin mic Laig xui a. r.
Lulach .u mis.
Maelcoluim mac Donnchatha iarsin.

As the foregoing list of kings is so nearly the same as that printed above, pp. 158–167, it has not been thought necessary to add a translation. It ends fol 87, *a*, *b*, and occupies two columns of the manuscript, which evidently contained a complete copy

[b] Read anni. It is curious that the same error is committed in the MS. from which the text is printed, see p. 164.

[c] The words "*uel Dub*" are written over the line by a later hand

copy of the Irish version of Nennius, although only a single page now remains   It is followed, as in the text (see p 168, *suprà*), by an abridged translation, in Irish, of the beginning of Bede's Church History

V   To the foregoing documents, which may be regarded as the principal *sources* of the history, may be added the narrative of Keating, which was compiled from them, but this is so accessible to students of Irish history, that it will not be necessary to reprint it here —(*T.*)

No. XIX   *See page 153.*

The vigorous Mac Brethach —The number of fifty kings demonstrates that Macbethach, i e, Macbeth, is the name here signified, the letter *r* having crept in by an error of transcription.   Macbeth Mac Finleg succeeded Donnchadh Mac Crinan in the united sovereignty of Fortren Mor and Dalriada   His contemporary and subject, the author of the Duan, calls him Macbeatha Mac Finlaoich, vv 102, 103   In the Nomina Regum Pictorum, Innes ii p. 803, Chron Regum Scotiæ, ib p 791, and Register of Loch Levin, his father is respectively called Finleg, Findleg, and Finlach The catalogue in Cambrensis Eversus writes Finlaigh   That which is given above, p 166, and p. lxxvii, absurdly says, Macbeathad, son of Fin, grandson of Laig!   This is the ancient Irish name of Finloga, borne by the fathers of Finnian of Clonard and Brendan of Clonfert, and it is the modern Scotch name Finlay   John of Fordun (with an ignorance, or contempt of truth, of which the former would be surprising) makes it the woman's name, Finele, of which hereafter.   Hector Boece, his right worthy follower (246 b 249 b), has changed her into a man, Synele, yet retains the locality of that famous woman in Angus, and he furnished the history to Holinshed and Shakspeare,

" By Sinel's death, I know, I am Thane of Glamis "

Among those hereditary lords of provinces, who were called in North Britain maormors or mormaers, and whom the Irish writers often called righ or ri, was a certain Rudri or Ruaidhre.   He had two sons, Malbrigid and Finleg.   The latter, whom Ulster Annals describe simply as being a " ri Alban," was, according to Tighernach, " the mormaer of the sons of Croeb;" but I cannot find it stated what territory that clan possessed; and he was, in 1020, "slain by the sons of his brother Malbrigid "   In 1029, one of his nephews and destroyers, Maelcolaim Mac Maelbrigdi Mac Ruadri, called by Tighernach a ' ri Alban," died   And, in 1032, another nephew, " Gilla-Comgan mac Maelbrigdi, Mormaer Murebe (of Moray or Murray), was burnt, and fifty others with him "   In 1040, Mac beth Mac Finleg MacRuadri became ardrigh of Albany, and was slain in the last days of 1056   In 1057, Lulach, son of Gilcomgan,

was

was reigning, and died ardrigh of Albany. And, in 1085, Maelsnectai, son of Lulach, and ri Muireb, died feliciter or in peace. Such, I believe, is the amount of the extant notices of the house of Ruadhri.

Finnleikr Jarl the Scot is mentioned at the close of the tenth age, as contending against Sigurd Hlodverson, Earl of Orkney (who afterwards fell in the battle of Clontarf), with superior forces but inferior fortune, in a battle fought at the Skidamyri[d] in Caithness. Olaf's Tryggvasonar Saga, i. p. 199. 1825. The same page mentions a previous victory gained in Caithness by Liot, Sigurd's uncle, over Margbiodr, another Scozkan jarl, or Scottish maormor. Macbeth Mac Finleg was too young for the tale to be *true* of him; yet I think it exhibits a Norse[e] corruption of some of the spellings of his name. The celebrity of Finleg's name among the Northmen may be argued from the fabulous romance entitled Samson Fagra's Saga, where Finlaugr figures as a Jarl of Brettaland, Britain. See that Saga, e. v. p. 6, c. vii. p. 10, in Biorner's Nordiska Kampa Dater. We know that Moray was hereditary in the house of Malbrigid; and I suspect the mic Croeb were seated in Crombath or Cromarty, or more generally in Ross. For in Macbeth's dream of the weird sisters, the first of the three salutations, descriptive of his natural and first estate, was, "Lo! yonder the Thane of Crwmbawehty!"—*Wyntown's Cron.* vi. cap. xviii. Crombath, as now limited, is the eastern angle and estuary of the extensive Land of Ross; in which territory it is, therefore, probable, that Finleg Mac Ruadri had his estates or dominions.

I think that his brother, Malbrigid (whose death is unchronicled, but seems to have occurred anterior to 1020), was probably that jarl of the Scots, Melbrigda Tönn, or Malbrigid of the Long Tooth, treacherously slain at a parley by Sigurd, the Norwegian Earl of Orkney, who had overrun Caithness, Sutherland, and Ross, and even built a fort in the Australis Moravia.—Olaf. Trygg. cap. xcv. p. 194; Torf. Orc. i. cap. iv. But this story is told of Sigurd, son of Eystein; whereas the date of Malbrigid, as well as the magnitude of this Sigurd's encroachments upon Scotland, would rather require it to be understood of Sigurd Hlodverson. We collect elsewhere who that Maormor was whom Sigurd Eysteinson had put to death; it was Malduin (Meldunus comes e Scotiâ) father of Erp, and husband to Mirgiol, daughter of Gliomal, an Irish rex.—Torf. Orc. i. cap. v. p. 16.

Macbeth

[d] Marsh of Skida.

[e] Torfæus had somewhere found it written Magbragda, which comes nearer to Mac, in the first syllable, while the residue is borrowed from Melbrigda. And he represents the defeat of this maormor as occurring at the same Skidamyri.—Orcades, c. ix. p. 25.

Macbeth Mac Finleg was certainly married to the lady Gruoch, daughter of Bodhe or Boidhe.—Chartulary of Dunfermlin cit Pink ii p 197; Reg of St. And cit. Chalmers Cal i 397, n ; " Dame Grwok," Wynt vi. p 18, 35. That Bodhe is supposed to have been son to Kenneth III [f] or IV whom Malcolm II slew and succeeded in 1003 Ulster Annals, at 1033, say, Mac mic ꝺoeƈhe mic Cineaꝺa ꝺo mapbaꝺ la Maelcolaim Mac Cinaeꝺa The son of the son of Boethe, son of Kenneth, was slain by Malcolm, son of Kenneth —Dublin MS This unnamed man, grandson of Boethe, nephew of Gruoch, and great grandson of Kenneth IV, was slain in 1033, but nothing is known of his grandfather's fate The violent death of Gilcomgan and his friends, in 1032 (and perhaps the death of his brother Malcolm, in 1029), was, probably, the penalty of Finleg's blood, which the young Macbeth would naturally desire, and, I think, did not want the power, to revenge. That Gruoch was his widow may be conjectured on the following ground Gilcomgan was maormor or ri of Moray and that province descended peaceably, through his son Lulach, to his posterity Yet her husband Macbeth, Maormor of Cromarty, was reputed to have somehow acquired the government of Moray, inasmuch as the second of the " werd systrys," saluted him as the *future*[g] thane of Morave —Wyntown, tom i p 216 The intimate connexion between Lulach and Macbeth will appear presently

The claims of Finleg's son to the united crowns of Dunstaffnage and Scone remain unknown and unexplained Donnchadh, daughter's son and successor to Malcolm II. and son to Criman Abbot of Dunkeld and Abthane[h] of Dull, was, as the Annalists write, a suis occisus, or, as the Nomina Regum say, was slain by Macbeth at Bethgowanan (Lochgosnane ap Fordun) near Elgin or, according to the Elgiac Chronicle,

> " A Finleg natus percussit eum Macabeta,
> Vulnere lethali rex apud Elgin obit "

However Marianus, who was about twelve years old when it happened, acquits Macbeth

[f] Kenneth Grim Mac Duff, cousin-german to Malcolm II

[g] In that legend, the existing and apparent fact is elegantly distinguished from the second sight, or vision of things future I Lo! yonder *the* thane of Crwmbawehty! II Of Morave yonder *I see* the thane III *I see* the king By what lying folly Angus or Glammis was, in later times, substituted for Cromarty, will appear in season Calder or Cawdor, now situate in Nairn and Inverness, was in ancient Moray , and that modern salutation is equivalent to the ancient, describing the Moravian Mormaer by one of his principal fastnesses, as the Angusian is described by that of Glammis See Rhind's Sketches of Moray, p 1 The modern division into counties is of no use for those times

[h] For the Abthanate of Dull, see Macpherson's notes to Wyntown, and the authorities there cited

beth of direct agency in that bloodshed, saying: " 1040, Donchad king of Scotia is slain a duce suo Mag-Finloech succeeded to his kingdom." For here the *dux* and the successor seem distinct persons. Duncan had succeeded Malcolm in 1033, and therefore, when the blood of the Lady Gruoch's nephew was still fresh; but nothing, unless it be his perishing by her husband's means, points to him as guilty of it. But if we may credit an ancient tradition (not to surmise any lost compositions in prose or verse) which flows through channels rather friendly than neutral, and comes to us conjoined with virulent abuse of his destroyer, the son of Crinan had provoked his fate by vicious and impolitic behaviour. For Wyntown tells us, that he made the miller's daughter[1] of Forteviot " his lemman luwyd," and begat on her a bastard son who afterwards reigned as Malcolm Ceannmor After Duncan's death (so the story runs) she married a boatman or *batward*, whose piece of land was transmitted to their posterity, and called the Batwardis land. Wyntown proceeds to boast that the Empress Maud, many kings of England and Scotland, and Pope Clement II., were descended from the miller of Forteviot He certainly knew nothing of what his contemporary, John of Fordun, had written, or was just about to write, that Duncan's[k] wife, " consanguinea Sywardi comitis," bore him Malcolm and Donald. iv. c. 44 The early writers assign no sort of domestic or personal motives for Earl Siward's march into Scotland, which was simply made jussu Eadwardi regis Simeon Dunelm in 1054 Duncan proceeded to load this girl with honour and dignity,

> " This woman he would have put til hycht,
> Til great state, and til mekyl mycht ,"

but that bad policy was put down by the revolt of the son of Finleg,

> " But Macbeth-Fynlak, his syster sowne,
> That purpose letted til be downe,"

and the crown was transferred to his head, on the death of Duncan at Elgin —cap. xiv p 206 These events happened in 1039 or 1040 Macbeth then reigned for seventeen years in prosperity and affluence,

> " Rex Macabeta decem Scotiæ septemque fit annis,
> In cujus regno fertile tempus eiat "— *Chron Eleg*

I think

[1] Perhaps the fame of it reached the northern kingdoms For the Samson Saga mentions, that Finlog, the Jarl of Brettaland, had among his subjects a miller Galin, and a giantess living under the mill stream, by whom, and by their son, all the distresses of that wild romance are brought about The miller and giantess are destroyed, but the wicked son survives Farther than as above, the matters are totally irrelevant

[k] He does not say " wife," but it is sufficiently implied Boece and Buchanan improve consanguinea into filia

I think the death of Malcolm II, leaving only grandchildren through his daughters, produced a disputed succession ab initio Simeon of Durham was perhaps born about the time of Macbeth's death, since he died about seventy-two years later He lived near the Scottish border at the time Duncan's sons were reigning, and ignorance on his part is hard to suppose Yet he takes no notice of any King Duncan, and says, "anno 1034, Malcolm rex Scotorum obiit, cui Machetad successit."—Sim in anno in Twisden This is the more remarkable, because Marian, of whose work Simeon made use, had said, "1033–34, Masleoluim, king of Scotia, died, Donchad, son of his daughter, succeeded him for five years" Simeon must have held with some persons who counted Duncan as an intrusive pretender; and implies that Finleg's son asserted his rights during the whole time This becomes clearer at the accession of Malcolm III, whom Simeon describes as "son of the king of Cumberland," thus owning that Duncan had been appointed tanist under his maternal grandfather, and entitling him accordingly, but denying that he had ever been king of Scots. Sim Dunelm et Florent. Wigorn in 1054 It is recorded by the Northmen that, at this same epoch of the second Malcolm's death, one Karl Hundason "took the kingdom[l] of Scotland," that is to say, assumed the style of ardrigh, and they appeal to[m] the contemporary and undeniable authority of the Orkney bard, Arnor Jarlaskald, of whose poems the authenticity will hardly be questioned He appeared as king of Scots in Caithness, supported by the forces of an Irishman acting in Caithness, named Moddan of Duncansby, and called[n] brother (in the sense, I suppose, of brother-in-law) to the king of the Scots, whom Karl appointed to be his general, and, on Thorfinn's refusal of tribute, to be Jarl of Katanes. He appears to be described as cousin-german of Karl. But in various actions Moddan was defeated, and slain, by Thorfinn Sigurdson (daughter's son to Malcolm II), and by his tutor, Thorkell-Fostri; and Karl, equally unsuccessful in his own subsequent efforts, disappeared from those parts, and his fate was never ascertained —Orkneyinga Saga, p 31. Karl's forces, besides those from Ireland, were raised both in East and West Scotland, and especially in Cantire[o]. He was son to Hundi, i.e. Canis, otherwise Hvelpr, i e Catulus.

Sigurd,

---

[l] Tok tha riki i Skotlandi Karl Hundason

[m] Pinkerton has the arrogance to say, " this fable needs only to be read to be rejected "—ii p 196

[n] Skotakonung's brodur —Nial's Saga, cap 86 Moddan is the same Irish name, as that of Modan of Kilmodan Abbey in Longford (doubtful whether saint or reprobate,—Lanigan ii 325–6), and that of a Scotch saint,

" Some to St Modan pay their vows,
Some to St Mary of the Lowes "
Lay of Last Minstrel, vi st. 27

[o] Called in the Norse tongue Satira See Orkn Saga, p 39, p 115

micum (before 1291) it is, absurdly, Lahoulan; MSS. of the Duan have Lulagh and Lugaidh[u] The Mac Gilcomgain of Ulster Annals is nepos filii Boidhe in Chron. Reg Scotorum. Perhaps it should be filiae Boidhe, as Gruoch was termed; and the nepos is ambiguous in the Latin of those days Whatever it means, the traditional filiation in Mac is of a greater weight than such a passage can have. But in that passage (howsoever we should correct either the copy or the author) we have Lulach's only title in blood, that I am aware of, to become tanist of the supreme crown, namely his descent, probably maternal, and through the lady Gruoch[v], from Boidhe, son of Kenneth Macduff. His reign was of four months (Nomina Regum), or of four and a half (Chron Reg. Scot., and the prose dates in Chron. Elegiacum); but in the elegy itself,

> " Mensibus infelix Lulach tribus extiterat rex

Nevertheless, the old Mr. O'Conor's copy of the Duan Albanach says expressly,

> " Seacht mbliadhna i bfhlaitheas Lulaigh,"
> " Seven years was the reign of Lulagh "—v. 104.

Another copy of that poem has seven months, seacht mis. He was overpowered and slain by Malcolm at a place called Essei in Strathbogie (Nom. Reg. Pict) in 1057. Though accounted daft or fatuus, headlong temerity was probably his defect, rather than supine imbecility His want of prudence was fatal to his cause, for Tighernach states that he was slain *per dolum*, and the Chron. Eleg. runs thus,

> " Armis ejusdem Malcolomi cecidit,
> Fata viri fuerant in Strathbolgin apud Esseg,
> Heu ! sic *incautè* rex miser occubuit "

He was buried along with Macbeth in Iona,

> " Hos in pace viros tenet insula Iona, sepultos
> In tumulo regum, Judicis usque diem "

And the consideration of his case is essential to the reign of Macbeth, the topic of this note

His reigning seven years can only be true, in case he was associated to the crown during the seven last years of Macbeth's reign, and died in or after the seventh year of his own kingship, but only in the fourth or fifth month of his own *separate* reign.

I would

---

[u] The latter malè, for it is a distinct name

[v] This lady left a sinister reputation. For not only does Boece charge her with instigating the usurpation he imputes to Macbeth, but Wyntown

lxxxii

I think the death of Malcolm II, leaving only grandchildren through his daughters, produced a disputed succession ab initio   Simeon of Durham was perhaps born about the time of Macbeth's death, since he died about seventy-two years later   He lived near the Scottish border at the time Duncan's sons were reigning, and ignorance on his part is hard to suppose   Yet he takes no notice of any King Duncan, and says, " anno 1034, Malcolm rex Scotorum obiit, cui Machetad successit."—Sim in anno in Twisden   This is the more remarkable, because Marian, of whose work Simeon made use, had said, " 1033-34, Masleoluim, king of Scotia, died, Donchad, son of his daughter, succeeded him for five years"   Simeon must have held with some persons who counted Duncan as an intrusive pretender; and implies that Finleg's son asserted his rights during the whole time   This becomes clearer at the accession of Malcolm III, whom Simeon describes as " son of the king of Cumberland," thus owning that Duncan had been appointed tanist under his maternal grandfather, and entitling him accordingly, but denying that he had ever been king of Scots.   Sim Dunelm et Florent. Wigorn in 1054   It is recorded by the Northmen that, at this same epoch of the second Malcolm's death, one Karl Hundason " took the kingdom[l] of Scotland," that is to say, assumed the style of ardrigh, and they appeal to[m] the contemporary and undeniable authority of the Orkney bard, Arnor Jarlaskald, of whose poems the authenticity will hardly be questioned   He appeared as king of Scots in Caithness, supported by the forces of an Irishman acting in Caithness, named Moddan of Duncansby, and called[n] brother (in the sense, I suppose, of brother-in-law) to the king of the Scots, whom Karl appointed to be his general, and, on Thorfinn's refusal of tribute, to be Jarl of Katanes.   He appears to be described as cousin-german of Karl.   But in various actions Moddan was defeated, and slain, by Thorfinn Sigurdson (daughter's son to Malcolm II), and by his tutor, Thorkell-Fostri; and Karl, equally unsuccessful in his own subsequent efforts, disappeared from those parts, and his fate was never ascertained.—Orkneyinga Saga, p 31.   Karl's forces, besides those from Ireland, were raised both in East and West Scotland, and especially in Cantire[o].   He was son to Hundi, i e. Canis, otherwise Hvelpr, i e Catulus.

Sigurd,

---

[l] Tok tha riki i Skotlandi Karl Hundason

[m] Pinkerton has the arrogance to say, " this fable needs only to be read to be rejected "—II p 196

[n] Skotakonung's brodur —Nial's Saga, cap 86 Moddan is the same Irish name, as that of Modan of Kilmodan Abbey in Longford (doubtful whether saint or reprobate,—Lanigan II 325-6), and that of a Scotch saint,

" Some to St Modan pay their vows,
Some to St Mary of the Lowes "
Lay of Last Minstrel, vi st. 27

[o] Called in the Norse tongue Satiria   See Orkn Saga, p 39, p 115

Sigurd, before marrying that king's daughter, had defeated the two Scottish jarls, Hundi and Melsnaddi or Melsnata[p] (Maelsnectai), not far from Duncansby, and slain the latter   See Nial's Saga, cc 86, 87   This Hundi should be Karl's father   Sigurd also himself had a son Hvelpr or Hundi, whom Olaf son of Tryggvi took to Norway as a hostage, and christened Hlodver.   These events happened from twelve to thirteen years after Finleg's death, and when Karl[q] was quite in his youth, for Arnor Jarlas-kald, Earl Thorfinn's bard, says of him and the war he carried on,

> " Ungr olli[r] thvi theingill,"
> " The youthful king was the cause thereof,"

Therefore Karl coincides with Macbeth in these points   in his probable age, in that he was a claimant of the crown on Malcolm's death, that he did not then succeed in his claims, and that he is not averred to have perished in the attempt   But he differs in the names, Karl Hundason being very different from Macbeth Mac Finleg.   The difference however is evanescent; for the Norse word Karl is no more of a Scoto-Pictish name, than Philadelphus or Soter were Coptic names.   And the Norse word Hundi was not any name at all, but a nick-name, being given (both to this Celt, and to Hlodver Sigurdson) in the alternative, Hvelpr edr Hundi, Hundi etha Hvelpr, anglicè, "either hound or puppy."   We chiefly, if not solely, meet with it for a name[s] in Orkney and Caithness, and perhaps it was adopted from the Gaelic appella-tion by which alone a king of Scots of the tenth century (a vile person, but whether so called on that account I do not say) is known to us, Culen or Catulus.   Vide Olaf. Trygg cap xcviii. tom. i. p. 202, ed 1825; et ap Snorio, cap. xi. p. 145, Torfæi Orc 1, cap x cap xiii. Considering the synchronism of Simeon Dunelmensis, that Malcolm II could scarcely have any claimant of his inheritance *named Karl*, otherwise than through his daughter, Sigurd's wife; that no idea of a Norse claim to the succession, through Sigurd, is anywhere hinted, and that the right and might of such a claim, had it been raised, would have been with Malcolm's grandson, the valiant Thorfinn Sigurdson, Earl of Orkney and Katanes, I am induced to the belief, that Macbeth in his youth was known in the northern jarldoms by the Teutonic appellation of Karl, *man*, and that his father, Finnleiki Jarl, who fled before Sigurd Hlodveison at the
Skidamyii,

---

[p] Mel is the regular equivalent of the Gaelic Maol or Mal

[q] Therefore I have rendered the ambiguous word systrson, applied to Moddan (Orkn p 30), by cousin-german, and not nephew

[r] Olli, in causâ fuit, from the verb velld, efficere, in causâ esse

[s] I mean standing by itself, for, added on to other names, we find Sigurd Hund and Thorer Hund in Norway

Skidamyri, was likewise the Hundi Jarl, *dog*, whom the same prince defeated, also in Caithness; the son's title standing in favourable antithesis to the father's   Finleg did not fall by northern hands, neither did this Hundi or Hvelpr, and' Maelsnectai, the name of this Hundi's colleague in the war, was a name used in the house of Ruadri

The most violent domestic occurrence of Macbeth's reign happened in 1045, namely, the bloody battle in which Crinan, father of the deceased Duncan, fell, prælium inter Albanenses invicem, in quo occisus est Crinan Abbas Dunceldensis et multi alii cum eo, i e. novies viginta heroes.—Tigh   It is written, that Macbet fihus Finlach gave lands to the Culdees, i e the Chapter, of Lochlevin.—Regr of Lochl But very few of his acts have been permitted to survive   In 1054, Siward, Earl of Northumberland, was sent into Scotland by the Confessor, and gained a battle over Macbeth, whom he put to flight, fugavit —Sim Dun. in anno. Chron. Sax. ibid., Flor Wig. ibid.   Two Norman nobles who had found refuge at his court in 1052, by name Osbern and Hugo, fought on Macbeth's side and were slain.—Roger Hoveden in anno   Ulster Annals describe it as a battle between the men of Albany and the Saxons, in which 3000 of the former and 1500 of the latter fell, and on the Saxon side a certain Albanian (to judge from his name) called Dolfinn, son of Finntur.—Ann. Ult. in 1054. By like order of King Edward, the Earl constituted Malcolm Ceannmor king —Sim et Flor ibid. It cannot be said what portion of the country he succeeded in conquering   But whatever Siward may have proclaimed after gaining the battle, the accession of Malcolm is universally dated more than two years later.   Siward died the next year, and Malcolm resumed the war in 1056. On the 5th of December 1056 (Fordun) Macbeth was slain in a battle fought against Malcolm, at Lumphannan in Aberdeenshire, and he was buried in the royal cemetery of Iona His fame has been both obscured and magnified through a mist of lies, partly fabricated in honour of the house of Stuart, but now immortalized and enshrined for ever.

After the battle of Lumphannan, Lulach Mac Gilcomgain, son to the burnt Maormor of Moray, first cousin once removed from Macbeth, and perhaps his stepson and ward, was proclaimed King at Scone by the opponents of Malcolm   In the Nomina Regum he is Lulach Fatuus; in Wyntown, vi. 19, Lulawch Fule; in the Chron. Regum Scotiæ, temp Willelm. filii David, simply Lulach, and in the Chron Rhythmicum

' It may be answered, that perhaps Macbeth did not claim from the Malcolms, but from the competing line of Indulf   If so, there would remain just the synchronism of Simeon, and whatever is conformable in the circumstances of Finleg.

micum (before 1291) it is, absurdly, Lahoulan; MSS. of the Duan have Lulagh and Lugaidh[u] The Mac Gilcomgain of Ulster Annals is nepos filii Boidhe in Chron. Reg. Scotorum. Perhaps it should be filiæ Boidhe, as Gruoch was termed; and the nepos is ambiguous in the Latin of those days Whatever it means, the traditional filiation in Mac is of a greater weight than such a passage can have. But in that passage (howsoever we should correct either the copy or the author) we have Lulach's only title in blood, that I am aware of, to become tanist of the supreme crown, namely his descent, probably maternal, and through the lady Gruoch[v], from Boidhe, son of Kenneth Macduff. His reign was of four months (Nomina Regum), or of four and a half (Chron Reg. Scot., and the prose dates in Chron. Elegiacum); but in the elegy itself,

> " Mensibus infelix Lulach tribus extiterat rex

Nevertheless, the old Mr. O'Conor's copy of the Duan Albanach says expressly,

> " Seacht mbhadhna i bfhlaitheas Lulaigh,"
> " Seven years was the reign of Lulagh "—v. 104.

Another copy of that poem has seven months, seacht mis. He was overpowered and slain by Malcolm at a place called Essei in Strathbogie (Nom. Reg. Pict) in 1057. Though accounted daft or fatuus, headlong temerity was probably his defect, rather than supine imbecility His want of prudence was fatal to his cause, for Tighernach states that he was slain *per dolum*, and the Chron. Eleg. runs thus,

> " Armis ejusdem Malcolomi cecidit,
> Fata viri fuerant in Strathbolgin apud Esseg,
> Heu ! sic *incautè* rex miser occubuit "

He was buried along with Macbeth in Iona,

> " Hos in pace viros tenet insula Iona, sepultos
> In tumulo regum, Judicis usque diem "

And the consideration of his case is essential to the reign of Macbeth, the topic of this note

His reigning seven years can only be true, in case he was associated to the crown during the seven last years of Macbeth's reign, and died in or after the seventh year of his own kingship, but only in the fourth or fifth month of his own *separate* reign.

I would

---

[u] The latter malè, for it is a distinct name

[v] This lady left a sinister reputation. For not only does Boece charge her with instigating the usurpation he imputes to Macbeth, but Wyntown

I would fling it aside as a clerical error, did I not meet with circumstances, indicating both that he so reigned, and for that number of years. Ulster Annals say, at 1058, " Lulach Mac Gilcomgain, arch-king of Albany, was slain in battle by Maelcolaim Mac Doncha," and Tighernach had said at the same year, " Lulach, king of Albany, was slain by Colum Mac Donchada, by stratagem." Then come other intervening events; after which, in the same year, " Macbeth Mac Finnlaich, arch-king of Albany, was slain in battle by Maelcholaim Mac Doncha;" and in Tighernach, " Macbetad Mac Finlai was slain by Maelcolaim Mac Donchada." These statements declare that, though one year killed both kings, Lulach died first. Now Tighernach O Brain died at Clon-macnois in A. D 1088 (Ann. Inisfal.), thirty-one years after Macbeth and Lulach. And he was not born later than about 1020, though perhaps earlier, for Marianus was born in 1028, and spoke[w] of him as " Tighernach senior meus' And, therefore, the latter is likely to have been Lulach's senior himself But Tighernach could scarce have been ignorant[x] that Macbeth had ruled the whole of Albany during seven-teen years of his own lifetime. Therefore when he represented Lulach (no matter if incorrectly) as dying king of Albany before Macbeth, who had been such for so many years, he did, in effect, declare that they had been kings together. He did, in effect, deny that Lulach was, in the common sense of it, Macbeth's successor; for had he been such, the very phrase, *Lulach, king of Albany*, previously unheard of, must have first reached the ears of Tighernach, together with the news of Macbeth's death Con-joint reigns occur among the Picts, num. 43, 48, 63, 73, and of the Scoto-Picts, Eochaidh and Grig reigned together for eleven years Such authors as Boece and Buchanan are not to be quoted as evidence *per se*, but their unexplained statement, that Macbeth reigned for ten years like the best of kings, and for seven years like the worst of tyrants, strangely coincides with the premises.—Boetius, xii fol. 246, b, Buchanan,

even imagined she was Duncan's widow, and mar-ried his slayer, who

> " Dame Grwok his emys wyf
> Tuk, and led with her his lyf

The truth may be, that she *was* privy to her husband's death and *did* marry with his destroyer, in 1032, when Gilcomgan was burned

[w] See O'Conor not in Ann Ult., p 327 If this were understood of some other Tighernach, the case would yet stand well For sixty-eight years was no long life for an ancient man of re-ligion, and celebrated for learning But if the historian died at fifty-five, he was twenty-four at the death of Macbeth

[x] It would be captious to reply, that this an-nalist has mistaken the year, putting 1058, for December, 1056, and April or May, 1057. For it is one thing to misdate slightly the occurrences of a foreign kingdom, and another to ignore a long and famous contemporary reign The priest may now live at Clonmacnois, who will say, that Louis Philippe acceded in 1831, for 1830, but not he that will say, that he acceded four months ago

Buchanan, vii 85 It divides his reign at the precise point of *seven years*, and changes
its temper, with no alleged reason, but in harmony with that of a Fatuus. We
read in a text of the contemporary Duan, that Lulach *did* reign seven years; we
collect from his other contemporary, Tighernach, that he *must* have reigned before the
death of Macbeth , and have found in historians the assertion, that Macbeth's last
seven years strangely differed from the prior ten. It remains to corroborate the latter
by the testimony of worthier authors   Marianus Scotus (born in 1028, as he states,
p. 450, ed. Pistorii, 1613, and twenty-nine years old when Macbeth died) says, at the
year 1050, Rex Scotiæ Machetad Romæ argentum seminando pauperibus distribuit
Simeon of Durham, who died about half a century later than Marian, at the same
year says the same, only putting the word *spargendo* for the words *seminando pauperibus.*
Lulach died in 1057, and 1050 is the year at which his Duan reign commenced, and
at which the historians date the change in Macbeth's administration   Marianus
neither avers that he took the money to Rome, nor that he sent it, but he couples
the ambiguous word distribuit with the gerund seminando, which graphically exhibits him casting his largesses among the crowd   Wyntown, a simple and faithful
writer, so understood the matter.

> " Quhen Leo the Tend [ninth] was Pape of Rome,
> As pylgryne to the curt he come,
> And in his almus he sew [seminavit] sylver
> Til all pure folk that had myster [need] "—vi. p 226

But he was again in Scotland before the end of the year 1052 —Hoveden in anno.
Certainly the fact of his pilgrimage to Rome (of which Canute the Great had set the
example some twenty years before) can only be denied by putting a harsh construction on the words of Marianus, or by rejecting his testimony, than which we cannot
look for better, as he had not emigrated to Germany in 1050   But that fact, if admitted, remarkably confirms the premises, for it shews him actually quitting for a
time, and therefore intrusting to another, the helm of government in the year in
question.   And, if he intrusted it to another, then to what other than him, who is
asserted to have come to the crown at that very date, and who is assumed to have
been king of Albany before Macbeth's death?   Likewise the reading of the Duan,
which confines him to months, gives *seven* months, a number quite different from all
the other accounts of his sole reign   It may therefore well be credited, that his
entire reign was seven years, and his sole reign of three or four months.   For the
authority of the Scottish documents in general leads us to suppose, in opposition to
the Irish annalists, that Lulach did survive Macbeth.

I am

I am not only at a loss for Macbeth's claim (hereditary or' tanastic) to the crown, but am unable to satisfy myself as to his appellation   I do not understand how the son of Finleg is called son of Beth; or how a filiation, even if true, could supply the place of a name in the ancient mode of nomenclature. Yet we read of his contemporary, Macbeathaidh M'Ainmirech and in the ninth century St. Macbethu and two other Irish pilgrims visited England —Sax Chron in 891   Probably it expresses the mother's name, and so resembles the use of Mac Erc, with this difference, that the great fame of Erca, the mother of kings, partly superseded Muirchertach's own name, but Macbeth had no other.   The name Beathaig is said, in Armstrong's Dictionary, to be Gaelic for Sophia, and the Gaelic Society's Dictionary says that Beathag means Rebecca. As wisdom is blessed, and Rebecca was blessed, this curious identity of dissimilar names resolves itself into the Latin *Beata*   We know not who Macbeth's mother was ; for Wyntown's tale, that she was Duncan's sister, and that of Boece, that she was Doada, Duncan's maternal aunt, have no firm basis in history   But the name Beathaig, or Beata in Latin, is the same with that of Bethoc (as the older Latin documents' term her), daughter to Malcolm II , wife to Crinan of Dunkeld, and mother of Duncan, the Beatrix of Fordun, Boece, and Buchanan   That is apparent from the Elegiacal Chronicles of Melrose, for I cannot understand them otherwise than by taking Bethoc to mean Beata

" Abbatis Crini, jam dicti filia régis,
　　Uxor erat Bethoc, *nomine digna sibi* "

The name is formed on the types, Beathaidh, Bethad, or Betad, and, by contemporary clerical error, Hetad , and Beathaigh, Bethach, or Betac, for the Bethu of the Saxon, though curious, cannot be relied on.   This oscitancy may be referred to its irregular and exotic origin   It is singular that the very same alternation shews itself in Daoda and Doaca, Macbeth's mother in Boece and in Buchanan; being, as it were, decapitations of Bethod and Bethoc.   Therefore I take Macbethach, Macbeathaidh, Micbeatha, Macbeth, Macbethu, &c , to mean Filius Beatæ, and suspect it to signify, in this particular instance, that Bethoc, daughter of Malcolm, gave birth to Finleg's son. either before or during her union with Crinan, or after some dissolution thereof. The legend that he was son to Duncan's sister, would make him a grandson of Bethoc, while Boece makes him her nephew.—Wynt vi 16, v. 47, Boetius, 246, b   But the

same

---

[y] Since the time of Kenneth III or IV , son of Malcolm, the two principles of succession had been conflicting, and the former gaining upon the latter, to the prejudice of both Indulf's line and the nearer line of Duff

[z] And as other women were called   See Chartul of Jedburg, ap. Pink ii 192

same fable of his birth supposes the incontinence[a] of his mother; for she sauntered into a wood, where she met

> " A fayr man
> Of bewtè plesand, and of hycht
> Proportiowned well in all mesoure, &c
> Thar in thar gamyn and thar play
> That persown by that woman lay,
> And on her that tyme to sowne gat
> This Makbeth."—vi 18, vv. 59-74

That lover, it is added, was the Devil himself; which accounts for Wyntown always calling him Makbeth-Fynlak, not son of Fynlak; but does not equally agree with his Latin quotation,

> " Of this matere are thire wers
> In Latyne wryttene to rehers
> A Fynlake natus percussit eum Macabeda "

But if we substitute Finleg for Satan, and Duncan's mother for his sister, Macbeatach in one word becomes Mac Beatach in two, and the whole affair receives elucidation.   The blood of Malcolm II. is as good in Macbeth as in his half brother Duncan, legitimacy excepted, and if it was proposed to make the bastard of the miller's daughter tanist of all Albany, that argument was abandoned

In A D. 994, Kenneth III. or IV. father of Malcolm II, grandfather of Bethoc and great-grandfather of Duncan, was a suis occisus, and per dolum —Tigh. and Ann. Ult   It is said, the lady Fincle or Fenella, daughter of Cruchne or Cruthneth, thane of Angus or Forfar, and mother to Cruthlint, chieftain of Mearns, instigated her son to murder her father, for which he was put to death by Kenneth   To revenge his death and to advance the rival interests of the families of Culen and Duff, she allured Kenneth into her house (probably Glammis castle) and there assassinated him   It

may

[a] Who, therefore, could *not* be " nomine digna " But it is very plain, that the Scoto-Saxon successors of Ceannmor, and their writers, delivered a different sort of history, both in statement and in suppression, from the previous traditions   Till Fordun had established the manufacture of Scotch history, both modes of thinking continued alive, and between them Wyntown's honest mind was bewildered, and so are our's In the Scoto-Saxon era, the history of the house of Ruadri in the lines of Finleg and Gilcomgan was obscured, partly by silence and partly by falsehood, and to us remains the amusement of conjecture, but we may as well judge the case of Warbeck by Tudor testimony, as that of Macbeth and Ceannmor by the language of the Duncanites of that era

may be supposed, from their names, that this family (otherwise unknown) were Picts[b] In 1033-4 a similar fate befell his son Malcolm II, who was treacherously slain at Glammis by the same Angusian family. See Fordun, iv 32, 41, 44, Boetius, 233, 234, 246; Buchanan, vi. pp 105, 110 John of Fordun, availing himself of that lady's name and of its resemblance to Finleg, has published this account of Duncan's death " He was slain by the crime of that family who had killed both his grandfather and his great-grandfather, of whom the chief was Machabeus, son of Finele[c] "—iv cap 44. By transforming Mac Finleg into Mac Finele, Son of Fenella, he sought to load Macbeth with odium as an hereditary murderer of kings And in this knavery of Fordun originated the whole notion of his being thane of Angus, or, as it is sometimes styled, thane of Glammis, a residence of the lords[d] of Angus, very near Forfar Boece, who could not stomach the fiction of Mac Finele, reverted to the traditions which made him the near connexion of Malcolm and Duncan, but disguised his paternal origin under the fictitious name of Synele, and, with Fordun, placed him in the thanedom of Angus In this manner the old, and probably true, traditions of Cromarty were upset Thane of Angus or Glammis merely signifies son of Fenella But Finleg, Malbrigid, and Macbeth were mormaers of the North, or country above the Grampians. See above, p lxxx, note [g].

However, without detracting from the infamy of these liars, I would offer this remark All parties seem agreed to regard Macbeth, considered as an aspirant to the crown, as *the son of a woman*, and to find in *her* blood, either his claim to the crown, or his hostility to it And if in fact it were not so, I do not clearly see how that idea should have established itself Though Finleg M'Ruadh, mormaer of Crombath and the Crocb, was a powerful toparch, nothing indicates him, and no one considered him, as contributing to the fulfilment of the third salutation —(*II*)

No XX

[b] These who record them having no such knowledge or intention But, on the other hand, the father is called Cunechat in the Nom Regum

[c] Mr Chalmers asserts (Caled 1 406), that Fordun calls him son of Finlegh, and that he mentions nothing of him or his father being maormor or thane of Angus It seems that he had not read Fordun, who never mentions Finlegh, but calls his mother filia Cruchne, *comitis de Angus*, cui nomen Finele —c. 32.

[d] Shakspeare, from topographical ignorance, has introduced (in Act v. scene 2) a thane of Angus bearing arms against the thane of Glammis

No XX   *See page* 153

The section " on the origin of the Cruithnians," occurs in the Book of Ballymote, immediately after the opening section, beginning, Є̄ʒo Ñenniur, which I have numbered sec I (see above, p 26) It is as follows

De bunaꝺ Cꞃuiꞇneach anꝺ ꞃeo

Cꞃuiꞇhne mac Cinʒe, mic Lucꞇai, mic Paꞃꞇalan, mic Aʒnoin, mic ꝺuain, mic Maiꞃ, mic Faꞇhecꞇ, mic Iaꝼeꞇh, mic Noe.

Iꞃe aꞇhaiꞃ Cꞃuiꞇneach ⁊ céꞇ bliaꝺan ꝺo iꞃꞃiʒe. Secꞇ meic Cꞃuiꞇhneaċ annꞃo .i Fib, Fiꝺach, Foꝺla, Foꞃꞇꞃenꝺ, Caꞇhach, Caiꞇce, Ciꞃiʒ, ⁊ ꞃecꞇ ꞃanꝺaib ꞃo ꞃoinꝺꞃeꞇ in ꝼeaꞃanꝺ, uꞇ ꝺixiꞇ Colum cilli

Moiꞃꝼeiꞃeꞃ ꝺo Cꞃuiꞇhne clainn,
Ꞃ ainꝺꞃeꞇ Albain i ꞃecꞇ ꞃ ainꝺ,
Caiꞇce, Ciꞃiʒ, Ceꞇhac clann,
Fib, Fiꝺac, Foꞇla, Foꞃꞇꞃeann.

Ocuꞃ iꞃ é ainm ʒac ꝼiꞃ ꝺib ꝼil ꝼoꞃ a ꝼeaꞃanꝺ, uꞇ eꞃꞇ Fib ⁊ Ce ⁊ Caiꞇ, ⁊ ꞃeliqua

Fib xxiiii. bliaꝺia iꞃꞃiʒe Fiꝺac xl. bliaꝺan. ꝺꞃuiꝺe Ponꞇ. Foꞃꞇꞃeanꝺ lxx. Foꞃꞇꞃeann .lxx. ꝺ. Uꞃꞃonꞇ Caiꞇ ꝺa bliaꝺan aꞃ.xx Uleo Ciꞃiʒ .lxxx. b ꝺ. Ʒanꞇ. Ce xii. bliaꝺan ꝺ. Uleo Aenbeccan, iꝬ. ꝺ. Uꞃʒanꞇ. Caiꞇ xxx bliaꝺan

Of the origin of the Cruithnians here

Cruithne, son of Cing, son of Luchta, son of Partholan, son of Buan, son of Mas, son of Fathecht, son of Japheth, son of Noe[e]

He was the father of the Cruithnians, and reigned an hundred years. These are the seven sons of Cruithne, viz . Fib, Fidach, Fodla, Fortrenn, Cathach, Caitce, Cirig, and they divided the land into seven divisions, ut dixit Colum-cille

Seven of the children of Cruithne
Divided Alba into seven portions,
Caitce, Cirig, Cetach of children[f],
Fib, Fidach, Fotla, Fortreann.

And it is a name of each man of them that is *given* to their *respective* portions, ut est, Fib, and Ce, and Cait, et reliqua.

Fib reigned xxiv. years.   Fidach xl. years   Bruide Pont.   Fortreann lxx. Fortreann lxx.   B. Urpont   Cait two years and xx.   Uleo   Cirig lxxx years   B Gant   Ce xii. years   B Uleo Aenbeccan, iꝬ[s]   B Urpont. Cait xxx years   B Gnith.

---

[e] See above, p 51, where the genealogy of Cruithne is somewhat differently given

[f] See above, p 155, note [t]

[s] *Aenbeccan* iꝬ.—The scribe appears to have taken the numeral denoting the year of the reign, for iꝬ the usual contraction for imoꞃꞃo In the

bliaoan ō Ᵹníɥ. Fineɥɥa .lx. bliaoan   B. Gnith. Fineɥta lx. years. B. Urgnith.
ō. Upᵹniɥh Ᵹuioiō. Ᵹaōbpe ō Feɥh .i.   Guididh. Gadbre. B. Feth i. Geis i. year.
Ᵹeiꝛ i b. ō Uꝛꝼeiciꝛ Ᵹeꝛɥᵹnuio .xl.   B. Urfeichir. Gestgruid xl B. Cab.
xl. ō Cab

The remainder of the list is so corrupt that it would be useless to attempt a translation. It is thus given in the manuscript:

Uꝛᵹeꝛ .xxx. b.   ō Uꝛcal.   ōꝛuioe Ponɥ xxx. b.   Cníɥ ꝛi Ulao li.   Uꝛcinɥ oe
aobeꝛɥea ꝼi b. ꝼeɥ ᵹaɥ ꝼiꝛ oib. ⁊ b   Uꝛꝼeɥ ꝛanōa na ꝼeaꝛ b.   Ruaile ꝛo ᵹab-
ꝛaoaꝛ .l. uɥ eꝛɥ illeabꝛaiō na Cꝛuiɥneac ōꝛuioe Eꝛo b Ᵹaꝛɥ b Aꝛᵹaꝛɥ b. cino
b. Uꝛcino. b. Uiꝛ b. Uꝛuiꝛ b. Ᵹníɥ. b Uꝛᵹniɥh b. Muin b Uꝛmuin

The gross inaccuracies of the list of kings can only be accounted for on the supposition that the transcriber (not perhaps the transcriber of the Book of Ballymote, but
some former copyist) found the names written in double columns (a thing very common in ancient Irish manuscripts), and, not perceiving that the columns were distinct,
he copied them in one continuous line. On this supposition the list may be corrected
as follows

Fib xxiiii bliaōna iꝛꝛiᵹe
Fioac xl. bliaōnu   ō Ponɥ
Foꝛɥeano lix   ō Uꝛponɥ.
Caiɥ oa bliaoan aꝛ .xx.   ō Leo.
Ciꝛiᵹ lxxx bl   ō Ᵹanɥ

And so on, where the reader will observe that the intermixture of the Bruides
with the other names will be fully explained until we come to the paragraph which
has been given above without a translation; in it the corruption is much greater
but it is also explained by supposing the manuscript from which the transcriber
copied to have been written thus

Uꝛᵹeꝛ .xxx. bliaoan   ō Uꝛcal.
ōꝛuioe Ponɥ .xxx bli   ō. Cinɥ.
ꝛi Ulao . . . . . [bꝛui]   ō. Uꝛcinɥ
oe aobeꝛɥea ꝼi [i e ꝼꝛi]   ō Feɥ.
ᵹaɥ ꝼiꝛ oib ⁊   ō. Uꝛꝼeɥ.

Ranōa

former copy of this list of kings Oenbegan is as-   But the present copy is so full of errors and cor-
signed a reign of 100 years; see above, p 155   ruptions that it is of no value

ꝛanꝺa na ꝼeaꝛ	ꝺ. Ruaile
ꝛo ᵹabꝛaꝺaꝛ l uᴄ eꝛᴄ	
illeabꝛaib na Cꝛuiᴄneaᴄ	ꝺ. Єꝛo
	ꝺ. Ᵹaꝛᴄ.
	ꝺ. Aꝛᵹaꝛᴄ
	ꝺ Ciꝺ.

And so on. The transcriber ought to have written down the first column, until he came to the words illeabꝛaib na Cꝛuiᴄneaᴄ, and then to have begun the second column, ꝺ Ponᴄ, ꝺ Uꝛponᴄ, &c If this conjecture be well founded, it will follow that Bruide Pont was the last of the first series, and the first of the kings who took the common title of Bruide. The words ꝛi Ulaꝺ would seem to imply that B. Pont was King of Uladh, or of the Dalaradian Picts, but it is more probable that for ꝛi ulaꝺ we should read ano uaꝺ. (See above, p 156)

The Book of Lecan contains three different copies of this section. In fact, as I have already remarked (see p. 154, *supra*, note ꝙ), the Book of Lecan contained two copies of the Irish Nennius. In the first of these the chapter which I have marked sect I. p. 25, *supra*, is omitted, and the work begins with sect II., "Britonia insola," &c, down to the word "Saxons" (sect. III p. 29, *supra*), omitting, however, the list of British cities. Then follows

Ꝺo bunaꝺ Cꝛuiᴄneᴄ ꝛo

Cꝛuiᴄhne maᴄ Ciᵹe, miᴄ Luᴄᴄa, miᴄ Paꝛᴄalon, miᴄ Aᵹnon, miᴄ ꝺuain, miᴄ Maiꝛ, miᴄ Faᴄheᴄᴄ, miᴄ Iauaꝺ, miᴄ Iaᴄhꝼeꝺ, miᴄ Nue, miᴄ Laimiach.

Iꝛhe aᴄhaiꝛ Cꝛuiᴄhneᴄh ꝛ ᴄeꝺ bliaꝺain ꝺo iꝛꝛiᵹi amail a ꝺeaꝛaꝛ ꝛeamainꝺ. Seaᴄhᴄ meiᴄ Cꝛuiᴄhneᴄh inꝛo i. Fiꝺ, ꝛ Fiꝺach, Folᴄla, Foꝛᴄꝛenꝺ, Caiᴄ, Ce, Ciꝛiᵹ, ꝛ i .uii. ꝛeanꝺaib ꝛanꝺꝛaᴄ a ꝼeaꝛanꝺ, amail aꝺbeꝛᴄ in ᴄ-eolach.

Moiꝛꝼeiꝛeꝛ ꝺo Cꝛuiᴄhne ᴄlainꝺ
Rainn Albain iꝛꝛeaᴄhᴄ ꝛainꝺ;

Caiᴄ,

Of the origin of the Cruithni this

Cruithne *uas* the son of Cinge, son of Luchta, son of Parthalon, son of Agnon, son of Buan, son of Mas, son of Fathecht, son of Jadud, son of Jathfed, son of Nea, son of Lamech.

He was the father of the Cruithnians, and he reigned an hundred years, as was said before The seven sons of Cruithne *are* these Fid, and Fidach, Foltla, Fortrenn, Cait, Ce, Cirig; and they divided his land into seven parts, as the learned man said:

Seven of the children of Cruithne
Divided Alban into seven portions,

Cait,

Caιτ, Ce, Cιριʒ ceτach claιnn
Fιb, Fιoach, Folτla, Fοιρτρeanο

Caιt, Ce, Cιrιgh of the hundred children
Fιb, Fιdach, Foltla, Foirtrann

Ocuρ ιρe aιnm cach fιρ οιb fιl ρoρ a
feaρanο, uτ Fιb, ⁊ Ce, ⁊ Caιτ, ⁊τc. .xιιι.
ριοe c οο ʒobρaο οιb.

And each gave his name to his own land;
as Fib. and Ce, and Cait, &c Thirteen
kings of them possessed [ι e. reigned]

Bρuοa Ponτ .xxxᵃ ριʒ uaο, ⁊ Bρuιοe
aοbeρτe fρι cach feaρ οιb, ⁊ ρanna na
feaρ aιlι, ρo ʒubρaοaρ τρe .l. aρ. c. uτ
eρτ ιllebρaιb na Cρuιτhnech

Bruda Pont, thirty kings afterwards,
and Bruide was the name of each man of
them, and they took the portions of the
other men [ι. e. of the former kings] for
one hundred and fifty years, as it is in the
books of the Cruithnians

The second form of this ancient fragment of history occurs in the same connexion,
and is, for substance, the same as that given above, pp. 50, 51. After the same account
of the children of Galeoin, son of Hercules, who seized upon the islands of Orkney,
there follows the genealogy of Cruithne, as quoted already, note ᵏ, p. 50, and then
we have

Iρ he aτhaιρ Cρuιτhnech, ⁊ ceτ blιa-
οaιn ιρριʒe. Seachτ meιc Cρuιτhne
ιnορο ι Fιο, ⁊ Fιοach, ⁊ Foτla, ⁊ Foρτ-
ρeann, Caιτ, ⁊ Ce, ⁊ Cιριc , uτ οιxιτ
Colam cιllι.

He was the father of the Cruithnians,
and reigned an hundred years. These
are the seven sons of Cruithne, Fid,
and Fidach, and Fotla, and Fortreann,
Cait, and Ce, and Ciric, as Columbcille
said.

Then follow the verses, as given. p. 50. after which we read

Co ρo ρoιnορeaτ ι uιι ρannaιb ιn
feaρann, ⁊ ιρ e aιnm cach fιρ οιb fιl ρoρ
a ρeaρanο, uτ eρτ Fιb, Ce, Caιτ, ⁊τc
.xιιι. ρι con ʒobρaο οιb foρρo; ⁊ ʒabaιρ
Onbecan mac Caιτ mιc Cρuιτhne aιρο-
ριʒι na ρecτ ρann ριn

So that they divided the land into
seven portions, and each man gave his
name to his own territory· as Fib, Ce,
Cait, &c. Thirteen kings of them possessed [ι. e. reigned]; and Onbecan, son
of Cait, son of Cruithne, seized upon the
supreme sovereignty of those seven divisions

Then follows, as in the text (p 50, *supra*), Fιnοacτa fa flaιτh n-Eρenn, &c
The third copy of the same document occurs in the beginning of what I suppose

to have been a second transcript[h] of the Irish Nennius, which begins as in the Book of Ballymote, and the manuscript from which the text of the present work is taken, with the section, *Ego Nennius*, &c.

After that section we have the following

Do bunaδaιb na Cpuιᴄhneach anδpo boδeapoa.

Cpuιᴄhne mac Inᵹe mic Lucᴄa mic Pappᴄhalon mic δuam mic Maιp mic Faᴄheᴄhᴄ mic Iaᴄhfeᴄ mic Naeι Ip h-e aᴄhaιp Cpuιᴄhnech ⁊ ceδ bᴄ. δo ι pιᵹe. Seᴄhᴄ meιc Cpuιᴄhne anδpo .ι. Fιb ⁊ ce ⁊ Cιpιch, pᴄ. ⁊ ι peaᴄhᴄ panδaιb po pannpaδ a feapanδ, ⁊ ιpe aιmm cach fιp διb fιl fop a feapann anιuᵹ. Fιb ιmoppo ceaᴄhpa blιaδaιa pιchιᴄ δo ι pιᵹι Fιδach ᕁl. bᴄ. δpuιδ Puιnᴄ Foιpᴄpenn ᒶᕁᕁ b. Uppoιnncaιᴄ ᕁᕁιι. Upleoce .ᕁι Upleocιpιch ᒶᕁᕁ. b. Ᵹanᴄaenbeccan m̄ b. Upᵹanᴄ caιᴄ .ᕁᕁᕁ b. Ᵹιιᴄh fιnδacᴄa ᒶᕁ δpuᵹnιᴄh ᵹuιδιδ ᵹaδbpe, b. Feᴄh .ι Ᵹep .ι.b .b. Uppeᴄhᴄaιp ᵹepᴄᵹuιpιδ .ι ᕁl. b, Claupᵹapᴄ ᴄpιcha b .b Uppeal δpuιδι Ponᴄ ᴄpιcha .b. pιᵹulaδ δe aδbepᴄhea fpι cach feap διb ⁊ panδa na feap. δ Cιnᴄ. δ Upchιnoᴄ δ. Feaᴄ. δ. Uppeaδ δ. Ruale po ᵹabpaδapι. δ. ap bᴄ uᴄ διcιᴄup a lebpaιb na Cpuιᴄhneach. δpuιδ Epo. δ Ᵹapᴄ δ Apᵹapᴄ δ Cιnn δ. Upchιnδ. δ. Uιp δ Upuιp δ Ᵹpoᴄh. δ. Upᵹpoᴄh. δ Muιn δ. Upumaιn. δ Ip amlaιδ pιn fo fpιᴄ.

This is also very corrupt; and as it adds nothing to what we have learned from the former copies, it is not worth our while to attempt a translation or a correction of it. The scribe appears to have been sensible of its incorrectness when he adds the apology, Ip amlaιδ pιn fo fpιᴄ, "Thus it was found." It is followed by the section beginning, δpιᴄanιa ιnδpola, &c., as given above, p. 27 —(*T*)

No. XXI   *See page* 154

Since the note vi. p. x. was printed, I have learned that the gloss scuite, wanderer, is not found to exist elsewhere, and that suspicion therefore arises of dictionaries having been interpolated, with a view to that very purpose to which I have applied them. This has induced me to expend some further observations on the subject.

The first point in it is, that an indigenous etymology produced the word Scoti, having one T, and the O long by nature Though Isidore's direct assertion, that Scotus was a word *in their own language*, may lose weight from his making it equivalent to Pictus, and explaining it to mean punctured with the painting needle,

yet

---

[h] This second transcript begins immediately after the Wonders of Britain and Man, with which the first copy seems to have concluded See above, p. 120.

yet it shows that he knew of no origin for it *out of their own language.* Isid. Hisp Etymol. ix. tom. iii p 414 Ed Areval. It is not a Latin word, it is not British, nor did it even become such by adoption, nor is it fetched from the Teutonic tribes, in any form that I can esteem specious But the name came up under Julian at latest, when those tribes were scarce beginning to move upon the empire's western shores and ocean to which date other weighty considerations may be joined. Firstly, it is absurd, and out of nature, that the Roman authors should exchange a name handed down by Pytheas, Eratosthenes, Cæsar, Strabo, Pliny, Tacitus, Ptolemy, &c., to adopt one freshly introduced by Saxons, Franks, and Alans, supposing their dialects had furnished it Secondly, the Irish historians restrict the use of it to one of their races, while foreigners employ it generally, which exhibits the usual difference between the native and foreign, proper and improper, use of a term Let us therefore pronounce, with Isidorus, that whosoever were called Scoti were so called propriâ linguâ.

It remains doubtful who they were that were so styled, and when, and why. That Porphyry, an Asiatic sophist of the third century, had used the word Σκώτικα or Σκωτῶν, where Jerome put Scoticæ gentes, seems to me very unlikely The third of the fragments of geography[1] by different authors, but ascribed to one Æthicus, is a mere extract from the first book of Orosius, and Hegesippus is a composition of the twelfth century Therefore Ammianus, circa 390, is our first written authority, but we cannot otherwise understand him, than that those marauders were known by that name in the year *of* which, as well as that *in* which, he wrote, viz, in A D 360. That Constans in 343 had been opposed to Scoti may be conjectured; but it cannot be inferred from the expressions of Ammian When the name in question began to be used in Ireland is unknown, and *how* it was there used is important. If it were an ancient name of the Irish for themselves, unknown to foreigners until they had improved their acquaintance with Ireland, but then adopted by them generally (as foreigners know the names German or Allemand, but have to learn the name Deutsch), it follows that the name is vernacular among the Irish people. But such (I believe) it neither is, nor ever was. Unwritten discourse does not so style them, nor does that of the Celts of Britain. Then as to writers, their date is late in Ireland, and their manner of using the word perhaps unsatisfactory They almost all possessed some Latin learning, and a Gaelicized adoption of the Latin word Scotus may prove no more than is proved by Tighernach's plain Latin "monumenta Scotorum" It is not evident what word we are to accept for it in Irish The poem ascribed to St Fiech of Sletty, st. 18, employs the dative plural Scotuibh, than which an earlier instance may (perhaps) not

readily

[1] Ad Calcem Pomp Melæ, p 62 Ed. Grooovii, 1772

readily be found   That is Scotus with an Erse inflexion   But others have Cineadh Scuit.   And a chronicle cited by Dr O'Conor varies in the name, speaking of Rifath Scuit or Scot, from whom proceeded the Scuit —Proleg 11, lxxvi.   But this name is taken from Mount Riphæus, the Scythian mythus, garnished with a scrap of Scythian geography. That either the Irish nation, or that major portion of it with which their mythologists connect the Scythian mythus, ever called or knew themselves by such a name, either generally, or vernacularly, or otherwise, than as some aborigines of America have learned to call themselves *Indians*, is opposed to the evidences of fact

The derivation from Scythæ is strictly impossible, for no nation so styled itself, though the Greeks did so call a large body of tribes or nations —Herod. iv c 6. Dr. O'Conor observing this, and that their true name was Scoloti (Herod. ibid.), tried to deduce Scoti from Scoloti; thus obstinately maintaining the historical derivation of the mythologists, but upon a different verbal etymology, and with the disadvantage of the additional and immutable consonant L.   But it is the wildest excess of credulity, and the lowest prostration of the critical faculty, to believe that the equestrian nomades of the East galloped away to the shores of Gaul, and there dismounted, and took boats, to go and tramp the forests and bogs of Erin,—for no other reason than because semi-barbarous writers, of a class well-known throughout all Europe, have played some tricks with the letters S, C, and T, and (what is more) with *the wrong* S, C, T.   The Scytho-Scolotian theory must rest on the basis of Scot having been the national and vernacular name, without interruption, from the first beginning downwards, than which nothing can appear more untrue.   That very portion of the fable which insinuates truth, by making the Scot colony *the latest* of the Irish denominations, proves it to be a fable, because the recency of the Firbolgian name, *which preceded it*, is proveable, as I shall show, but will not waste more words on such a topic as this.

I have observed that Scoti was the name of the Scoti in their own language, and I have also observed, that it neither is, nor ever was (to our knowledge) the name of the Gaoidhil, or Irish nation, in their own discourse, and can scarce be said to have established itself in their writings, always excepting such as treat of the Scythian mythus   Here is something to explain, if not to reconcile.

Since the name is Irish, and the Irish nation did not call themselves so, who did? Those to whom the Romans first applied it.   But who were they?   The armaments of marauders who came over from Ireland to ravage the province of Britannia   Such is our original date and application of the word.   The question is, whether it was an exclusive application.   And the affirmative may be supposed, from its not being any-

where found earlier, and not being found national in Erin   Thus it would seem as if Irishmen were not Scoti, but expeditions of Irish warriors and pirates were   It may be here well to remind the reader, that many names more or less famous in history were not the names of nations or countries, but those of belligerent associations of men.   Such were the Bagaudæ, the Vargi, the Aiteach-Tuatha, the Maroons, the Chouans, and the Pindarrees; but none more to our purpose than the Vikingar, and the Buccaneers, names terrible in the ears of foreigners, yet belonging to no nation. The first instance I know of the territorial phrase, Scotia, is in Isidore of Seville, whom David Rothe of Ossory cites at the year 630 —Tractatus, sect. iv. ap. Messingham, Flor. Insulæ SS ; Isidori Orig xiv. cap 6, tom. iv. p 171. Arevali

The same Isidorus has flatly affirmed, that Scoti signfied men stained by acupuncture. And it were wrong, in our state of ignorance, to reject with flippancy a positive assertion, which may have been derived from the lost books of Ammian, or some other grave authority.   Nor is the statement absurd, either in word or in matter   For scoth and sgoth are genuine Irish glosses for *a flower*, which will either apply to a people painted[k] with flowers, as the Britons opposed to Severus were with animals, γραφαῖς ποικίλων ζωων, or generally, to ornament by diversity of colour , ἀνθιζω, varietate distinguo.—E Lluyd; O'Reilly, Scapulæ Lex.   This laxer sense shews itself in scoth, morbus (Lluyd), and sgôt, " common speech" for spot or blemish, macula (ap. Gael Soc Dict., and Macleod and Dewar's), seemingly in allusion to exanthematous or efflorescent maladies   And as regards the matter, it would not be improbable, but the reverse, that those Irish marauders, who first came over in fleets of coracles to support the Gwyddyl Fichti in their depredations, were of the Crutheni ; and this being probable in itself, it is possible that the name thus originating may have inured to subsequent expeditions of the red Irish.

But the same gloss hath other idioms, flowing (I believe) out of the idea of *flower*. Scoth, chosen, selected (O'Reilly and O'Brien); scoth, choice or best of any thing, rcoth na brean, best part of the army (G Soc Dict) To the same idea belongs scoth, a youth, a young lad, a son, a young shoot of a plant , and, perhaps, also scotha and scuite, said by Mr. O'Reilly to mean " brambles used for fences." Now it is certainly no violent supposition, that the bands, who sallied forth from Erin in her piratical era, both were, and called themselves, her rcoth na brean, the flower of her warriors.

Besides this masculine noun, we have the same word in the feminine, *scoth*, *sgoth*, a boat, or small vessel; *scoth-long* (boat-ship), a yacht.—O'Reilly ; Gael. Soc., Armstrong.

---

[k] *Scotha* Hibernis idem sonat quod *flores* seu *florum variegatio*, et *scotadh* idem quod *celeritas* —Colgan in Vit S Seutini vel Scothini, 11 Jan , p. 10

strong. This will scarcely arise out of the first intention of *flower* But if the " flower
of warriors" had so adopted that description as to make a very name of it, then the
vessels in which they plied their lawless business would, in the usual idiom of sailors,
receive the same appellation, together with the gender commonly ascribed to ships
What is yon vessel? *She* is a pirate What is her captain? *He* is a pirate And so
forth. Should any one say, that Isidore had lightly assumed *Scoti* to be an Erse
synonyme for the Latin *Picti*, that the general use of the name (so rapidly diffused
through the West) agrees but ill with a narrow derivation from the Crutheni; and that
the desperate adventures of the Flower of Erin, in their pirate or flower boats, introduced this late but famous name. he would (as the case now stands) carry my humble
approbation. When people get a new name, we may also suppose new circumstances
The Hiberni did greatly change, viz., from mere landsmen to a race of pirates under sea-
kings. No light reasoning in the abstract, and reinforced by the fact, that those
belligerents were the first (within our knowledge) that obtained the appellation In
considering Irish words with a view to the elucidation of ancient history, it will be
right to bear in mind, that letters, as well as signs of aspiration, were always introduced
into the writing of words for the purpose of being pronounced: and that any eclipsing
or obliterated pronunciation of a letter is necessarily an idiom of speech, subsequent
in date not only to the word, but to the act of writing it.

I have withheld, in No V p ix, my own firm belief concerning the Tuatha De,
because the argumentation of it is long, and incapable of compression, but, upon
second thought, I will here briefly state my persuasion that they were the great order
or college of British Druids, flying before the face of the Romans into Ireland; and
will, with equal brevity, set forth my general notion of Irish origins.

Hiberni of the ancients Emigrations from Great Britain, made at dates unknown,
but old enough for the two dialects to have diverged from their common type, of
course fed from time to time by the arrival of other adventurers or refugees, and
forming a population of the extremest ferity.

Firbolg. A colony of Gaulish tribes planted along South Britain, and retaining
the same names they had borne in Belgium. Cæsar speaks of it as a known and historical fact, which remote facts in those countries were not—B G v. 12. Within
living memory Divitiacus, king of the Suessones and other Belgians, had reigned
also over a great part of Britain.—B. G II. 4. That is to say, British and Gaulish
Belgium were remembered as forming one sovereignty. Within eighty-seven years of
their planting in Britain, the Fergusian Scots denied the superiority of the kings of
Tara. And we shall make liberal allowance, if we say the Belgæ had held South
Britain 150 years before Cæsar assailed it, a century would, perhaps, satisfy the truth

c

The Firbolg invaded Ireland from Britain, not from Soissons or any other part of
Belgium   Because the Dumnonii of Solinus and Ptolemy (popularly misspelt Damnonii), were the Domhnon or Domhnan of the Irish Firbolg But they had their name
from the *dyvnon*, i e. deeps, little valleys among steep hills,—from which their country
is still called *Devon*,—and in Welsh *Dyvnaint* , the permutation of the V, otherwise
single F, with the M, being of perpetual occurrence, and the two consonants used
indifferently in manuscripts of no vast age. See Lhuyd's Archæologia, pp. 221, 228.
So the Irish MII sounds V   The same word is Doumn, Douvn, and Doun, in the
Armorican, and Dom Lepelletier found, in three lives of St. Gwenolè, pars Domnonica,
pagos Domnonicos, and rura Domnoniensia, from which he collects that there was
also a Domnonia among the hills and vales of the Armorican Cornwall—Dict. Bret. in
Doun The name of the Firdomhnan described the surface of a particular district in
the greater island; while the Firbolgian tribe Firbolg, or Belgæ by excellence, were,
I suppose, from the royal demesnes of Belgica, near the Venta Belgarum.

But a people do not thus indelibly receive a name from the face of their country,
till they have been long and fully settled there.   Therefore the Firbolgian conquest
was not much older than Cæsar's time, if it were not a good bit later.   And it
was the first influx of a civilization, rude indeed, but much superior to that of the
Hiberni, the first emerging of a gens effera towards the higher rank of the gentes
barbaræ.

Tuatha De The people of Gods, or the people of the [i e. dear and sacred to the]
Gods   When the druidic college could no longer maintain in Britain its vast power
and mysterious rites, it removed them to Erin, their only sure asylum.   They obtained superiority in that island more by their treasures, arts, and learning, and the
engines of religious awe, and as gods or divine men, a tribe sacer interpresque Deorum,
than as men, by arms and numbers.   At this date, the druidical magic was systematically organized in Ireland   They have been called Danann, either falsely, from the
more modern Dani, or ancient Danai, but rather from *dan*, art, poem, song (see Keating, p 48, O'Connor's ed.), which derivation, if it do not express the Druids, sufficiently
expresses the Bards

The time of the removal of the hierarchy was after the unsuccessful wars of Cynobeline's sons against the Romans; of which events the capture of Caractacus, in A D
50, was the cardinal point   I have already said that the argument vastly exceeds the
space now at my disposal, and I must, therefore, be excused for speaking meo periculo
But Firbolg, saith Gilda Coeman, ruled during thirty-seven[1] years.   Therefore, with
their

[1] A poem, cited by Keating, p 39, but of no comparable authority, says fifty-six years

their fulcrum in A. D. 50, our compasses will sweep through A. D. 13 for the advent of the Firbolg; and I suppose it was thereabouts. The magical dynasty prevailed, according to the Psalter of Cashel, during 197 years, when the era of the Gaoidhil[m] arises. That is to say, the Hiberni, or general population, quasi-indigenous, of Ireland, resumed that superiority which the Brito-Belgic and Druidical migrations of Britons had wrested from them, changed and improved in its social energies by the infusion of those more advanced races. This falls, as it were, upon the year 247, according to the Irish chronologers, combined with my date of the transfer of Druidism. But the emancipation of the Gaoidhil from the yoke of the Tuatha De is myth-historically identified with the rise and establishment of the Scoti. And the year 247 is only seven years before the accession of Cormac M'Art, to whom I have (by a curious coincidence, for I had not made this computation) conjecturally assigned the beginnings of the Scoti, as being the first recorded sea-king. But the year 50 was only named as the cardinal year in the misfortunes of Cynobeline's house, and not with any idea of its being the actual year of that great transaction. Therefore there is not really any discrepancy at all. I cannot refrain from thinking, that the durations assigned by the seannachies to these fabulous dynasties (durations as short and modest as the dates are remote and extravagant) were based in truth, and may serve us for clues to its investigation.—(II.)

No. XXII. *See page* 180.

The following documents seem worthy of preservation, and will give the reader some of the principal authorities for the history of the parties mentioned in the legend of St. Cairnech:

I. The first is a legend preserved in the book of Dubhaltach, or Dudley Mac Firbis, in the possession of the Earl of Roden, p. 112. It relates to the history of Muredhach Mac Eoghan, and his wife, Erc, the maternal aunt of St. Carnech.

Muıreaóac mac Eoġaın ceṫre mec laır, ꝺ aon maṫaır leo; Muıréırṫaċ, Moen, Fĭraóaċ, ꝺ Tıġṡınac. Eapc ınġean	Muireadhach, son of Eoghan, had four sons, who had one mother: Muircheartach, Moen, Fearadach, and Tighearnach. Earc, daughter

---

[m] Nomen quo Hibernenses se ab immemorabili distinguunt.—O'Con. Proleg. ii. lxxxviii.

But its history, meaning, and affinities, seem quite unascertained; it belongs only to the original Irish (and their colonies in North Britain), as distinct from the Belgians and Danauns; and its etymological affinity to Galli and Galatæ appears to me devoid of solid foundation.

ȝean Lóaiṗn ṗiȝ Alban maṫaiṗ an cṡṫṗaiṗ ṗin, uṫ ḋixiṫ,

> Ceṫṗe mec la Muiṗḃac
> Fṗia h-Eṗc ṗa ṗaoṗ ṗéun,
> Muiṗceaṗṫac, Tiȝṡṗnac,
> Fṡṗaḃoc aȝuṡ Moeun.

Iaṗ n-euȝ mec Eoȝain, ṫuȝ Fṗȝuṡ, mac Conuill Ȝulban, Eaṗc iṅȝean Lóaiṗn, ȝo ṗuȝ ṗi ceṫṗe mec ele ḋó .i. Feḋlim, Loaṗn, Ḃṗennainn, ⁊ Seuḋna, amail aṗpeaṗṫ,

> Ceṫṗe mec aȝ Fṗȝuṡ Fṗia h-Eṗc
> Cħubuiḋ ceuḋna,
> Feḋlimiḋ aȝuṡ Loaṗn,
> Ḃṗennainn aȝuṡ Seuḋna,

Ṫainiȝ Eaṗc ṗṡmṗaṫe ȝo Caiṗnṡc ṗo ċiṫṗiȝe, aȝuṡ ḋob é meuḋ a h-aiṫṗiȝe, ȝo ṗleuċṫaḋ ȝaċa ḋaṗa h-iomaiṗe ó Ṫóṗaiȝ ȝo h-aiṗin i m-baoi Caiṗnṡc naom i cᴄṗic Roiṡ Oiliȝ (no Ailiȝ), maile ṗe oṗuċṫ ṗola aȝ ṗṅiȝe ṫṗé báiṗ ȝaċ mṡoiṗ ḋi aȝ ṗoċṫain Ċaiṗniȝ Mo ᴄṡn ḋuiṫ aṗ Caiṗnṡc, a Eaṗc, ⁊ ṗoḋṗia nṡm, aȝuṡ ȝaċ ḋaṗa Ṗí buṡ áiṗmṡc ȝeuḃuṡ Eṗinn ȝo bṗaṫ ȝuṗoḃ ḋoḃ ṗiol, ⁊ buaiḋ mná, ⁊ cleṗiȝ ḋiḃ, ⁊ buaiḋ caṫa ⁊ comloinn

daughter of Loarn, King of Alba, was the mother of those four, ut dixit [*poeta*],

> Four sons had Muireadhach
> By Earc, of noble worthiness,
> Muircheartach, Tigearnach,
> Fearadhach, and Moen

After the death of the son of Eoghan, Fergus, son of Conal Gulban, espoused Earc, the daughter of Loarn, and she bore four sons more for him, viz., Fedhlim, Loarn, Brennainn, and Seudna, as was said,

> Four sons had Fergus by Erc,
> The same *were* worthy:
> Fedlhimidh, and Loarn,
> Brennainn, and Seudna.

The aforesaid Earc came to Cairneach in penitence, and such was the greatness of her penitence that she knelt at every second ridge from Tory *island* to where Saint Cairneach was, in the district of Ross Oiligh (or Ailigh[n]), at the same time that a dew of blood was issuing from the top of every one of her fingers as she approached Cairneach I hail thee, said Cairneach, O Earc, and thou shalt go to heaven, and one of every two[o] worthy kings

---

[n] *Ross Oiligh or Ailigh —*This was the celebrated palace of Aileach, near Londonderry, for a full account of which see the Ordnance Memoir of the parish of Templemore, p 27, *sq* The whole district was anciently called Tir-Ailigh (ibid, p 207), and probably Ross Ailigh was the place now called the Rosses, on the Foyle, near Derry Erc is said to have passed in penitential pilgrimage from Tory island to Ross Ailigh, i e from one extremity to the other of the district belonging to her race.

[o] *Every two —*Colgan says " Hi octo Ercæ filii in adeo magnam temporis successu crevere gentem et potentiam, ut ex eis, viginti sex universæ Hiberniæ monarchæ, et omnes Tir-eoganiæ (vulgo Tyroniæ) et Tirconalliæ Principes, hi ex Sedna,

ꞇ comloinn ꝼoꝛꝛa , ꞇ ιaꝛ ꝼꝛιoꞇaιlⸯm eaᵹ-
luꝛꝺacꞇa o Caιꝛnꝼc ꝺι ιaꝛum, ꝼaoιꝺiᵹ
a ꞃꝛιoꝛaꝺ ꝺocum na ᵹloιꝛe ꞃιoꝛuιꝺe.

ꝺeanꝺaċuꝛ Cáιꝛnꝼc an maιᵹιꝛꝛιn,
cona ꝺe aιnmnιᵹꞇⸯꝛι .ι. Ceall Eaꝛca,
aιꞇ ιonꝺoꝛċaιꝛ Eaꝛc, ꞇ ꝼáᵹbaιꝺ Caιꝛnꝼc caιmeúꝺ ιnꞇe .ι. Cꝛιoꝺan Eꝛꞃcoꝛ.

Ꝯ maιcleaⸯaꝛ Lecan Mhec Fhιꝛbι-
ꞃᵹ ꞃιn.

Eaꝛc, umoꝛꝛo, aꝛ ꝺaιꞇe ꝛloιnnꞇⸯꝛ a
mac Muιꝛꞃꝛꞇac mac Eꝛca.

Muιꝛꞃꞃꞇac mac Muιꝛꝛꝺoιᵹ ꞇ Eaꝛca, coιᵹ mec leꝛ .ι. Fꞃꝛᵹuꝛ, Ꝺomnall,
ⸯaoꝺan, Nellιn, ꞇ Sᵹanꝺal, amuιl aꝛ-
ꝺeaꝛꞇ,

    Coιᵹ mec Muιꝛꞃꝛꞃaιᵹ ᵹo m-blaιꝺ
    Mec Muιꝛꝛꝺaιᵹ mιc Eoᵹaιn.
    Ꝺomnall, Nellιn ᵹaꝛᵹ ᵹo n-ᵹuꝛ
    ⸯaoꝺan, Sᵹanꝺal ιꝛ Fꞃꝛᵹuꝛ (no Feoꝛ-
    ᵹuꝛ).

Ꝯꝺeꝛ

kings who shall ever reign over Erin shall
be of thy seed , and the best women, and
the best clerics, shall be theirs, and success in battle and combat shall be upon
them. And after ecclesiastical ministra-
tions from Cairneach, her spirit passed
into eternal glory.

Cairneach blessed that spot, and hence
its name, viz., Ccall Earca [Earc's cell],
where Earc died ; and Cairneach left a
person in charge of the place, viz., Criodan[p] the Bishop.

This *is* from the copy of the Book of
Lecan Meic Firbisigh.

Earc then, from her is her son Muircheartach Mac Earca named

Muircheartach, the son of Muireadhach
and of Earc, had five sons, viz., Fearghus,
Domhnall, Baodan, Nellin, and Scannal,
as was said,

    The five sons of famous Muircheartach,
    The son of Muireadhach, son of Eoghan.
    Domhnall, Nellin, the fierce and puis-
      sant,
    Baodan, Sgannal, and Fearghus (or
      Feorghus)

It

---

illi ex Murchertacho prodierunt."—Vit. S. Carnech, 2 Mart p 782, c. 4. And in a note
he adds . " Hæc colliguntur ex Ketenno, lib. 2,
ex Quatuor Magistris in Annalibus, Gilda Mo-
duda in Catalogo Regum Hiberniæ, et aliis pas-
sim scriptoribus qui de eisdem Regibus agunt
Omnes enim numerant 16 Reges ex Eugenio et
decem ex Conalli posteris oriundos, quorum ge-
nealogiam referunt ad Murchertachum ex Mure-

dacio, et ad Sednam ex Fergussio Ercæ filios "

[p] *Criodan* —Perhaps this is the same whom
Colgan mentions as a disciple of St Petroc, or
Pereuse, abbot of Padstow (i e. Petrocstowe), in
Cornwall, who died about A. D 564. Of Crio-
dan Colgan says " Cridanus .   colitur in
Lagenia in ecclesia de Acadh Biuuich, die 11
Maii "—Acta Sanctorum, p' 586 *n* 11, 12, 13

Aʙeᵽ ᵽlɩoct ᵽenleabaɩᵽ cɩanaoᵽʙa (nac aɩcne a uᵹʙaᵽ) clann ele ʙo bec aᵹ Muɩᵽeᵽcac mac Eaᵽca, maᵽ ᵽo aʙeᵽ, Ice annᵽo na ʙᵽᵽcaɩn acáʙ aᵽ ᵽlɩoct cuɩnn ceuʙcacaɩᵹ ɩ. ʙɩa ccuᵹ Muɩᵽceaᵽ-cac mac [Eaᵽca] bean Cuɩᵽɩᵹ ᵹo ᵽuᵹ cecᵽe maca ʙo ɩ Conᵽaɩcɩn ᵹ Ꙅaɩʙɩl-Ficht, o ccá ᵽuɩᵽɩᵹ ᵹ ᵽíᵹ ʙᵽeacan Coᵽn, ᵹ Nellɩn a quo uɩ Néllɩn

Nɩ abaɩᵽ an ᵽenlebaᵽ aɩᵽ acc ᵽɩn Ꙅɩʙeaʙ ᵹɩbe lenab aɩl ɩaᵽᵽmoᵽacc aᵽ ᵽíoᵹᵽaɩʙ ʙᵽᵽcon-Coᵽn ᵽeucaɩʙ an ᵽonn ɩ Saᵹaɩb ʙá n-ᵹoɩᵽɩʙ ɩ Saɩᵹ *Cornwall*, uaɩᵽ aᵹᵽɩn ʙᵽᵽcaɩncoᵽn.

It is said in a very ancient book (the author of which is not known) that Muircheartach Mac Earca had other children. Thus does it say " These are the Britons who descended from Conn of the Hundred Battles, viz, Muircheartach Mac (Earca) having espoused the wife of Luirig, she bore him four sons, viz, Consaitin, and Gaidil-Ficht, from whom *descended* the chiefs and kings of Britain-Corn, Neillin a quo Ui Neillin."[q]

The old book says no more about him than this. But whosoever wishes to inquire about the kings of Britain-Corn, let him search the country in Saxonland, and which in Saxon is called Cornwall, for that is Britain-Corn

There can be very little doubt that " the old book," whose author was unknown, which is spoken of and quoted in the foregoing passage, is the identical legend of St. Carnech, which is for the first time printed above, p 172, *seq.*, but whether Mac Firbis quoted it from the book of Ballymote, or from an older copy, which contained also other similar matter, we have now no means of ascertaining

II The following curious verses will also throw light on the history of Muredach and Erc, the daughter of Loarn. They are taken from a poem beginning Enna ʙalca Chaɩᵽbᵽe cᵽuaɩʙ, " Enna, the pupil of hardy Cairbre," of which there is a very good copy in p 163 of a manuscript volume of bardic poetry, of great interest and historical value, the property of the late O'Conor Don, by whose kindness it was deposited in trust with the Royal Irish Academy, that its contents might be examined and transcribed by Irish scholars

Eaᵽc ɩnᵹean Coáɩᵽn ᵹan lén
macoɩᵽ na n-occaɩᵽ mac moɩᵽ-cᵽén

ɩᵽa

Earc, the daughter of unsubdued Loarn,
The mother of the eight great brave sons,

Whose

[q] Only three of the sons are here mentioned, but the fourth, " Scannall, a quo gens Scannail," is given above, pp 187, 189, where the passage here quoted occurs

ıṗa ṗıol ıṗ ꞇṗeoṗaċ ꞇall
ıꝺeṗ Eoġan ıṗ Conall.

Ꞇıġeṗnaċ ba ꞇṗén a ṗí
ıṗ Ƒeaṗaꝺaċ ꝟo bƒlaıꞇṗí
Muıṗċeaṗꞇaċ, Moan meaꝺaċ
Clann Eıṗce ṗe Muıṗeaꝺaċ.

Clann Ꞇıġeaṗnaıġ an ꞇaoıḃ ꞇe
ṗıl Ꞇıġeaṗnaıġ ṁıc Eıṗce
Ƒeaṗaꝺaċ ṗéın ṗlaıꞇ abaıꝺ
ó ꞇáıꝺ Cenel Ƒeaṗaꝺaıġ.

[Cenel Moaın co meaꝺaıḃ
o Moan mac Muıṗeaꝺaıġ
Muıṗċeaṗꞇaċ co meaꝺaıṗ mín
ıṗ ꝟaꝺ aıṗoṗıġnaꝺ Oılıġ.]

Sıl ṗın na ᵹ-ceıꞇṗe mac mín
ꝺo ṗáᵹ Eaṗc a n-Eoġan ꞇíṗ
ṗloınnṗıoꝺ ꝺaoıḃ anoıṗ ᵹan ṗaıll
ṗıl mac n-Eıṗc a ccṗíċ Conaıll.

Un Eaṗca ıṗa clanna ṗın
ınġean Loaıṗn a h-Ulbaın
ꞇuᵹ Ƒeaṗᵹuṗ mac Conaıll caın
ı aṗ cṗaꝺ ꞇaṗeıṗ Muıṗeaꝺaıġ.

Seaꝺna, Ƒeıꝺlımıꝺ ṗo ṗeaṗ
ḃṗeanaınn ıṗ Loaṗn laıṁꝺeaṗ
clann

Whose seed has been powerful within[r],
Between Eoghan and Conall[s].

Tigernach, who ruled with bravery,
    And Fearadhach of kingly power,
    Muircheartach, and Moan, rich in mead,
    Were the sons of Earc by Muireadach.

The race of Tighearnach of rich domains,
    Are the Siol Tighernaigh Mic Eirce,
    Fearadhach too, a full ripe chief,
    From whom are the Cenel Fearadhaigh.

[Cenel Moain[t] of the mead,
    From Moan, son of Muireadhach,
    Muircheartach, the gentle and merry,—
    From him descend the kings of Aileach.]

Those are the descendants of the four
    gentle sons
    Whom Earc left in Tir-Eoghain;
    Now I shall name for you without fail
    The descendants of Earc's sons in Tir
    Chonaill.

The Earc, whose sons these were,
    Was the daughter of Loarn of Alba;
    Whom Fearghus, the son of Conall, took
    To wife, for dowry[u], after Muireadhach.

Seadna, Feidhlimidh, well do I know,
    Breanainn and Loarn, the right-handed,
        Were

---

[r] Ꞇall is a Brehon law term, signifying within the tribe or territory.

[s] *Eoghan and Conall:* i. e. Eoghan son of Niall, of the Nine Hostages, the father of Muireadach, her first husband, and Conall Gulban, the father of Fergus, her second husband.

---

[t] *Cenel Moain.*—The four lines enclosed in brackets are supplied by Mr. Curry from another copy of this poem in the Book of Fenagh.

[u] *For dowry:* i. e. he gave her a dowry; which, according to ancient custom, was the proof of an honourable marriage.

clann Eince velbġoṗa an oṗuinġ,
aġuṗ Ḟeaṗġuiṗ mic Conuill.

Were the sons of Earc, valorous the band,
And of Fearghus, the son of Conall.

Niṗ ḟaġaiḃ Ḟeilim vo cloinn
áct Eoġan beaġ iṗ Coluim,
niṗ ḟáġ Ḃṗenainn, ṗeim ġo ṗat
act mav vaoitin ḟṗitḃeaṗtaċ (no
ḟṗitt ṗtaċ).

Feilim left no children,
Except Eoghan the little, and Colum[v].
Breanainn of happy career left not,
But only Baoithin[w] of the goodly deeds

Loaṗn ba laivin a ġlac
ṗob uaṗal pṗimġeine a mac
Ronan ataiṗ na mac meann
Colman Seiġinn iṗ Laiṗṗeann

Loarn, whose hand was strong,
Illustrious was the first-born of his sons,
Ronan, the father of the powerful sons[x],
Colman, Seighinn, and Laisreann

Na tṗi mic ṗin o'ḟáġaiḃ Eaṗc
ġan t-ṗil uct naoim ġo naoimneaṗt,
Seavna aice ṗé ṗiolav
tuat taoiṗeac tṗén ṗioġṗav

These three sons which Earc left,
Were without issue[y], except saints of saintly power
Seadna was her's for the propagation
Of people, chiefs, and brave kings

Seavna mac Ḟeaṗġuṗa Ḟáil
o ḟuil ṗiol Seavna ṗaoṗnáiṗ

Seadna, the son of Fearghus of Fail[z],
From whom descended the Siol Seadna
noble and brave,

Cinel

Cenel

---

[v] *Colum* —This was the celebrated St. Columba, or Columb-Kille See Colgan, Trias Th, p. 477 Eoghan, his younger brother, was the father of St Ernan, abbot of Druim-thuama in Tirconnell —Colgan, Acta SS in 1 Jan p 7

[w] *Baoithin* —This was the successor of St Columba in the government of the monastery of Iona, and founder of the church of Tigh-baoithin in Tirconnell —Colgan, Trias Thaum., p 480, n. 4

[x] *Powerful sons* i e saints. For St. Colman, who is also called Columbanus, see Colgan,

Tr Th, p 480, n 8. For St Seighin, or Segineus, ibid p 482, n 38   It is doubtful whether this was the Segineus who was abbot of Bangor, and died A D 664, according to the Four Masters, or the Segineus who was Archbishop of Armagh, and died A D 687. For St Laisreann, see Colgan, ib p 481, n 26

[y] *Without issue* i e Fedlim, Brenainn, and Loarn, left no posterity except saints, but Seadna was the ancestor of kings and people

[z] *Fail* i e of Ireland

Cinel Luġoac coiṗ 'ṗa ḃuṗ
ṗluaᵹ Fánao ᵹo ṗíoṗ ḟolluṗ.

Cenel Lughdach in the East[a] and here,
And the hosts of Fanad[b], 'tis clearly true.

Clann Ciaṗáin, clann Cṗonnmaoil
cáin
iṗ clann Loinᵹṗiᵹ ᵹo ṗioᵹaiḃ
iṗ iaoṗin ᵹo n-ᵹnioṁ n-ᵹuṗa
ṗiol Seaona mic Feaṗᵹuṗa.

The Clann Ciarain, and the fair Clann Crunnmaoil,
And the kingly Clann Loingsigh,
They,—the distinguished for valiant deeds,—
Are the descendants of Seadna, the son of Fearghus.

Siol mic n-Eiṗce ṗin ᵹan ail
a ciṗ Conuill iṗ Eoᵹain
olc ṗéan a ccaiṗoiṗ boí lá
oo ṗiol cCoṗmaic mic Enna.

These are the descendants of Earc's sons without reproach,
In the countries of Conall and of Loghan[c],
Ill did their friendship work
To the descendants of Cormac, son of Enna.

Do cuinniᵹ Eaṗc comaio cáio
aṗ a h-occaṗ mac moṗ blaiz
ṗeaṗonn ṗuice nac Fṗiz ṗaill
ṗiol mic n-Eiṗc a cciṗé Conaill.

Earc besought a noble gift
From her eight sons of great renown,
A territory, free of all claim[d], to depend,
From the descendants of Earc's sons in Tir Conaill.

Cuᵹṗac mic Feaṗᵹuṗa oí
Dṗuim Liᵹean aṗ a uaiṗle

The sons of Fearghus gave unto her
Druim Lighean[e], because of its nobleness,

aṗ

For

---

[a] *In the East* i. e. in Scotland, and *here*, in Ireland

[b] *Fanad* —A territory in the north of Tirconnell, extending from Lough Swilly to Mulroy Lough, and from the sea to Rathmelton It comprised the parish of Cloondawadoge, and Rathmullen was its chief residence

[c] *Eoghan·* i e Tir Connell and Tir Eoghain (Tyrone).

[d] *Free of all claim.*—Fṗiz ṗaill, a Brehon law term nearly equivalent to our *fee simple*

[e] *Druim Lighean*, or *Cruachan Lighean*, now Drumleene, on the western bank of Lough Foyle, near Lifford, is still the name of a townland in the barony of Raphoe, parish of Clonleigh, or Clonlaodh, county Donegal A monastery was

ap a coimveipi ap ip zall
ioen Eozan if Conall.

For its convenient situation within the
land,
Between Tir Eoghain and Tir Conaill.

Oo pizne a ziomna pe n-éz
Eapc aluinn, ní h-iomapbpéz
a cpíoc oo Caipneac miao n-zal
oo veazmac a oepbpeapan

She made her will before her death—
Earc, the beautiful, it is no falsehood—
She bequeathed her territory to the ve-
nerated, powerful Cairneach,
The goodly son of her sister.

A h-eic, a h-óp, a h-éavac,
a zioolacao cpoimcéavac,
a ppeapoal póp az pleazaib
vaize ap macaib Muipeavaiz.

Her horses, her gold, her apparel,
Her presents of many heavy hundreds,
And that he be entertained at ban-
quets,
For her, by the sons of Muireadhach

A h-eappao zaca bliaona
map oo biao beo péim piazla
up céo oa zac cpao iappin
oo Chaipneac ó piol Eozain.

Her suit of apparel every year,
As if she were alive, by strict injunction,
And an hundred of every kind of cattle,
To Cairneach, from the seed of Eoghan

Tuzpaz piol Eozain an cíop
fpí pé Caipniz zan azpzip,
azup oo paopaz, miao n-zal,
'na oiaiz pé piciod bliaoan.

The seed of Eoghan paid the tribute
During Cairneach's life without mur-
mur,
And they paid it,—noble deed,—
After him for the term of twenty years

Mappán ip Cappán iappin,
oá comapba o'eip Caipniz

Massan and Cassan[f] then
Were the two coarbs after Cairneach;

zucpaz

They

founded by St Columba at Clonleigh (Colgan,
Trias Thaum p 435, n 33), over which St
Carnech perhaps afterwards presided Colgan,
Acta SS p 782 See above, p 241, n *, and
O'Donovan's Four Masters, at the year 1522
(p 1357), 1524 (p 1371), and 1538 (p. 1813)

[f] *Massan and Cassan*—Colgan says · " Forte
hic Cassanus fuit unus ex quatuor Sanctis Cas-
sanis, de quibus egimus supra hac die [28 Martii]
in vita S Cassani Episcopi, et fortasse quartus qui
20 Junii colitur Item eum qui hic Massanus ap-
pellatur, existimo esse, qui ab aliis *Assanus* vocatur; et colitur 27 April, secundum Marianum et
alios Solent enim nostrates præfigere particulam
Mo, vel solum *M* nominibus Sanctorum a vocali
incipientibus, ut antea sæpe monui "—Acta SS.,
p. 783, n 8

tucrat Ɖnuim Liʒean ʒan ċáin
ap ċíor Caipniʒ ɒo conʒmáil.

They gave away Druim Lighean freely,
Upon condition of receiving Cairneach's
tribute.

Tucrat clanna Néill co paċ
ʒan cíor ʒan feaċt ʒan t-rluaiʒ-
eaɒ,
ciɒ cia po conʒbaiɒ ʒan t-ral
cíor Caipniʒ a ɒuɓpuɒap.

The prosperous Clann Néill gave,
Free of expeditions or of hostings[g],
Although they might have kept it
without reproach,
Cairneach's tribute as they asked.

Feapʒur mac Muipċeaptaiʒ móip
cona cloinn uapail apomóip
ʒabrat an Ɖnuim fa cíor ɒe
Fip Ɖpoma iaɒ ɒa éire.

Fearghus, the son of great Muircheartach,
With his noble, illustrious, great sons,
Took the Druim[h] subject to this tri-
bute,
And hence they were called Fir Droma[i].

Although the foregoing curious poem was never before published, yet it was not unknown to the indefatigable Colgan[k]; and it evidently forms the authority for the following historical narrative, which he has given in his Life of St. Carnech: " Mortuo deinde secundo conjuge Fergussio, Erca a quatuor filiis, quos eidem genuerat, in suæ viduitatis solatium et sustentationem donatur supramemorato prædio nunc *Druim-ligean* nunc Cruchan-ligean appellari solito: quod et ipsa sub mortem condito testamento S. Carnecho sobrino, de filiorum consensu perpetuo legavit; relictáque Murchertacho cæterisque filiis ex priori thoro susceptis suâ regiâ suppellectile, eosdem, ultro ad hoc se offerentes, obligavit ad centum capita ex quolibet armentorum genere eidem S. Carnecho ejusve successori quotannis in perpetuum numeranda. Hæc autem pia et perampla devotæ Principis legata, toto tempore, quo S. Carnechus supervixit,

et

---

[g] *Hostings.*—The successors of St. Carnech, it appears, preferred the tribute to the land, which was at that time burdened with the charges of expeditions and hostings, the maintenance of troops, and also the obligation of serving personally in the wars, from which the ecclesiastical character of the owners did not protect them.

[h] *The Druim :* i. e. Druim Lighean.

[i] *Fir Droma.*—They were called Uí Ethach

Droma Lighean, the descendants of Eochaidh of Druim Lighean, or Feara Droma Lighean, the men of Drum-Lighean. See the genealogy of the O'Donnellys, who were the chiefs of the Fir Droma, in the Appendix to O'Donovan's Four Masters, p. 2426.

[k] Colgan speaks of the author of this poem only under the general terms of " author quidam anonymus, qui videtur ante octingentos vel amplius annos vixisse."

et annis insuper viginti ab ejus morte, rata et firma manserunt, et fideliter solveban-
tur. Verum postea Cassanus et Massanus qui S Carnecho in monasterii regimine suc-
cesserant, negligentiam aliquam in annuâ illâ armentorum pensione solvendâ, vel jam
commissam videntes, vel ne in posterum committeretur metuentes, consenserunt ad
dominium prædicti prædii in filios posterosve Muredacii ea conditione transferendum,
quod dudum statuta pensio, quotannis, ut olim consuevit, integre solveretur. Hac
ergo transactione peracta, Fergussius supra memorato Murchertacho natus, ejusque filii
prædictum prædium possidendum susceperunt, et annis pluribus retinuerunt, usque
scilicet ad tempora Domnaldi filii Aidi Hiberniæ Monarchæ, qui ex supra memorati
Conalli semine oriundus, ab anno Domini 623 ad 639 regnavit."—Acta SS., p. 782

From the foregoing documents it would seem that, at the time when Erc became
St Carnech's penitent, he was at Ross-Ailigh   That after the liberal endowments
bequeathed to him by Erc, he established a monastery at Drium Lighean, or perhaps
enlarged and enriched that which had been founded by St Columba at Cluain Laodh,
now Clonleigh[1].

There are also some data furnished in the poem for determining the year of St. Carnech's death. The bard tells us that the successors of St Carnech, twenty years after
his death, consented to give up the manor of Drum-Lighean, and that Fergus, the son
of Muircheartach, was the sovereign who accepted this surrender, and resumed possession of the Drum, from which his posterity were termed Fir-Droma

But Fergus, according to O'Flaherty's Chronology, reigned conjointly with his
brother Domhnall for one year only, viz , A D 565-6 The Four Masters place the
commencement of the reign of Domhnall and Fergus in 559, and their death in 561
But the Annals of Ulster favour O'Flaherty's date It is probable, however, that Fergus entered into possession of Drum-Lighean when he was chief of Tyrone, and before
he became king of Ireland Therefore St Carnech must have died before the year 545,
if we adopt the dates of O'Flaherty, or before the year 539, if we adopt, with Colgan,
the chronology of the Four Masters.

There is another St. Carnech mentioned in Irish history, who is said to have been
bishop of Tuilen, now Dulane, near Kells. in the county of Meath; but his memory is
now altogether forgotten there Colgan is of opinion that this is not the same as the
Carnech who is the subject of the foregoing remarks For his day is not the 28th of
March,

---

[1] Colgan says " Unde cum duæ ecclesiæ, una
Domhnac-mor, de Magh-Ith, appellata, altera
Cluain Laodh dicta, sint illi prædio [scil de
Druim-ligean], una ad occidentem, altera ad
septentrionem, satis vicinæ , in alterutra ipsum
Abbatis, et per consequens Episcopi munus ex-
ercuisse existimo "—Acta SS , p 782, c. 2

March, but the 16th of May, under which date his death is thus recorded in the Feilire of Aenghus:

ɮαꞅ cαιꝺ chαrniᵹ ꝼirꝺαꞁc.

"The illustrious death of Carnech the truly powerful."

And the gloss adds:

.ı. Caıpnech o Ꞇuılen ı ꝼaıl Che- nannꞃa, ⁊ ꝺo ꞷꞃeaꞇnaıꞷ Copn ꝺo.

i. e. Carnech of Tuilen, in the neigh- bourhood of Cenannas [Kells], and he is of the Britons of Corn [Cornwall].

By this it appears that St. Carnech of Tuilen was not a native of Ireland, but of Cornwall, and therefore Colgan supposes him to be the same as St. Cernach or Caran- tach, whose day in the Calendar of the British Church is the 16th of May, and who flourished about a century before the other St. Carnech, having been, as it is said, a contemporary of St. Patrick.—Trias. Thaum., p. 231. (Acta SS., p. 783, c. 8). It is pro- bable that his memory was introduced into Ireland, and a church dedicated to him at Tuilen, by the three tuatha or septs of the British, i. e. Welshmen, who settled there, according to the topographical poem of O'Dugan, and who were called Comꞇionol Chaıpnıᵹ, or Cairnech's Congregation.

It is of this Carnech, or Carantoch of Tuilen, that Dudley Mac Firbis probably speaks when he says (p. 749, MS. Royal Irish Academy):

Caıpnecc, ꝺo ꞷꞃecnuıꞷ Copn ꝺo, aꞃ uıme ꞃın a oꞅꞃaꞃ Caıpneċ ꝼıꞃ .ı. Caıp- neċ mac Ꞁuıꞇủıc, mıc Ꞁuıᵹıꝺ, mıc Chα- luım, mıc Ioꞇαċaıꞃ, mıc Cꞁꞇα. Cꞃ αṁluıꝺ ꞃın nıꞃıoꞃ Ꝺıolla Caoṁaın ı Soaınıꞷ na m-ꞷꞃꞅꞇon.

Cairnech, he was of the Britons of Corn, and hence he is called Cairnech [Cornish]; viz., Cairnech, son of Luitech, son of Luighidh, son of Talum, son of Jothacar, son of Alt. This is what Giolla Caomhain relates in the Histories of the Britons.

The History of the Britons by Giolla Caomhain, who died about A. D. 1072, is a work which is not now known to exist, unless it be the same as the Leabhar Breathnach, or Irish version of Nennius, here published: for O'Reilly states (Trans. Iberno-Gælic Society, p. cxxii.), that in the Book of Hy-Many there was a copy of the Leabhar Breathnach, at the head of which was a memorandum stating that Nen- nius was the author, but that Giolla Caomhain had translated it into Irish. The genealogy of St. Cairnech, however, as quoted by Dudley Mac Firbis, does not now occur in any of the copies of this work which exist in Dublin.—(T.)

No. XXIII.

No XXIII *Giraldus Cambrensis on the Picts and Scots*

In the course of the year 1846, the Second and Third Distinctions of the work of Giraldus Cambrensis, de Instructione Principis, have been printed, with only excerpta from the First Distinction   The editors excuse this mode of publication, by alleging that the first portion is chiefly ethical, but the words of the following curious extract shew that some historical notices have been omitted.

Excerptum vi p. 188.

" But since the Picti and Scoti have here been mentioned, I have thought it relevant to explain who these nations were, and whence, and why, they were brought into Britannia, as I have gathered it from divers histories.

" Histories relate that the Picti, whom Virgil also calls Agatirsi[m], had their dwellings near the Scitic marshes   And Servius, commenting upon Virgil, and expounding that place[n] ' Picti Agatirsi,' says   ' We call the same people Picti whom we call Agatirsi, and they are called Picti as being stigmatized, since they are wont to be stigmatized and cauterized for the abundance of phlegm   And these people are the same as the Gothi Since, then, the continual punctures superinduce scars, their bodies become, as it were, painted, and they are called Picti from these cauteries overgrown[o] with scars '

" So, when that tyrant Maximus went over from Britannia to Francia, with all the men and forces and arms of the island, to assume the empire, Gratian and Valentinian, brothers and partners in the empire, transported[p] this Gothic nation, brave and strong in war, either allied or subject to themselves, and [won][q] by imperial benefits, from the boundaries of Scitia to the northern parts of Britannia, to infest the Britons, and

call

---

[m] Contrariwise, he gives to the Agathyrsi the epithet of Picti

[n] Neither there nor elsewhere hath the extant Servius (Edit. Masvici) one syllable of this, nor has he anywhere any mention of the Gothi

[o] This disfiguring of the features by cicatrization was an entirely distinct practice, and limited to the face.   The Hunnish tribes were those who delighted in such deformity   Ammianus says they cicatrized their new-born infants —xxxi. cap 2   Others relate that they inflicted these scars on occasion of grief and mourning   But the statements are not incompatible.   The poet Sidonius only means *bloody when inflicted by red,—*

—————————————— " vultuque minaci
Rubra cicatricum vestigia defodisse "—*Ad Avitum*, 239

[p] Manifestly false, for Eumenius of Autun, in the year 297, spoke of the Picti in Britannia   Paneg Constantio cap xi

[q] Imperialibus .   tam beneficiis, *tam* being the last syllable of some passive participle

call home the tyrant with all the youth of the island, which he had taken away never destined to return.

" But they, being strong in the warlike valour natural to Goths, nevertheless finding the island stript (as I have said) of men and forces, occupied no small part of its northern provinces, never meaning to revisit their own country, and of pirates becoming settlers.

" In process of time (having married wives from the neighbouring Hybernia since they could have none from the Britons) they took into alliance the Hybernic nation, also called Scotian ; and gave them the maritime part of the land they had occupied, and the nearest to their own country, where the sea is narrow, which is called[r] Galweidia, where they afterwards became unanimous in infesting the Britons, and advancing their own frontiers. And it is of them that Gildas, in his treatise de Excidio Britonum, says: ' Then Britannia, destitute of armed soldiers, and deprived of the vigorous young men of the country, who, having followed the above-mentioned tyrant, never returned home, being now entirely ignorant of the use of war, began first to be oppressed and trampled by two very fierce nations, the Picti from the north, and the Scoti from the north-west.' &c., &c[s]. And now I will briefly relate how the mighty nation of Picti, after so many victories, has come to nothing.

" When the Saxons had occupied the island, as I have said, and concluded a stable peace with the Picti, the Scoti (who had been joined to the Picti, and invited by them to inhabit their country) seeing that the Picti (although now fewer[t], because of the affinity of Hibernia) were yet much their superiors in arms and courage, had recourse to their wonted and, as it were, innate treacheries[u] [*prædictiones*], in which they surpass other nations. They invited[v] all the magnates of the Picti to a banquet, and when an excess and profusion of meat and drink had been taken, and they perceived their opportunity, they removed the pegs which supported the planks, whereby they all

[r] Galloway. Here Giraldus evinces his complete ignorance of the history and geography of the Scots colony.

[s] The Editor has omitted much of the quotations from Gildas.

[t] If the text is sound, it probably means that the Pictish *superiority of numbers* was diminished by the succours which the Scots obtained from their mother country.

[u] For this word, *prædictiones*, which occurs twice, and is not intelligible to me, I suppose we ought to read *proditiones*.

[v] This tale, howsoever fabulous, and borrowed from the story of Hengist, puts on its true footing the pretended total extirpation of the Picts by Kenneth M'Alpin. It was an extirpation of the *righs*, or royal Picts, in whom the crown was heritable, of the whole tanistry (if I may so term it) of the realm.

all fell, by a wonderful stratagem, up to their hams into the hollow of the benches whereon they were sitting, so that they could by no means rise; and then straight-way they slaughtered them all, taken by surprise, and fearing no such treatment from their kinsfolk and confederates, whom they had joined in fealty to their own enfeoff-ment[w], and who were their allies in war In this manner the more warlike and pow-erful of the two nations entirely disappeared, but the other, in all respects far inferior, having gained the advantage in the moment of so great a treachery [*prædiction*], obtained even unto this day the whole of that country, from sea to sea, which after their own name they called Scotia "—(*H.*)

No. XXIV   *Addenda et Corrigenda*

Page 26, note [m], "*The Welsh also call themselves Gwydhil, and their country Tir Gwydhil.*" This is a mistake A part of Anglesea (or the whole) was in the posses-sion of the Irish in the fifth and sixth centuries, and certain monuments there are called *Carrig y Wyddyl,* "Stones of the Gael;" some rude old houses are called *tre'r Wydde-lodd,* "Houses of the Gael," and a prince of Mona living in those times was styled the *Brenn o Wyddelodd* If there ever was a *Tir y Gwyddyl,* out of Albany, it was probably that colony in Mona But that places the name in opposition to Cymmry, and not in synonyme with it The statement that the Welsh call *themselves* Gwyddyl, or their country Tir y Gwyddyl, is altogether a mistake

P 30, note [f], line 18. It is, however, possible that the discreditable sense of the word havren may be a secondary and modern one, its older meaning having been void of reproach. During the long time since I penned this note, I have concluded this much, that Geoffrey's original was neither brought from, nor written in, Armo-rica.—(*H*)

P 103, note [s], col 1, line 8, for "*is usually attributed to the year 473,*" read, "is variously dated from 456 to 473"

P 111, line 6, "*his shoulder*" That *ysguyd,* a shield, was mistaken for *ysgwydd,* a shoulder, is the convincing remark of Mr Price in his Hanes Cymru —See the notes to Schulz on Welsh tradition, p. 10 This easy mistake was probably fur-ther facilitated by the use of both words. Geoffrey says "adaptat *humeris* quoque suis *clypeum*" Two of his Welsh translators have tarian ar ysgwydd, but we find poets affecting the gingle of ysgwyd ar ysgwydd.—(*H*)

P 130, line (of the poem) 18 am pano Ɛpcail-icbi This is very obscure and corrupt, am pano is not properly "in the portion," although it has been so conjec-turally

[w] Suo beneficio confeodatis

jecturally rendered: to be so it ought to be ιɲpoιnꝺ, or ιɲɲanꝺ. Mr. Curry proposes to read αm ɲαnꝺ eɲcαιlιꝅ bι, for αm ɲon eɲcαιleαꝺ αmbιꝅ, "when *first* their existence was discovered." Eɲcαιleαꝺ is an old word which is thus explained in a Glossary in the Library of Trinity College: .ι. eιɲneαꝺ, uꝅ eɲꝅ, ιn bι bɲeꝅeαm nα bι eɲcαιlꝅeꝅ ꝛc. αɲ ιɼ ꝅɲe eɲcαιleαꝺ ꝼαιllɼιꝶꝅeαɲ αιnꝅeαɼ ní beαꝅαꝺ .ι. αɲιɼ ꝅɲια ɼιn eɲneαꝺ ꝼuɲɼαmαιꝶꝅeαɲ, ɲo ꝼαιllɼιꝶꝅeɲ αιnꝅeαɼ ιn beαꝅα. "*Ercaileadh*, i. e. *eirneadh* (solution), as in *the saying*, 'There will be no judge who will not be able to solve (*ercail-tech*), &c.;' *and*, 'For it is by solution (*ercaileadh*) that all the difficult questions of life are made clear,' i. e. through *erneadh* (solution), all the questions of life are made clear or explained."—(*T*).

Ibid., line 22 (of the poem), ꝅαιꝅne. This word is translated *understood*, on the authority of the following passage from the Leabhar Breac, fol. 27, *b. a.*

Αlιι ů eoɼ Ebɼιcα lιnꝶα locuꝅoɼ ꝼuιɼɼe αɲbιꝅɲαnꝅuɲ. Seo ιꝅα αb omnιbuɼ ēē ιnꝅellecꝅα eα ꝗ ꝺꝅα ɼunꝅ ꝗ̄ ɼιnꝶulιɼ pɲopɲια ɼuα loꝗueɲeꝅuɲ. Ꝼαιɲenꝺ αιle ů. ιɼɼeꝺ αꝺbɲeuꝅ conιꝺ on beɲlα Ebɲαιꝺe nαmα ɲo lαbαιɲɼeꝅ ꝶ conιꝺ αιɼɼιꝺe ꝺo ꝅαιꝅne αeb α m-beɲlα ꝺιlιɼ ꝺo ꝅαch.

Alii vero eos [sc. Apostolos] Hebraica lingua locutos fuisse arbitrantur. Sed ita ab omnibus esse intellecta ea quæ dicta sunt, quia singulis propria sua loqueretur (*sic*). Others think that they spake in the Hebrew language, and that it sounded with the sweet accent of his own language to each.

The allusion, as the reader will evidently perceive, is to Acts, ii. 4–11.

Ibid., line 26 (of the poem), ꝼɲιlαꝅαɲ ꝶun lιun. In the same glossary already quoted lαꝅαɲ is explained by ιnꝺιll, ready prepared: and lιun by leαn no ꝼαιll, defect or neglect.—See line 54.

P. 284, note ¹. The word bɲeαcαιꝺ may be the third person plural of the verb bɲecαιm, to variegate, adorn, illustrate, colour with spots: and the meaning is, that Malcolm was king thirty years, a period that has been celebrated or illustrated, blazoned in poems or verses.—(*T.*)

P. liv, Additional Notes, line 26, "*Or silver-hip.*" Observe the strictly analogous names of the Danaunian king, Nuadh Silver-hand. Compare also the Druidess Geal-cosach, or white-legs, whose tomb is shewn in Inishowen.—(*H.*)

P. xlviii, lines 5, 6, "*We read in Lib. Ballymote, that Bruide Cnit. . . . was King of Ulster.—Ap. Pinkerton, i. 502–504.*" The passage certainly does so stand in the Book of Ballymote, Cnιꝅ ɲι ulαꝺ; "Cnit [or Cint], King of Uladh."—See p. xcii. And it is also stated in the Book of Lecan (see p. lxvii. *supra*), that Urchal Bruidi-pont was

thirty

thirty years King of Uladh.   But these passages, particularly the former, are so corrupt, that no safe inference can be drawn from them.

There is in the Book of Lecan another copy of the Cruithnian story, besides those given above, p lxv. *et seq.*, and p. xciii. *et seq.*; but it is so nearly the same as the others, that it has not been thought worth while to transcribe it, especially as it is very corrupt, and adds nothing to the information given us in the copies which have been printed   It occurs in the history of the reign of Herimon, in a long account of the Milesian invasion of Ireland[1]

The allusion to the King of Uladh, or Uhdia, in this tract, is as follows

Uρealbρuıɀe poνɀ χχχ b ıρρıɀe nuɀ Iρoe uρbeaρɀa bρuıɀe Fρı ɀac Feaρ oıb ꝺ ρeνꝺa νa Feaρ.	Urealbruide Pont thirty years in the kingdom of Uladh It is from him the name of Bruide is given to every man of them and to the divisions of their lands.

In this list of the kings the same confused mixture of the Bruides with the other names occurs which has been already noticed in the Book of Ballymote, and originated, probably, in the same cause —See p. xcii , *supra*

Hence, although the name is written above Urealbruide Pont, yet it is clear that two names, Ureal and Bruide Pont, are run together, and that the observation applies properly to Pont, or Bont (see above, p 156), who is called Bout by Pinkerton

It will be seen also, that in the reading of this passage, as given above, p 156, and also in that given from another part of the Book of Lecan (p. xci , *supra*), there is no mention of Uladh.   There we find, instead of ıρρıɀe nuɀ or nulaꝺ, as in the former place, χχχ. aνꝺ uaꝺ, and in the latter, χχχ ᵃ ρıɀ uaꝺ, intimating that after Bruide Pont there were thirty kings, who bore the common title of Bruide.

Which of these was the true reading it is now impossible to say, but it is evident that we must be very cautious in drawing any inference from the mention of Uladh in so very corrupt a passage —(*T*)

P cviii, note ᶠ, *Massan* and *Cassan*   These saints are mentioned in the poem on the Saints of the Cinel Laeghaire, in a poem beginning Naem ρeνcaρ naem ıννρı Faıl (Book of Ballymote, fol. 126, *b b*)

ꝺeoaν, Aρρaν, Caρaν ɀρıuρ, ucuρ Rıchell a νꝺeρꝺρıuρ, Aρɀρaıɀ mıc Aeꝺa aıν, mıc ρeıνɀ Lıbıρ mıc Ꝺallaıν	Beoan, Assan, Cassan three, and Richell their sister, Artraigh, son of noble Aedh, son of chaste Liber, son of Dallan —(*T*)

INDEX.

---

[1] Book of Lecan, fol 13, *b. b*

INDEX.

cxxiii

q 2

FINIS

IRISH

ARCHÆOLOGICAL SOCIETY.

At a General Meeting of the Irish Archæological Society, held in the Board Room of the Royal Irish Academy, on Saturday, the 19th day of December, 1846,

The Most Noble the Marquis of Kildare in the Chair,

The Secretary read the following Report from the Council:

" The month of December being the time of the year in which the Council are bound, by the by-law passed on the 10th of July, 1844, to summon a General Meeting of the Society, they beg leave to lay before your Lordship, and the Members here present, a Report of the proceedings during the past year, and to congratulate the Society on being now met together to celebrate its *sixth* anniversary.

" Since the last General Meeting, held on the 19th of December, 1845, twenty-two new Members have been elected[a] ; whose names are as follows :

His Excellency the Earl of Bessborough, Lord Lieutenant of Ireland	Rev Beaver H. Blacker.
The Earl of Portarlington.	*Patrick Chalmers, Esq
Viscount Suirdale.	John David Chambers, Esq.
	William Chambers, Esq.

Thomas

[a] Those to whose names an asterisk is prefixed are Life Members.

a

Thomas Clarke, Esq.	John Nolan, Junior, Esq
*Rev Edward F Day.	Denis O'Conor, Esq
*William Donnelly, Esq.	R More O'Ferrall, Esq, M P.
John Flanedy, Esq.	Richard O'Reilly, Esq
John Hyde, Esq.	Henry Thompson Redmond, Esq
*The Right Hon. Henry Labouchere, M P.	John Sadleir, Esq.
	Rev. Charles Strong
The Rev. Daniel M'Carthy.	William Robert Wilde, Esq

" The Society has to lament the death, since the last Meeting, of the following seven Members, one of whom was a Member of the Council, and a zealous friend to the Society, at its original formation :

The Bishop of Kildare.	Thomas Goold, Esq, Master in Chancery.
Viscount Templetown	James A. Maconochie, Esq
Sir Aubrey de Vere, Bart	John Smith Furlong, Esq, Q C.
James Gibbons, Esq	

" The number of Members on the Books of the Society now amounts to 443, including 60 Life Members

" Since the last Annual Meeting, the Council have issued to all Members, who have subscribed for the year 1845, the valuable work edited by Mr Hardiman, from a MS in the Library of Trinity College, entitled, A Chorographical Description of West or H-iar Connaught, written, A. D 1684, by Roderick O'Flaherty, Esq, author of the 'Ogygia' This volume is illustrated with a map of West Connaught, and a fac-simile of O'Flaherty's hand-writing, and extends to 483 pages, including the Introduction

" The delay in the publication of this volume was chiefly owing to the editor's absence from Dublin, but also, in some degree, to his having discovered, after the work was far advanced, a great number of original documents connected with the history of West Connaught, which it seemed very desirable to print in the Appendix, as a more favourable opportunity of publishing these important records might not occur hereafter ; the Council, therefore, willingly acceded to Mr Hardiman's wishes, to whom they take this opportunity of returning their sincere thanks

" The volume contains a mass of topographical and historical matter of very unusual interest and value. It is highly creditable to Mr. Hardiman's learning
and

and research, and the Council are happy to find that it has been most favour-ably received by the Members of the Society.

"The Council had hoped to have been able to give, along with the foregoing volume, Cormac's Glossary. But in this intention, which was announced at the last annual Meeting, they have been doubly disappointed. The unex-pected size to which Mr. Hardiman's Appendix and notes extended, and the consequent expense of the work, render it impossible to put together, as an equivalent for one year's subscription, two such costly books. O'Flaherty's West Connaught has actually cost the Society sixteen shillings per copy ; and when to this are added the expenses of delivery, salaries, and other charges of the year, it will be seen that the Council would be wanting in their duty as Trustees of the Society's funds, if they should persevere in their original inten-tion of giving any additional volume, and especially one so costly as Cormac's Glossary, to the Members of the year 1845. They hope, therefore, that the Society will perceive the necessity which exists for a change in the arrange-ment proposed by the Council of that year, and announced in the last Annual Report.

"Another source of disappointment has arisen from the unexpected obstacles that have been experienced in the preparation of Cormac's Glossary for the Press. No person who has never actually engaged in such studies can ade-quately estimate the real difficulties of this work, filled as it is with obsolete words and obscure allusions, fragments of the languages spoken by Northmen, Picts, and British in the tenth century, and quotations from Brehon laws and ancient poems, all of which must be sought for in our manuscript libraries, without the aid of catalogue or index of any kind, except such as the private labours of Mr. O'Donovan and Mr. Curry have provided for themselves. These difficulties are so frequent, and arise so unexpectedly, that the Council feel it to be impossible to say when this important and laborious work will be ready for delivery ; but they can promise that no pains or labour shall be spared to bring it out as speedily as is consistent with the necessary attention to accuracy.

"The first volume of the Miscellany of the Irish Archæological Society, constituting the book for the present year, is now in course of distribution to the Members.

"In addition to the contents, as announced in the Report of last year, there have been added some short pieces, particularly The Annals of Ireland, from

the

the year 1443 to 1468, translated from the Irish, by Dudley Firbisse, or, as he is more usually called, Duald Mac Firbis, for Sir James Ware, in the year 1666

"These Annals, which have been quoted by Ware, Harris, and others, are of considerable value and importance, although never before published They have been translated from an Irish original, now lost, or at least unknown, which was evidently in the hands of the Four Masters, and has been made use of by them as an authority, for they have frequently transcribed it *verbatim* in their Annals.

"The Council propose to give for the year 1847, The Irish Version of the 'Historia Britonum' of Nennius, with a translation and notes, by the Secretary; and additional notes, and an Introduction, by the Hon Algernon Herbert A considerable portion of this work is printed, and it is hoped that nothing will prevent its completion in the course of a few months

"Of the projected publications of the Society, it will be necessary now to speak very briefly

"It was announced in the last Annual Report, that the Council had in view a collection of the Latin annalists of Ireland Of these there are already in the Press ·

"1 The Annals, by John Clyn, of Kilkenny, which have been transcribed from a MS in the Library of Trinity College, Dublin, collated with a copy in the Bodleian Library, Oxford, and will be edited, with notes, by the Rev. Richard Butler

"2. The Annals of Thady Dowling, Chancellor of Leighlin, which will be edited, with notes, by Aquilla Smith, Esq , M.D , from a MS in the Library of Trinity College, Dublin.

"3 The Annals of Henry Marlborough , from a MS in the Cottonian Library, British Museum, collated with an imperfect copy in the Library of Trinity College, Dublin.

"To these it is probable that one or two others of the minor Annals may be added, which, although in themselves of little moment, are valuable, as they have been quoted by our principal historians, and are an essential part of the original sources of Irish history

"Of the other works proposed for publication, the Council are happy to be able to state that one, which has been long announced, and which has been looked

for

it was, no doubt, transcribed from much earlier documents, it may be taken as representing the doctrine and devotion of the Irish Church in the age of St. Columba, when Ireland was so justly known throughout Europe as "Insula Sanctorum." A Hymnarium of the seventh century is a literary treasure that ought not to be left any longer in obscurity.

"Of the other works suggested for publication, the Council have nothing to say in addition to what was stated by their predecessors in the Report of last year; they are precluded by the deficiency of funds from undertaking any such expensive publications as the Dinnseanchus, or the Brehon Laws, which present difficulties of so peculiar a nature. For such great works, therefore, they can only hope to prepare the way, and they cannot but flatter themselves that the publications of this Society have already done much to awaken a taste for Irish literature, and to arouse the Public to some little sense of the national disgrace which rests upon us, for allowing these invaluable monuments of antiquity to slumber so long on the shelves of our libraries.

"The Council have it in contemplation to publish, as soon as they find it possible, the Topographical Poems of O'Dugan and O'Heerin, with illustrative notes by Mr. O'Donovan, a work that cannot fail to prove interesting to the Public; but so many circumstances, over which they have no control, may combine to delay this design, that they cannot undertake as yet to fix the time when this publication may be expected. The same remark applies to Duald Mac Firbis's Account of the Firbolgs and Danes of Ireland, and to the Naemh Seanchus, or History of the Saints of Ireland, attributed to Aengus the Culdee or some of his disciples, and preserved in the Book of Lecan. In short, there is the greatest abundance of interesting and important materials, and funds alone are wanting for giving them to the Public.

"It will be remembered by the Society that in former Reports the Council more than once declared that they were overdrawing the funds of the Society, and giving to the Members a higher value for their subscriptions than the disposable means of the Society justified. This was done for the purpose of bringing the Society into notice, and of enabling the Irish public to judge of the great abundance of the materials that exist, as well as of the manner in which it was proposed to render our ancient literature accessible to students. In this there

[b] See Report for 1842 (prefixed to the Battle of Magh Ragh), p. 4. Report for 1845 (prefixed to O'Flaherty's West Connaught), p. 6.

is no doubt the Council judged wisely; but the time is now come when a different course must be pursued   The experience of five years, during which the limited number of 500 members has never been obtained, proves clearly the small amount of interest that is felt for the objects of the Society, and it is, therefore, become the duty of the Council to announce, that the number of pages hitherto published in the year must henceforth be very seriously diminished, unless a large accession of additional Members can be obtained   If every Member would engage to procure one new Member in the course of the next year, the means of bringing out the works in preparation would be in a great measure supplied, but if the Society remains at its present limit, Members must be content to perceive a very sensible diminution in the bulk of our annual publications "

The Report having been read, it was moved by the Provost of Trinity College, seconded by Lieutenant General Birch, and

" RESOLVED,—That the Report now read be received and printed, and circulated amongst the Members of the Society "

Moved by N P O'Gorman, Esq, seconded by Charles Mac Donnell, Esq., and

" RESOLVED,—That the Rev. Charles Graves, and James McGlashan, Esq., be appointed Auditors for the ensuing year, and that their statement of the accounts of the Society be printed with the Report "

Moved by John O'Callaghan, Esq, seconded by Rev. Dr. Wilson, and

" RESOLVED,—That his Grace the Duke of Leinster be elected President of the Society for the ensuing year, and that the following Noblemen and Gentlemen be the Council

THE MOST NOBLE THE MARQUIS OF KILDARE, M R I A.
THE RIGHT HON THE EARL OF LEITRIM, M R I A.
THE RIGHT HON THE VISCOUNT ADARE, M P, M R I A
THE REV SAMUEL BUTCHER, A M, M R I A

JAMES HARDIMAN, ESQ, M R I. A.
THE REV J H TODD. D.D, M.R I.A.
WILLIAM E HUDSON, ESQ, M R I A
MAJOR LARCOM, R E., V P. R I A
J. MACCULLAGH, ESQ, LL D., M R I A
GEO PETRIE, ESQ, R H.A. V P R I A.
AQUILLA SMITH, ESQ, M D, M R I A.
J HUBAND SMITH, ESQ, A M., M R I A

Moved

IRISH

ARCHÆOLOGICAL SOCIETY.

At a General Meeting of the IRISH ARCHÆOLOGICAL SOCIETY, held in the Board Room of the Royal Irish Academy, on Wednesday, the 22nd day of December, 1847,

HIS GRACE THE DUKE OF LEINSTER in the Chair,

The Secretary read the following Report from the Council:

" The labours of the Irish Archæological Society have now been continued for a period of seven years, and the Council, on laying before you their annual Report of the progress and prospects of the Society, are compelled, with great regret, to abandon the tone of hope with which they have hitherto addressed you.

" They regret to say that the experience of the last seven years has forced upon them the conviction, that very little interest is felt by the Irish public for the publication of ancient Irish literature, or the preservation of the ancient Irish language. In seven years, during which this Society has been before the public, we have not succeeded in obtaining 500 subscribers, including those resident in England, in any one year, who have been willing to contribute an entrance fee of £3, and an annual subscription of £1, towards the objects of the Society; and yet, before the establishment of the Society, nothing was more common than declamations on the national disgrace of suffering our ancient Irish manuscripts to moulder in oblivion.

" Since

" Since the last Annual Meeting, twenty-five new members have been elected Their names are as follows.

His Excellency the Earl of Clarendon
Lord John Manners
Mons Le Comte O'Kelly Farrell
Robert Archbold, Esq
Rowland Bateman, Esq
Richard S. Bourke, Esq , M P.
W H Bradshaw, Esq.
John Wilham Browne, Esq
*R Clayton Browne, Esq
Rev George Crolly.
Rev John Dunne
Sir Thomas Esmonde, Bart
John Greene, Esq

Right Rev Dr. Haly, R C. Bishop of Kildare and Leighlin.
Rev. James Hamilton
The Kildare-street Club
G A M'Dermott, Esq , F G S
Right Rev Dr M'Nally, R. C Bishop of Clogher
Robert Power, Esq.
*Rev. G C Renouard, B D
John Reynolds, Esq., M P.
*George Smith. Esq , F R S
Michael Staunton, Esq.
Rev Dr. Walsh
The Very Rev. Dr. Yore, V G Dublin

" During the past year the Society has lost, by death, the following Members

The Duke of Northumberland.
The Earl of Bessborough
Right Hon. Thomas Grenville
*James Mac Cullagh, Esq
Joseph Nelson, Esq , Q C.

Daniel O'Connell, Esq., M P
The O'Conor Don , M. P.
William Potts, Esq
Remmy Sheehan, Esq
Rev Robert Trail, D D

' The number of Members now on the books of the Society amount to 458, of whom sixty-two are Life Members

" To show the progress of the Society, the Council think it right to lay before this Meeting the following tabular view of the number of Members on our books in each year since the commencement of our labours

Year	Annual Members	Life Members	Total	Annual Increase.
1841	221	11	232	
1842	239	19	258	26
1843	308	36	314	86
1844	337	48	385	41
1845	373	57	430	45
1846	383	60	443	13
1847	396	62	458	15

" From

* Those to whose names an asterisk is prefixed are Life Members

vanced.* The delay has been occasioned in a great measure by the necessity of sending each proof sheet, for Mr. Herbert's remarks and corrections, to England; but principally by the discovery of a most interesting ancient historical poem, which was necessary to the illustration of the work, and which the Editor is now adding to it from a MS. of the twelfth century in the Library of Trinity College, Dublin.

" The Council will not anticipate the duty of the Editor by describing more particularly the nature of this document, or the reasons which have induced them to delay the publication for the sake of admitting it. They feel assured that every Member of the Society will agree with them in thinking that it was better to incur the delay than to bring out the work in a less perfect form; they have little doubt that the *Historia* of Nennius in its Irish dress, with the curious illustrations of British, Scottish, and Welsh history with which it is accompanied, will be received by the learned world as a valuable addition to the *sources* of British history.

" The disappointments experienced by the Council from the circumstances already referred to, render it impossible for them to say much on the subject of future publications. For an account of the works already undertaken, and partly in progress, they have nothing to add to what was said in the Report presented to the Society last year. They may add, however, that the *Macariæ Excidium*, or Destruction of Cyprus, by Colonel Charles O'Kelly, is now completed, and ready for the press, and as soon as the funds at the disposal of the Council enable them to do so, it shall be placed in the hands of the printer. If any considerable portion of the arrears due to the Society should be collected, the Council would propose to give this work as the Society's publication for the year 1848.

" The Council have received from Mr. Shirley, the Rev. Mr. Graves of Kilkenny, Mr. O'Donovan, and other friends, some valuable contributions to the second volume of the Irish Archæological Miscellany; and they are in a condition, if funds permit, to bring out a fasciculus at least of this work during the ensuing year.

" Since the last meeting of the Society Mr. Reeves has published his Ecclesiastical

* The volume has been completed since the Annual Meeting was held, and is now in course of distribution to the Members.

siastical Taxation of the Dioceses of Down and Connor and Dromore, in a form exactly similar to the publications of this Society. This may be hailed as a satisfactory proof that the labours of the Society have excited in others, and in the public at large, a thirst for sound historical and topographical information. Mr. Reeves, it will be recollected, has undertaken to edit for the Society the whole of the important document, of which he has already brought out a part in the volume alluded to We have no hope that the Society's funds will enable the Council to undertake this work for some time to come , but it may, perhaps, be interesting to the Society to have on record the following account of his intended labours, with which Mr Reeves has kindly furnished the Council

" ' *Ecclesiastical Taxation of Ireland*, A D 1306 *Edited from the original Exchequer Rolls, London* By the Rev WILLIAM REEVES, M. B., M. R I. A., &c

" ' This Record notices all the dioceses of Ireland, and the several churches contained in them, arranged under rural deaneries, except the dioceses of Ferns, Ossory, and the upper part of Armagh The deficiency, however, as far as regards Ossory, may be fully supplied from the Red Book of Ossory, in which are two taxations of the diocese, anterior to 1320. In the Registry of Primate Sweteman is contained a catalogue of the churches in the upper or county of Louth part of Armagh, of about the same date So that Ferns is the only hiatus, for the repair of which there are no available materials.

" ' Though the recital extends only to the names and incomes of the benefices, so that the notice of each occupies but a single line, the bare text would fill a volume nearly as large as any of those yet published by the Society. It is therefore proposed that the work should appear in four parts, containing severally an ecclesiastical province, with brief notes, identifying each name with the corresponding modern one on the Ordnance Map, and noticing such authorities as illustrate the ancient history and modern condition of the churches

" ' This arrangement will enable the Editor to put to press the first part, which is the province of Armagh, as soon as the Council think fit ; and at the same time avoid the inconvenience of swelling a single volume to such a size as to be unwieldy, or to monopolize the resources of the Society

" ' WILLIAM REEVES

" ' *Dec* 16, 1847 ' "

The

The Report having been read, it was moved by the Rev. Richard Mac Donnell, D. D., Senior Fellow of Trinity College, Dublin, and

"RESOLVED,—That the Report now read be received and printed, and circulated amongst the Members of the Society."

Moved by the Very Rev. L. F. Renehan, D. D., President of the Royal College of St. Patrick, Maynooth, and

"RESOLVED,—That Sir Colman O'Loghlen and Mr. O'Donoghue be appointed Auditors for the ensuing year, and that the statement of the accounts of the Society be printed with the Report."

Moved by the Rev. James Wilson, D. D., Precentor of St. Patrick's Cathedral, Dublin, and

"RESOLVED,—That, in accordance with the recommendation of the Council, the following words in the 7th Fundamendal Law,—'Any Member who shall be one year in arrear of his subscription shall be considered as having resigned,'— be omitted; and that the following words be substituted instead thereof: 'Any Member who shall be one year in arrear of his subscription shall be liable to be removed by the Council from the books of the Society, after due notice served upon him to that effect.'"

Moved by George Petrie, Esq., LL.D., V. P. R. I. A, and

"RESOLVED,—That, in accordance with the recommendation of the Council, the 2nd Fundamental Law be altered to the following: 'The affairs of the Society shall be managed by a Council consisting of a President, three Vice-Presidents, and twelve other Members, to be annually elected by the Society.'"

Moved by the Rev. Charles Russell, D. D., Professor of Ecclesiastical History in the Royal College of St. Patrick, Maynooth, and

"RESOLVED,—That His Grace the Duke of Leinster be elected President of the Society for the following year: that the Most Noble the Marquis of Kildare, the Right Hon. the Earl of Leitrim, and the Right Hon. the Viscount

c   Adare

Adare, be the Vice-Presidents of the Society; and that the following be elected on the Council:

Rev. Sam Butcher, A M., F T.C D, M.R.I A.	Geo. Petrie, Esq., LL.D, V P R I A
Rev. Chas. Graves, A.M, F.T C.D., M.R.I.A.	Rev. Wm. Reeves, M.B, M. R. I. A.
	The Very Rev. L. F. Renehan, D D., President of Maynooth College.
James Hardiman, Esq, M. R. I A	Aquilla Smith, Esq, M.D., M.R.I.A.
W. E. Hudson, Esq, M. R. I A	Joseph Huband Smith, Esq., M. A., M R I A.
Thomas A. Larcom, Esq., R. E., V. P. R. I A.	
Charles MacDonnell, Esq., M.R.I.A.	Rev. J H. Todd, D. D, F. T. C D., M R. I. A "

Moved by John C O'Callaghan, Esq, and

" Resolved,—That the thanks of the Society be voted to the President and Council of the Royal Irish Academy, for their kindness in granting the use of their room for this meeting "

Moved by Sir Colman M O'Loghlen, Bart., and

" Resolved,—That the thanks of the Society be voted to His Grace the Duke of Leinster, for his kindness in accepting the office of President of the Society, and for his conduct in the Chair on this occasion "

27

John O'Connell, Esq., M. P., Gowran-hill, Dalkey.

Denis O'Connor, Esq., Mount Druid, Belenagare, County Roscommon.

John O'Donoghue, Esq., Dublin.

The O'Donovan, Montpelier, Douglas, Cork.

*John O'Donovan, Esq., Newcomen-place, Dublin.

The O'Dowda, Bonniconlan House, Ballina.

*Joseph Michael O'Ferrall, Esq., Rutlandsquare, West, Dublin.

The Right Hon. R. More O'Ferrall, Governor of Malta.

*William Ogilby, Esq., London.

Nicholas Purcell O'Gorman, Esq., Q. C., Blessington-street, Dublin.

Richard O'Gorman, Esq., Lower Dominickstreet, Dublin.

The O'Grady, Kilballyowen, Bruff.

Thomas O'Hagan, Esq., Great Charles-st., Dublin.

Major O'Hara, Annamoe, Collooney.

Sir Colman M. O'Loghlen, Bart., Merrionsquare South, Dublin.

Richard O'Reilly, Esq., Upper Sackvillestreet, Dublin.

Richard O'Shaughnessy, Esq., Lower Gardiner-street, Dublin.

Rev. Mortimer O'Sullivan, D. D., Killyman.

George Panton, Esq., Heriot's Hospital, Edinburgh.

Marcus Patterson, Esq., Clifden House, Curofin.

Right Hon. Sir Robert Peel, Bart., M. P., London.

Louis Hayes Petit, Esq., F. R. S., London.

George Petrie, Esq., LL. D., R. H. A. V. P. R. I. A., Great Charles-st., Dublin,

* Sir Thomas Phillipps, Bart., Middlehill, Broadway, Worcestershire.

John Edward Pigott, Esq., Merrion-square, South, Dublin.

Robert Pitcairn, Esq., Queen-street, Edinburgh.

*Rev. Charles Porter, Ballybay.

Rev. Classon Porter, Larne.

Colonel Henry Edward Porter, Minterne, Dorchester.

Robt. Power, Esq., Pembroke-place, Dublin.

Lieutenant-Colonel Joseph Pratt, Calra Castle, Kingscourt.

Hon. Edward Preston, Gormanstown Castle, Balbriggan.

Colonel J. Dawson Rawdon, M. P., Coldstream Guards, Stanhope-street, London.

Thomas M. Ray, Esq., Dublin.

Thomas N. Redington, Esq., M. R. I. A., Under Secretary for Ireland, Dublin Castle.

Henry Thompson Redmond, Esq., Carrick-on-Suir.

Rev. William Reeves, M. B., Ballymena.

Lewis Reford, Esq., Beechmount, Belfast.

W. Reilly, Esq., Belmont, Mullingar.

Rev. Laurence F. Renehan, D. D., President of St. Patrick's College, Maynooth.

Rev. G. C. Renouard, B. D., Dartford, Kent.

E. William Robertson, Esq., Breadsall Priory, Derby.

Rev. Thomas R. Robinson, D. D., M. R. I. A., Observatory, Armagh.

George Roe, Esq., Nutley, Dublin.

Richard Rothwell, Esq., Rockfield, Kells.

Rev. Charles Russell, D. D., St. Patrick's College, Maynooth.

Rev. Franc Sadleir, D. D., V. P. R. I. A., Provost of Trinity College, Dublin.

John Sadleir, Esq., Great Denmark-street, Dublin.

Rev.

28

Rev. George Salmon, A. M., Fellow of Trinity College, Dublin.

Rev. Francis A. Sanders, A. B., Lower Fitzwilliam-street, Dublin.

Robert Sharpe, Esq., Coleraine.

Right Hon. Frederick Shaw, Recorder of Dublin, Kimmage House.

Evelyn John Shirley, Esq., M. P., Carrickmacross.

Evelyn Philip Shirley, Esq., Eatington Park, Shipton-on-Stour.

Rev. Joseph H. Singer, D. D., M. R. I. A., Senior Fellow of Trinity College, Dublin.

W. F. Skene, Esq., Edinburgh.

Aquilla Smith, Esq., M. D., M. R. I. A., 121, Lower Baggot-street, Dublin.

*George Smith, Esq., Lower Baggot-street, Dublin.

*George Smith, F. R. S., Trevu, Camborne, England.

*Rev. J. Campbell Smith, A. B., Rome.

J. Huband Smith, Esq., A. M., M. R. I. A., Holles-street, Dublin.

Wm. Smith, Esq., Carbeth, Guthrie, Glasgow.

John Smith, Esq., LL. D., Secretary to the Maitland Club, Glasgow.

John G. Smyly, Esq., Upper Merrion-street, Dublin.

George Lewis Smyth, Esq., Derby street, London.

The Right Hon. Sir Wm. Meredyth Somerville, Bart., M. P., Somerville, Drogheda.

Rev. Thomas Stack, A. M., M. R. I. A., Fellow of Trinity College, Dublin.

Augustus Stafford Esq., M. P., Blatherwycke Park, Northamptonshire.

Michael Staunton, Esq., Marlborough-street, Dublin.

John Vandeleur Stewart, Esq., Rockhill, Letterkenny.

Colonel William Stewart, Killymoon, Cookstown.

William Stokes, Esq., M. D., M. R. I. A., Regius Professor of Physic, Dublin.

The Ven. Charles Strong, A. M., M. R. I. A., Archdeacon of Glendalough, Cavendishrow, Dublin.

Hon. and Rev. Andrew Godfrey Stuart, Rectory of Cottesmore, Oakham.

William Villiers Stuart, Esq., Dromana, Cappoquin.

Rev. George Studdert, A. M., Dundalk.

*Thomas Swanton, Esq., Crannliath, Ballidahob, Skibbereen.

Walter Sweetman, Esq., Mountjoy-square, North, Dublin.

James Talbot, Esq., Evercreech House, Shepton Mallet, Somersetshire.

Bartholomew M. Tabuteau, Esq., Fitzwilliam-place, Dublin.

*Edward King Tenison, Esq., Castle Tenison, Keadue, Carrick-on-Shannon.

*Robert J. Tennent, Esq., Belfast.

*James Thompson, Esq., Ballysillan, Belfast.

Robert Tighe, Esq., M. R. I. A., Fitzwilliam-square, North Dublin.

*William Fownes Tighe, Esq., Woodstock, Inistiogue.

*Rev. James H. Todd, D. D., M. R. I. A., Fellow of Trinity College, Dublin.

James Ruddell Todd, Esq., London.

Rev. John M. Traherne, Coedriglan, Cardiff.

William B. C. C. Turnbull, Esq., Advocate, F. S. A., Edinburgh.

Travers Twiss, Esq., D. C. L., F. R. S., University College, Oxford.

*Henry Tyler, Esq., Newtown-Limavaddy.

Crofton Moore Vandeleur, Esq., Rutland-square, Dublin.

Edward Crips Villiers, Esq., Kilpeacon.

Rev.

XIII. A Treatise on the Ogham or occult Forms of Writing of the ancient Irish ; from a MS. in the Library of Trinity College, Dublin ; with a Translation and Notes, and preliminary Dissertation, by the REV. CHARLES GRAVES, A. M., M. R. I. A., Fellow of Trinity College, and Professor of Mathematics in the University of Dublin.

XIV. The Topographical Poems of O'Heerin and O'Duggan; with Notes by JOHN O'DONOVAN, Esq.

In addition to the foregoing projected Publications, there are many important works in the contemplation of the Council, which want of funds alone prevents the possibility of their undertaking, such as the Brehon Laws, the Dinnseanchus, the Feilire or Festilogium of Aengus the Culdee, the Annals of Connaught, the Annals of Tigernach, &c., &c.

CPSIA information can be obtained at www.ICGtesting.com
Printed in the USA
BVOW08s1437071014

369853BV00020B/399/P